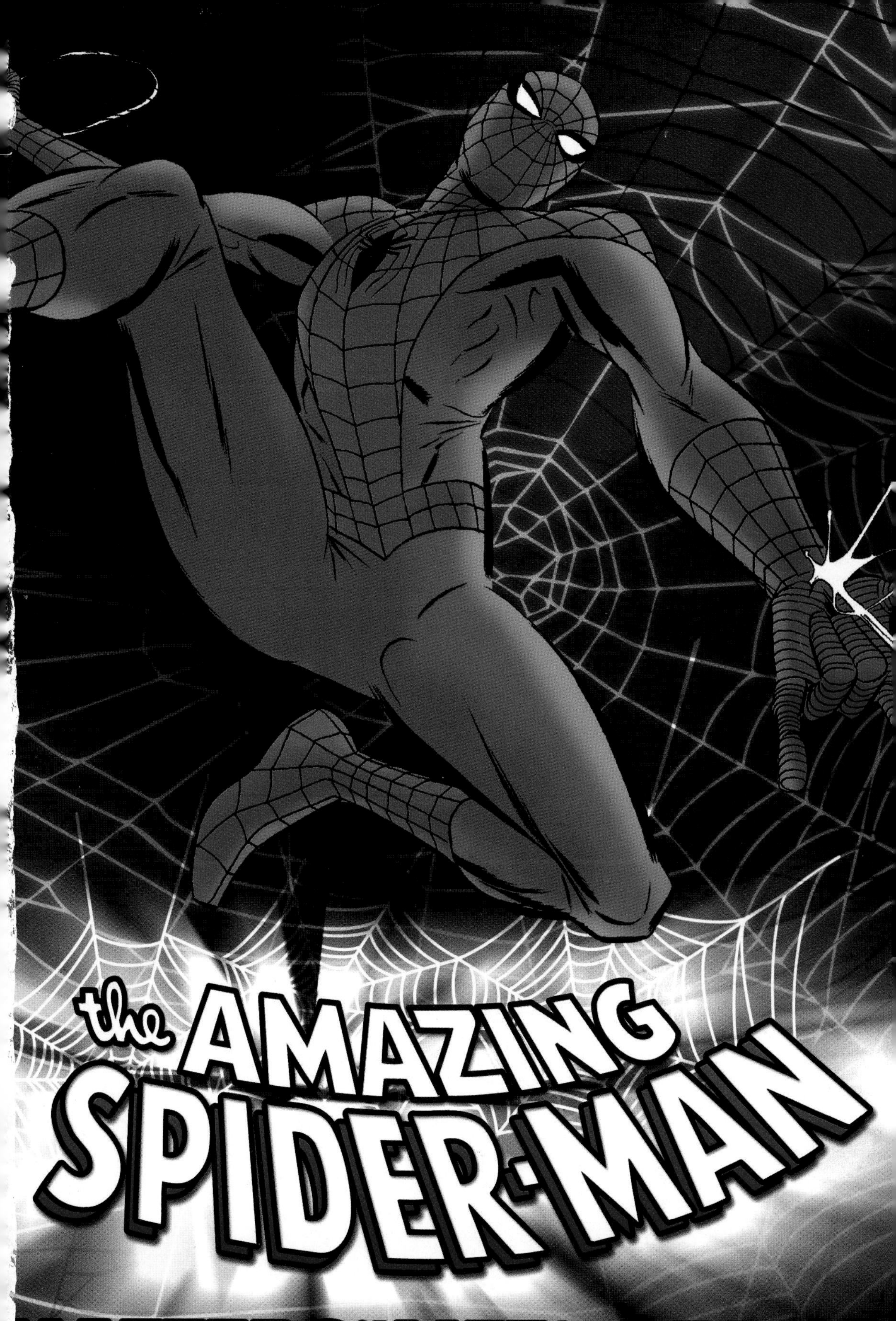
the AMAZING SPIDER-MAN

MATTERS OF LIFE AND DEATH

the AMAZING SPIDER-MAN

MATTERS OF LIFE AND DEATH

Writer: **DAN SLOTT**

ISSUES #652-654
Script, Issues #653-654: **FRED VAN LENTE**
Artist: **STEFANO CASELLI**
Colorists: **EDGAR DELGADO** & **MARTE GRACIA** (ISSUE #654)

"REBIRTH"
Pencilers: **PAULO SIQUEIRA** & **RONAN CLIQUET DE OLIVEIRA**
Inkers: **PAULO SIQUEIRA, ROLAND PARIS** & **GREG ADAMS**
Colorist: **FABIO D'AURIA**

ISSUE #654.1
Penciler: **HUMBERTO RAMOS**
Inker: **CARLOS CUEVAS**
Colorist: **EDGAR DELGADO**

ISSUES #655-657
Artist: **MARCOS MARTIN**
WITH **TY TEMPLETON, NUNO PLATI** & **STEFANO CASELLI** (ISSUE #657)
Colorist: **EDGAR DELGADO**
WITH **JAVIER RODRIGUEZ, NUNO PLATI** & **MARTE GRACIA** (ISSUE #657)

"LOCK AND/OR KEY"
Writer: **FRED VAN LENTE**
Penciler: **REILLY BROWN**
Inker: **VICTOR OLAZABA**
Colorist: **ANDRES MOSSA**

Letterer: **VC'S JOE CARAMAGNA** • Assistant Editor: **ELLIE PYLE** • Senior Editor: **STEPHEN WACKER**

Collection Editor: **JENNIFER GRÜNWALD** • Editorial Assistants: **JAMES EMMETT** & **JOE HOCHSTEIN**
Assistant Editors: **ALEX STARBUCK** & **NELSON RIBEIRO** • Editor, Special Projects: **MARK D. BEAZLEY**
Senior Editor, Special Projects: **JEFF YOUNGQUIST** • Senior Vice President of Sales: **DAVID GABRIEL**

Editor in Chief: **AXEL ALONSO** • Chief Creative Officer: **JOE QUESADA** • Publisher: **DAN BUCKLEY** • Executive Producer: **ALAN FINE**

SPIDER-MAN: MATTERS OF LIFE AND DEATH. Contains material originally published in magazine form as AMAZING SPIDER-MAN #652-657 and #654.1. First printing 2011. Hardcover ISBN# 978-0-7851-5102-9. Softcover ISBN# 978-0-7851-5103-6. Published by MARVEL WORLDWIDE, INC., a subsidiary of MARVEL ENTERTAINMENT, LLC. OFFICE OF PUBLICATION: 135 West 50th Street, New York, NY 10020. Copyright © 2011 Marvel Characters, Inc. All rights reserved. Hardcover: $24.99 per copy in the U.S. and $27.99 in Canada (GST #R127032852). Softcover: $19.99 per copy in the U.S. and $21.99 in Canada (GST #R127032852). Canadian Agreement #40668537. All characters featured in this issue and the distinctive names and likenesses thereof, and all related indicia are trademarks of Marvel Characters, Inc. No similarity between any of the names, characters, persons, and/or institutions in this magazine with those of any living or dead person or institution is intended, and any such similarity which may exist is purely coincidental. **Printed in the U.S.A.** ALAN FINE, EVP - Office of the President, Marvel Worldwide, Inc. and EVP & CMO Marvel Characters B.V.; DAN BUCKLEY, Publisher & President - Print, Animation & Digital Divisions; JOE QUESADA, Chief Creative Officer; JIM SOKOLOWSKI, Chief Operating Officer; DAVID BOGART, SVP of Business Affairs & Talent Management; TOM BREVOORT, SVP of Publishing; C.B. CEBULSKI, SVP of Creator & Content Development; DAVID GABRIEL, SVP of Publishing Sales & Circulation; MICHAEL PASCIULLO, SVP of Brand Planning & Communications; JIM O'KEEFE, VP of Operations & Logistics; DAN CARR, Executive Director of Publishing Technology; JUSTIN F. GABRIE, Director of Publishing & Editorial Operations; SUSAN CRESPI, Editorial Operations Manager; ALEX MORALES, Publishing Operations Manager; STAN LEE, Chairman Emeritus. For information regarding advertising in Marvel Comics or on Marvel.com, please contact Ron Stern, VP of Business Development, at rstern@marvel.com or 800-217-9158.

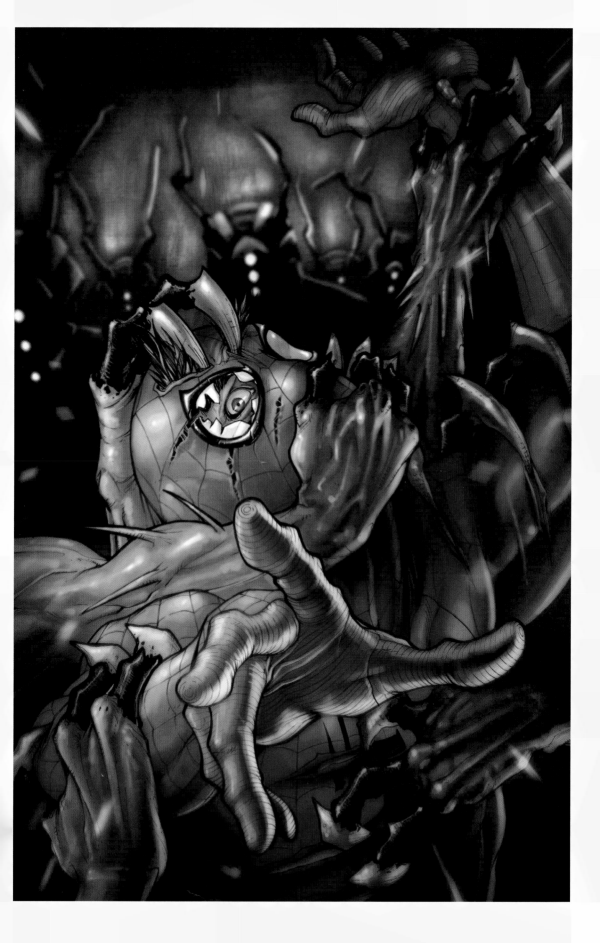

FOOLPROOF PLANS:
SUPER-VILLAIN MESSAGE BOARD

| AUTHOR | MESSAGE |

SPIDER-SLAYER
Alistair Smythe

J. Jonah Jameson must pay for his crimes! My father slaved over spider-slayers for Jameson for years and died an agonizing death from radiation exposure. But soon, Jameson too will know that there are pains worse than death! I will kill everyone he loves!

His son:
Colonel John Jameson

Space Pilot.

His wife:
Dr. Marla Jameson

She recently used her connections to get Peter Parker his dream job in the think tank at Horizon Labs.

And (most importantly) his father: Jay Jameson Sr.

Married to Peter Parker's Aunt May.

As well as anyone else Jameson cares about who dares to get in my way! And I am not alone. There are others Jameson has wronged:

Mac Gargan – Formerly Venom, once again Scorpion, victim of Jameson's experiments

Not even Jameson's enhanced security as mayor will protect him from my INSECT ARMY!

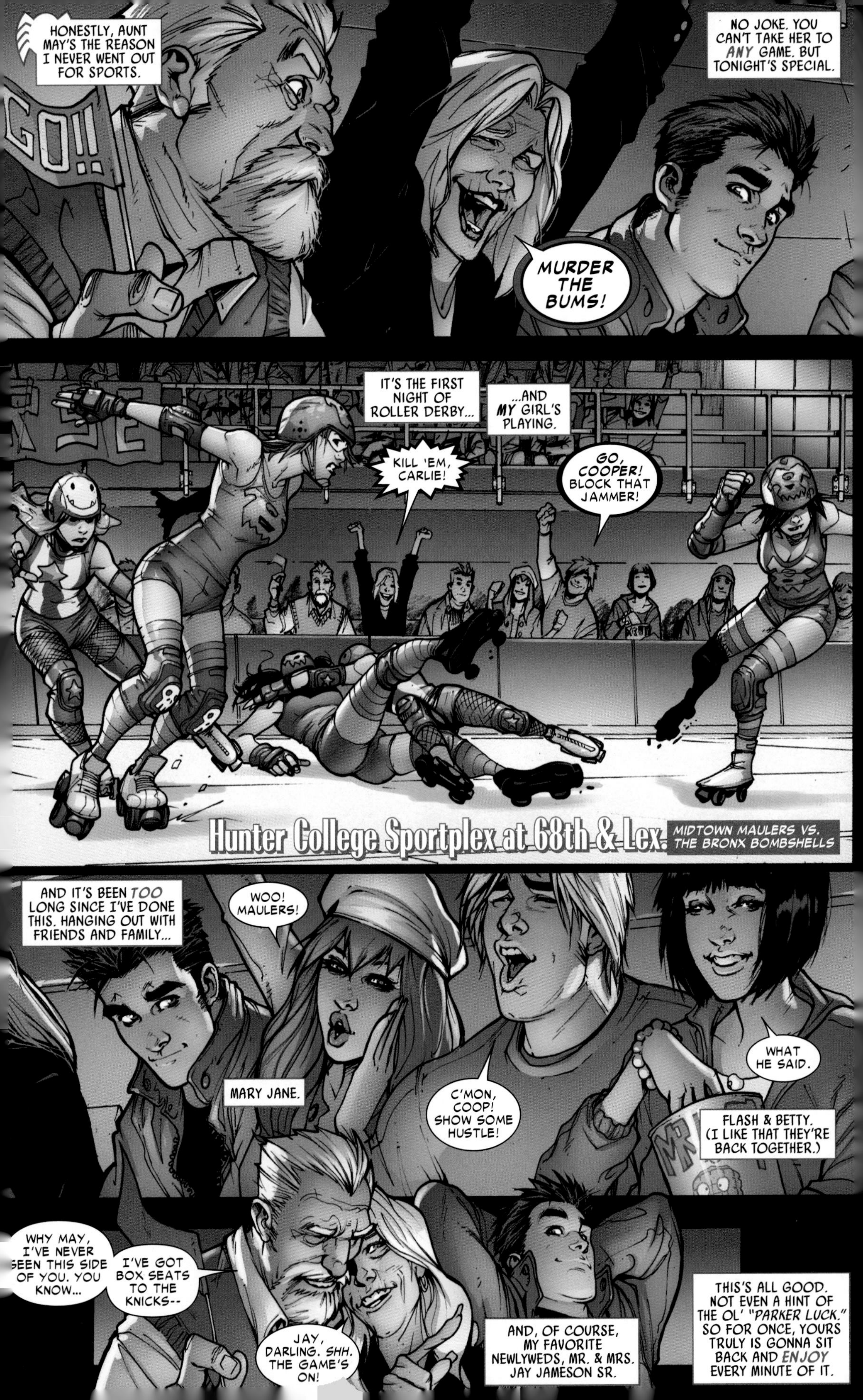
HONESTLY, AUNT MAY'S THE REASON I NEVER WENT OUT FOR SPORTS.
NO JOKE. YOU CAN'T TAKE HER TO ANY GAME. BUT TONIGHT'S SPECIAL.
GO!!
MURDER THE BUMS!
IT'S THE FIRST NIGHT OF ROLLER DERBY...
...AND MY GIRL'S PLAYING.
KILL 'EM, CARLIE!
GO, COOPER! BLOCK THAT JAMMER!
Hunter College Sportplex at 68th & Lex.
MIDTOWN MAULERS VS. THE BRONX BOMBSHELLS
AND IT'S BEEN TOO LONG SINCE I'VE DONE THIS. HANGING OUT WITH FRIENDS AND FAMILY...
WOO! MAULERS!
MARY JANE.
C'MON, COOP! SHOW SOME HUSTLE!
WHAT HE SAID.
FLASH & BETTY. (I LIKE THAT THEY'RE BACK TOGETHER.)
WHY MAY, I'VE NEVER SEEN THIS SIDE OF YOU. YOU KNOW...
I'VE GOT BOX SEATS TO THE KNICKS--
JAY, DARLING. SHH. THE GAME'S ON!
AND, OF COURSE, MY FAVORITE NEWLYWEDS, MR. & MRS. JAY JAMESON SR.
THIS'S ALL GOOD. NOT EVEN A HINT OF THE OL' "PARKER LUCK." SO FOR ONCE, YOURS TRULY IS GONNA SIT BACK AND ENJOY EVERY MINUTE OF IT.

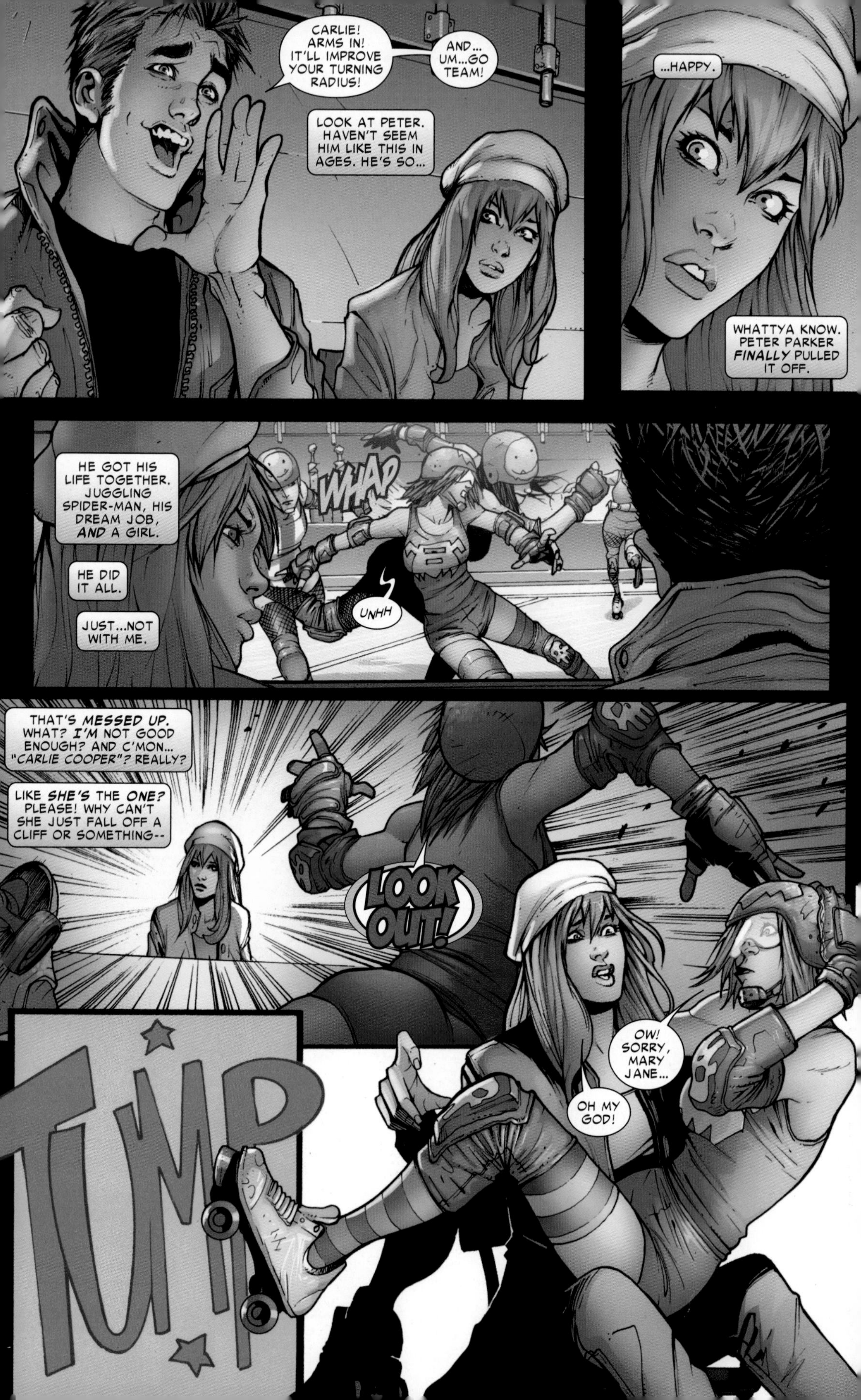
CARLIE! ARMS IN! IT'LL IMPROVE YOUR TURNING RADIUS!
AND... UM...GO TEAM!
LOOK AT PETER. HAVEN'T SEEM HIM LIKE THIS IN AGES. HE'S SO...
...HAPPY.
WHATTYA KNOW. PETER PARKER FINALLY PULLED IT OFF.
HE GOT HIS LIFE TOGETHER. JUGGLING SPIDER-MAN, HIS DREAM JOB, AND A GIRL.
WHAP
HE DID IT ALL.
UNHH
JUST...NOT WITH ME.
THAT'S MESSED UP. WHAT? I'M NOT GOOD ENOUGH? AND C'MON... "CARLIE COOPER"? REALLY?
LIKE SHE'S THE ONE? PLEASE! WHY CAN'T SHE JUST FALL OFF A CLIFF OR SOMETHING--
LOOK OUT!
TUMP
OW! SORRY, MARY JANE...
OH MY GOD!

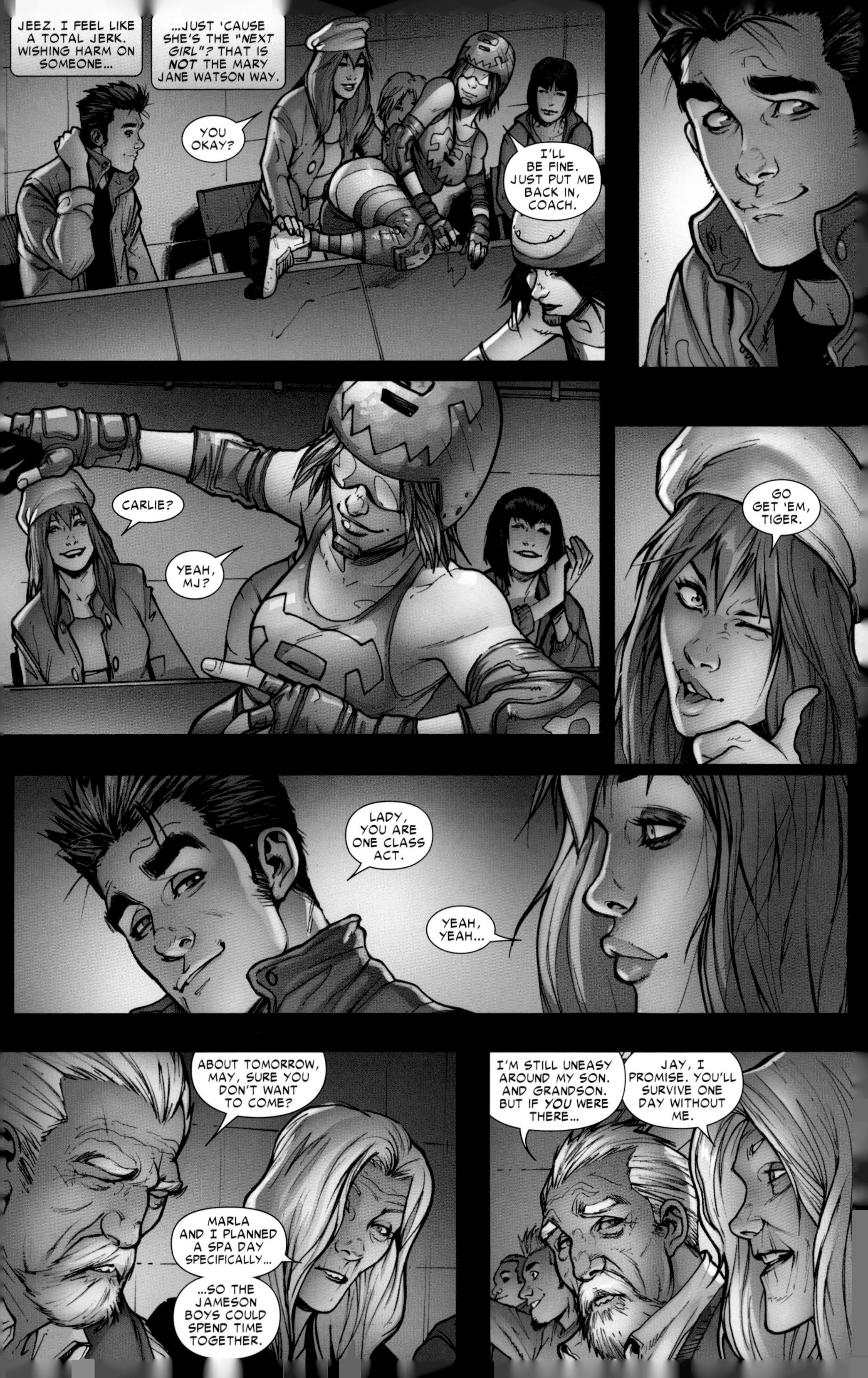
JEEZ. I FEEL LIKE A TOTAL JERK. WISHING HARM ON SOMEONE...
...JUST 'CAUSE SHE'S THE "NEXT GIRL"? THAT IS NOT THE MARY JANE WATSON WAY.
YOU OKAY?
I'LL BE FINE. JUST PUT ME BACK IN, COACH.
CARLIE?
YEAH, MJ?
GO GET 'EM, TIGER.
LADY, YOU ARE ONE CLASS ACT.
YEAH, YEAH...
ABOUT TOMORROW, MAY, SURE YOU DON'T WANT TO COME?
MARLA AND I PLANNED A SPA DAY SPECIFICALLY...
...SO THE JAMESON BOYS COULD SPEND TIME TOGETHER.
I'M STILL UNEASY AROUND MY SON. AND GRANDSON. BUT IF YOU WERE THERE...
JAY, I PROMISE. YOU'LL SURVIVE ONE DAY WITHOUT ME.

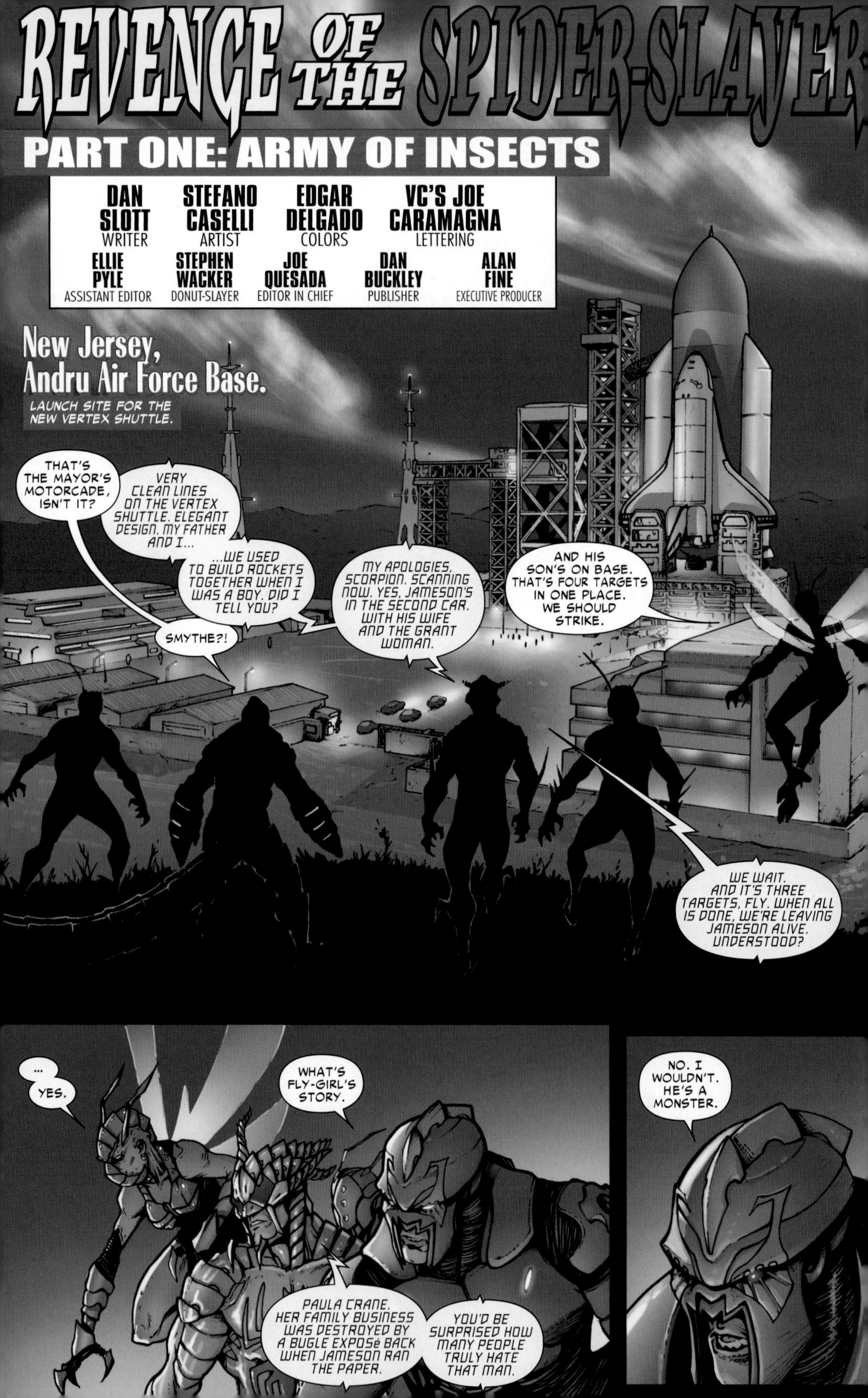
REVENGE OF THE SPIDER-SLAYER
PART ONE: ARMY OF INSECTS
DAN SLOTT WRITER
STEFANO CASELLI ARTIST
EDGAR DELGADO COLORS
VC'S JOE CARAMAGNA LETTERING
ELLIE PYLE ASSISTANT EDITOR
STEPHEN WACKER DONUT-SLAYER
JOE QUESADA EDITOR IN CHIEF
DAN BUCKLEY PUBLISHER
ALAN FINE EXECUTIVE PRODUCER
New Jersey, Andru Air Force Base.
LAUNCH SITE FOR THE NEW VERTEX SHUTTLE.
THAT'S THE MAYOR'S MOTORCADE, ISN'T IT?
VERY CLEAN LINES ON THE VERTEX SHUTTLE. ELEGANT DESIGN. MY FATHER AND I...
...WE USED TO BUILD ROCKETS TOGETHER WHEN I WAS A BOY. DID I TELL YOU?
SMYTHE?!
MY APOLOGIES, SCORPION. SCANNING NOW. YES, JAMESON'S IN THE SECOND CAR. WITH HIS WIFE AND THE GRANT WOMAN.
AND HIS SON'S ON BASE. THAT'S FOUR TARGETS IN ONE PLACE. WE SHOULD STRIKE.
WE WAIT. AND IT'S THREE TARGETS, FLY. WHEN ALL IS DONE, WE'RE LEAVING JAMESON ALIVE. UNDERSTOOD?
... YES.
WHAT'S FLY-GIRL'S STORY.
PAULA CRANE. HER FAMILY BUSINESS WAS DESTROYED BY A BUGLE EXPOSé BACK WHEN JAMESON RAN THE PAPER.
YOU'D BE SURPRISED HOW MANY PEOPLE TRULY HATE THAT MAN.
NO. I WOULDN'T. HE'S A MONSTER.

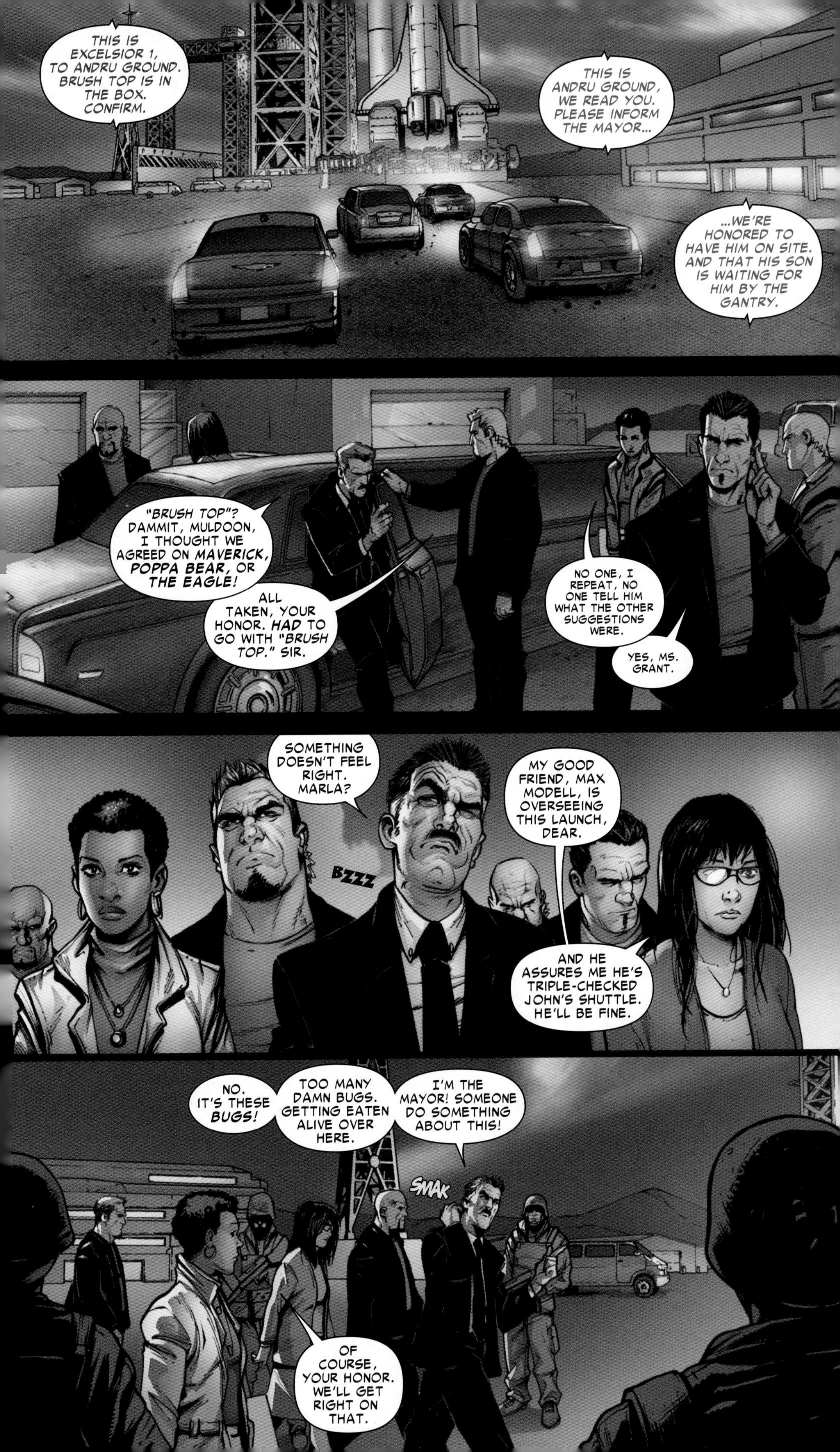
THIS IS EXCELSIOR 1, TO ANDRU GROUND. BRUSH TOP IS IN THE BOX. CONFIRM.
THIS IS ANDRU GROUND, WE READ YOU. PLEASE INFORM THE MAYOR...
...WE'RE HONORED TO HAVE HIM ON SITE. AND THAT HIS SON IS WAITING FOR HIM BY THE GANTRY.
"BRUSH TOP"? DAMMIT, MULDOON, I THOUGHT WE AGREED ON MAVERICK, POPPA BEAR, OR THE EAGLE!
ALL TAKEN, YOUR HONOR. HAD TO GO WITH "BRUSH TOP." SIR.
NO ONE, I REPEAT, NO ONE TELL HIM WHAT THE OTHER SUGGESTIONS WERE.
YES, MS. GRANT.
SOMETHING DOESN'T FEEL RIGHT. MARLA?
BZZZ
MY GOOD FRIEND, MAX MODELL, IS OVERSEEING THIS LAUNCH, DEAR.
AND HE ASSURES ME HE'S TRIPLE-CHECKED JOHN'S SHUTTLE. HE'LL BE FINE.
NO. IT'S THESE BUGS!
TOO MANY DAMN BUGS. GETTING EATEN ALIVE OVER HERE.
I'M THE MAYOR! SOMEONE DO SOMETHING ABOUT THIS!
SMAK
OF COURSE, YOUR HONOR. WE'LL GET RIGHT ON THAT.

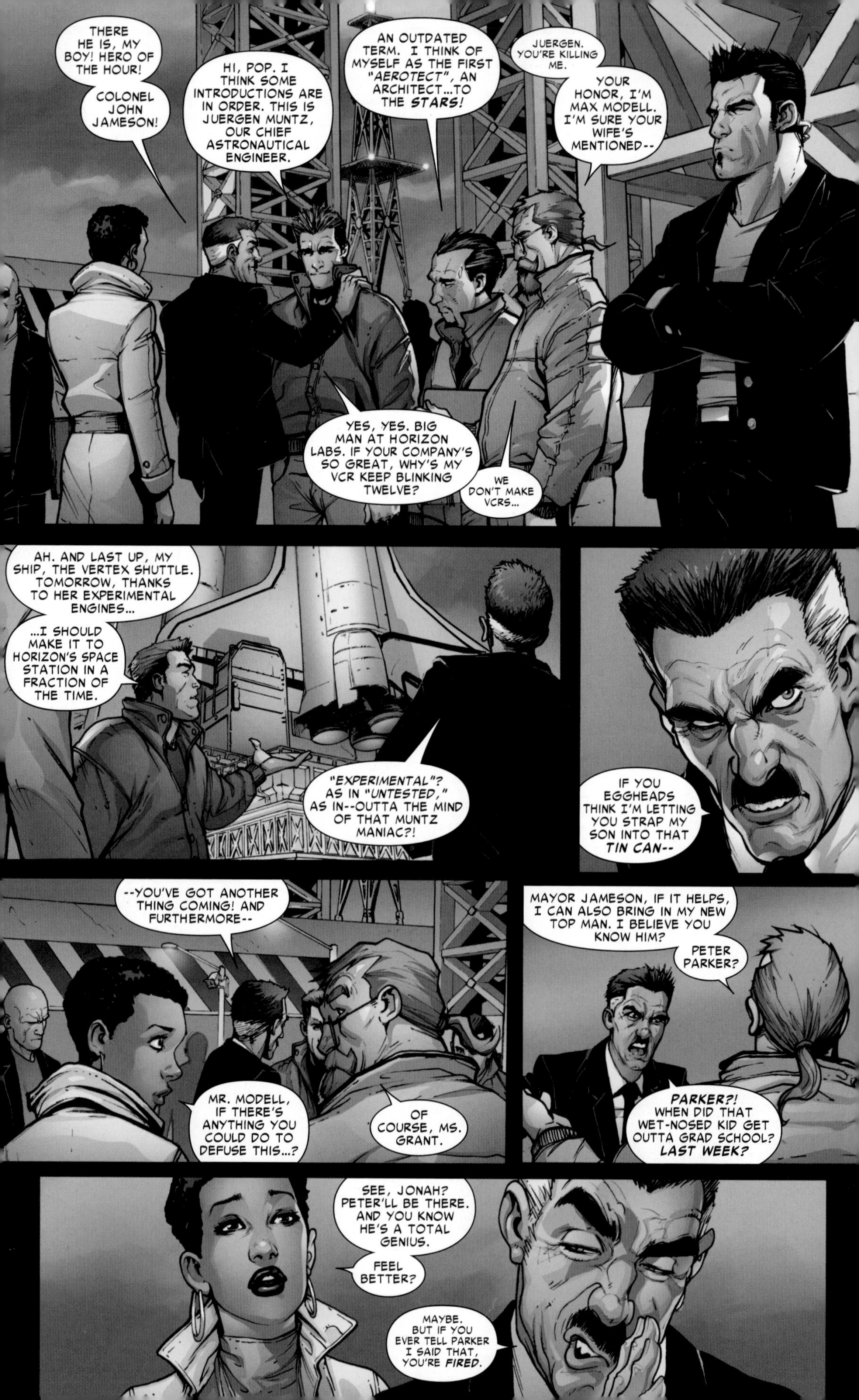
THERE HE IS, MY BOY! HERO OF THE HOUR!
COLONEL JOHN JAMESON!
HI, POP. I THINK SOME INTRODUCTIONS ARE IN ORDER. THIS IS JUERGEN MUNTZ, OUR CHIEF ASTRONAUTICAL ENGINEER.
AN OUTDATED TERM. I THINK OF MYSELF AS THE FIRST "AEROTECT", AN ARCHITECT...TO THE STARS!
JUERGEN. YOU'RE KILLING ME.
YOUR HONOR, I'M MAX MODELL. I'M SURE YOUR WIFE'S MENTIONED--
YES, YES. BIG MAN AT HORIZON LABS. IF YOUR COMPANY'S SO GREAT, WHY'S MY VCR KEEP BLINKING TWELVE?
WE DON'T MAKE VCRS...
AH. AND LAST UP, MY SHIP, THE VERTEX SHUTTLE. TOMORROW, THANKS TO HER EXPERIMENTAL ENGINES...
...I SHOULD MAKE IT TO HORIZON'S SPACE STATION IN A FRACTION OF THE TIME.
"EXPERIMENTAL"? AS IN "UNTESTED," AS IN--OUTTA THE MIND OF THAT MUNTZ MANIAC?!
IF YOU EGGHEADS THINK I'M LETTING YOU STRAP MY SON INTO THAT TIN CAN--
--YOU'VE GOT ANOTHER THING COMING! AND FURTHERMORE--
MR. MODELL, IF THERE'S ANYTHING YOU COULD DO TO DEFUSE THIS...?
OF COURSE, MS. GRANT.
MAYOR JAMESON, IF IT HELPS, I CAN ALSO BRING IN MY NEW TOP MAN. I BELIEVE YOU KNOW HIM?
PETER PARKER?
PARKER?! WHEN DID THAT WET-NOSED KID GET OUTTA GRAD SCHOOL? LAST WEEK?
SEE, JONAH? PETER'LL BE THERE. AND YOU KNOW HE'S A TOTAL GENIUS.
FEEL BETTER?
MAYBE. BUT IF YOU EVER TELL PARKER I SAID THAT, YOU'RE FIRED.

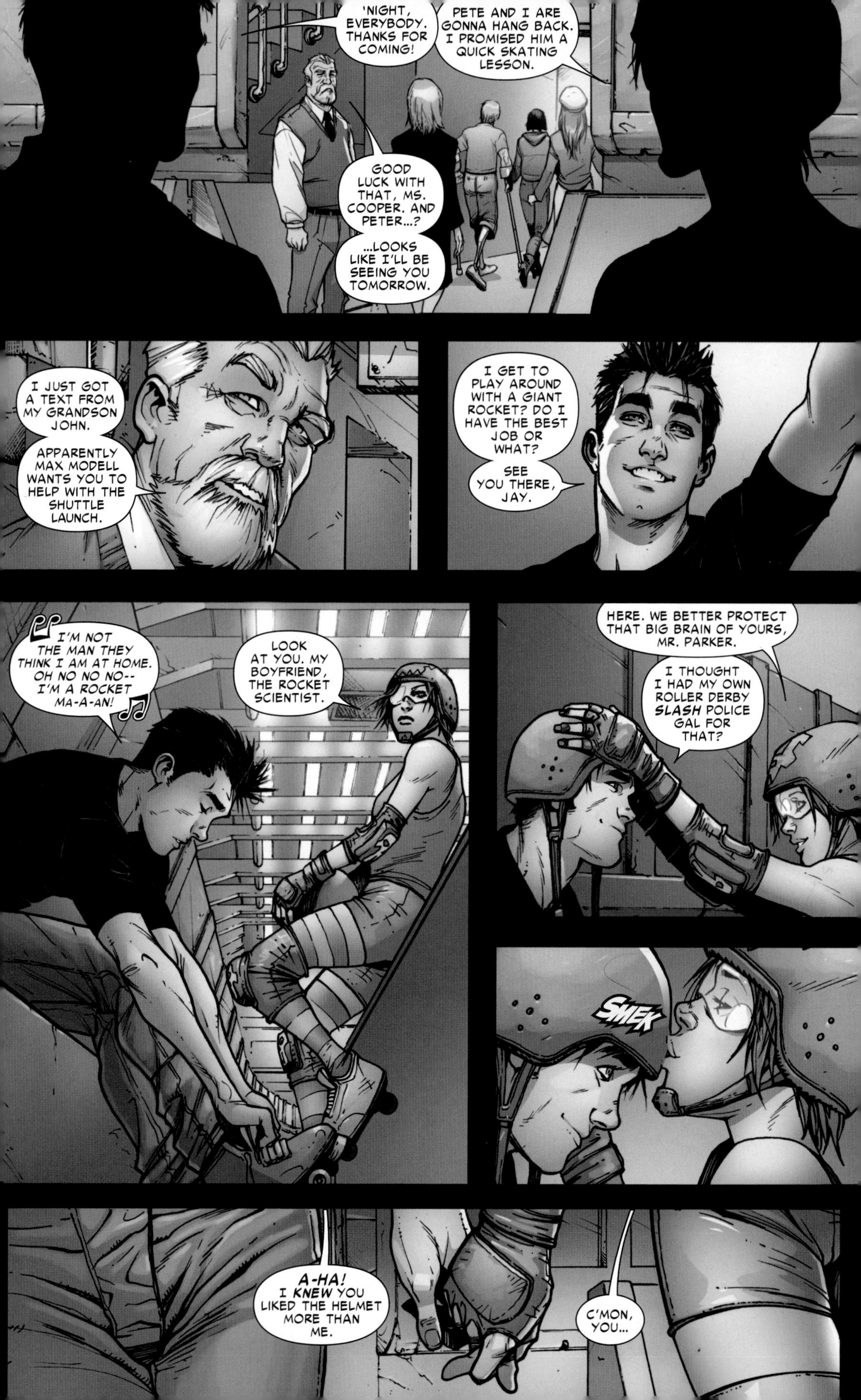
'NIGHT, EVERYBODY. THANKS FOR COMING!
PETE AND I ARE GONNA HANG BACK. I PROMISED HIM A QUICK SKATING LESSON.
GOOD LUCK WITH THAT, MS. COOPER. AND PETER...?
...LOOKS LIKE I'LL BE SEEING YOU TOMORROW.
I JUST GOT A TEXT FROM MY GRANDSON JOHN.
APPARENTLY MAX MODELL WANTS YOU TO HELP WITH THE SHUTTLE LAUNCH.
I GET TO PLAY AROUND WITH A GIANT ROCKET? DO I HAVE THE BEST JOB OR WHAT?
SEE YOU THERE, JAY.
I'M NOT THE MAN THEY THINK I AM AT HOME. OH NO NO NO-- I'M A ROCKET MA-A-AN!
LOOK AT YOU. MY BOYFRIEND, THE ROCKET SCIENTIST.
HERE. WE BETTER PROTECT THAT BIG BRAIN OF YOURS, MR. PARKER.
I THOUGHT I HAD MY OWN ROLLER DERBY SLASH POLICE GAL FOR THAT?
SMEK
A-HA! I KNEW YOU LIKED THE HELMET MORE THAN ME.
C'MON, YOU...

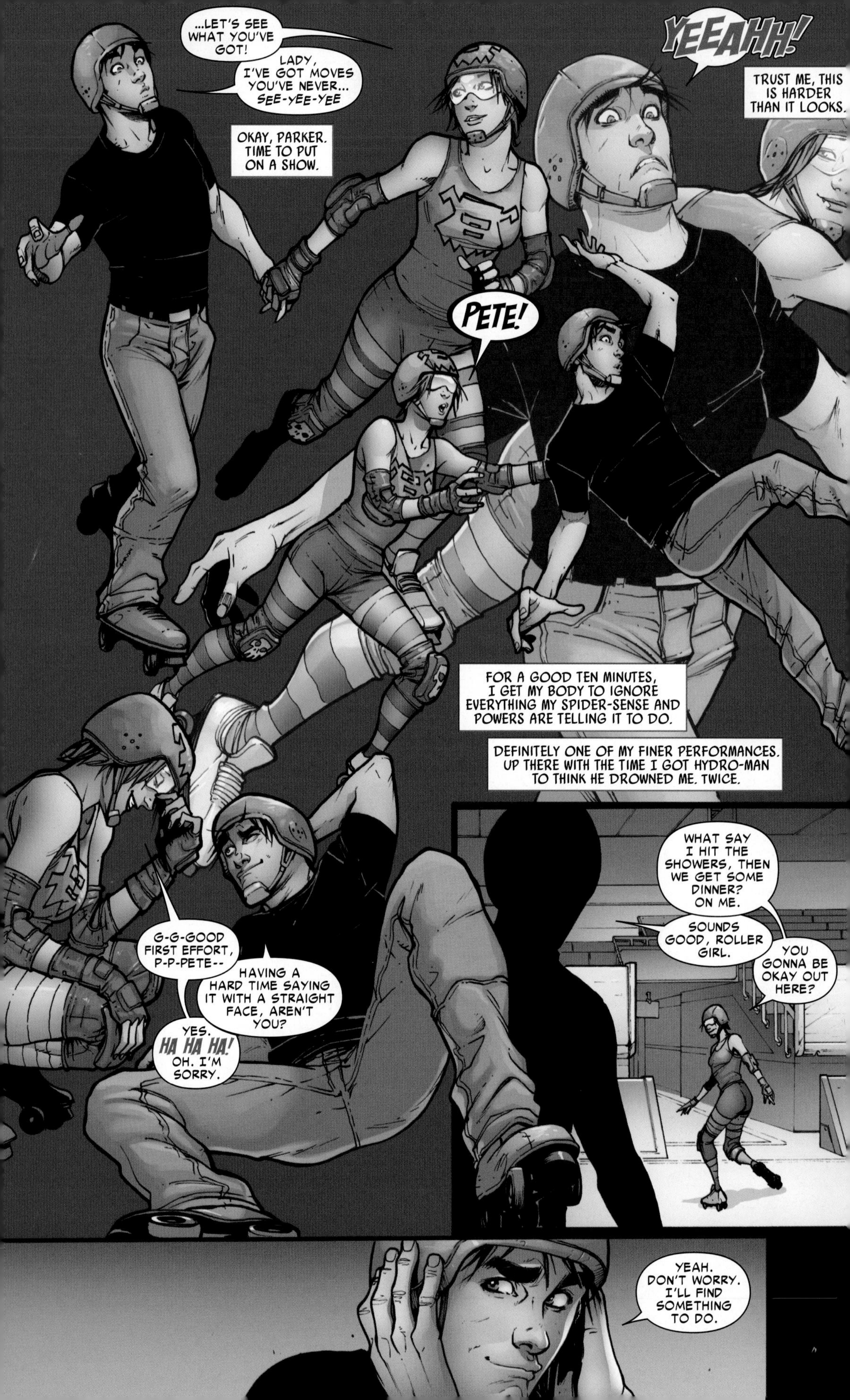

...LET'S SEE WHAT YOU'VE GOT!
LADY, I'VE GOT MOVES YOU'VE NEVER... SEE-YEE-YEE
OKAY, PARKER. TIME TO PUT ON A SHOW.
YEEAHH!
TRUST ME, THIS IS HARDER THAN IT LOOKS.
PETE!
FOR A GOOD TEN MINUTES, I GET MY BODY TO IGNORE EVERYTHING MY SPIDER-SENSE AND POWERS ARE TELLING IT TO DO.
DEFINITELY ONE OF MY FINER PERFORMANCES. UP THERE WITH THE TIME I GOT HYDRO-MAN TO THINK HE DROWNED ME. TWICE.
G-G-GOOD FIRST EFFORT, P-P-PETE--
HAVING A HARD TIME SAYING IT WITH A STRAIGHT FACE, AREN'T YOU?
YES. HA HA HA! OH. I'M SORRY.
WHAT SAY I HIT THE SHOWERS, THEN WE GET SOME DINNER? ON ME.
SOUNDS GOOD, ROLLER GIRL.
YOU GONNA BE OKAY OUT HERE?
YEAH. DON'T WORRY. I'LL FIND SOMETHING TO DO.

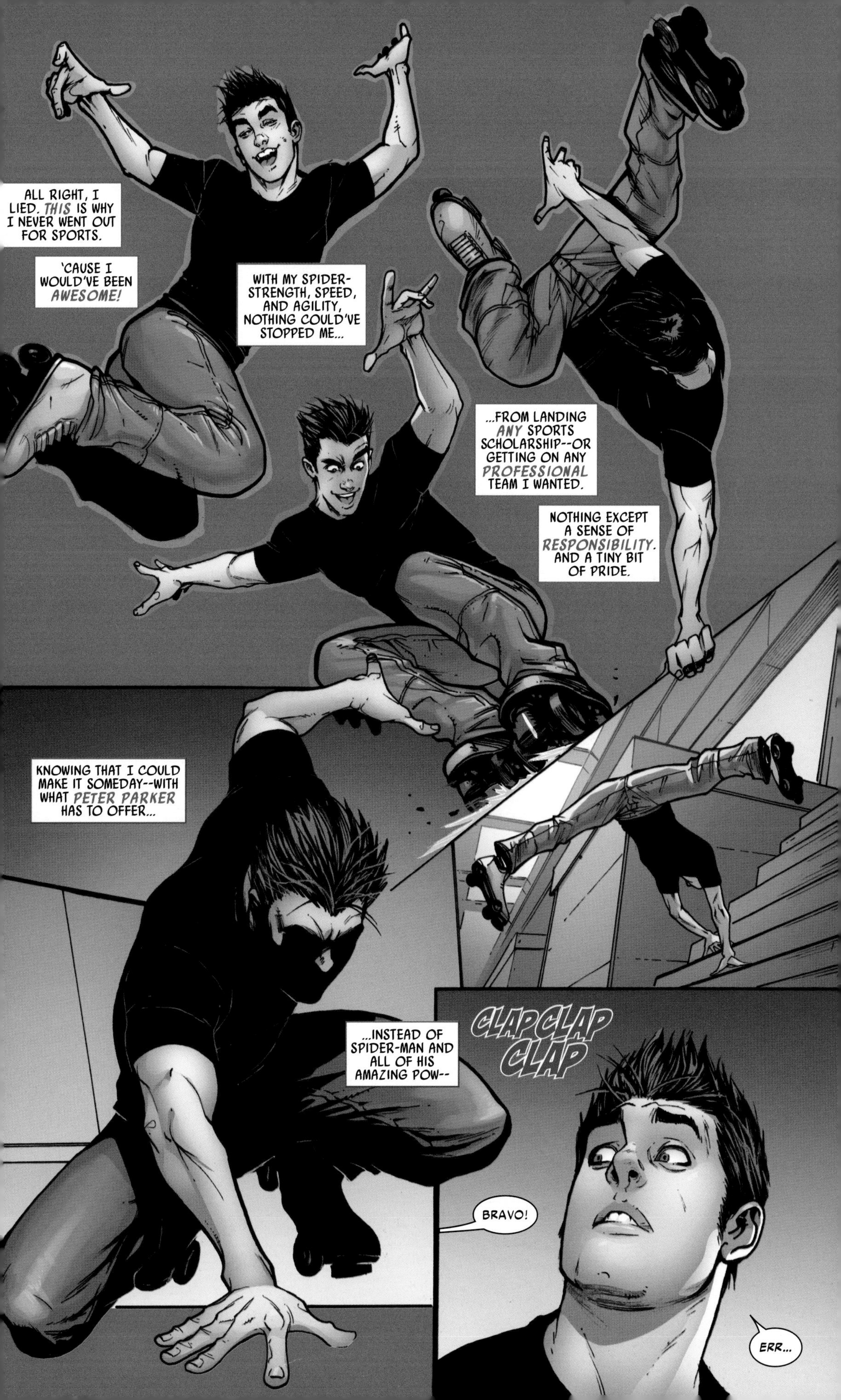
ALL RIGHT, I LIED. THIS IS WHY I NEVER WENT OUT FOR SPORTS.
'CAUSE I WOULD'VE BEEN AWESOME!
WITH MY SPIDER-STRENGTH, SPEED, AND AGILITY, NOTHING COULD'VE STOPPED ME...
...FROM LANDING ANY SPORTS SCHOLARSHIP--OR GETTING ON ANY PROFESSIONAL TEAM I WANTED.
NOTHING EXCEPT A SENSE OF RESPONSIBILITY. AND A TINY BIT OF PRIDE.
KNOWING THAT I COULD MAKE IT SOMEDAY--WITH WHAT PETER PARKER HAS TO OFFER...
...INSTEAD OF SPIDER-MAN AND ALL OF HIS AMAZING POW--
CLAP CLAP CLAP
BRAVO!
ERR...

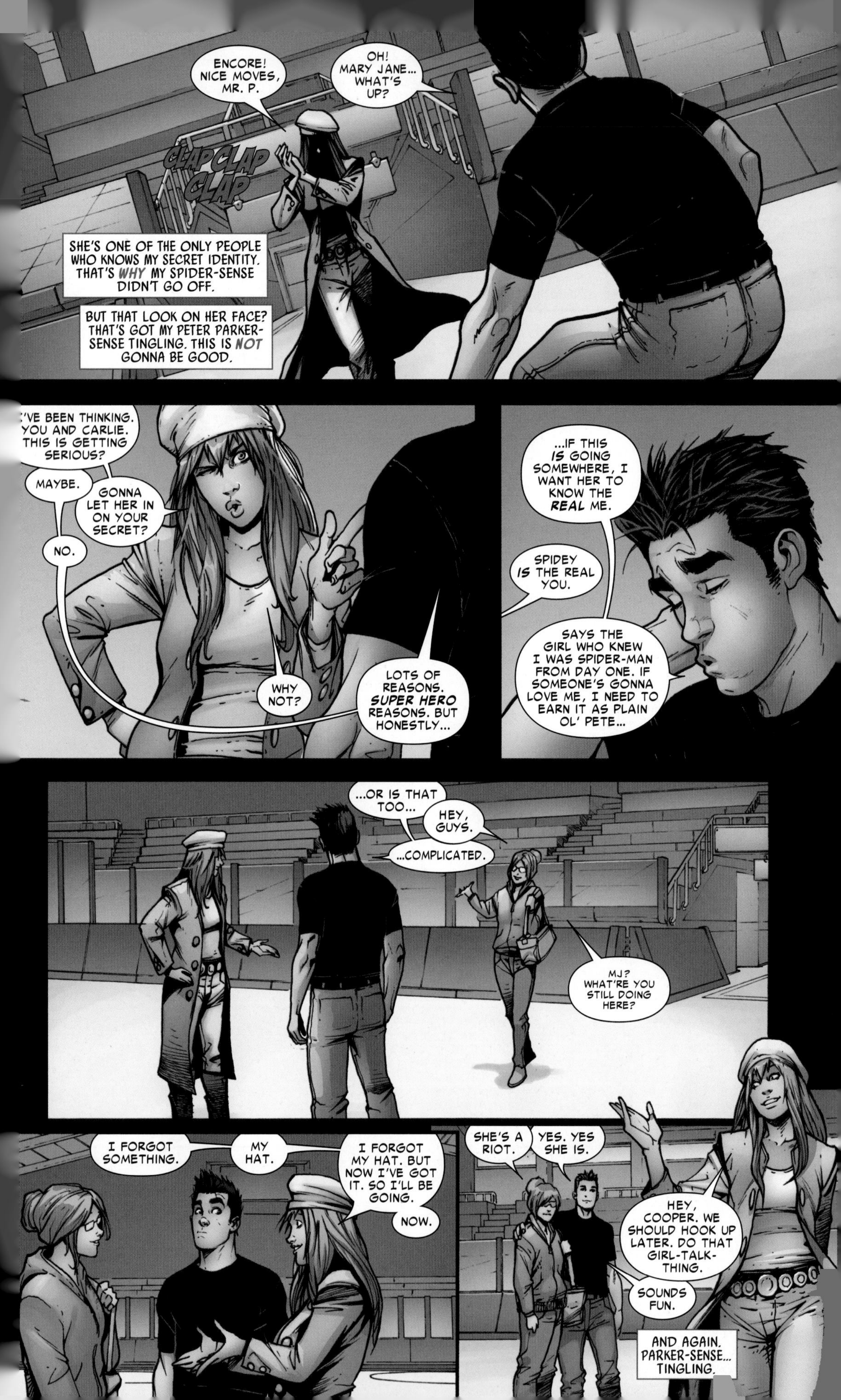
ENCORE! NICE MOVES, MR. P.
CLAP CLAP CLAP
OH! MARY JANE... WHAT'S UP?
SHE'S ONE OF THE ONLY PEOPLE WHO KNOWS MY SECRET IDENTITY. THAT'S WHY MY SPIDER-SENSE DIDN'T GO OFF.
BUT THAT LOOK ON HER FACE? THAT'S GOT MY PETER PARKER-SENSE TINGLING. THIS IS NOT GONNA BE GOOD.
'VE BEEN THINKING. YOU AND CARLIE. THIS IS GETTING SERIOUS?
MAYBE.
GONNA LET HER IN ON YOUR SECRET?
NO.
WHY NOT?
LOTS OF REASONS. SUPER HERO REASONS. BUT HONESTLY...
...IF THIS IS GOING SOMEWHERE, I WANT HER TO KNOW THE REAL ME.
SPIDEY IS THE REAL YOU.
SAYS THE GIRL WHO KNEW I WAS SPIDER-MAN FROM DAY ONE. IF SOMEONE'S GONNA LOVE ME, I NEED TO EARN IT AS PLAIN OL' PETE...
...OR IS THAT TOO...
...COMPLICATED.
HEY, GUYS.
MJ? WHAT'RE YOU STILL DOING HERE?
I FORGOT SOMETHING.
MY HAT.
I FORGOT MY HAT. BUT NOW I'VE GOT IT. SO I'LL BE GOING.
NOW.
SHE'S A RIOT.
YES. YES SHE IS.
HEY, COOPER. WE SHOULD HOOK UP LATER. DO THAT GIRL-TALK-THING.
SOUNDS FUN.
AND AGAIN. PARKER-SENSE... TINGLING.

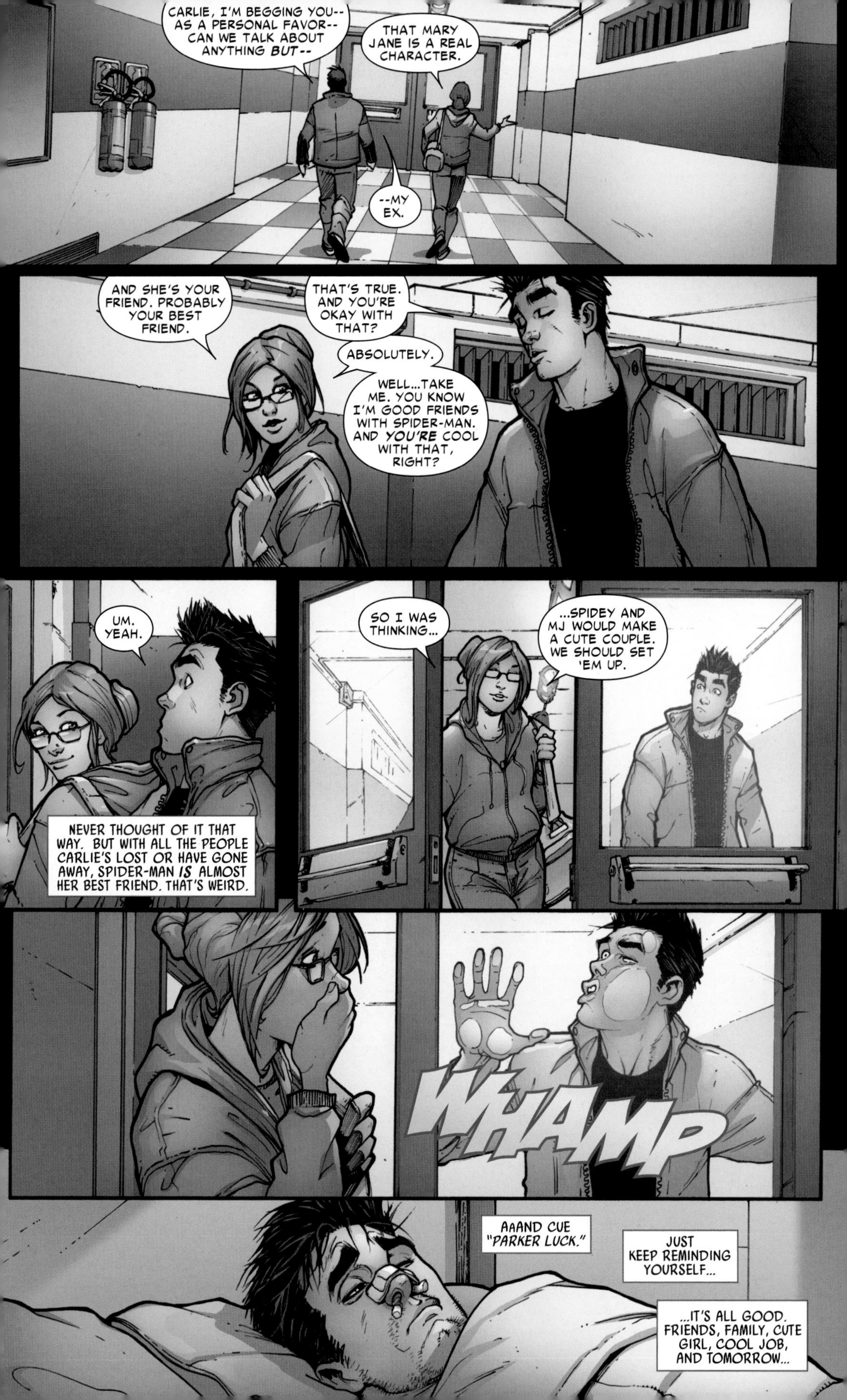
CARLIE, I'M BEGGING YOU-- AS A PERSONAL FAVOR-- CAN WE TALK ABOUT ANYTHING BUT--
THAT MARY JANE IS A REAL CHARACTER.
--MY EX.
AND SHE'S YOUR FRIEND. PROBABLY YOUR BEST FRIEND.
THAT'S TRUE. AND YOU'RE OKAY WITH THAT?
ABSOLUTELY.
WELL...TAKE ME. YOU KNOW I'M GOOD FRIENDS WITH SPIDER-MAN. AND YOU'RE COOL WITH THAT, RIGHT?
UM. YEAH.
NEVER THOUGHT OF IT THAT WAY. BUT WITH ALL THE PEOPLE CARLIE'S LOST OR HAVE GONE AWAY, SPIDER-MAN IS ALMOST HER BEST FRIEND. THAT'S WEIRD.
SO I WAS THINKING...
...SPIDEY AND MJ WOULD MAKE A CUTE COUPLE. WE SHOULD SET 'EM UP.
WHAMP
AAAND CUE "PARKER LUCK."
JUST KEEP REMINDING YOURSELF...
...IT'S ALL GOOD. FRIENDS, FAMILY, CUTE GIRL, COOL JOB, AND TOMORROW...

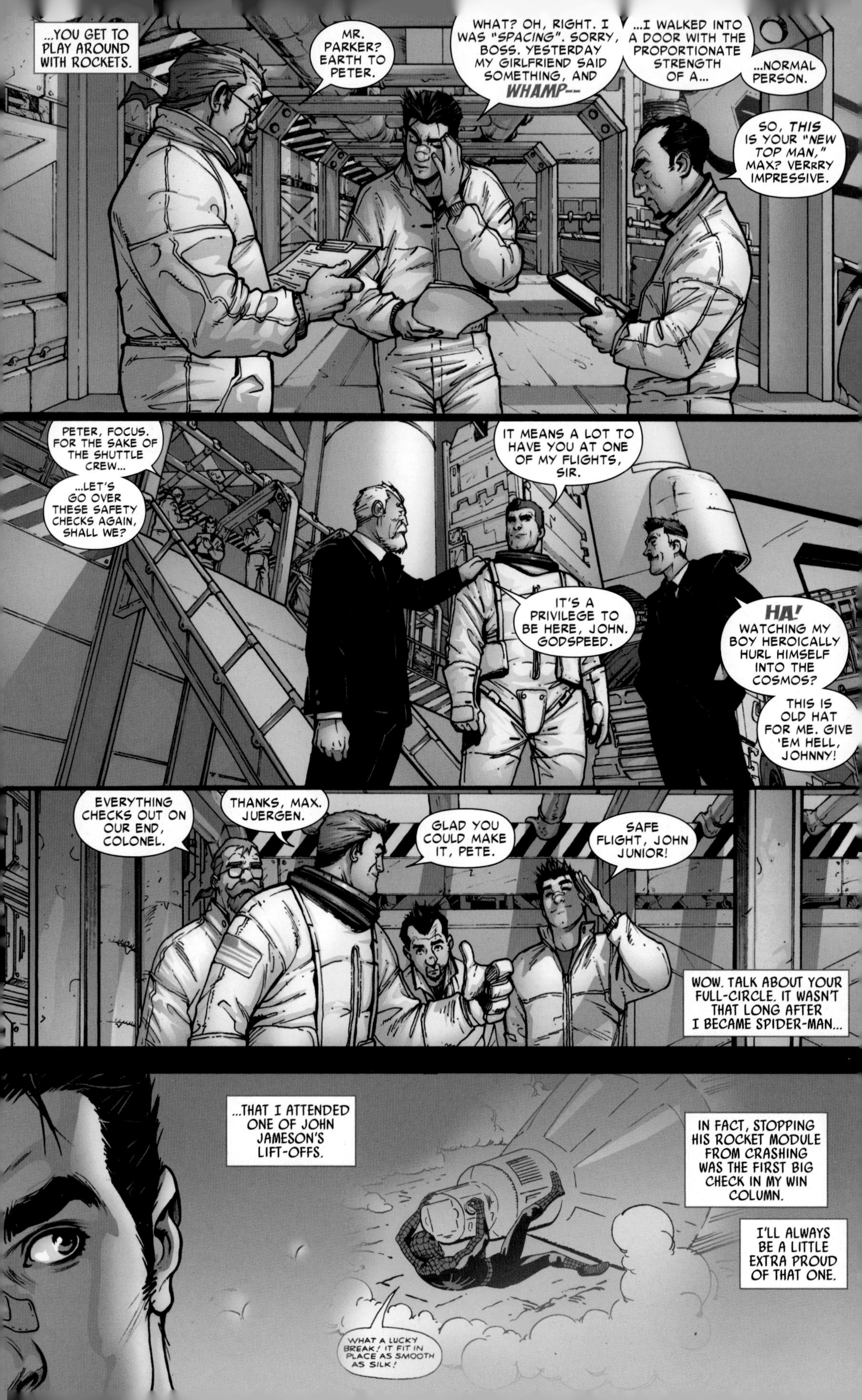
...YOU GET TO PLAY AROUND WITH ROCKETS.
MR. PARKER? EARTH TO PETER.
WHAT? OH, RIGHT. I WAS "SPACING". SORRY, BOSS. YESTERDAY MY GIRLFRIEND SAID SOMETHING, AND WHAMP--
...I WALKED INTO A DOOR WITH THE PROPORTIONATE STRENGTH OF A...
...NORMAL PERSON.
SO, THIS IS YOUR "NEW TOP MAN," MAX? VERRRY IMPRESSIVE.
PETER, FOCUS. FOR THE SAKE OF THE SHUTTLE CREW...
...LET'S GO OVER THESE SAFETY CHECKS AGAIN, SHALL WE?
IT MEANS A LOT TO HAVE YOU AT ONE OF MY FLIGHTS, SIR.
IT'S A PRIVILEGE TO BE HERE, JOHN. GODSPEED.
HA! WATCHING MY BOY HEROICALLY HURL HIMSELF INTO THE COSMOS?
THIS IS OLD HAT FOR ME. GIVE 'EM HELL, JOHNNY!
EVERYTHING CHECKS OUT ON OUR END, COLONEL.
THANKS, MAX. JUERGEN.
GLAD YOU COULD MAKE IT, PETE.
SAFE FLIGHT, JOHN JUNIOR!
WOW. TALK ABOUT YOUR FULL-CIRCLE. IT WASN'T THAT LONG AFTER I BECAME SPIDER-MAN...
...THAT I ATTENDED ONE OF JOHN JAMESON'S LIFT-OFFS.
IN FACT, STOPPING HIS ROCKET MODULE FROM CRASHING WAS THE FIRST BIG CHECK IN MY WIN COLUMN.
I'LL ALWAYS BE A LITTLE EXTRA PROUD OF THAT ONE.
WHAT A LUCKY BREAK! IT FIT IN PLACE AS SMOOTH AS SILK!

'CAUSE NO MATTER WHAT J. JONAH JAMESON SAYS ABOUT ME, NOTHING WILL EVER CHANGE THE FACT...

...THAT THE FIRST GUY I EVER SAVED WAS HIS ONE AND ONLY--

AHH!

SPIDER-SENSE! GOING OFF LIKE CRAZY! DANGER... EVERYWHERE!

PETER?

GOTTA GO. MUST'VE HURT MYSELF MORE THAN I THOUGHT.

UM... WHATEVER YOU DO, MAX, DON'T START THE LAUNCH WITHOUT ME, OKAY? SOMETHING'S OFF!

HMM.

MR. MODELL, TELL ME YOU'RE NOT TAKING THAT--FLAKE SERIOUSLY.

WE'VE GONE OVER THESE SYSTEMS A DOZEN TIMES.

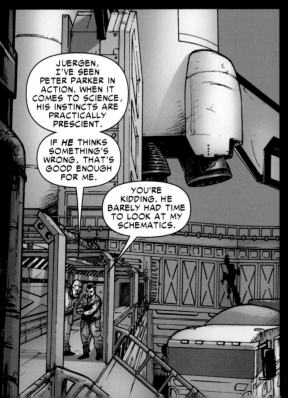

JUERGEN, I'VE SEEN PETER PARKER IN ACTION. WHEN IT COMES TO SCIENCE, HIS INSTINCTS ARE PRACTICALLY PRESCIENT.

IF HE THINKS SOMETHING'S WRONG, THAT'S GOOD ENOUGH FOR ME.

YOU'RE KIDDING. HE BARELY HAD TIME TO LOOK AT MY SCHEMATICS.

EXACTLY. WE'VE PORED OVER THIS DATA FOR MONTHS. HE'S A FRESH SET OF EYES. PERHAPS WE'RE TOO CLOSE TO IT.

PLEASE, IF ANYTHING WERE OUT OF PLACE, I'D NOTICE.

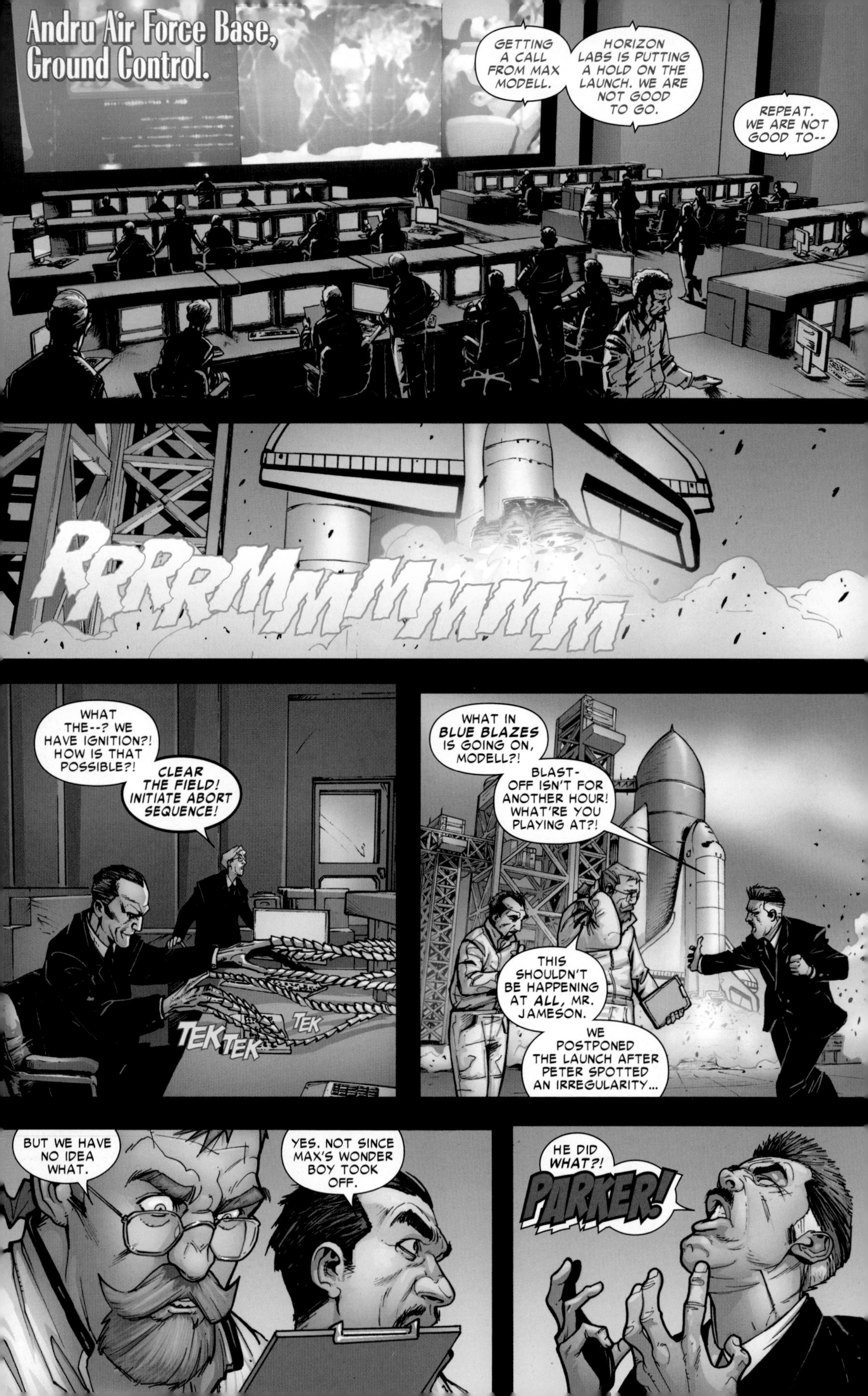
Andru Air Force Base, Ground Control.
GETTING A CALL FROM MAX MODELL.
HORIZON LABS IS PUTTING A HOLD ON THE LAUNCH. WE ARE NOT GOOD TO GO.
REPEAT. WE ARE NOT GOOD TO--
RRRRMMMMMMM
WHAT THE--? WE HAVE IGNITION?! HOW IS THAT POSSIBLE?!
CLEAR THE FIELD! INITIATE ABORT SEQUENCE!
TEK TEK TEK
WHAT IN BLUE BLAZES IS GOING ON, MODELL?!
BLAST-OFF ISN'T FOR ANOTHER HOUR! WHAT'RE YOU PLAYING AT?!
THIS SHOULDN'T BE HAPPENING AT ALL, MR. JAMESON.
WE POSTPONED THE LAUNCH AFTER PETER SPOTTED AN IRREGULARITY...
BUT WE HAVE NO IDEA WHAT.
YES. NOT SINCE MAX'S WONDER BOY TOOK OFF.
HE DID WHAT?!
PARKER!

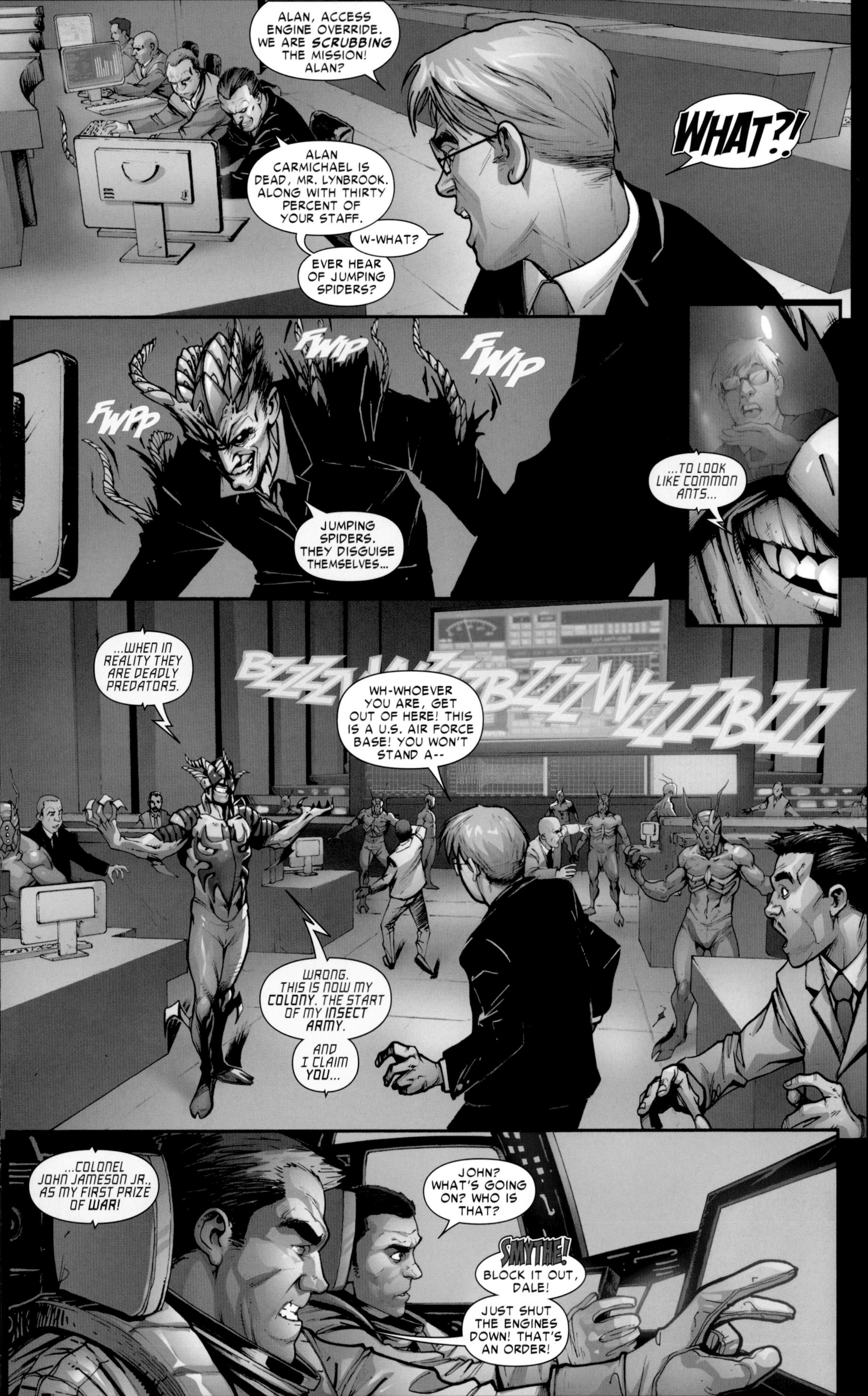
ALAN, ACCESS ENGINE OVERRIDE. WE ARE SCRUBBING THE MISSION! ALAN?
WHAT?!
ALAN CARMICHAEL IS DEAD, MR. LYNBROOK. ALONG WITH THIRTY PERCENT OF YOUR STAFF.
W-WHAT?
EVER HEAR OF JUMPING SPIDERS?
FWIP
FWIP
FWPP
JUMPING SPIDERS. THEY DISGUISE THEMSELVES...
...TO LOOK LIKE COMMON ANTS...
...WHEN IN REALITY THEY ARE DEADLY PREDATORS.
WH-WHOEVER YOU ARE, GET OUT OF HERE! THIS IS A U.S. AIR FORCE BASE! YOU WON'T STAND A--
WRONG. THIS IS NOW MY COLONY. THE START OF MY INSECT ARMY.
AND I CLAIM YOU...
...COLONEL JOHN JAMESON JR., AS MY FIRST PRIZE OF WAR!
JOHN? WHAT'S GOING ON? WHO IS THAT?
SMYTHE!
BLOCK IT OUT, DALE!
JUST SHUT THE ENGINES DOWN! THAT'S AN ORDER!

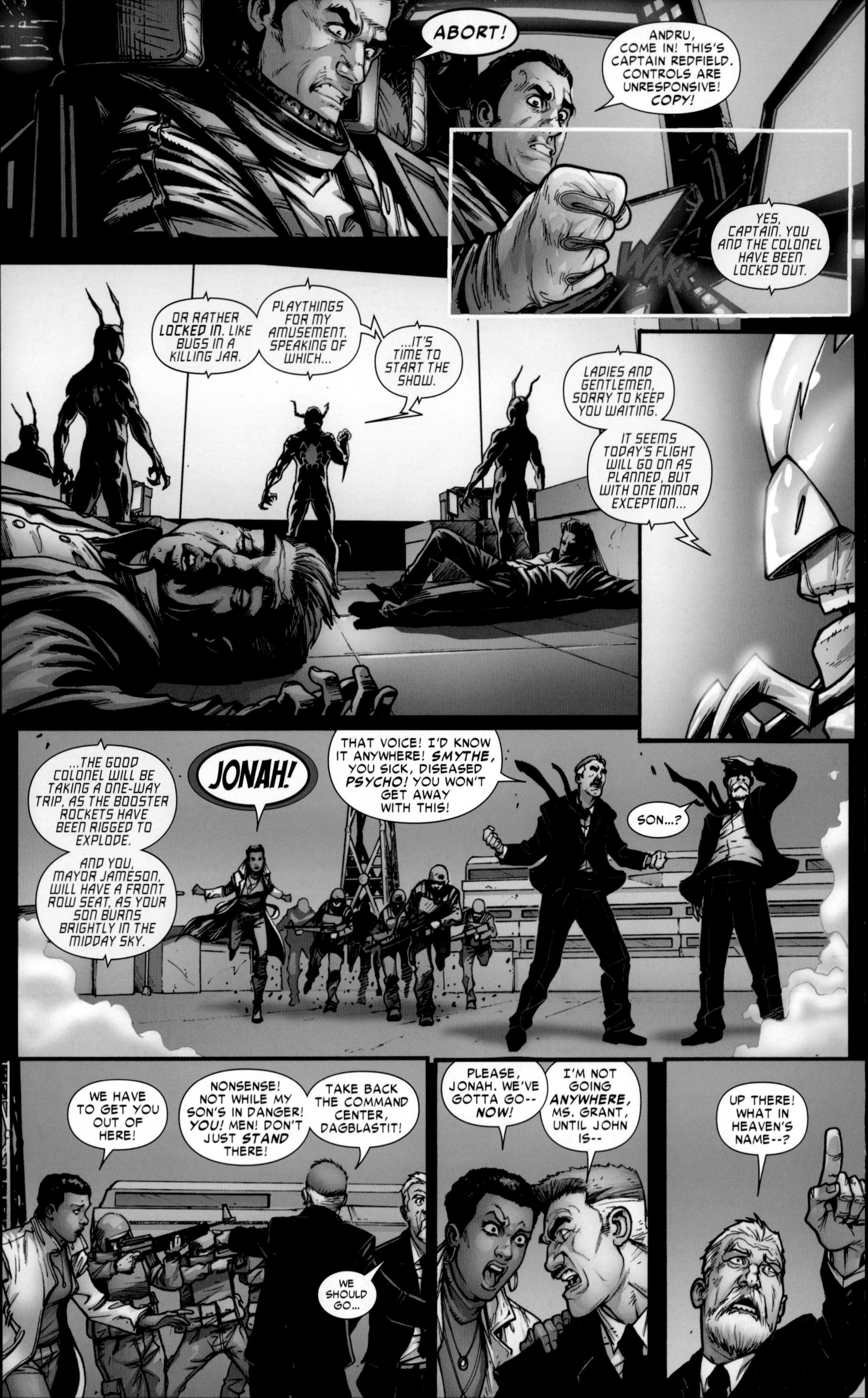
ABORT!
ANDRU, COME IN! THIS'S CAPTAIN REDFIELD. CONTROLS ARE UNRESPONSIVE! COPY!
WAKK
YES, CAPTAIN. YOU AND THE COLONEL HAVE BEEN LOCKED OUT.
OR RATHER LOCKED IN. LIKE BUGS IN A KILLING JAR.
PLAYTHINGS FOR MY AMUSEMENT. SPEAKING OF WHICH...
...IT'S TIME TO START THE SHOW.
LADIES AND GENTLEMEN, SORRY TO KEEP YOU WAITING.
IT SEEMS TODAY'S FLIGHT WILL GO ON AS PLANNED, BUT WITH ONE MINOR EXCEPTION...
...THE GOOD COLONEL WILL BE TAKING A ONE-WAY TRIP, AS THE BOOSTER ROCKETS HAVE BEEN RIGGED TO EXPLODE.
AND YOU, MAYOR JAMESON, WILL HAVE A FRONT ROW SEAT, AS YOUR SON BURNS BRIGHTLY IN THE MIDDAY SKY.
JONAH!
THAT VOICE! I'D KNOW IT ANYWHERE! SMYTHE, YOU SICK, DISEASED PSYCHO! YOU WON'T GET AWAY WITH THIS!
SON...?
WE HAVE TO GET YOU OUT OF HERE!
NONSENSE! NOT WHILE MY SON'S IN DANGER! YOU! MEN! DON'T JUST STAND THERE!
TAKE BACK THE COMMAND CENTER, DAGBLASTIT!
WE SHOULD GO...
PLEASE, JONAH. WE'VE GOTTA GO-- NOW!
I'M NOT GOING ANYWHERE, MS. GRANT, UNTIL JOHN IS--
UP THERE! WHAT IN HEAVEN'S NAME--?

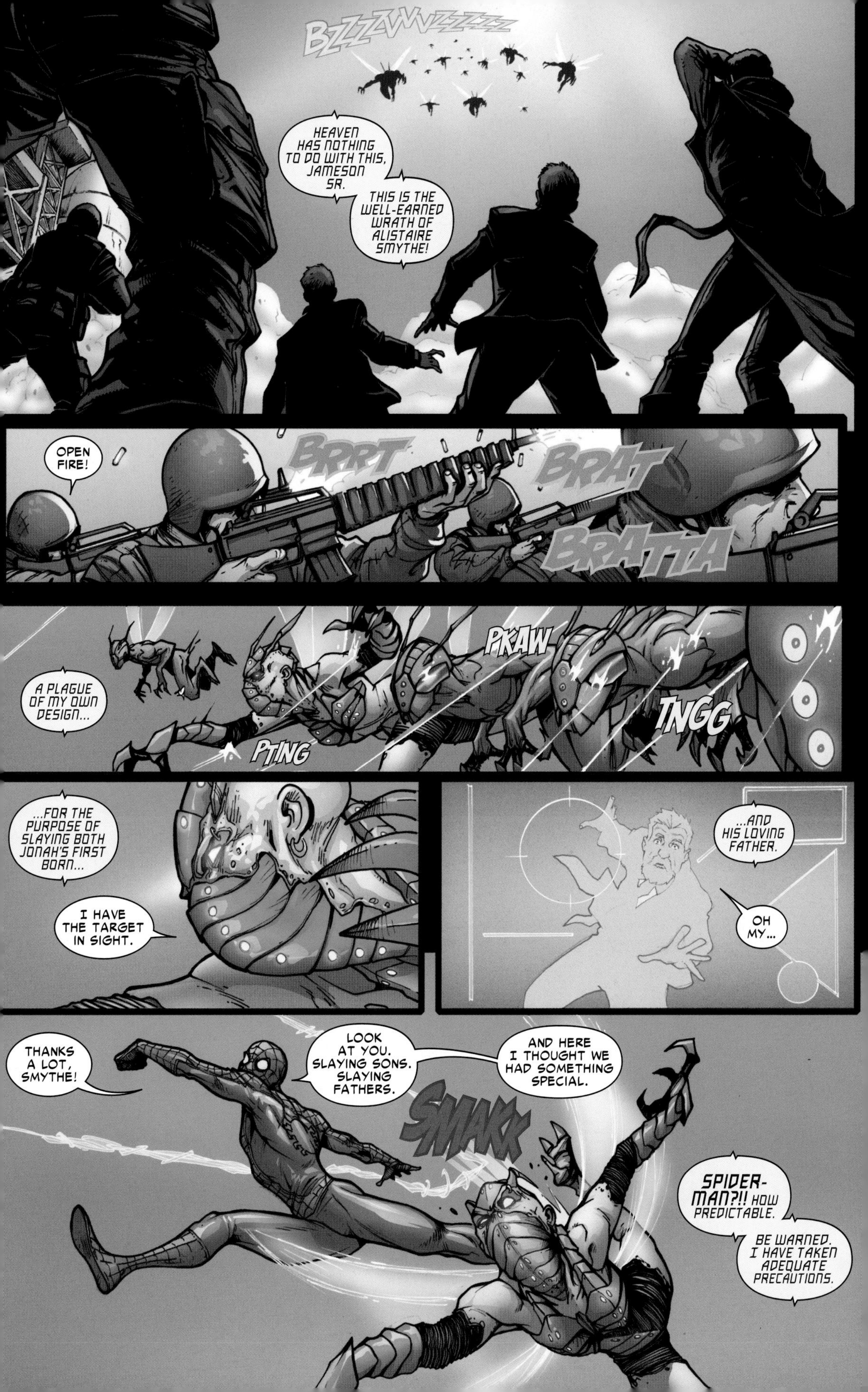
BZZZVVVZZZZZ
HEAVEN HAS NOTHING TO DO WITH THIS, JAMESON SR.
THIS IS THE WELL-EARNED WRATH OF ALISTAIRE SMYTHE!
OPEN FIRE!
BRRT
BRAT
BRATTA
A PLAGUE OF MY OWN DESIGN...
PKAW
TNGG
PTING
...FOR THE PURPOSE OF SLAYING BOTH JONAH'S FIRST BORN...
I HAVE THE TARGET IN SIGHT.
...AND HIS LOVING FATHER.
OH MY...
THANKS A LOT, SMYTHE!
LOOK AT YOU. SLAYING SONS. SLAYING FATHERS.
AND HERE I THOUGHT WE HAD SOMETHING SPECIAL.
SMAKK
SPIDER-MAN?!! HOW PREDICTABLE.
BE WARNED. I HAVE TAKEN ADEQUATE PRECAUTIONS.

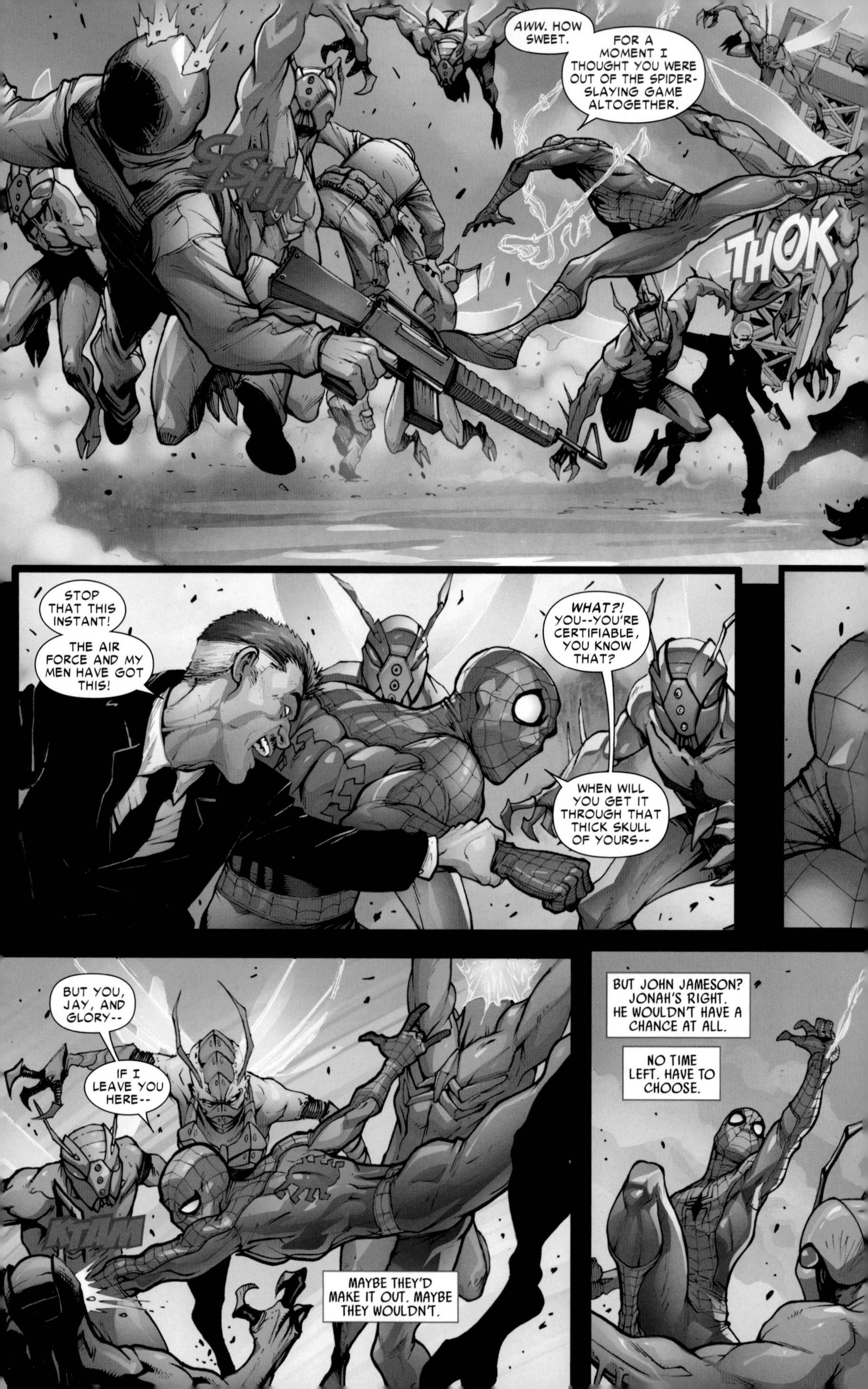
AWW. HOW SWEET.
FOR A MOMENT I THOUGHT YOU WERE OUT OF THE SPIDER-SLAYING GAME ALTOGETHER.
SISHH
THOK
STOP THAT THIS INSTANT!
THE AIR FORCE AND MY MEN HAVE GOT THIS!
WHAT?! YOU--YOU'RE CERTIFIABLE, YOU KNOW THAT?
WHEN WILL YOU GET IT THROUGH THAT THICK SKULL OF YOURS--
BUT YOU, JAY, AND GLORY--
IF I LEAVE YOU HERE--
KTAM
MAYBE THEY'D MAKE IT OUT. MAYBE THEY WOULDN'T.
BUT JOHN JAMESON? JONAH'S RIGHT. HE WOULDN'T HAVE A CHANCE AT ALL.
NO TIME LEFT. HAVE TO CHOOSE.

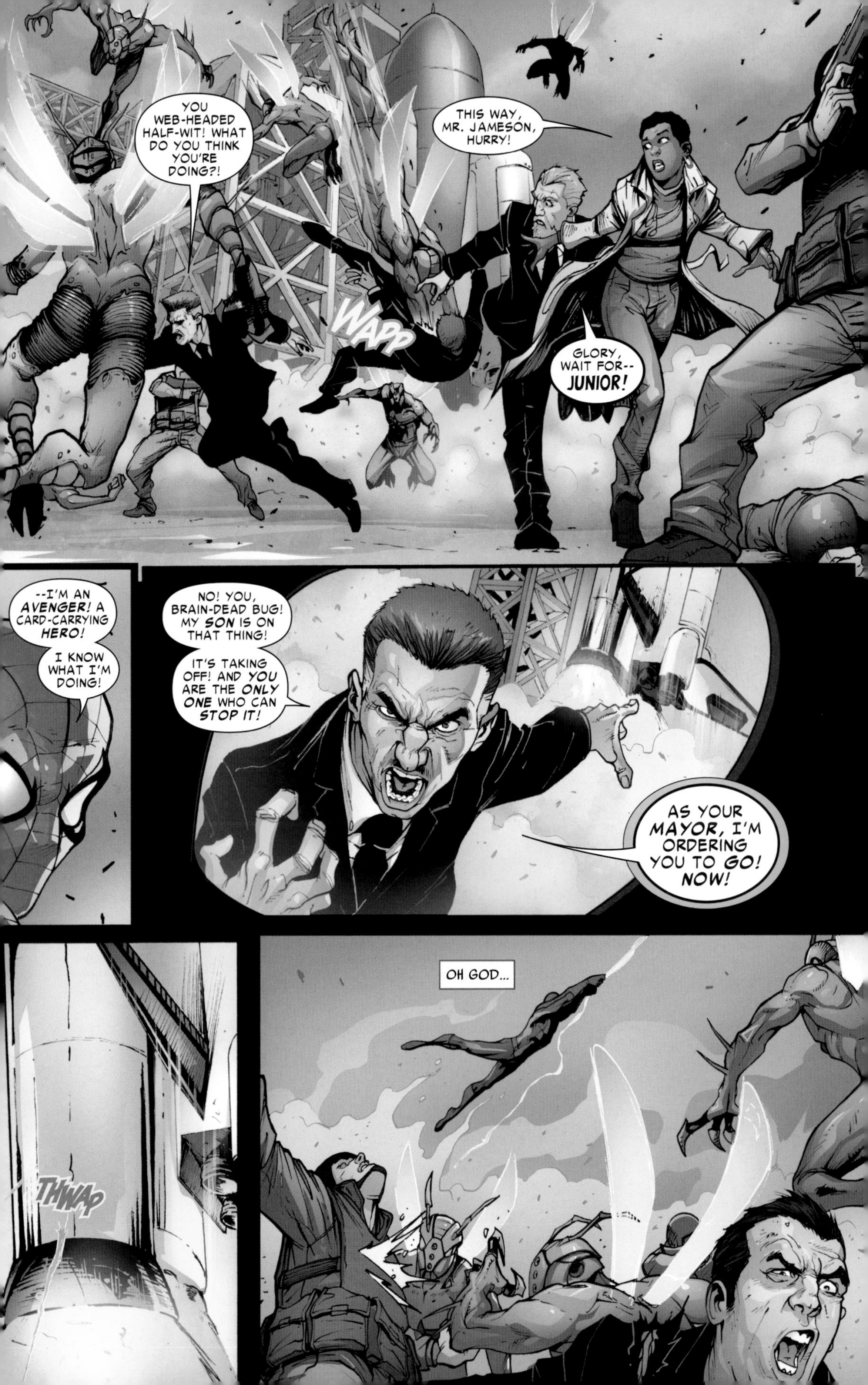
YOU WEB-HEADED HALF-WIT! WHAT DO YOU THINK YOU'RE DOING?!
THIS WAY, MR. JAMESON, HURRY!
WAPP
GLORY, WAIT FOR-- JUNIOR!
--I'M AN AVENGER! A CARD-CARRYING HERO!
I KNOW WHAT I'M DOING!
NO! YOU, BRAIN-DEAD BUG! MY SON IS ON THAT THING!
IT'S TAKING OFF! AND YOU ARE THE ONLY ONE WHO CAN STOP IT!
AS YOUR MAYOR, I'M ORDERING YOU TO GO! NOW!
THWAP
OH GOD...

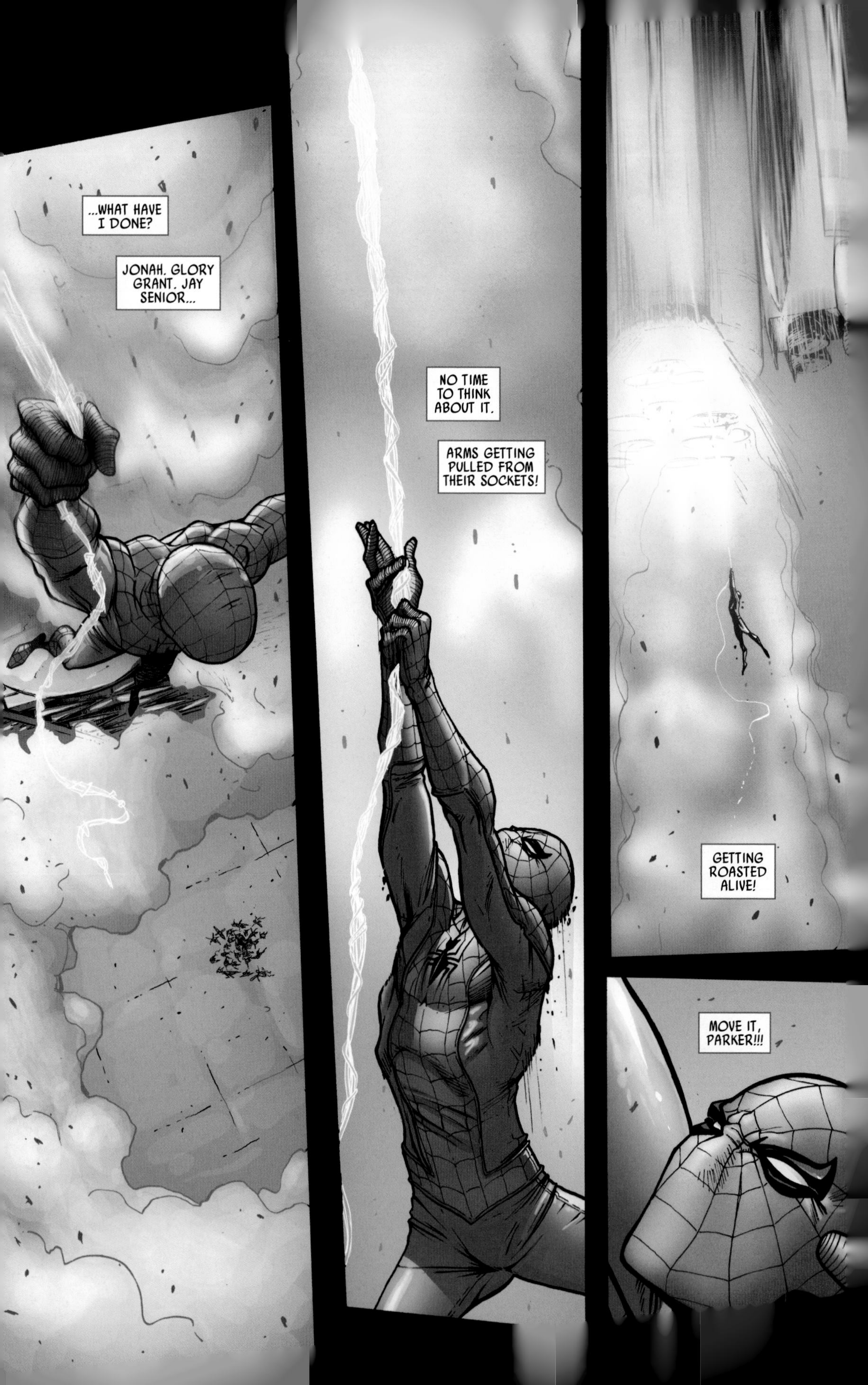
...WHAT HAVE I DONE?
JONAH, GLORY GRANT, JAY SENIOR...
NO TIME TO THINK ABOUT IT.
ARMS GETTING PULLED FROM THEIR SOCKETS!
GETTING ROASTED ALIVE!
MOVE IT, PARKER!!!

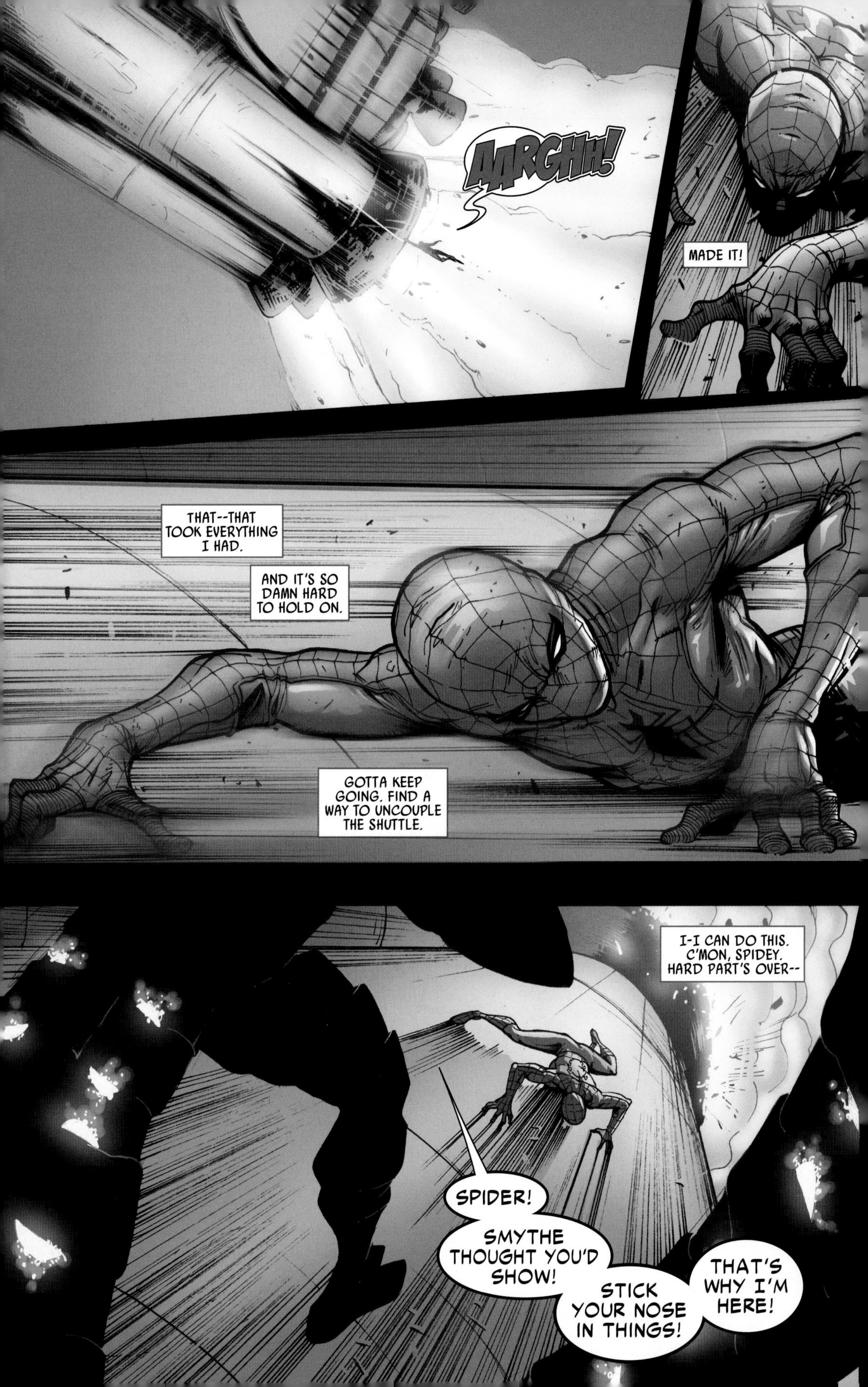
AARGHH!
MADE IT!
THAT--THAT TOOK EVERYTHING I HAD.
AND IT'S SO DAMN HARD TO HOLD ON.
GOTTA KEEP GOING. FIND A WAY TO UNCOUPLE THE SHUTTLE.
I-I CAN DO THIS. C'MON, SPIDEY. HARD PART'S OVER--
SPIDER!
SMYTHE THOUGHT YOU'D SHOW!
STICK YOUR NOSE IN THINGS!
THAT'S WHY I'M HERE!

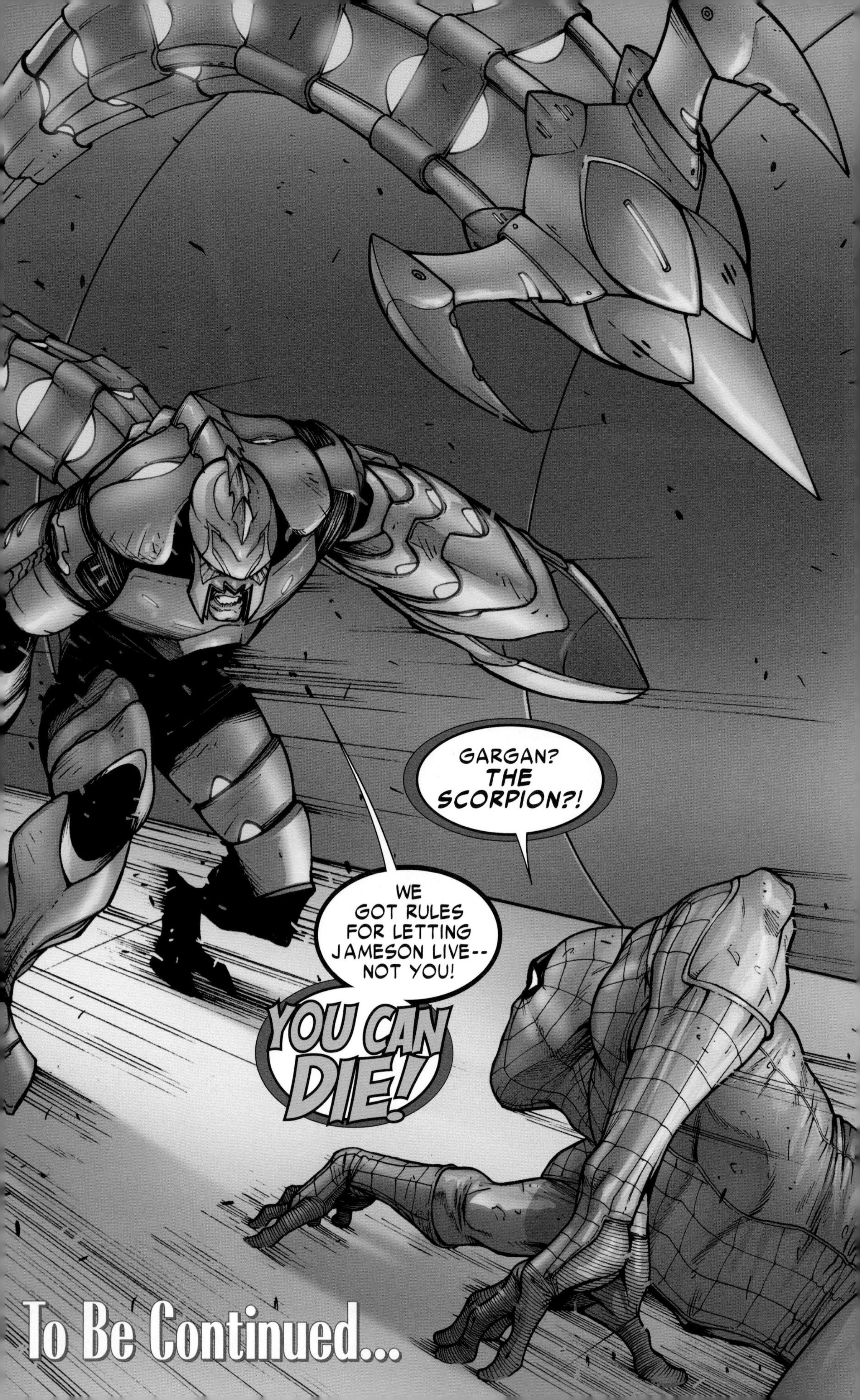
GARGAN? THE SCORPION?!
WE GOT RULES FOR LETTING JAMESON LIVE-- NOT YOU!
YOU CAN DIE!
To Be Continued...

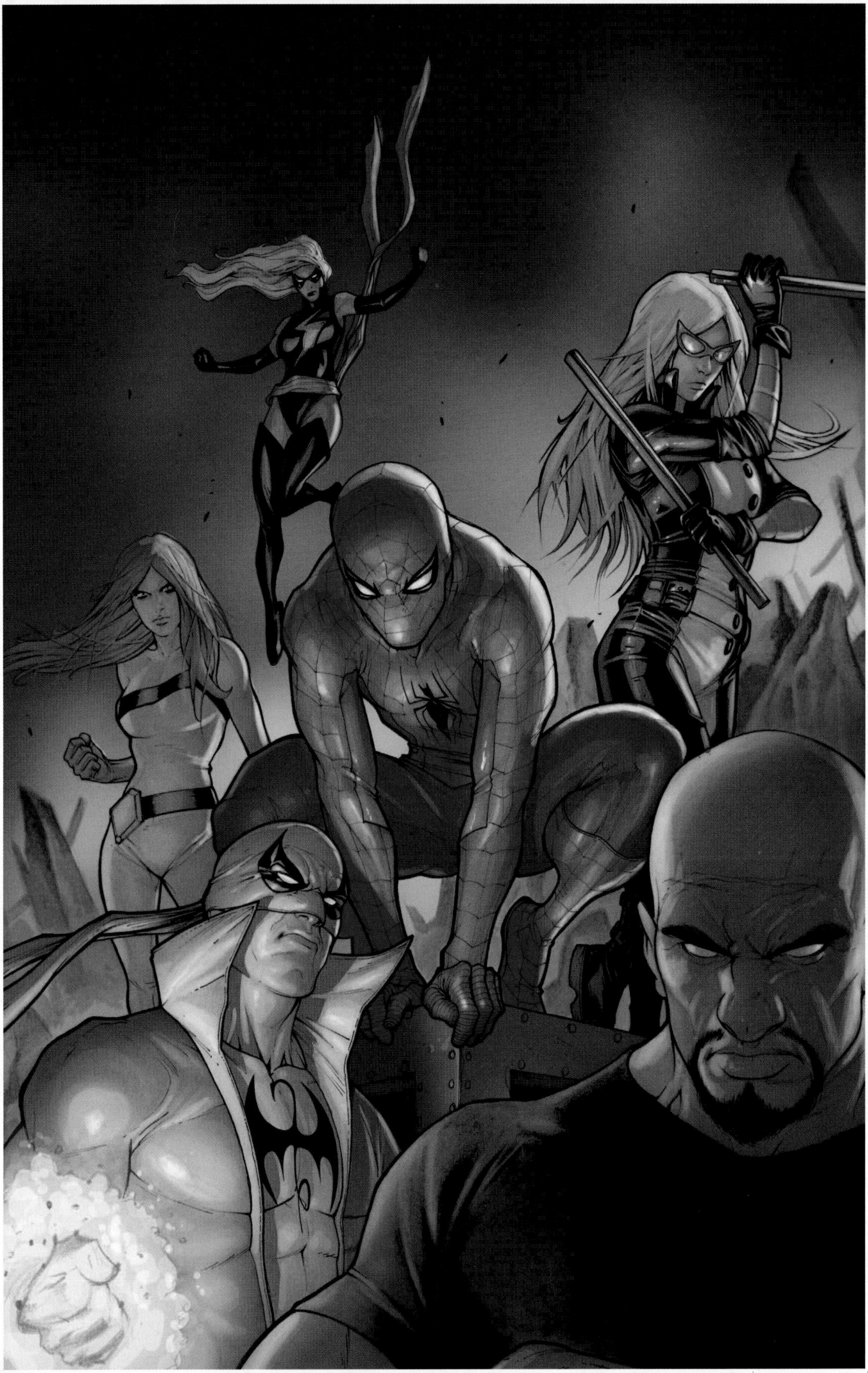

SPIDER-MAN #653
& EDGAR DELGADO

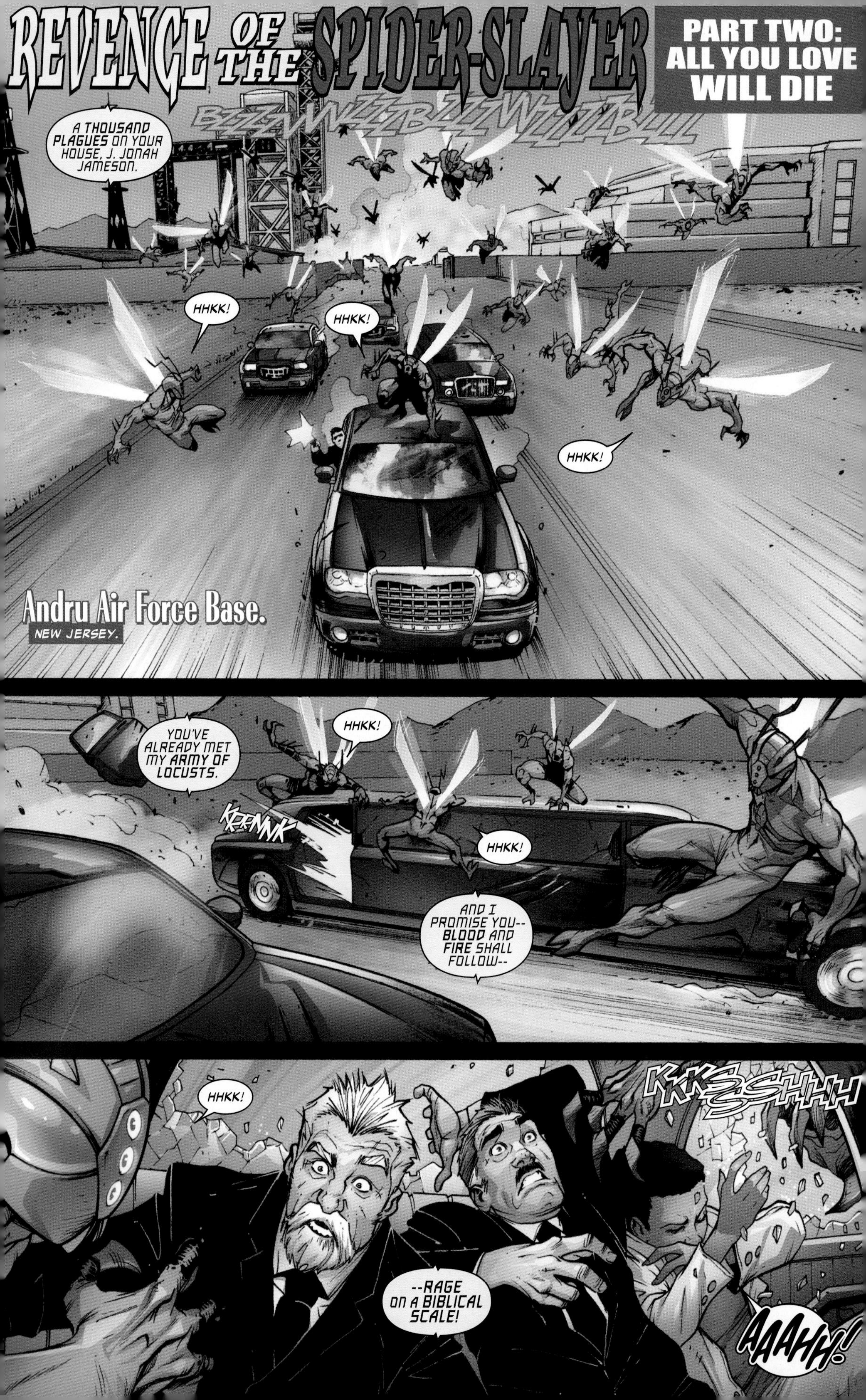
REVENGE OF THE SPIDER-SLAYER
PART TWO: ALL YOU LOVE WILL DIE
BZZZVWZZZBZZZVWZZZBZZZ
A THOUSAND PLAGUES ON YOUR HOUSE, J. JONAH JAMESON.
HHKK!
HHKK!
HHKK!
Andru Air Force Base.
NEW JERSEY.
YOU'VE ALREADY MET MY ARMY OF LOCUSTS.
HHKK!
KRRNNK
HHKK!
AND I PROMISE YOU-- BLOOD AND FIRE SHALL FOLLOW--
HHKK!
KKKSSHHH
--RAGE ON A BIBLICAL SCALE!
AAAHH!

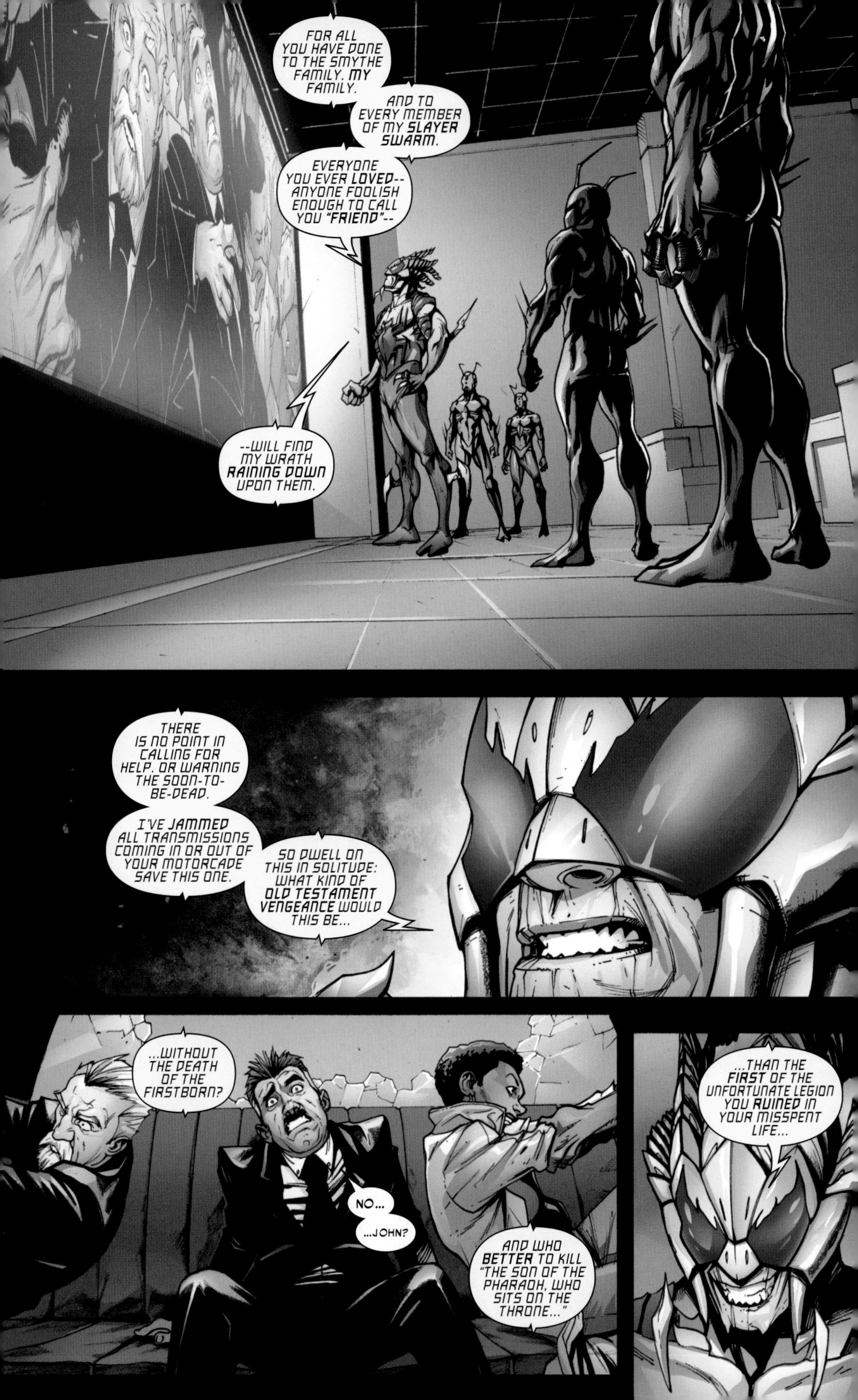
FOR ALL YOU HAVE DONE TO THE SMYTHE FAMILY. MY FAMILY.
AND TO EVERY MEMBER OF MY SLAYER SWARM.
EVERYONE YOU EVER LOVED-- ANYONE FOOLISH ENOUGH TO CALL YOU "FRIEND"--
--WILL FIND MY WRATH RAINING DOWN UPON THEM.
THERE IS NO POINT IN CALLING FOR HELP. OR WARNING THE SOON-TO-BE-DEAD.
I'VE JAMMED ALL TRANSMISSIONS COMING IN OR OUT OF YOUR MOTORCADE SAVE THIS ONE.
SO DWELL ON THIS IN SOLITUDE: WHAT KIND OF OLD TESTAMENT VENGEANCE WOULD THIS BE...
...WITHOUT THE DEATH OF THE FIRSTBORN?
NO...
...JOHN?
AND WHO BETTER TO KILL "THE SON OF THE PHARAOH, WHO SITS ON THE THRONE..."
...THAN THE FIRST OF THE UNFORTUNATE LEGION YOU RUINED IN YOUR MISSPENT LIFE...

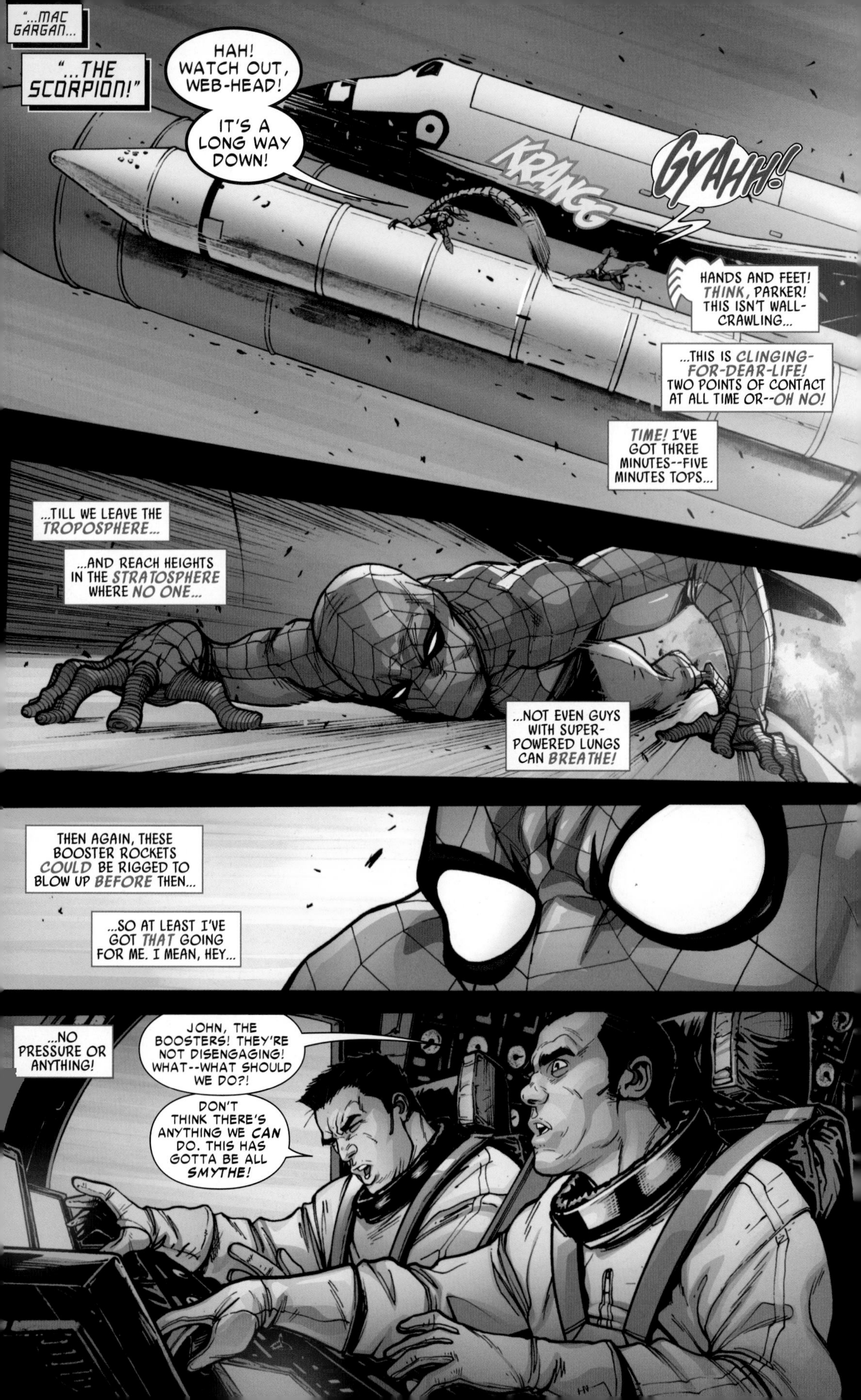
"...MAC GARGAN...
"...THE SCORPION!"
HAH! WATCH OUT, WEB-HEAD!
IT'S A LONG WAY DOWN!
KRANGG
GYAHH!
HANDS AND FEET! THINK, PARKER! THIS ISN'T WALL-CRAWLING...
...THIS IS CLINGING-FOR-DEAR-LIFE! TWO POINTS OF CONTACT AT ALL TIME OR--OH NO!
TIME! I'VE GOT THREE MINUTES--FIVE MINUTES TOPS...
...TILL WE LEAVE THE TROPOSPHERE...
...AND REACH HEIGHTS IN THE STRATOSPHERE WHERE NO ONE...
...NOT EVEN GUYS WITH SUPER-POWERED LUNGS CAN BREATHE!
THEN AGAIN, THESE BOOSTER ROCKETS COULD BE RIGGED TO BLOW UP BEFORE THEN...
...SO AT LEAST I'VE GOT THAT GOING FOR ME. I MEAN, HEY...
...NO PRESSURE OR ANYTHING!
JOHN, THE BOOSTERS! THEY'RE NOT DISENGAGING! WHAT--WHAT SHOULD WE DO?!
DON'T THINK THERE'S ANYTHING WE CAN DO. THIS HAS GOTTA BE ALL SMYTHE!

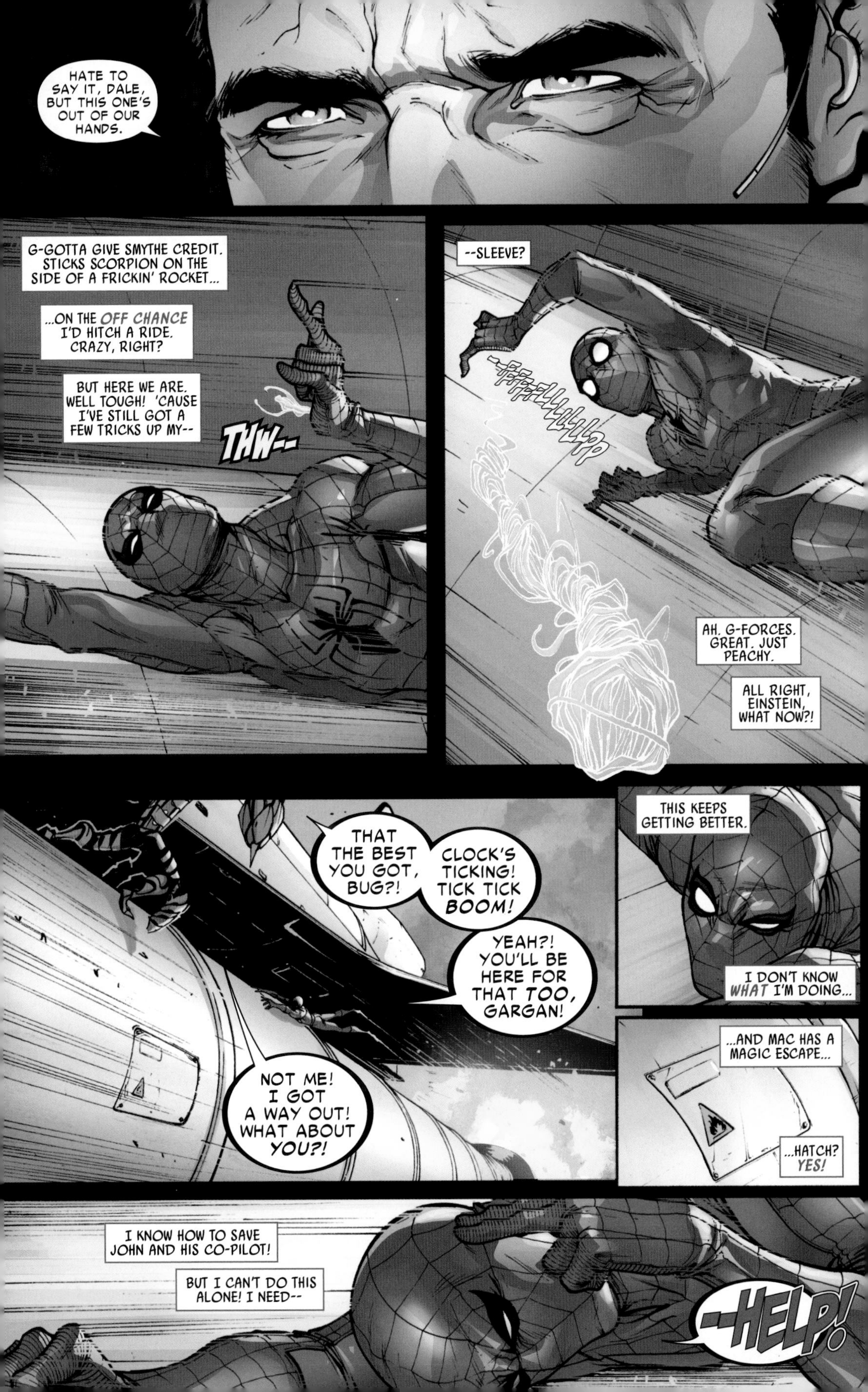
HATE TO SAY IT, DALE, BUT THIS ONE'S OUT OF OUR HANDS.
G-GOTTA GIVE SMYTHE CREDIT. STICKS SCORPION ON THE SIDE OF A FRICKIN' ROCKET...
...ON THE OFF CHANCE I'D HITCH A RIDE. CRAZY, RIGHT?
BUT HERE WE ARE. WELL TOUGH! 'CAUSE I'VE STILL GOT A FEW TRICKS UP MY--
THW--
--SLEEVE?
FFFFLLLLLP
AH. G-FORCES. GREAT. JUST PEACHY.
ALL RIGHT, EINSTEIN, WHAT NOW?!
THAT THE BEST YOU GOT, BUG?!
CLOCK'S TICKING! TICK TICK BOOM!
YEAH?! YOU'LL BE HERE FOR THAT TOO, GARGAN!
NOT ME! I GOT A WAY OUT! WHAT ABOUT YOU?!
THIS KEEPS GETTING BETTER.
I DON'T KNOW WHAT I'M DOING...
...AND MAC HAS A MAGIC ESCAPE...
...HATCH? YES!
I KNOW HOW TO SAVE JOHN AND HIS CO-PILOT!
BUT I CAN'T DO THIS ALONE! I NEED--
--HELP!

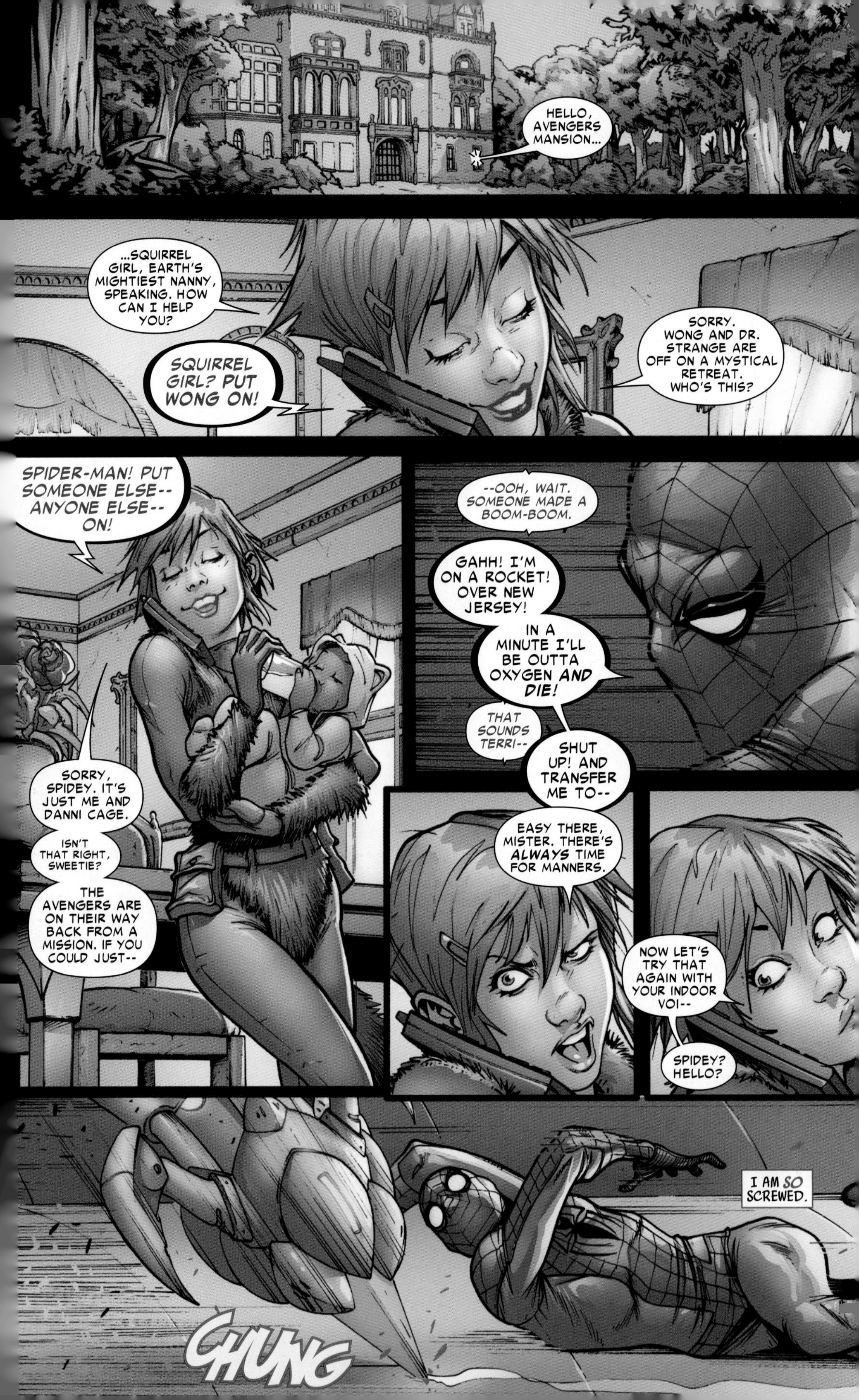

HELLO, AVENGERS MANSION...
...SQUIRREL GIRL, EARTH'S MIGHTIEST NANNY, SPEAKING. HOW CAN I HELP YOU?
SQUIRREL GIRL? PUT WONG ON!
SORRY. WONG AND DR. STRANGE ARE OFF ON A MYSTICAL RETREAT. WHO'S THIS?
SPIDER-MAN! PUT SOMEONE ELSE-- ANYONE ELSE-- ON!
SORRY, SPIDEY. IT'S JUST ME AND DANNI CAGE.
ISN'T THAT RIGHT, SWEETIE?
THE AVENGERS ARE ON THEIR WAY BACK FROM A MISSION. IF YOU COULD JUST--
--OOH, WAIT. SOMEONE MADE A BOOM-BOOM.
GAHH! I'M ON A ROCKET! OVER NEW JERSEY!
IN A MINUTE I'LL BE OUTTA OXYGEN AND DIE!
THAT SOUNDS TERRI--
SHUT UP! AND TRANSFER ME TO--
EASY THERE, MISTER. THERE'S ALWAYS TIME FOR MANNERS.
NOW LET'S TRY THAT AGAIN WITH YOUR INDOOR VOI--
SPIDEY? HELLO?
I AM SO SCREWED.
CHUNG

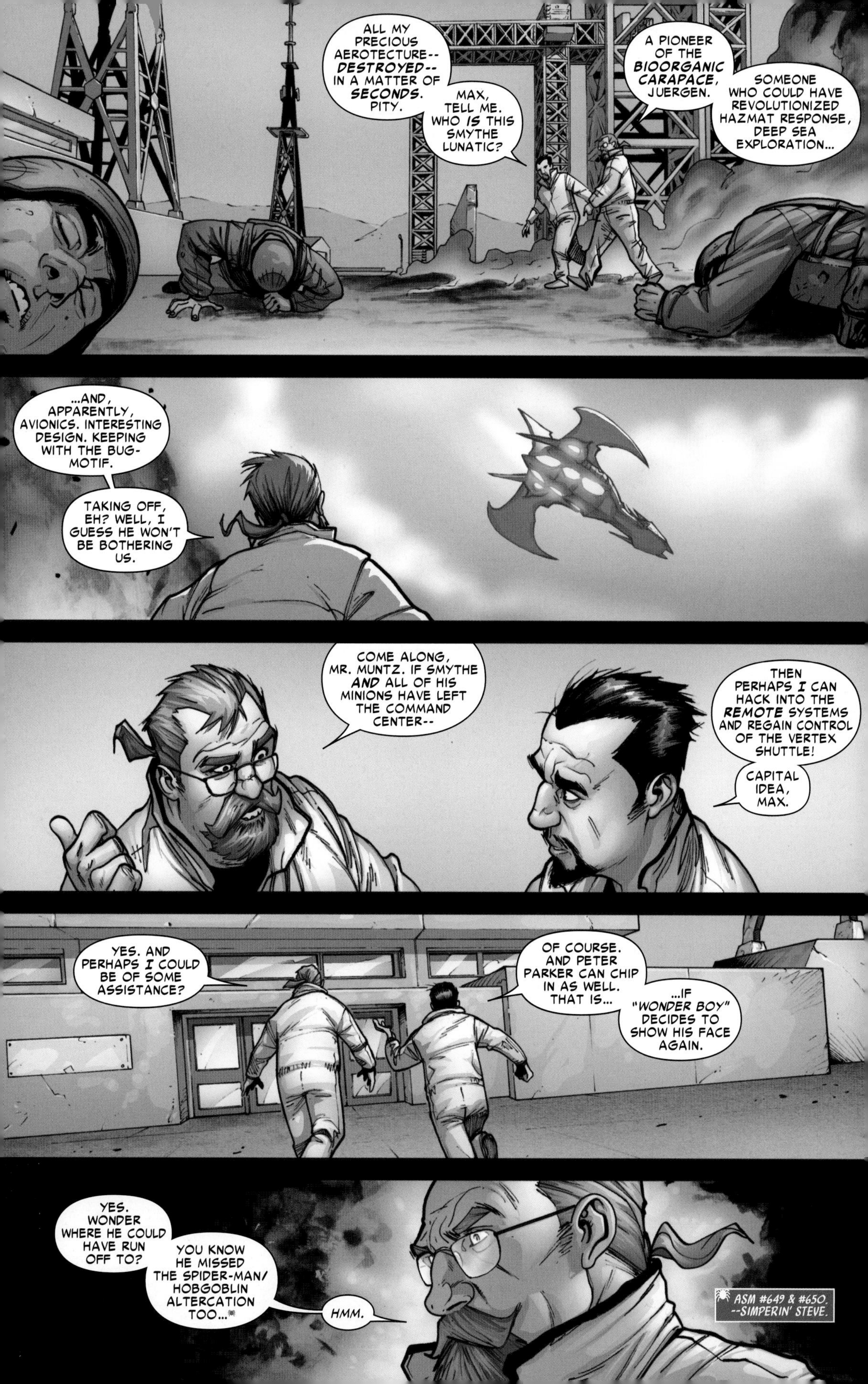
ALL MY PRECIOUS AEROTECTURE-- DESTROYED-- IN A MATTER OF SECONDS. PITY.
MAX, TELL ME. WHO IS THIS SMYTHE LUNATIC?
A PIONEER OF THE BIOORGANIC CARAPACE, JUERGEN.
SOMEONE WHO COULD HAVE REVOLUTIONIZED HAZMAT RESPONSE, DEEP SEA EXPLORATION...
...AND, APPARENTLY, AVIONICS. INTERESTING DESIGN. KEEPING WITH THE BUG-MOTIF.
TAKING OFF, EH? WELL, I GUESS HE WON'T BE BOTHERING US.
COME ALONG, MR. MUNTZ. IF SMYTHE AND ALL OF HIS MINIONS HAVE LEFT THE COMMAND CENTER--
THEN PERHAPS I CAN HACK INTO THE REMOTE SYSTEMS AND REGAIN CONTROL OF THE VERTEX SHUTTLE!
CAPITAL IDEA, MAX.
YES. AND PERHAPS I COULD BE OF SOME ASSISTANCE?
OF COURSE. AND PETER PARKER CAN CHIP IN AS WELL. THAT IS...
...IF "WONDER BOY" DECIDES TO SHOW HIS FACE AGAIN.
YES. WONDER WHERE HE COULD HAVE RUN OFF TO?
YOU KNOW HE MISSED THE SPIDER-MAN/HOBGOBLIN ALTERCATION TOO...
HMM.
ASM #649 & #650. --SIMPERIN' STEVE.

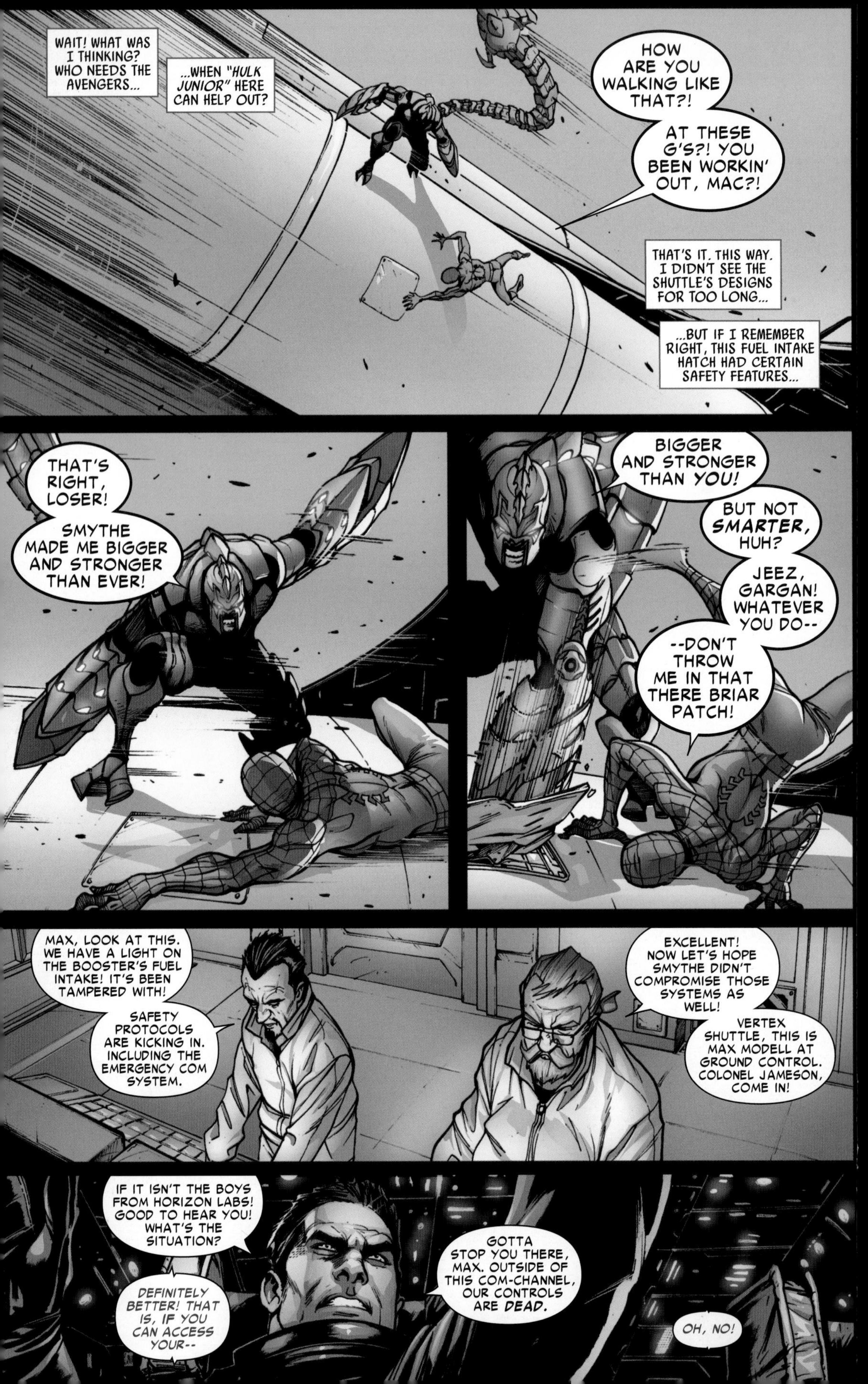
WAIT! WHAT WAS I THINKING? WHO NEEDS THE AVENGERS...
...WHEN "HULK JUNIOR" HERE CAN HELP OUT?
HOW ARE YOU WALKING LIKE THAT?!
AT THESE G'S?! YOU BEEN WORKIN' OUT, MAC?!
THAT'S IT. THIS WAY. I DIDN'T SEE THE SHUTTLE'S DESIGNS FOR TOO LONG...
...BUT IF I REMEMBER RIGHT, THIS FUEL INTAKE HATCH HAD CERTAIN SAFETY FEATURES...
THAT'S RIGHT, LOSER!
SMYTHE MADE ME BIGGER AND STRONGER THAN EVER!
BIGGER AND STRONGER THAN YOU!
BUT NOT SMARTER, HUH?
JEEZ, GARGAN! WHATEVER YOU DO--
--DON'T THROW ME IN THAT THERE BRIAR PATCH!
MAX, LOOK AT THIS. WE HAVE A LIGHT ON THE BOOSTER'S FUEL INTAKE! IT'S BEEN TAMPERED WITH!
SAFETY PROTOCOLS ARE KICKING IN. INCLUDING THE EMERGENCY COM SYSTEM.
EXCELLENT! NOW LET'S HOPE SMYTHE DIDN'T COMPROMISE THOSE SYSTEMS AS WELL!
VERTEX SHUTTLE, THIS IS MAX MODELL AT GROUND CONTROL. COLONEL JAMESON, COME IN!
IF IT ISN'T THE BOYS FROM HORIZON LABS! GOOD TO HEAR YOU! WHAT'S THE SITUATION?
DEFINITELY BETTER! THAT IS, IF YOU CAN ACCESS YOUR--
GOTTA STOP YOU THERE, MAX. OUTSIDE OF THIS COM-CHANNEL, OUR CONTROLS ARE DEAD.
OH, NO!

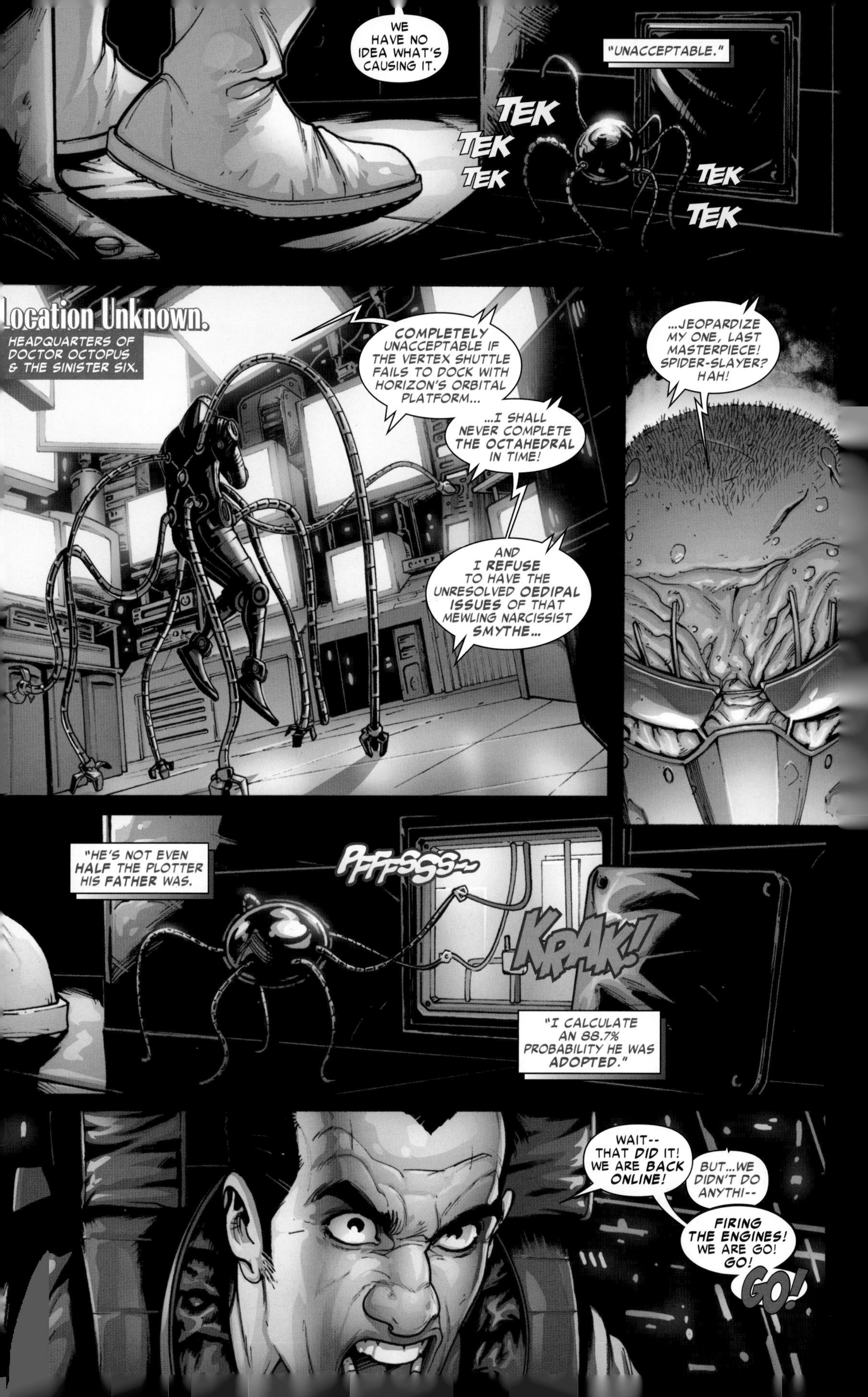

WE HAVE NO IDEA WHAT'S CAUSING IT.
"UNACCEPTABLE."
TEK TEK TEK
TEK TEK
Location Unknown.
HEADQUARTERS OF DOCTOR OCTOPUS & THE SINISTER SIX.
COMPLETELY UNACCEPTABLE IF THE VERTEX SHUTTLE FAILS TO DOCK WITH HORIZON'S ORBITAL PLATFORM...
...I SHALL NEVER COMPLETE THE OCTAHEDRAL IN TIME!
AND I REFUSE TO HAVE THE UNRESOLVED OEDIPAL ISSUES OF THAT MEWLING NARCISSIST SMYTHE...
...JEOPARDIZE MY ONE, LAST MASTERPIECE! SPIDER-SLAYER? HAH!
"HE'S NOT EVEN HALF THE PLOTTER HIS FATHER WAS.
PFFFSSS--
KRAK!
"I CALCULATE AN 88.7% PROBABILITY HE WAS ADOPTED."
WAIT-- THAT DID IT! WE ARE BACK ONLINE!
BUT...WE DIDN'T DO ANYTHI--
FIRING THE ENGINES! WE ARE GO! GO!
GO!

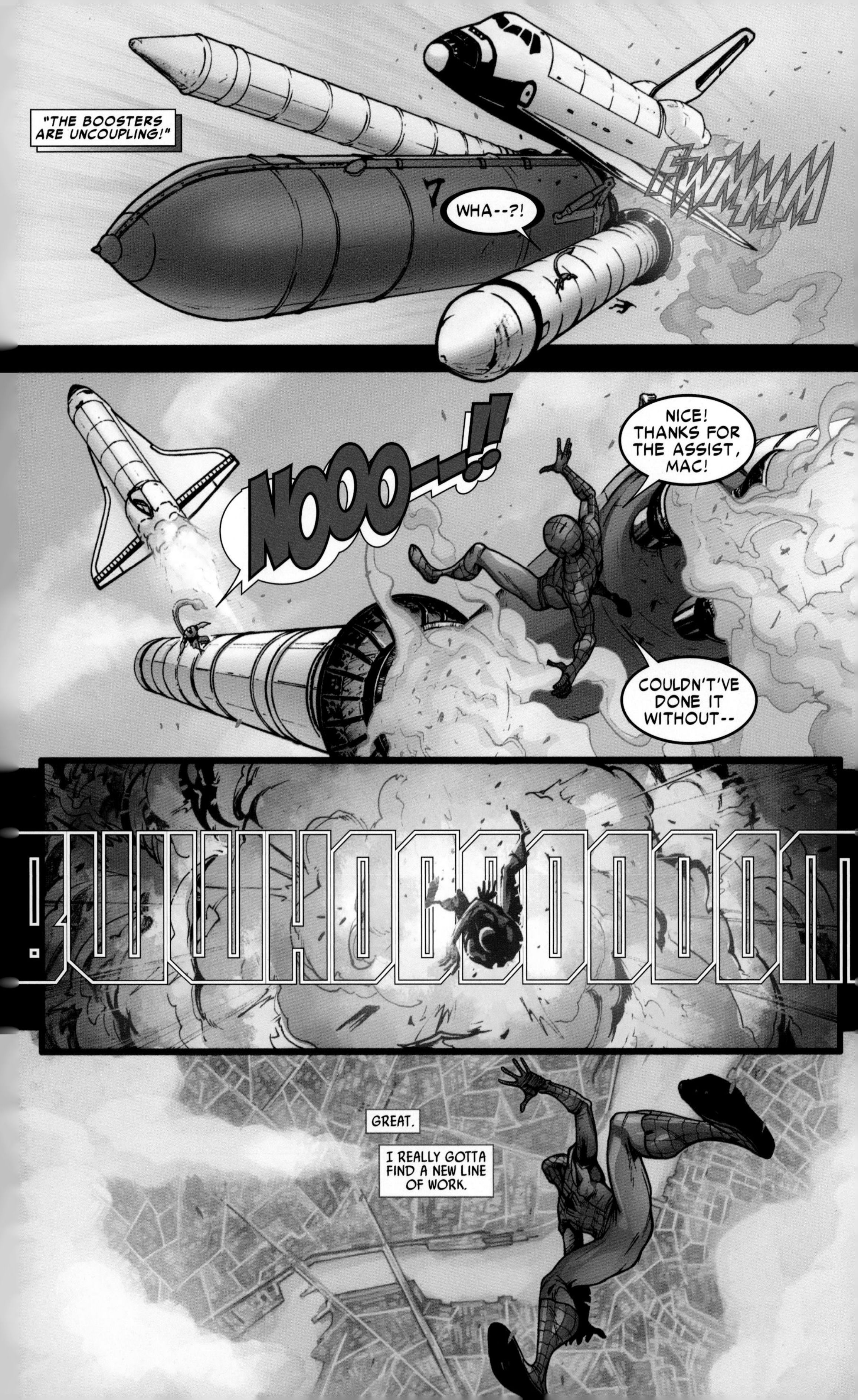
"THE BOOSTERS ARE UNCOUPLING!"
WHA--?!
NOOO--!!
NICE! THANKS FOR THE ASSIST, MAC!
COULDN'T'VE DONE IT WITHOUT--
GREAT.
I REALLY GOTTA FIND A NEW LINE OF WORK.

THIS CAN'T BE HAPPENING!

IT'S NOT--

HOW DID THE ROCKETS--

SPIDER-MAN GOT NOWHERE *NEAR* THE OVERRIDE--

HA HA HAHAHA HA!

MY *SON* DID IT! I *KNOW* HE DID! HE'S ALWAYS BEEN THE *REAL* HERO!

YOU BETTER HOPE YOUR SON CAN BE TWO PLACES AT ONCE, THEN.

"BECAUSE MY SLAYER SWARM WILL BE."

"THEY ARE WATCHING YOUR LOVED ONES..."

WHAT DO YOU THINK, MAY? SHOULD WE SPRING FOR THE HOT ROCKS?

I'M LETTING YOU GUIDE ME, MARLA--

--BUT THAT SOUNDS MORE LIKE A *TORTURE TECHNIQUE* THAN A *MASSAGE* TO ME...

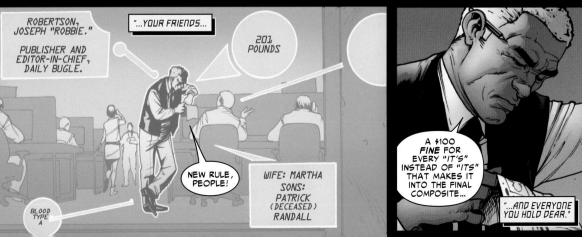

ROBERTSON, JOSEPH "ROBBIE."

PUBLISHER AND EDITOR-IN-CHIEF, DAILY BUGLE.

"...YOUR FRIENDS..."

201 POUNDS

NEW RULE, PEOPLE!

WIFE: MARTHA
SONS:
PATRICK (DECEASED)
RANDALL

BLOOD TYPE A

A $100 *FINE* FOR EVERY "IT'S" INSTEAD OF "ITS" THAT MAKES IT INTO THE FINAL COMPOSITE...

"...AND EVERYONE YOU HOLD DEAR."

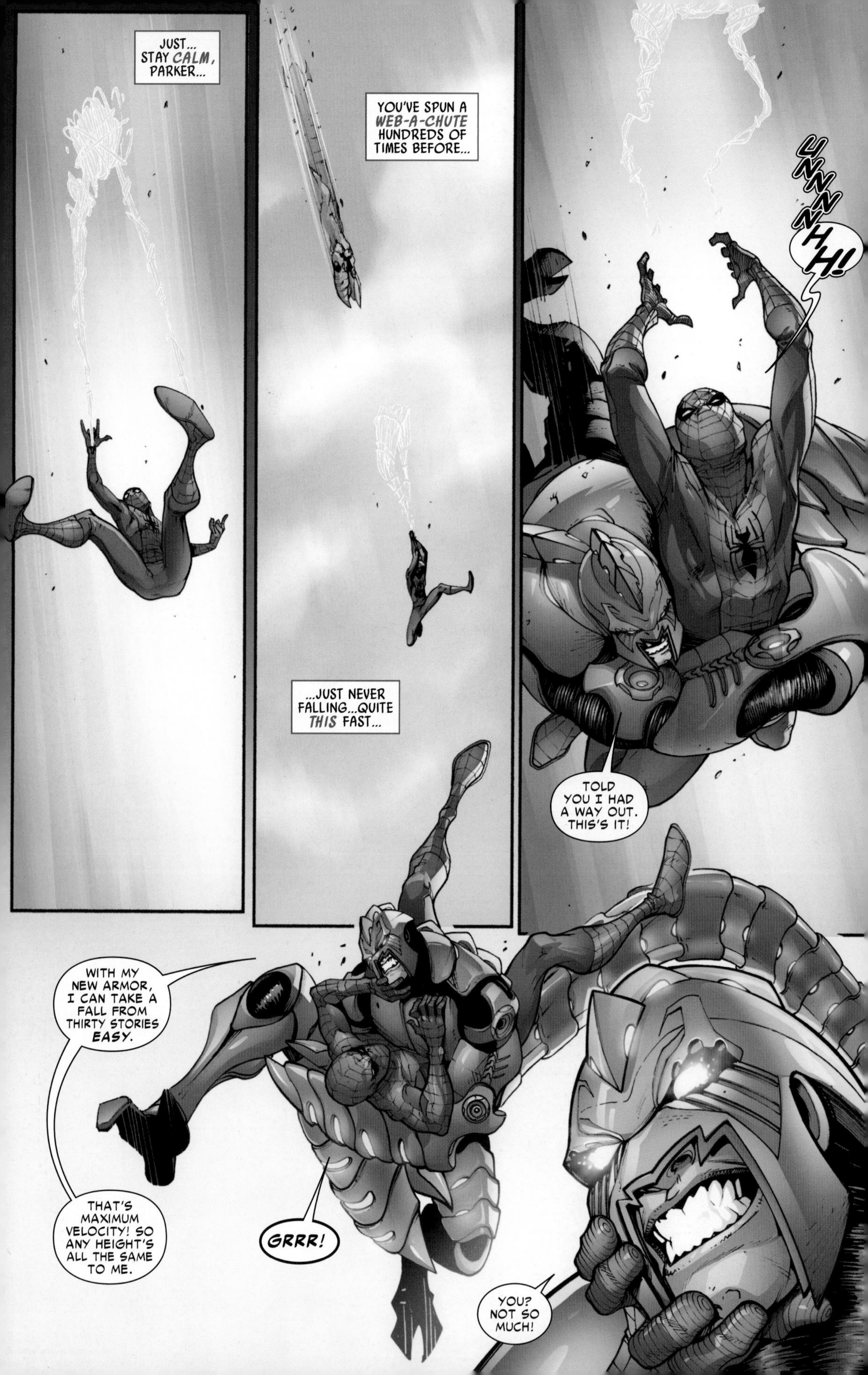
JUST... STAY CALM, PARKER...
YOU'VE SPUN A WEB-A-CHUTE HUNDREDS OF TIMES BEFORE...
...JUST NEVER FALLING...QUITE THIS FAST...
UNNNNHH!
TOLD YOU I HAD A WAY OUT. THIS'S IT!
WITH MY NEW ARMOR, I CAN TAKE A FALL FROM THIRTY STORIES EASY.
THAT'S MAXIMUM VELOCITY! SO ANY HEIGHT'S ALL THE SAME TO ME.
GRRR!
YOU? NOT SO MUCH!

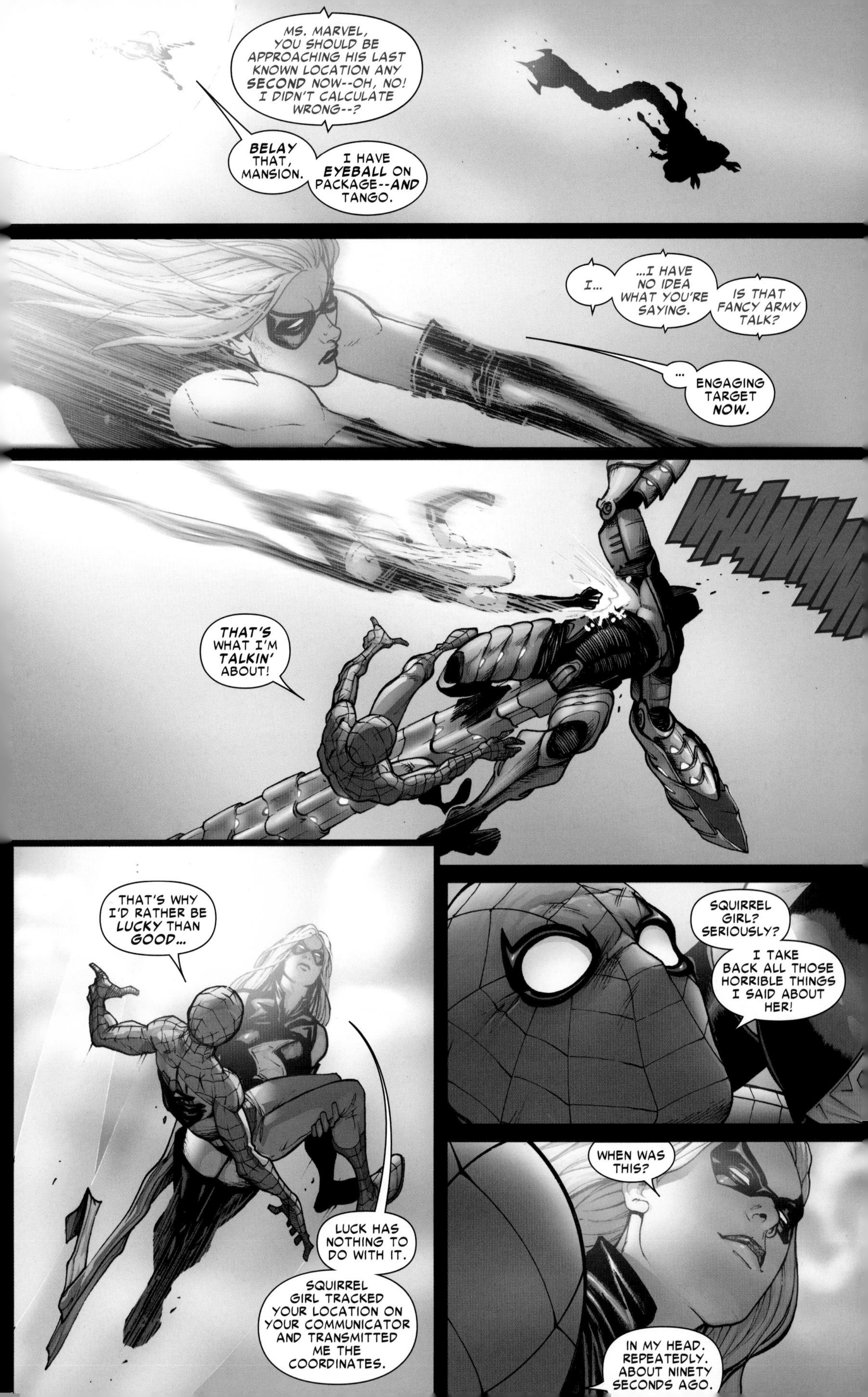
MS. MARVEL, YOU SHOULD BE APPROACHING HIS LAST KNOWN LOCATION ANY SECOND NOW--OH, NO! I DIDN'T CALCULATE WRONG--?
BELAY THAT, MANSION.
I HAVE EYEBALL ON PACKAGE--AND TANGO.
I...
...I HAVE NO IDEA WHAT YOU'RE SAYING.
IS THAT FANCY ARMY TALK?
... ENGAGING TARGET NOW.
THAT'S WHAT I'M TALKIN' ABOUT!
THAT'S WHY I'D RATHER BE LUCKY THAN GOOD...
LUCK HAS NOTHING TO DO WITH IT.
SQUIRREL GIRL TRACKED YOUR LOCATION ON YOUR COMMUNICATOR AND TRANSMITTED ME THE COORDINATES.
SQUIRREL GIRL? SERIOUSLY?
I TAKE BACK ALL THOSE HORRIBLE THINGS I SAID ABOUT HER!
WHEN WAS THIS?
IN MY HEAD. REPEATEDLY. ABOUT NINETY SECONDS AGO.

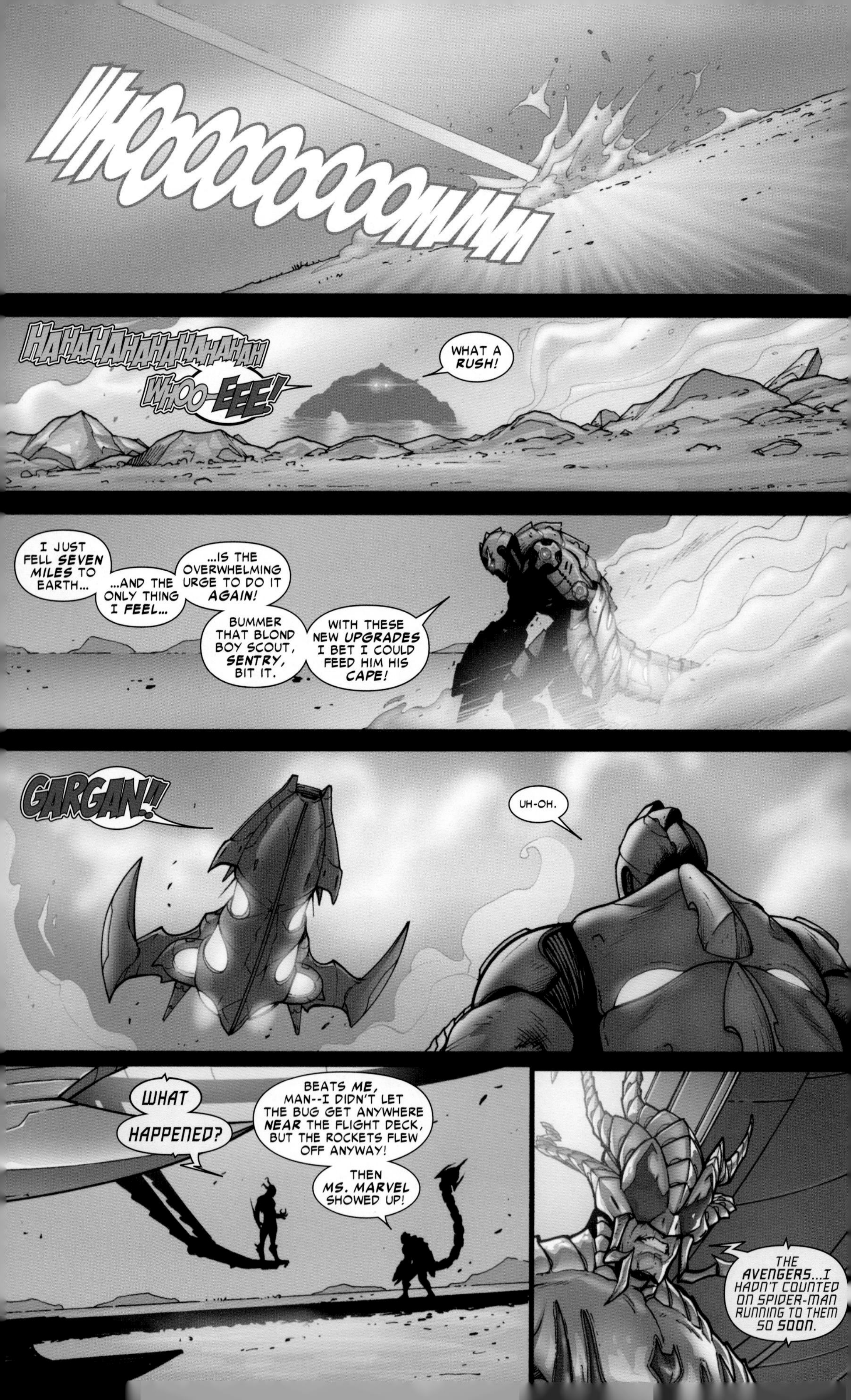
WHOOOOOOOOOOMMM
HAHAHAHAHAHAHAHAH
WHOO-EEE!
WHAT A RUSH!
I JUST FELL SEVEN MILES TO EARTH...
...AND THE ONLY THING I FEEL...
...IS THE OVERWHELMING URGE TO DO IT AGAIN!
BUMMER THAT BLOND BOY SCOUT, SENTRY, BIT IT.
WITH THESE NEW UPGRADES I BET I COULD FEED HIM HIS CAPE!
GARGAN!!
UH-OH.
WHAT HAPPENED?
BEATS ME, MAN--I DIDN'T LET THE BUG GET ANYWHERE NEAR THE FLIGHT DECK, BUT THE ROCKETS FLEW OFF ANYWAY!
THEN MS. MARVEL SHOWED UP!
THE AVENGERS...I HADN'T COUNTED ON SPIDER-MAN RUNNING TO THEM SO SOON.

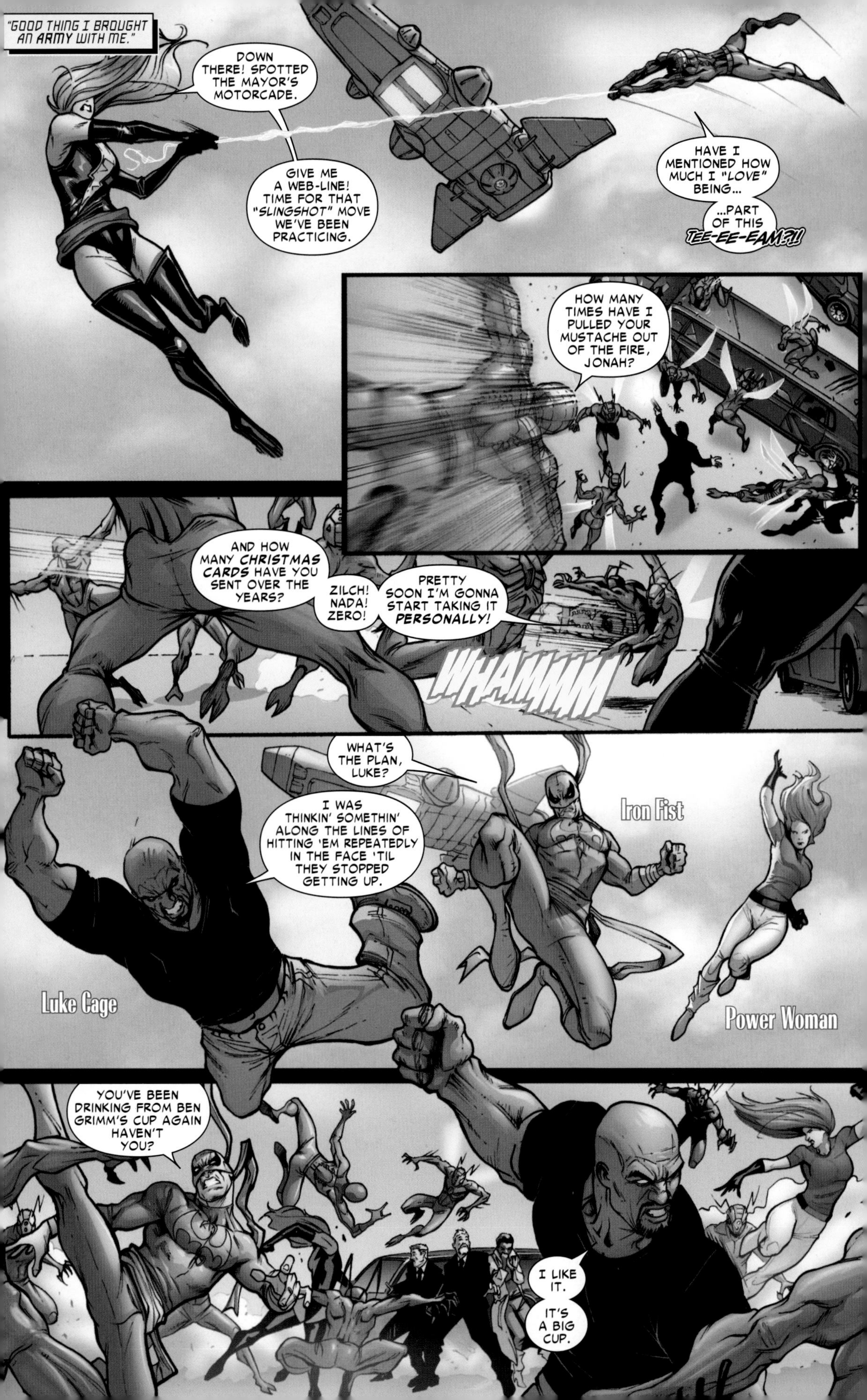
"GOOD THING I BROUGHT AN ARMY WITH ME."
DOWN THERE! SPOTTED THE MAYOR'S MOTORCADE.
GIVE ME A WEB-LINE! TIME FOR THAT "SLINGSHOT" MOVE WE'VE BEEN PRACTICING.
HAVE I MENTIONED HOW MUCH I "LOVE" BEING...
...PART OF THIS TEE-EE-EAM?!!
HOW MANY TIMES HAVE I PULLED YOUR MUSTACHE OUT OF THE FIRE, JONAH?
AND HOW MANY CHRISTMAS CARDS HAVE YOU SENT OVER THE YEARS?
ZILCH! NADA! ZERO!
PRETTY SOON I'M GONNA START TAKING IT PERSONALLY!
WHAMMMM
WHAT'S THE PLAN, LUKE?
I WAS THINKIN' SOMETHIN' ALONG THE LINES OF HITTING 'EM REPEATEDLY IN THE FACE 'TIL THEY STOPPED GETTING UP.
Iron Fist
Luke Cage
Power Woman
YOU'VE BEEN DRINKING FROM BEN GRIMM'S CUP AGAIN HAVEN'T YOU?
I LIKE IT.
IT'S A BIG CUP.

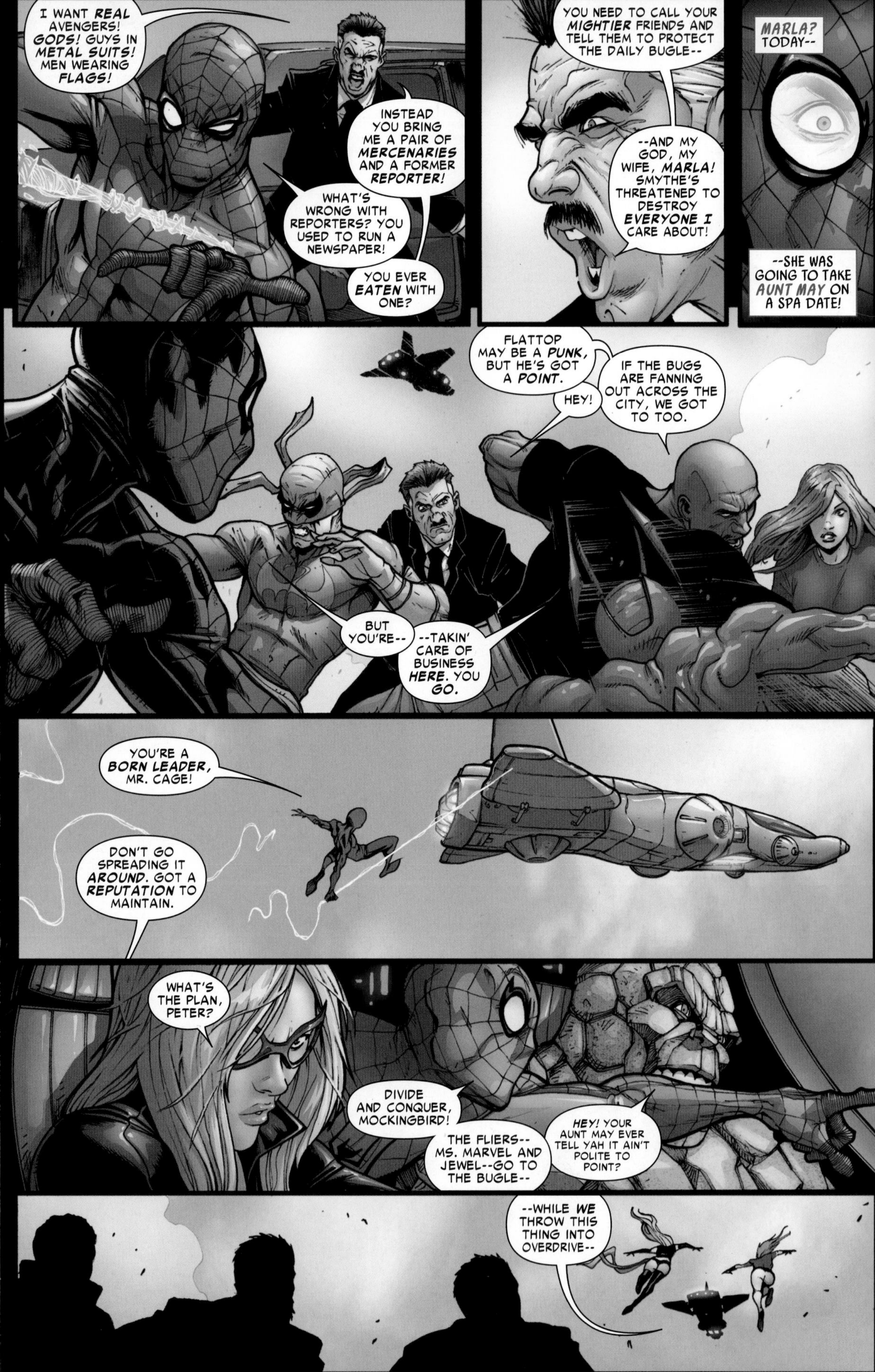
I WANT REAL AVENGERS! GODS! GUYS IN METAL SUITS! MEN WEARING FLAGS!
INSTEAD YOU BRING ME A PAIR OF MERCENARIES AND A FORMER REPORTER!
WHAT'S WRONG WITH REPORTERS? YOU USED TO RUN A NEWSPAPER!
YOU EVER EATEN WITH ONE?
YOU NEED TO CALL YOUR MIGHTIER FRIENDS AND TELL THEM TO PROTECT THE DAILY BUGLE--
--AND MY GOD, MY WIFE, MARLA! SMYTHE'S THREATENED TO DESTROY EVERYONE I CARE ABOUT!
MARLA? TODAY--
--SHE WAS GOING TO TAKE AUNT MAY ON A SPA DATE!
FLATTOP MAY BE A PUNK, BUT HE'S GOT A POINT.
HEY!
IF THE BUGS ARE FANNING OUT ACROSS THE CITY, WE GOT TO TOO.
BUT YOU'RE--
--TAKIN' CARE OF BUSINESS HERE. YOU GO.
YOU'RE A BORN LEADER, MR. CAGE!
DON'T GO SPREADING IT AROUND. GOT A REPUTATION TO MAINTAIN.
WHAT'S THE PLAN, PETER?
DIVIDE AND CONQUER, MOCKINGBIRD!
THE FLIERS-- MS. MARVEL AND JEWEL--GO TO THE BUGLE--
HEY! YOUR AUNT MAY EVER TELL YAH IT AIN'T POLITE TO POINT?
--WHILE WE THROW THIS THING INTO OVERDRIVE--

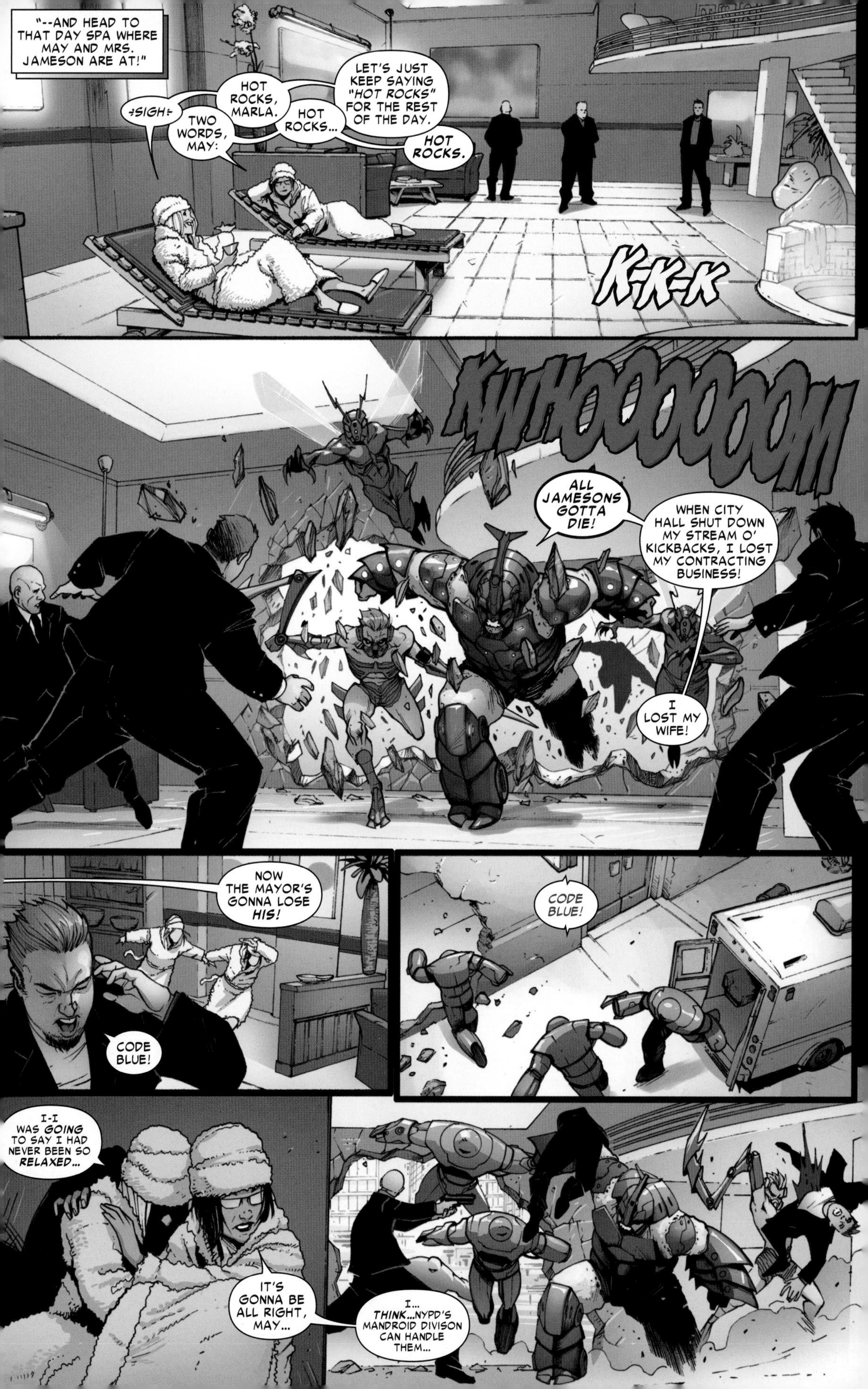
"--AND HEAD TO THAT DAY SPA WHERE MAY AND MRS. JAMESON ARE AT!"
≈SIGH≈
TWO WORDS, MAY:
HOT ROCKS, MARLA.
HOT ROCKS...
LET'S JUST KEEP SAYING "HOT ROCKS" FOR THE REST OF THE DAY.
HOT ROCKS.
K-K-K
KWHOOOOOOOM
ALL JAMESONS GOTTA DIE!
WHEN CITY HALL SHUT DOWN MY STREAM O' KICKBACKS, I LOST MY CONTRACTING BUSINESS!
I LOST MY WIFE!
NOW THE MAYOR'S GONNA LOSE HIS!
CODE BLUE!
CODE BLUE!
I-I WAS GOING TO SAY I HAD NEVER BEEN SO RELAXED...
IT'S GONNA BE ALL RIGHT, MAY...
I... THINK...NYPD'S MANDROID DIVISON CAN HANDLE THEM...

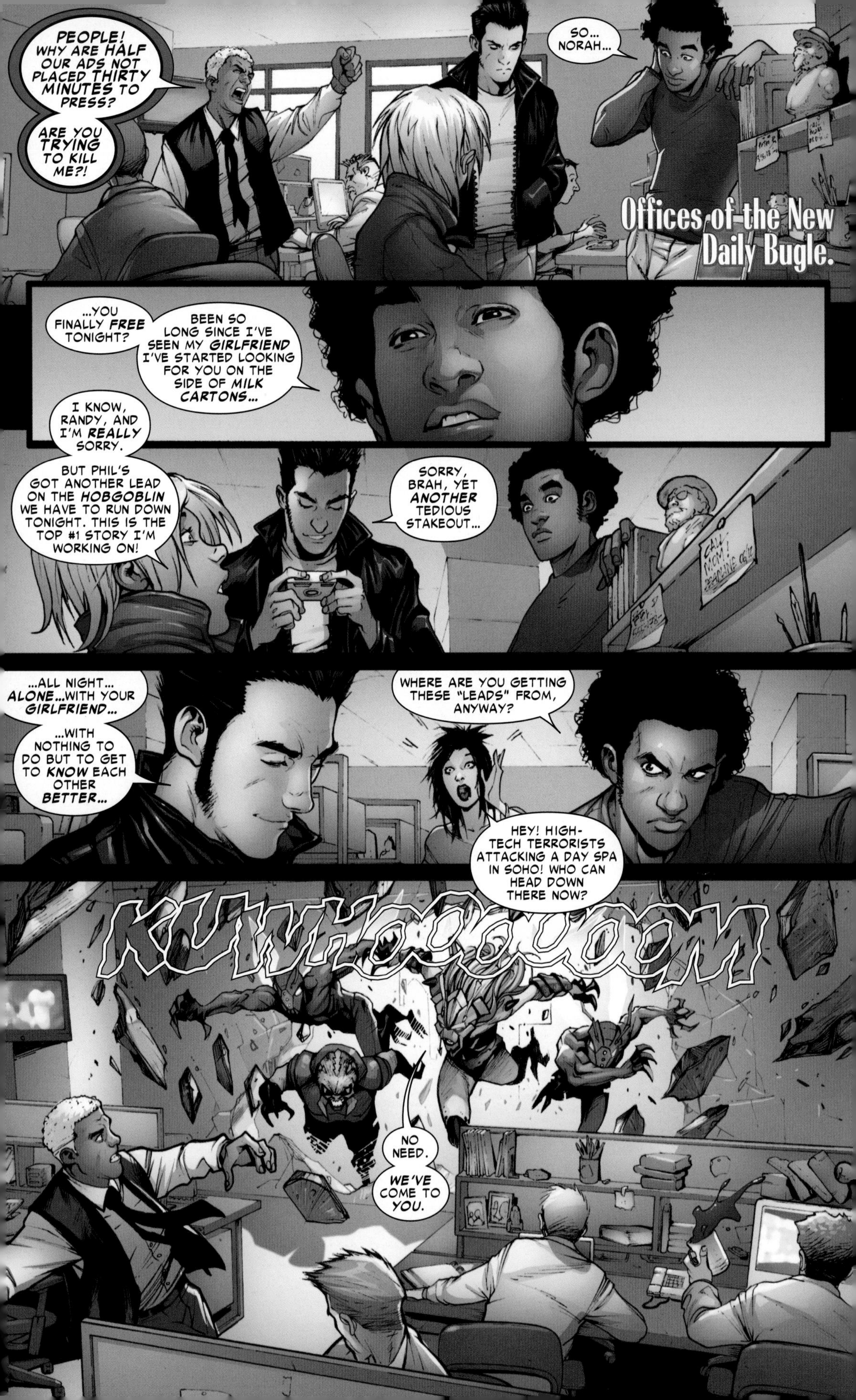
PEOPLE! WHY ARE HALF OUR ADS NOT PLACED THIRTY MINUTES TO PRESS?
ARE YOU TRYING TO KILL ME?!
SO... NORAH...
Offices of the New Daily Bugle.
...YOU FINALLY FREE TONIGHT?
BEEN SO LONG SINCE I'VE SEEN MY GIRLFRIEND I'VE STARTED LOOKING FOR YOU ON THE SIDE OF MILK CARTONS...
I KNOW, RANDY, AND I'M REALLY SORRY.
BUT PHIL'S GOT ANOTHER LEAD ON THE HOBGOBLIN WE HAVE TO RUN DOWN TONIGHT. THIS IS THE TOP #1 STORY I'M WORKING ON!
SORRY, BRAH, YET ANOTHER TEDIOUS STAKEOUT...
...ALL NIGHT... ALONE...WITH YOUR GIRLFRIEND...
...WITH NOTHING TO DO BUT TO GET TO KNOW EACH OTHER BETTER...
WHERE ARE YOU GETTING THESE "LEADS" FROM, ANYWAY?
HEY! HIGH-TECH TERRORISTS ATTACKING A DAY SPA IN SOHO! WHO CAN HEAD DOWN THERE NOW?
KUNHOOOOOOM
NO NEED.
WE'VE COME TO YOU.

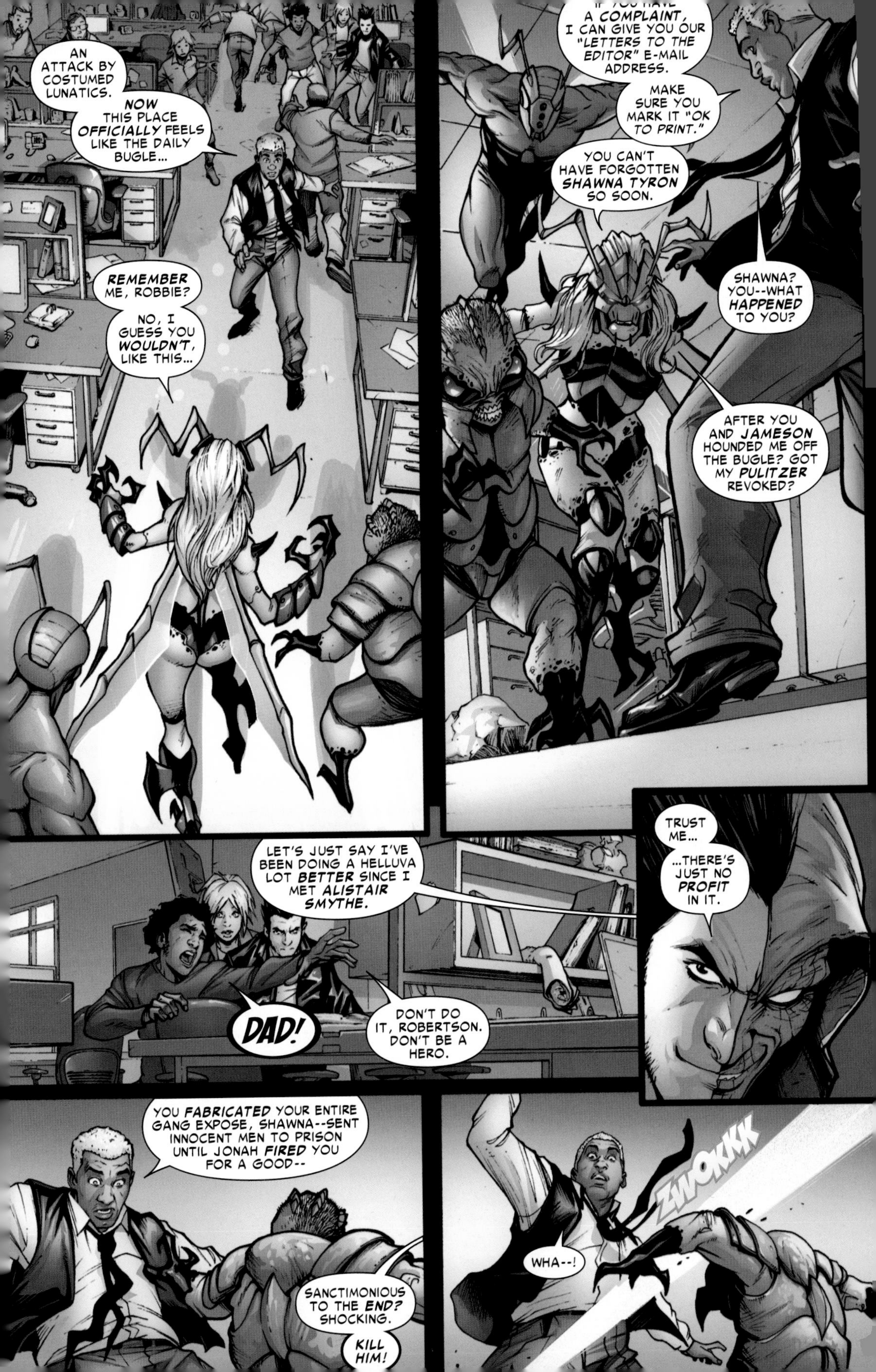
AN ATTACK BY COSTUMED LUNATICS.
NOW THIS PLACE OFFICIALLY FEELS LIKE THE DAILY BUGLE...
REMEMBER ME, ROBBIE?
NO, I GUESS YOU WOULDN'T, LIKE THIS...
IF YOU HAVE A COMPLAINT, I CAN GIVE YOU OUR "LETTERS TO THE EDITOR" E-MAIL ADDRESS.
MAKE SURE YOU MARK IT "OK TO PRINT."
YOU CAN'T HAVE FORGOTTEN SHAWNA TYRON SO SOON.
SHAWNA? YOU--WHAT HAPPENED TO YOU?
AFTER YOU AND JAMESON HOUNDED ME OFF THE BUGLE? GOT MY PULITZER REVOKED?
LET'S JUST SAY I'VE BEEN DOING A HELLUVA LOT BETTER SINCE I MET ALISTAIR SMYTHE.
DAD!
DON'T DO IT, ROBERTSON. DON'T BE A HERO.
TRUST ME...
...THERE'S JUST NO PROFIT IN IT.
YOU FABRICATED YOUR ENTIRE GANG EXPOSE, SHAWNA--SENT INNOCENT MEN TO PRISON UNTIL JONAH FIRED YOU FOR A GOOD--
SANCTIMONIOUS TO THE END? SHOCKING.
KILL HIM!
ZWOKKK
WHA--!

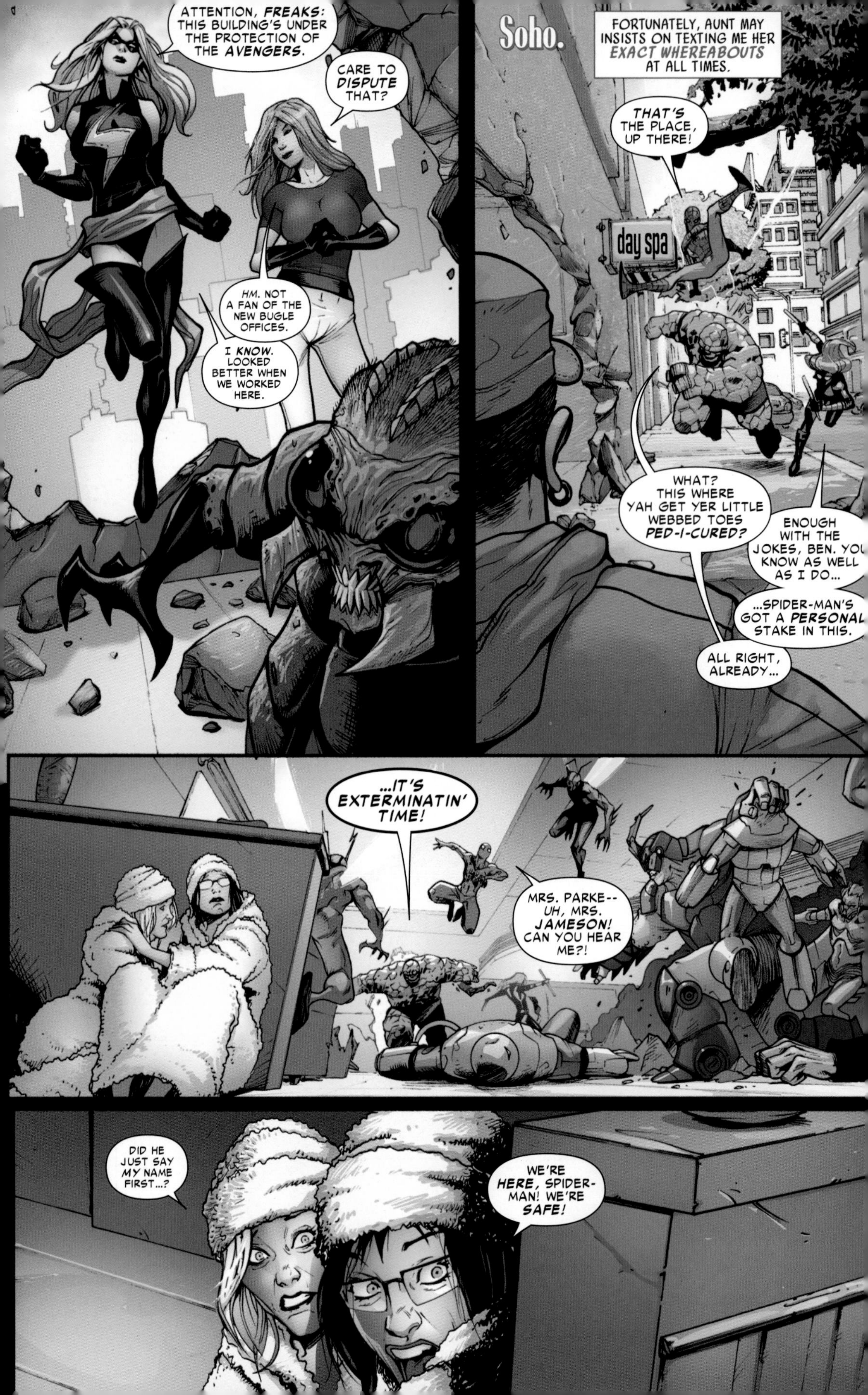
ATTENTION, FREAKS: THIS BUILDING'S UNDER THE PROTECTION OF THE AVENGERS.
CARE TO DISPUTE THAT?
HM. NOT A FAN OF THE NEW BUGLE OFFICES.
I KNOW. LOOKED BETTER WHEN WE WORKED HERE.
Soho.
FORTUNATELY, AUNT MAY INSISTS ON TEXTING ME HER EXACT WHEREABOUTS AT ALL TIMES.
THAT'S THE PLACE, UP THERE!
day spa
WHAT? THIS WHERE YAH GET YER LITTLE WEBBED TOES PED-I-CURED?
ENOUGH WITH THE JOKES, BEN. YOU KNOW AS WELL AS I DO...
...SPIDER-MAN'S GOT A PERSONAL STAKE IN THIS.
ALL RIGHT, ALREADY...
...IT'S EXTERMINATIN' TIME!
MRS. PARKE-- UH, MRS. JAMESON! CAN YOU HEAR ME?!
DID HE JUST SAY MY NAME FIRST...?
WE'RE HERE, SPIDER-MAN! WE'RE SAFE!

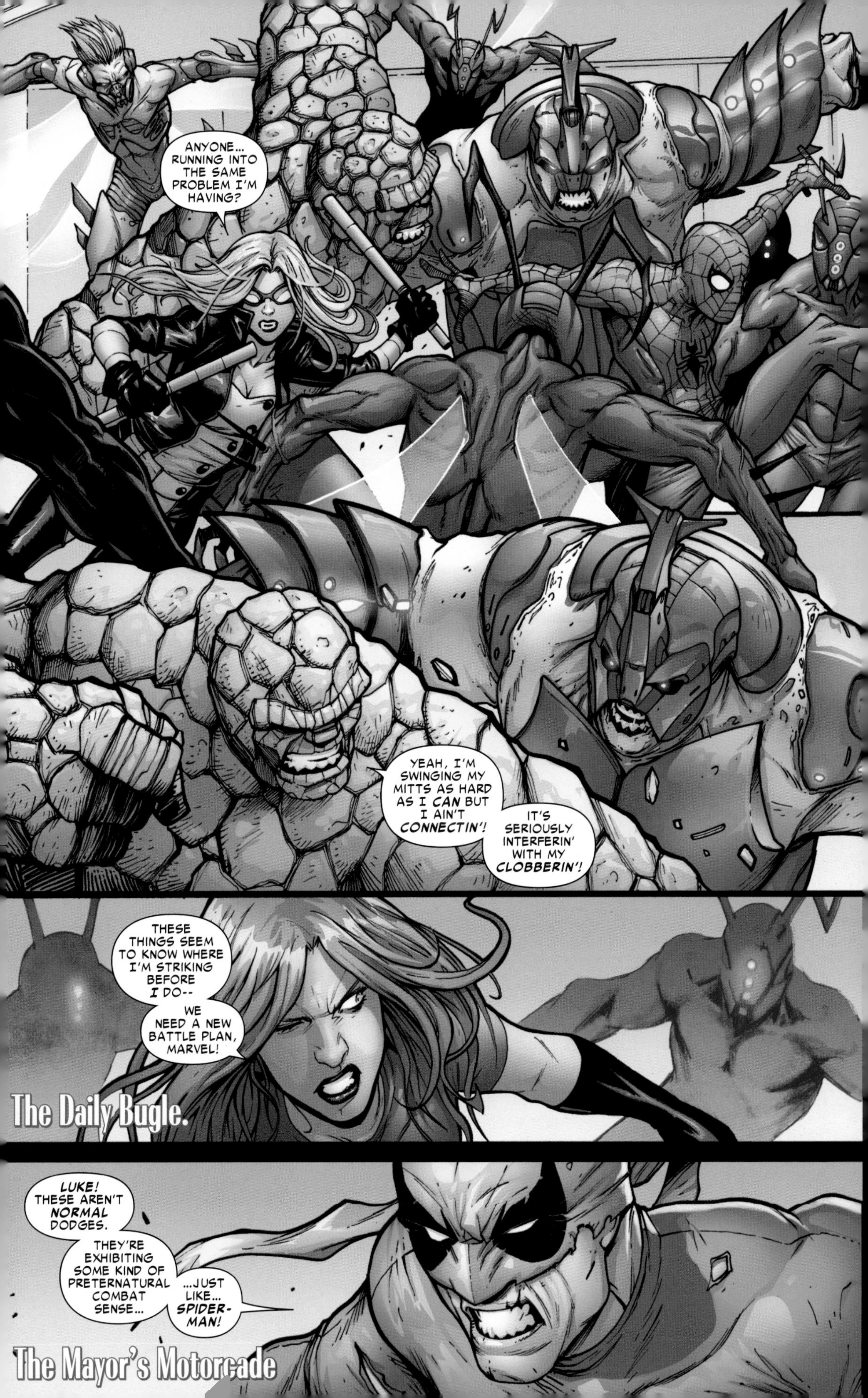
ANYONE... RUNNING INTO THE SAME PROBLEM I'M HAVING?
YEAH, I'M SWINGING MY MITTS AS HARD AS I *CAN* BUT I AIN'T *CONNECTIN'*!
IT'S SERIOUSLY INTERFERIN' WITH MY *CLOBBERIN'*!
THESE THINGS SEEM TO KNOW WHERE I'M STRIKING BEFORE *I* DO--
WE NEED A NEW BATTLE PLAN, MARVEL!
The Daily Bugle.
LUKE! THESE AREN'T *NORMAL* DODGES.
THEY'RE EXHIBITING SOME KIND OF PRETERNATURAL COMBAT SENSE...
...JUST LIKE... *SPIDER-MAN!*
The Mayor's Motorcade

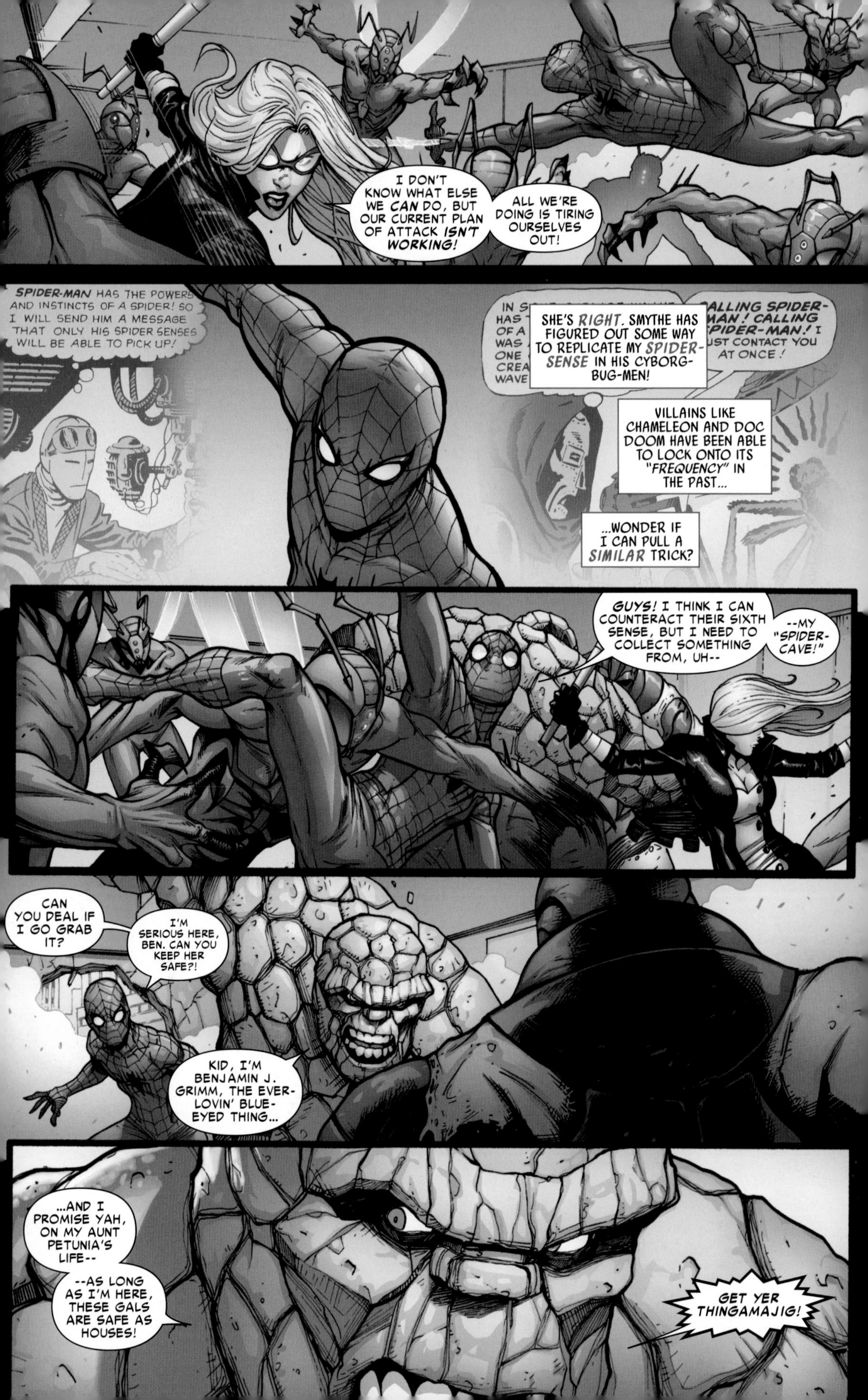
I DON'T KNOW WHAT ELSE WE CAN DO, BUT OUR CURRENT PLAN OF ATTACK ISN'T WORKING!
ALL WE'RE DOING IS TIRING OURSELVES OUT!
SPIDER-MAN HAS THE POWERS AND INSTINCTS OF A SPIDER! SO I WILL SEND HIM A MESSAGE THAT ONLY HIS SPIDER SENSES WILL BE ABLE TO PICK UP!
SHE'S RIGHT. SMYTHE HAS FIGURED OUT SOME WAY TO REPLICATE MY SPIDER-SENSE IN HIS CYBORG-BUG-MEN!
VILLAINS LIKE CHAMELEON AND DOC DOOM HAVE BEEN ABLE TO LOCK ONTO ITS "FREQUENCY" IN THE PAST...
...WONDER IF I CAN PULL A SIMILAR TRICK?
GUYS! I THINK I CAN COUNTERACT THEIR SIXTH SENSE, BUT I NEED TO COLLECT SOMETHING FROM, UH--
--MY "SPIDER-CAVE!"
CAN YOU DEAL IF I GO GRAB IT?
I'M SERIOUS HERE, BEN. CAN YOU KEEP HER SAFE?!
KID, I'M BENJAMIN J. GRIMM, THE EVER-LOVIN' BLUE-EYED THING...
...AND I PROMISE YAH, ON MY AUNT PETUNIA'S LIFE--
--AS LONG AS I'M HERE, THESE GALS ARE SAFE AS HOUSES!
GET YER THINGAMAJIG!

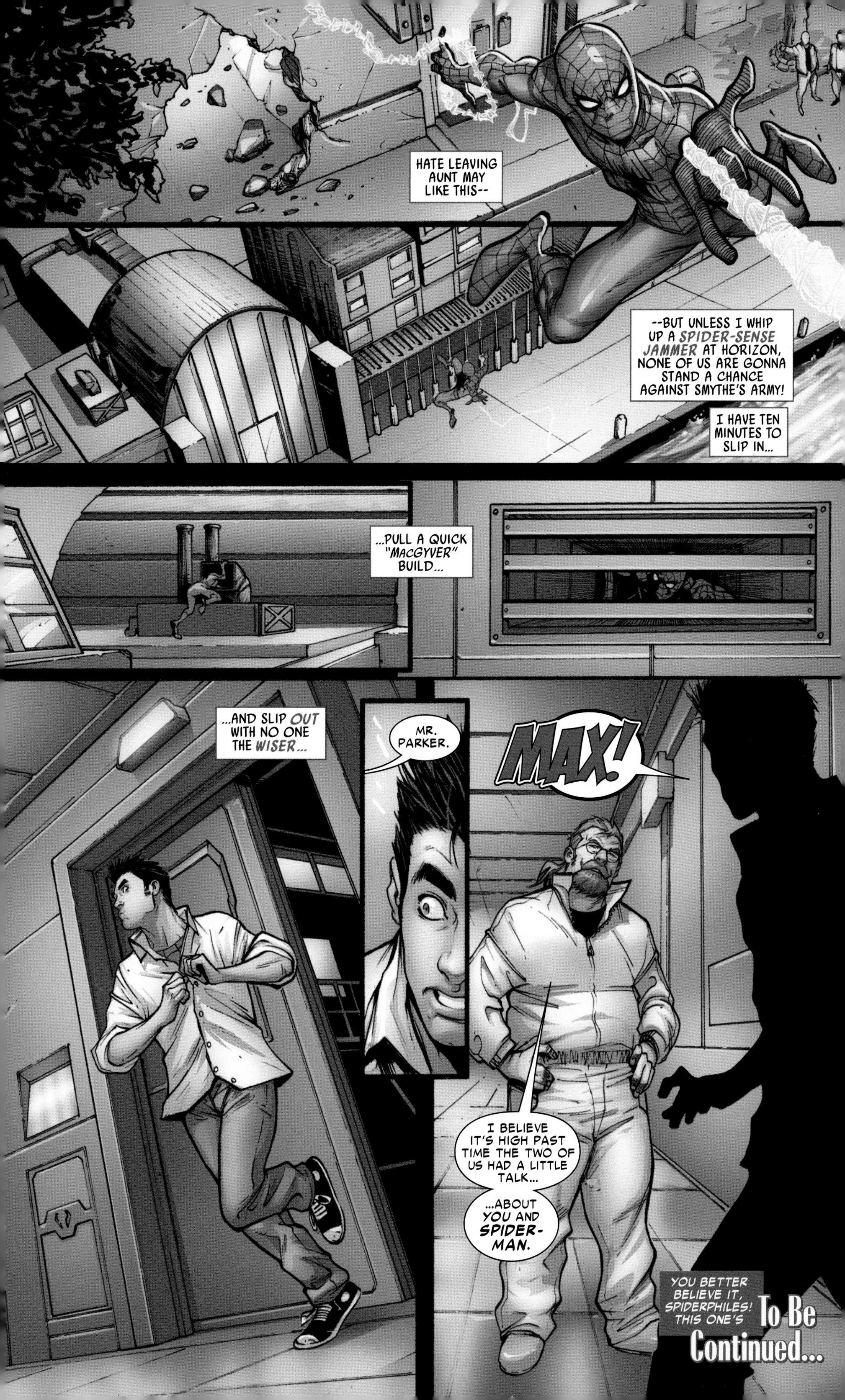
HATE LEAVING AUNT MAY LIKE THIS--
--BUT UNLESS I WHIP UP A SPIDER-SENSE JAMMER AT HORIZON, NONE OF US ARE GONNA STAND A CHANCE AGAINST SMYTHE'S ARMY!
I HAVE TEN MINUTES TO SLIP IN...
...PULL A QUICK "MACGYVER" BUILD...
...AND SLIP OUT WITH NO ONE THE WISER...
MR. PARKER.
MAX!
I BELIEVE IT'S HIGH PAST TIME THE TWO OF US HAD A LITTLE TALK...
...ABOUT YOU AND SPIDER-MAN.
YOU BETTER BELIEVE IT, SPIDERPHILES! THIS ONE'S
To Be Continued...

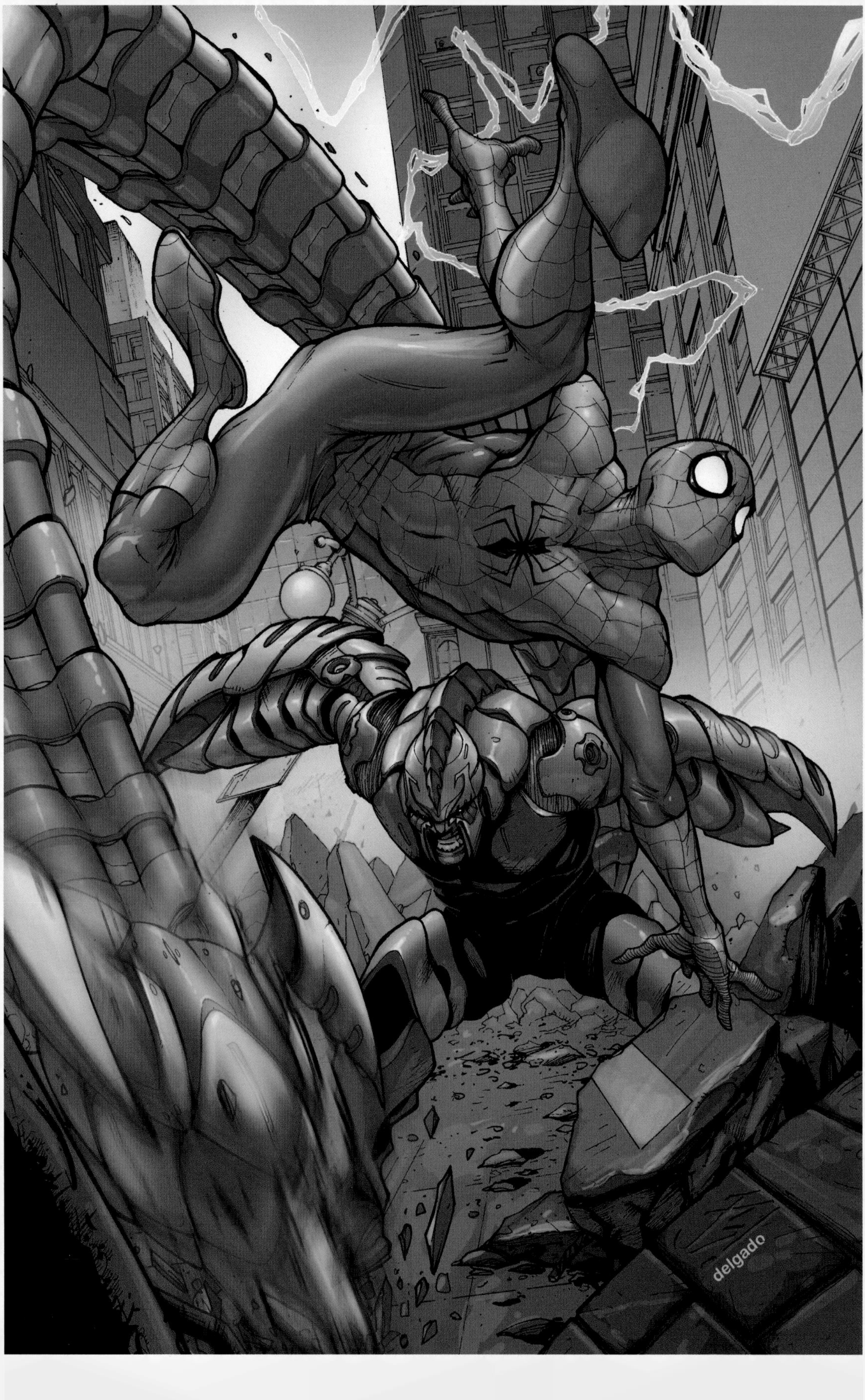
delgado

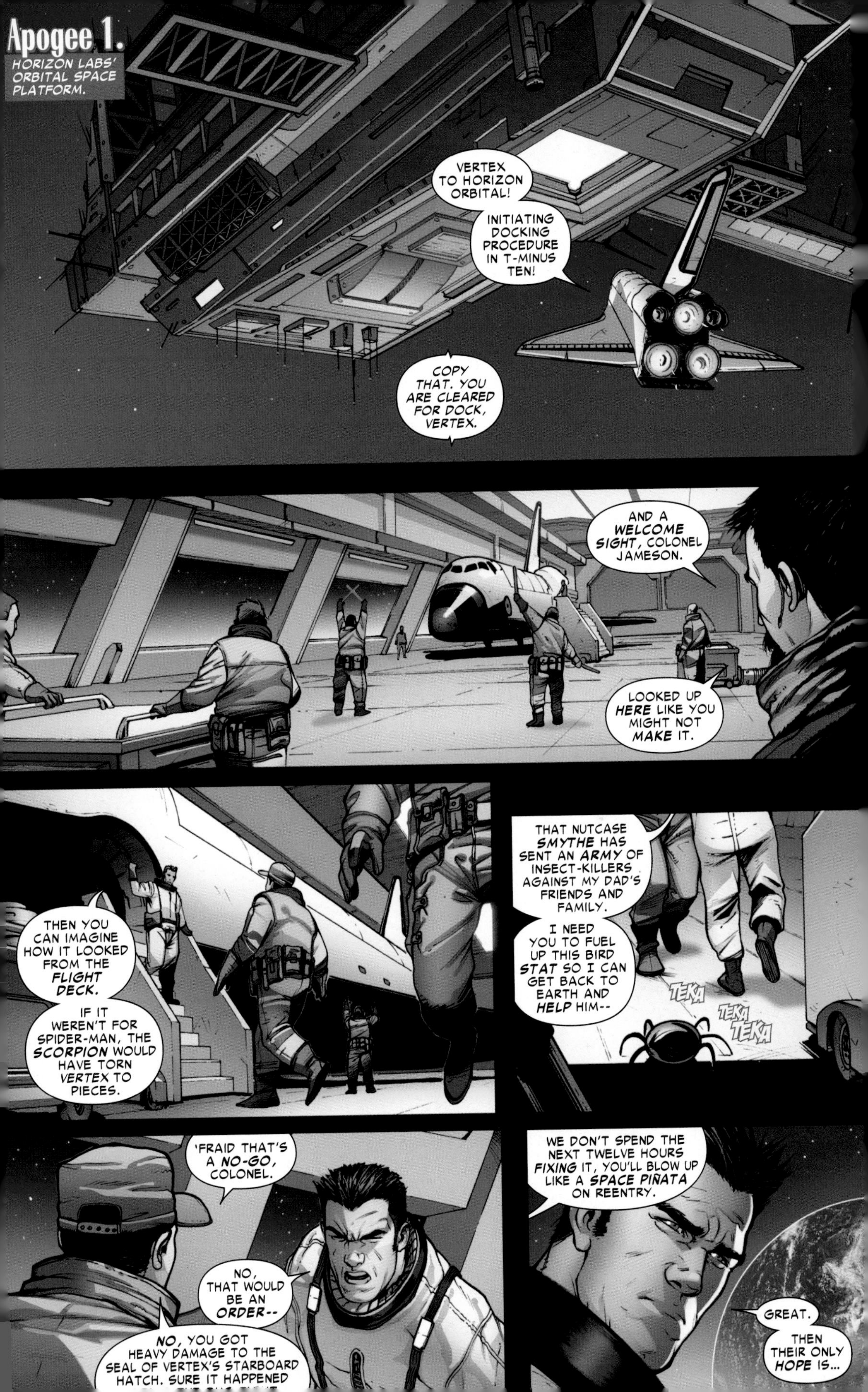
Apogee 1.
HORIZON LABS' ORBITAL SPACE PLATFORM.
VERTEX TO HORIZON ORBITAL!
INITIATING DOCKING PROCEDURE IN T-MINUS TEN!
COPY THAT. YOU ARE CLEARED FOR DOCK, VERTEX.
AND A WELCOME SIGHT, COLONEL JAMESON.
LOOKED UP HERE LIKE YOU MIGHT NOT MAKE IT.
THEN YOU CAN IMAGINE HOW IT LOOKED FROM THE FLIGHT DECK.
IF IT WEREN'T FOR SPIDER-MAN, THE SCORPION WOULD HAVE TORN VERTEX TO PIECES.
THAT NUTCASE SMYTHE HAS SENT AN ARMY OF INSECT-KILLERS AGAINST MY DAD'S FRIENDS AND FAMILY.
I NEED YOU TO FUEL UP THIS BIRD STAT SO I CAN GET BACK TO EARTH AND HELP HIM--
TEKA
TEKA TEKA
'FRAID THAT'S A NO-GO, COLONEL.
NO, THAT WOULD BE AN ORDER--
NO, YOU GOT HEAVY DAMAGE TO THE SEAL OF VERTEX'S STARBOARD HATCH. SURE IT HAPPENED
WE DON'T SPEND THE NEXT TWELVE HOURS FIXING IT, YOU'LL BLOW UP LIKE A SPACE PIÑATA ON REENTRY.
GREAT.
THEN THEIR ONLY HOPE IS...

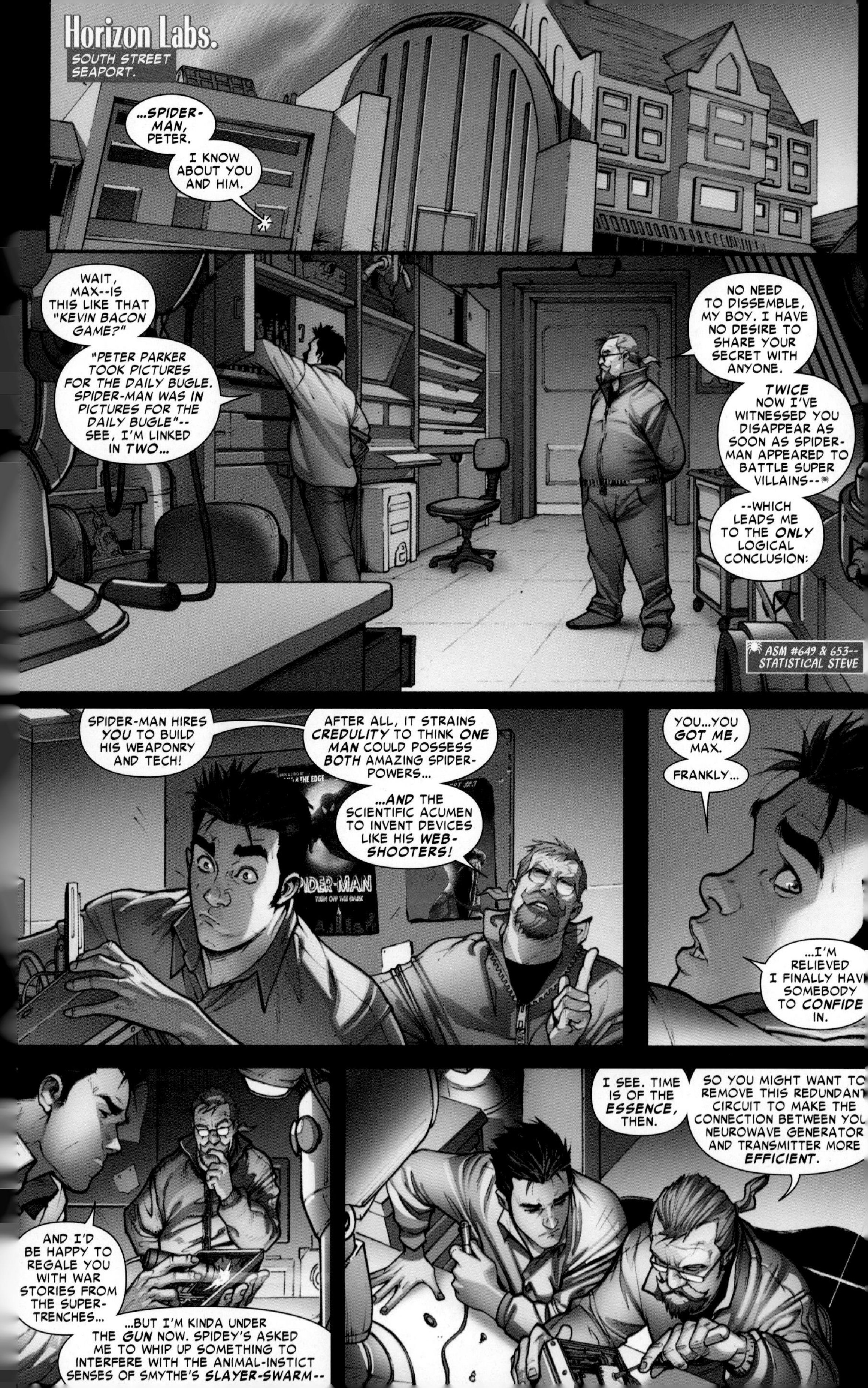
Horizon Labs.
SOUTH STREET SEAPORT.
...SPIDER-MAN, PETER.
I KNOW ABOUT YOU AND HIM.
WAIT, MAX--IS THIS LIKE THAT "KEVIN BACON GAME?"
"PETER PARKER TOOK PICTURES FOR THE DAILY BUGLE. SPIDER-MAN WAS IN PICTURES FOR THE DAILY BUGLE"--SEE, I'M LINKED IN TWO...
NO NEED TO DISSEMBLE, MY BOY. I HAVE NO DESIRE TO SHARE YOUR SECRET WITH ANYONE.
TWICE NOW I'VE WITNESSED YOU DISAPPEAR AS SOON AS SPIDER-MAN APPEARED TO BATTLE SUPER VILLAINS--
--WHICH LEADS ME TO THE ONLY LOGICAL CONCLUSION:
ASM #649 & 653--STATISTICAL STEVE
SPIDER-MAN HIRES YOU TO BUILD HIS WEAPONRY AND TECH!
AFTER ALL, IT STRAINS CREDULITY TO THINK ONE MAN COULD POSSESS BOTH AMAZING SPIDER-POWERS...
...AND THE SCIENTIFIC ACUMEN TO INVENT DEVICES LIKE HIS WEB-SHOOTERS!
SPIDER-MAN
TURN OFF THE DARK
YOU...YOU GOT ME, MAX.
FRANKLY...
...I'M RELIEVED I FINALLY HAV SOMEBODY TO CONFIDE IN.
AND I'D BE HAPPY TO REGALE YOU WITH WAR STORIES FROM THE SUPER-TRENCHES...
...BUT I'M KINDA UNDER THE GUN NOW. SPIDEY'S ASKED ME TO WHIP UP SOMETHING TO INTERFERE WITH THE ANIMAL-INSTICT SENSES OF SMYTHE'S SLAYER-SWARM--
I SEE. TIME IS OF THE ESSENCE, THEN.
SO YOU MIGHT WANT TO REMOVE THIS REDUNDANT CIRCUIT TO MAKE THE CONNECTION BETWEEN YOU NEUROWAVE GENERATOR AND TRANSMITTER MORE EFFICIENT.

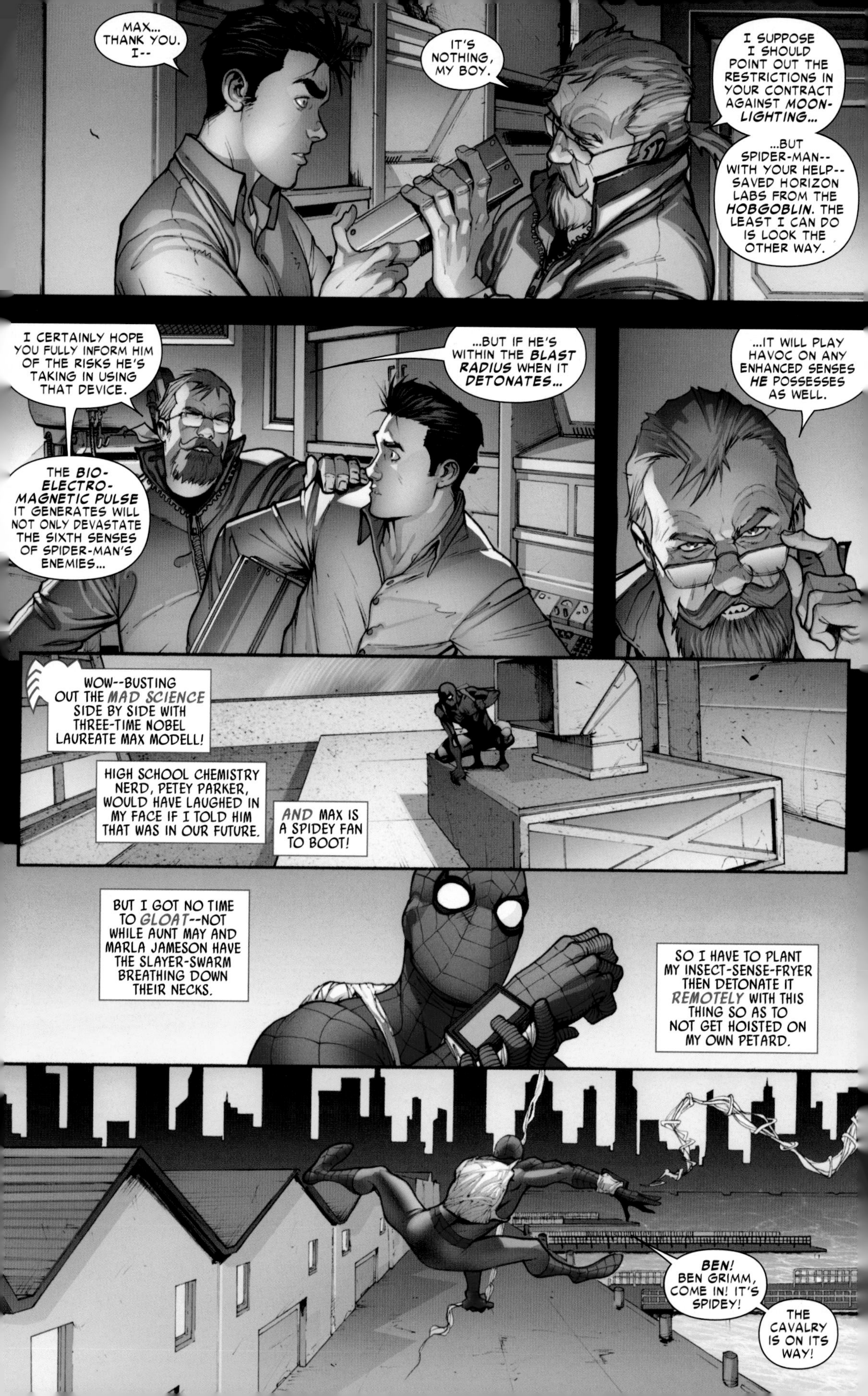
MAX... THANK YOU. I--
IT'S NOTHING, MY BOY.
I SUPPOSE I SHOULD POINT OUT THE RESTRICTIONS IN YOUR CONTRACT AGAINST MOON-LIGHTING...
...BUT SPIDER-MAN--WITH YOUR HELP--SAVED HORIZON LABS FROM THE HOBGOBLIN. THE LEAST I CAN DO IS LOOK THE OTHER WAY.
I CERTAINLY HOPE YOU FULLY INFORM HIM OF THE RISKS HE'S TAKING IN USING THAT DEVICE.
THE BIO-ELECTRO-MAGNETIC PULSE IT GENERATES WILL NOT ONLY DEVASTATE THE SIXTH SENSES OF SPIDER-MAN'S ENEMIES...
...BUT IF HE'S WITHIN THE BLAST RADIUS WHEN IT DETONATES...
...IT WILL PLAY HAVOC ON ANY ENHANCED SENSES HE POSSESSES AS WELL.
WOW--BUSTING OUT THE MAD SCIENCE SIDE BY SIDE WITH THREE-TIME NOBEL LAUREATE MAX MODELL!
HIGH SCHOOL CHEMISTRY NERD, PETEY PARKER, WOULD HAVE LAUGHED IN MY FACE IF I TOLD HIM THAT WAS IN OUR FUTURE.
AND MAX IS A SPIDEY FAN TO BOOT!
BUT I GOT NO TIME TO GLOAT--NOT WHILE AUNT MAY AND MARLA JAMESON HAVE THE SLAYER-SWARM BREATHING DOWN THEIR NECKS.
SO I HAVE TO PLANT MY INSECT-SENSE-FRYER THEN DETONATE IT REMOTELY WITH THIS THING SO AS TO NOT GET HOISTED ON MY OWN PETARD.
BEN! BEN GRIMM, COME IN! IT'S SPIDEY!
THE CAVALRY IS ON ITS WAY!

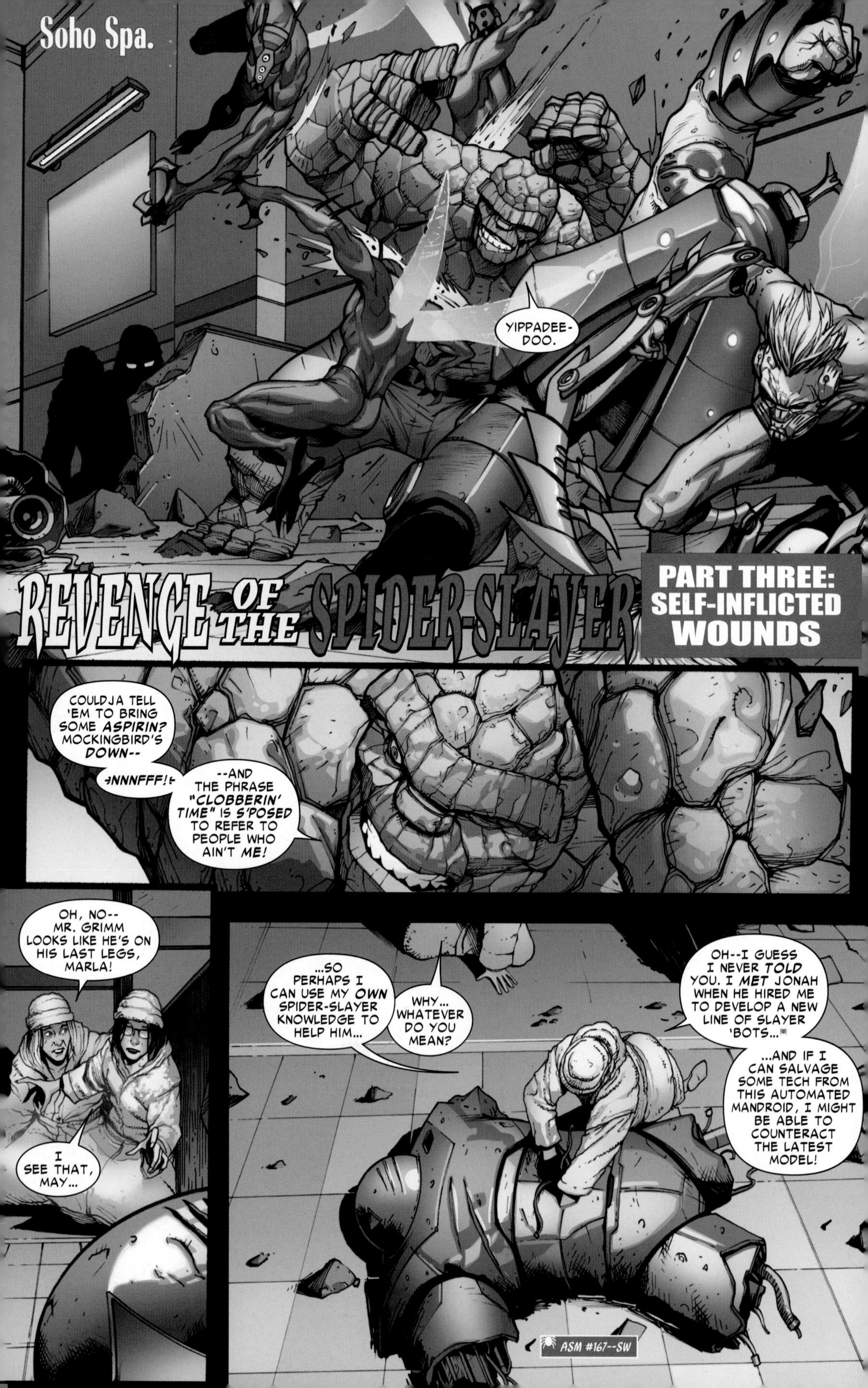
Soho Spa.
YIPPADEE-DOO.
REVENGE OF THE SPIDER-SLAYER
PART THREE: SELF-INFLICTED WOUNDS
COULDJA TELL 'EM TO BRING SOME ASPIRIN? MOCKINGBIRD'S DOWN--
NNNFFF!
--AND THE PHRASE "CLOBBERIN' TIME" IS S'POSED TO REFER TO PEOPLE WHO AIN'T ME!
OH, NO-- MR. GRIMM LOOKS LIKE HE'S ON HIS LAST LEGS, MARLA!
I SEE THAT, MAY...
...SO PERHAPS I CAN USE MY OWN SPIDER-SLAYER KNOWLEDGE TO HELP HIM...
WHY... WHATEVER DO YOU MEAN?
OH--I GUESS I NEVER TOLD YOU. I MET JONAH WHEN HE HIRED ME TO DEVELOP A NEW LINE OF SLAYER 'BOTS...
...AND IF I CAN SALVAGE SOME TECH FROM THIS AUTOMATED MANDROID, I MIGHT BE ABLE TO COUNTERACT THE LATEST MODEL!
ASM #167--SW

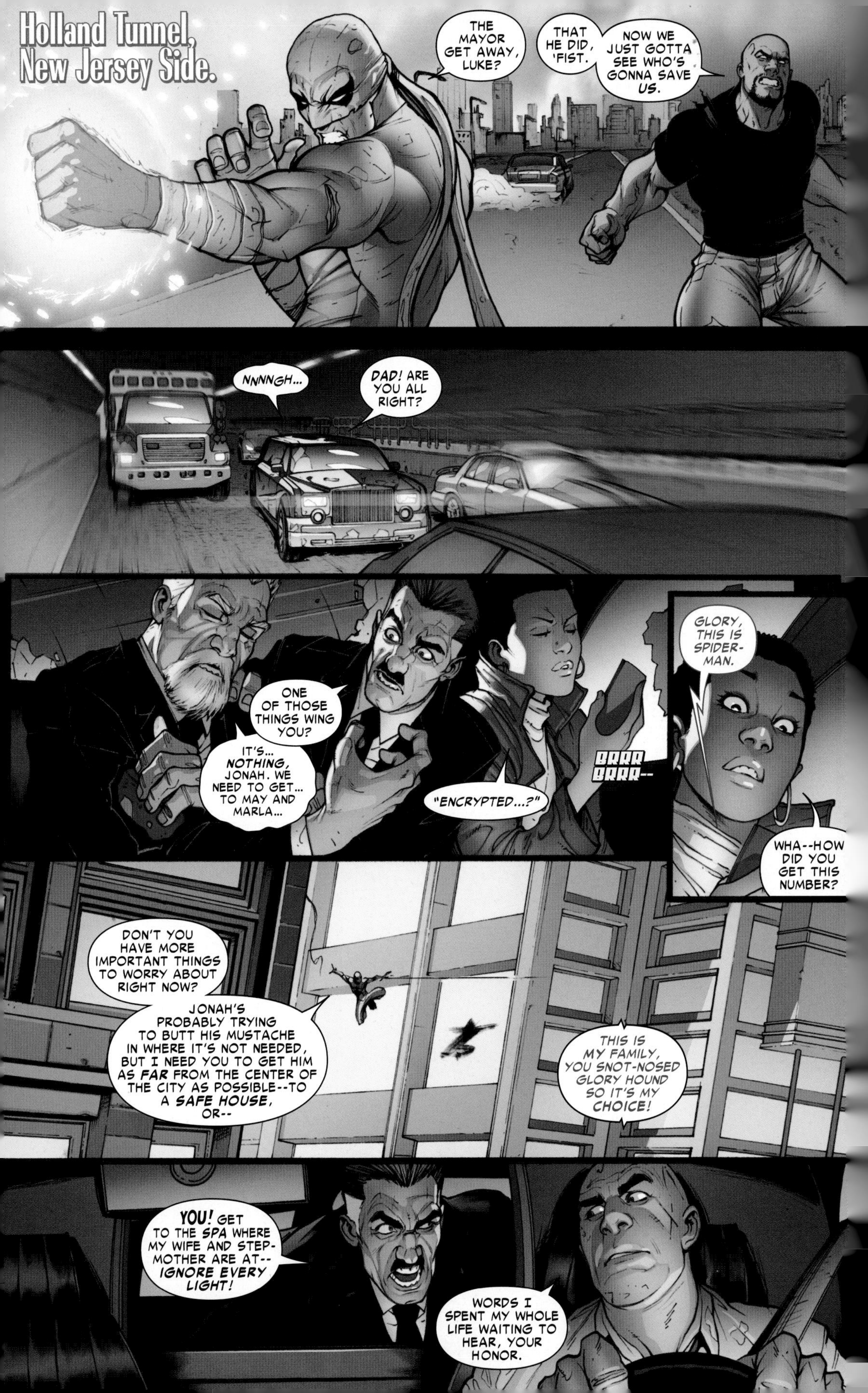
Holland Tunnel, New Jersey Side.
THE MAYOR GET AWAY, LUKE?
THAT HE DID, 'FIST.
NOW WE JUST GOTTA SEE WHO'S GONNA SAVE US.
NNNNGH...
DAD! ARE YOU ALL RIGHT?
ONE OF THOSE THINGS WING YOU?
IT'S... NOTHING, JONAH. WE NEED TO GET... TO MAY AND MARLA...
"ENCRYPTED...?"
BRRR BRRR--
GLORY, THIS IS SPIDER-MAN.
WHA--HOW DID YOU GET THIS NUMBER?
DON'T YOU HAVE MORE IMPORTANT THINGS TO WORRY ABOUT RIGHT NOW?
JONAH'S PROBABLY TRYING TO BUTT HIS MUSTACHE IN WHERE IT'S NOT NEEDED, BUT I NEED YOU TO GET HIM AS FAR FROM THE CENTER OF THE CITY AS POSSIBLE--TO A SAFE HOUSE, OR--
THIS IS MY FAMILY, YOU SNOT-NOSED GLORY HOUND SO IT'S MY CHOICE!
YOU! GET TO THE SPA WHERE MY WIFE AND STEP-MOTHER ARE AT-- IGNORE EVERY LIGHT!
WORDS I SPENT MY WHOLE LIFE WAITING TO HEAR, YOUR HONOR.

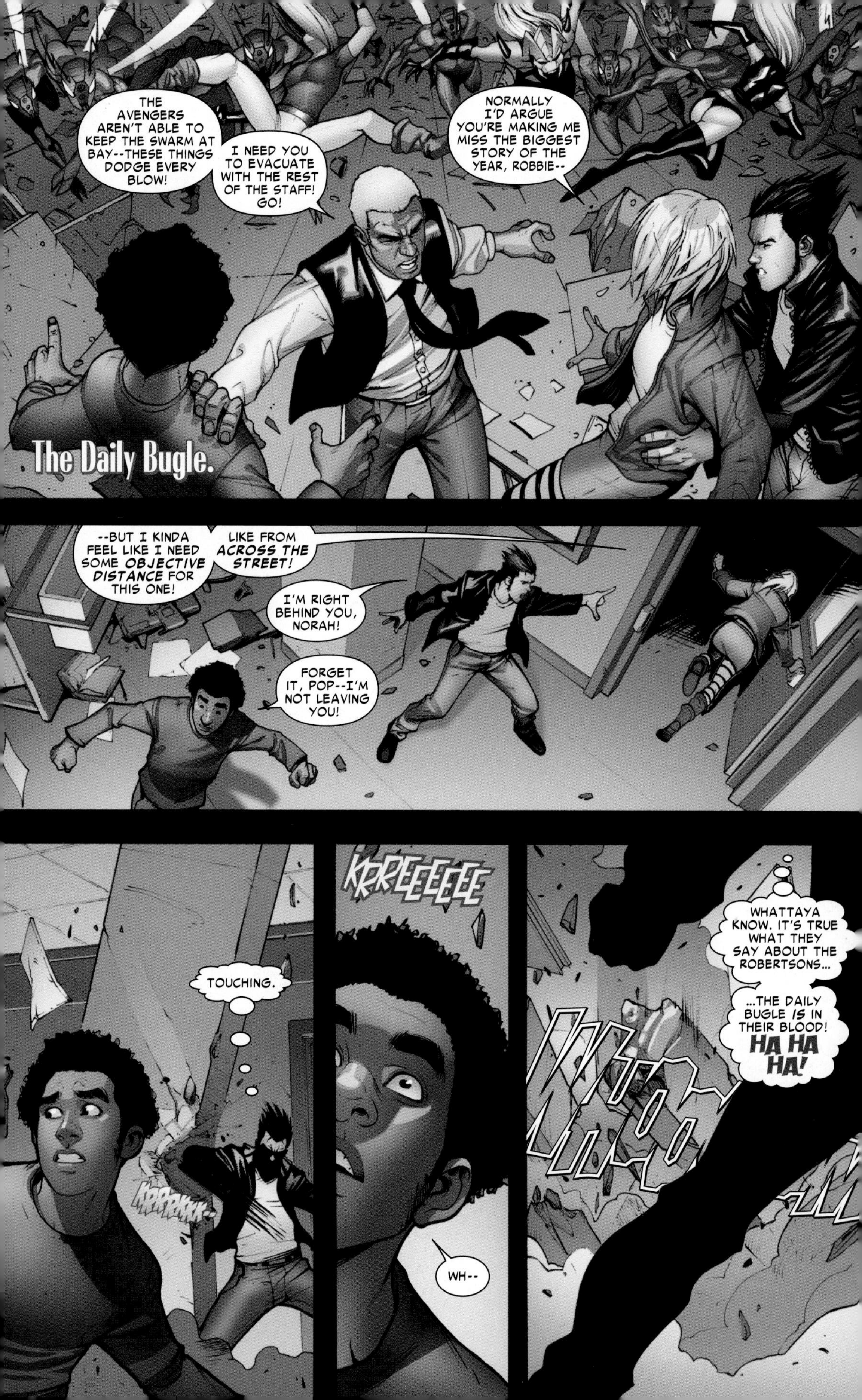

THE AVENGERS AREN'T ABLE TO KEEP THE SWARM AT BAY--THESE THINGS DODGE EVERY BLOW!
I NEED YOU TO EVACUATE WITH THE REST OF THE STAFF! GO!
NORMALLY I'D ARGUE YOU'RE MAKING ME MISS THE BIGGEST STORY OF THE YEAR, ROBBIE--
The Daily Bugle.
--BUT I KINDA FEEL LIKE I NEED SOME *OBJECTIVE DISTANCE* FOR THIS ONE!
LIKE FROM *ACROSS THE STREET!*
I'M RIGHT BEHIND YOU, NORAH!
FORGET IT, POP--I'M NOT LEAVING YOU!
TOUCHING.
KRRRKKK--
KRREEEEEEE
WH--
WHATTAYA KNOW. IT'S TRUE WHAT THEY SAY ABOUT THE ROBERTSONS...
...THE DAILY BUGLE *IS* IN THEIR BLOOD! HA HA HA!

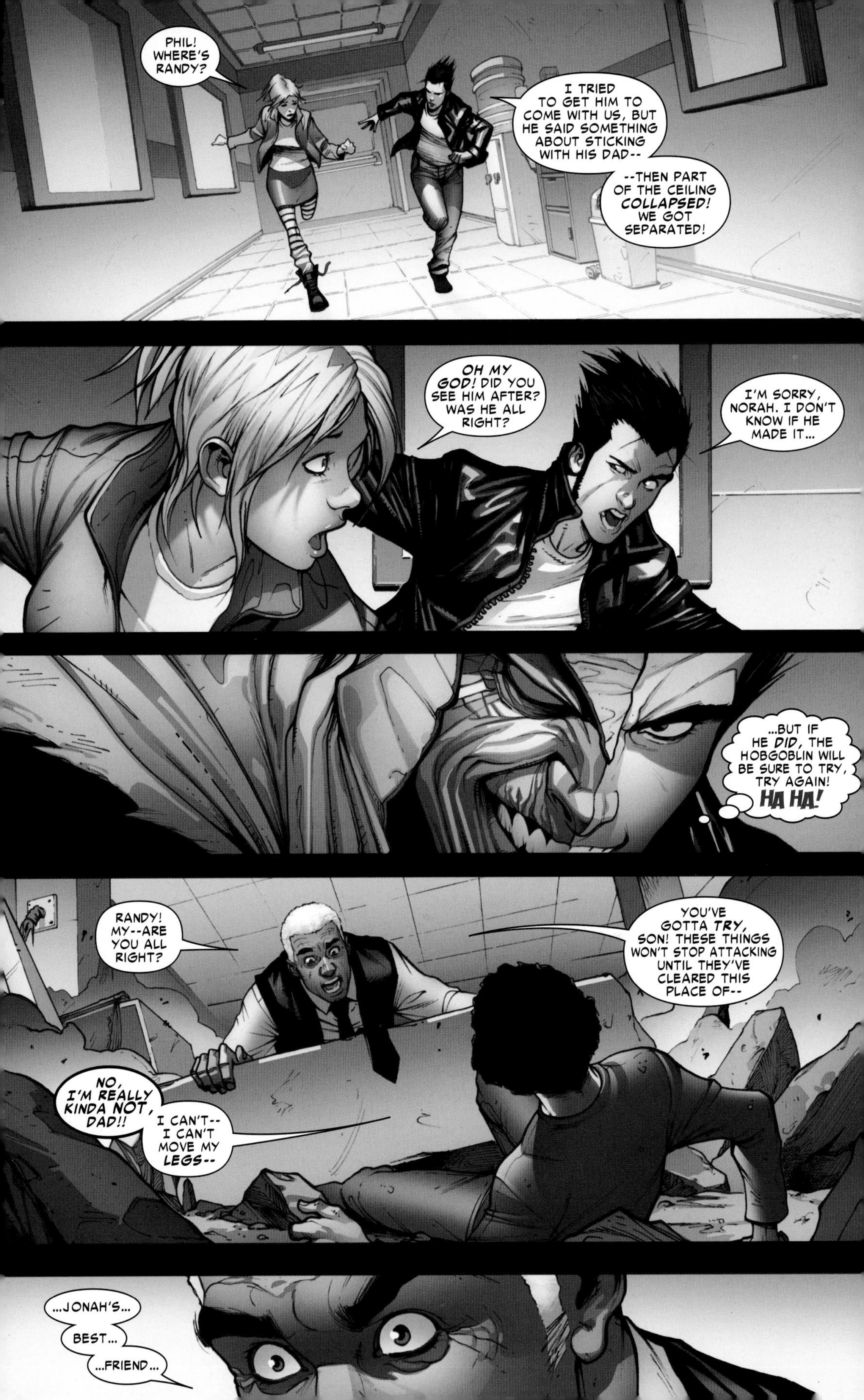
PHIL! WHERE'S RANDY?
I TRIED TO GET HIM TO COME WITH US, BUT HE SAID SOMETHING ABOUT STICKING WITH HIS DAD--
--THEN PART OF THE CEILING COLLAPSED! WE GOT SEPARATED!
OH MY GOD! DID YOU SEE HIM AFTER? WAS HE ALL RIGHT?
I'M SORRY, NORAH. I DON'T KNOW IF HE MADE IT...
...BUT IF HE DID, THE HOBGOBLIN WILL BE SURE TO TRY, TRY AGAIN! HA HA!
RANDY! MY--ARE YOU ALL RIGHT?
NO, I'M REALLY KINDA NOT, DAD!!
I CAN'T-- I CAN'T MOVE MY LEGS--
YOU'VE GOTTA TRY, SON! THESE THINGS WON'T STOP ATTACKING UNTIL THEY'VE CLEARED THIS PLACE OF--
...JONAH'S...
BEST...
...FRIEND...

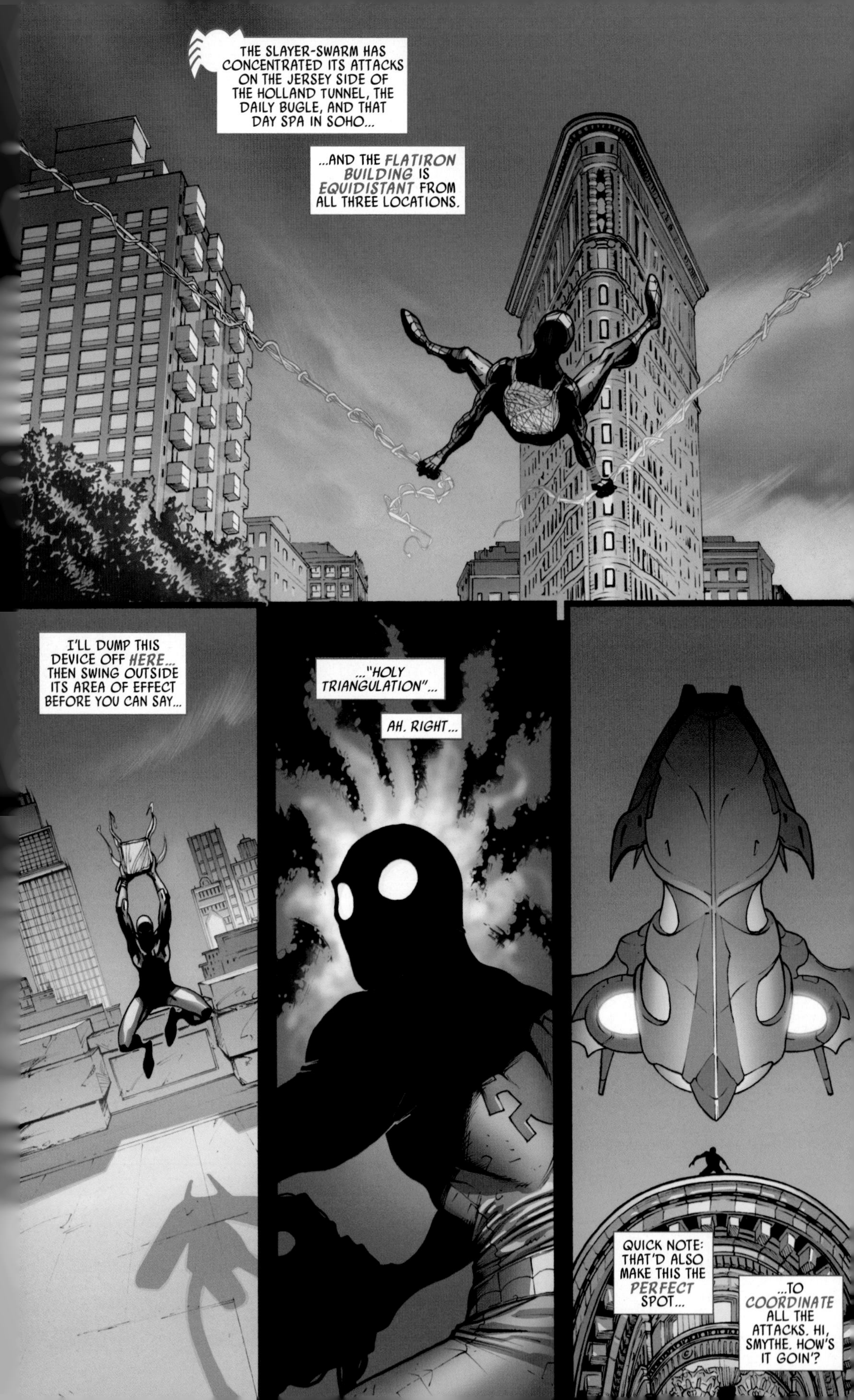

THE SLAYER-SWARM HAS CONCENTRATED ITS ATTACKS ON THE JERSEY SIDE OF THE HOLLAND TUNNEL, THE DAILY BUGLE, AND THAT DAY SPA IN SOHO...
...AND THE FLATIRON BUILDING IS EQUIDISTANT FROM ALL THREE LOCATIONS.
I'LL DUMP THIS DEVICE OFF HERE... THEN SWING OUTSIDE ITS AREA OF EFFECT BEFORE YOU CAN SAY...
..."HOLY TRIANGULATION"...
AH. RIGHT...
QUICK NOTE: THAT'D ALSO MAKE THIS THE PERFECT SPOT...
...TO COORDINATE ALL THE ATTACKS. HI, SMYTHE. HOW'S IT GOIN'?

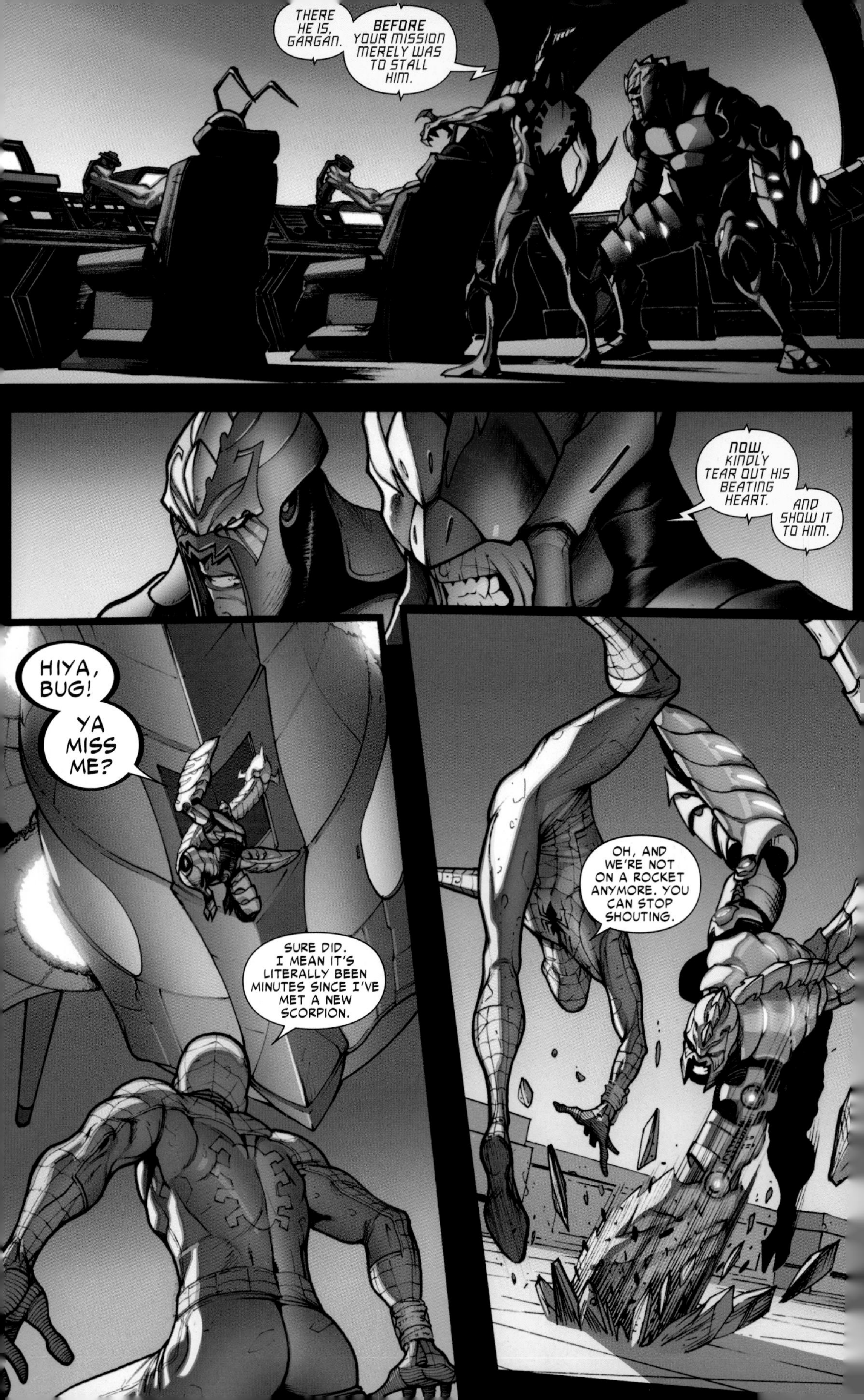
THERE HE IS, GARGAN.
BEFORE YOUR MISSION MERELY WAS TO STALL HIM.
NOW, KINDLY TEAR OUT HIS BEATING HEART.
AND SHOW IT TO HIM.
HIYA, BUG!
YA MISS ME?
SURE DID. I MEAN IT'S LITERALLY BEEN MINUTES SINCE I'VE MET A NEW SCORPION.
OH, AND WE'RE NOT ON A ROCKET ANYMORE. YOU CAN STOP SHOUTING.

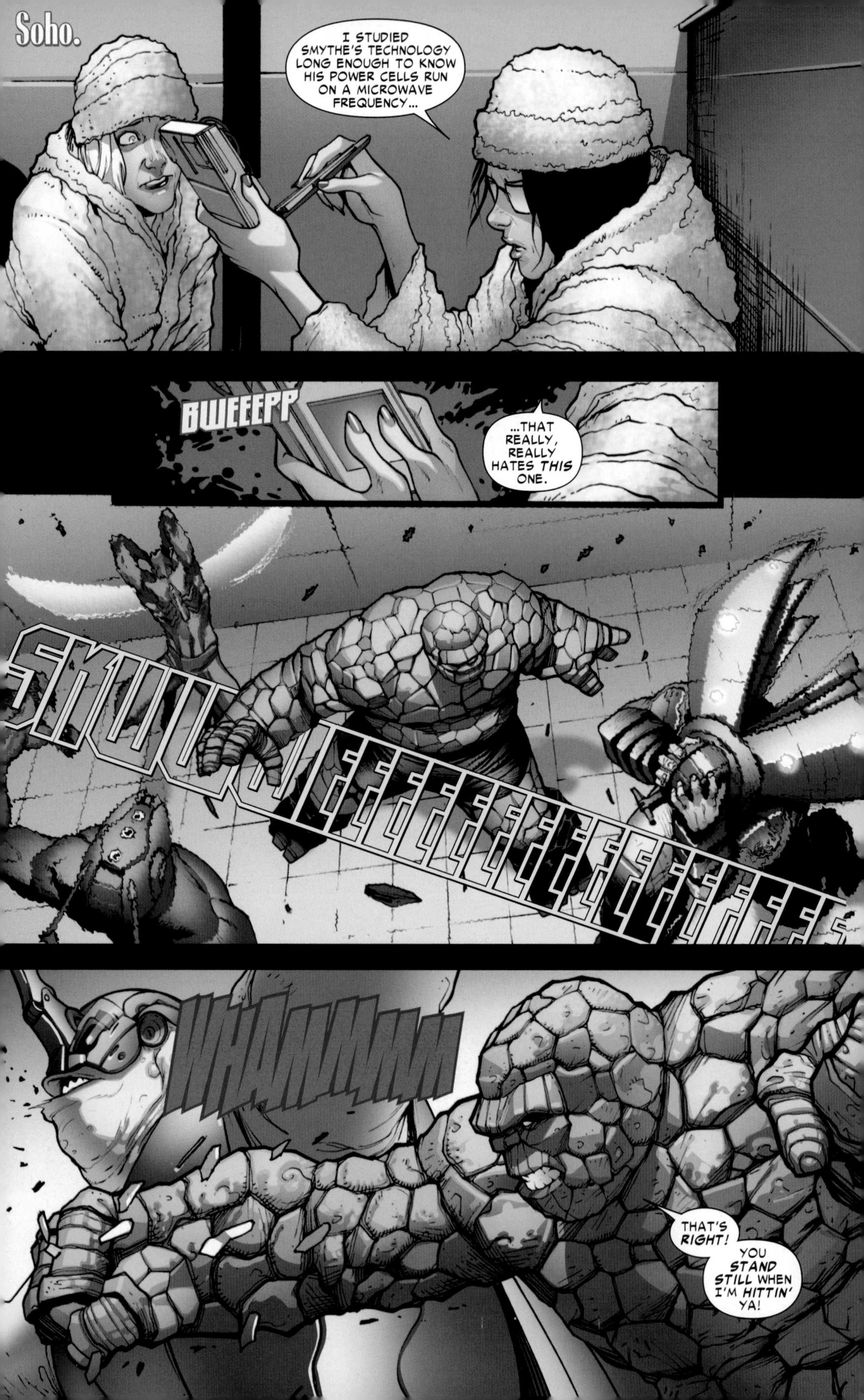
Soho.
I STUDIED SMYTHE'S TECHNOLOGY LONG ENOUGH TO KNOW HIS POWER CELLS RUN ON A MICROWAVE FREQUENCY...
BWEEEPP
...THAT REALLY, REALLY HATES THIS ONE.
WHAMMMM
THAT'S RIGHT!
YOU STAND STILL WHEN I'M HITTIN' YA!

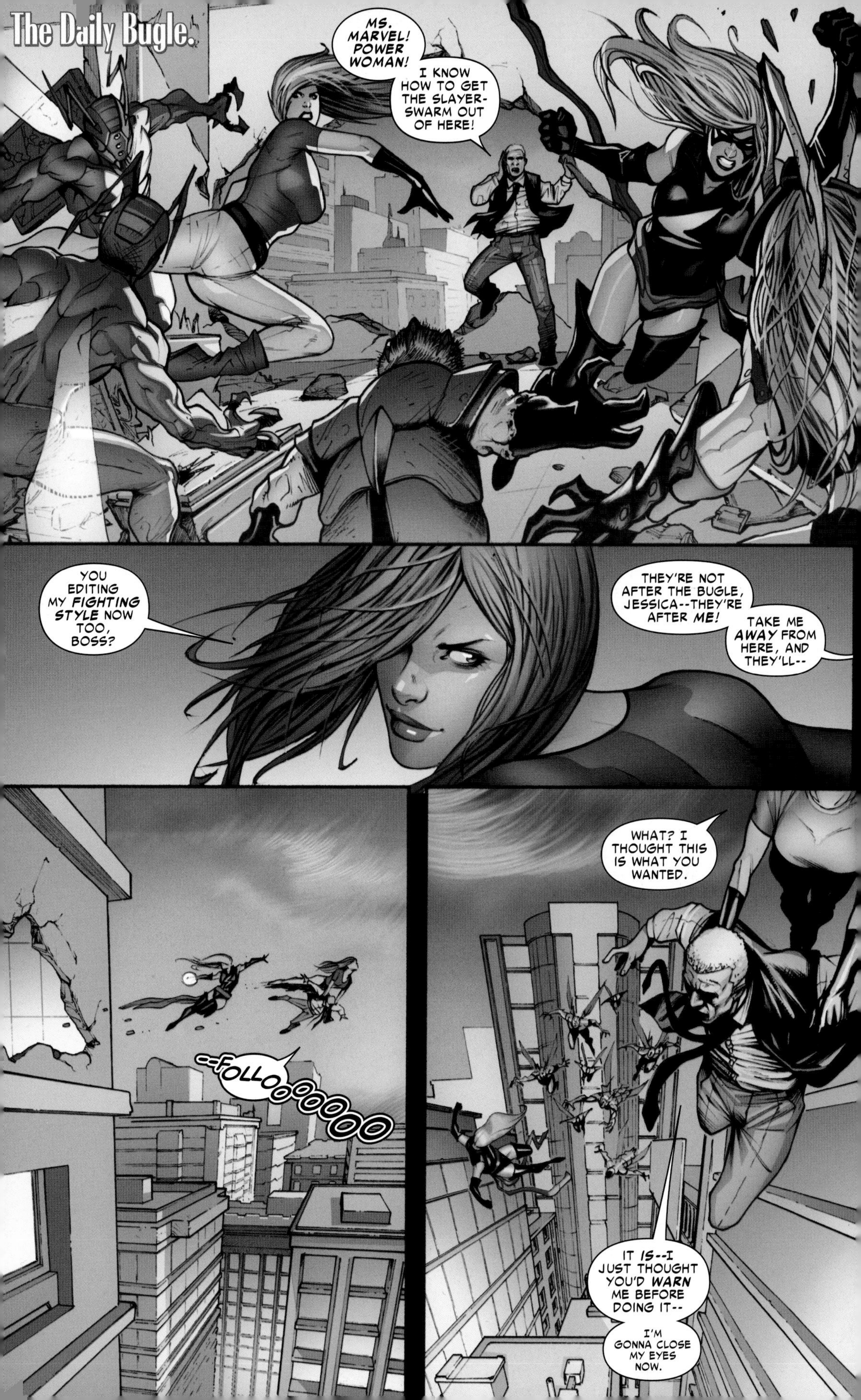

The Daily Bugle.
MS. MARVEL! POWER WOMAN!
I KNOW HOW TO GET THE SLAYER-SWARM OUT OF HERE!
YOU EDITING MY FIGHTING STYLE NOW TOO, BOSS?
THEY'RE NOT AFTER THE BUGLE, JESSICA--THEY'RE AFTER ME!
TAKE ME AWAY FROM HERE, AND THEY'LL--
--FOLLOOOOOOO
WHAT? I THOUGHT THIS IS WHAT YOU WANTED.
IT IS--I JUST THOUGHT YOU'D WARN ME BEFORE DOING IT--
I'M GONNA CLOSE MY EYES NOW.

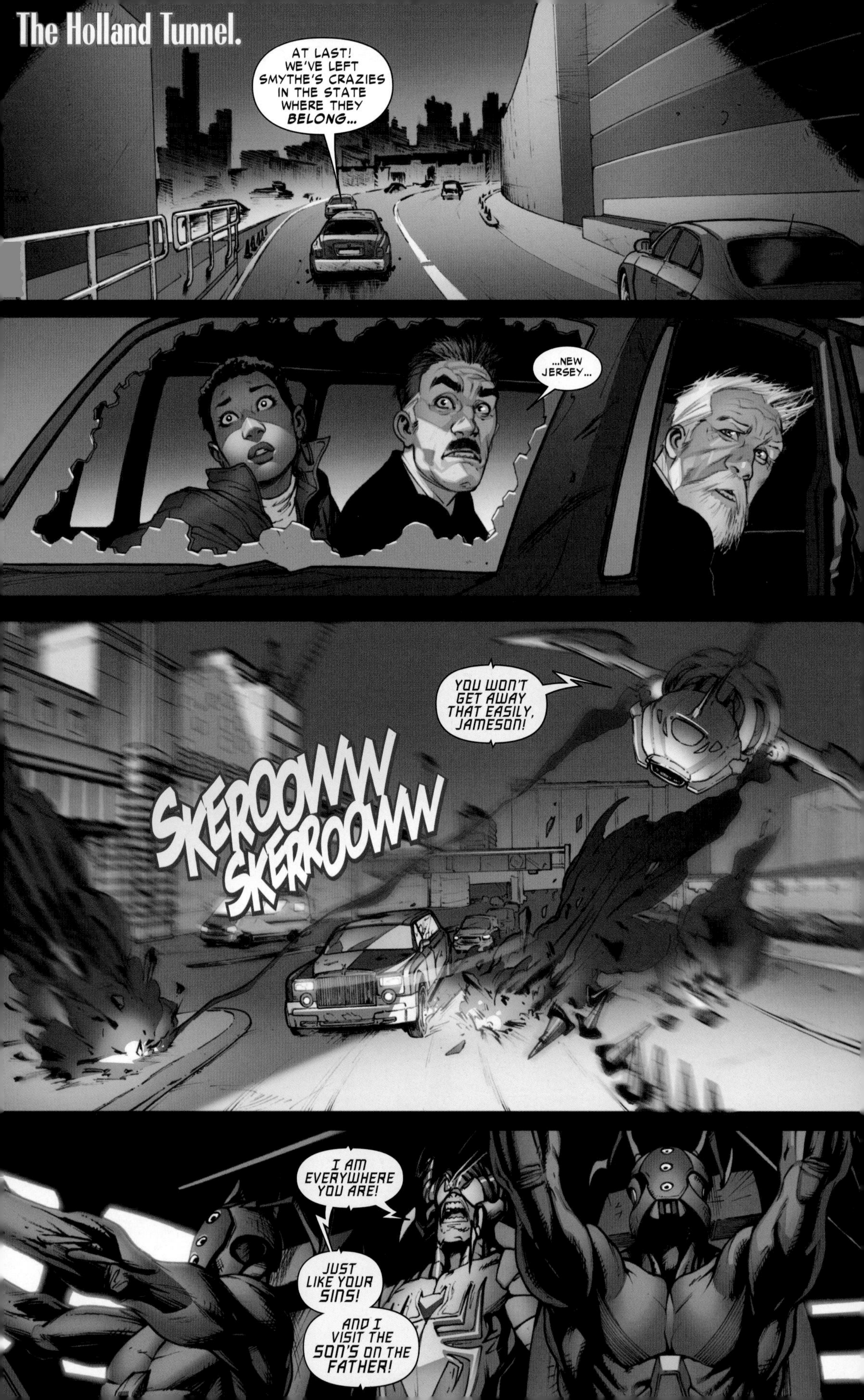
The Holland Tunnel.
AT LAST! WE'VE LEFT SMYTHE'S CRAZIES IN THE STATE WHERE THEY BELONG...
...NEW JERSEY...
YOU WON'T GET AWAY THAT EASILY, JAMESON!
SKEROOWW
SKERROOWW
I AM EVERYWHERE YOU ARE!
JUST LIKE YOUR SINS!
AND I VISIT THE SON'S ON THE FATHER!

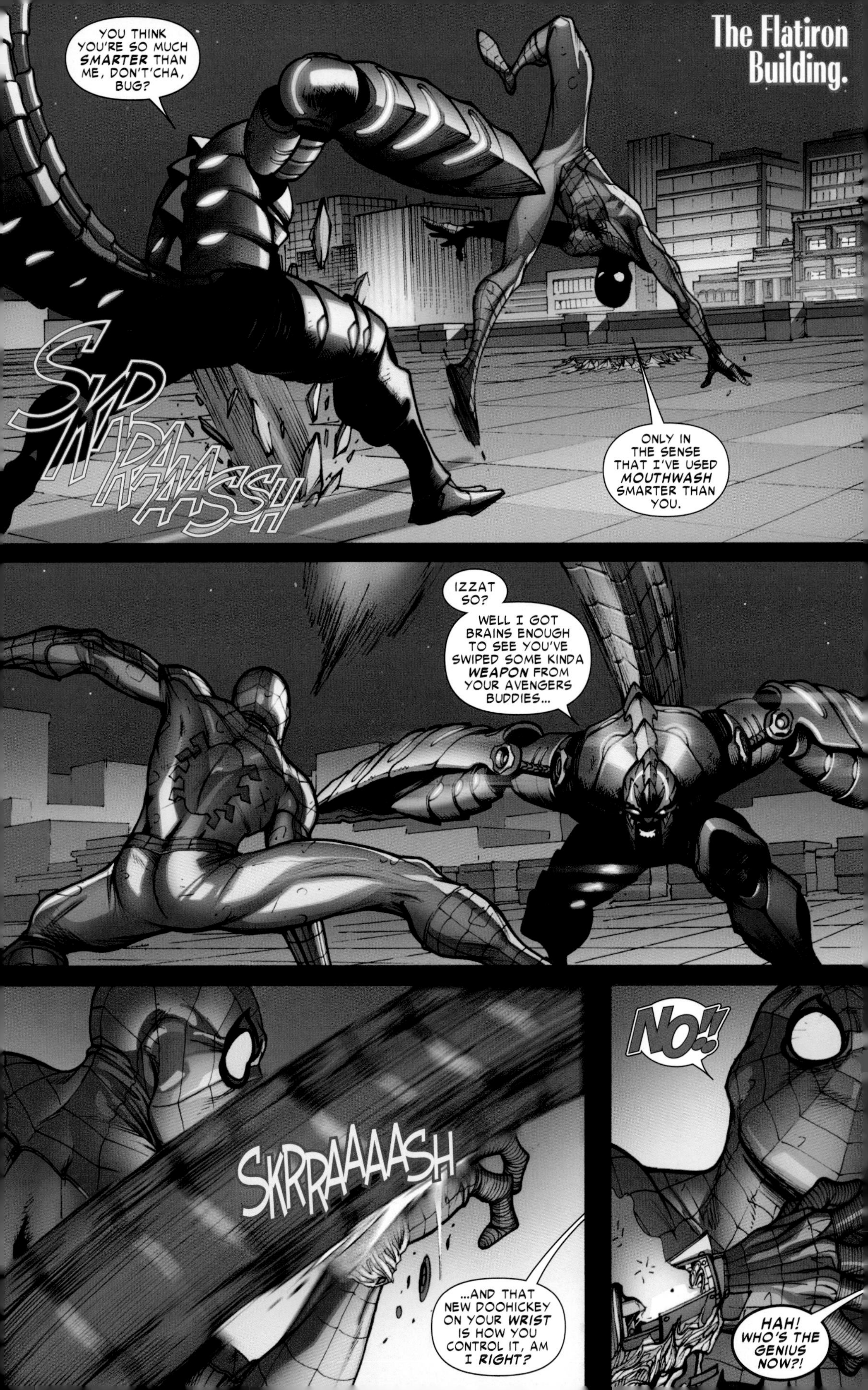
The Flatiron Building.
YOU THINK YOU'RE SO MUCH SMARTER THAN ME, DON'T'CHA, BUG?
SKRAAASH
ONLY IN THE SENSE THAT I'VE USED MOUTHWASH SMARTER THAN YOU.
IZZAT SO?
WELL I GOT BRAINS ENOUGH TO SEE YOU'VE SWIPED SOME KINDA WEAPON FROM YOUR AVENGERS BUDDIES...
SKRRAAAASH
...AND THAT NEW DOOHICKEY ON YOUR WRIST IS HOW YOU CONTROL IT, AM I RIGHT?
NO!!
HAH! WHO'S THE GENIUS NOW?!

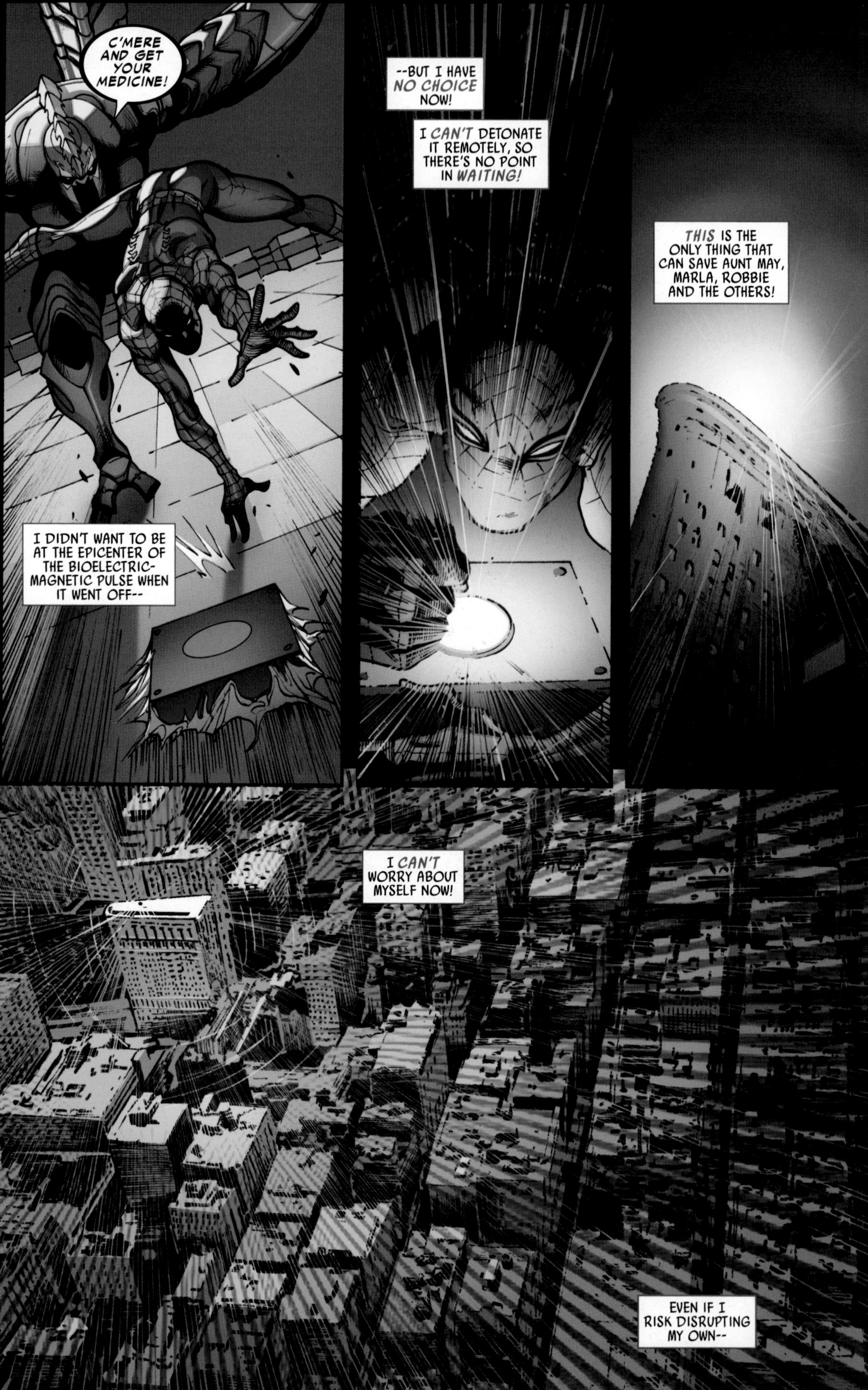
C'MERE AND GET YOUR MEDICINE!
I DIDN'T WANT TO BE AT THE EPICENTER OF THE BIOELECTRIC-MAGNETIC PULSE WHEN IT WENT OFF--
--BUT I HAVE NO CHOICE NOW!
I CAN'T DETONATE IT REMOTELY, SO THERE'S NO POINT IN WAITING!
THIS IS THE ONLY THING THAT CAN SAVE AUNT MAY, MARLA, ROBBIE AND THE OTHERS!
I CAN'T WORRY ABOUT MYSELF NOW!
EVEN IF I RISK DISRUPTING MY OWN--

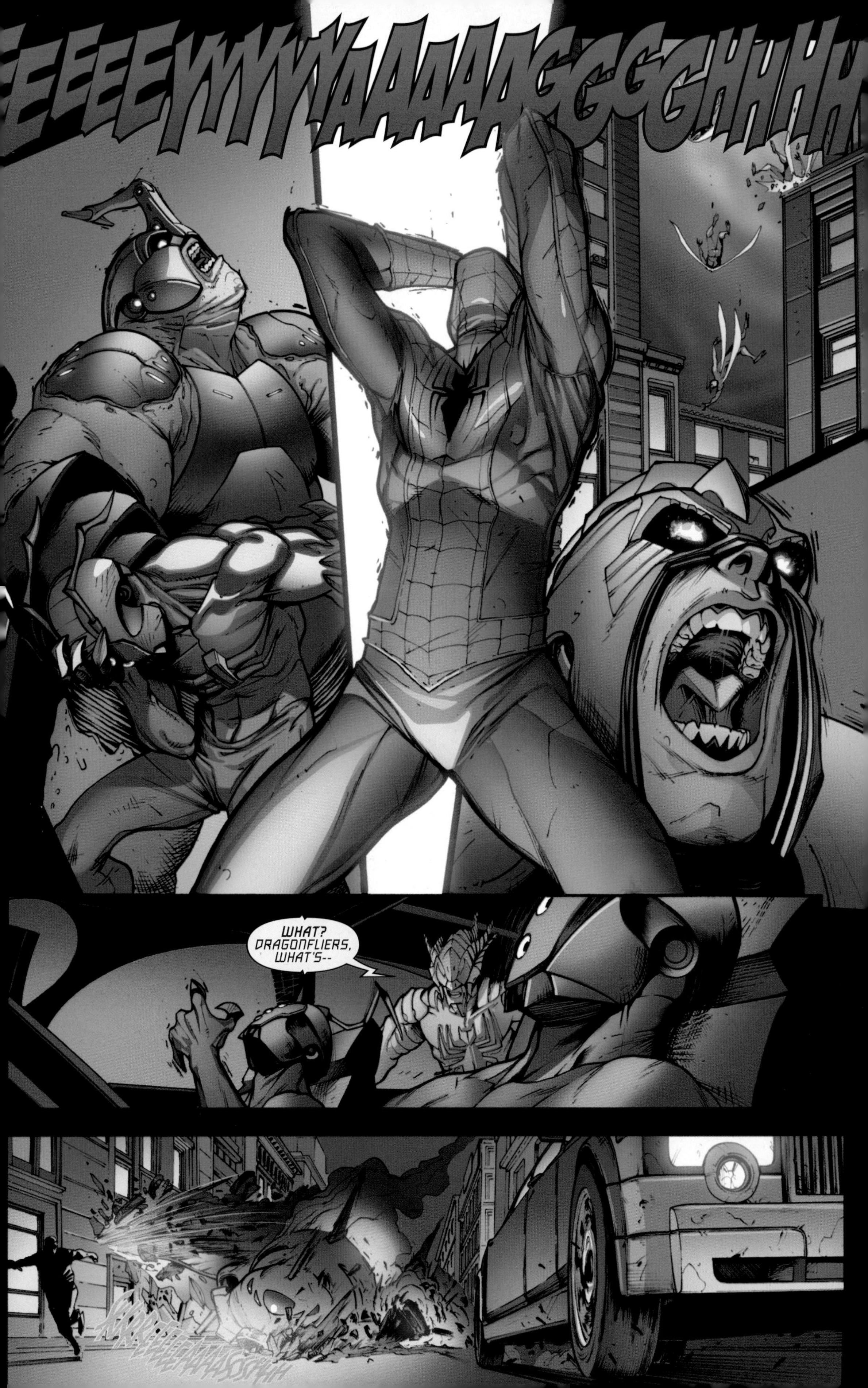
EEEEYYYYAAAAAGGGHHHH
WHAT? DRAGONFLIERS, WHAT'S--

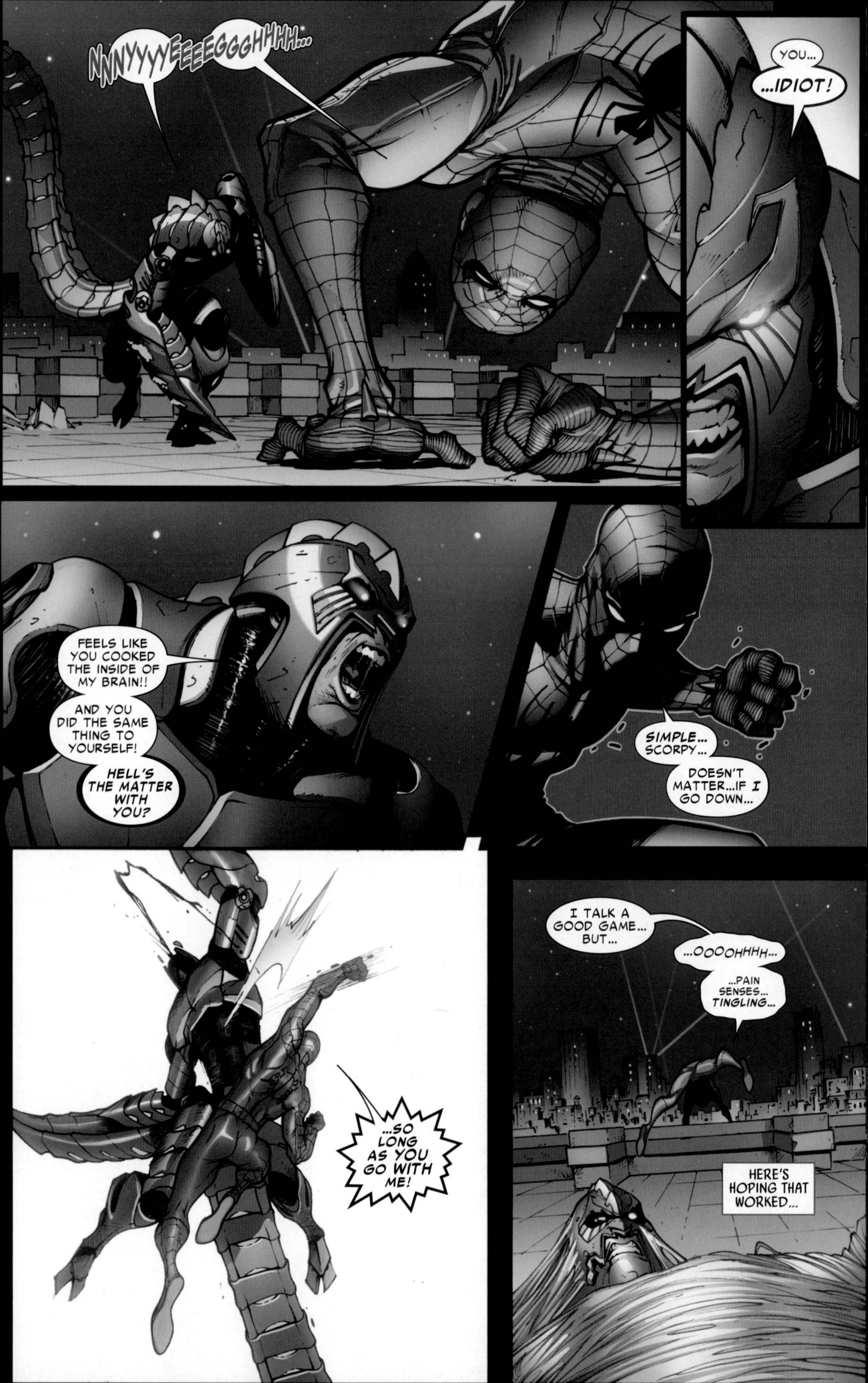

NNNYYYYEEEEGGGHHHH...
YOU...
...IDIOT!
FEELS LIKE YOU COOKED THE INSIDE OF MY BRAIN!!
AND YOU DID THE SAME THING TO YOURSELF!
HELL'S THE MATTER WITH YOU?
SIMPLE... SCORPY...
DOESN'T MATTER...IF I GO DOWN...
...SO LONG AS YOU GO WITH ME!
I TALK A GOOD GAME... BUT...
...OOOOHHHH...
...PAIN SENSES... TINGLING...
HERE'S HOPING THAT WORKED...

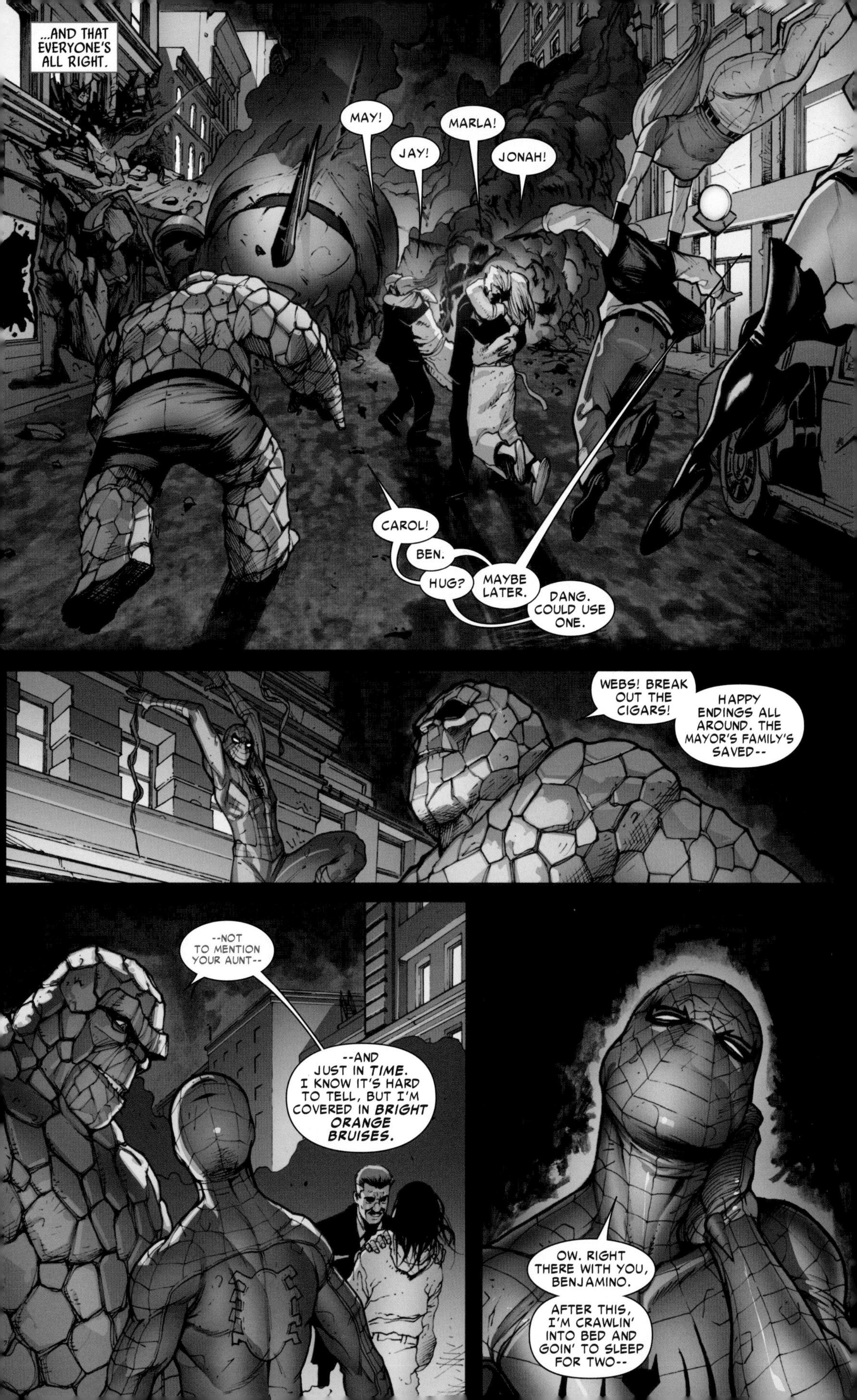
...AND THAT EVERYONE'S ALL RIGHT.
MAY!
JAY!
MARLA!
JONAH!
CAROL!
BEN.
HUG?
MAYBE LATER.
DANG. COULD USE ONE.
WEBS! BREAK OUT THE CIGARS!
HAPPY ENDINGS ALL AROUND. THE MAYOR'S FAMILY'S SAVED--
--NOT TO MENTION YOUR AUNT--
--AND JUST IN TIME. I KNOW IT'S HARD TO TELL, BUT I'M COVERED IN BRIGHT ORANGE BRUISES.
OW. RIGHT THERE WITH YOU, BENJAMINO.
AFTER THIS, I'M CRAWLIN' INTO BED AND GOIN' TO SLEEP FOR TWO--

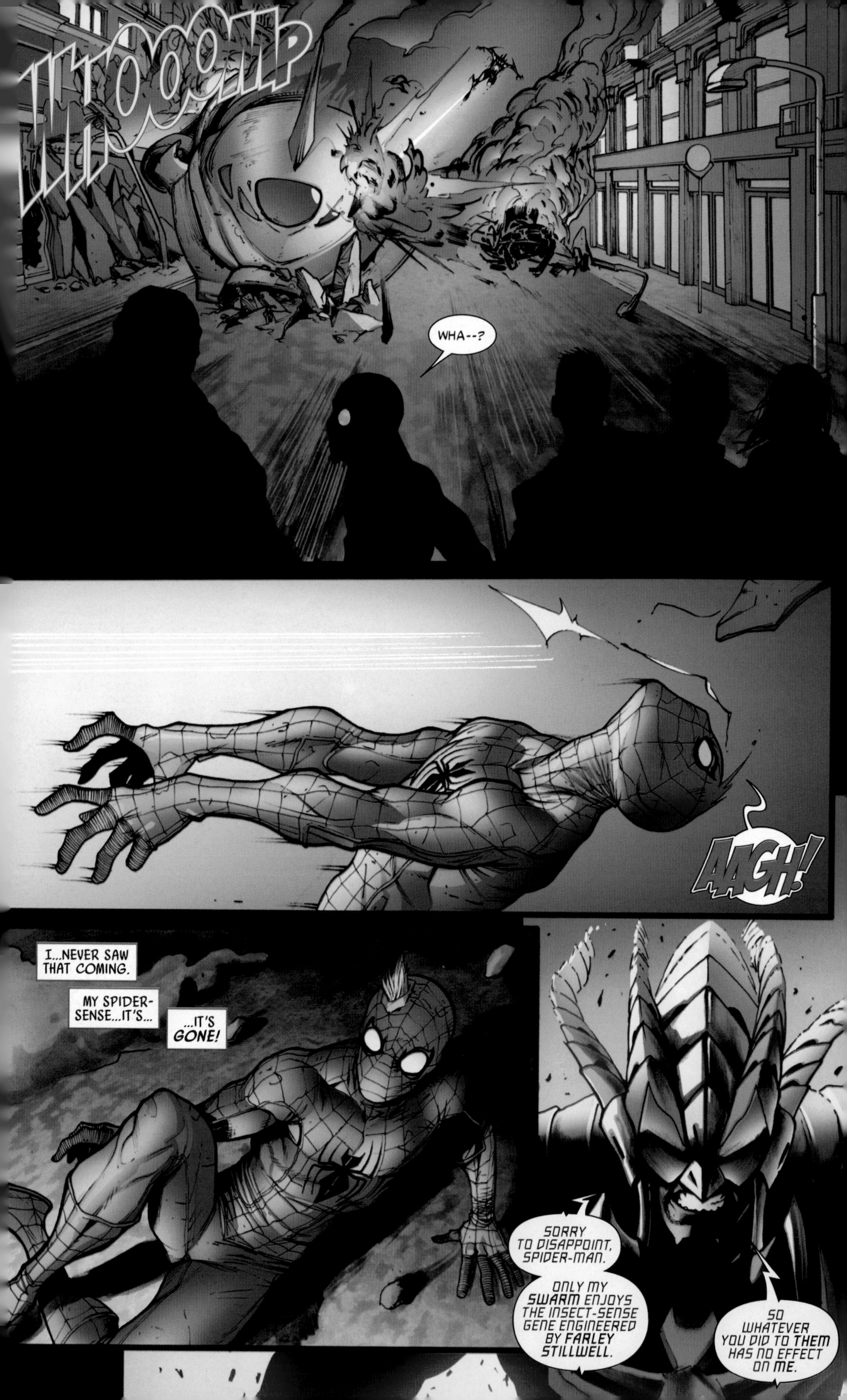

WHOOOMP
WHA--?
AAGH!
I...NEVER SAW THAT COMING.
MY SPIDER-SENSE...IT'S...
...IT'S GONE!
SORRY TO DISAPPOINT, SPIDER-MAN.
ONLY MY SWARM ENJOYS THE INSECT-SENSE GENE ENGINEERED BY FARLEY STILLWELL.
SO WHATEVER YOU DID TO THEM HAS NO EFFECT ON ME.

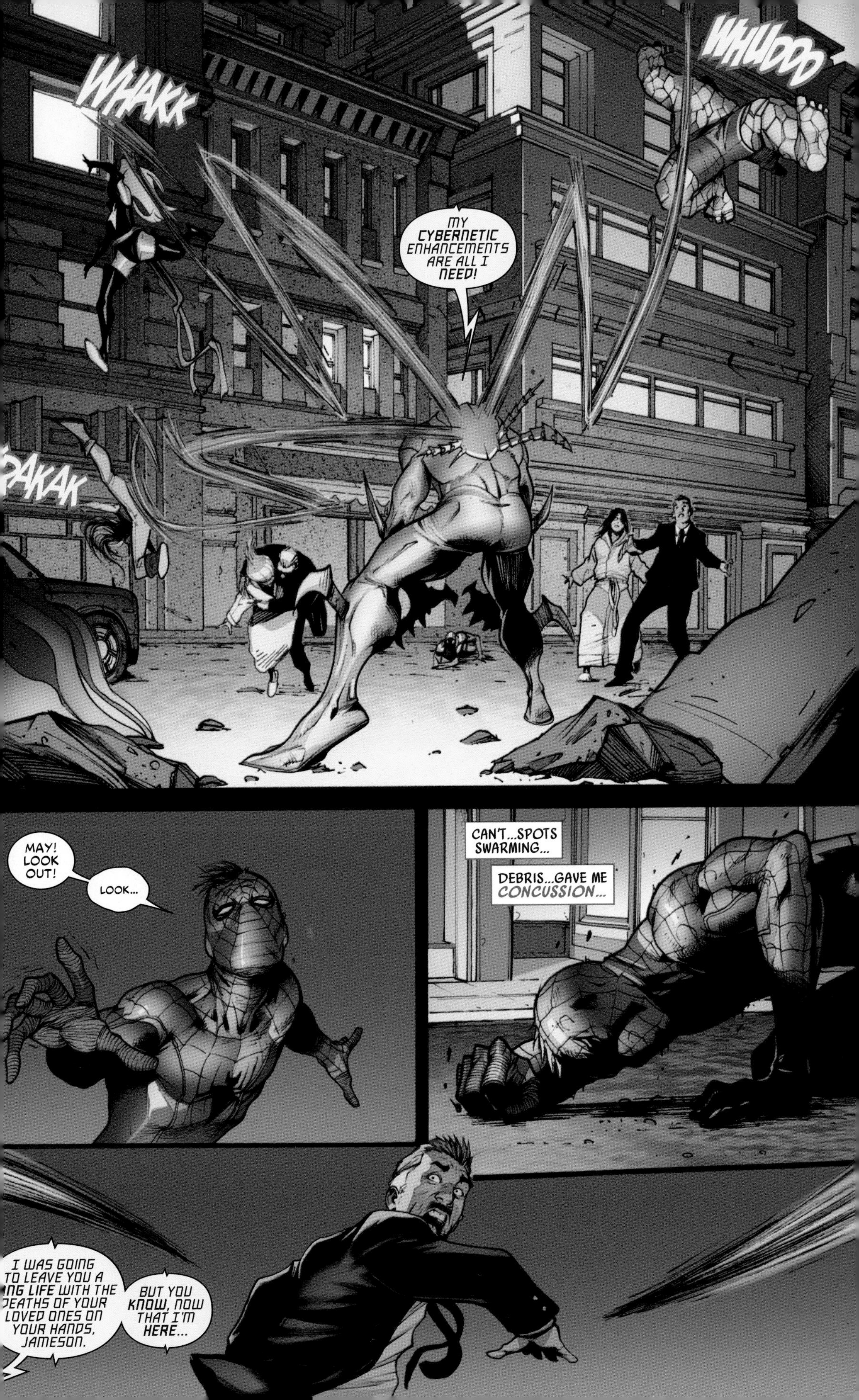
WHAKK
WHUDOO
MY CYBERNETIC ENHANCEMENTS ARE ALL I NEED!
PAKAK
MAY! LOOK OUT!
LOOK...
CAN'T...SPOTS SWARMING...
DEBRIS...GAVE ME CONCUSSION...
I WAS GOING TO LEAVE YOU A NG LIFE WITH THE DEATHS OF YOUR LOVED ONES ON YOUR HANDS, JAMESON.
BUT YOU KNOW, NOW THAT I'M HERE...

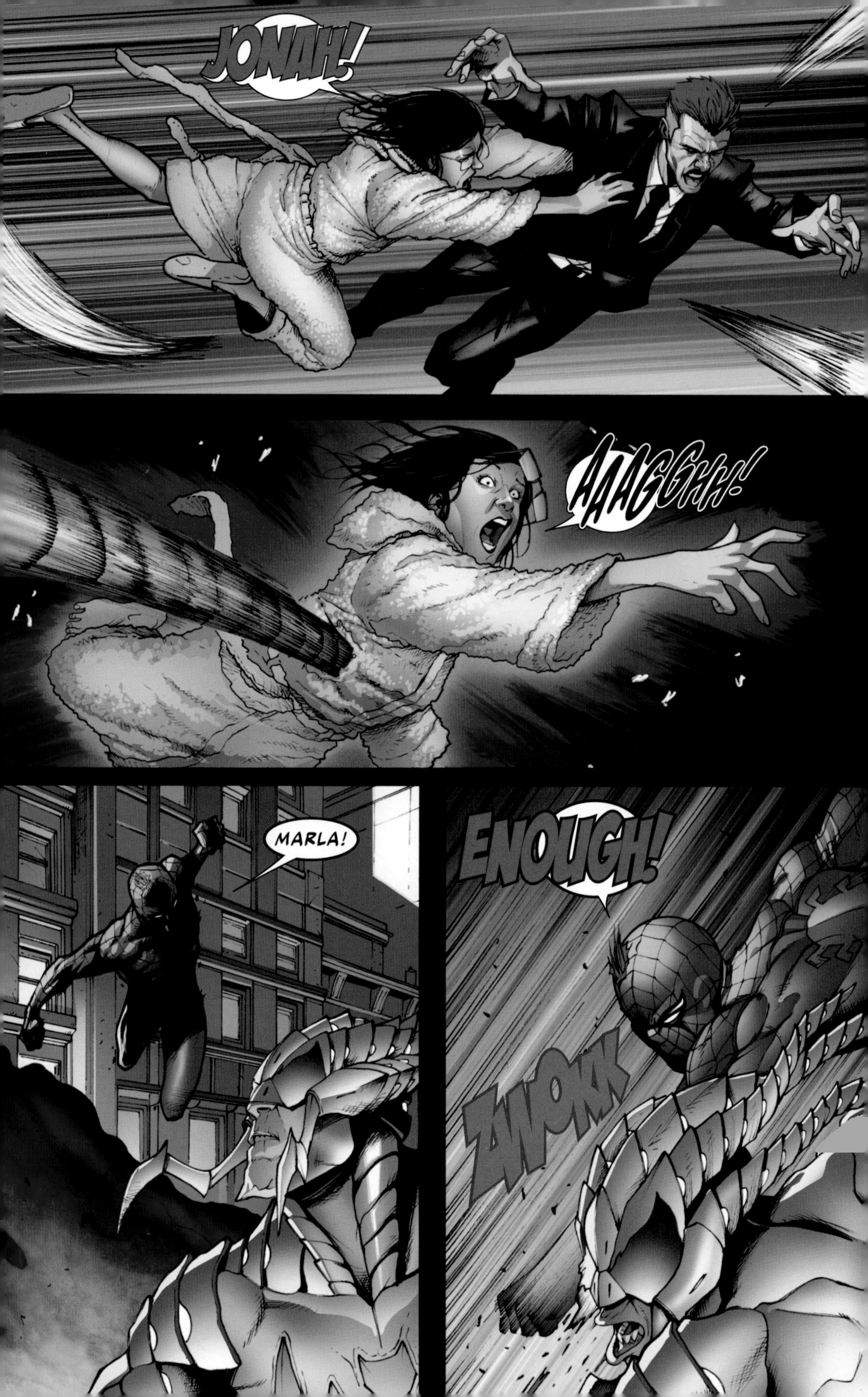
JONAH!
AAAGGHH!
MARLA!
ENOUGH!
ZWOKK

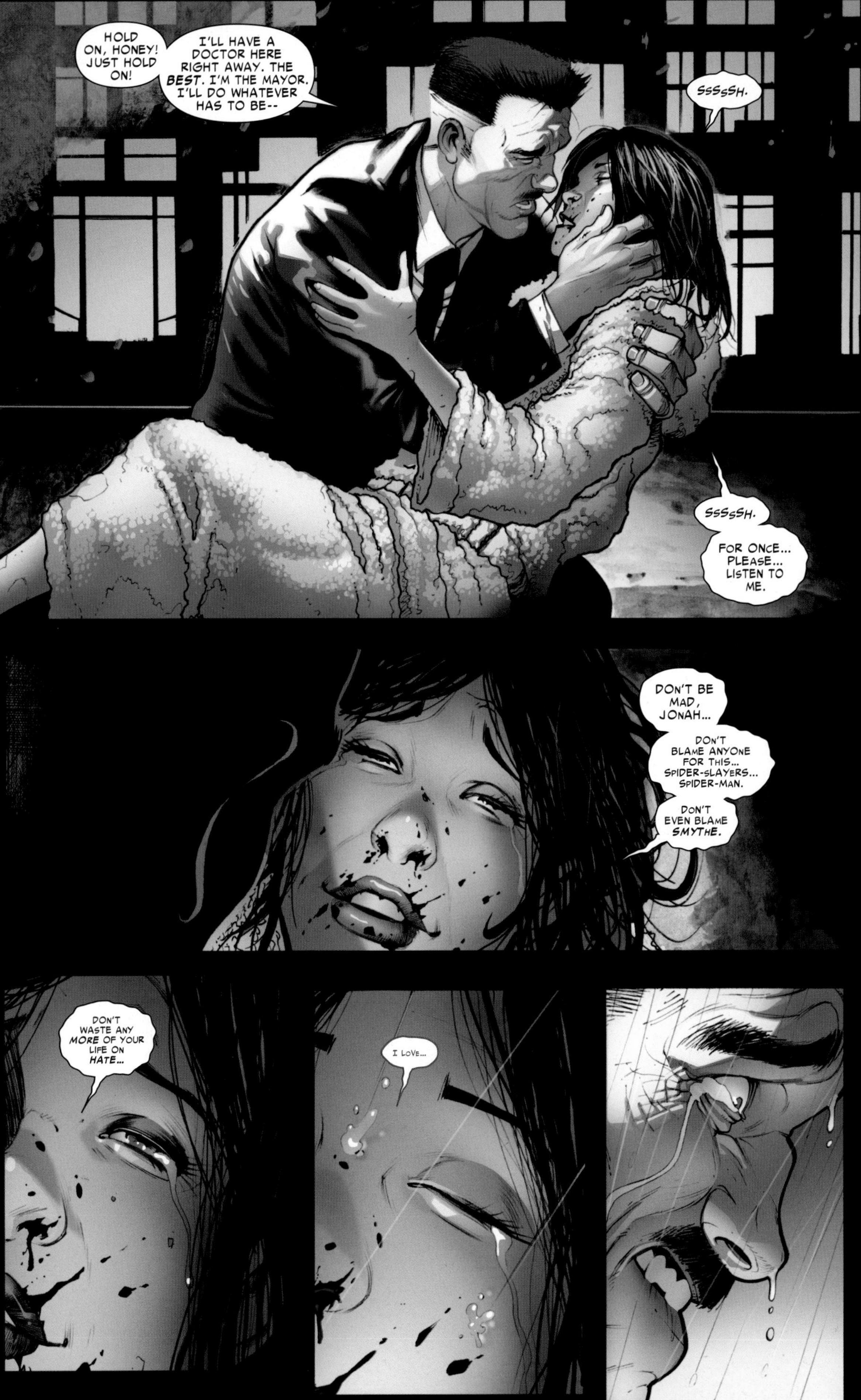
HOLD ON, HONEY! JUST HOLD ON!
I'LL HAVE A DOCTOR HERE RIGHT AWAY. THE BEST. I'M THE MAYOR. I'LL DO WHATEVER HAS TO BE--
SSSSSH.
SSSSSH.
FOR ONCE... PLEASE... LISTEN TO ME.
DON'T BE MAD, JONAH...
DON'T BLAME ANYONE FOR THIS... SPIDER-SLAYERS... SPIDER-MAN.
DON'T EVEN BLAME SMYTHE.
DON'T WASTE ANY MORE OF YOUR LIFE ON HATE...
I LOVE...

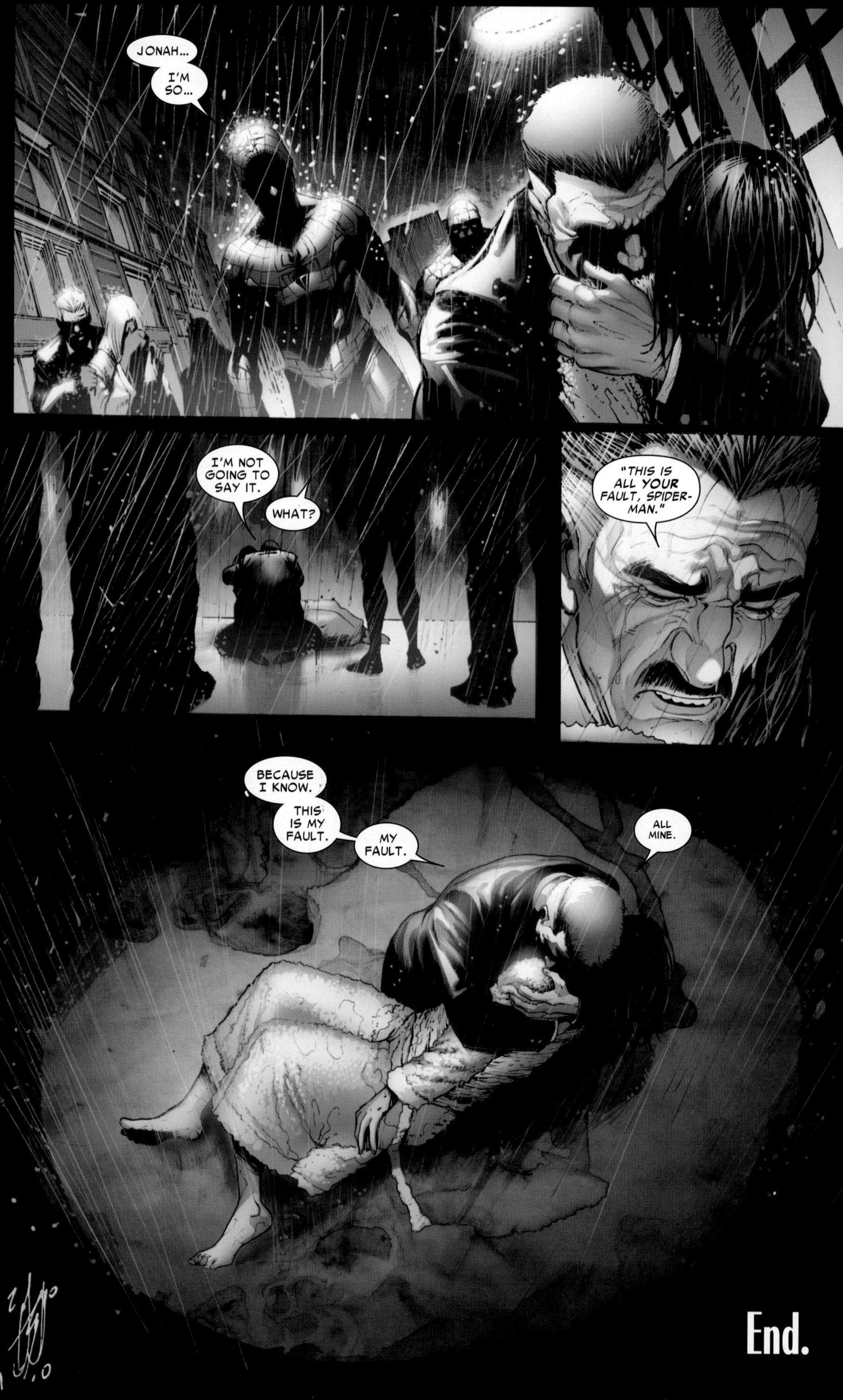
JONAH...
I'M SO...
I'M NOT GOING TO SAY IT.
WHAT?
"THIS IS ALL YOUR FAULT, SPIDER-MAN."
BECAUSE I KNOW.
THIS IS MY FAULT.
MY FAULT.
ALL MINE.
End.

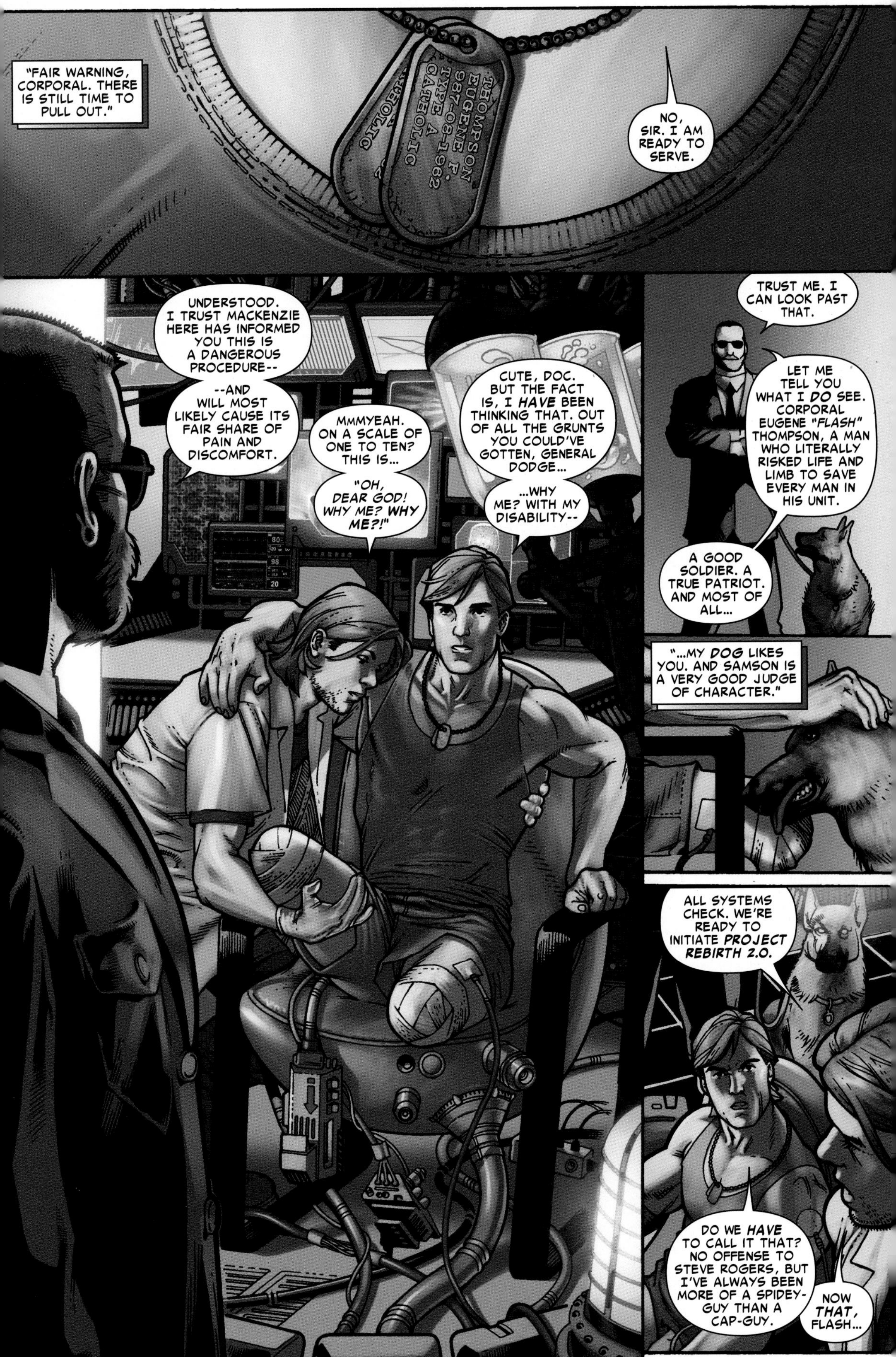

"FAIR WARNING, CORPORAL. THERE IS STILL TIME TO PULL OUT."
THOMPSON EUGENE F. 987-08-1982 TYPE A CATHOLIC
NO, SIR. I AM READY TO SERVE.
UNDERSTOOD. I TRUST MACKENZIE HERE HAS INFORMED YOU THIS IS A DANGEROUS PROCEDURE--
--AND WILL MOST LIKELY CAUSE ITS FAIR SHARE OF PAIN AND DISCOMFORT.
MMMYEAH. ON A SCALE OF ONE TO TEN? THIS IS...
"OH, DEAR GOD! WHY ME? WHY ME?!"
CUTE, DOC. BUT THE FACT IS, I HAVE BEEN THINKING THAT. OUT OF ALL THE GRUNTS YOU COULD'VE GOTTEN, GENERAL DODGE...
...WHY ME? WITH MY DISABILITY--
TRUST ME. I CAN LOOK PAST THAT.
LET ME TELL YOU WHAT I DO SEE. CORPORAL EUGENE "FLASH" THOMPSON, A MAN WHO LITERALLY RISKED LIFE AND LIMB TO SAVE EVERY MAN IN HIS UNIT.
A GOOD SOLDIER. A TRUE PATRIOT. AND MOST OF ALL...
"...MY DOG LIKES YOU. AND SAMSON IS A VERY GOOD JUDGE OF CHARACTER."
ALL SYSTEMS CHECK. WE'RE READY TO INITIATE PROJECT REBIRTH 2.0.
DO WE HAVE TO CALL IT THAT? NO OFFENSE TO STEVE ROGERS, BUT I'VE ALWAYS BEEN MORE OF A SPIDEY-GUY THAN A CAP-GUY.
NOW THAT, FLASH...

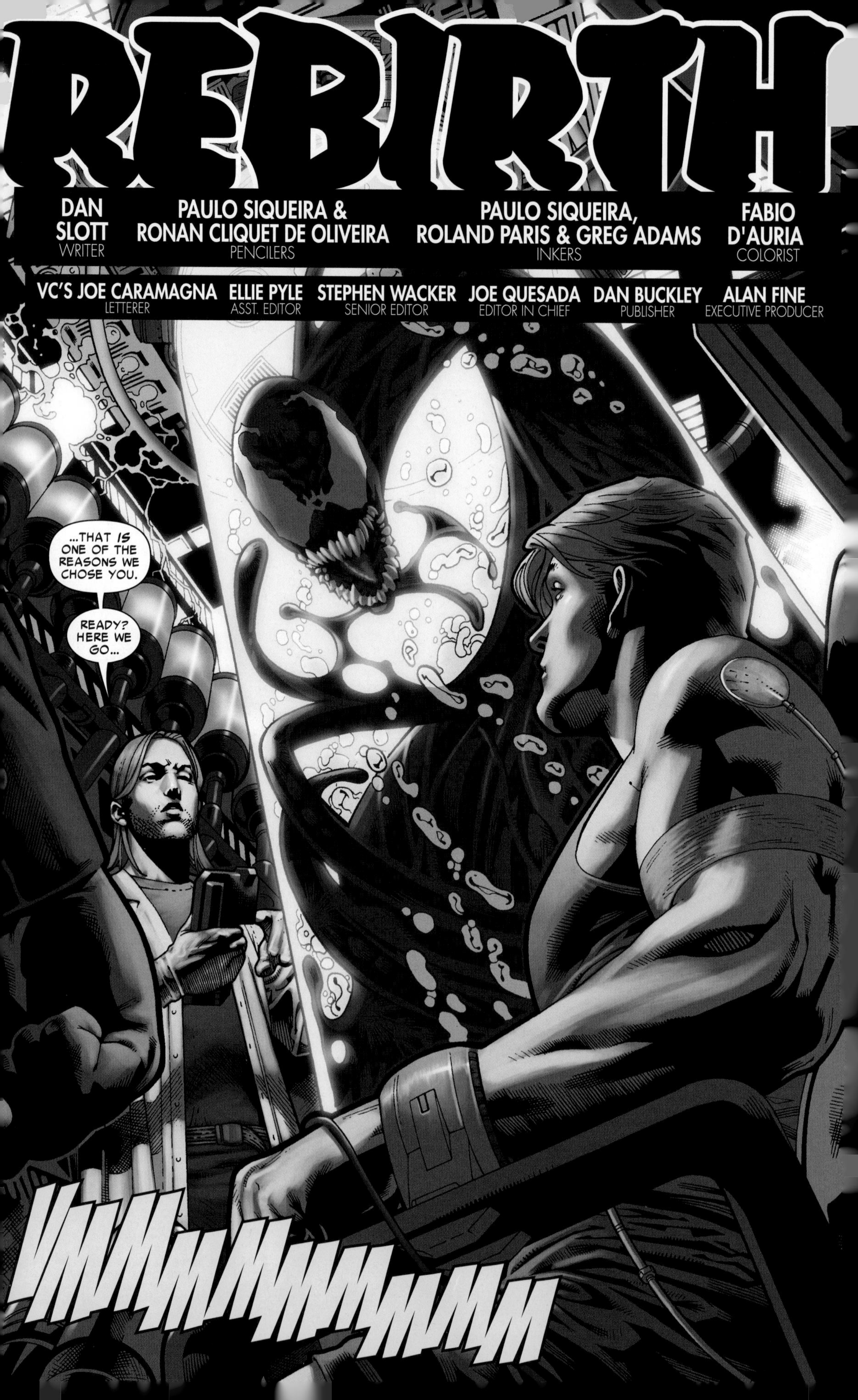
REBIRTH
DAN SLOTT WRITER
PAULO SIQUEIRA & RONAN CLIQUET DE OLIVEIRA PENCILERS
PAULO SIQUEIRA, ROLAND PARIS & GREG ADAMS INKERS
FABIO D'AURIA COLORIST
VC'S JOE CARAMAGNA LETTERER
ELLIE PYLE ASST. EDITOR
STEPHEN WACKER SENIOR EDITOR
JOE QUESADA EDITOR IN CHIEF
DAN BUCKLEY PUBLISHER
ALAN FINE EXECUTIVE PRODUCER
...THAT *IS* ONE OF THE REASONS WE CHOSE YOU.
READY? HERE WE GO...

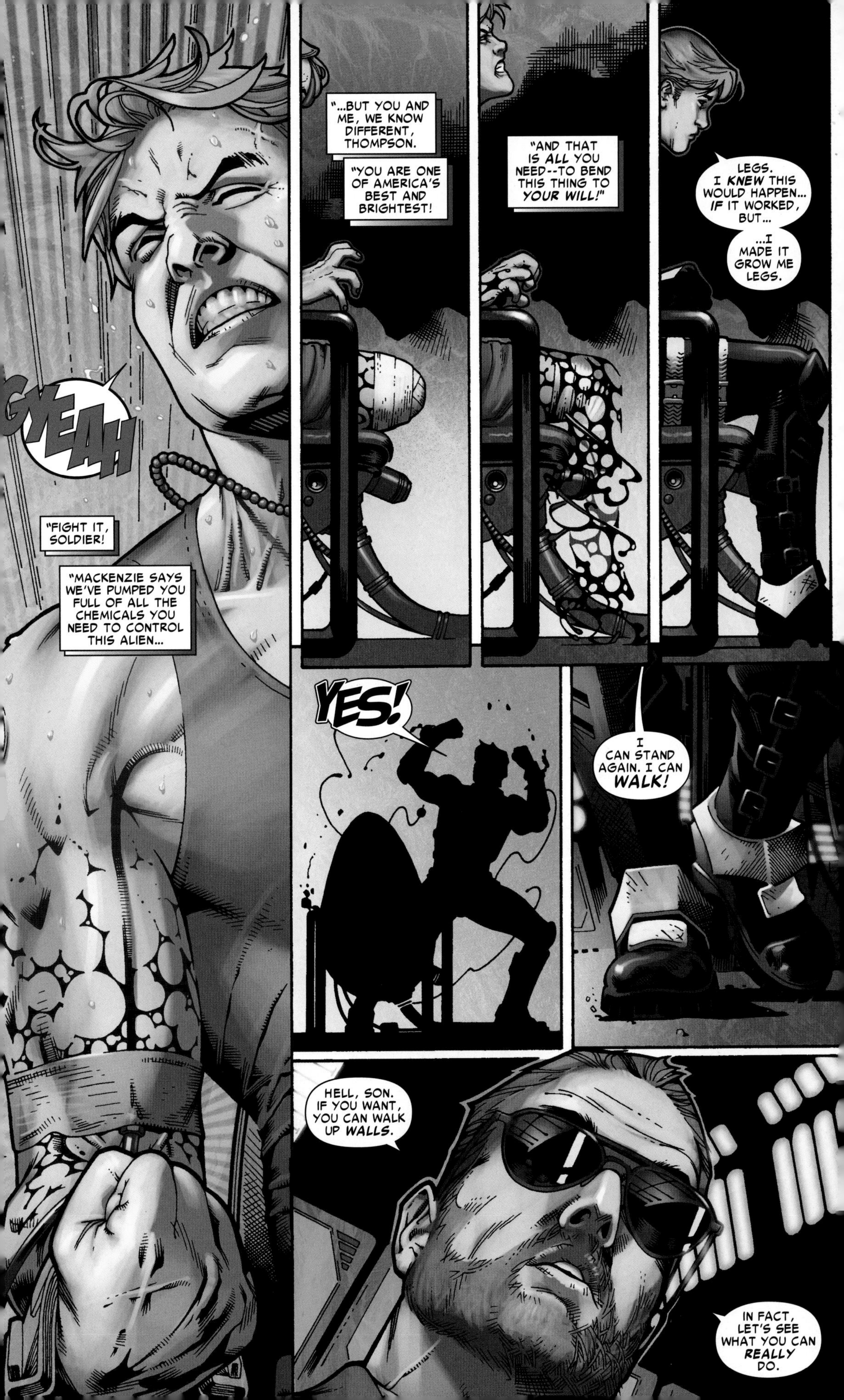
GYEAH
"FIGHT IT, SOLDIER!
"MACKENZIE SAYS WE'VE PUMPED YOU FULL OF ALL THE CHEMICALS YOU NEED TO CONTROL THIS ALIEN...
"...BUT YOU AND ME, WE KNOW DIFFERENT, THOMPSON.
"YOU ARE ONE OF AMERICA'S BEST AND BRIGHTEST!
"AND THAT IS ALL YOU NEED--TO BEND THIS THING TO YOUR WILL!"
LEGS. I KNEW THIS WOULD HAPPEN... IF IT WORKED, BUT...
...I MADE IT GROW ME LEGS.
YES!
I CAN STAND AGAIN. I CAN WALK!
HELL, SON. IF YOU WANT, YOU CAN WALK UP WALLS.
IN FACT, LET'S SEE WHAT YOU CAN REALLY DO.

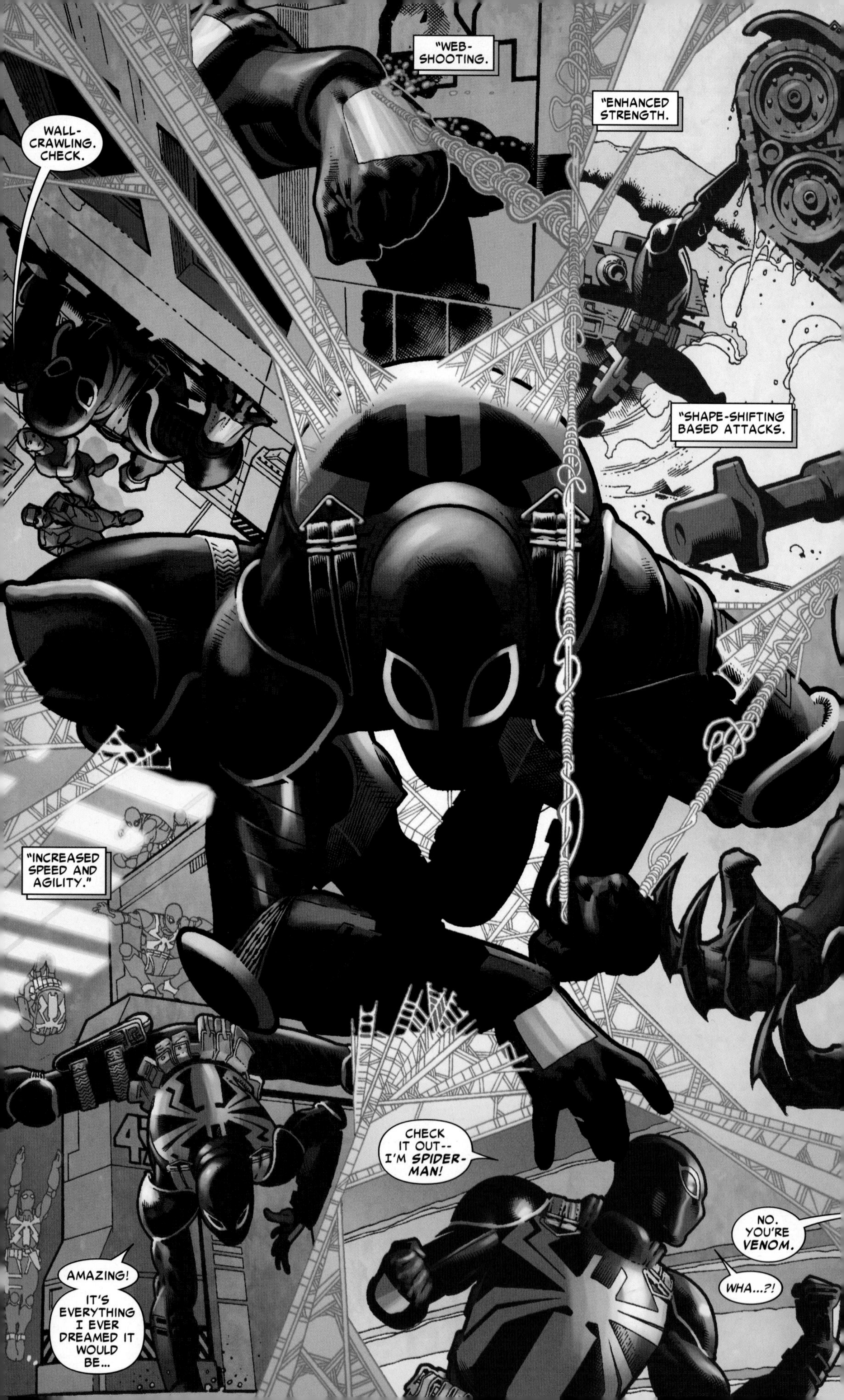
WALL-CRAWLING. CHECK.
"WEB-SHOOTING.
"ENHANCED STRENGTH.
"SHAPE-SHIFTING BASED ATTACKS.
"INCREASED SPEED AND AGILITY."
AMAZING!
IT'S EVERYTHING I EVER DREAMED IT WOULD BE...
CHECK IT OUT-- I'M SPIDER-MAN!
NO. YOU'RE VENOM.
WHA...?!

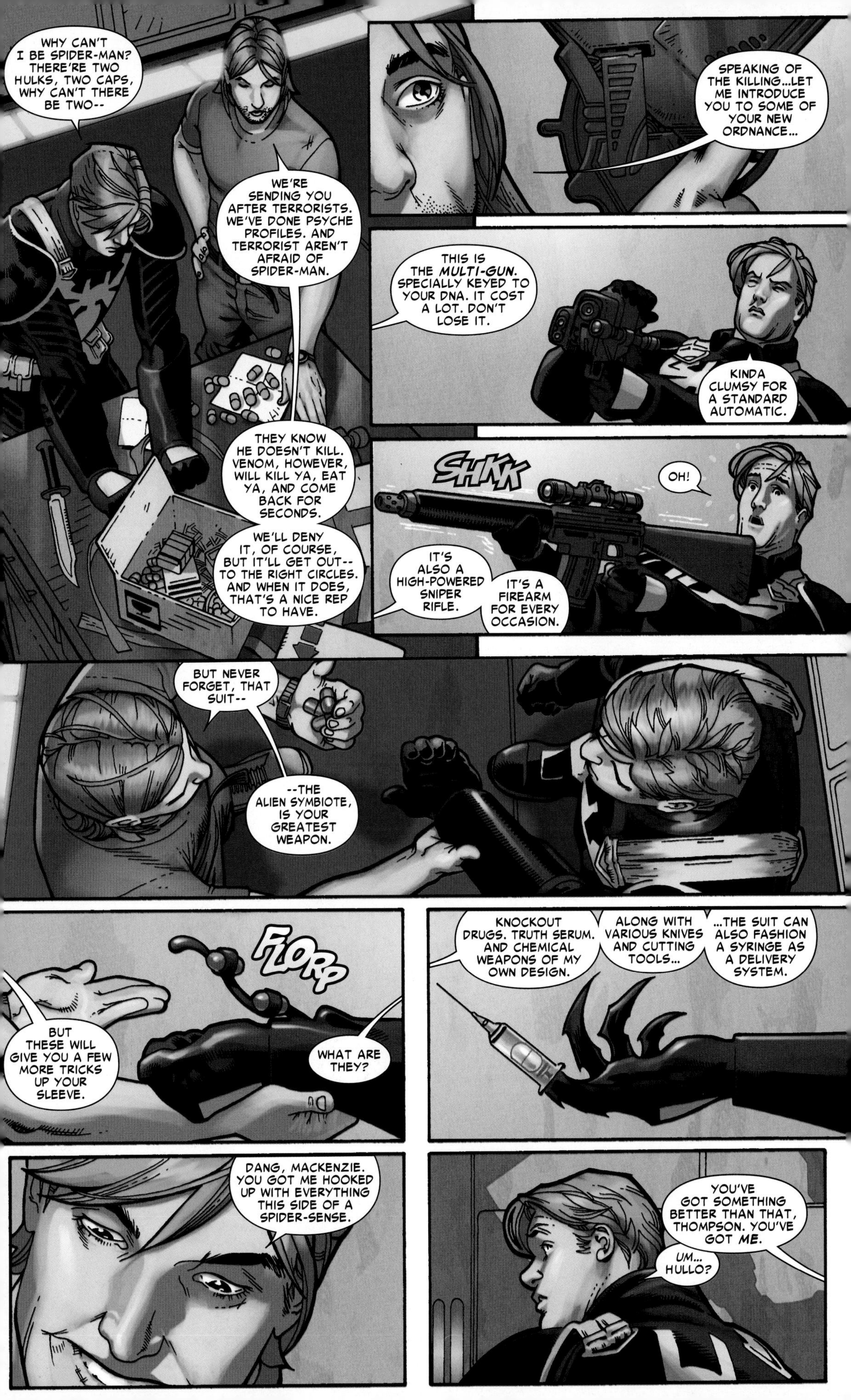
WHY CAN'T I BE SPIDER-MAN? THERE'RE TWO HULKS, TWO CAPS, WHY CAN'T THERE BE TWO--
WE'RE SENDING YOU AFTER TERRORISTS. WE'VE DONE PSYCHE PROFILES. AND TERRORIST AREN'T AFRAID OF SPIDER-MAN.
THEY KNOW HE DOESN'T KILL. VENOM, HOWEVER, WILL KILL YA, EAT YA, AND COME BACK FOR SECONDS.
WE'LL DENY IT, OF COURSE, BUT IT'LL GET OUT-- TO THE RIGHT CIRCLES. AND WHEN IT DOES, THAT'S A NICE REP TO HAVE.
SPEAKING OF THE KILLING...LET ME INTRODUCE YOU TO SOME OF YOUR NEW ORDNANCE...
THIS IS THE MULTI-GUN. SPECIALLY KEYED TO YOUR DNA. IT COST A LOT. DON'T LOSE IT.
KINDA CLUMSY FOR A STANDARD AUTOMATIC.
SHKK
OH!
IT'S ALSO A HIGH-POWERED SNIPER RIFLE.
IT'S A FIREARM FOR EVERY OCCASION.
BUT NEVER FORGET, THAT SUIT--
--THE ALIEN SYMBIOTE, IS YOUR GREATEST WEAPON.
FLORP
BUT THESE WILL GIVE YOU A FEW MORE TRICKS UP YOUR SLEEVE.
WHAT ARE THEY?
KNOCKOUT DRUGS. TRUTH SERUM. AND CHEMICAL WEAPONS OF MY OWN DESIGN.
ALONG WITH VARIOUS KNIVES AND CUTTING TOOLS...
...THE SUIT CAN ALSO FASHION A SYRINGE AS A DELIVERY SYSTEM.
DANG, MACKENZIE. YOU GOT ME HOOKED UP WITH EVERYTHING THIS SIDE OF A SPIDER-SENSE.
YOU'VE GOT SOMETHING BETTER THAN THAT, THOMPSON. YOU'VE GOT ME.
UM... HULLO?

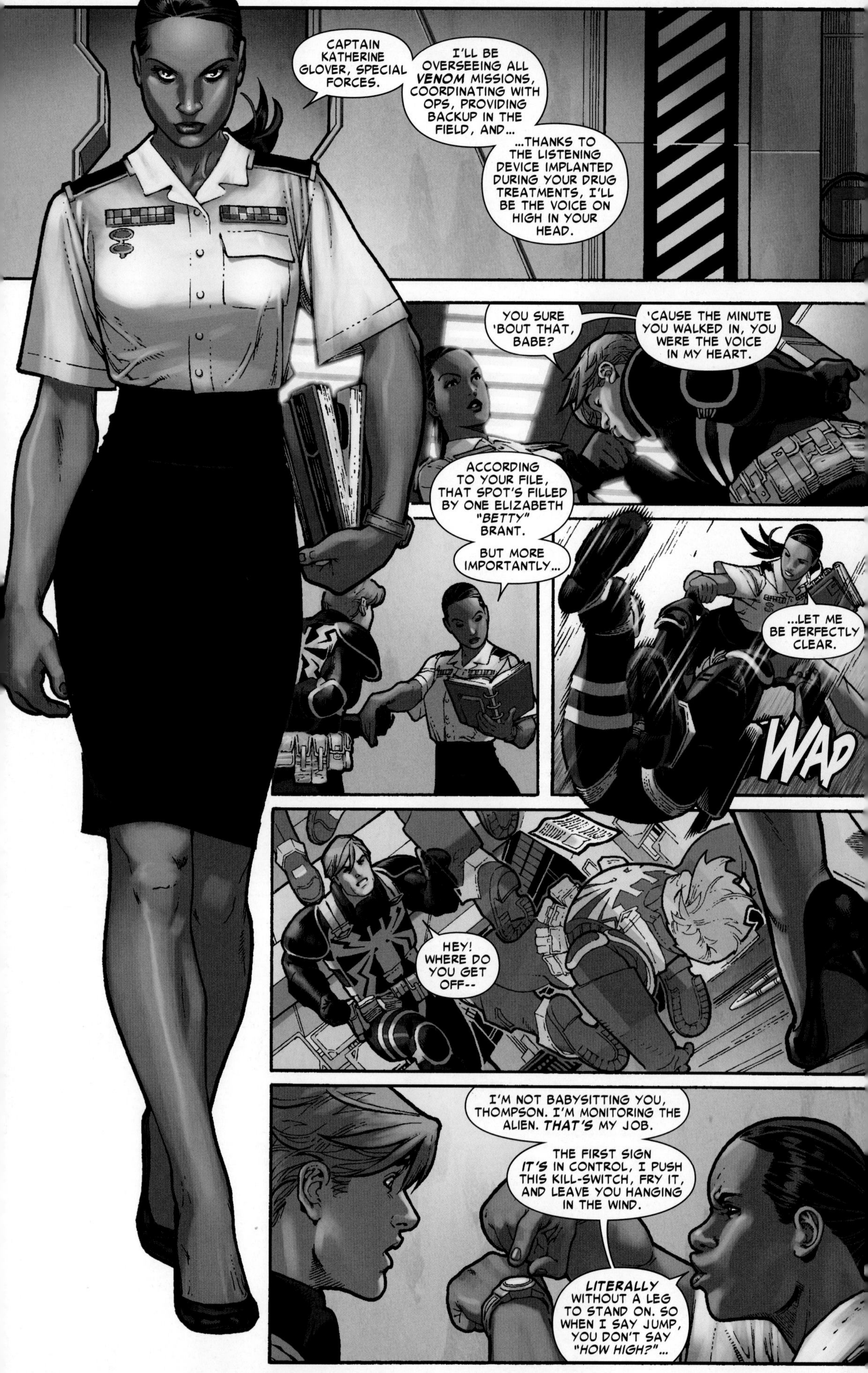
CAPTAIN KATHERINE GLOVER, SPECIAL FORCES.
I'LL BE OVERSEEING ALL *VENOM* MISSIONS, COORDINATING WITH OPS, PROVIDING BACKUP IN THE FIELD, AND...
...THANKS TO THE LISTENING DEVICE IMPLANTED DURING YOUR DRUG TREATMENTS, I'LL BE THE VOICE ON HIGH IN YOUR HEAD.
YOU SURE 'BOUT THAT, BABE?
'CAUSE THE MINUTE YOU WALKED IN, YOU WERE THE VOICE IN MY HEART.
ACCORDING TO YOUR FILE, THAT SPOT'S FILLED BY ONE ELIZABETH "*BETTY*" BRANT.
BUT MORE IMPORTANTLY...
...LET ME BE PERFECTLY CLEAR.
WAP
HEY! WHERE DO YOU GET OFF--
I'M NOT BABYSITTING YOU, THOMPSON. I'M MONITORING THE ALIEN. *THAT'S* MY JOB.
THE FIRST SIGN *IT'S* IN CONTROL, I PUSH THIS KILL-SWITCH, FRY IT, AND LEAVE YOU HANGING IN THE WIND.
LITERALLY WITHOUT A LEG TO STAND ON. SO WHEN I SAY JUMP, YOU DON'T SAY "*HOW HIGH?*"...

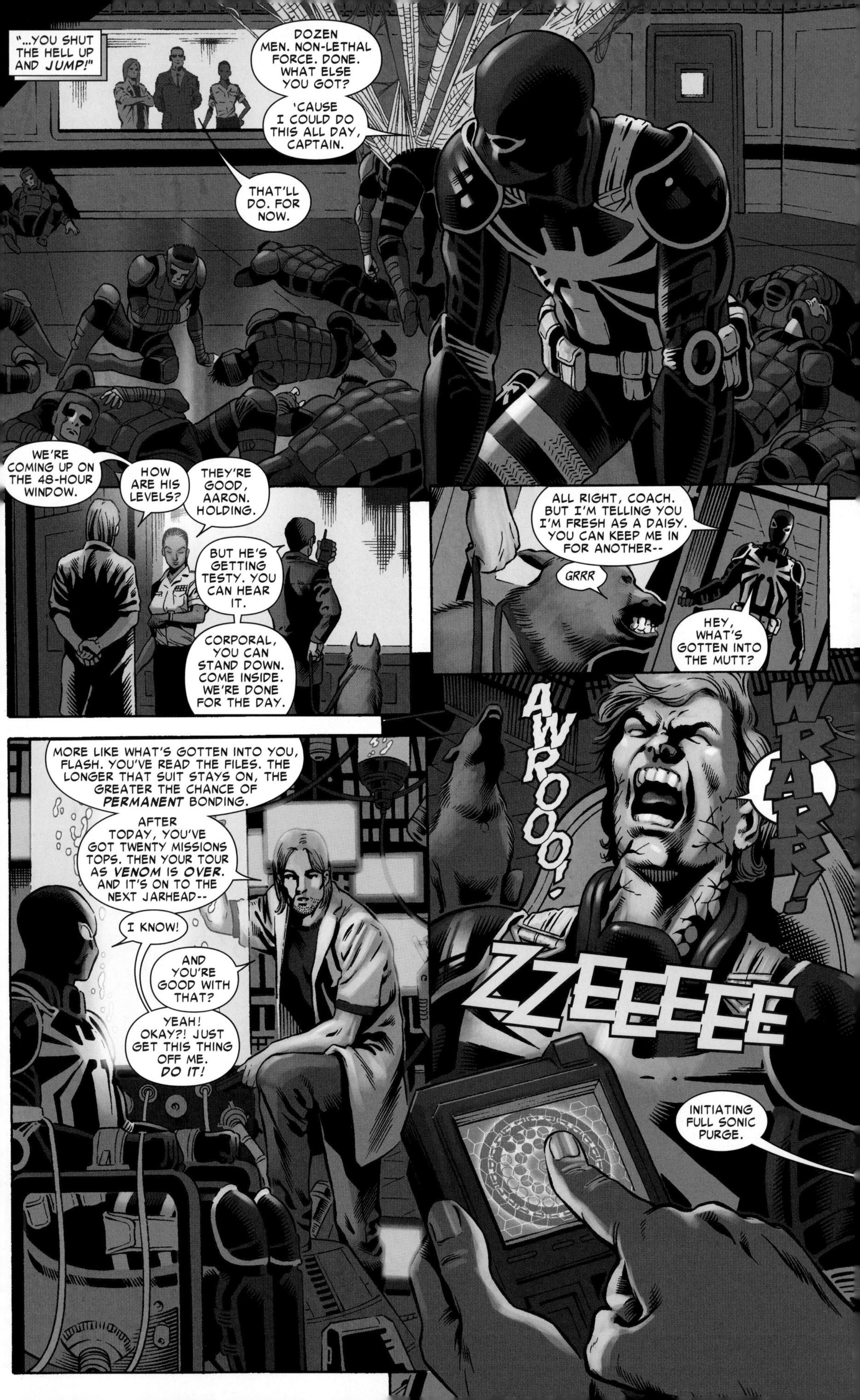
"...YOU SHUT THE HELL UP AND *JUMP!*"
DOZEN MEN. NON-LETHAL FORCE. DONE. WHAT ELSE YOU GOT?
'CAUSE I COULD DO THIS ALL DAY, CAPTAIN.
THAT'LL DO. FOR NOW.
WE'RE COMING UP ON THE 48-HOUR WINDOW.
HOW ARE HIS LEVELS?
THEY'RE GOOD, AARON. HOLDING.
BUT HE'S GETTING TESTY. YOU CAN HEAR IT.
CORPORAL, YOU CAN STAND DOWN. COME INSIDE. WE'RE DONE FOR THE DAY.
ALL RIGHT, COACH. BUT I'M TELLING YOU I'M FRESH AS A DAISY. YOU CAN KEEP ME IN FOR ANOTHER--
GRRR
HEY, WHAT'S GOTTEN INTO THE MUTT?
MORE LIKE WHAT'S GOTTEN INTO YOU, FLASH. YOU'VE READ THE FILES. THE LONGER THAT SUIT STAYS ON, THE GREATER THE CHANCE OF *PERMANENT* BONDING.
AFTER TODAY, YOU'VE GOT TWENTY MISSIONS TOPS. THEN YOUR TOUR AS *VENOM* IS *OVER*. AND IT'S ON TO THE NEXT JARHEAD--
I KNOW!
AND YOU'RE GOOD WITH THAT?
YEAH! OKAY?! JUST GET THIS THING OFF ME. *DO IT!*
AWROOO!
WRARR!
ZZEEEEE
INITIATING FULL SONIC PURGE.

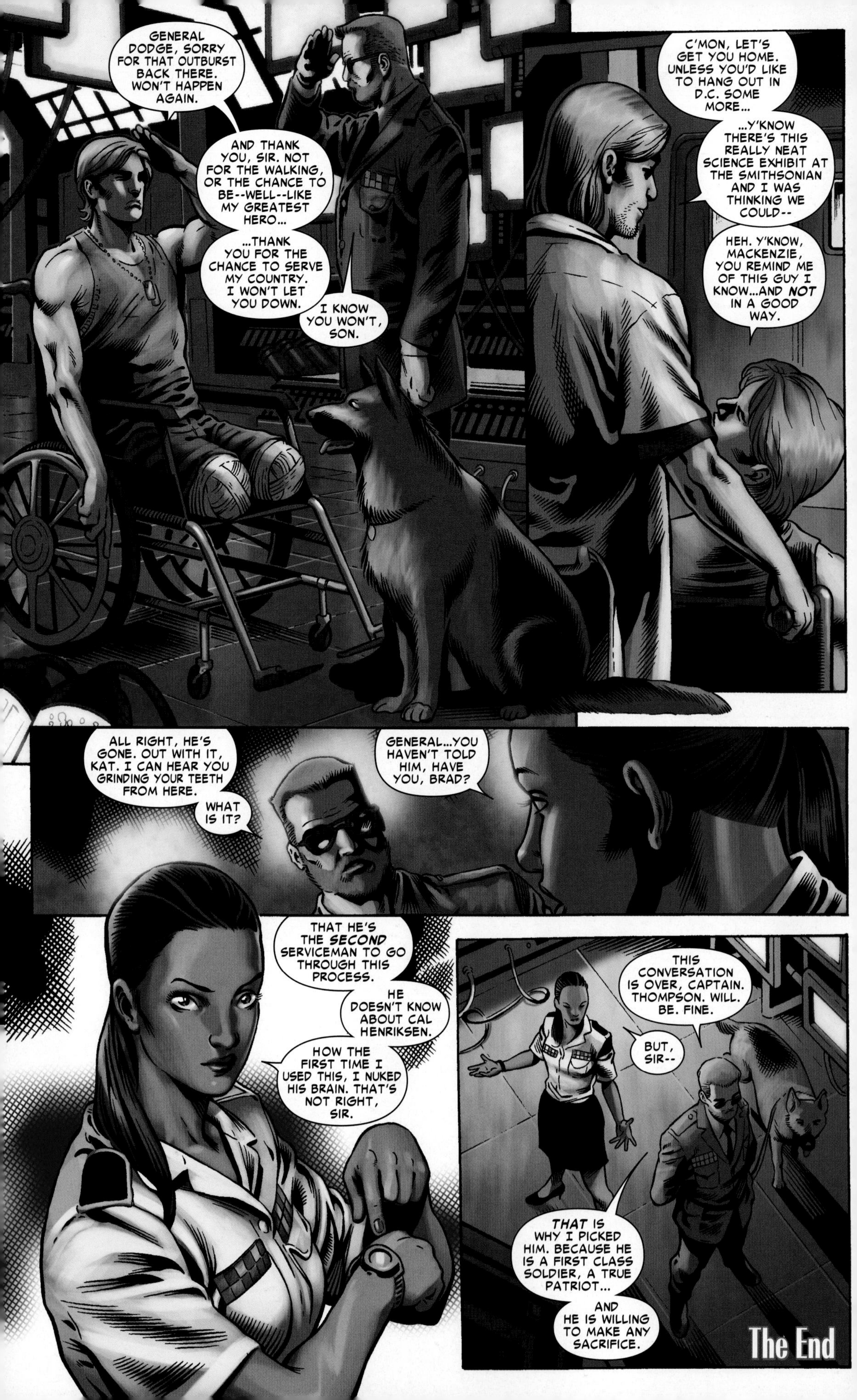
GENERAL DODGE, SORRY FOR THAT OUTBURST BACK THERE. WON'T HAPPEN AGAIN.
AND THANK YOU, SIR. NOT FOR THE WALKING, OR THE CHANCE TO BE--WELL--LIKE MY GREATEST HERO...
...THANK YOU FOR THE CHANCE TO SERVE MY COUNTRY. I WON'T LET YOU DOWN.
I KNOW YOU WON'T, SON.
C'MON, LET'S GET YOU HOME. UNLESS YOU'D LIKE TO HANG OUT IN D.C. SOME MORE...
...Y'KNOW THERE'S THIS REALLY NEAT SCIENCE EXHIBIT AT THE SMITHSONIAN AND I WAS THINKING WE COULD--
HEH. Y'KNOW, MACKENZIE, YOU REMIND ME OF THIS GUY I KNOW...AND *NOT* IN A GOOD WAY.
ALL RIGHT, HE'S GONE. OUT WITH IT, KAT. I CAN HEAR YOU GRINDING YOUR TEETH FROM HERE.
WHAT IS IT?
GENERAL...YOU HAVEN'T TOLD HIM, HAVE YOU, BRAD?
THAT HE'S THE *SECOND* SERVICEMAN TO GO THROUGH THIS PROCESS.
HE DOESN'T KNOW ABOUT CAL HENRIKSEN.
HOW THE FIRST TIME I USED THIS, I NUKED HIS BRAIN. THAT'S NOT RIGHT, SIR.
THIS CONVERSATION IS OVER, CAPTAIN. THOMPSON. WILL. BE. FINE.
BUT, SIR--
THAT IS WHY I PICKED HIM. BECAUSE HE IS A FIRST CLASS SOLDIER, A TRUE PATRIOT...
AND HE IS WILLING TO MAKE ANY SACRIFICE.
The End

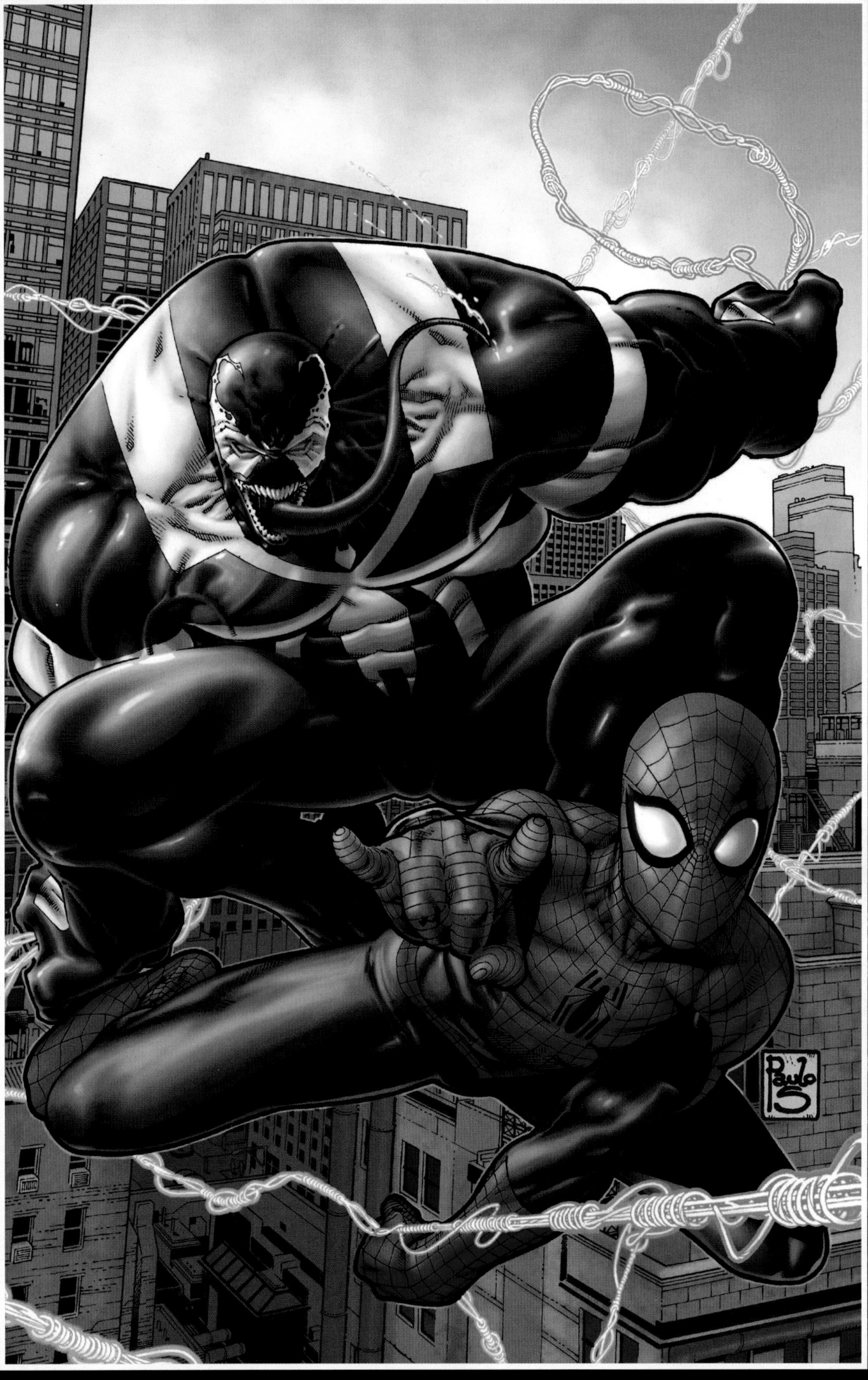
Paulo S

AMAZING SPIDER-MAN #654.1
COVER BY PAULO SIQUEIRA, CARLOS CUEVAS & MORRY HOLLOWELL

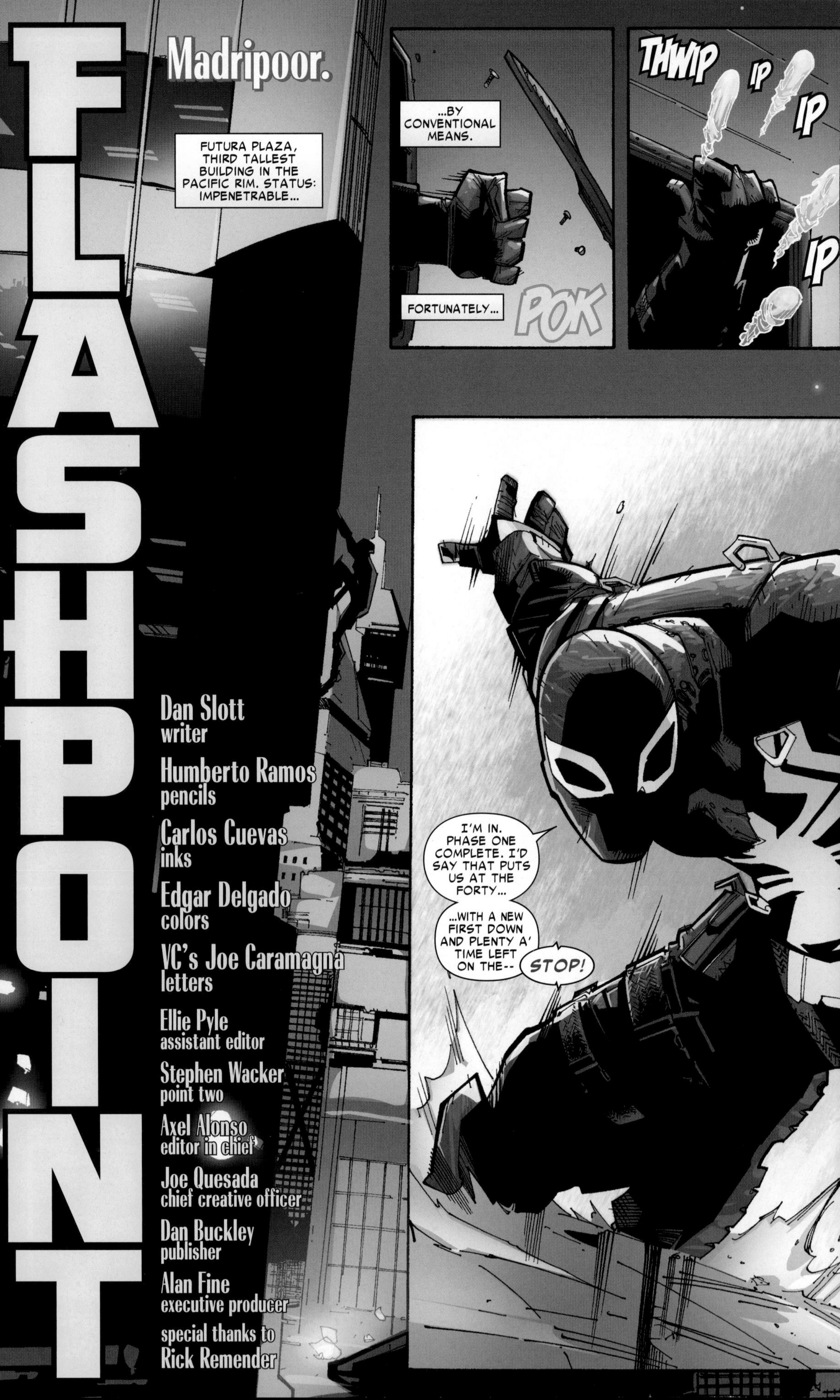
FLASHPOINT
Madripoor.
FUTURA PLAZA, THIRD TALLEST BUILDING IN THE PACIFIC RIM. STATUS: IMPENETRABLE...
...BY CONVENTIONAL MEANS.
FORTUNATELY...
POK
THWIP
IP
IP
IP
I'M IN. PHASE ONE COMPLETE. I'D SAY THAT PUTS US AT THE FORTY...
...WITH A NEW FIRST DOWN AND PLENTY A' TIME LEFT ON THE--
STOP!
Dan Slott
writer
Humberto Ramos
pencils
Carlos Cuevas
inks
Edgar Delgado
colors
VC's Joe Caramagna
letters
Ellie Pyle
assistant editor
Stephen Wacker
point two
Axel Alonso
editor in chief
Joe Quesada
chief creative officer
Dan Buckley
publisher
Alan Fine
executive producer
special thanks to
Rick Remender

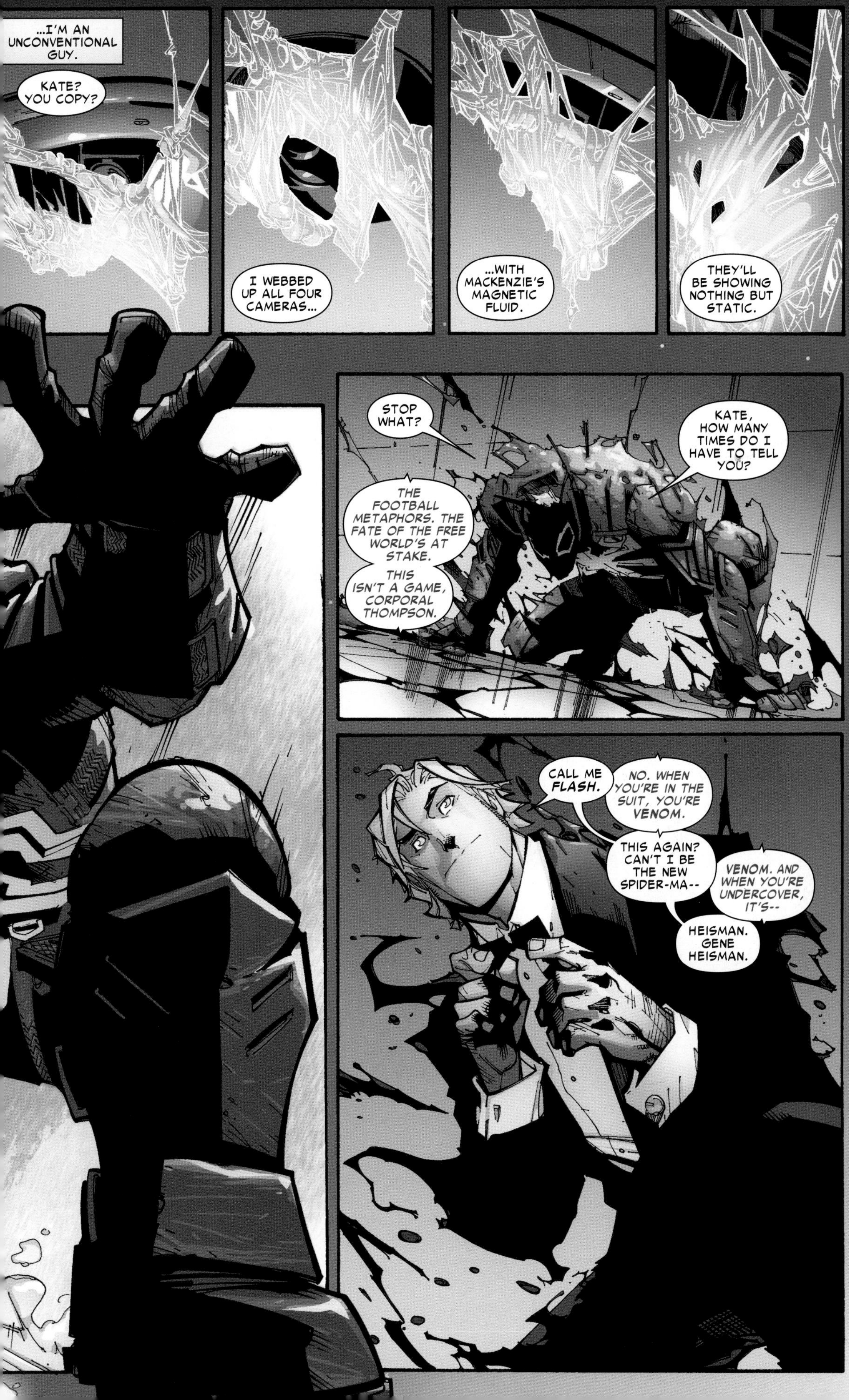
...I'M AN UNCONVENTIONAL GUY.
KATE? YOU COPY?
I WEBBED UP ALL FOUR CAMERAS...
...WITH MACKENZIE'S MAGNETIC FLUID.
THEY'LL BE SHOWING NOTHING BUT STATIC.
KATE, HOW MANY TIMES DO I HAVE TO TELL YOU?
STOP WHAT?
THE FOOTBALL METAPHORS. THE FATE OF THE FREE WORLD'S AT STAKE.
THIS ISN'T A GAME, CORPORAL THOMPSON.
CALL ME FLASH.
NO. WHEN YOU'RE IN THE SUIT, YOU'RE VENOM.
THIS AGAIN? CAN'T I BE THE NEW SPIDER-MA--
VENOM. AND WHEN YOU'RE UNDERCOVER, IT'S--
HEISMAN. GENE HEISMAN.

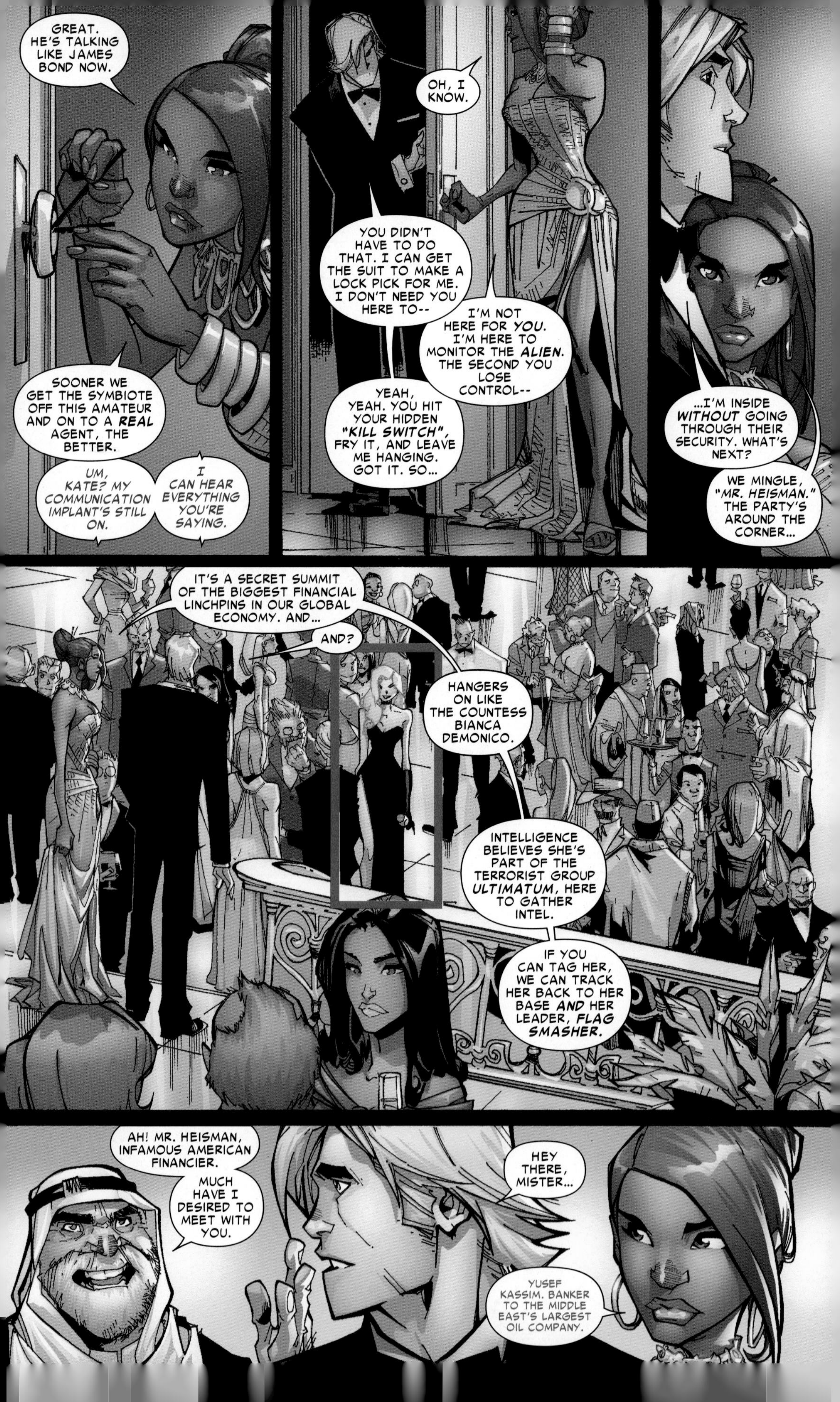
GREAT. HE'S TALKING LIKE JAMES BOND NOW.
SOONER WE GET THE SYMBIOTE OFF THIS AMATEUR AND ON TO A REAL AGENT, THE BETTER.
UM, KATE? MY COMMUNICATION IMPLANT'S STILL ON.
I CAN HEAR EVERYTHING YOU'RE SAYING.
OH, I KNOW.
YOU DIDN'T HAVE TO DO THAT. I CAN GET THE SUIT TO MAKE A LOCK PICK FOR ME. I DON'T NEED YOU HERE TO--
I'M NOT HERE FOR YOU. I'M HERE TO MONITOR THE ALIEN. THE SECOND YOU LOSE CONTROL--
YEAH, YEAH. YOU HIT YOUR HIDDEN "KILL SWITCH", FRY IT, AND LEAVE ME HANGING. GOT IT. SO...
...I'M INSIDE WITHOUT GOING THROUGH THEIR SECURITY. WHAT'S NEXT?
WE MINGLE, "MR. HEISMAN." THE PARTY'S AROUND THE CORNER...
IT'S A SECRET SUMMIT OF THE BIGGEST FINANCIAL LINCHPINS IN OUR GLOBAL ECONOMY. AND...
AND?
HANGERS ON LIKE THE COUNTESS BIANCA DEMONICO.
INTELLIGENCE BELIEVES SHE'S PART OF THE TERRORIST GROUP ULTIMATUM, HERE TO GATHER INTEL.
IF YOU CAN TAG HER, WE CAN TRACK HER BASE BACK TO HER BASE AND HER LEADER, FLAG SMASHER.
AH! MR. HEISMAN, INFAMOUS AMERICAN FINANCIER.
MUCH HAVE I DESIRED TO MEET WITH YOU.
HEY THERE, MISTER...
YUSEF KASSIM. BANKER TO THE MIDDLE EAST'S LARGEST OIL COMPANY.

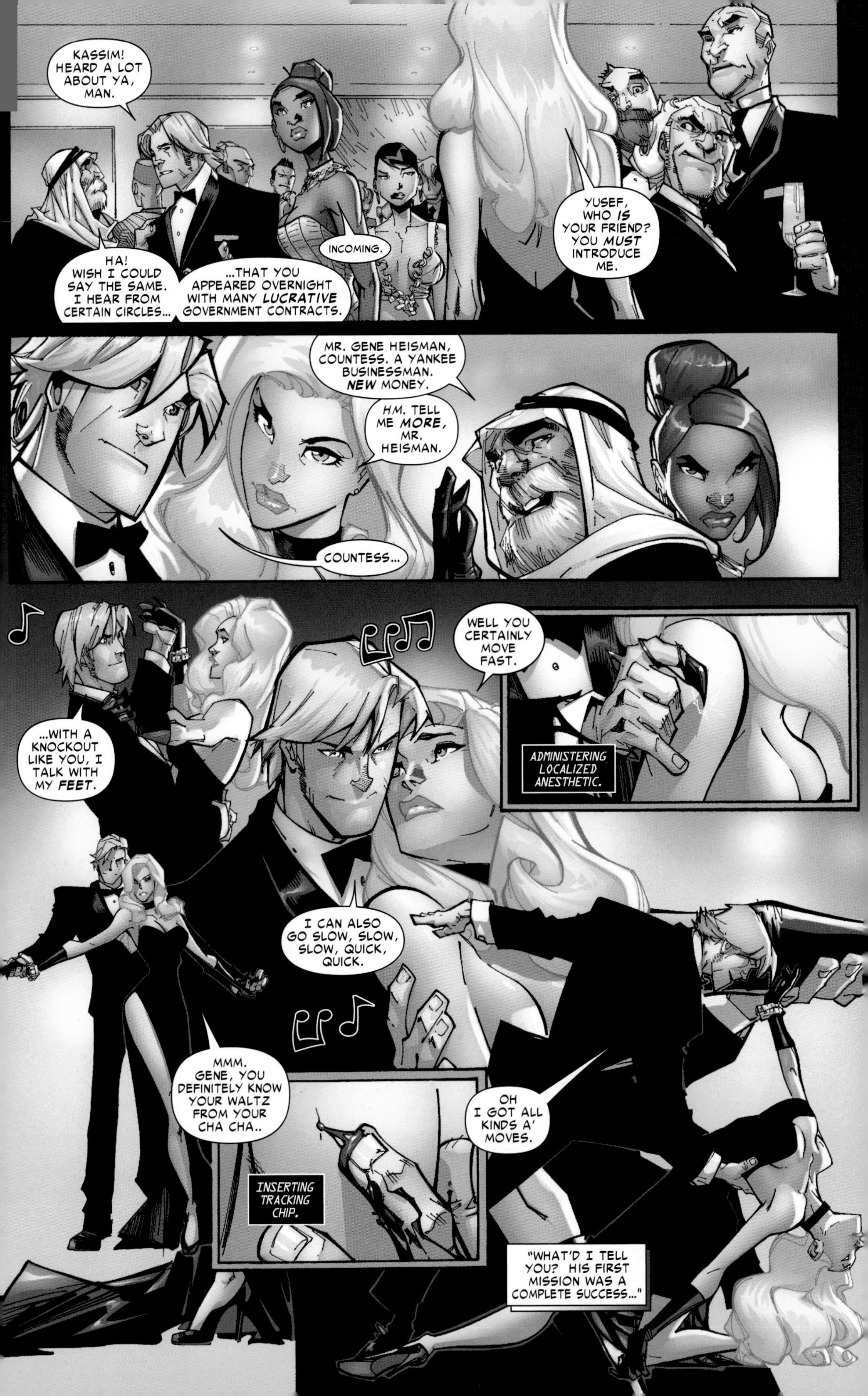
KASSIM! HEARD A LOT ABOUT YA, MAN.
HA! WISH I COULD SAY THE SAME. I HEAR FROM CERTAIN CIRCLES...
...THAT YOU APPEARED OVERNIGHT WITH MANY LUCRATIVE GOVERNMENT CONTRACTS.
INCOMING.
YUSEF, WHO IS YOUR FRIEND? YOU MUST INTRODUCE ME.
MR. GENE HEISMAN, COUNTESS. A YANKEE BUSINESSMAN. NEW MONEY.
HM. TELL ME MORE, MR. HEISMAN.
COUNTESS...
...WITH A KNOCKOUT LIKE YOU, I TALK WITH MY FEET.
WELL YOU CERTAINLY MOVE FAST.
ADMINISTERING LOCALIZED ANESTHETIC.
I CAN ALSO GO SLOW, SLOW, SLOW, QUICK, QUICK.
MMM. GENE, YOU DEFINITELY KNOW YOUR WALTZ FROM YOUR CHA CHA..
INSERTING TRACKING CHIP.
OH I GOT ALL KINDS A' MOVES.
"WHAT'D I TELL YOU? HIS FIRST MISSION WAS A COMPLETE SUCCESS..."

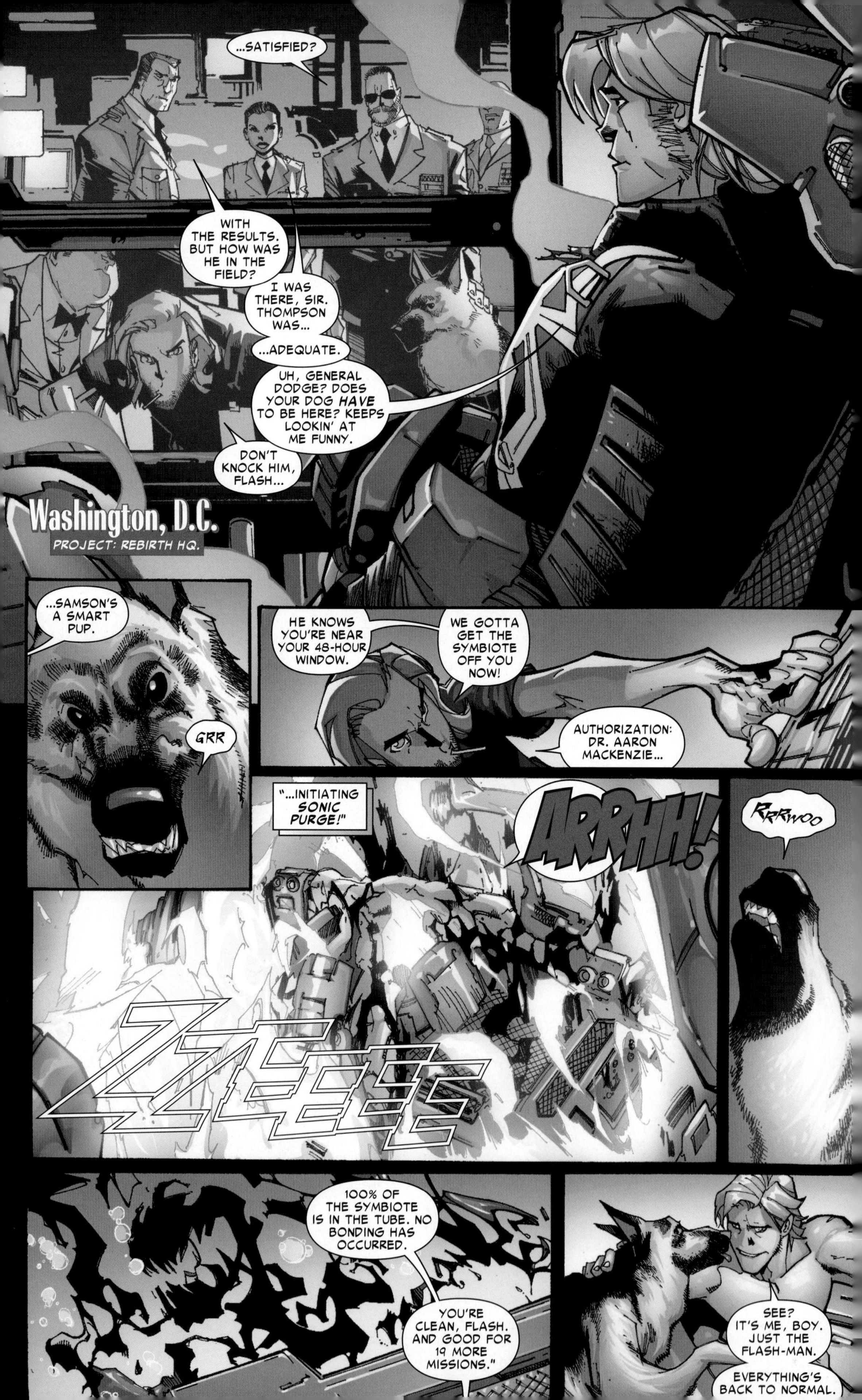

...SATISFIED?
WITH THE RESULTS. BUT HOW WAS HE IN THE FIELD?
I WAS THERE, SIR. THOMPSON WAS...
...ADEQUATE.
UH, GENERAL DODGE? DOES YOUR DOG HAVE TO BE HERE? KEEPS LOOKIN' AT ME FUNNY.
DON'T KNOCK HIM, FLASH...
Washington, D.C.
PROJECT: REBIRTH HQ.
...SAMSON'S A SMART PUP.
GRR
HE KNOWS YOU'RE NEAR YOUR 48-HOUR WINDOW.
WE GOTTA GET THE SYMBIOTE OFF YOU NOW!
AUTHORIZATION: DR. AARON MACKENZIE...
"...INITIATING SONIC PURGE!"
ARRHH!
RRRWOO
100% OF THE SYMBIOTE IS IN THE TUBE. NO BONDING HAS OCCURRED.
YOU'RE CLEAN, FLASH. AND GOOD FOR 19 MORE MISSIONS."
SEE? IT'S ME, BOY. JUST THE FLASH-MAN.
EVERYTHING'S BACK TO NORMAL.

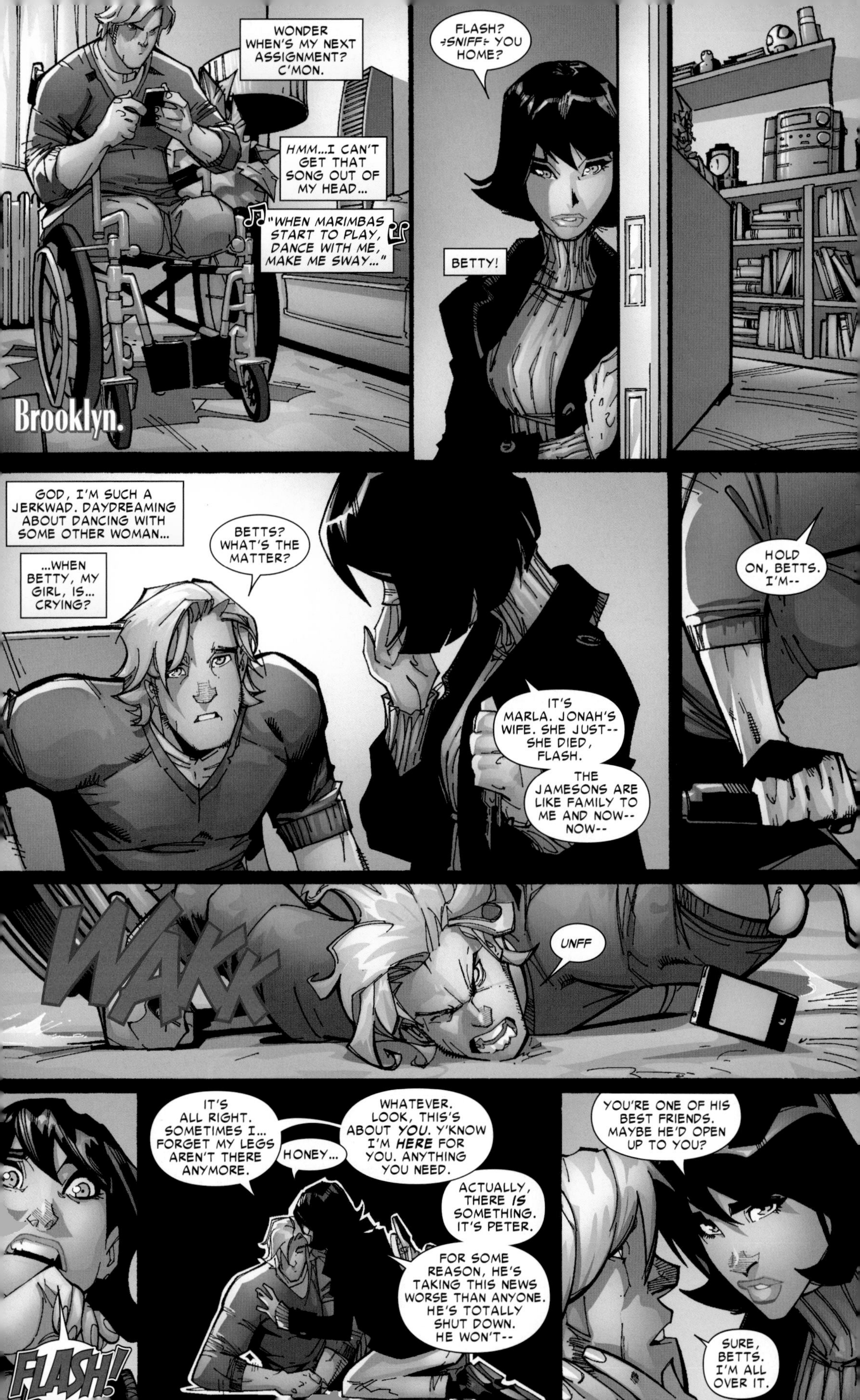
WONDER WHEN'S MY NEXT ASSIGNMENT? C'MON.
HMM...I CAN'T GET THAT SONG OUT OF MY HEAD...
"WHEN MARIMBAS START TO PLAY, DANCE WITH ME, MAKE ME SWAY..."
Brooklyn.
FLASH? *SNIFF* YOU HOME?
BETTY!
GOD, I'M SUCH A JERKWAD. DAYDREAMING ABOUT DANCING WITH SOME OTHER WOMAN...
...WHEN BETTY, MY GIRL, IS... CRYING?
BETTS? WHAT'S THE MATTER?
IT'S MARLA. JONAH'S WIFE. SHE JUST-- SHE DIED, FLASH.
THE JAMESONS ARE LIKE FAMILY TO ME AND NOW-- NOW--
HOLD ON, BETTS. I'M--
WAKK
UNFF
FLASH!
IT'S ALL RIGHT. SOMETIMES I... FORGET MY LEGS AREN'T THERE ANYMORE.
HONEY...
WHATEVER. LOOK, THIS'S ABOUT YOU. Y'KNOW I'M HERE FOR YOU. ANYTHING YOU NEED.
ACTUALLY, THERE IS SOMETHING. IT'S PETER.
FOR SOME REASON, HE'S TAKING THIS NEWS WORSE THAN ANYONE. HE'S TOTALLY SHUT DOWN. HE WON'T--
YOU'RE ONE OF HIS BEST FRIENDS. MAYBE HE'D OPEN UP TO YOU?
SURE, BETTS. I'M ALL OVER IT.

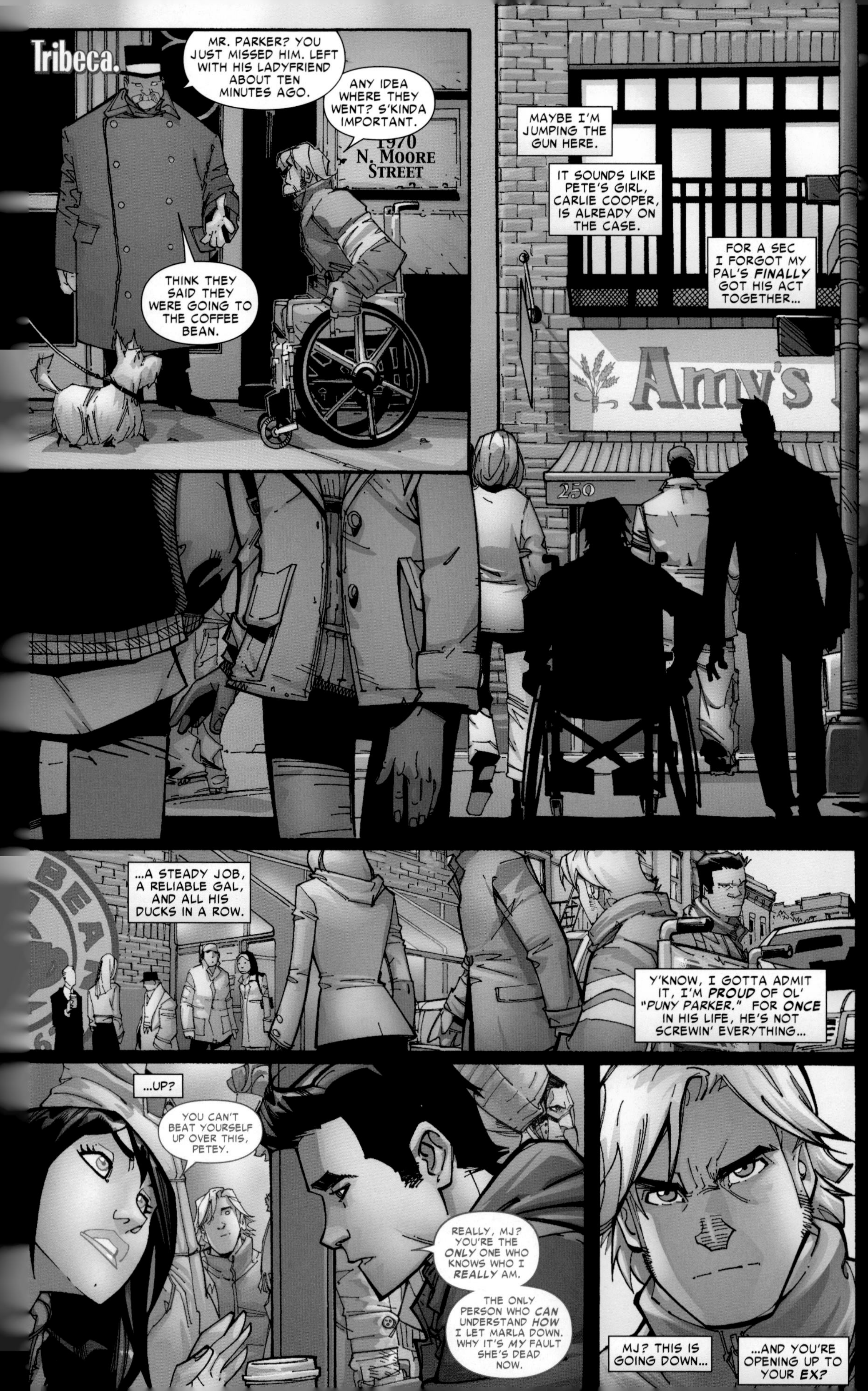
Tribeca.
MR. PARKER? YOU JUST MISSED HIM. LEFT WITH HIS LADYFRIEND ABOUT TEN MINUTES AGO.
ANY IDEA WHERE THEY WENT? S'KINDA IMPORTANT.
1970 N. MOORE STREET
THINK THEY SAID THEY WERE GOING TO THE COFFEE BEAN.
MAYBE I'M JUMPING THE GUN HERE.
IT SOUNDS LIKE PETE'S GIRL, CARLIE COOPER, IS ALREADY ON THE CASE.
FOR A SEC I FORGOT MY PAL'S FINALLY GOT HIS ACT TOGETHER...
Amy's
250
...A STEADY JOB, A RELIABLE GAL, AND ALL HIS DUCKS IN A ROW.
Y'KNOW, I GOTTA ADMIT IT, I'M PROUD OF OL' "PUNY PARKER." FOR ONCE IN HIS LIFE, HE'S NOT SCREWIN' EVERYTHING...
...UP?
YOU CAN'T BEAT YOURSELF UP OVER THIS, PETEY.
REALLY, MJ? YOU'RE THE ONLY ONE WHO KNOWS WHO I REALLY AM.
THE ONLY PERSON WHO CAN UNDERSTAND HOW I LET MARLA DOWN. WHY IT'S MY FAULT SHE'S DEAD NOW.
MJ? THIS IS GOING DOWN...
...AND YOU'RE OPENING UP TO YOUR EX?

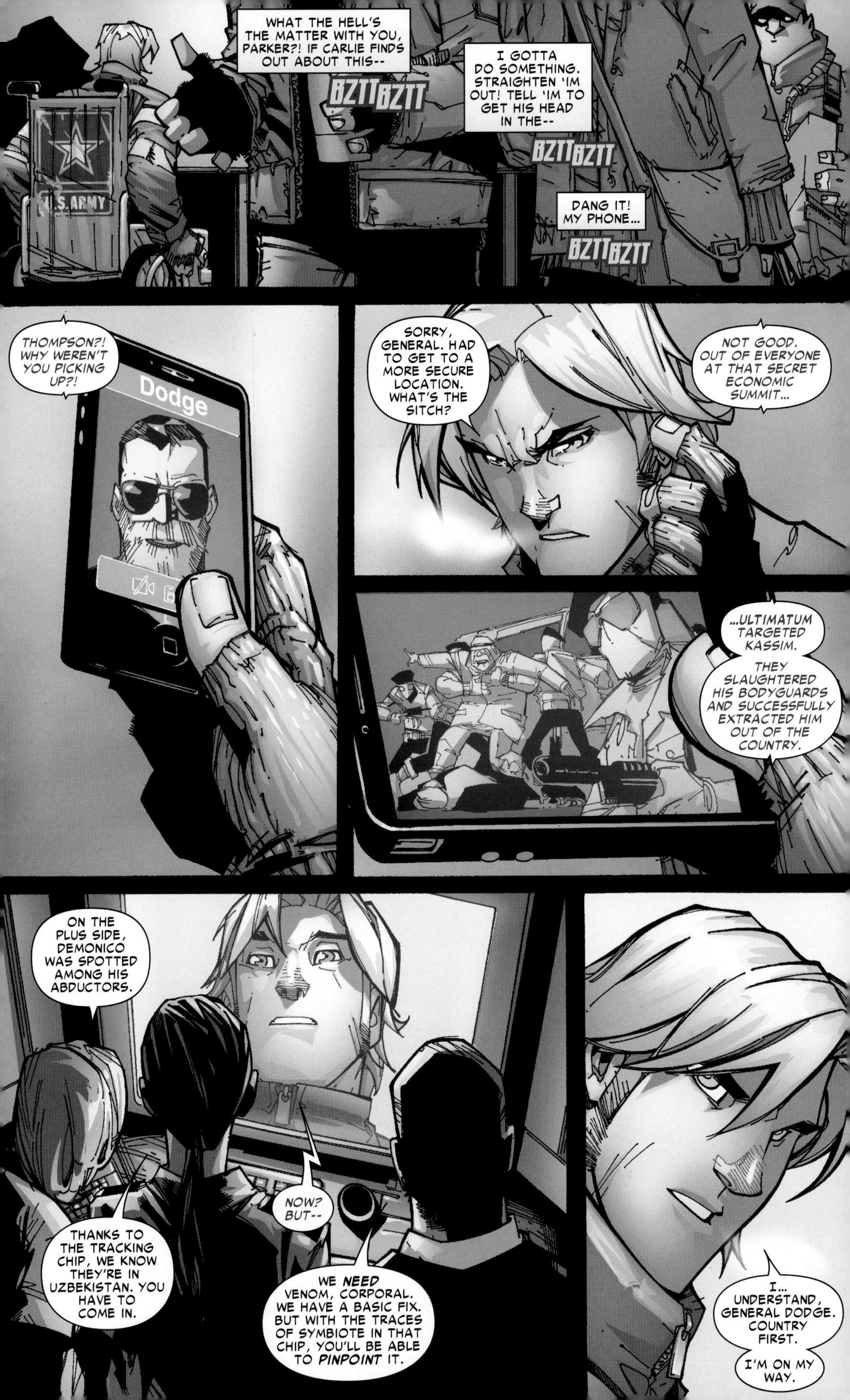
WHAT THE HELL'S THE MATTER WITH YOU, PARKER?! IF CARLIE FINDS OUT ABOUT THIS--
BZTT BZTT
I GOTTA DO SOMETHING. STRAIGHTEN 'IM OUT! TELL 'IM TO GET HIS HEAD IN THE--
BZTT BZTT
DANG IT! MY PHONE...
BZTT BZTT
U.S. ARMY
THOMPSON?! WHY WEREN'T YOU PICKING UP?!
Dodge
SORRY, GENERAL. HAD TO GET TO A MORE SECURE LOCATION. WHAT'S THE SITCH?
NOT GOOD. OUT OF EVERYONE AT THAT SECRET ECONOMIC SUMMIT...
...ULTIMATUM TARGETED KASSIM.
THEY SLAUGHTERED HIS BODYGUARDS AND SUCCESSFULLY EXTRACTED HIM OUT OF THE COUNTRY.
ON THE PLUS SIDE, DEMONICO WAS SPOTTED AMONG HIS ABDUCTORS.
THANKS TO THE TRACKING CHIP, WE KNOW THEY'RE IN UZBEKISTAN. YOU HAVE TO COME IN.
NOW? BUT--
WE NEED VENOM, CORPORAL. WE HAVE A BASIC FIX. BUT WITH THE TRACES OF SYMBIOTE IN THAT CHIP, YOU'LL BE ABLE TO PINPOINT IT.
I... UNDERSTAND, GENERAL DODGE. COUNTRY FIRST.
I'M ON MY WAY.

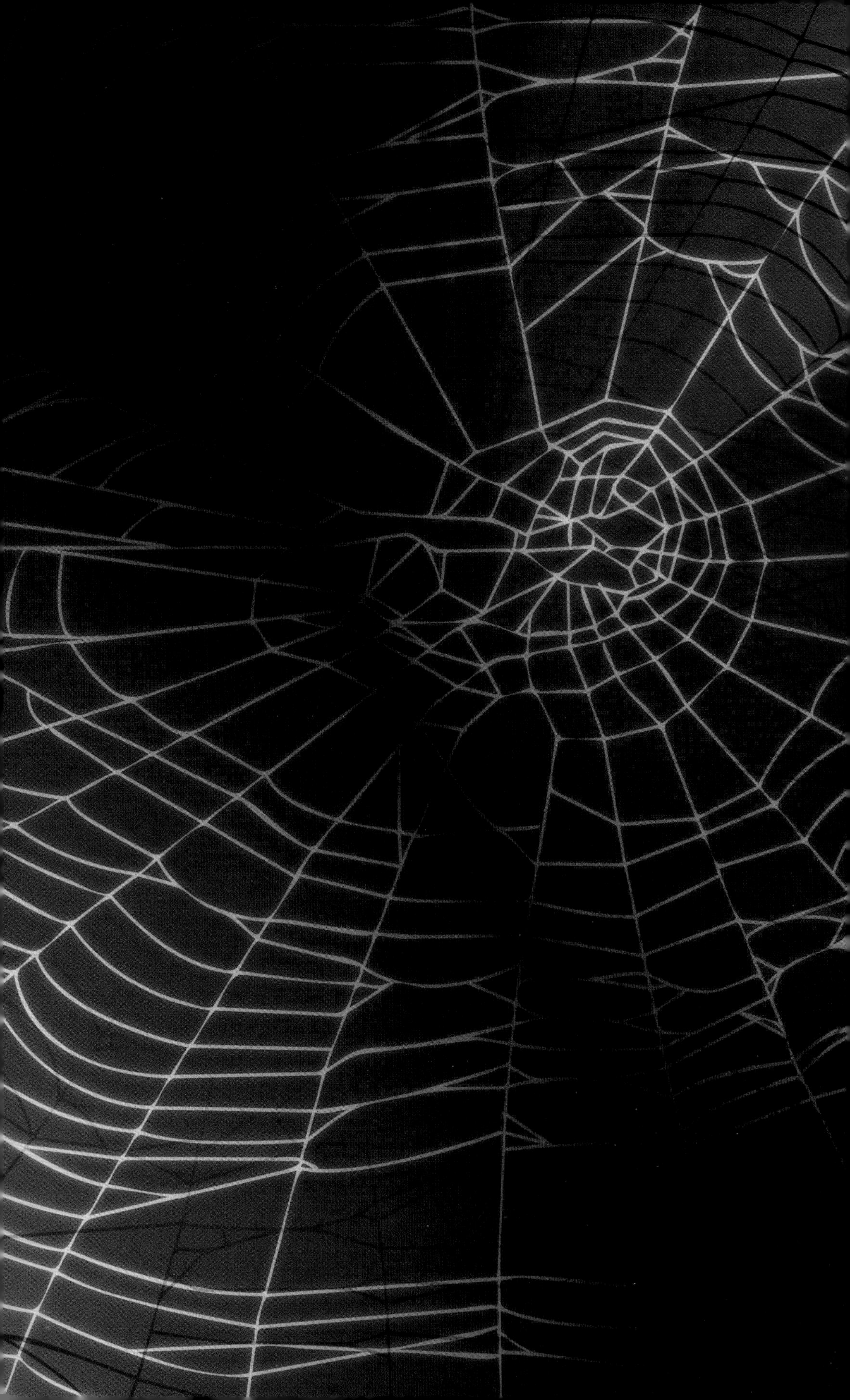

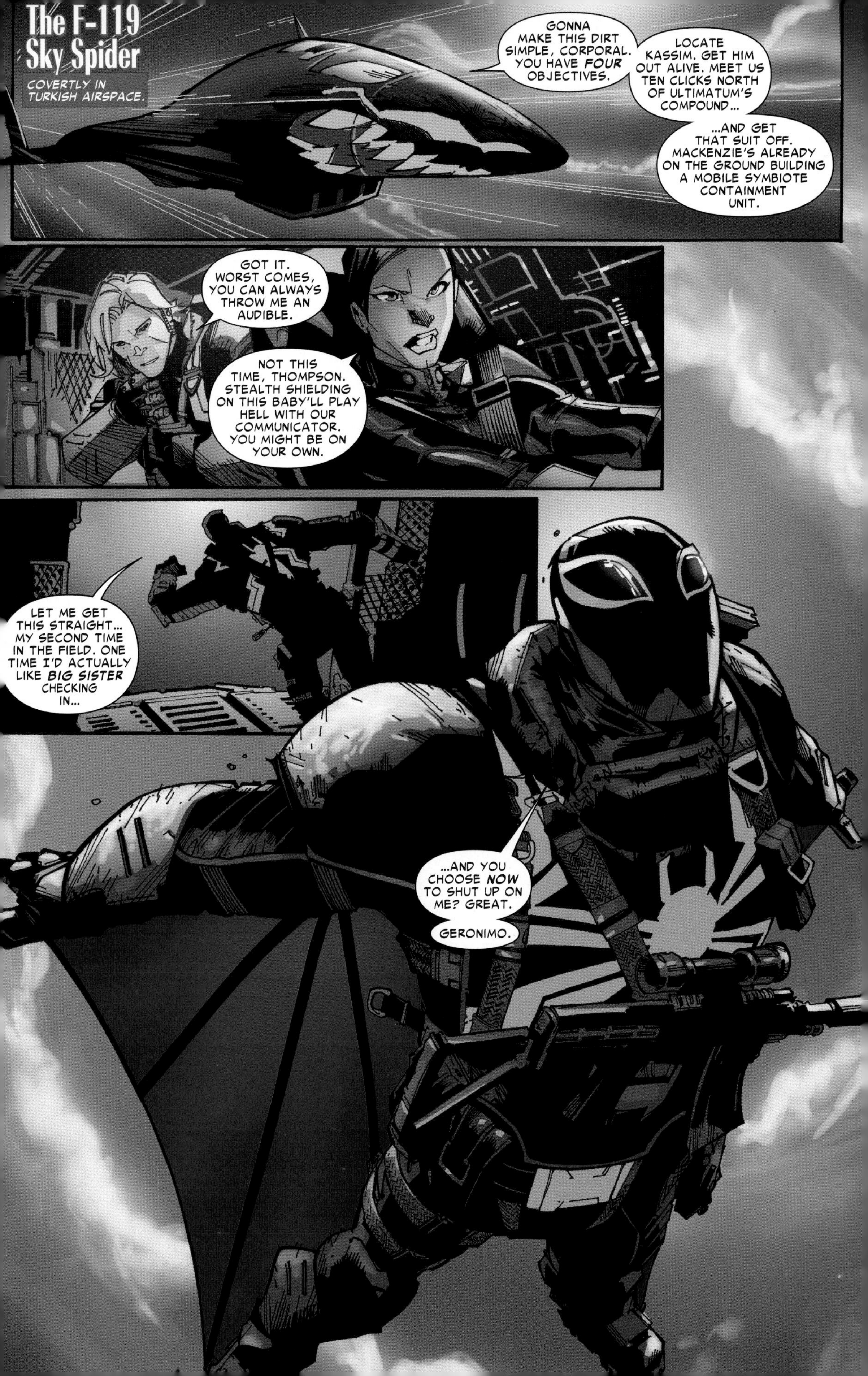
The F-119 Sky Spider
COVERTLY IN TURKISH AIRSPACE.
GONNA MAKE THIS DIRT SIMPLE, CORPORAL. YOU HAVE FOUR OBJECTIVES.
LOCATE KASSIM. GET HIM OUT ALIVE. MEET US TEN CLICKS NORTH OF ULTIMATUM'S COMPOUND...
...AND GET THAT SUIT OFF. MACKENZIE'S ALREADY ON THE GROUND BUILDING A MOBILE SYMBIOTE CONTAINMENT UNIT.
GOT IT. WORST COMES, YOU CAN ALWAYS THROW ME AN AUDIBLE.
NOT THIS TIME, THOMPSON. STEALTH SHIELDING ON THIS BABY'LL PLAY HELL WITH OUR COMMUNICATOR. YOU MIGHT BE ON YOUR OWN.
LET ME GET THIS STRAIGHT... MY SECOND TIME IN THE FIELD. ONE TIME I'D ACTUALLY LIKE BIG SISTER CHECKING IN...
...AND YOU CHOOSE NOW TO SHUT UP ON ME? GREAT.
GERONIMO.

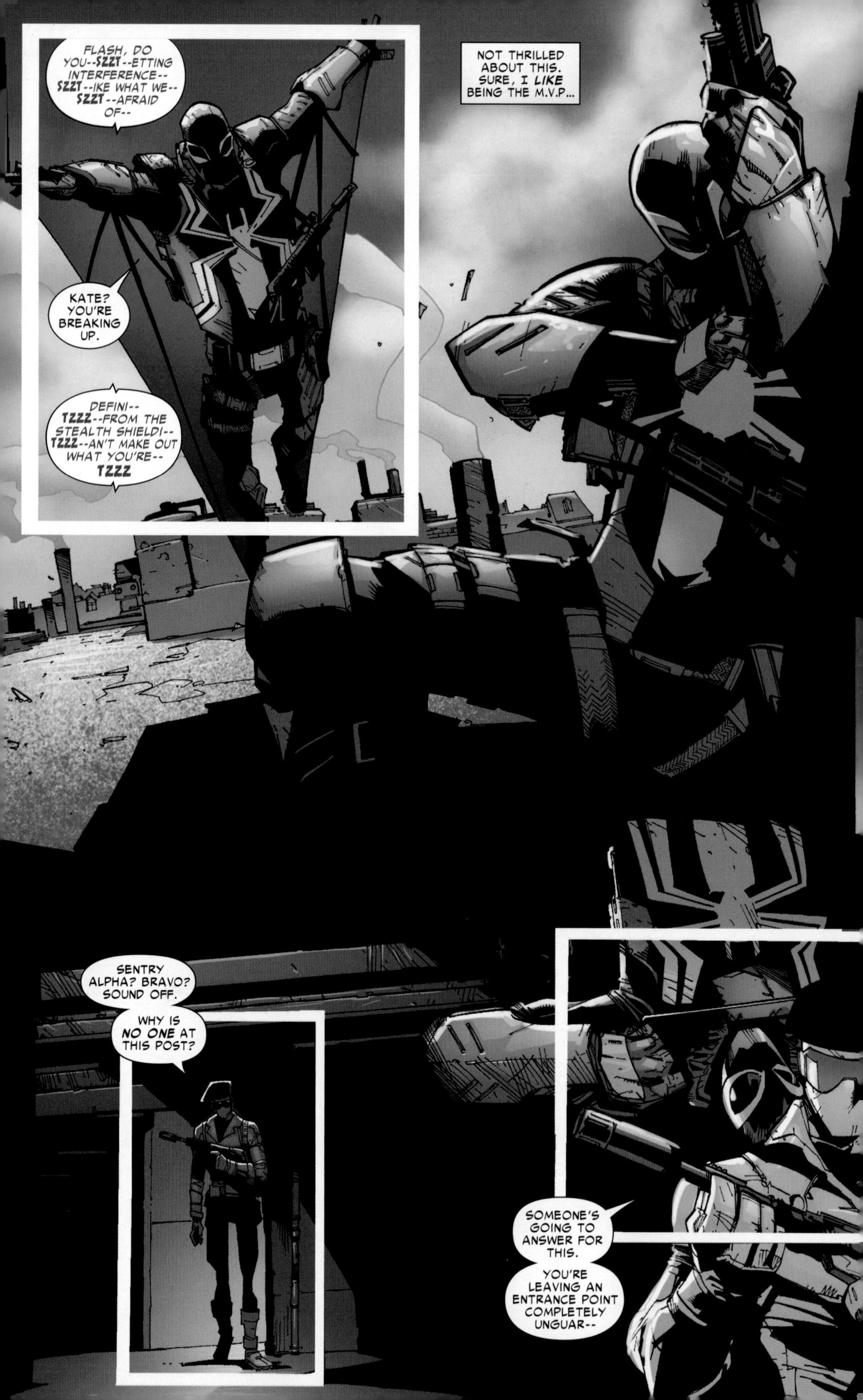
FLASH, DO YOU--SZZT--ETTING INTERFERENCE--SZZT--IKE WHAT WE--SZZT--AFRAID OF--
KATE? YOU'RE BREAKING UP.
DEFINI--TZZZ--FROM THE STEALTH SHIELDI--TZZZ--AN'T MAKE OUT WHAT YOU'RE--TZZZ
NOT THRILLED ABOUT THIS. SURE, I LIKE BEING THE M.V.P...
SENTRY ALPHA? BRAVO? SOUND OFF.
WHY IS NO ONE AT THIS POST?
SOMEONE'S GOING TO ANSWER FOR THIS.
YOU'RE LEAVING AN ENTRANCE POINT COMPLETELY UNGUAR--

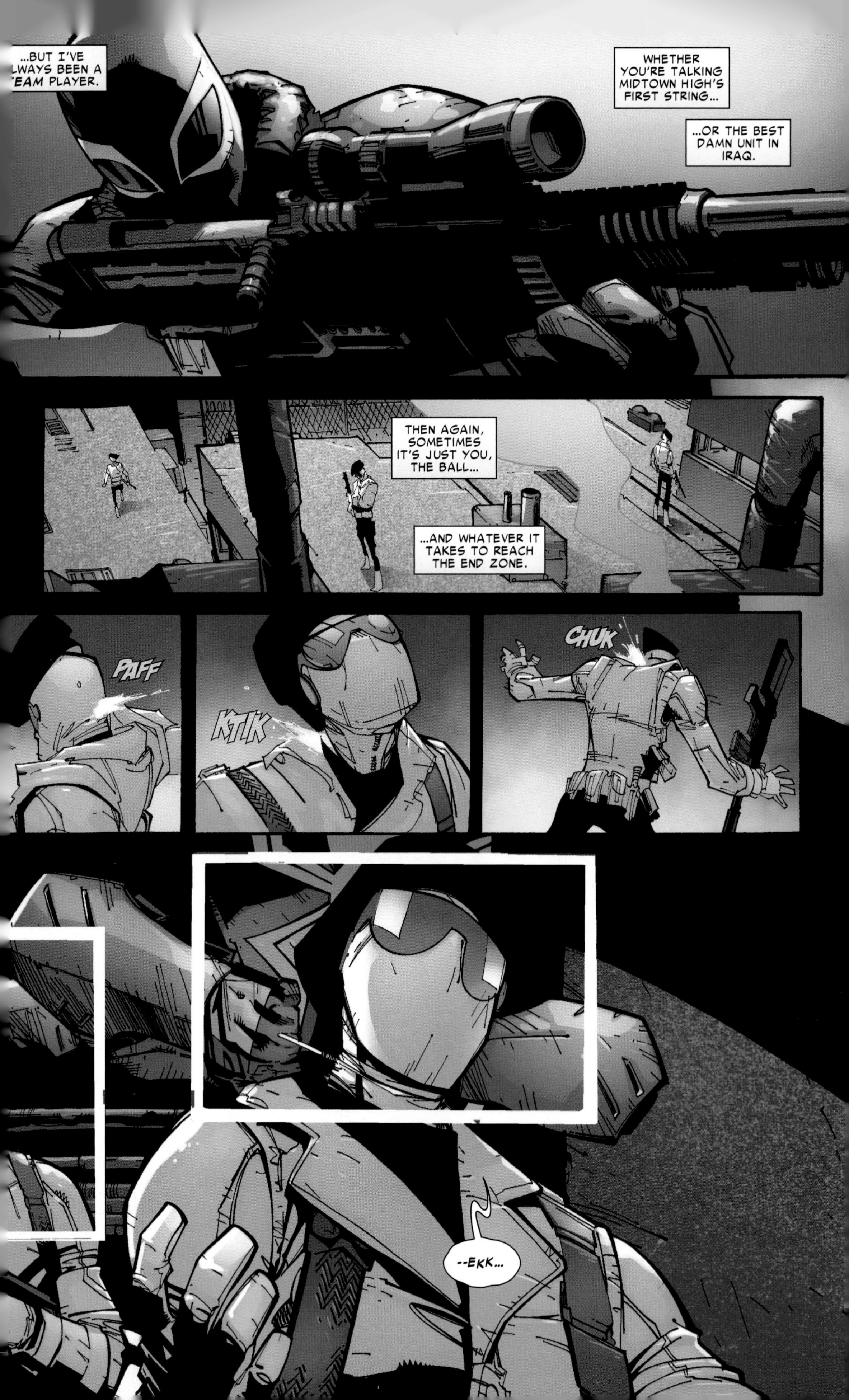

...BUT I'VE ALWAYS BEEN A TEAM PLAYER.
WHETHER YOU'RE TALKING MIDTOWN HIGH'S FIRST STRING...
...OR THE BEST DAMN UNIT IN IRAQ.
THEN AGAIN, SOMETIMES IT'S JUST YOU, THE BALL...
...AND WHATEVER IT TAKES TO REACH THE END ZONE.
PAFF
KTIK
CHUK
--EKK...

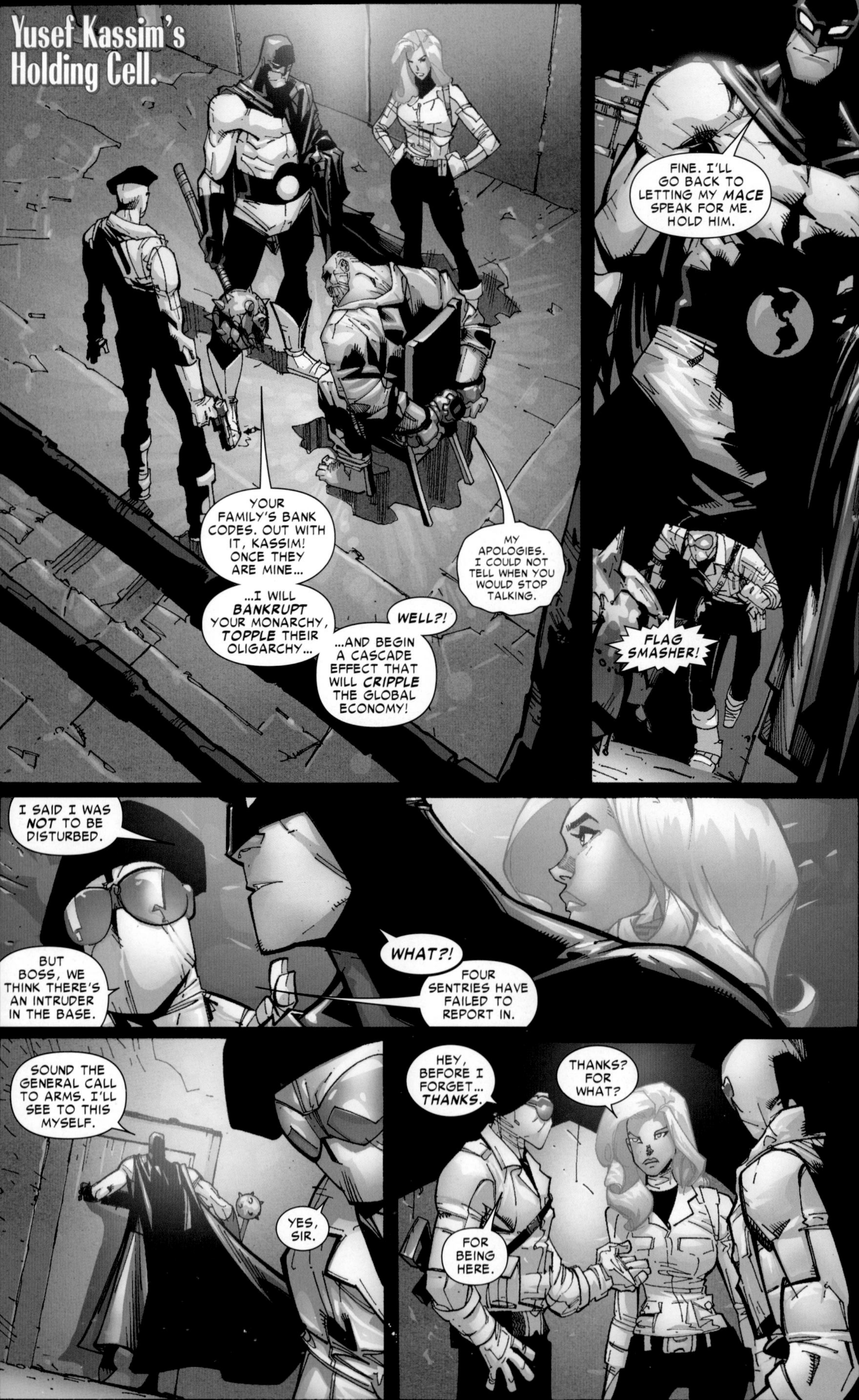
Yusef Kassim's Holding Cell.
YOUR FAMILY'S BANK CODES. OUT WITH IT, KASSIM! ONCE THEY ARE MINE...
...I WILL BANKRUPT YOUR MONARCHY, TOPPLE THEIR OLIGARCHY...
...AND BEGIN A CASCADE EFFECT THAT WILL CRIPPLE THE GLOBAL ECONOMY!
WELL?!
MY APOLOGIES. I COULD NOT TELL WHEN YOU WOULD STOP TALKING.
FINE. I'LL GO BACK TO LETTING MY MACE SPEAK FOR ME. HOLD HIM.
FLAG SMASHER!
I SAID I WAS NOT TO BE DISTURBED.
BUT BOSS, WE THINK THERE'S AN INTRUDER IN THE BASE.
WHAT?!
FOUR SENTRIES HAVE FAILED TO REPORT IN.
SOUND THE GENERAL CALL TO ARMS. I'LL SEE TO THIS MYSELF.
YES, SIR.
HEY, BEFORE I FORGET... THANKS.
THANKS? FOR WHAT?
FOR BEING HERE.

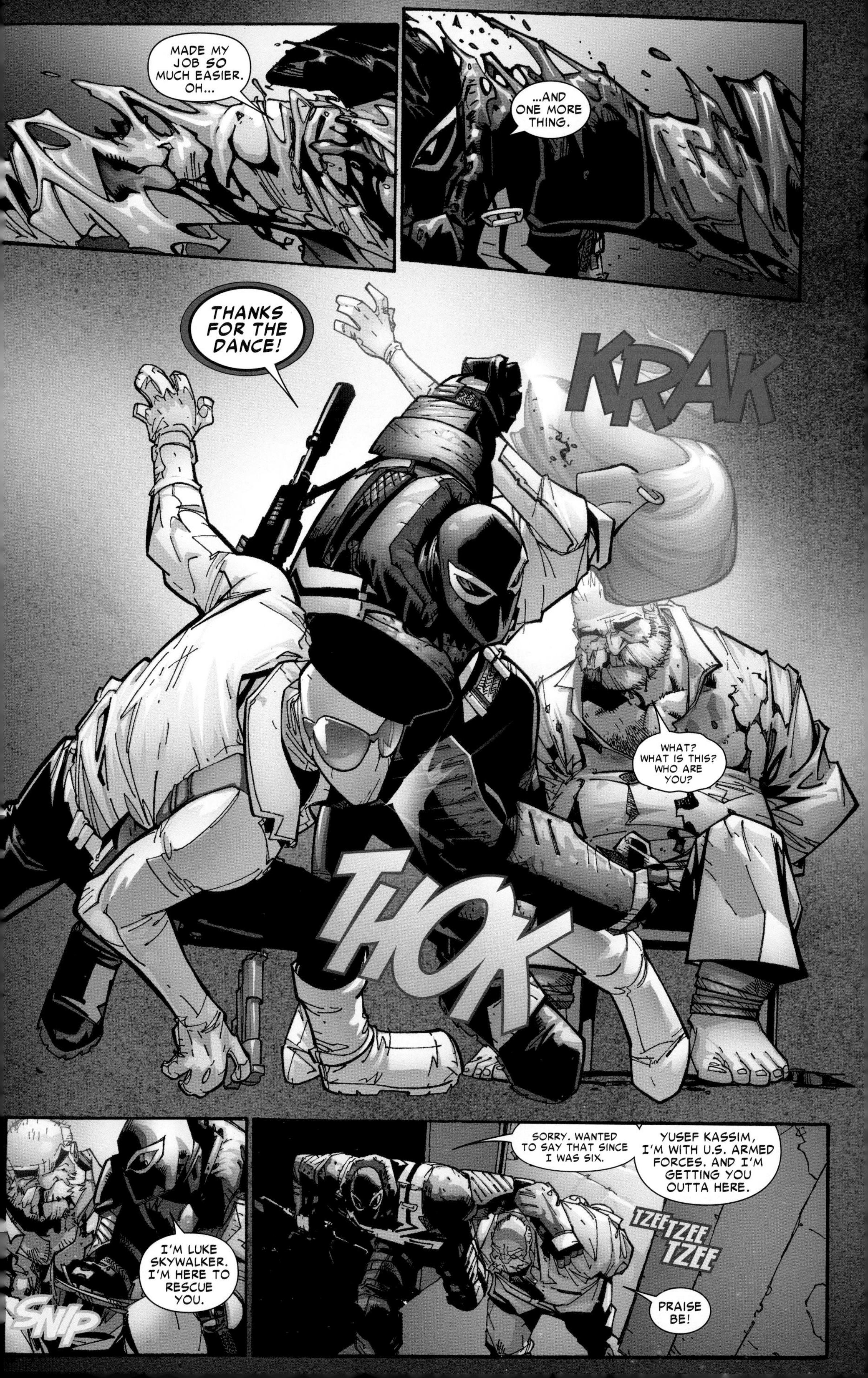
MADE MY JOB SO MUCH EASIER. OH...
...AND ONE MORE THING.
THANKS FOR THE DANCE!
KRAK
WHAT? WHAT IS THIS? WHO ARE YOU?
THOK
I'M LUKE SKYWALKER. I'M HERE TO RESCUE YOU.
SNIP
SORRY. WANTED TO SAY THAT SINCE I WAS SIX.
YUSEF KASSIM, I'M WITH U.S. ARMED FORCES. AND I'M GETTING YOU OUTTA HERE.
TZEE TZEE TZEE
PRAISE BE!

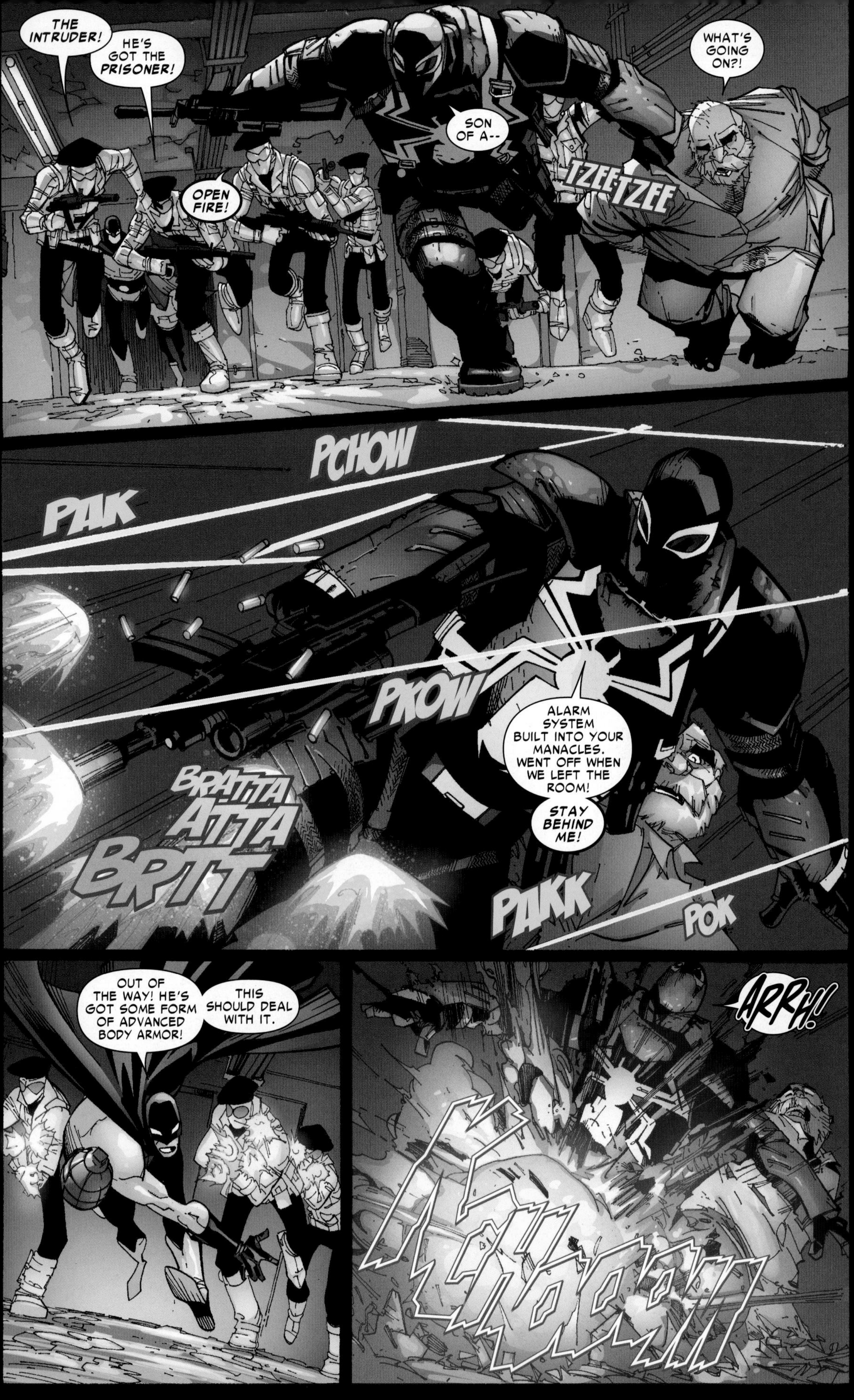
THE INTRUDER!
HE'S GOT THE PRISONER!
WHAT'S GOING ON?!
SON OF A--
OPEN FIRE!
TZEE TZEE
PCHOW
PAK
PKOW
ALARM SYSTEM BUILT INTO YOUR MANACLES. WENT OFF WHEN WE LEFT THE ROOM!
STAY BEHIND ME!
BRATTA ATTA BRTT
PAKK
POK
OUT OF THE WAY! HE'S GOT SOME FORM OF ADVANCED BODY ARMOR!
THIS SHOULD DEAL WITH IT.
ARRH!
KABOOM

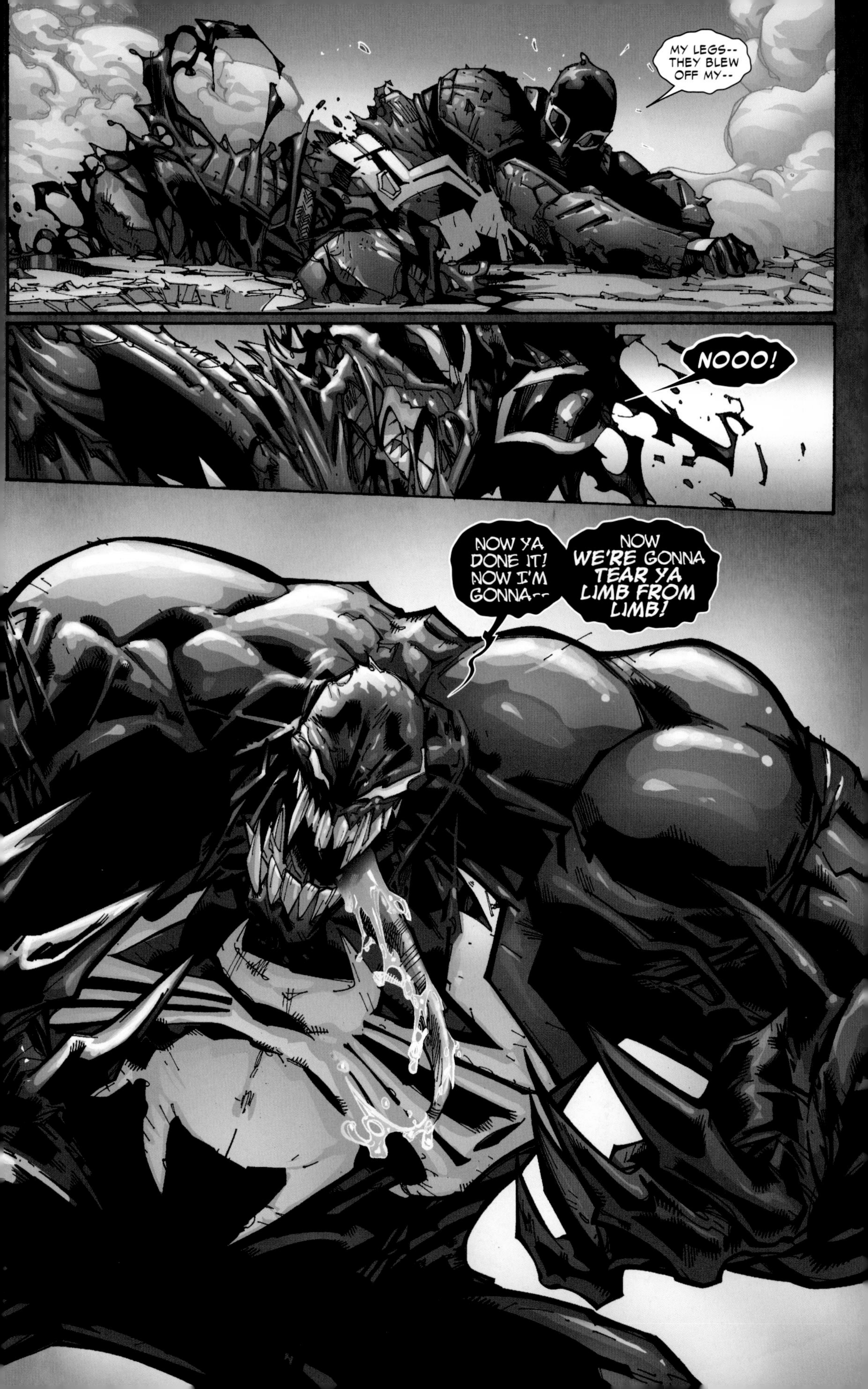
MY LEGS-- THEY BLEW OFF MY--
NOOO!
NOW YA DONE IT! NOW I'M GONNA--
NOW WE'RE GONNA TEAR YA LIMB FROM LIMB!

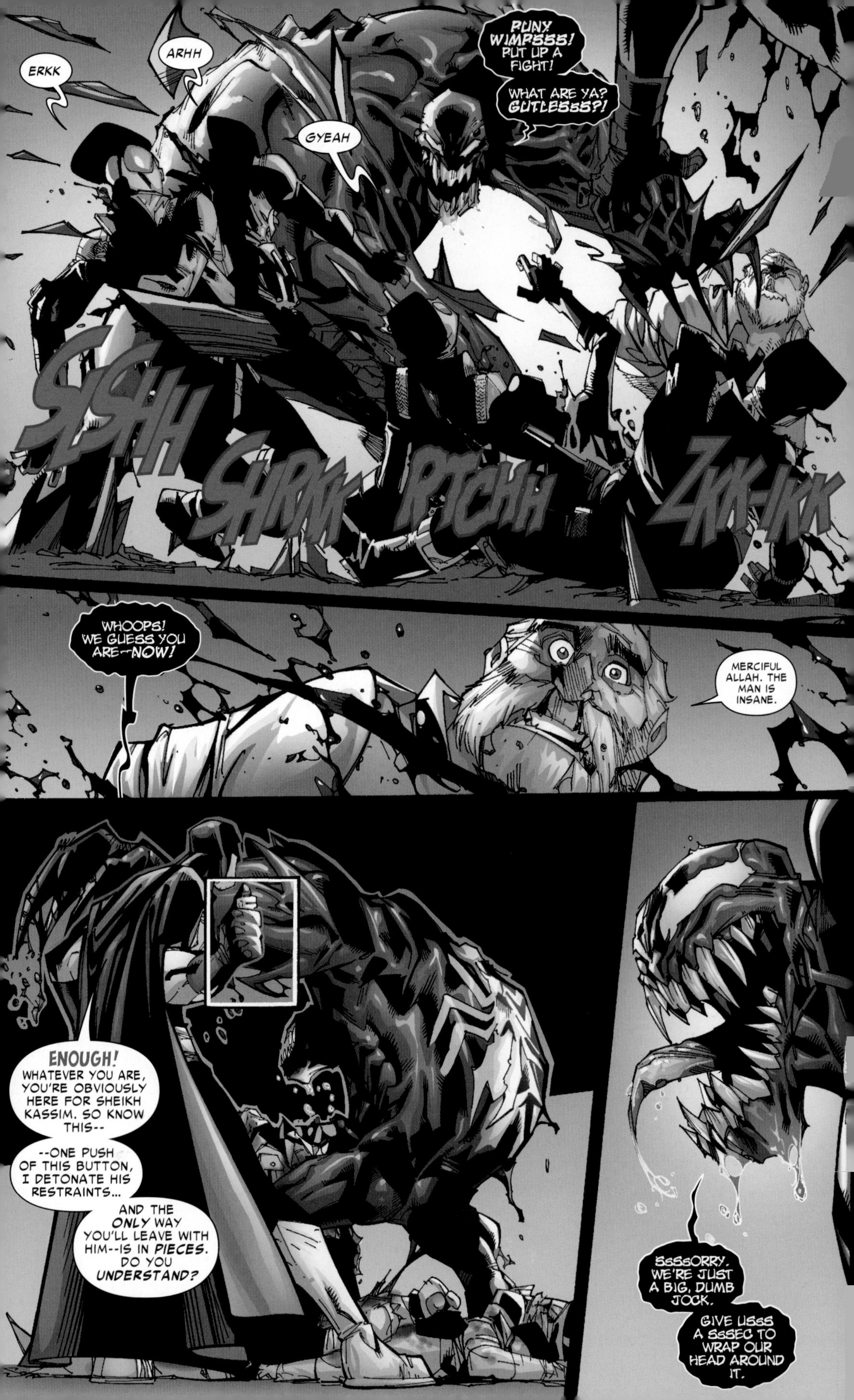
ERKK
ARHH
GYEAH
PUNY WIMPSSS! PUT UP A FIGHT!
WHAT ARE YA? GUTLESSS?!
SLSHH
SHRKK
RTCHH
ZKK-IKK
WHOOPS! WE GUESS YOU ARE--NOW!
MERCIFUL ALLAH. THE MAN IS INSANE.
ENOUGH! WHATEVER YOU ARE, YOU'RE OBVIOUSLY HERE FOR SHEIKH KASSIM. SO KNOW THIS--
--ONE PUSH OF THIS BUTTON, I DETONATE HIS RESTRAINTS...
AND THE ONLY WAY YOU'LL LEAVE WITH HIM--IS IN PIECES. DO YOU UNDERSTAND?
SsssORRY. WE'RE JUST A BIG, DUMB JOCK.
GIVE USSS A SSSEC TO WRAP OUR HEAD AROUND IT.

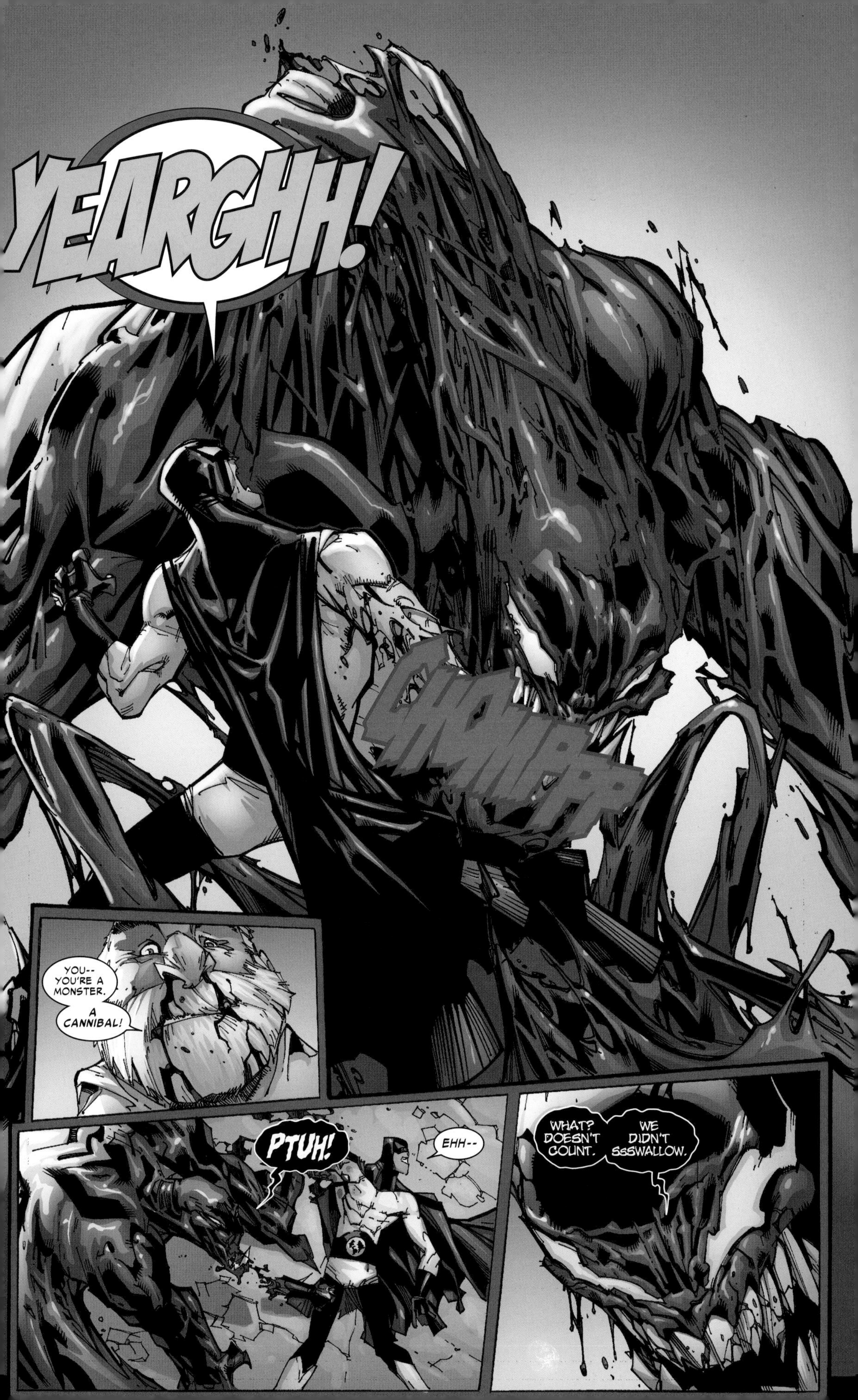
YEARGHH!
CHOMPP
YOU-- YOU'RE A MONSTER.
A CANNIBAL!
PTUH!
EHH--
WHAT? DOESN'T COUNT.
WE DIDN'T SSSWALLOW.

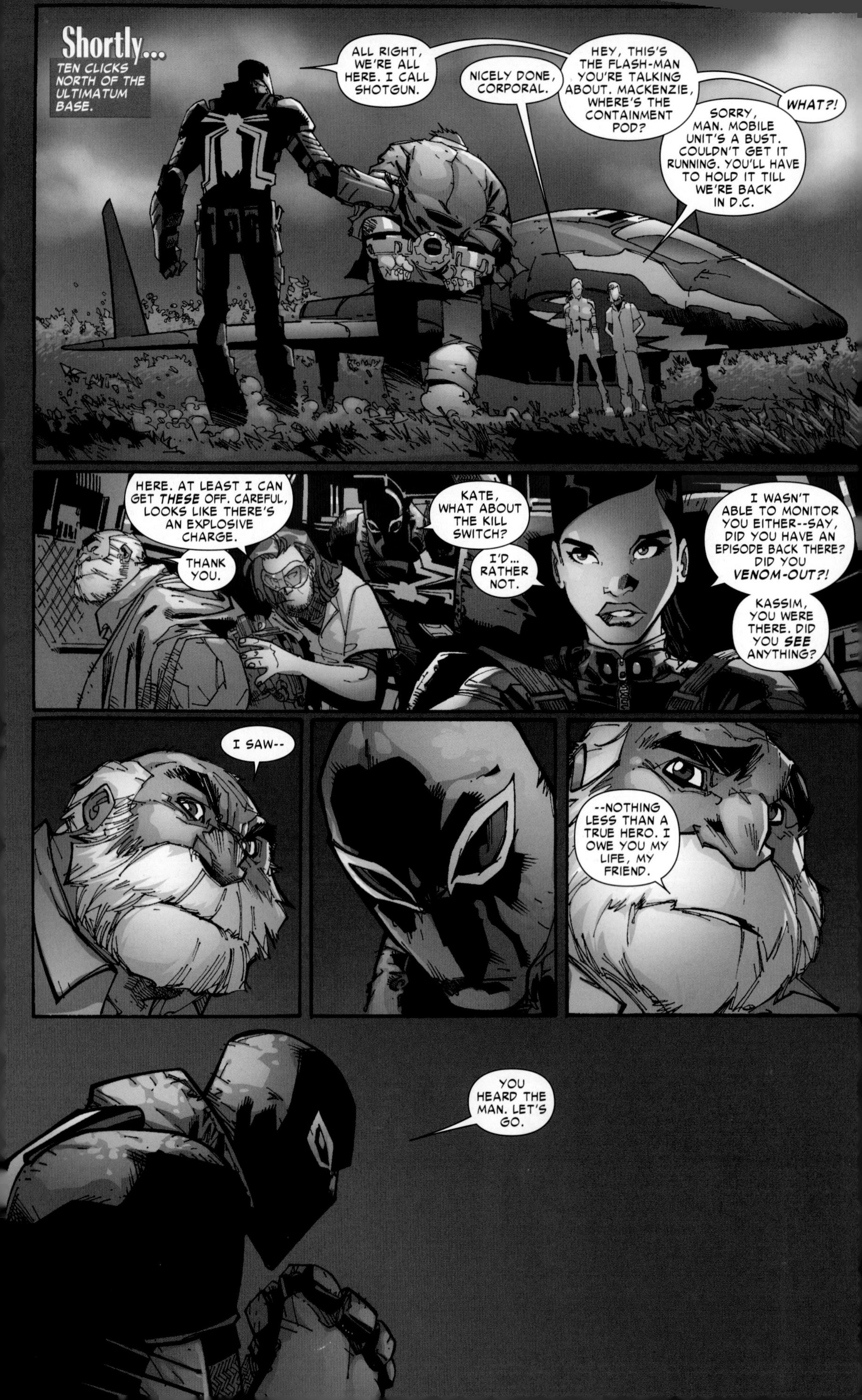
Shortly...
TEN CLICKS NORTH OF THE ULTIMATUM BASE.
ALL RIGHT, WE'RE ALL HERE. I CALL SHOTGUN.
NICELY DONE, CORPORAL.
HEY, THIS'S THE FLASH-MAN YOU'RE TALKING ABOUT. MACKENZIE, WHERE'S THE CONTAINMENT POD?
WHAT?!
SORRY, MAN. MOBILE UNIT'S A BUST. COULDN'T GET IT RUNNING. YOU'LL HAVE TO HOLD IT TILL WE'RE BACK IN D.C.
HERE. AT LEAST I CAN GET THESE OFF. CAREFUL, LOOKS LIKE THERE'S AN EXPLOSIVE CHARGE.
THANK YOU.
KATE, WHAT ABOUT THE KILL SWITCH?
I'D... RATHER NOT.
I WASN'T ABLE TO MONITOR YOU EITHER--SAY, DID YOU HAVE AN EPISODE BACK THERE? DID YOU VENOM-OUT?!
KASSIM, YOU WERE THERE. DID YOU SEE ANYTHING?
I SAW--
--NOTHING LESS THAN A TRUE HERO. I OWE YOU MY LIFE, MY FRIEND.
YOU HEARD THE MAN. LET'S GO.

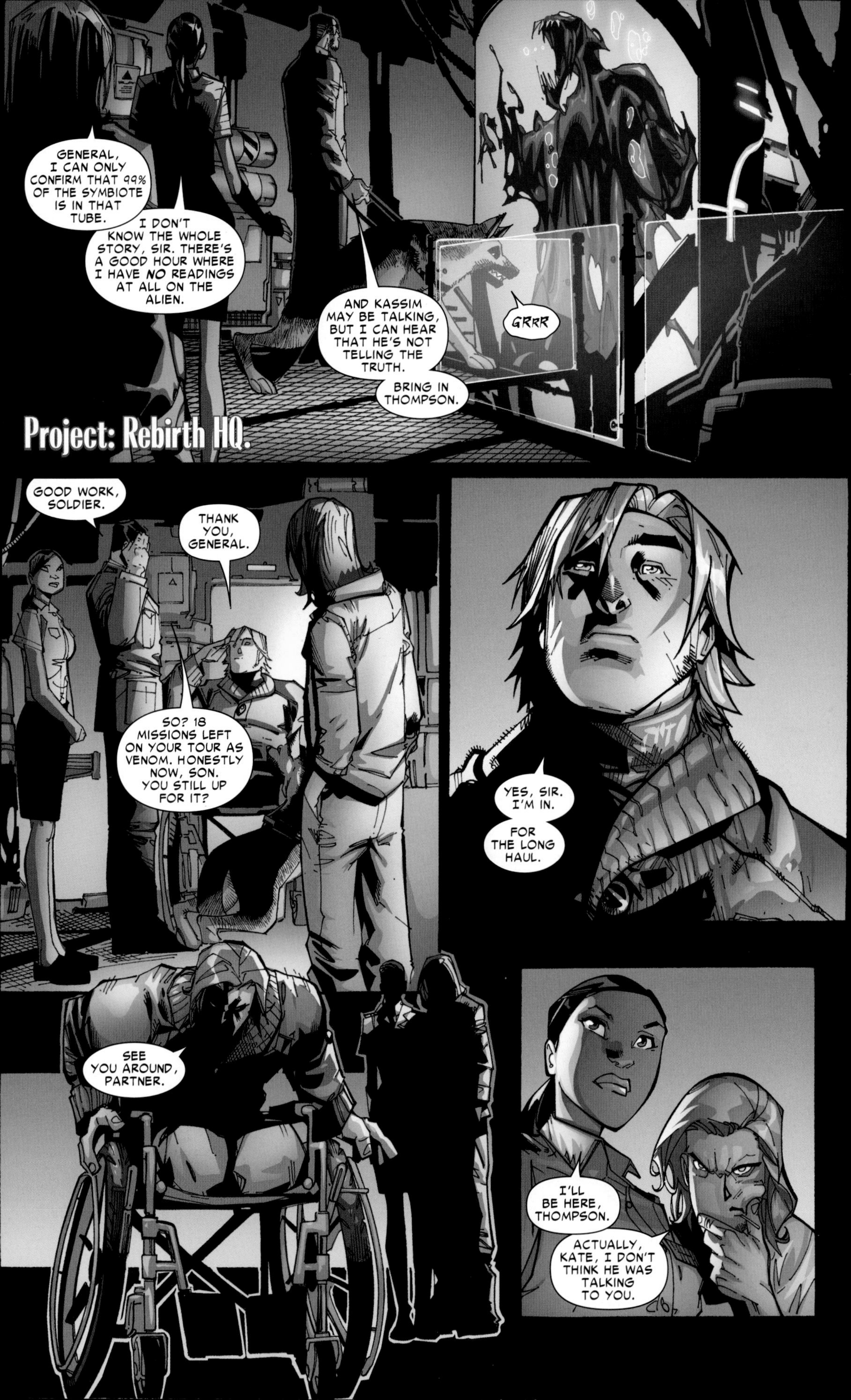
GENERAL, I CAN ONLY CONFIRM THAT 99% OF THE SYMBIOTE IS IN THAT TUBE.
I DON'T KNOW THE WHOLE STORY, SIR. THERE'S A GOOD HOUR WHERE I HAVE NO READINGS AT ALL ON THE ALIEN.
AND KASSIM MAY BE TALKING, BUT I CAN HEAR THAT HE'S NOT TELLING THE TRUTH.
BRING IN THOMPSON.
GRrR
Project: Rebirth HQ.
GOOD WORK, SOLDIER.
THANK YOU, GENERAL.
SO? 18 MISSIONS LEFT ON YOUR TOUR AS VENOM. HONESTLY NOW, SON. YOU STILL UP FOR IT?
YES, SIR. I'M IN.
FOR THE LONG HAUL.
SEE YOU AROUND, PARTNER.
I'LL BE HERE, THOMPSON.
ACTUALLY, KATE, I DON'T THINK HE WAS TALKING TO YOU.

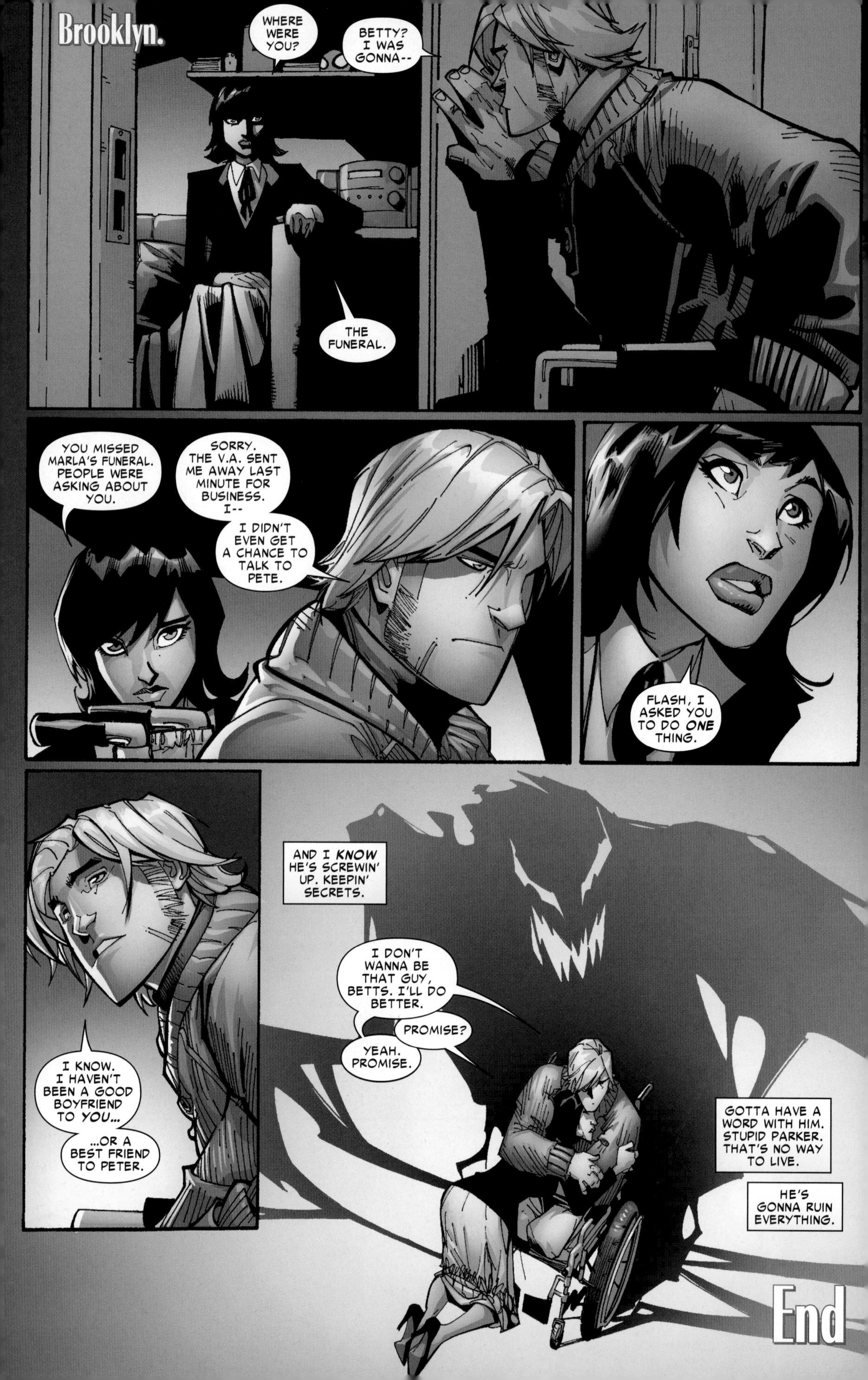
Brooklyn.
WHERE WERE YOU?
BETTY? I WAS GONNA--
THE FUNERAL.
YOU MISSED MARLA'S FUNERAL. PEOPLE WERE ASKING ABOUT YOU.
SORRY. THE V.A. SENT ME AWAY LAST MINUTE FOR BUSINESS. I--
I DIDN'T EVEN GET A CHANCE TO TALK TO PETE.
FLASH, I ASKED YOU TO DO ONE THING.
I KNOW. I HAVEN'T BEEN A GOOD BOYFRIEND TO YOU...
...OR A BEST FRIEND TO PETER.
AND I KNOW HE'S SCREWIN' UP. KEEPIN' SECRETS.
I DON'T WANNA BE THAT GUY, BETTS. I'LL DO BETTER.
PROMISE?
YEAH. PROMISE.
GOTTA HAVE A WORD WITH HIM. STUPID PARKER. THAT'S NO WAY TO LIVE.
HE'S GONNA RUIN EVERYTHING.
End

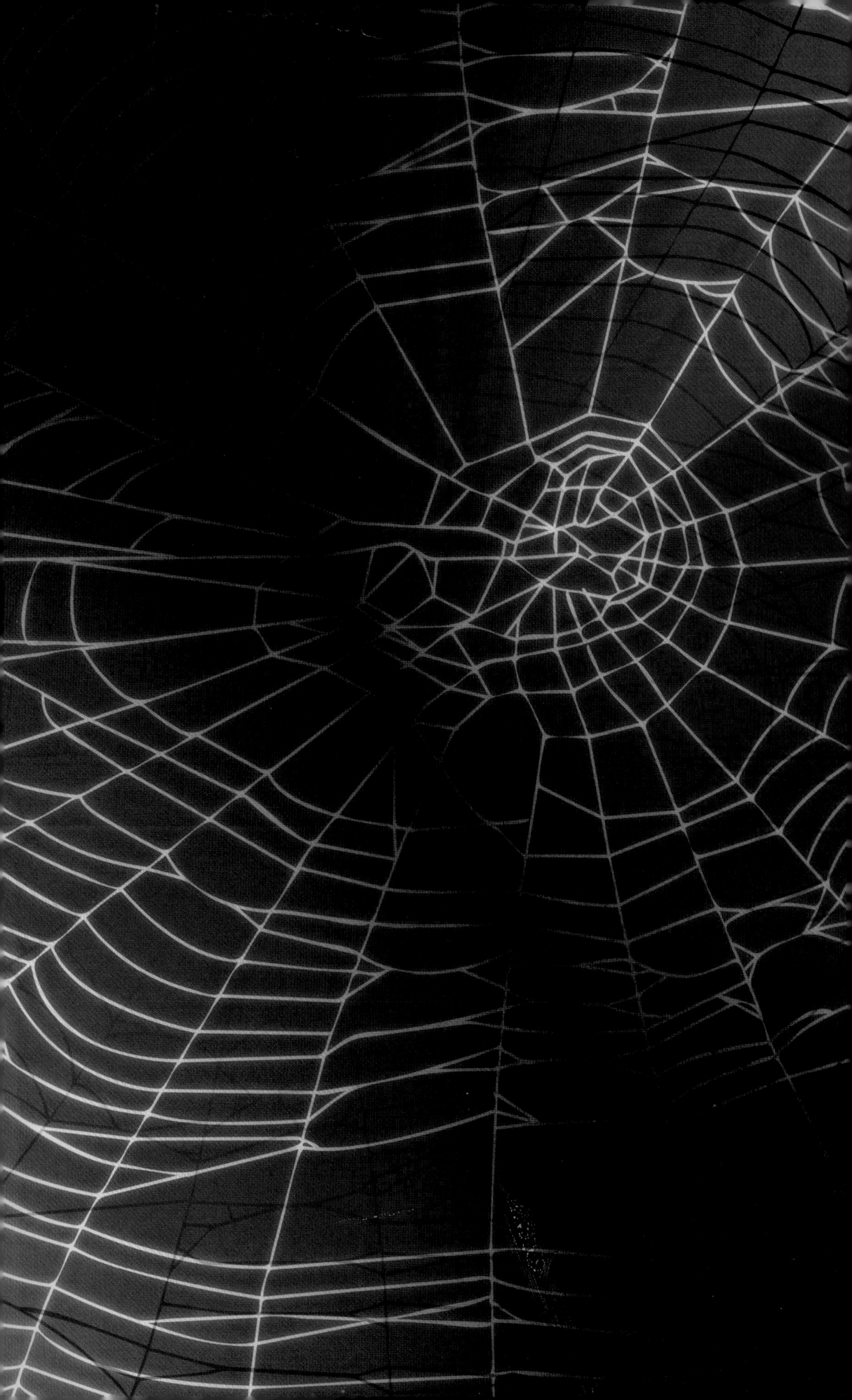

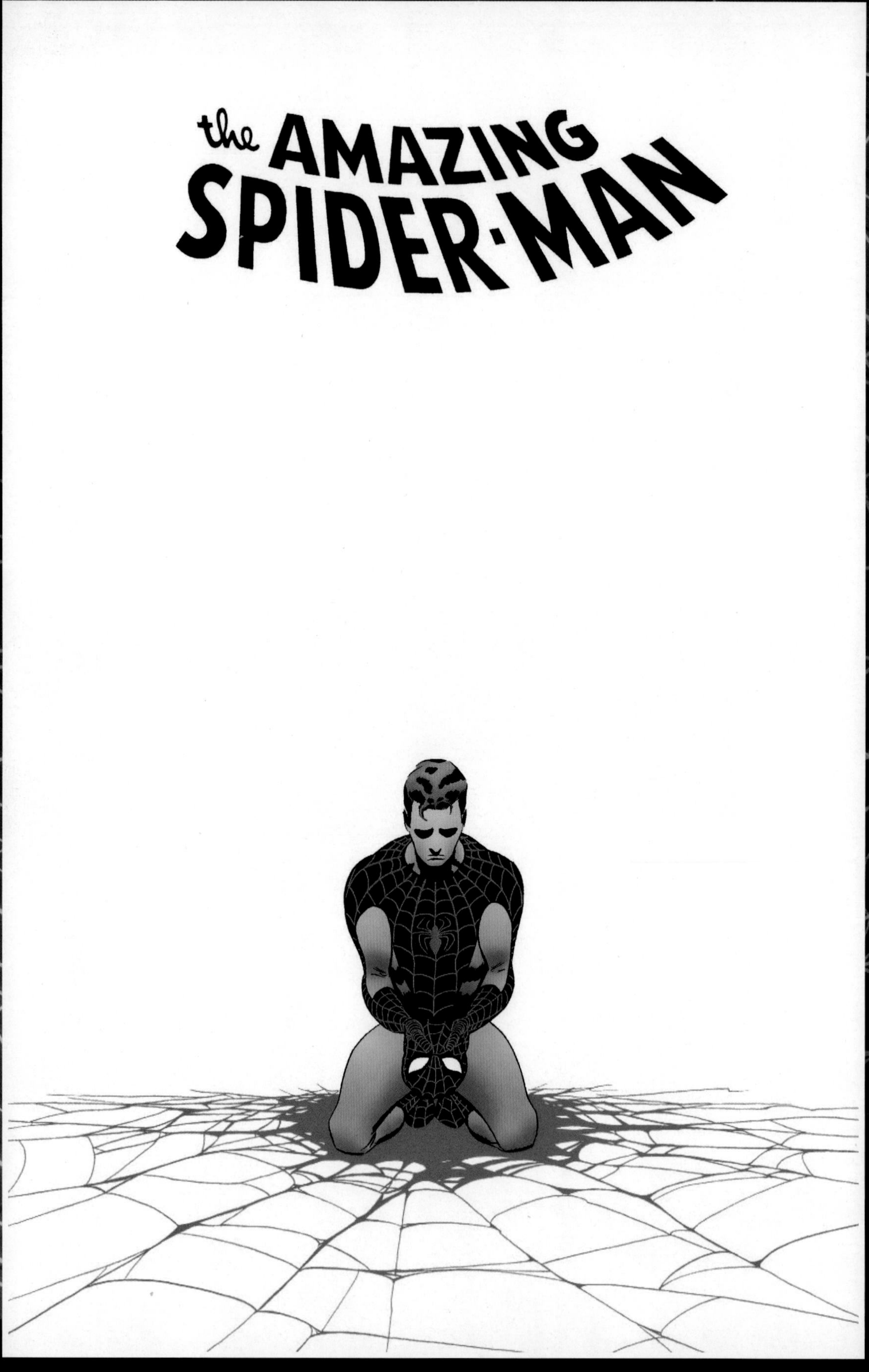
the AMAZING
SPIDER-MAN

AMAZING SPIDER-MAN #655

IN MEMORY OF MARLA JAMESON

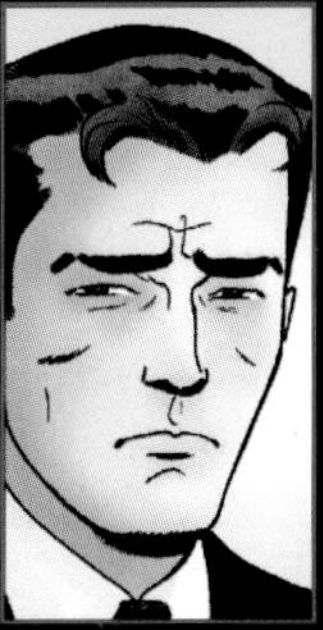

PETER PARKER
Spider-Man.

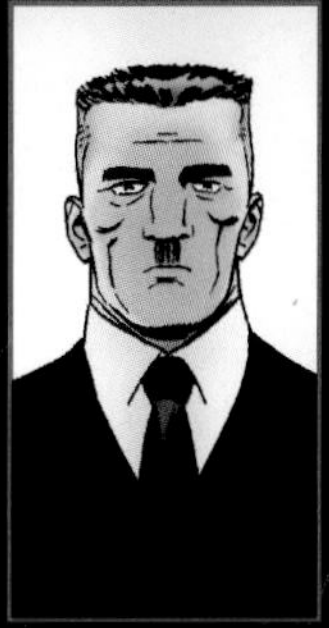

J. JONAH JAMESON
Marla's husband.
Mayor of NYC.

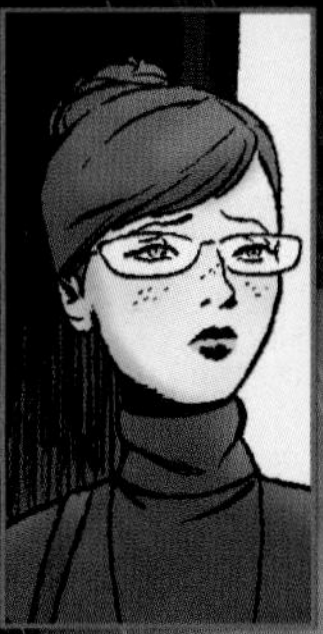

CARLIE COOPER
Peter's girlfriend.

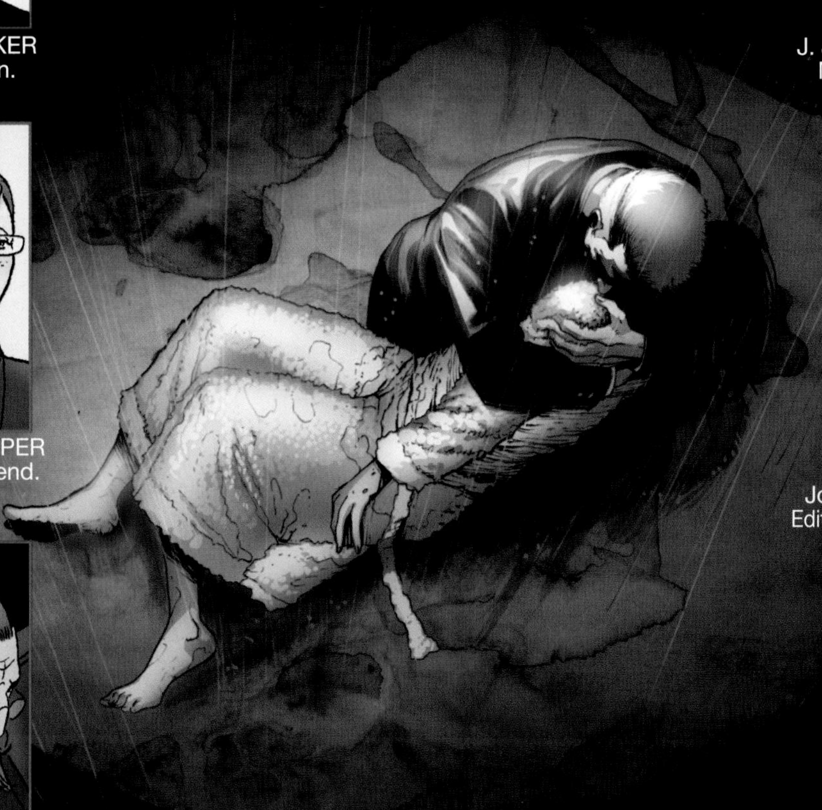

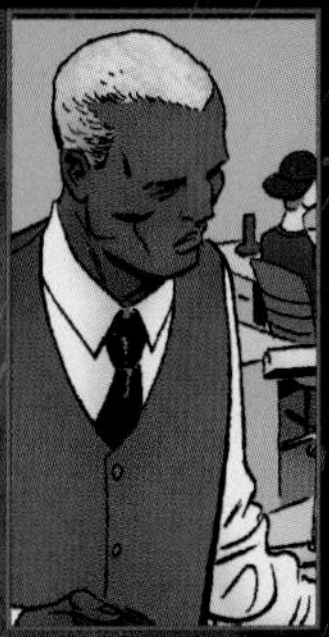

ROBBIE ROBERTSON
Jonah's best friend.
Editor of the Daily Bugle.

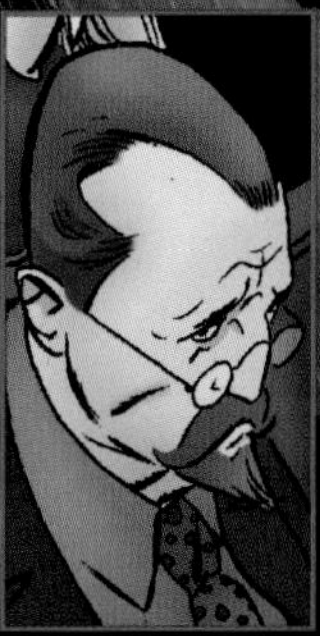

MAX MODELL
Marla's friend.
Peter's boss.

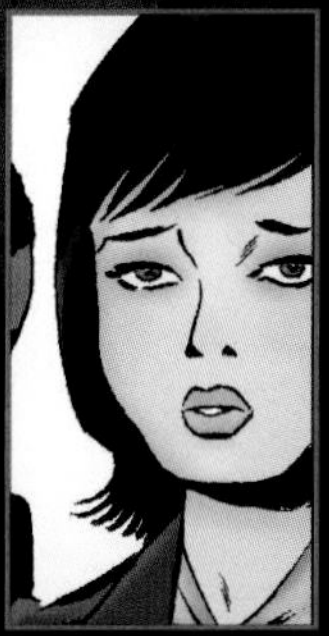

BETTY BRANT
Jonah's former secretary.

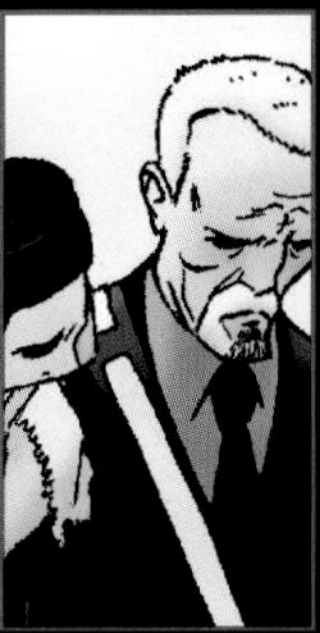

MAY & JAY JAMESON
Peter's aunt and
Jonah's father.

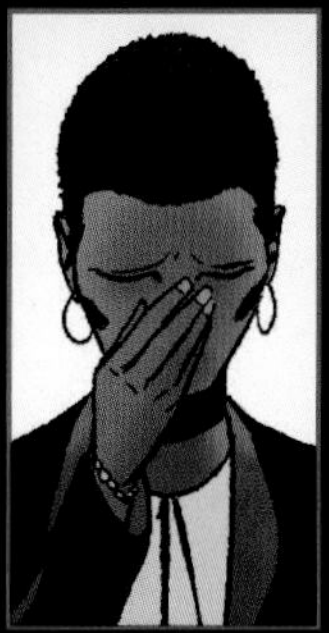

GLORY GRANT
Jonah's assistant.

DAN SLOTT – writer
MARCOS MARTIN – art
MUNTSA VICENTE – colors
VC's JOE CARAMAGNA – letters

ELLIE PYLE – assistant editor
STEPHEN WACKER – senior editor
AXEL ALONSO – editor in chief
JOE QUESADA – chief creative officer
DAN BUCKLEY – publisher
ALAN FINE – executive producer

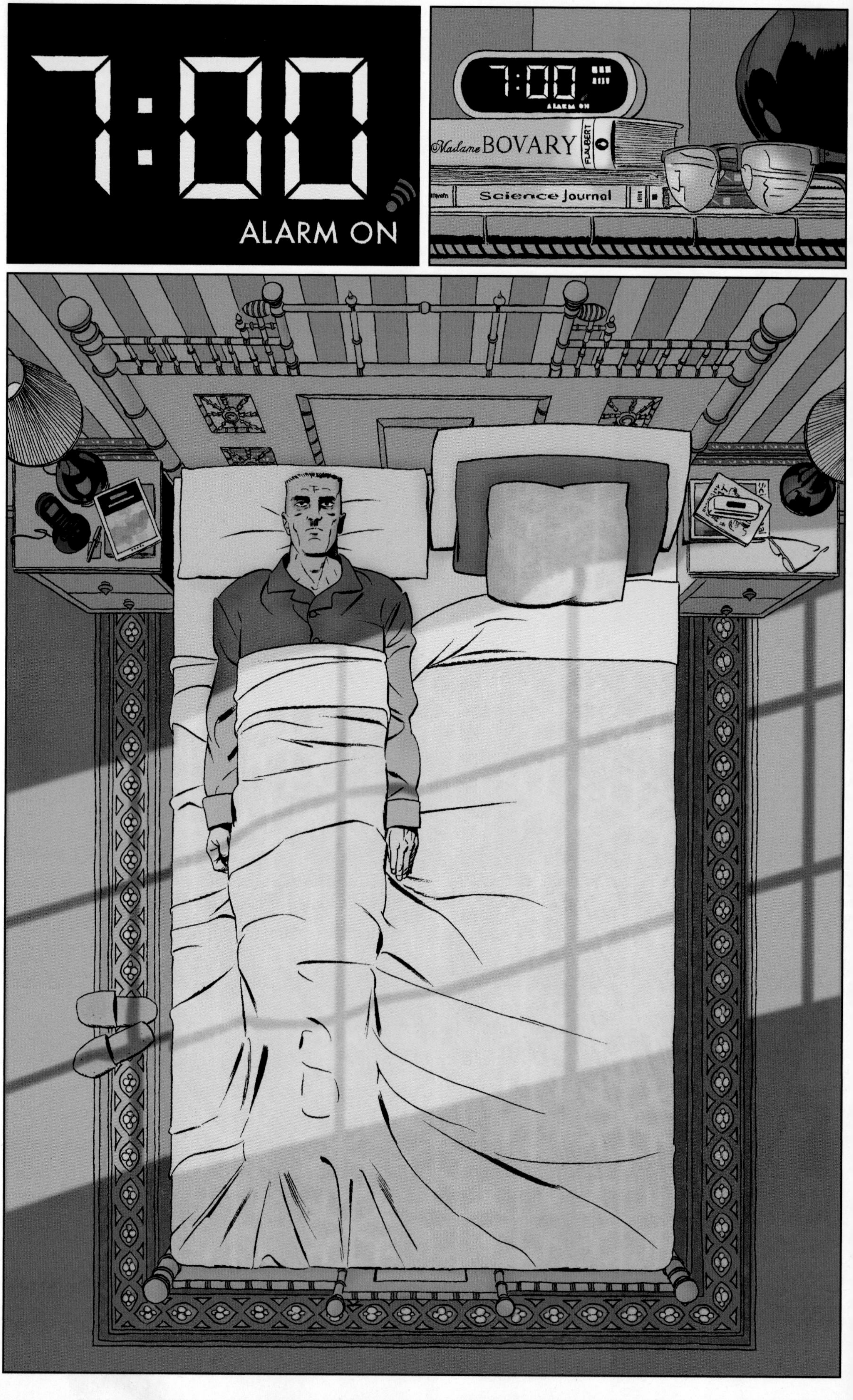
7:00
ALARM ON
7:00
ALARM ON
Madame BOVARY
FLAUBERT
Science Journal

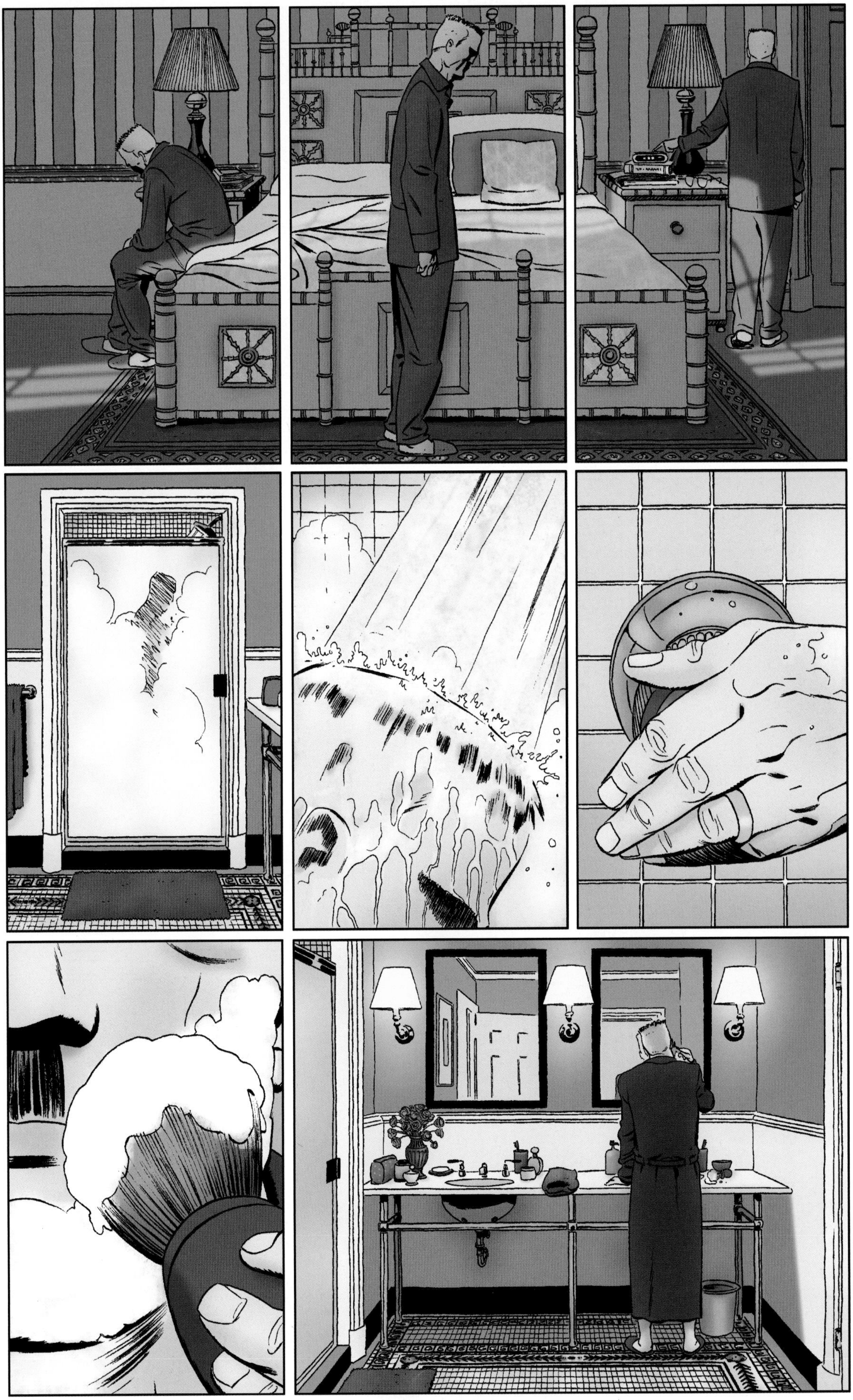

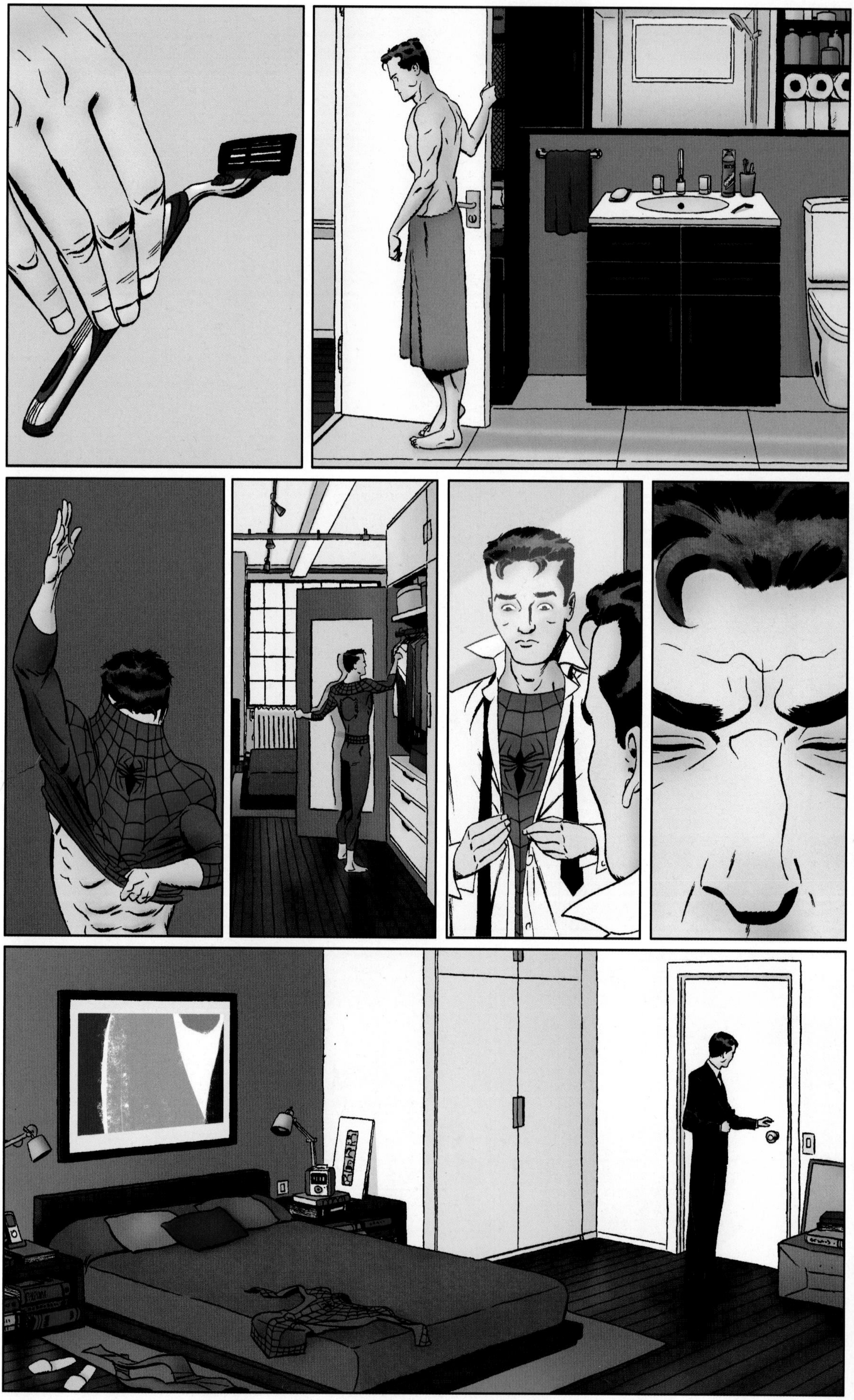

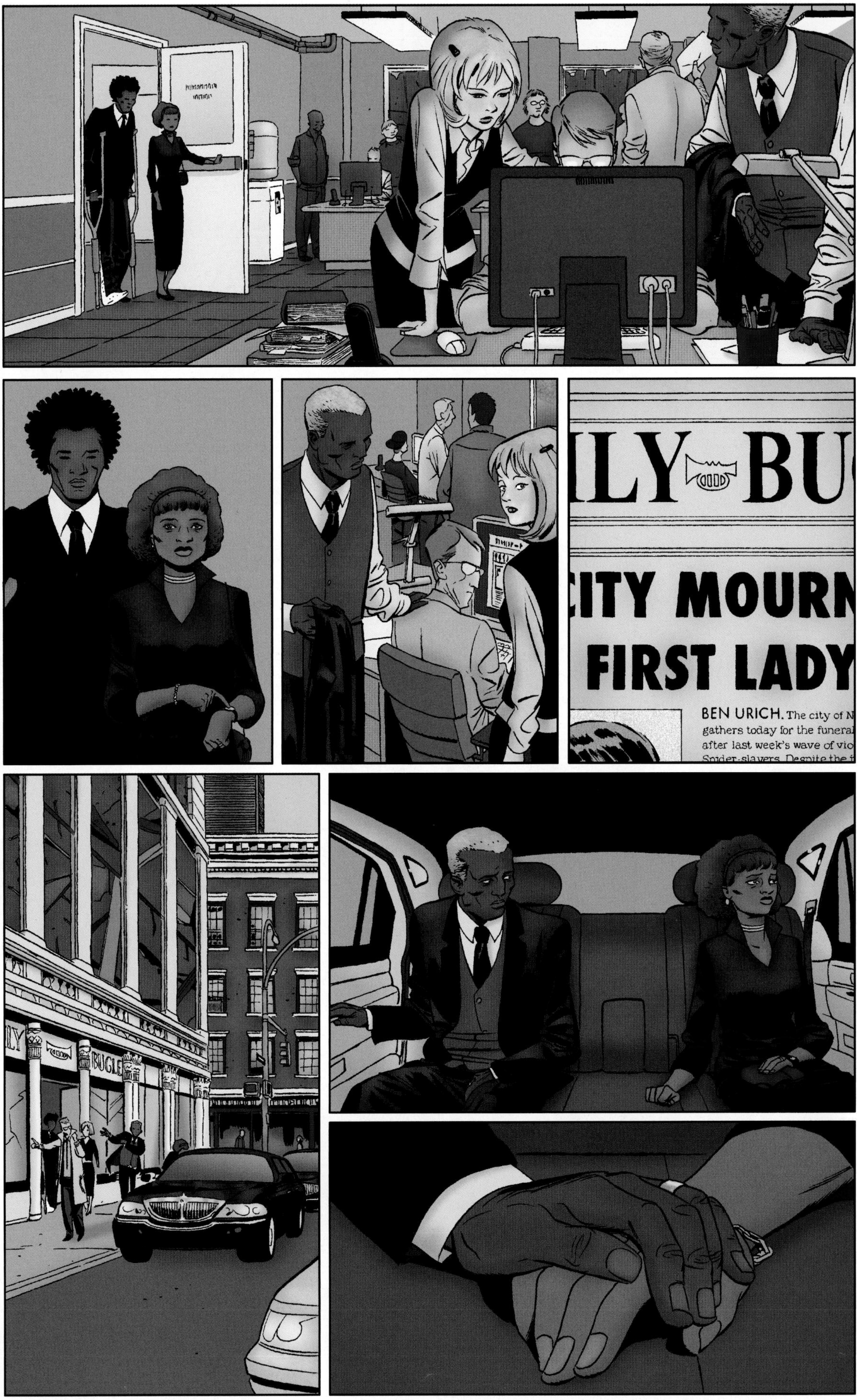

ILY BU
CITY MOURN
FIRST LADY
BEN URICH. The city of N
gathers today for the funeral
after last week's wave of vio
BUGLE

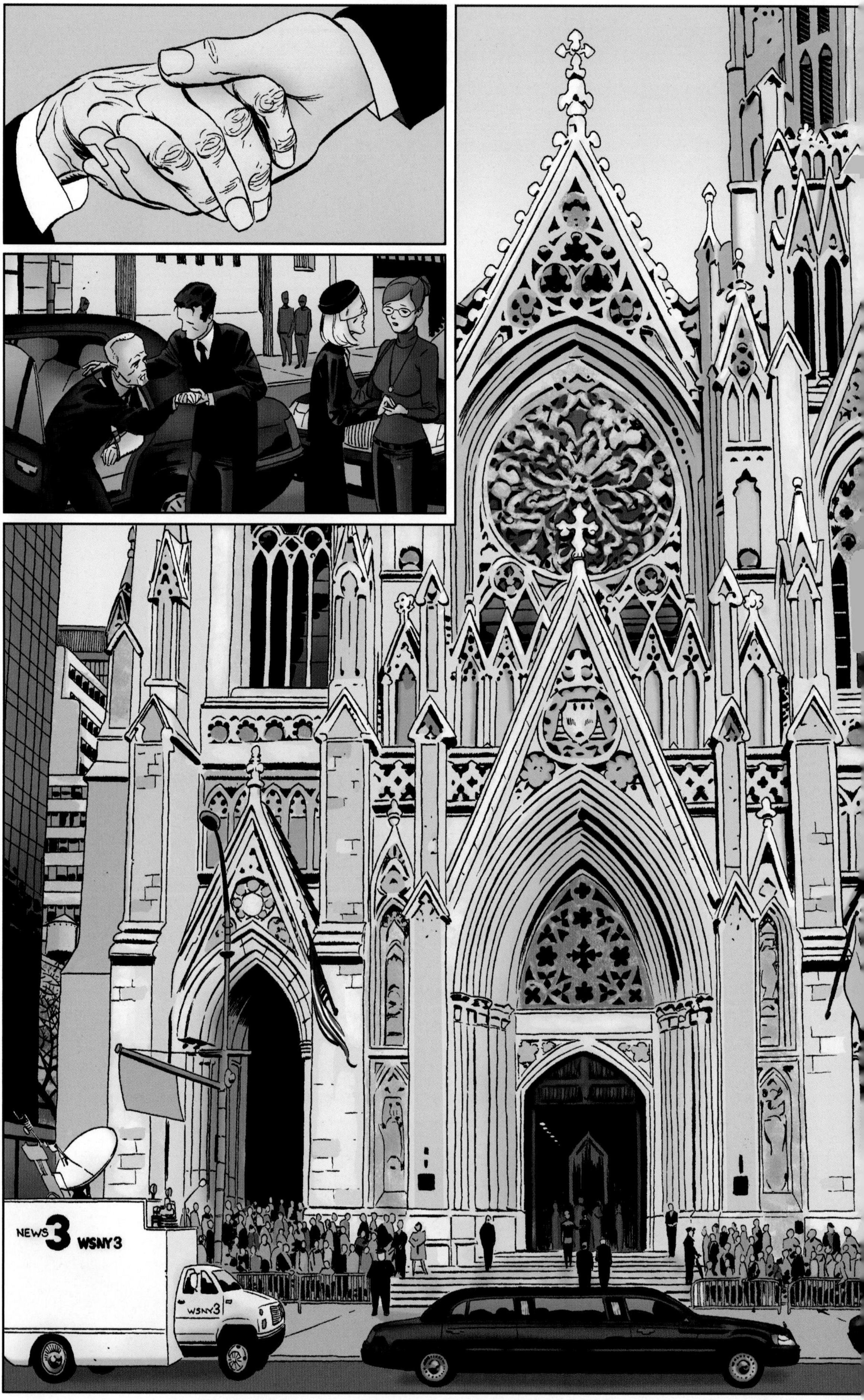
NEWS 3 WSNY3
WSNY3

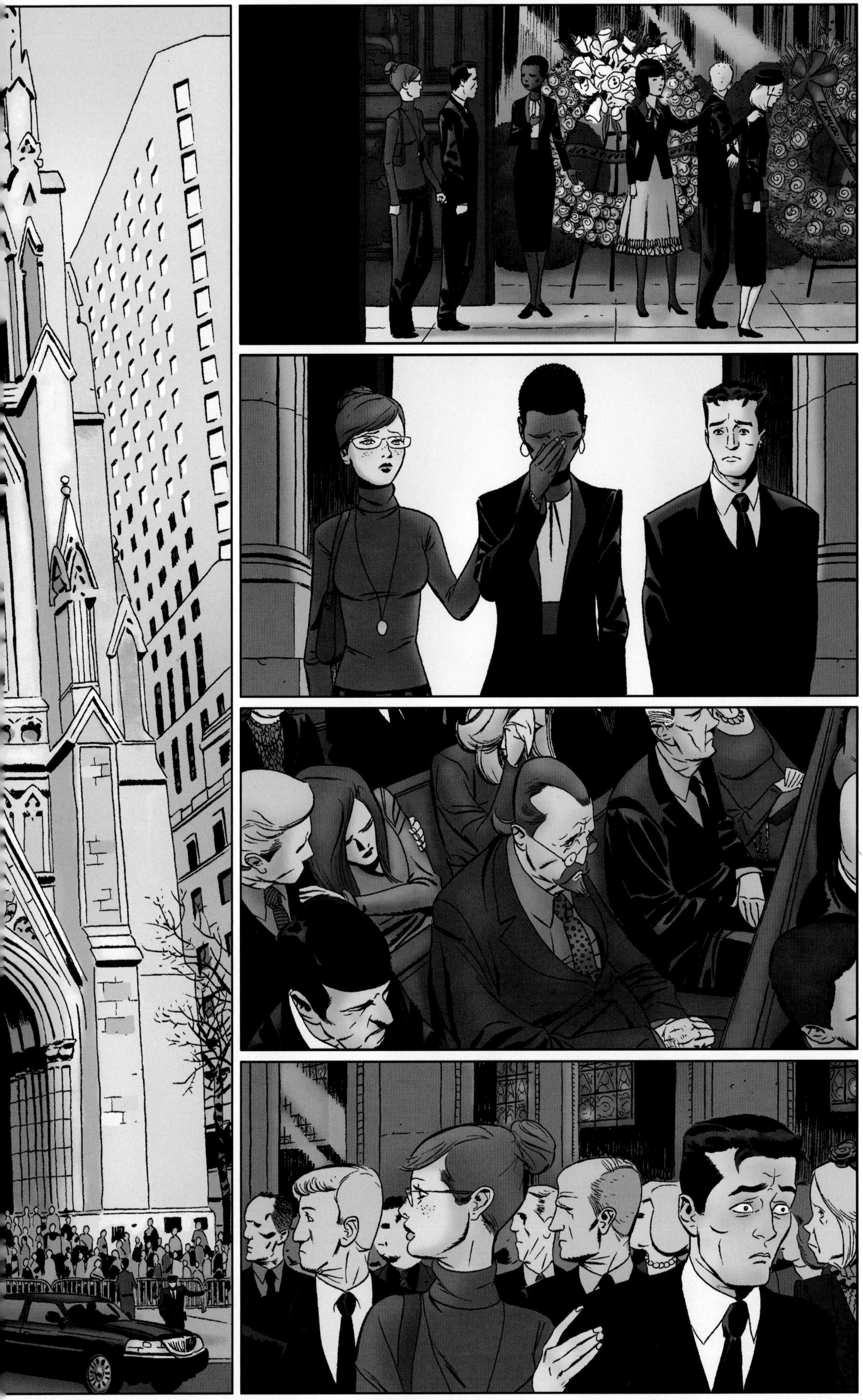

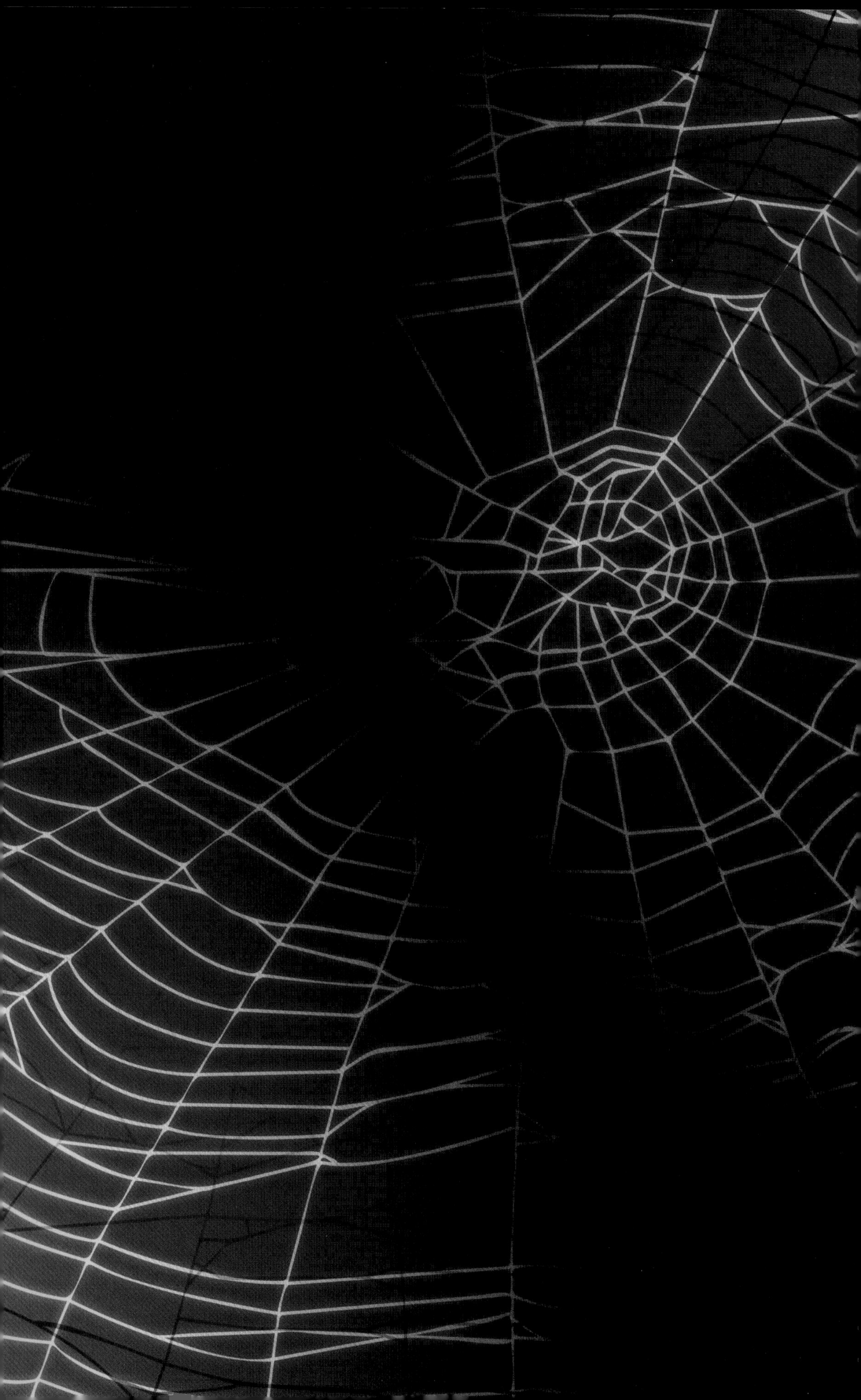

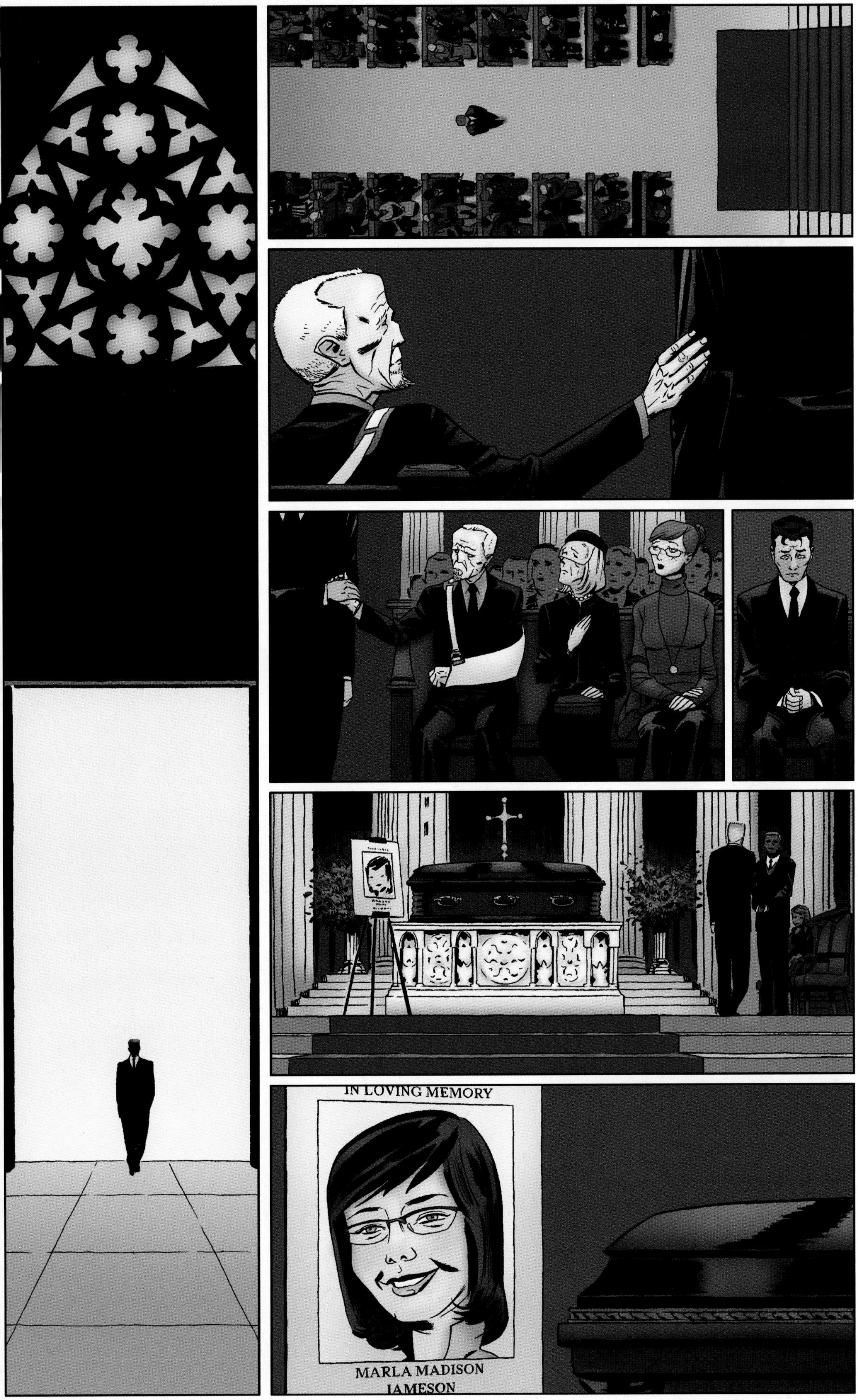
IN LOVING MEMORY
MARLA MADISON JAMESON

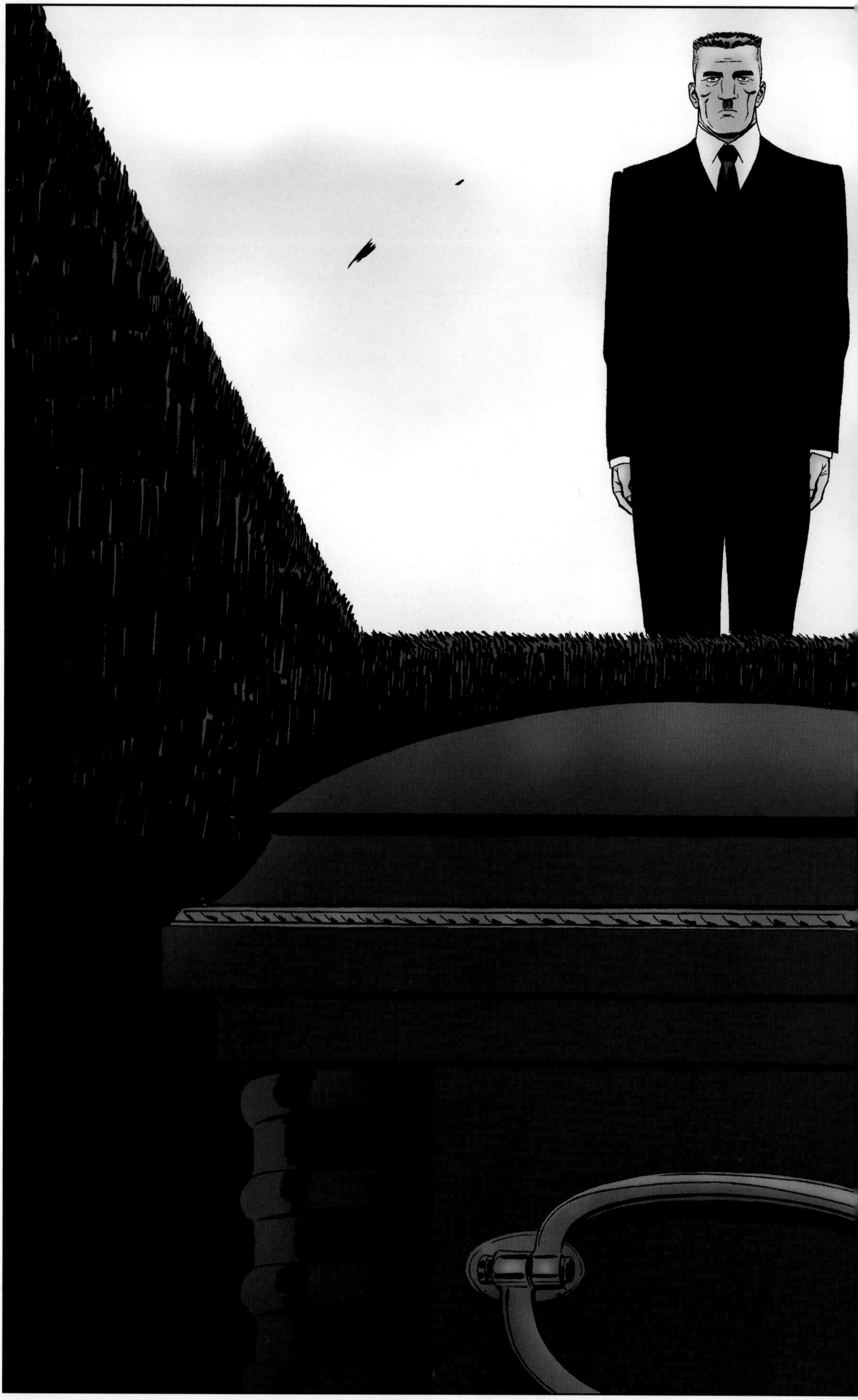

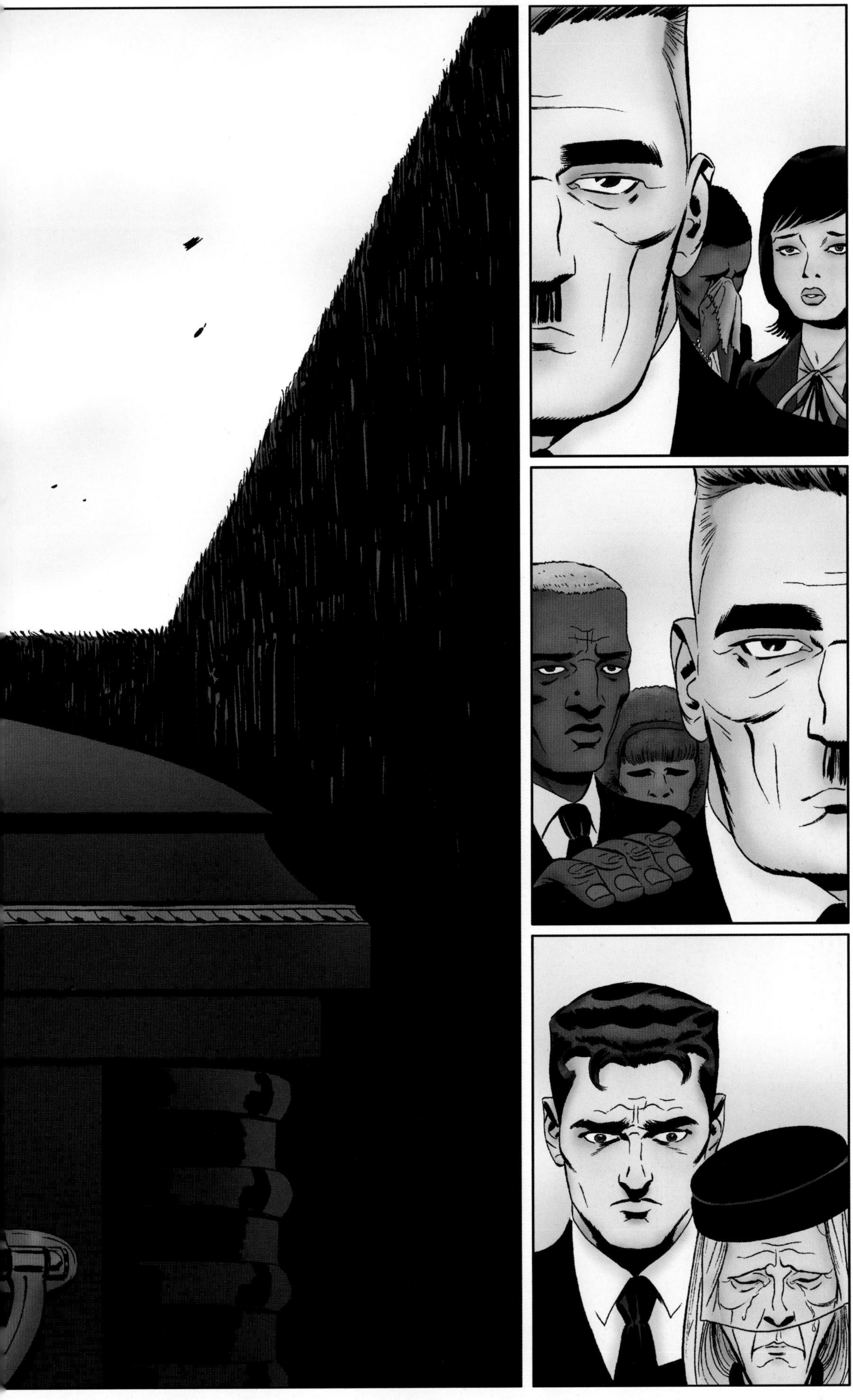

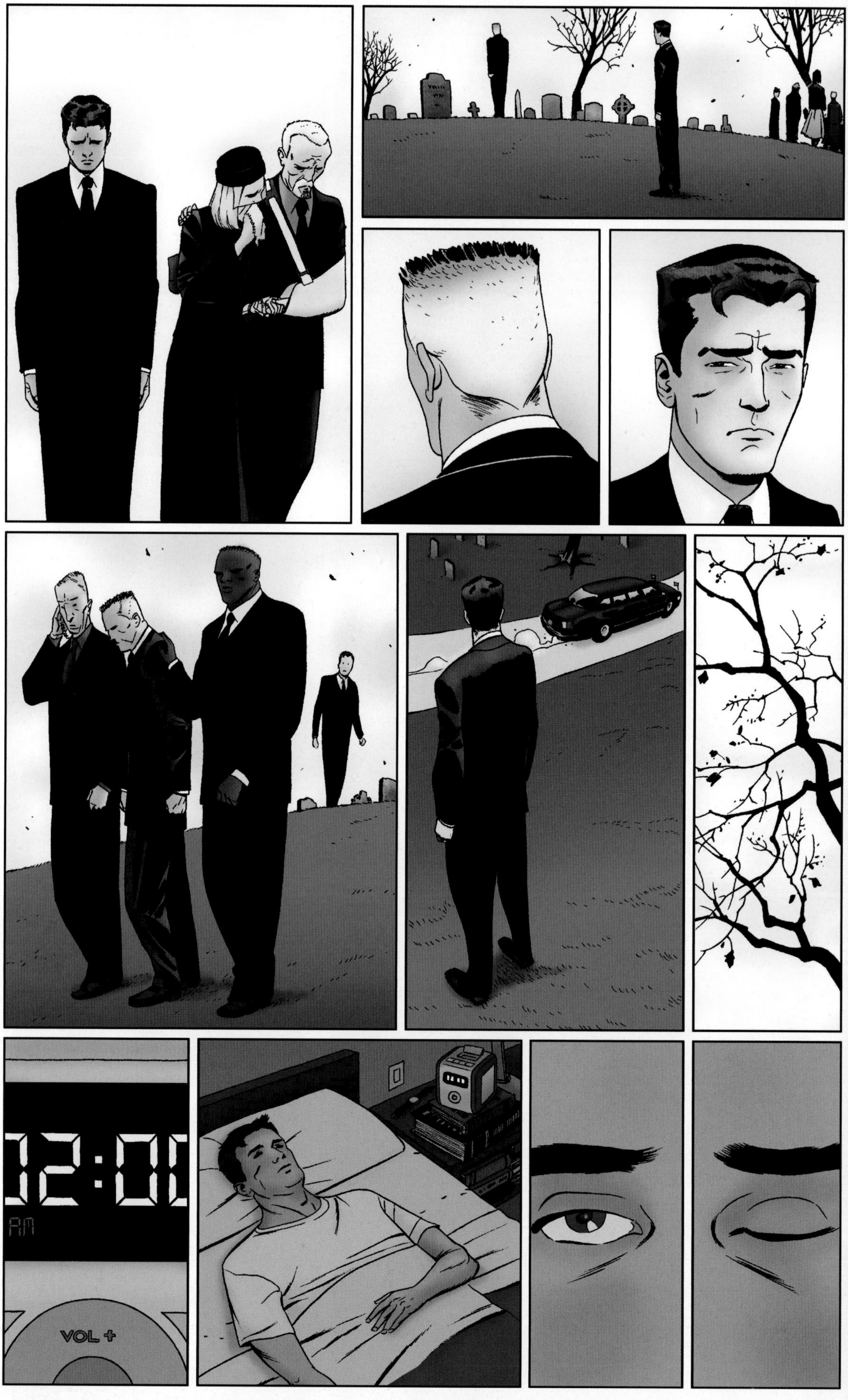
AM
VOL +

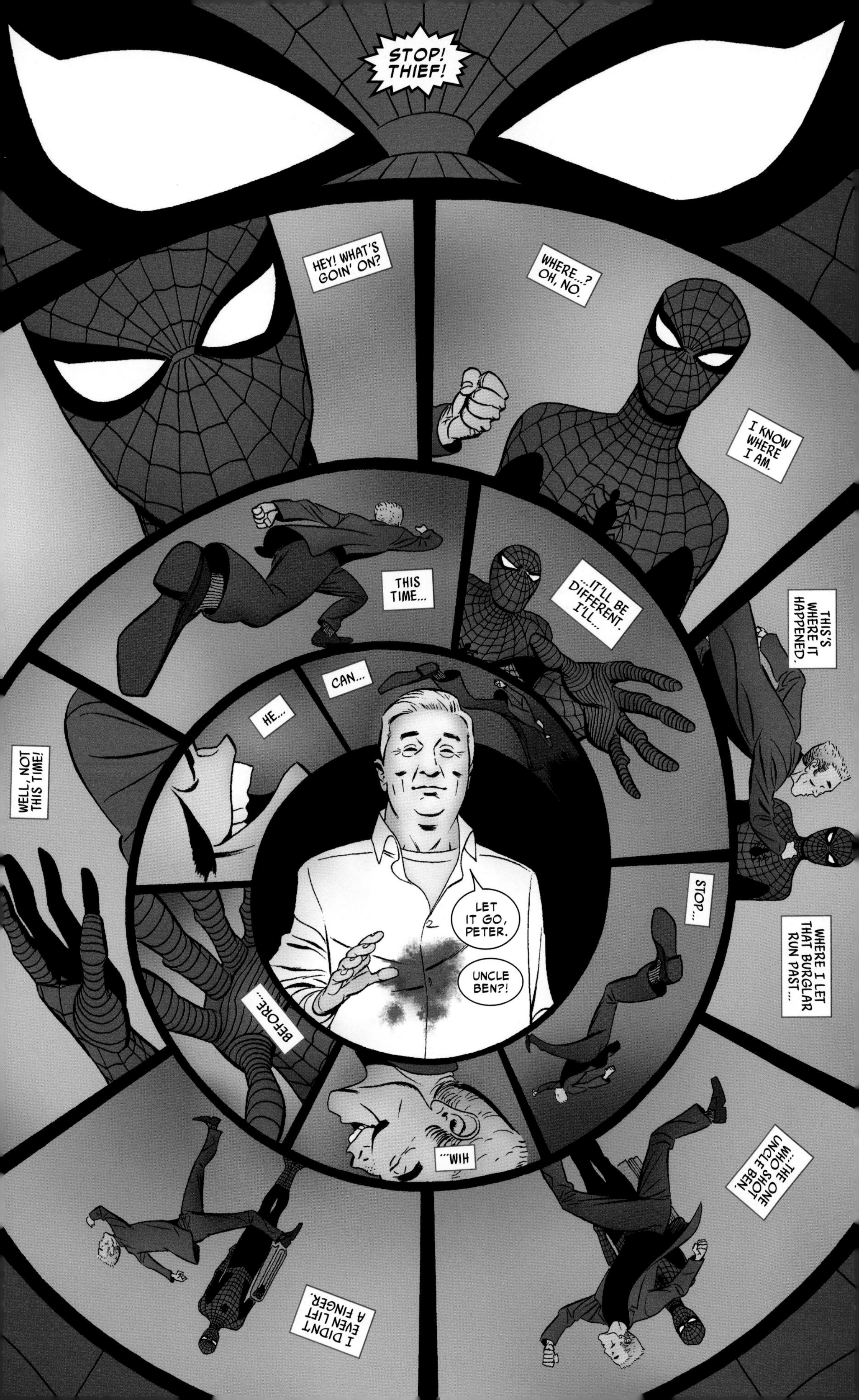
STOP! THIEF!
HEY! WHAT'S GOIN' ON?
WHERE...? OH, NO.
I KNOW WHERE I AM.
THIS'S WHERE IT HAPPENED.
WHERE I LET THAT BURGLAR RUN PAST...
...THE ONE WHO SHOT UNCLE BEN.
I DIDN'T EVEN LIFT A FINGER.
WELL, NOT THIS TIME!
THIS TIME...
...IT'LL BE DIFFERENT. I'LL...
STOP...
HIM...
BEFORE...
HE...
CAN...
LET IT GO, PETER.
UNCLE BEN?!

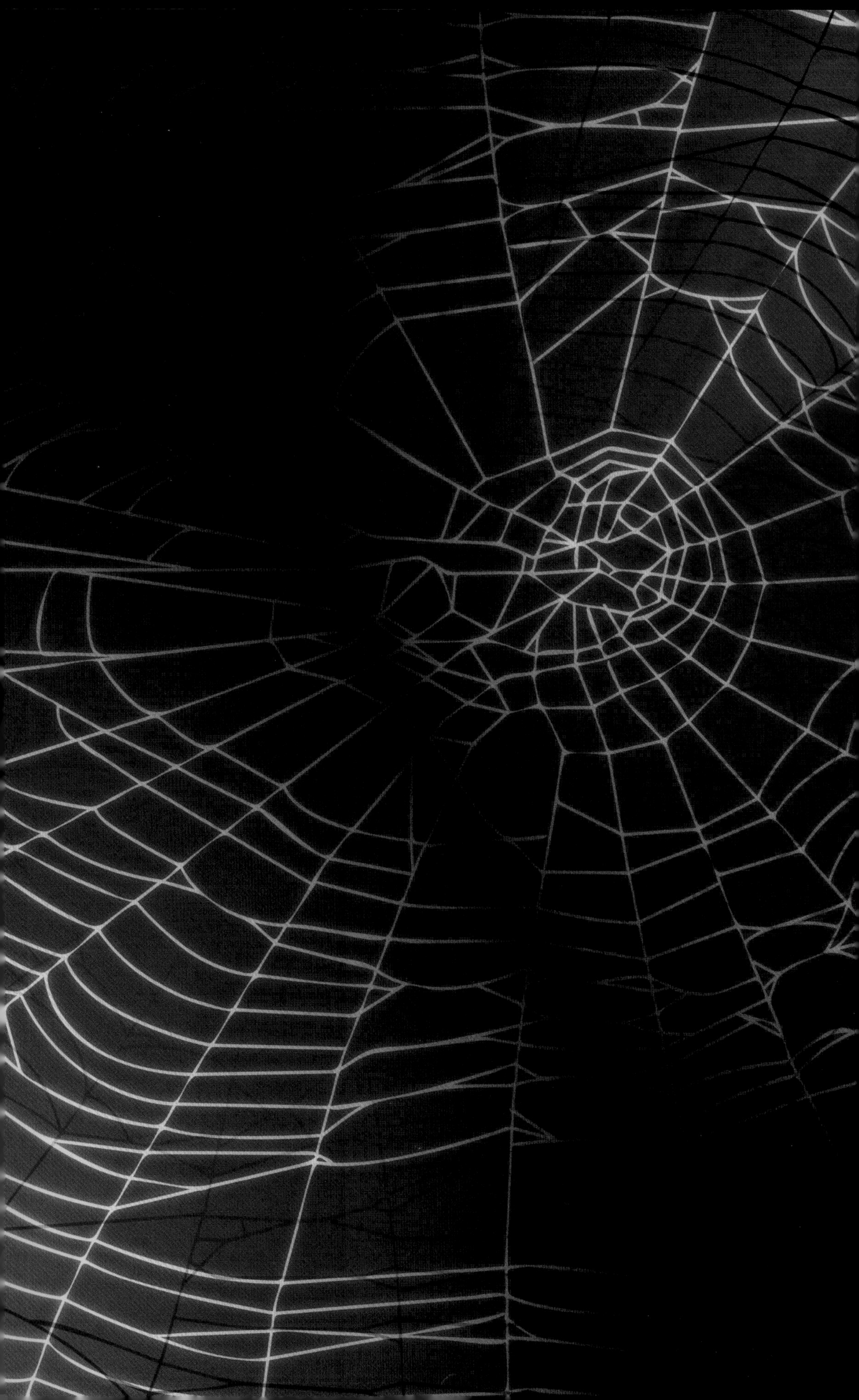

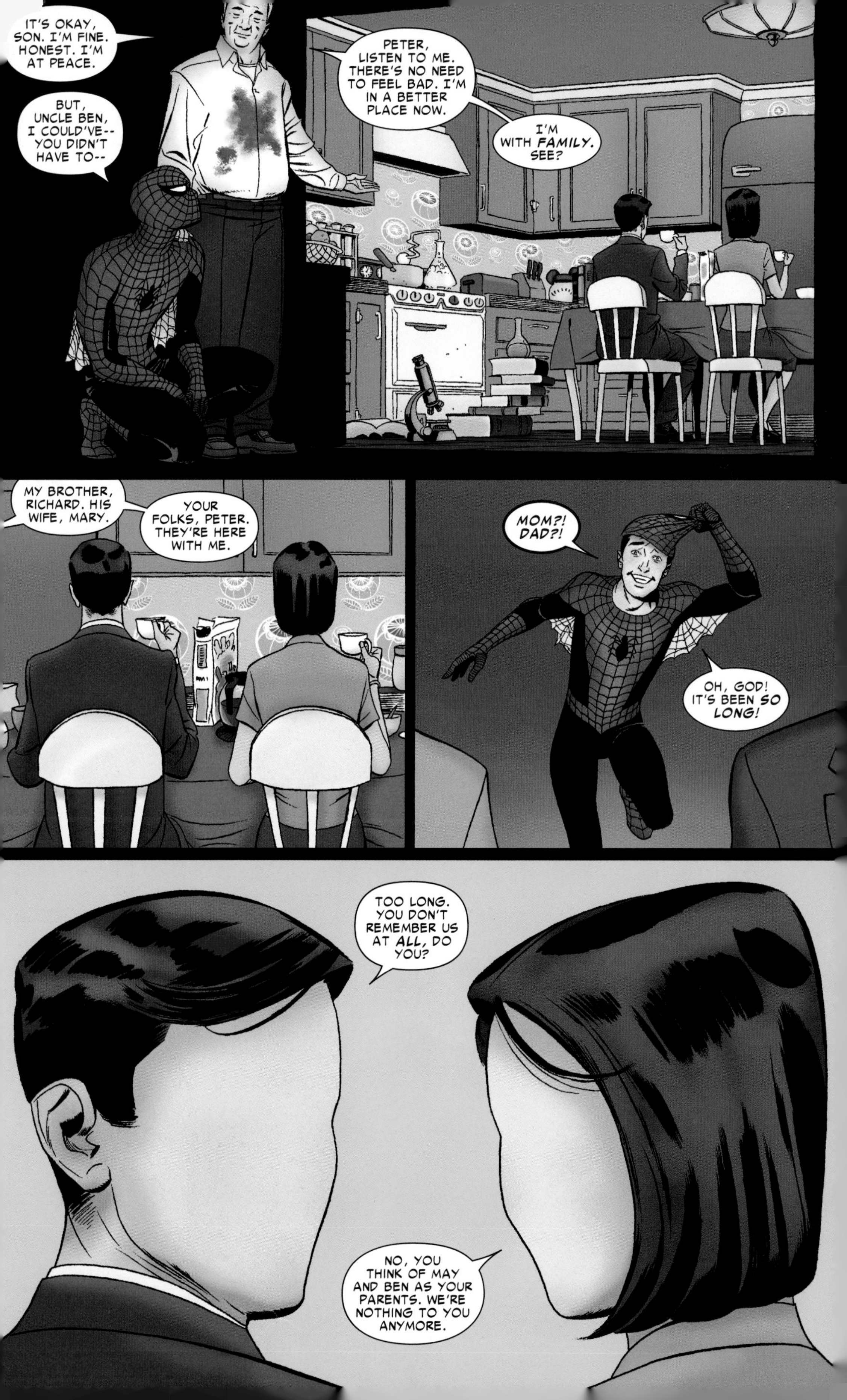
IT'S OKAY, SON. I'M FINE. HONEST. I'M AT PEACE.
BUT, UNCLE BEN, I COULD'VE-- YOU DIDN'T HAVE TO--
PETER, LISTEN TO ME. THERE'S NO NEED TO FEEL BAD. I'M IN A BETTER PLACE NOW.
I'M WITH FAMILY. SEE?
MY BROTHER, RICHARD. HIS WIFE, MARY.
YOUR FOLKS, PETER. THEY'RE HERE WITH ME.
MOM?! DAD?!
OH, GOD! IT'S BEEN SO LONG!
TOO LONG. YOU DON'T REMEMBER US AT ALL, DO YOU?
NO, YOU THINK OF MAY AND BEN AS YOUR PARENTS. WE'RE NOTHING TO YOU ANYMORE.

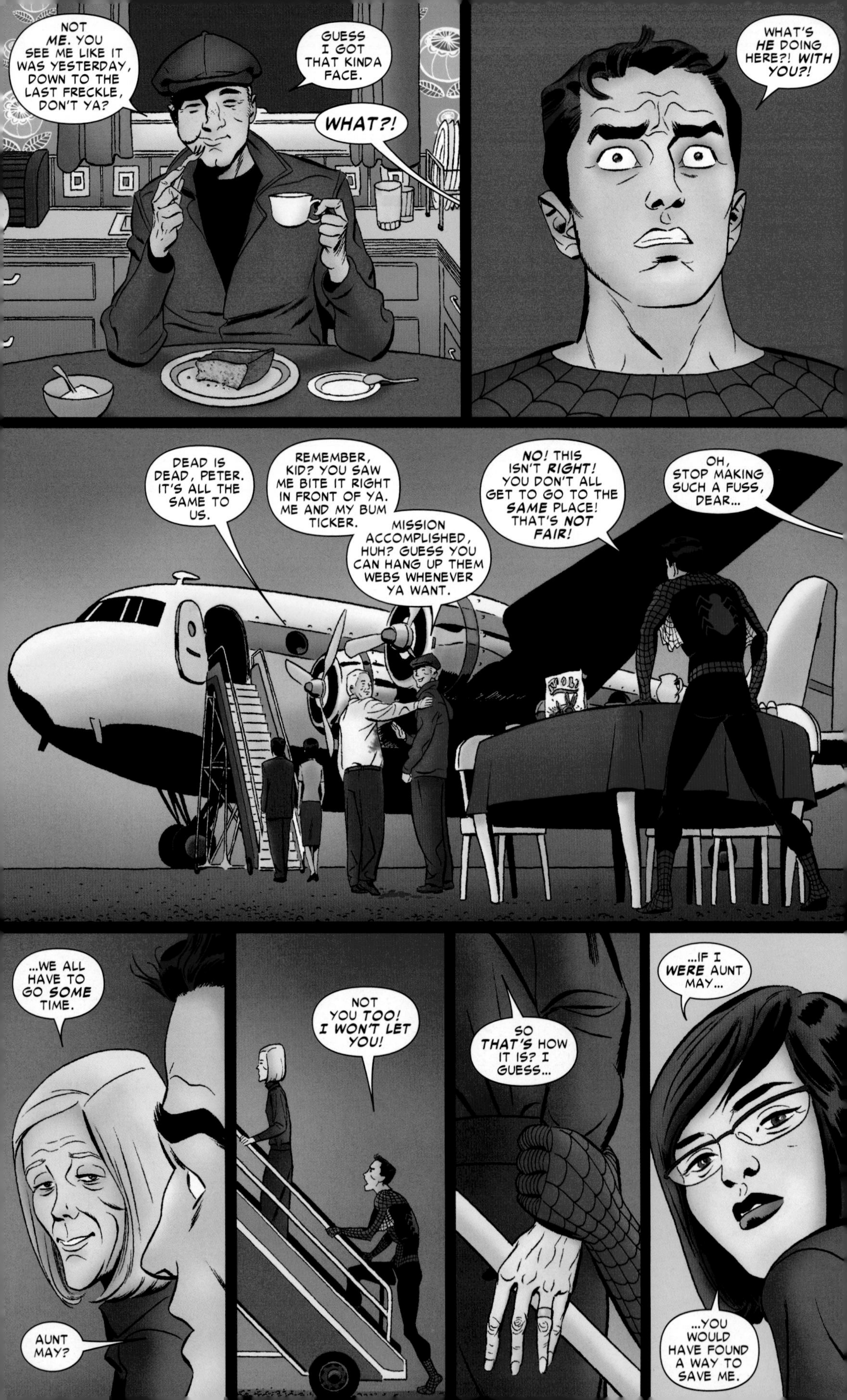
NOT ME. YOU SEE ME LIKE IT WAS YESTERDAY, DOWN TO THE LAST FRECKLE, DON'T YA?
GUESS I GOT THAT KINDA FACE.
WHAT?!
WHAT'S HE DOING HERE?! WITH YOU?!
DEAD IS DEAD, PETER. IT'S ALL THE SAME TO US.
REMEMBER, KID? YOU SAW ME BITE IT RIGHT IN FRONT OF YA. ME AND MY BUM TICKER.
MISSION ACCOMPLISHED, HUH? GUESS YOU CAN HANG UP THEM WEBS WHENEVER YA WANT.
NO! THIS ISN'T RIGHT! YOU DON'T ALL GET TO GO TO THE SAME PLACE! THAT'S NOT FAIR!
OH, STOP MAKING SUCH A FUSS, DEAR...
...WE ALL HAVE TO GO SOME TIME.
AUNT MAY?
NOT YOU TOO! I WON'T LET YOU!
SO THAT'S HOW IT IS? I GUESS...
...IF I WERE AUNT MAY...
...YOU WOULD HAVE FOUND A WAY TO SAVE ME.

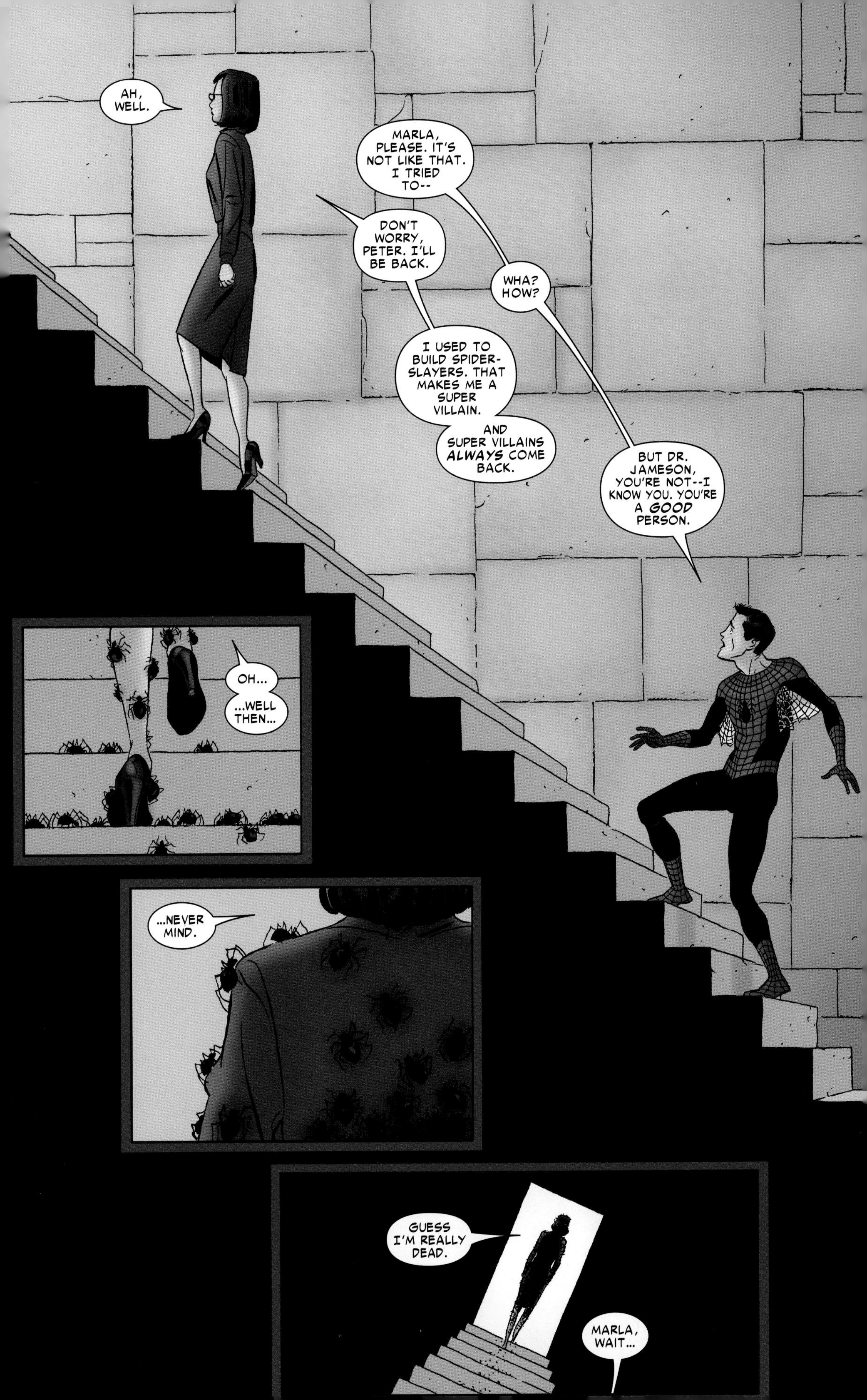
AH, WELL.
MARLA, PLEASE. IT'S NOT LIKE THAT. I TRIED TO--
DON'T WORRY, PETER. I'LL BE BACK.
WHA? HOW?
I USED TO BUILD SPIDER-SLAYERS. THAT MAKES ME A SUPER VILLAIN.
AND SUPER VILLAINS ALWAYS COME BACK.
BUT DR. JAMESON, YOU'RE NOT--I KNOW YOU. YOU'RE A GOOD PERSON.
OH...
...WELL THEN...
...NEVER MIND.
GUESS I'M REALLY DEAD.
MARLA, WAIT...

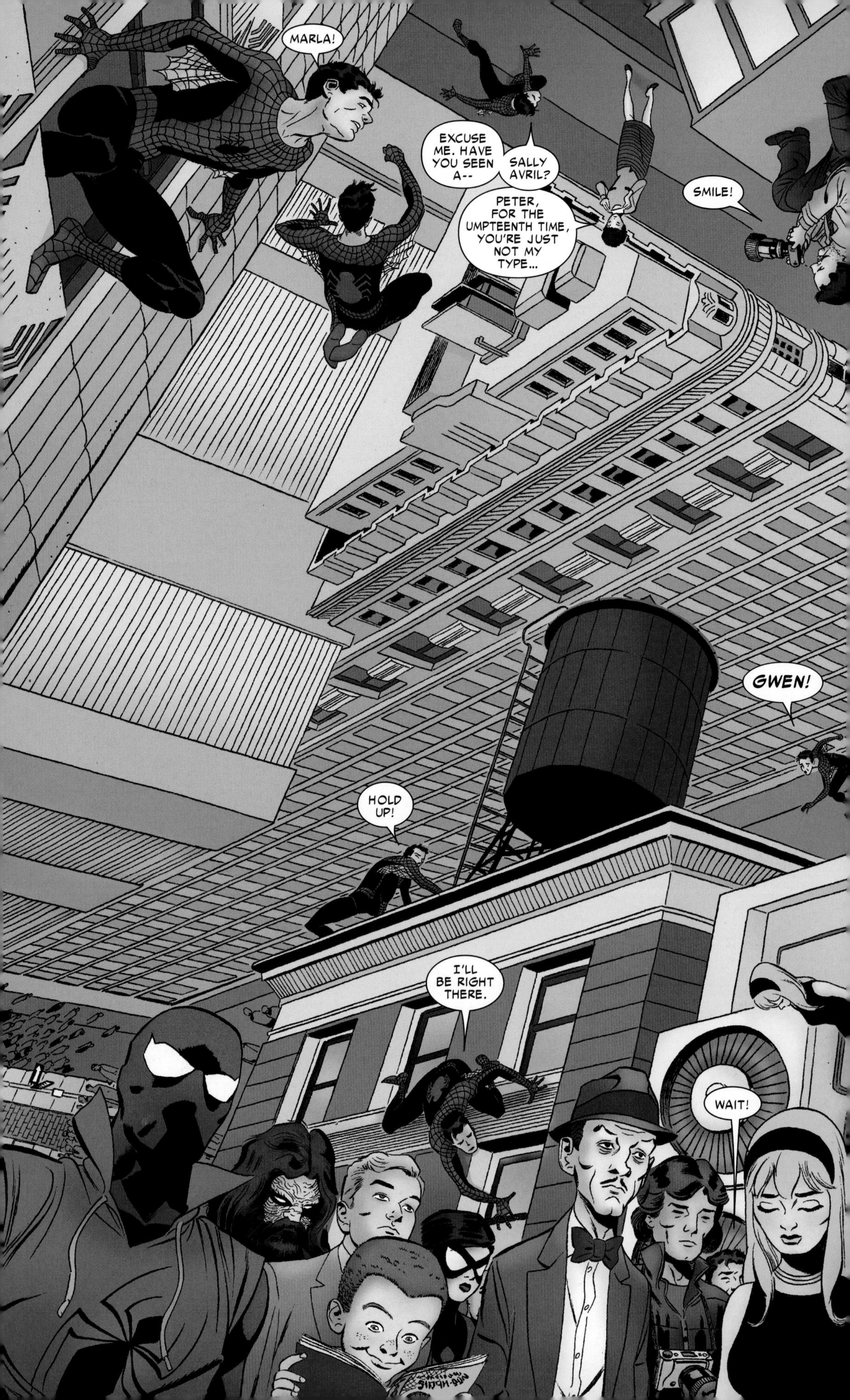
MARLA!
EXCUSE ME. HAVE YOU SEEN A--
SALLY AVRIL?
PETER, FOR THE UMPTEENTH TIME, YOU'RE JUST NOT MY TYPE...
SMILE!
GWEN!
HOLD UP!
I'LL BE RIGHT THERE.
WAIT!

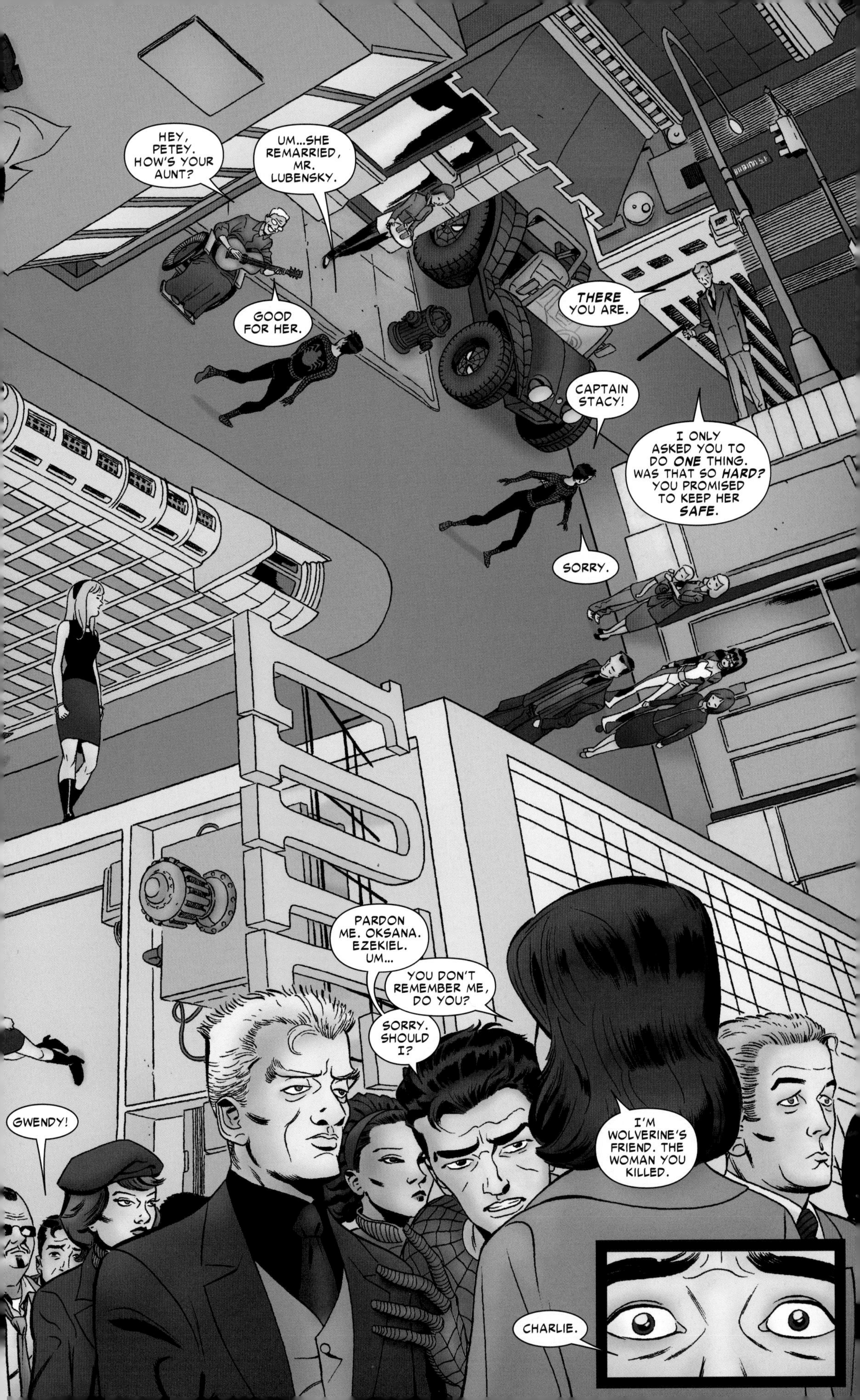
HEY, PETEY. HOW'S YOUR AUNT?
UM...SHE REMARRIED, MR. LUBENSKY.
GOOD FOR HER.
THERE YOU ARE.
CAPTAIN STACY!
I ONLY ASKED YOU TO DO ONE THING. WAS THAT SO HARD? YOU PROMISED TO KEEP HER SAFE.
SORRY.
PARDON ME. OKSANA. EZEKIEL. UM...
YOU DON'T REMEMBER ME, DO YOU?
SORRY. SHOULD I?
GWENDY!
I'M WOLVERINE'S FRIEND. THE WOMAN YOU KILLED.
CHARLIE.

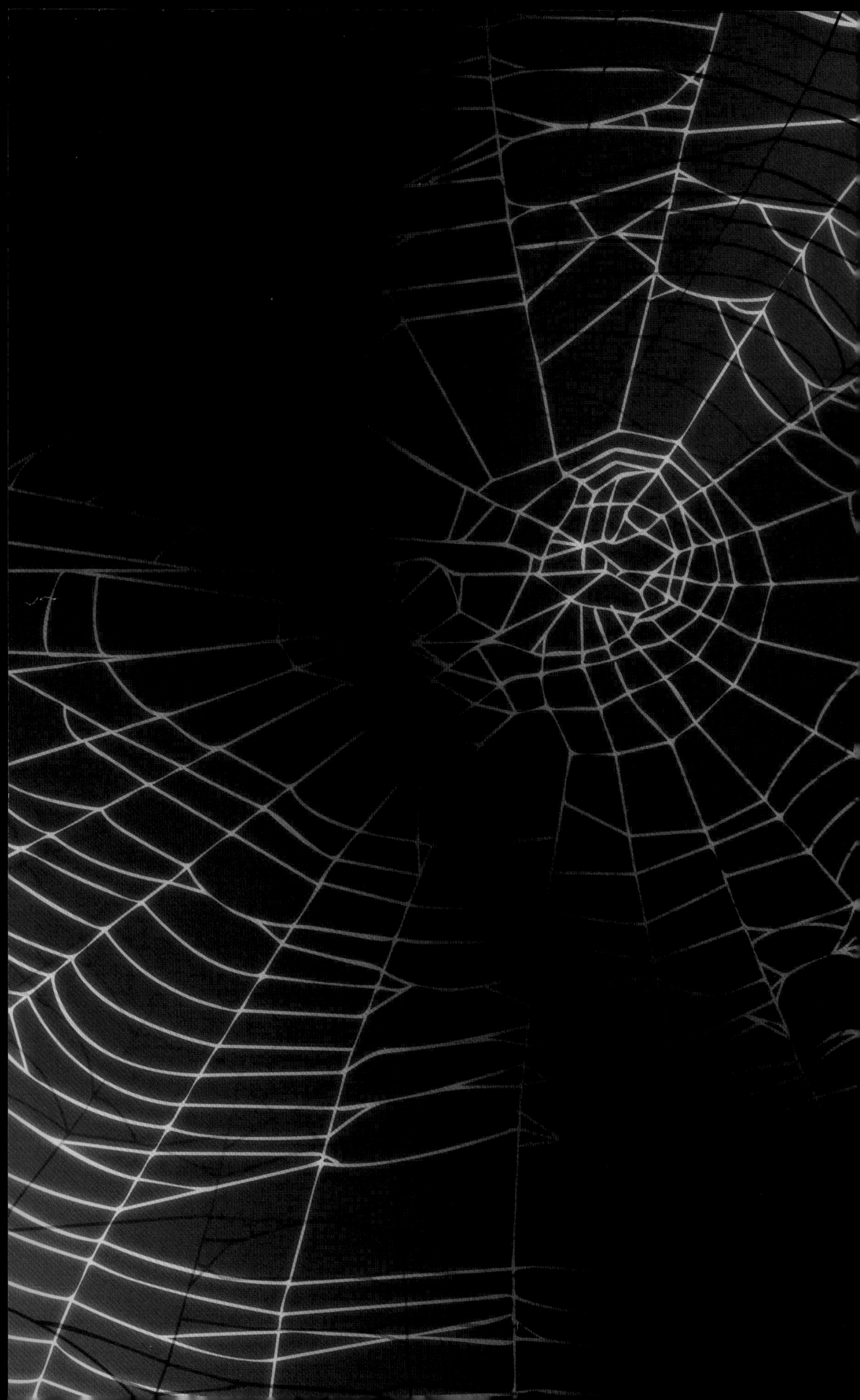

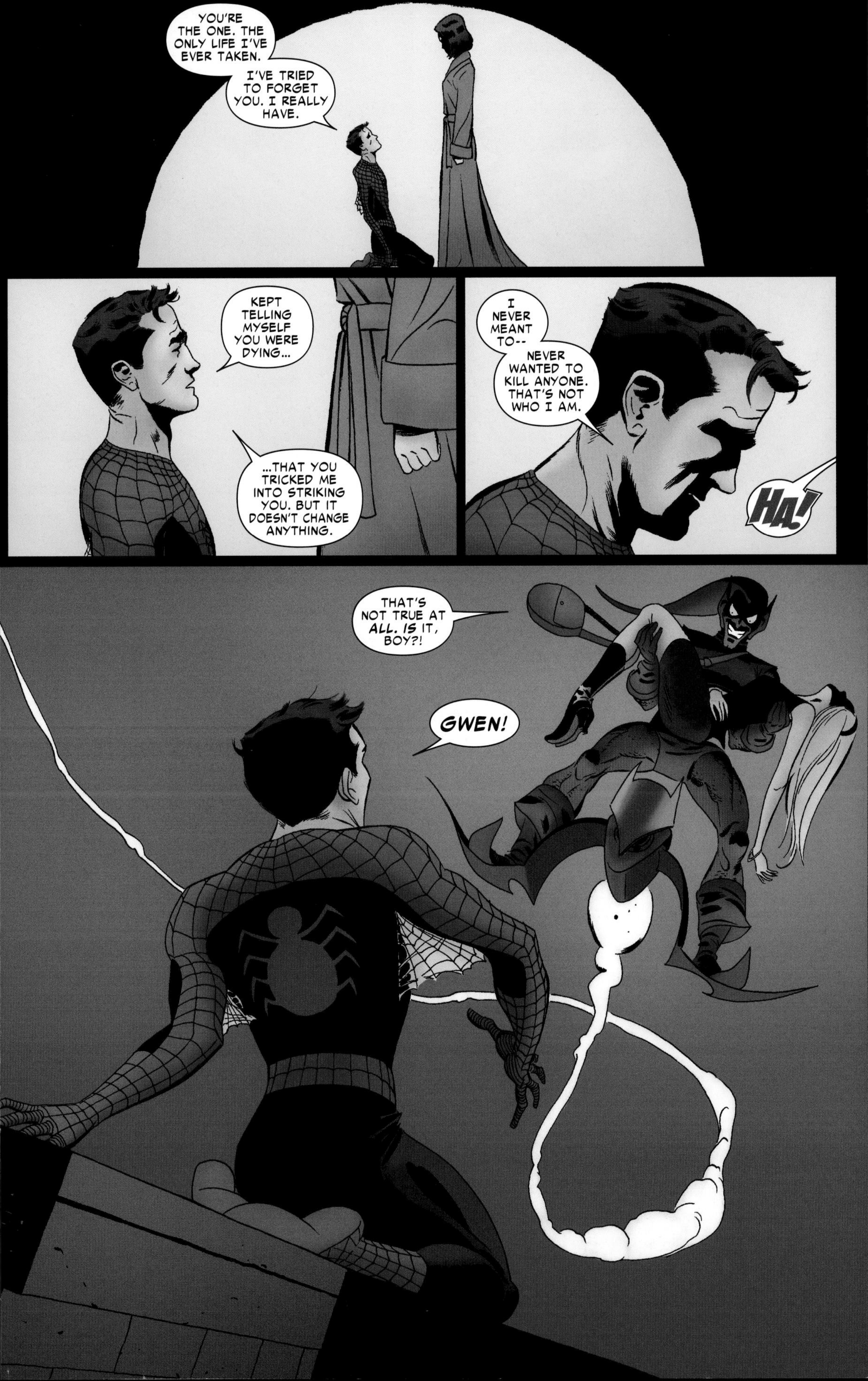
YOU'RE THE ONE. THE ONLY LIFE I'VE EVER TAKEN.
I'VE TRIED TO FORGET YOU. I REALLY HAVE.
KEPT TELLING MYSELF YOU WERE DYING...
...THAT YOU TRICKED ME INTO STRIKING YOU. BUT IT DOESN'T CHANGE ANYTHING.
I NEVER MEANT TO--
NEVER WANTED TO KILL ANYONE. THAT'S NOT WHO I AM.
HA!
THAT'S NOT TRUE AT ALL. IS IT, BOY?!
GWEN!

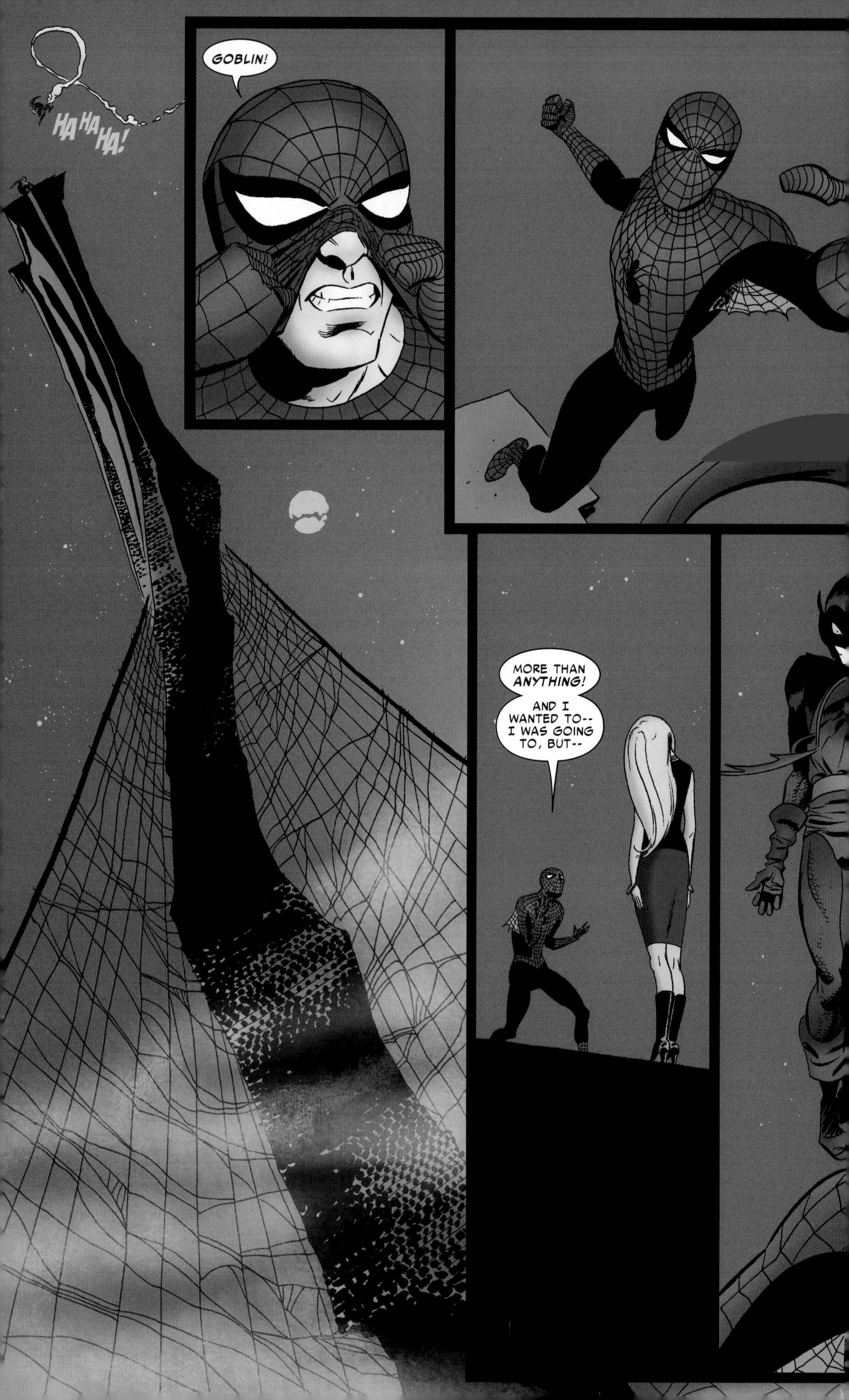
HA HA HA!
GOBLIN!
MORE THAN ANYTHING!
AND I WANTED TO-- I WAS GOING TO, BUT--

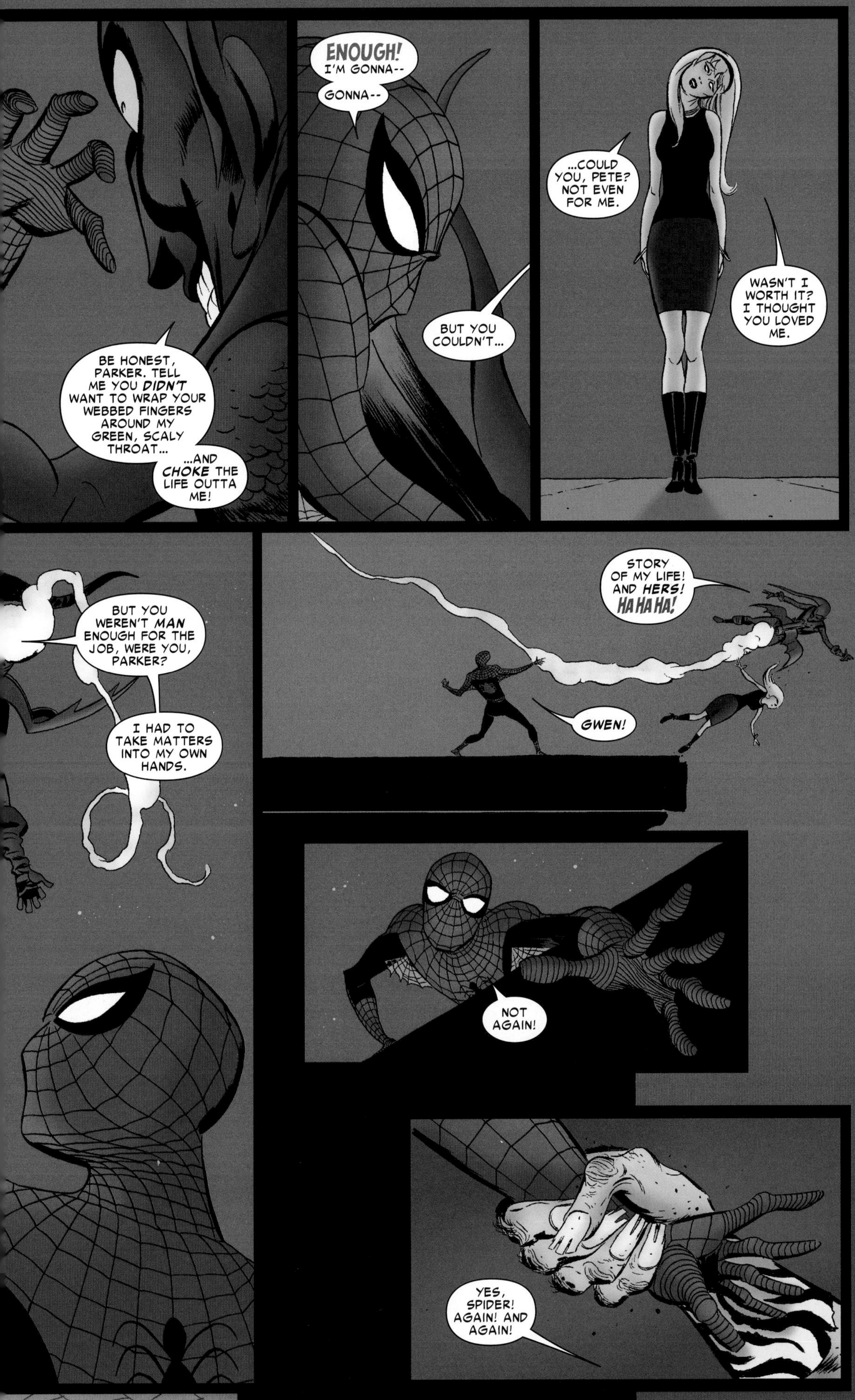
BE HONEST, PARKER. TELL ME YOU DIDN'T WANT TO WRAP YOUR WEBBED FINGERS AROUND MY GREEN, SCALY THROAT...
...AND CHOKE THE LIFE OUTTA ME!
ENOUGH! I'M GONNA--
GONNA--
BUT YOU COULDN'T...
...COULD YOU, PETE? NOT EVEN FOR ME.
WASN'T I WORTH IT? I THOUGHT YOU LOVED ME.
BUT YOU WEREN'T MAN ENOUGH FOR THE JOB, WERE YOU, PARKER?
I HAD TO TAKE MATTERS INTO MY OWN HANDS.
STORY OF MY LIFE! AND HERS! HA HA HA!
GWEN!
NOT AGAIN!
YES, SPIDER! AGAIN! AND AGAIN!

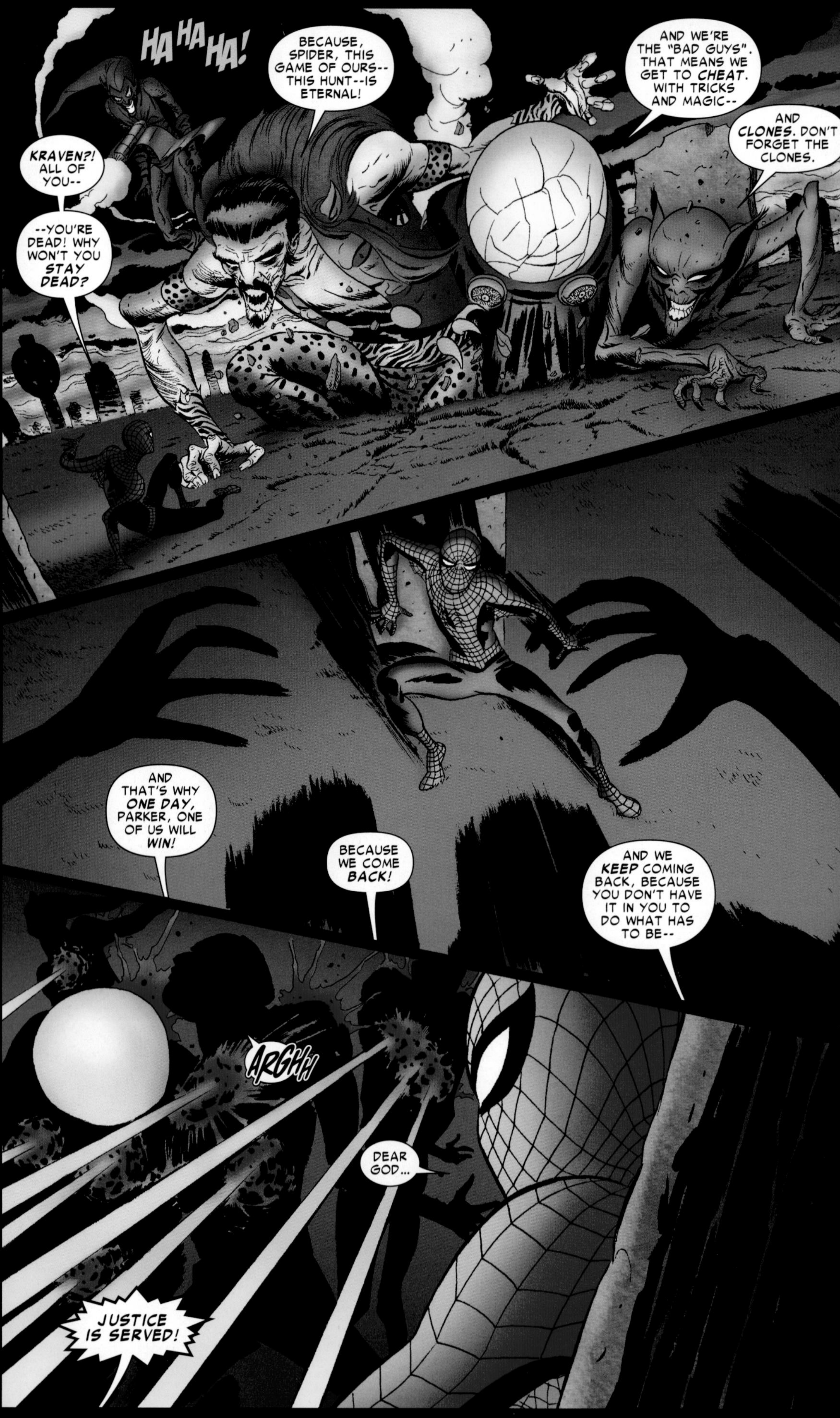
HA HA HA!
KRAVEN?! ALL OF YOU--
--YOU'RE DEAD! WHY WON'T YOU STAY DEAD?
BECAUSE, SPIDER, THIS GAME OF OURS-- THIS HUNT--IS ETERNAL!
AND WE'RE THE "BAD GUYS". THAT MEANS WE GET TO CHEAT. WITH TRICKS AND MAGIC--
AND CLONES. DON'T FORGET THE CLONES.
AND THAT'S WHY ONE DAY, PARKER, ONE OF US WILL WIN!
BECAUSE WE COME BACK!
AND WE KEEP COMING BACK, BECAUSE YOU DON'T HAVE IT IN YOU TO DO WHAT HAS TO BE--
ARGHH
DEAR GOD...
JUSTICE IS SERVED!

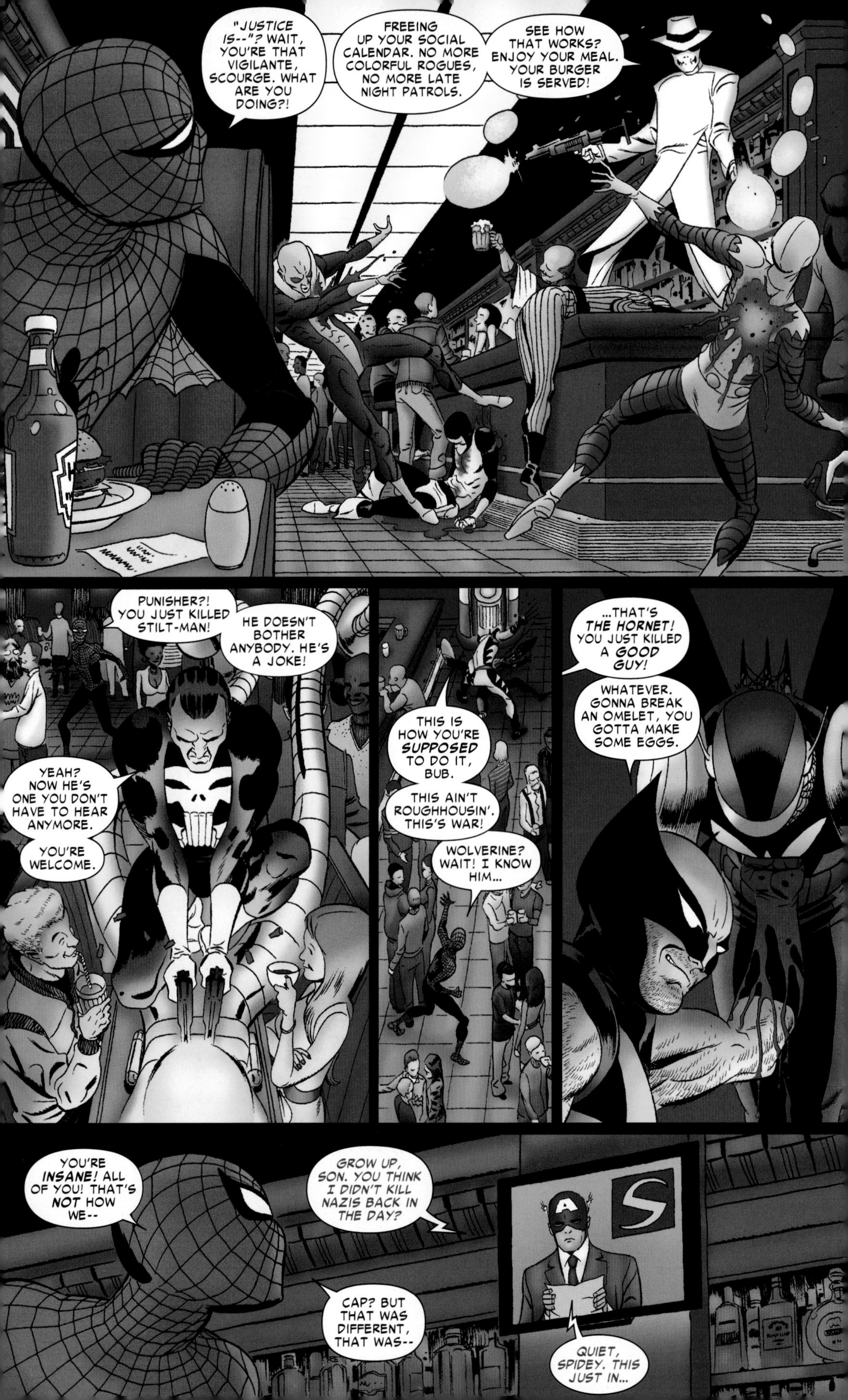
"JUSTICE IS--"? WAIT, YOU'RE THAT VIGILANTE, SCOURGE. WHAT ARE YOU DOING?!
FREEING UP YOUR SOCIAL CALENDAR. NO MORE COLORFUL ROGUES, NO MORE LATE NIGHT PATROLS.
SEE HOW THAT WORKS? ENJOY YOUR MEAL. YOUR BURGER IS SERVED!
PUNISHER?! YOU JUST KILLED STILT-MAN!
HE DOESN'T BOTHER ANYBODY. HE'S A JOKE!
YEAH? NOW HE'S ONE YOU DON'T HAVE TO HEAR ANYMORE.
YOU'RE WELCOME.
THIS IS HOW YOU'RE SUPPOSED TO DO IT, BUB.
THIS AIN'T ROUGHHOUSIN'. THIS'S WAR!
WOLVERINE? WAIT! I KNOW HIM...
...THAT'S THE HORNET! YOU JUST KILLED A GOOD GUY!
WHATEVER. GONNA BREAK AN OMELET, YOU GOTTA MAKE SOME EGGS.
YOU'RE INSANE! ALL OF YOU! THAT'S NOT HOW WE--
GROW UP, SON. YOU THINK I DIDN'T KILL NAZIS BACK IN THE DAY?
CAP? BUT THAT WAS DIFFERENT, THAT WAS--
QUIET, SPIDEY. THIS JUST IN...

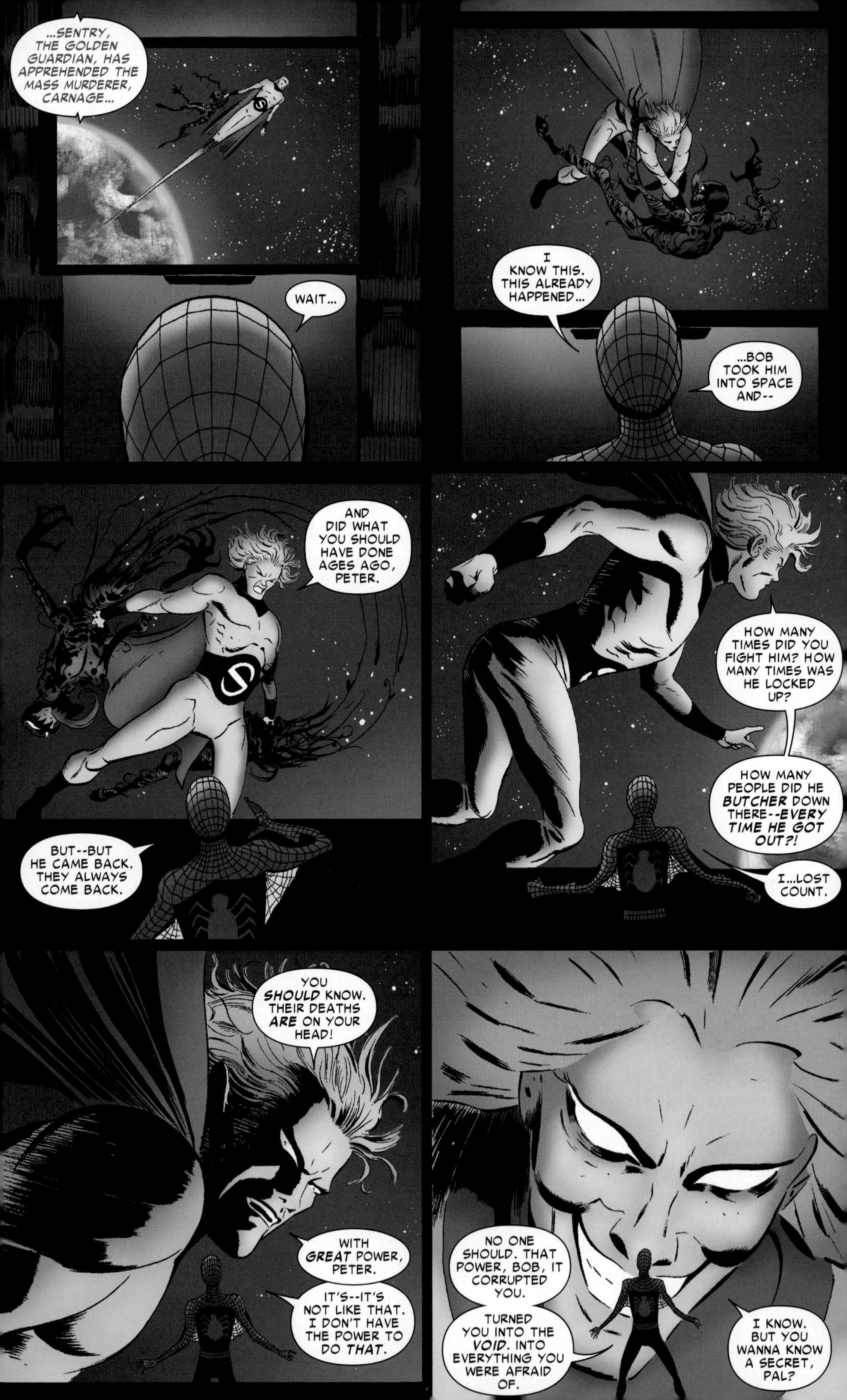
...SENTRY, THE GOLDEN GUARDIAN, HAS APPREHENDED THE MASS MURDERER, CARNAGE...
WAIT...
I KNOW THIS. THIS ALREADY HAPPENED...
...BOB TOOK HIM INTO SPACE AND--
AND DID WHAT YOU SHOULD HAVE DONE AGES AGO, PETER.
BUT--BUT HE CAME BACK. THEY ALWAYS COME BACK.
HOW MANY TIMES DID YOU FIGHT HIM? HOW MANY TIMES WAS HE LOCKED UP?
HOW MANY PEOPLE DID HE BUTCHER DOWN THERE--EVERY TIME HE GOT OUT?!
I...LOST COUNT.
YOU SHOULD KNOW. THEIR DEATHS ARE ON YOUR HEAD!
WITH GREAT POWER, PETER.
IT'S--IT'S NOT LIKE THAT. I DON'T HAVE THE POWER TO DO THAT.
NO ONE SHOULD. THAT POWER, BOB, IT CORRUPTED YOU.
TURNED YOU INTO THE VOID. INTO EVERYTHING YOU WERE AFRAID OF.
I KNOW. BUT YOU WANNA KNOW A SECRET, PAL?

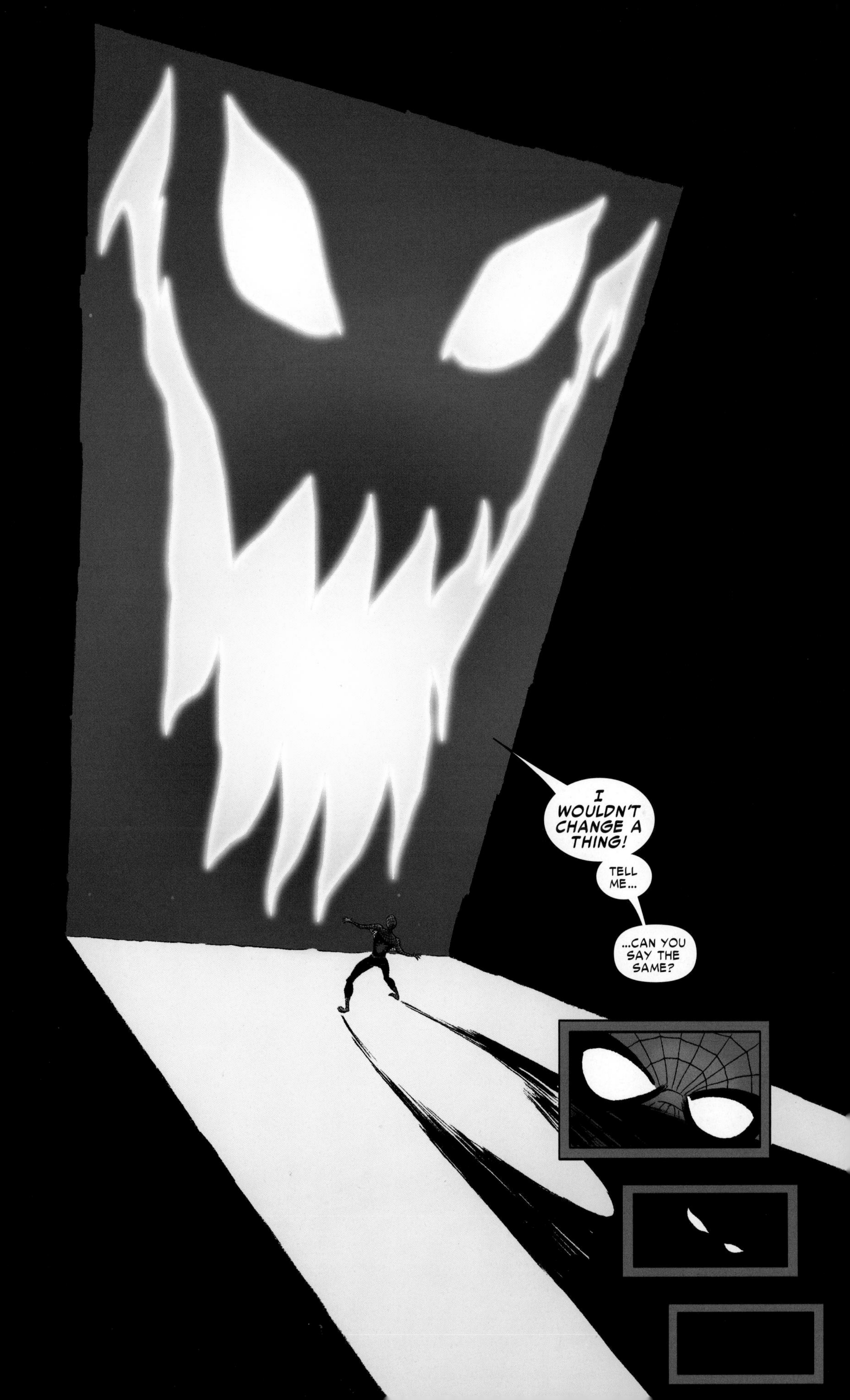
I WOULDN'T CHANGE A THING!
TELL ME...
...CAN YOU SAY THE SAME?

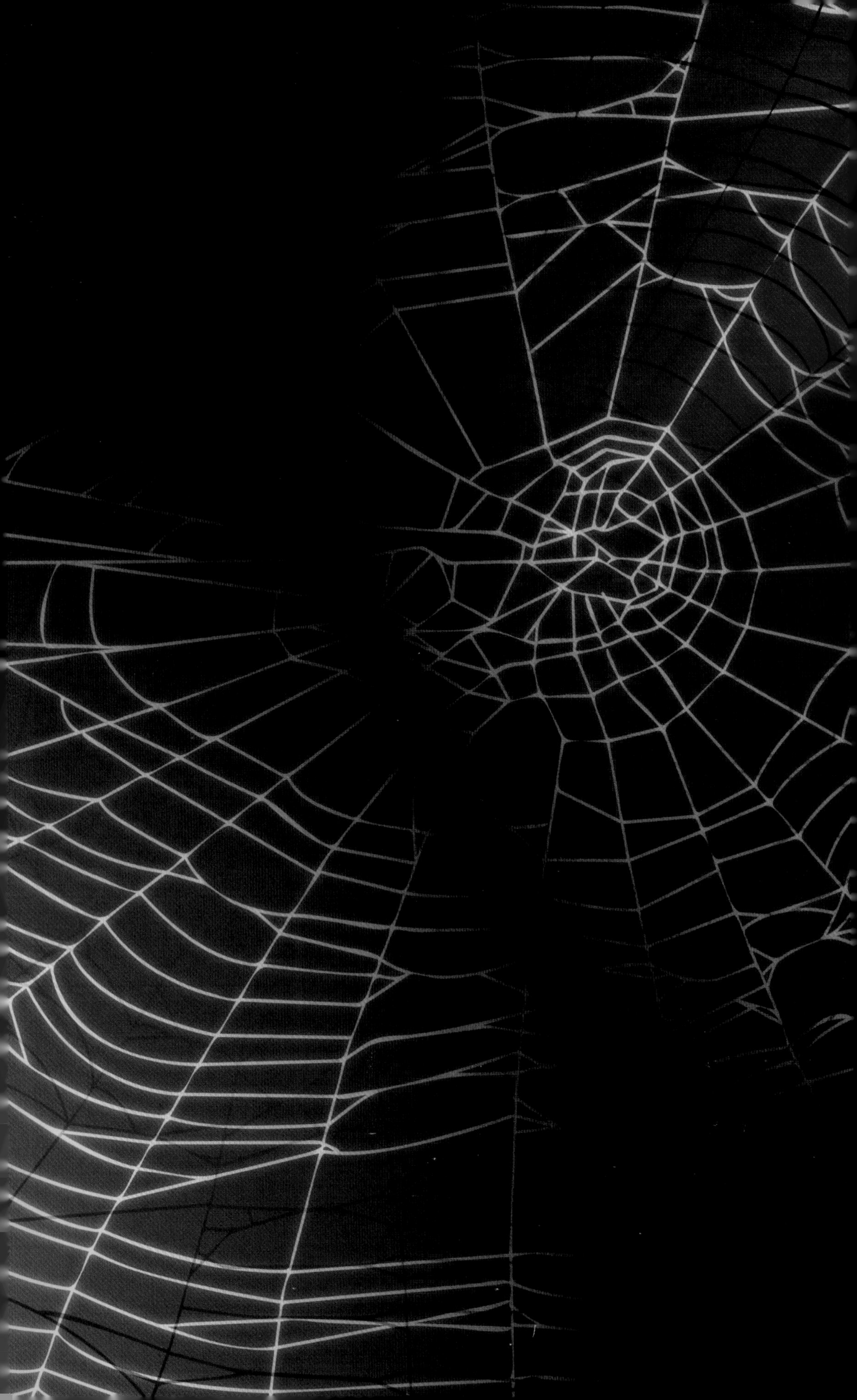

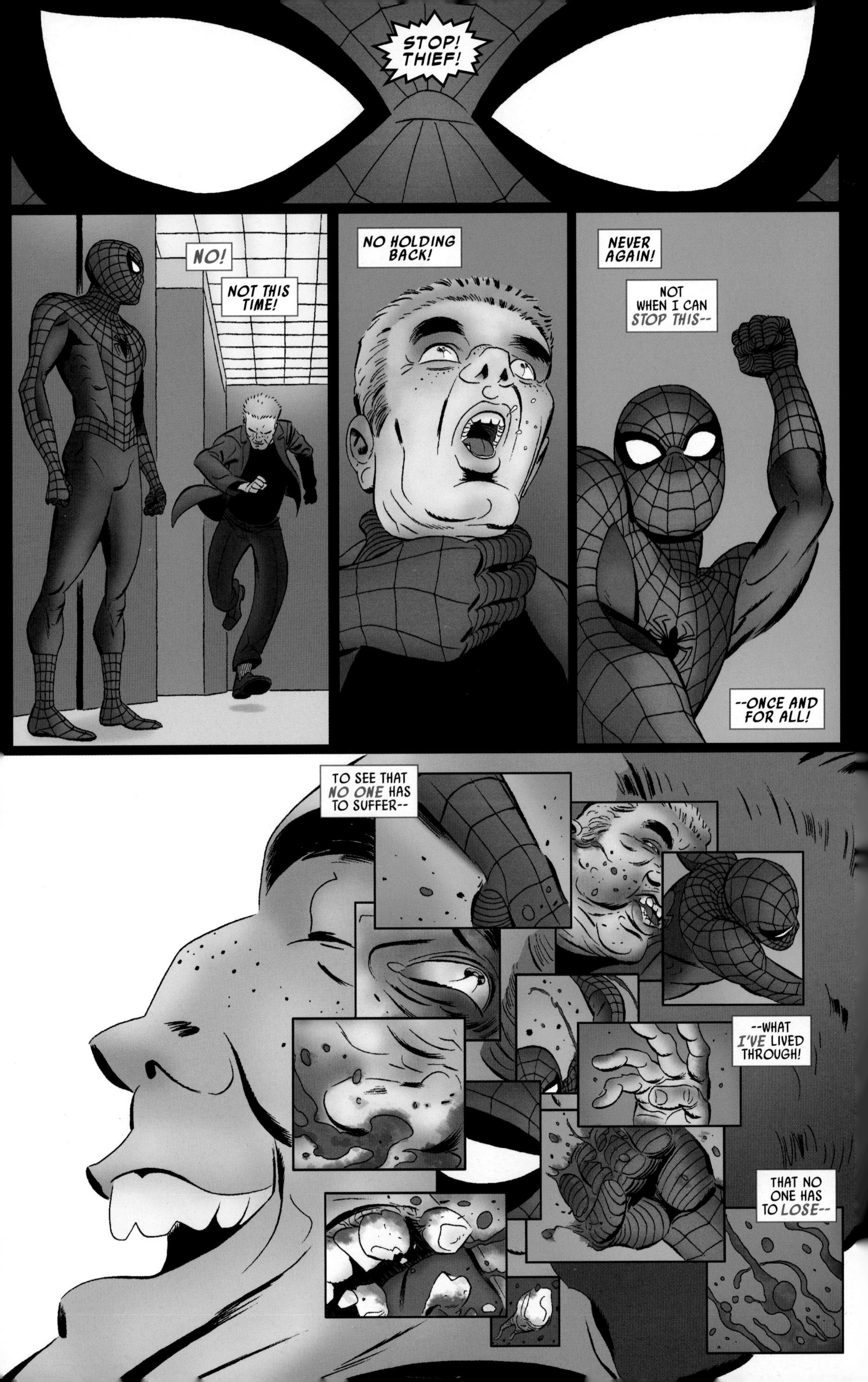
STOP! THIEF!
NO!
NOT THIS TIME!
NO HOLDING BACK!
NEVER AGAIN!
NOT WHEN I CAN STOP THIS--
--ONCE AND FOR ALL!
TO SEE THAT NO ONE HAS TO SUFFER--
--WHAT I'VE LIVED THROUGH!
THAT NO ONE HAS TO LOSE--

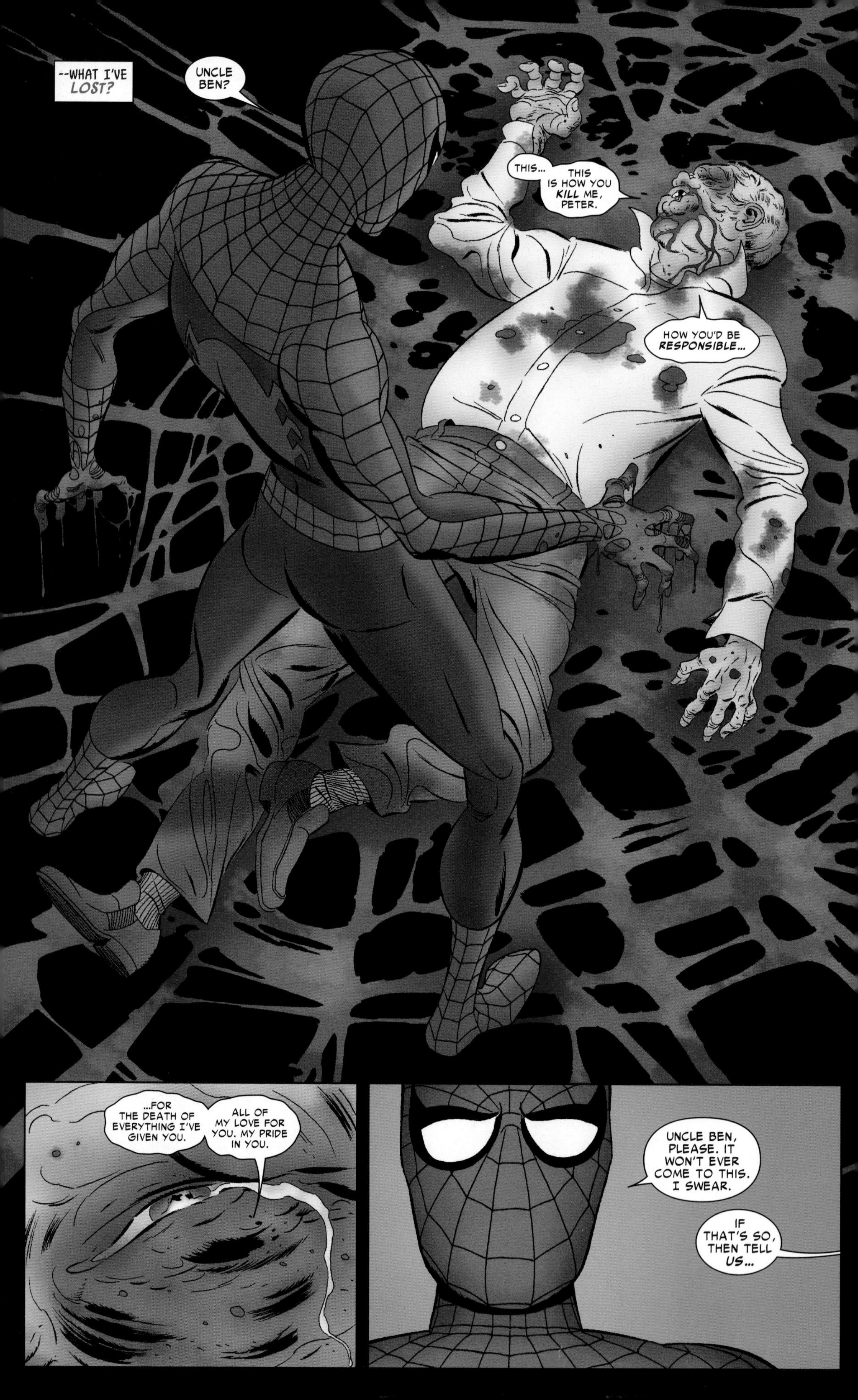
--WHAT I'VE LOST?
UNCLE BEN?
THIS...
THIS IS HOW YOU KILL ME, PETER.
HOW YOU'D BE RESPONSIBLE...
...FOR THE DEATH OF EVERYTHING I'VE GIVEN YOU.
ALL OF MY LOVE FOR YOU. MY PRIDE IN YOU.
UNCLE BEN, PLEASE. IT WON'T EVER COME TO THIS. I SWEAR.
IF THAT'S SO, THEN TELL US...

...WHAT WILL YOU DO NOW?

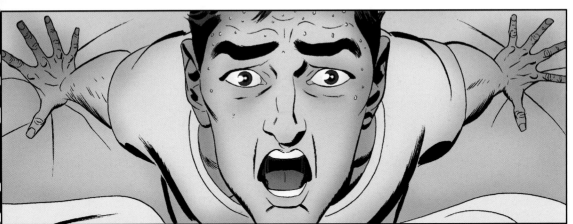

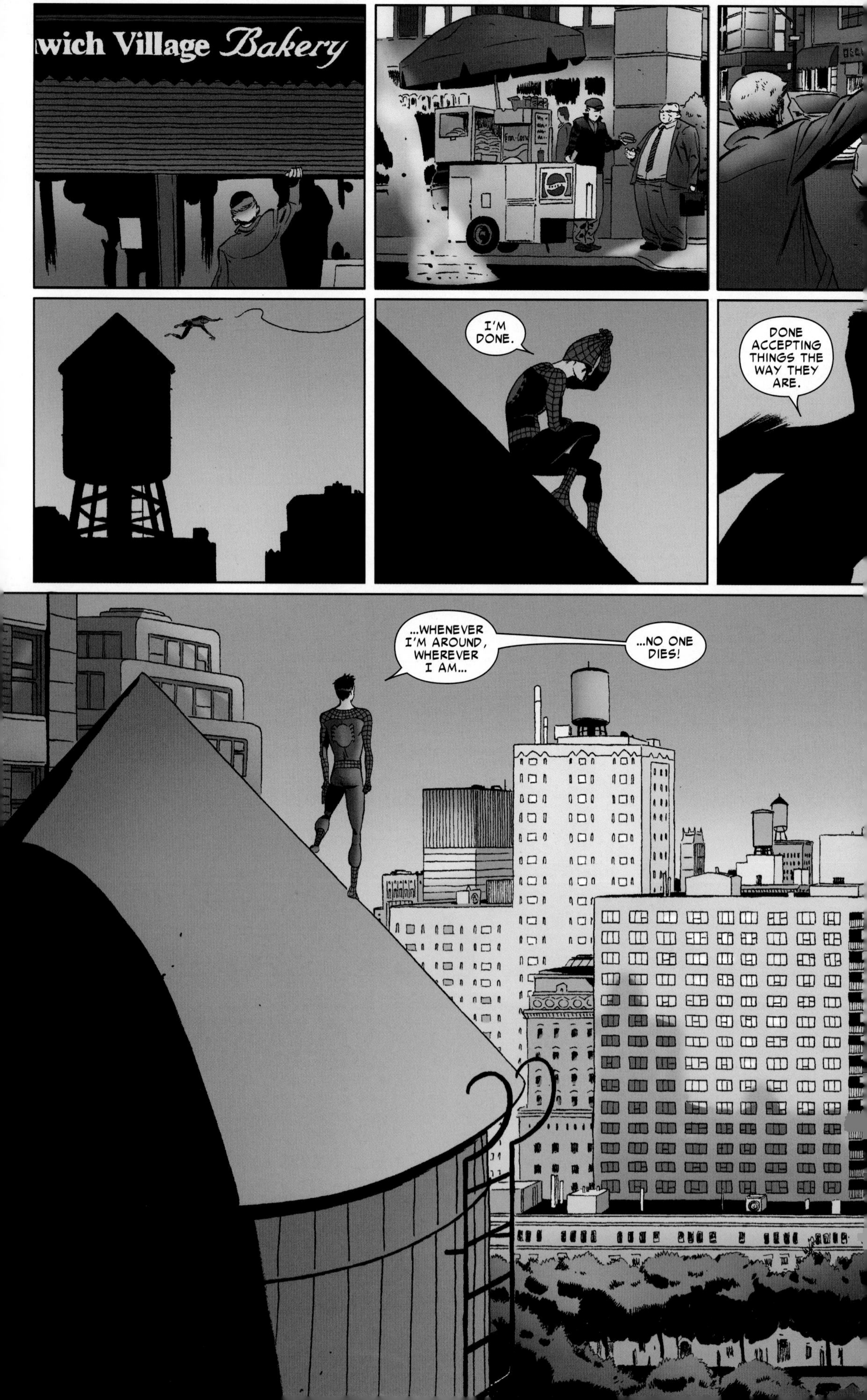
wich Village Bakery
I'M DONE.
DONE ACCEPTING THINGS THE WAY THEY ARE.
...WHENEVER I'M AROUND, WHEREVER I AM...
...NO ONE DIES!

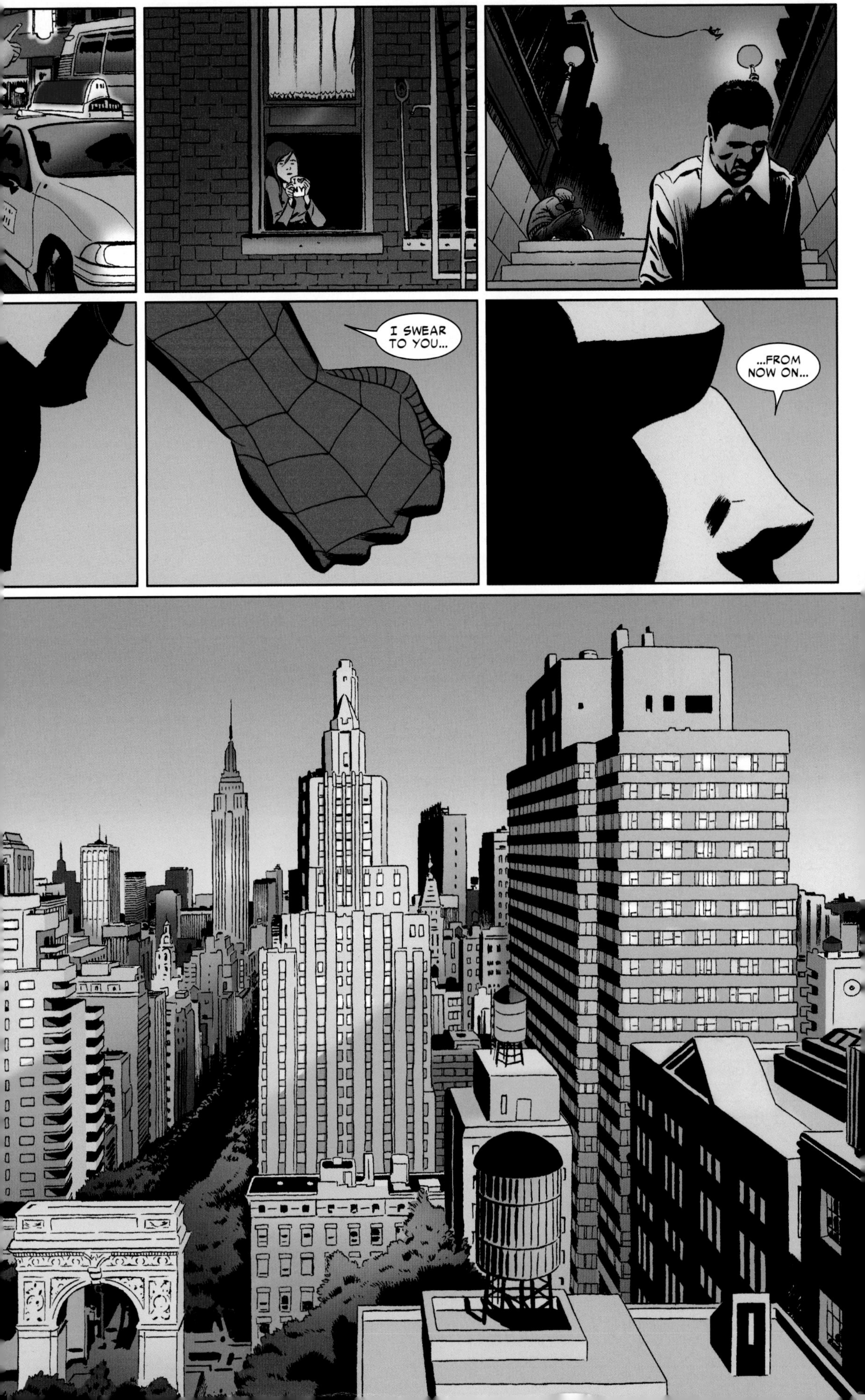
I SWEAR TO YOU...
...FROM NOW ON...

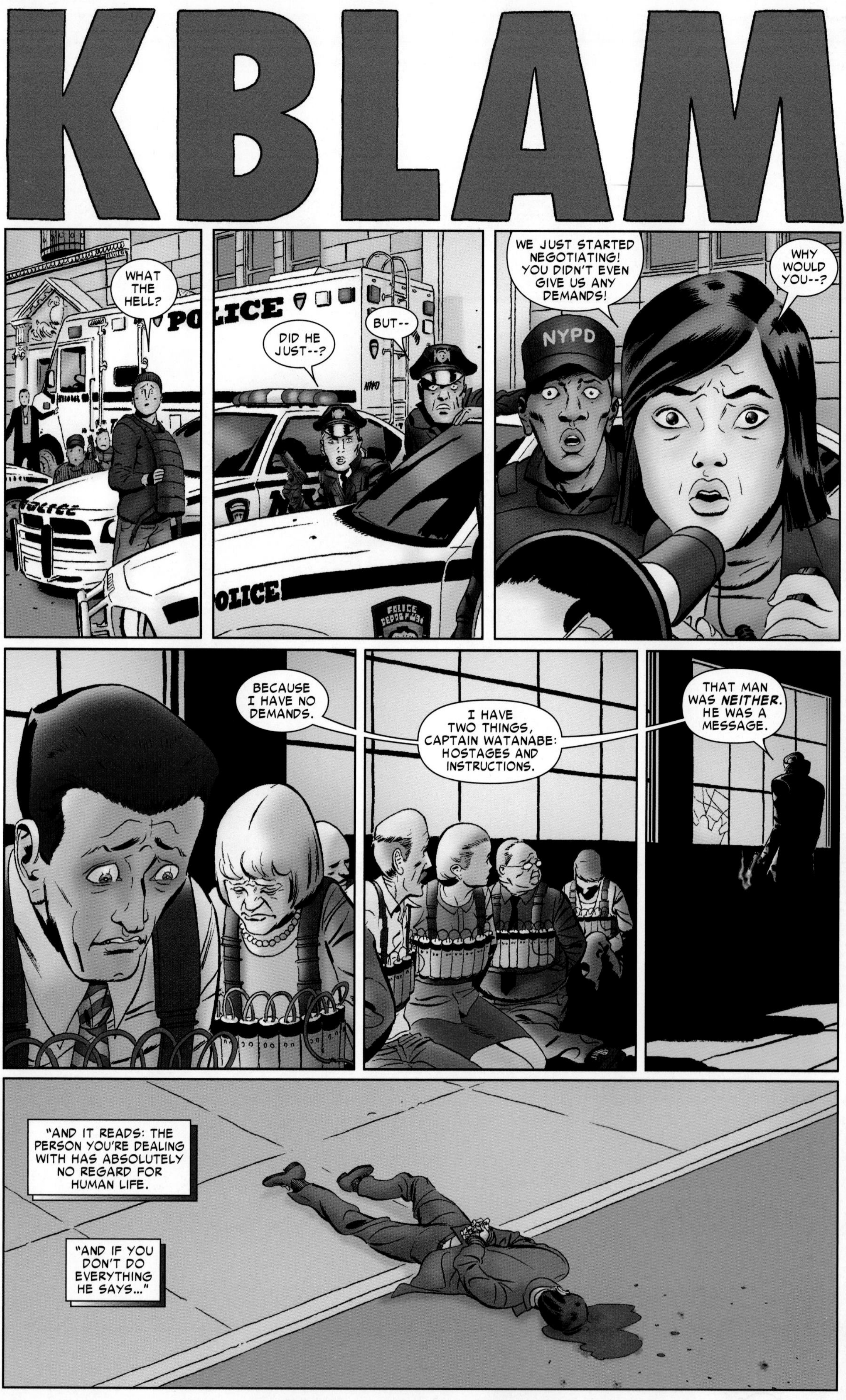
KBLAM
WHAT THE HELL?
POLICE
DID HE JUST--?
BUT--
WE JUST STARTED NEGOTIATING! YOU DIDN'T EVEN GIVE US ANY DEMANDS!
NYPD
WHY WOULD YOU--?
BECAUSE I HAVE NO DEMANDS.
I HAVE TWO THINGS, CAPTAIN WATANABE: HOSTAGES AND INSTRUCTIONS.
THAT MAN WAS NEITHER. HE WAS A MESSAGE.
"AND IT READS: THE PERSON YOU'RE DEALING WITH HAS ABSOLUTELY NO REGARD FOR HUMAN LIFE.
"AND IF YOU DON'T DO EVERYTHING HE SAYS..."

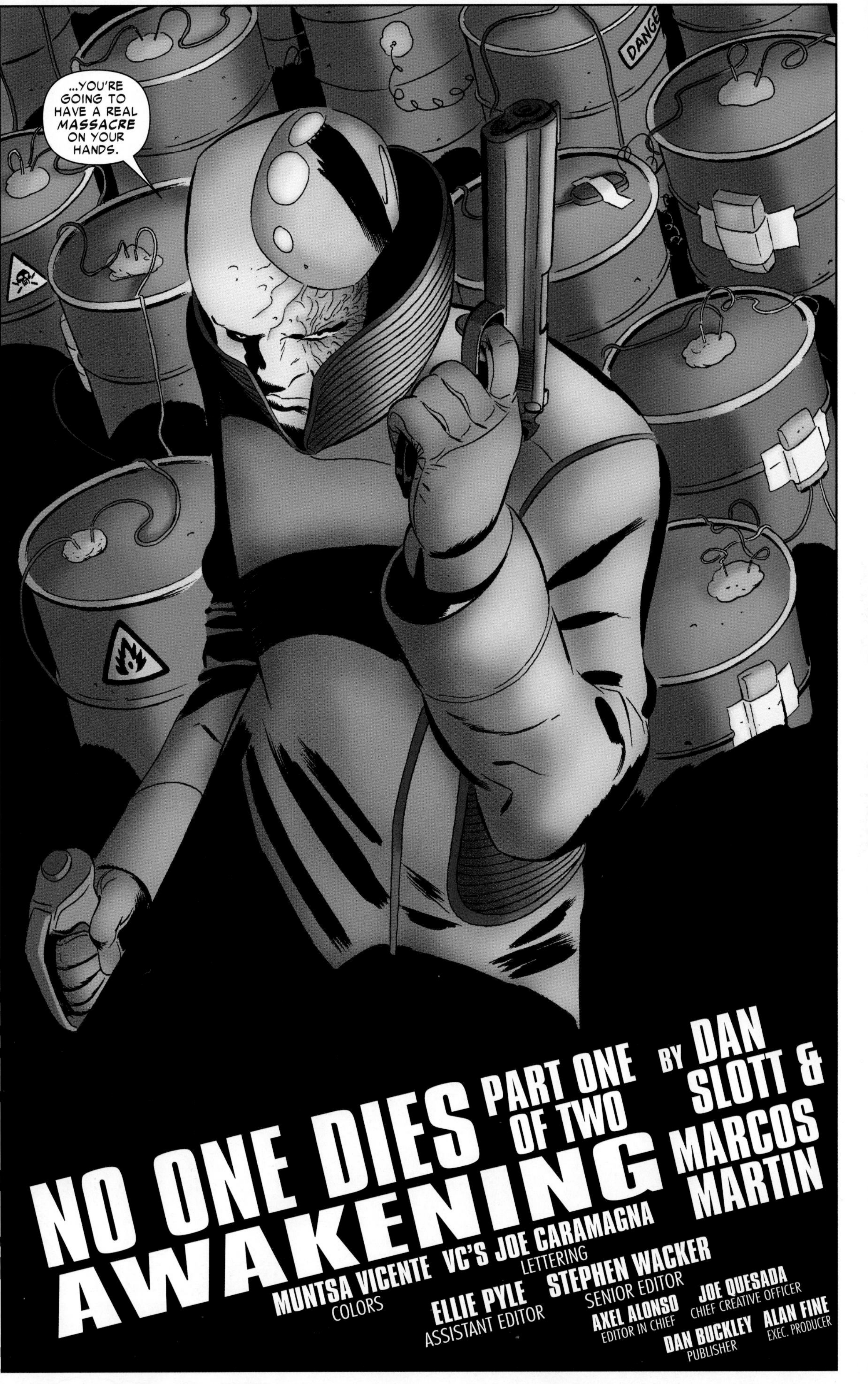
...YOU'RE GOING TO HAVE A REAL MASSACRE ON YOUR HANDS.
NO ONE DIES
PART ONE OF TWO
AWAKENING
BY DAN SLOTT & MARCOS MARTIN
MUNTSA VICENTE
COLORS
VC'S JOE CARAMAGNA
LETTERING
ELLIE PYLE
ASSISTANT EDITOR
STEPHEN WACKER
SENIOR EDITOR
AXEL ALONSO
EDITOR IN CHIEF
JOE QUESADA
CHIEF CREATIVE OFFICER
DAN BUCKLEY
PUBLISHER
ALAN FINE
EXEC. PRODUCER

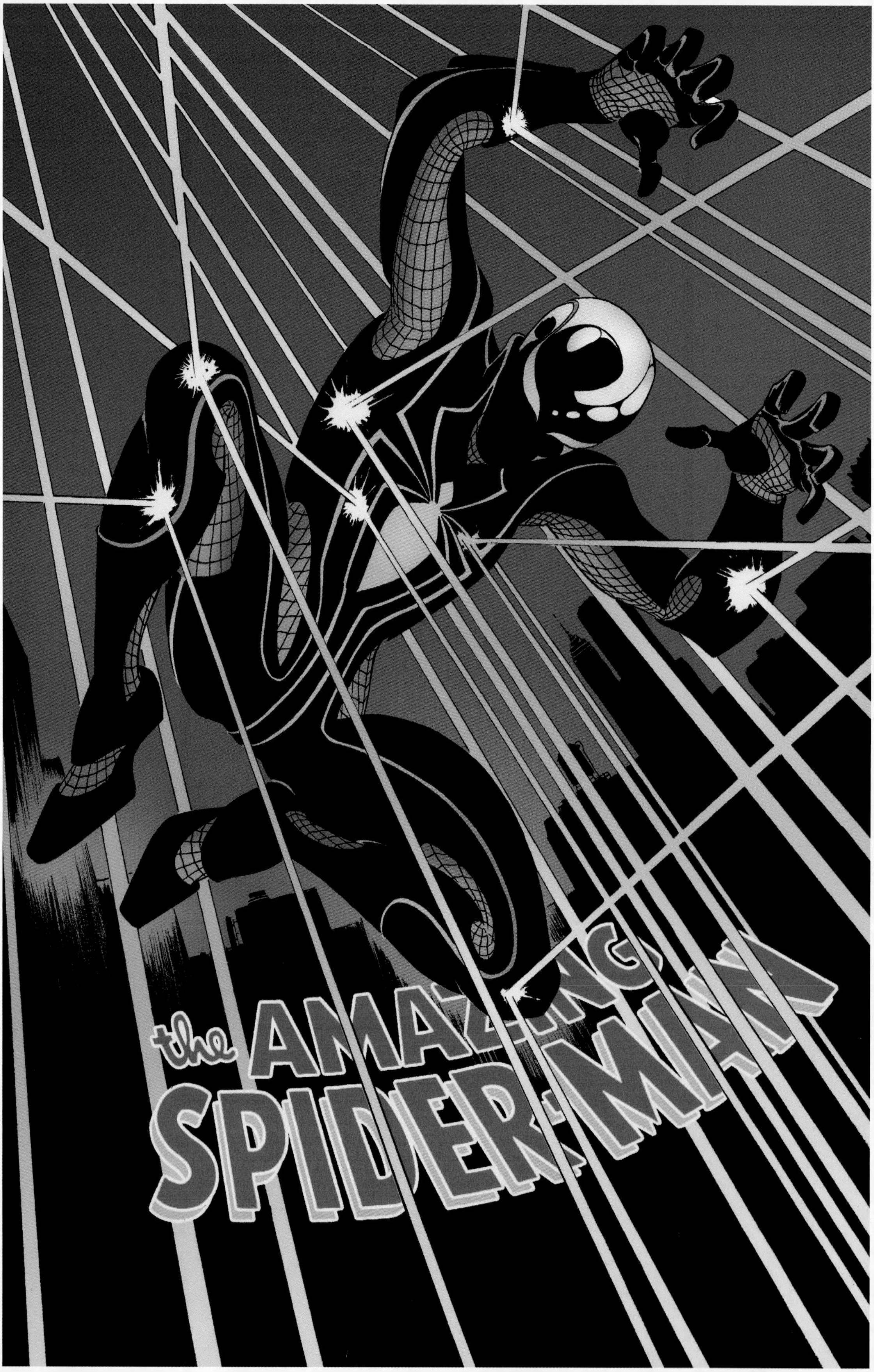
the AMAZING
SPIDER-MAN

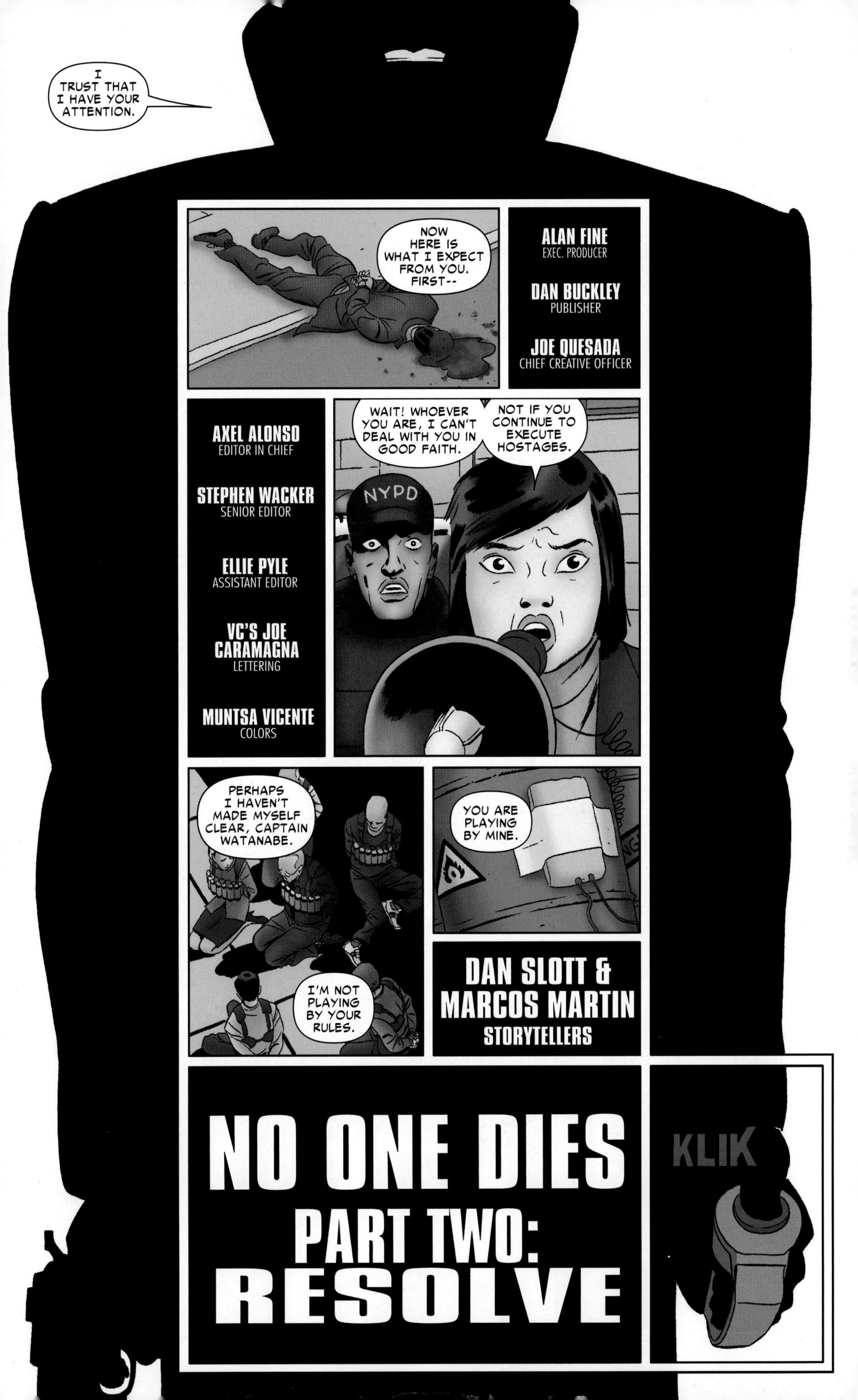

I TRUST THAT I HAVE YOUR ATTENTION.
NOW HERE IS WHAT I EXPECT FROM YOU. FIRST--
ALAN FINE
EXEC. PRODUCER
DAN BUCKLEY
PUBLISHER
JOE QUESADA
CHIEF CREATIVE OFFICER
AXEL ALONSO
EDITOR IN CHIEF
STEPHEN WACKER
SENIOR EDITOR
ELLIE PYLE
ASSISTANT EDITOR
VC'S JOE CARAMAGNA
LETTERING
MUNTSA VICENTE
COLORS
WAIT! WHOEVER YOU ARE, I CAN'T DEAL WITH YOU IN GOOD FAITH.
NOT IF YOU CONTINUE TO EXECUTE HOSTAGES.
NYPD
PERHAPS I HAVEN'T MADE MYSELF CLEAR, CAPTAIN WATANABE.
I'M NOT PLAYING BY YOUR RULES.
YOU ARE PLAYING BY MINE.
DAN SLOTT &
MARCOS MARTIN
STORYTELLERS
NO ONE DIES
PART TWO:
RESOLVE
KLIK

BOOM

THERE. I HAVE JUST TAKEN OUT THE WEST WING OF THIS BANK, ALONG WITH SEVEN MORE HOSTAGES INSIDE. DO WHAT I TELL YOU, OR MORE WILL DIE.

YOU WILL SHUT DOWN ALL CLOSED-CIRCUIT CAMERAS, ALARMS, AND SURVEILLANCE SYSTEMS IN THIS BUILDING--AND THE SURROUNDING FIVE BLOCKS.

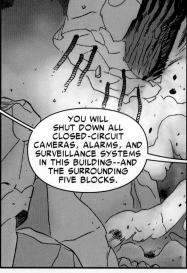

THEN ALL POLICE AND EMERGENCY SERVICES WILL PULL BACK THAT FAR AS WELL.

THIS IS NOT A NEGOTIATION. THESE ARE THE RULES. YOU HAVE TEN MINUTES AND COUNTING.

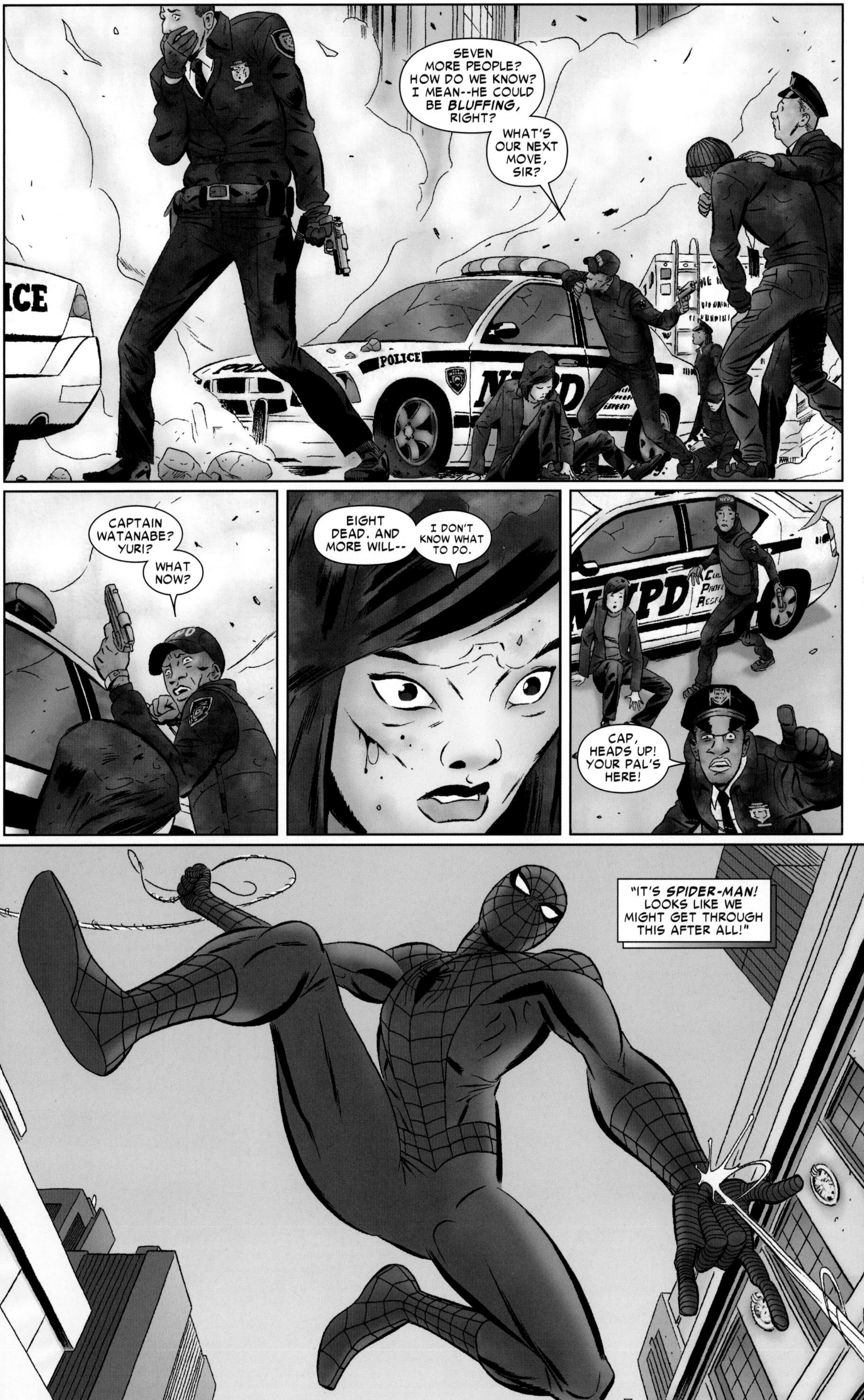
SEVEN MORE PEOPLE? HOW DO WE KNOW? I MEAN--HE COULD BE BLUFFING, RIGHT?
WHAT'S OUR NEXT MOVE, SIR?
CAPTAIN WATANABE? YURI?
WHAT NOW?
EIGHT DEAD. AND MORE WILL--
I DON'T KNOW WHAT TO DO.
CAP, HEADS UP! YOUR PAL'S HERE!
"IT'S SPIDER-MAN! LOOKS LIKE WE MIGHT GET THROUGH THIS AFTER ALL!"

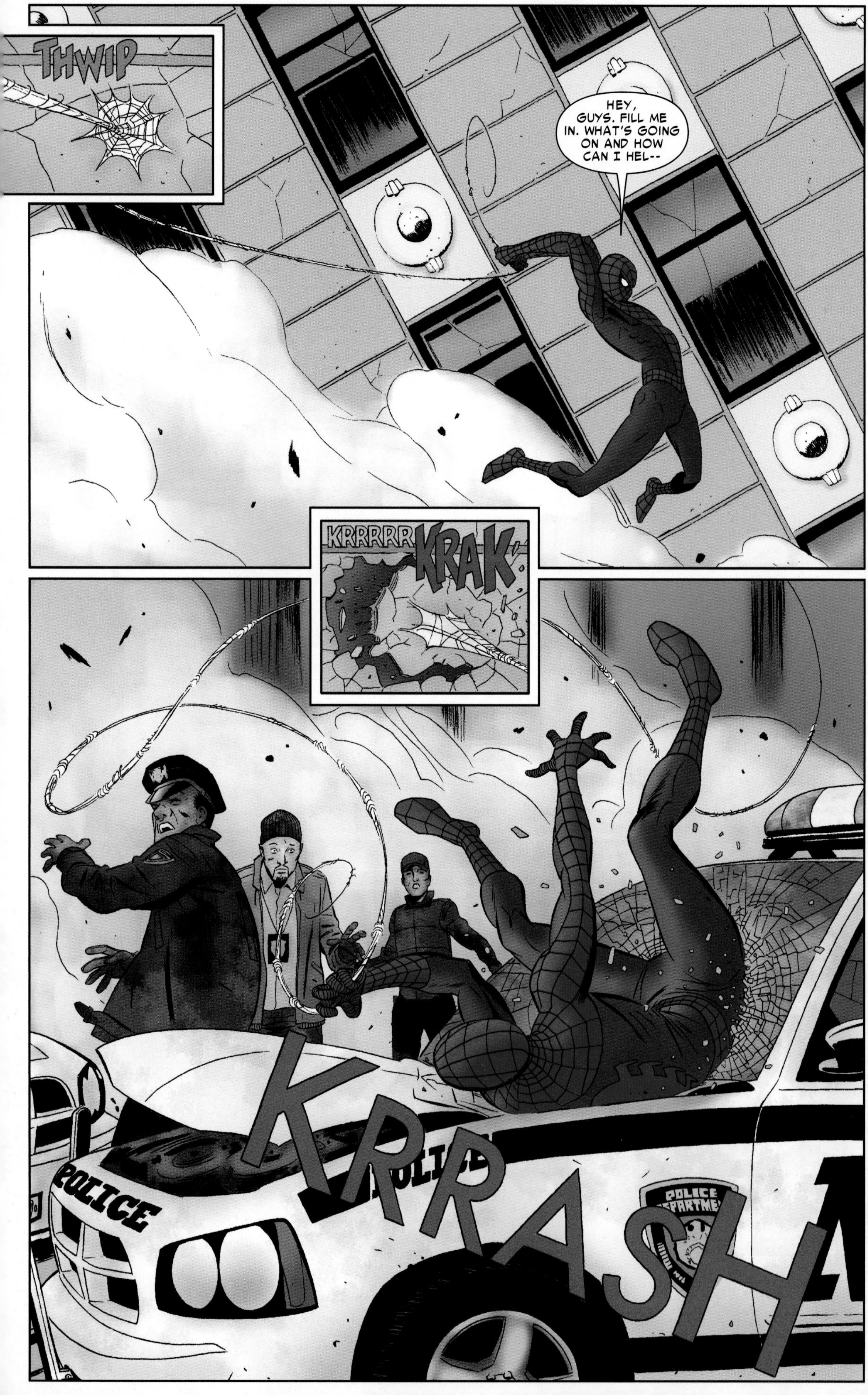
THWIP
HEY, GUYS. FILL ME IN. WHAT'S GOING ON AND HOW CAN I HEL--
KRRRRR KRAK
KRRASH
POLICE
POLICE DEPARTMENT

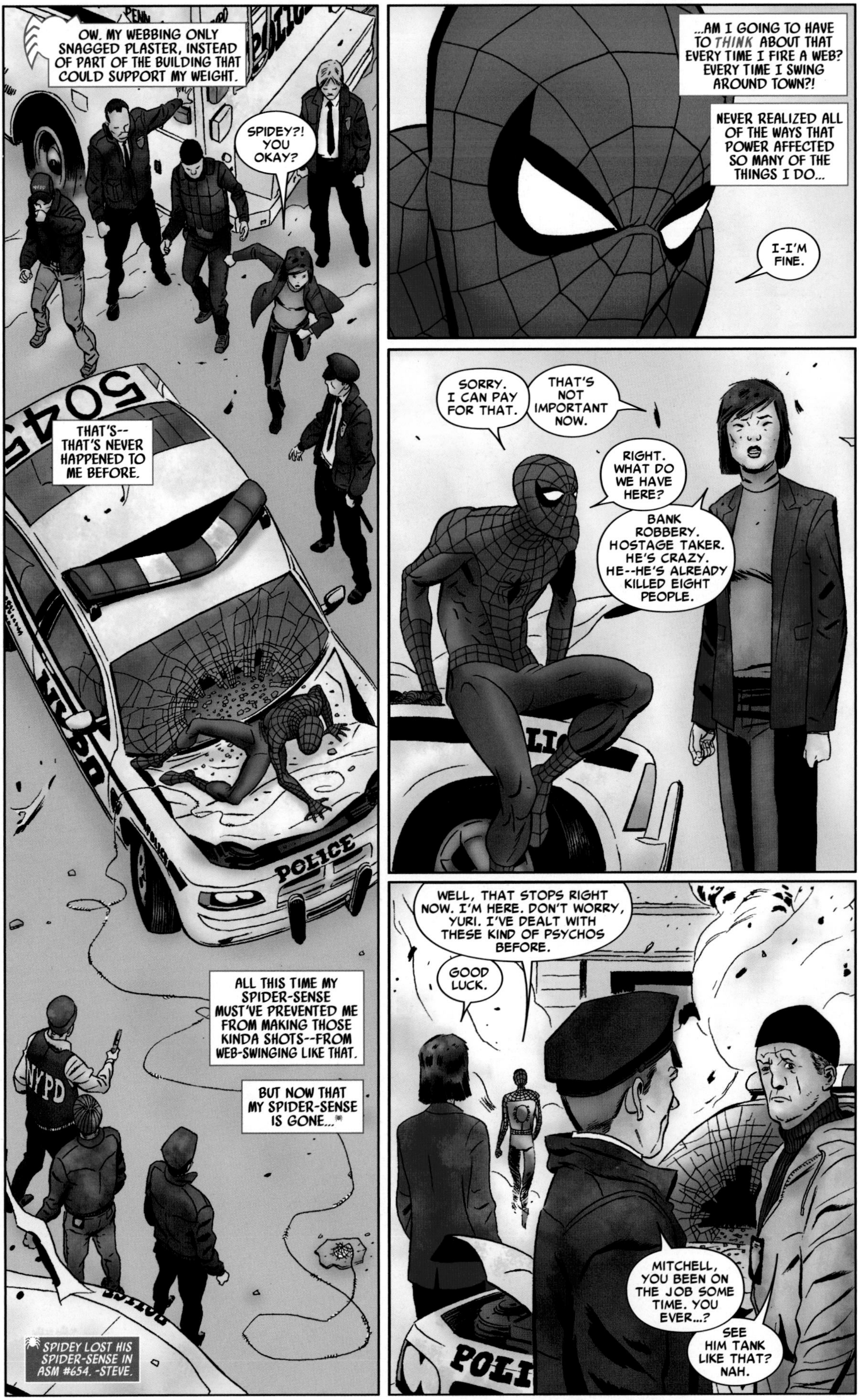
OW. MY WEBBING ONLY SNAGGED PLASTER, INSTEAD OF PART OF THE BUILDING THAT COULD SUPPORT MY WEIGHT.
SPIDEY?! YOU OKAY?
THAT'S-- THAT'S NEVER HAPPENED TO ME BEFORE.
ALL THIS TIME MY SPIDER-SENSE MUST'VE PREVENTED ME FROM MAKING THOSE KINDA SHOTS--FROM WEB-SWINGING LIKE THAT.
BUT NOW THAT MY SPIDER-SENSE IS GONE...*
SPIDEY LOST HIS SPIDER-SENSE IN ASM #654. -STEVE.
...AM I GOING TO HAVE TO THINK ABOUT THAT EVERY TIME I FIRE A WEB? EVERY TIME I SWING AROUND TOWN?!
NEVER REALIZED ALL OF THE WAYS THAT POWER AFFECTED SO MANY OF THE THINGS I DO...
I-I'M FINE.
SORRY. I CAN PAY FOR THAT.
THAT'S NOT IMPORTANT NOW.
RIGHT. WHAT DO WE HAVE HERE?
BANK ROBBERY. HOSTAGE TAKER. HE'S CRAZY. HE--HE'S ALREADY KILLED EIGHT PEOPLE.
WELL, THAT STOPS RIGHT NOW. I'M HERE. DON'T WORRY, YURI. I'VE DEALT WITH THESE KIND OF PSYCHOS BEFORE.
GOOD LUCK.
MITCHELL, YOU BEEN ON THE JOB SOME TIME. YOU EVER...?
SEE HIM TANK LIKE THAT? NAH.

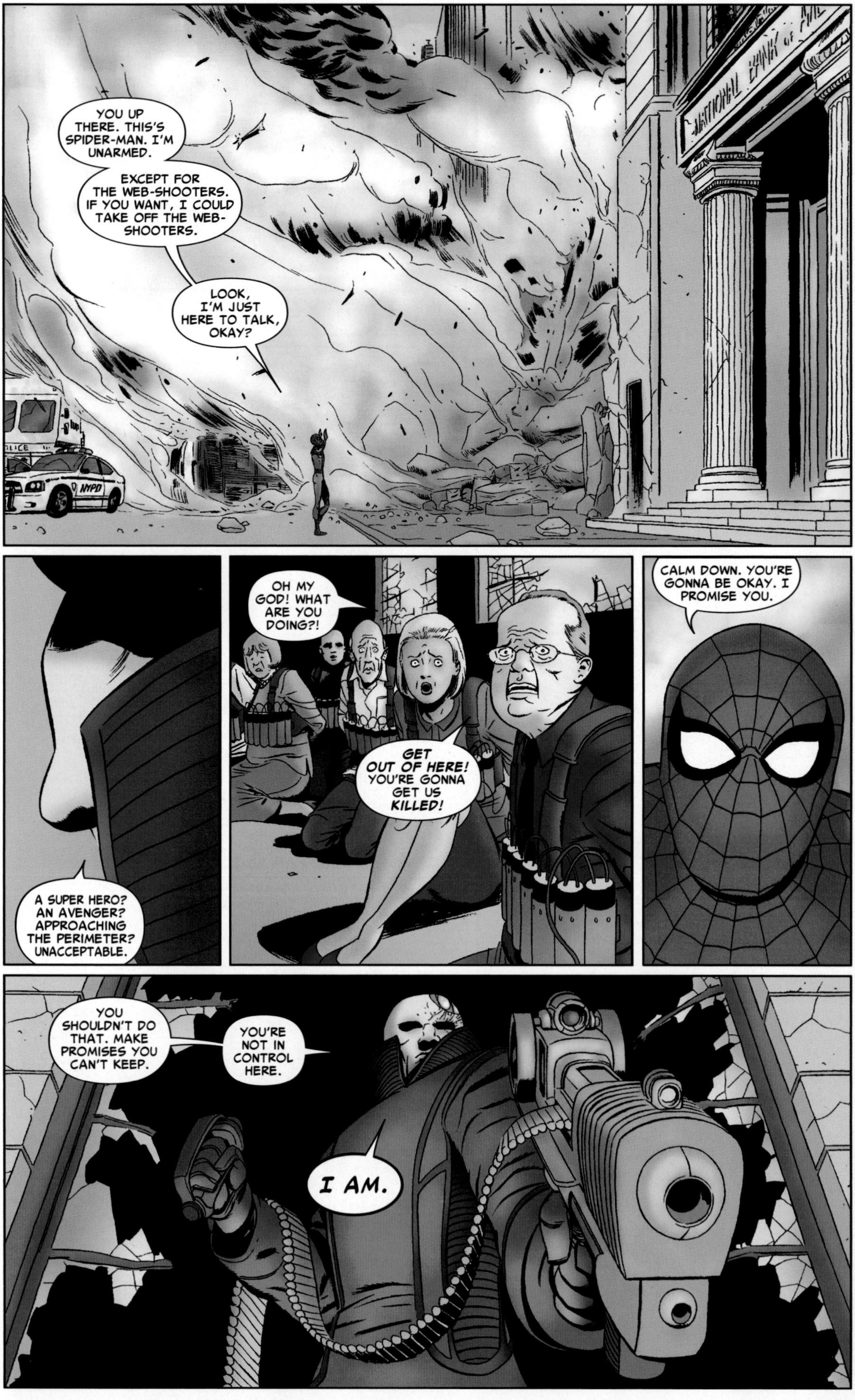

YOU UP THERE. THIS'S SPIDER-MAN. I'M UNARMED.
EXCEPT FOR THE WEB-SHOOTERS. IF YOU WANT, I COULD TAKE OFF THE WEB-SHOOTERS.
LOOK, I'M JUST HERE TO TALK, OKAY?
NYPD
A SUPER HERO? AN AVENGER? APPROACHING THE PERIMETER? UNACCEPTABLE.
OH MY GOD! WHAT ARE YOU DOING?!
GET OUT OF HERE! YOU'RE GONNA GET US KILLED!
CALM DOWN. YOU'RE GONNA BE OKAY. I PROMISE YOU.
YOU SHOULDN'T DO THAT. MAKE PROMISES YOU CAN'T KEEP.
YOU'RE NOT IN CONTROL HERE.
I AM.

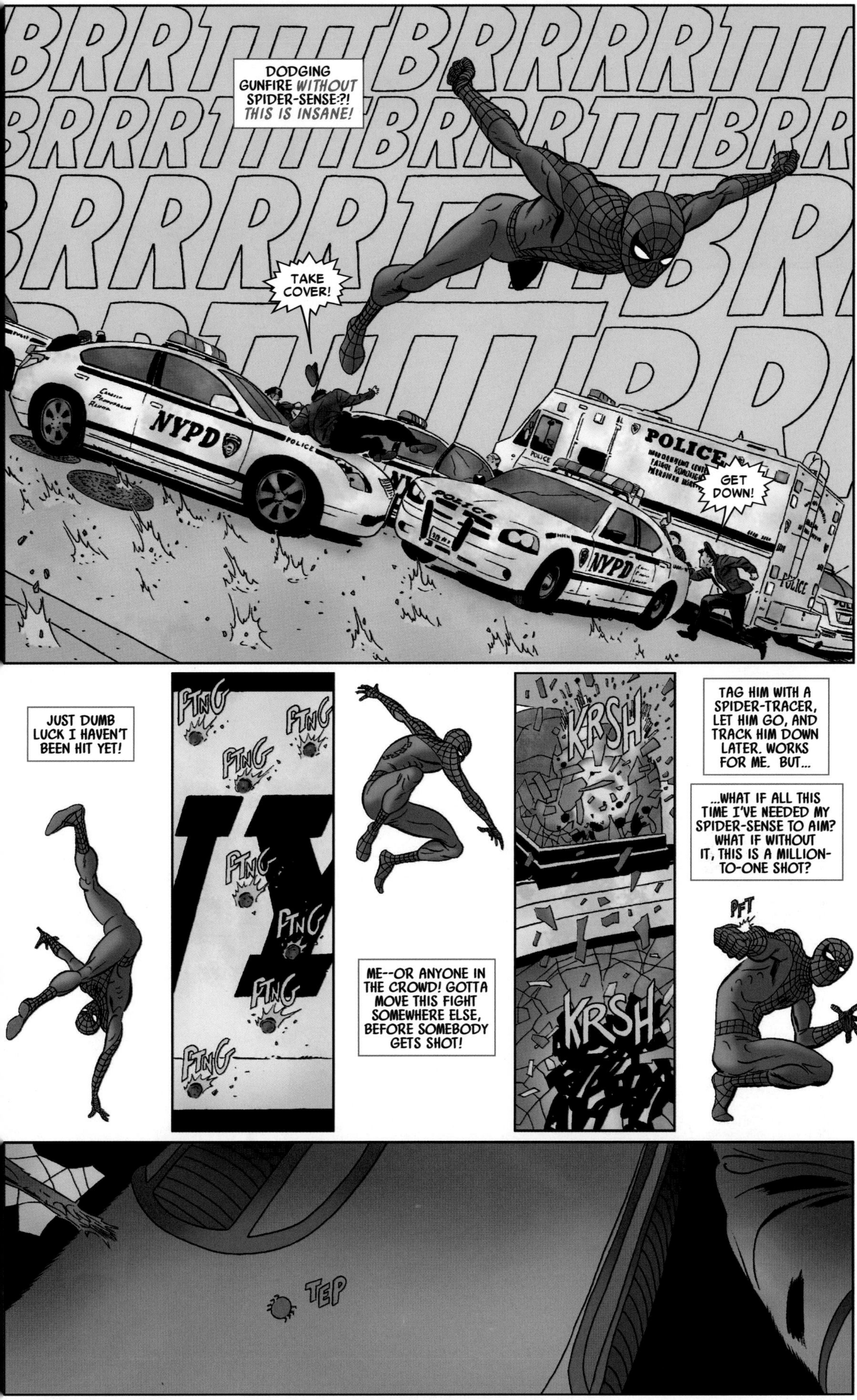
BRRTTTTBRRRRRTTTT
BRRRTTTTBRRRRTTTTBRR
BRRRRTTTTBRR
DODGING GUNFIRE WITHOUT SPIDER-SENSE:?! THIS IS INSANE!
TAKE COVER!
NYPD
POLICE
GET DOWN!
JUST DUMB LUCK I HAVEN'T BEEN HIT YET!
PTNG
PTNG
PTNG
PTNG
PTNG
PTNG
PTNG
ME--OR ANYONE IN THE CROWD! GOTTA MOVE THIS FIGHT SOMEWHERE ELSE, BEFORE SOMEBODY GETS SHOT!
KRSH
KRSH
TAG HIM WITH A SPIDER-TRACER, LET HIM GO, AND TRACK HIM DOWN LATER. WORKS FOR ME. BUT...
...WHAT IF ALL THIS TIME I'VE NEEDED MY SPIDER-SENSE TO AIM? WHAT IF WITHOUT IT, THIS IS A MILLION-TO-ONE SHOT?
PFT
TEP

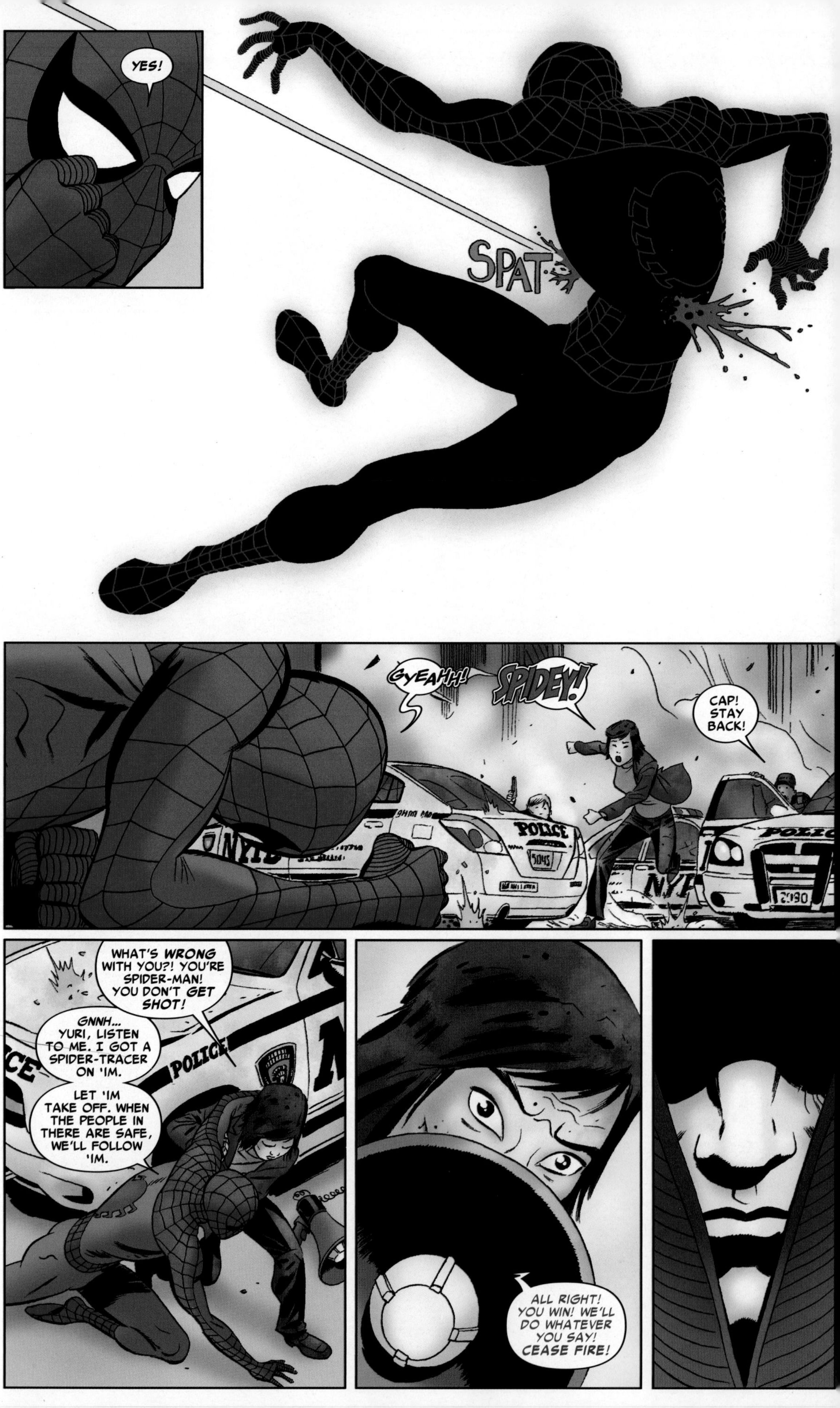
YES!
SPAT
GYEAHH!
SPIDEY!
CAP! STAY BACK!
WHAT'S WRONG WITH YOU?! YOU'RE SPIDER-MAN! YOU DON'T GET SHOT!
GNNH... YURI, LISTEN TO ME. I GOT A SPIDER-TRACER ON 'IM.
LET 'IM TAKE OFF. WHEN THE PEOPLE IN THERE ARE SAFE, WE'LL FOLLOW 'IM.
ALL RIGHT! YOU WIN! WE'LL DO WHATEVER YOU SAY! CEASE FIRE!

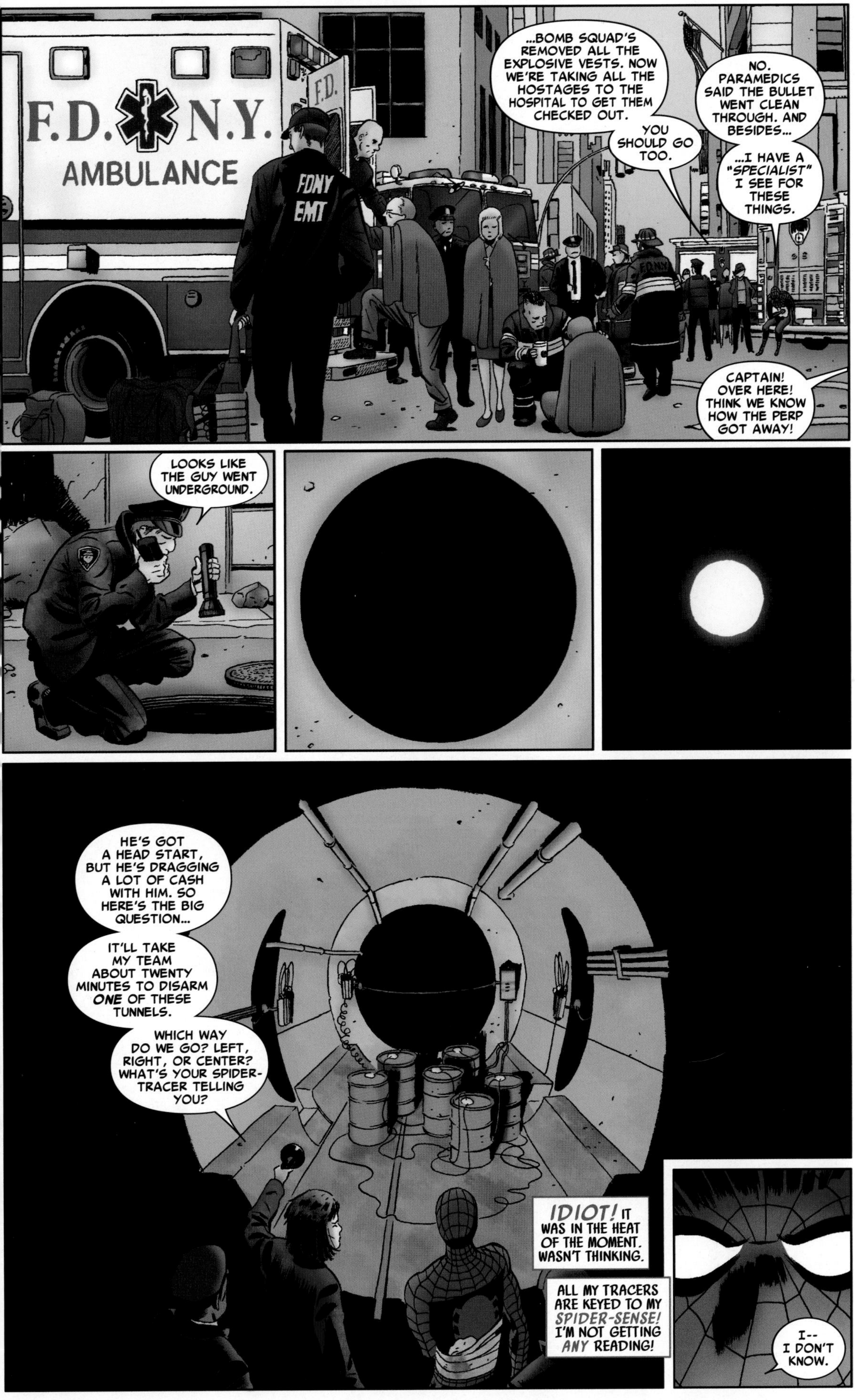
F.D. N.Y.
AMBULANCE
FDNY EMT
...BOMB SQUAD'S REMOVED ALL THE EXPLOSIVE VESTS. NOW WE'RE TAKING ALL THE HOSTAGES TO THE HOSPITAL TO GET THEM CHECKED OUT.
YOU SHOULD GO TOO.
NO. PARAMEDICS SAID THE BULLET WENT CLEAN THROUGH. AND BESIDES...
...I HAVE A "SPECIALIST" I SEE FOR THESE THINGS.
CAPTAIN! OVER HERE! THINK WE KNOW HOW THE PERP GOT AWAY!
LOOKS LIKE THE GUY WENT UNDERGROUND.
HE'S GOT A HEAD START, BUT HE'S DRAGGING A LOT OF CASH WITH HIM. SO HERE'S THE BIG QUESTION...
IT'LL TAKE MY TEAM ABOUT TWENTY MINUTES TO DISARM ONE OF THESE TUNNELS.
WHICH WAY DO WE GO? LEFT, RIGHT, OR CENTER? WHAT'S YOUR SPIDER-TRACER TELLING YOU?
IDIOT! IT WAS IN THE HEAT OF THE MOMENT. WASN'T THINKING.
ALL MY TRACERS ARE KEYED TO MY SPIDER-SENSE! I'M NOT GETTING ANY READING!
I-- I DON'T KNOW.

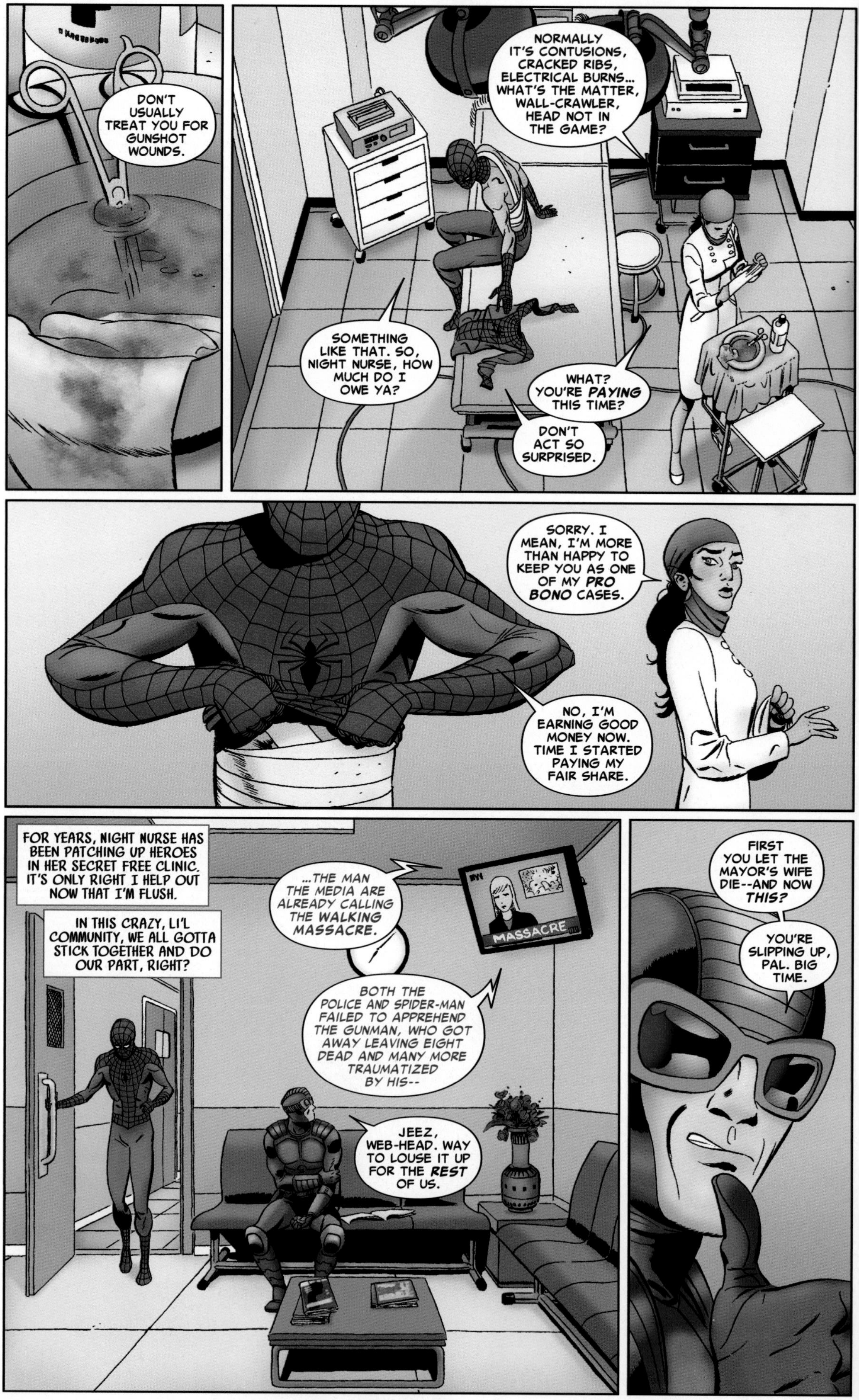

DON'T USUALLY TREAT YOU FOR GUNSHOT WOUNDS.
NORMALLY IT'S CONTUSIONS, CRACKED RIBS, ELECTRICAL BURNS... WHAT'S THE MATTER, WALL-CRAWLER, HEAD NOT IN THE GAME?
SOMETHING LIKE THAT. SO, NIGHT NURSE, HOW MUCH DO I OWE YA?
WHAT? YOU'RE PAYING THIS TIME?
DON'T ACT SO SURPRISED.
SORRY. I MEAN, I'M MORE THAN HAPPY TO KEEP YOU AS ONE OF MY PRO BONO CASES.
NO, I'M EARNING GOOD MONEY NOW. TIME I STARTED PAYING MY FAIR SHARE.
FOR YEARS, NIGHT NURSE HAS BEEN PATCHING UP HEROES IN HER SECRET FREE CLINIC. IT'S ONLY RIGHT I HELP OUT NOW THAT I'M FLUSH.
IN THIS CRAZY, LI'L COMMUNITY, WE ALL GOTTA STICK TOGETHER AND DO OUR PART, RIGHT?
...THE MAN THE MEDIA ARE ALREADY CALLING THE WALKING MASSACRE.
MASSACRE
BOTH THE POLICE AND SPIDER-MAN FAILED TO APPREHEND THE GUNMAN, WHO GOT AWAY LEAVING EIGHT DEAD AND MANY MORE TRAUMATIZED BY HIS--
JEEZ, WEB-HEAD. WAY TO LOUSE IT UP FOR THE REST OF US.
FIRST YOU LET THE MAYOR'S WIFE DIE--AND NOW THIS?
YOU'RE SLIPPING UP, PAL. BIG TIME.

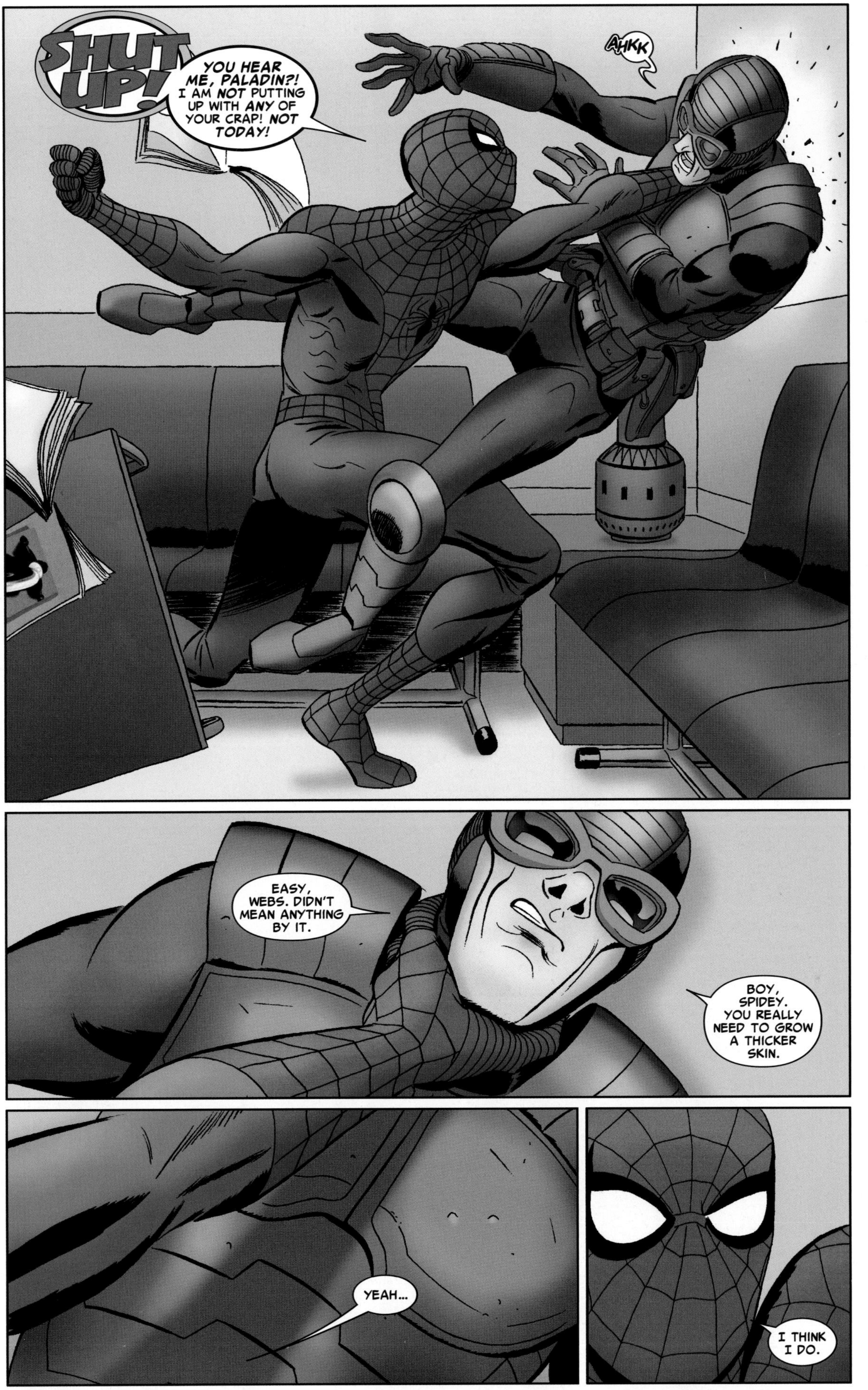
SHUT UP!
YOU HEAR ME, PALADIN?! I AM NOT PUTTING UP WITH ANY OF YOUR CRAP! NOT TODAY!
AHKK
EASY, WEBS. DIDN'T MEAN ANYTHING BY IT.
BOY, SPIDEY. YOU REALLY NEED TO GROW A THICKER SKIN.
YEAH...
I THINK I DO.

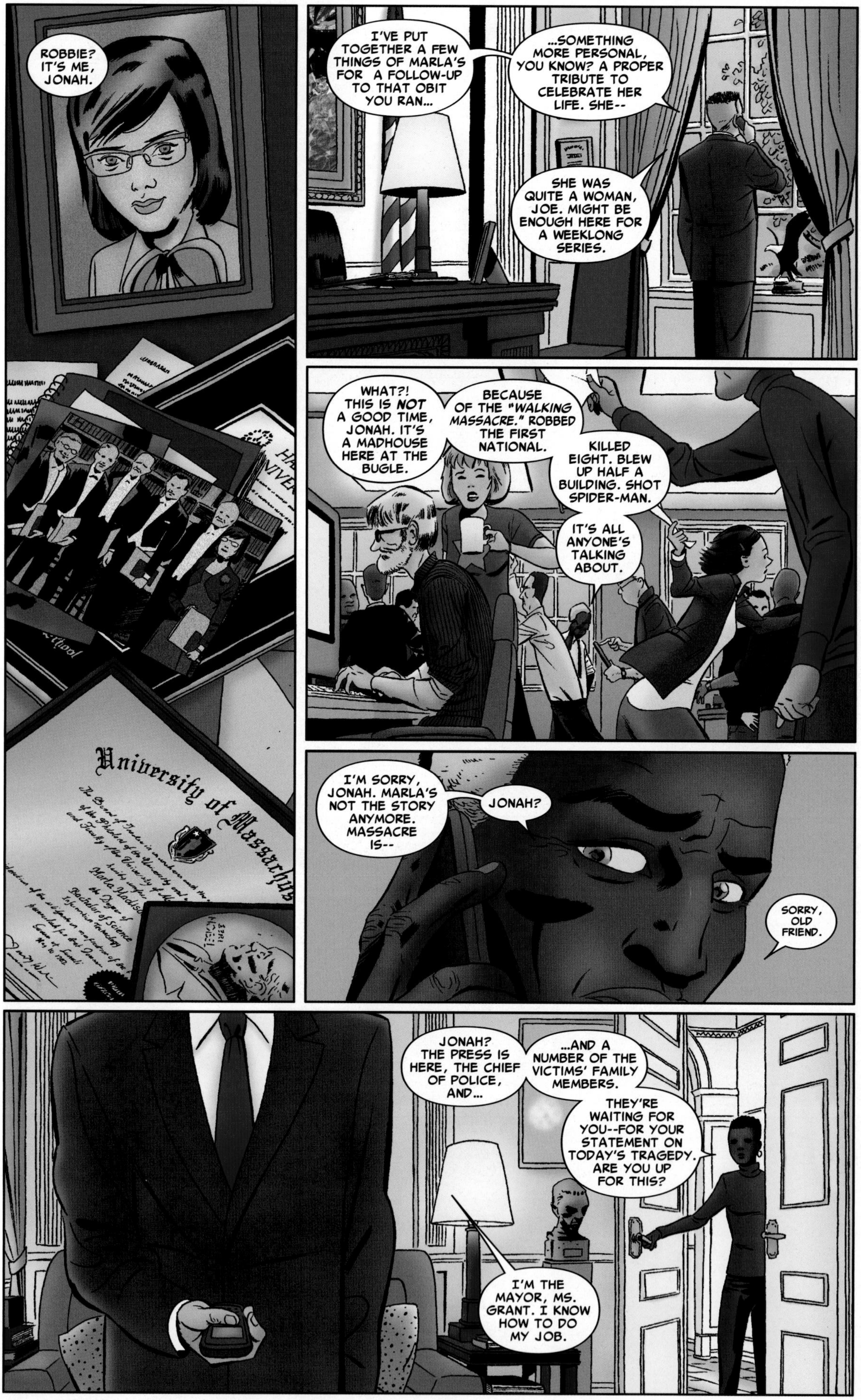
ROBBIE? IT'S ME, JONAH.
I'VE PUT TOGETHER A FEW THINGS OF MARLA'S FOR A FOLLOW-UP TO THAT OBIT YOU RAN...
...SOMETHING MORE PERSONAL, YOU KNOW? A PROPER TRIBUTE TO CELEBRATE HER LIFE. SHE--
SHE WAS QUITE A WOMAN, JOE. MIGHT BE ENOUGH HERE FOR A WEEKLONG SERIES.
University of Massachus
WHAT?! THIS IS *NOT* A GOOD TIME, JONAH. IT'S A MADHOUSE HERE AT THE BUGLE.
BECAUSE OF THE "*WALKING MASSACRE.*" ROBBED THE FIRST NATIONAL.
KILLED EIGHT. BLEW UP HALF A BUILDING. SHOT SPIDER-MAN.
IT'S ALL ANYONE'S TALKING ABOUT.
I'M SORRY, JONAH. MARLA'S NOT THE STORY ANYMORE. MASSACRE IS--
JONAH?
SORRY, OLD FRIEND.
JONAH? THE PRESS IS HERE, THE CHIEF OF POLICE, AND...
...AND A NUMBER OF THE VICTIMS' FAMILY MEMBERS.
THEY'RE WAITING FOR YOU--FOR YOUR STATEMENT ON TODAY'S TRAGEDY. ARE YOU UP FOR THIS?
I'M THE MAYOR, MS. GRANT. I KNOW HOW TO DO MY JOB.

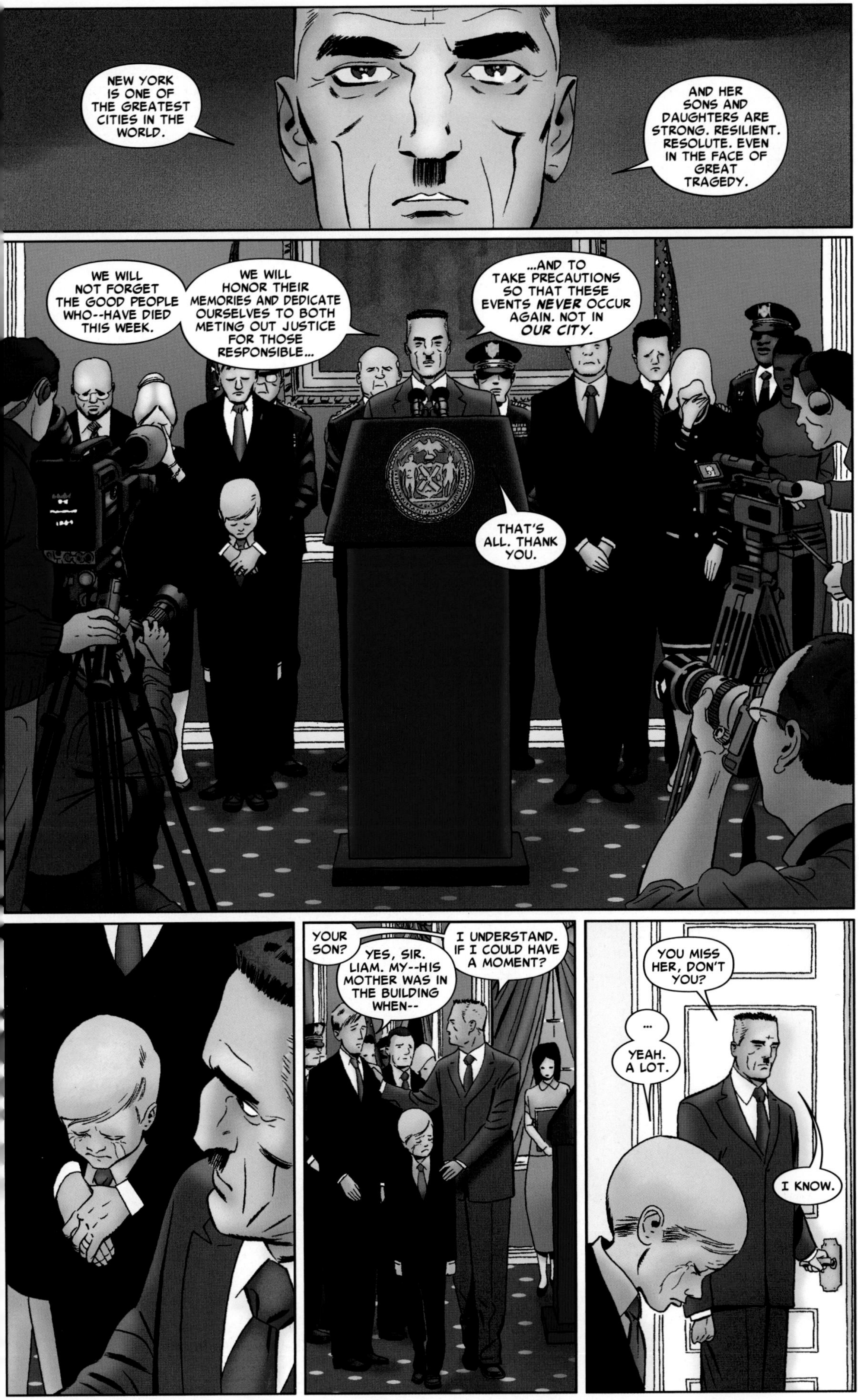
NEW YORK IS ONE OF THE GREATEST CITIES IN THE WORLD.
AND HER SONS AND DAUGHTERS ARE STRONG. RESILIENT. RESOLUTE. EVEN IN THE FACE OF GREAT TRAGEDY.
WE WILL NOT FORGET THE GOOD PEOPLE WHO--HAVE DIED THIS WEEK.
WE WILL HONOR THEIR MEMORIES AND DEDICATE OURSELVES TO BOTH METING OUT JUSTICE FOR THOSE RESPONSIBLE...
...AND TO TAKE PRECAUTIONS SO THAT THESE EVENTS NEVER OCCUR AGAIN. NOT IN OUR CITY.
THAT'S ALL. THANK YOU.
YOUR SON?
YES, SIR. LIAM. MY--HIS MOTHER WAS IN THE BUILDING WHEN--
I UNDERSTAND. IF I COULD HAVE A MOMENT?
YOU MISS HER, DON'T YOU?
...
YEAH. A LOT.
I KNOW.

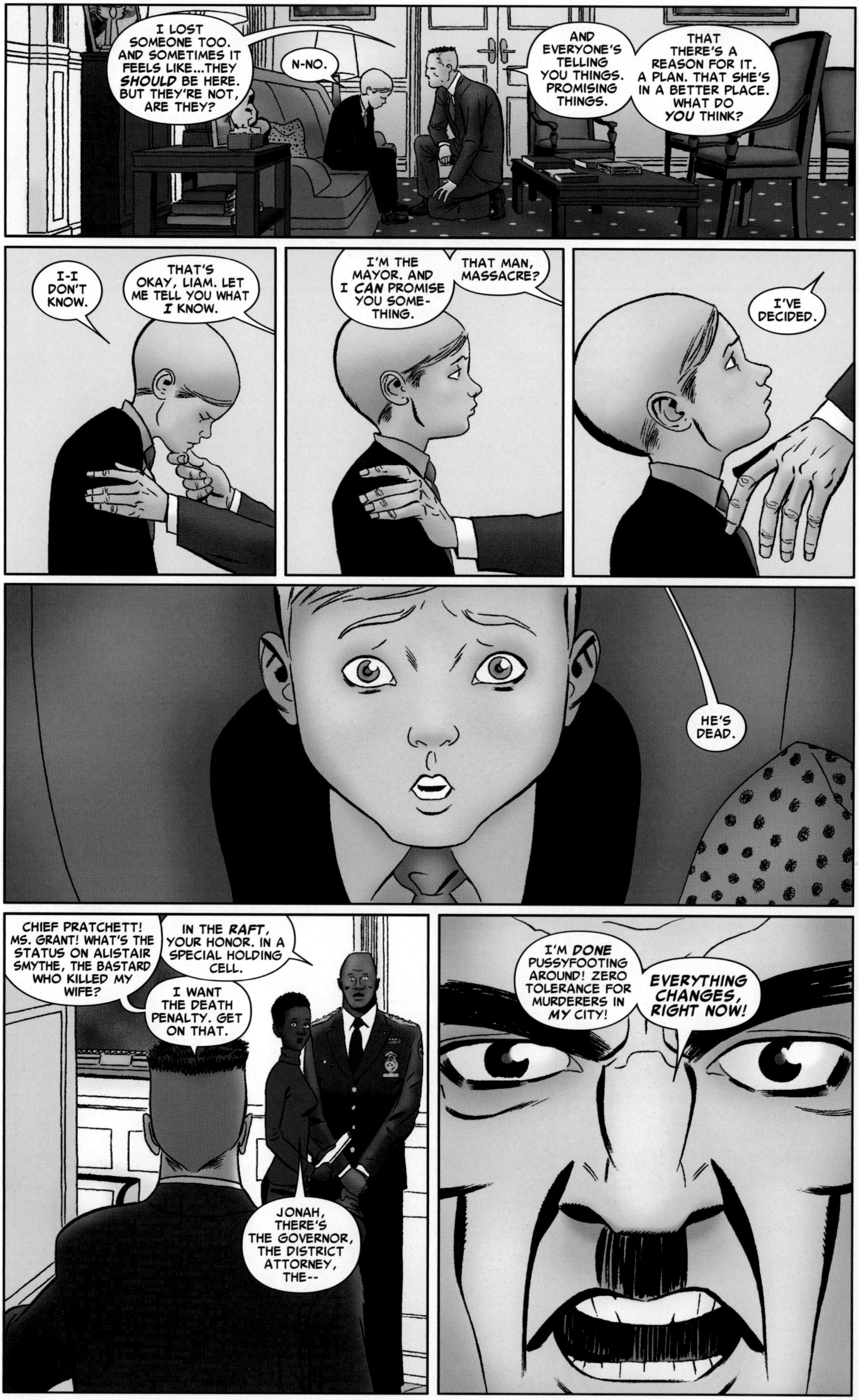

I LOST SOMEONE TOO. AND SOMETIMES IT FEELS LIKE...THEY SHOULD BE HERE. BUT THEY'RE NOT, ARE THEY?
N-NO.
AND EVERYONE'S TELLING YOU THINGS. PROMISING THINGS.
THAT THERE'S A REASON FOR IT. A PLAN. THAT SHE'S IN A BETTER PLACE. WHAT DO YOU THINK?
I-I DON'T KNOW.
THAT'S OKAY, LIAM. LET ME TELL YOU WHAT I KNOW.
I'M THE MAYOR. AND I CAN PROMISE YOU SOME-THING.
THAT MAN, MASSACRE?
I'VE DECIDED.
HE'S DEAD.
CHIEF PRATCHETT! MS. GRANT! WHAT'S THE STATUS ON ALISTAIR SMYTHE, THE BASTARD WHO KILLED MY WIFE?
IN THE RAFT, YOUR HONOR. IN A SPECIAL HOLDING CELL.
I WANT THE DEATH PENALTY. GET ON THAT.
JONAH, THERE'S THE GOVERNOR, THE DISTRICT ATTORNEY, THE--
I'M DONE PUSSYFOOTING AROUND! ZERO TOLERANCE FOR MURDERERS IN MY CITY!
EVERYTHING CHANGES, RIGHT NOW!

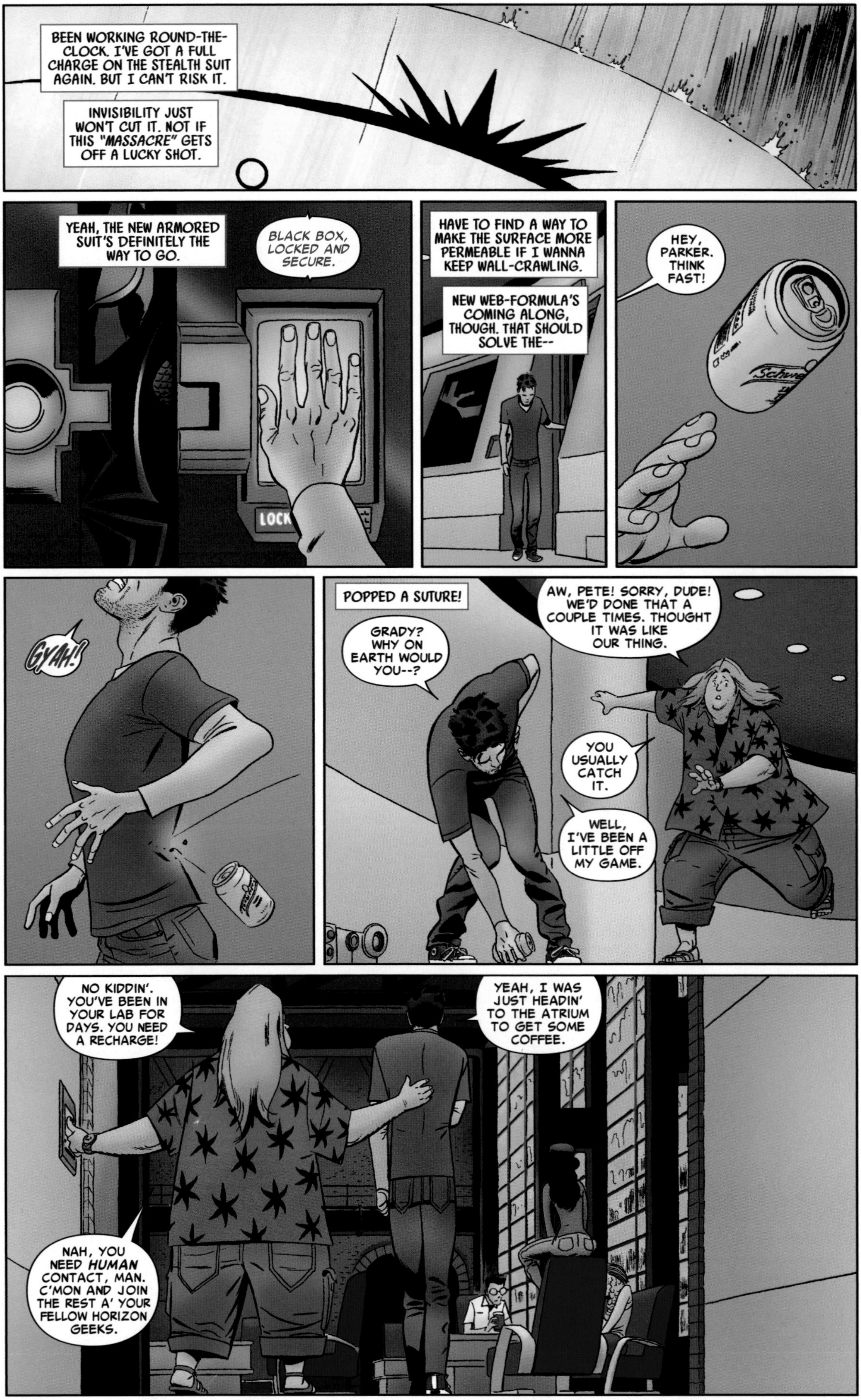

BEEN WORKING ROUND-THE-CLOCK. I'VE GOT A FULL CHARGE ON THE STEALTH SUIT AGAIN. BUT I CAN'T RISK IT.
INVISIBILITY JUST WON'T CUT IT. NOT IF THIS "MASSACRE" GETS OFF A LUCKY SHOT.
YEAH, THE NEW ARMORED SUIT'S DEFINITELY THE WAY TO GO.
BLACK BOX, LOCKED AND SECURE.
LOCK
HAVE TO FIND A WAY TO MAKE THE SURFACE MORE PERMEABLE IF I WANNA KEEP WALL-CRAWLING.
NEW WEB-FORMULA'S COMING ALONG, THOUGH. THAT SHOULD SOLVE THE--
HEY, PARKER. THINK FAST!
GYAH!
POPPED A SUTURE!
GRADY? WHY ON EARTH WOULD YOU--?
AW, PETE! SORRY, DUDE! WE'D DONE THAT A COUPLE TIMES. THOUGHT IT WAS LIKE OUR THING.
YOU USUALLY CATCH IT.
WELL, I'VE BEEN A LITTLE OFF MY GAME.
NO KIDDIN'. YOU'VE BEEN IN YOUR LAB FOR DAYS. YOU NEED A RECHARGE!
YEAH, I WAS JUST HEADIN' TO THE ATRIUM TO GET SOME COFFEE.
NAH, YOU NEED HUMAN CONTACT, MAN. C'MON AND JOIN THE REST A' YOUR FELLOW HORIZON GEEKS.

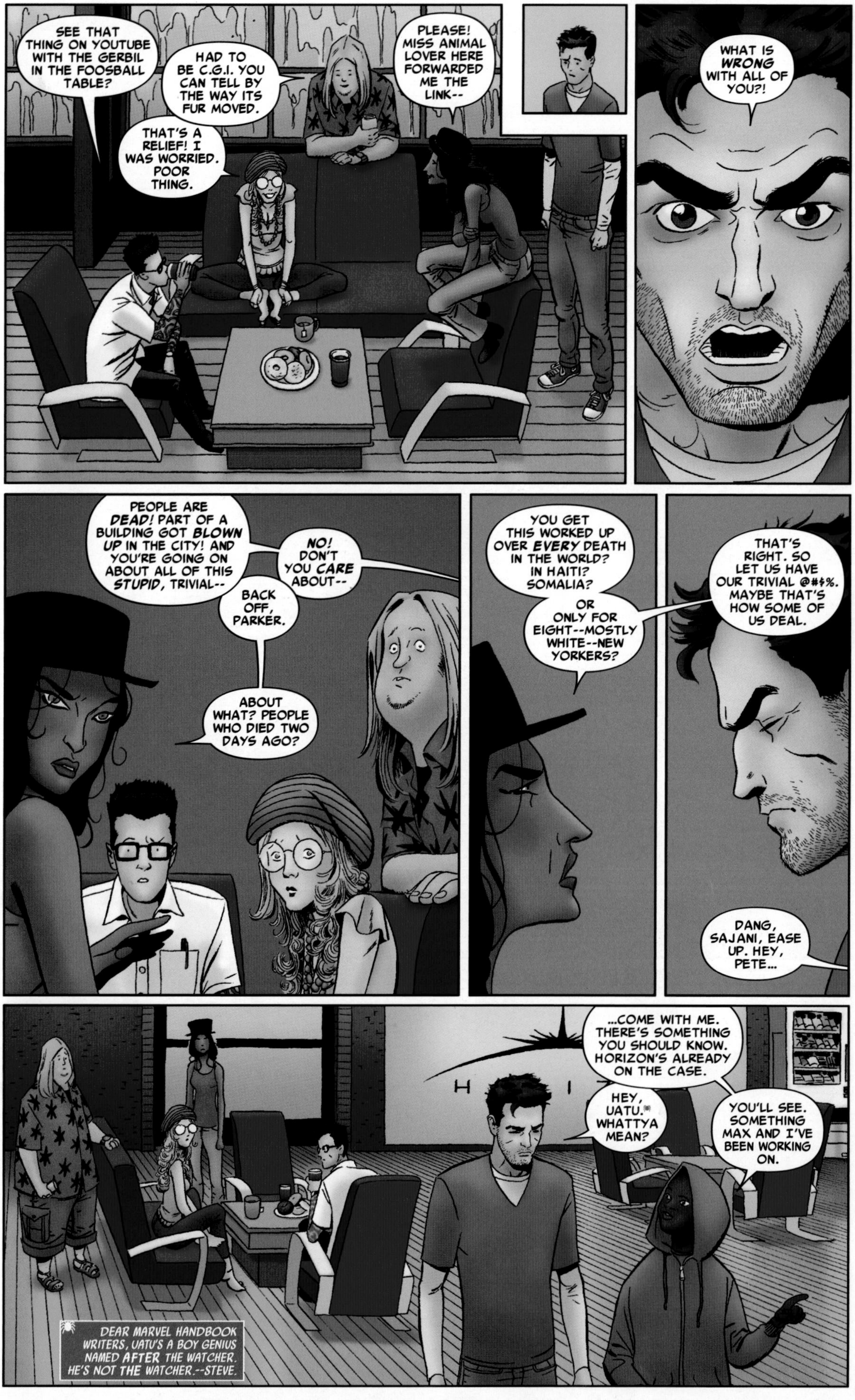
SEE THAT THING ON YOUTUBE WITH THE GERBIL IN THE FOOSBALL TABLE?
HAD TO BE C.G.I. YOU CAN TELL BY THE WAY ITS FUR MOVED.
THAT'S A RELIEF! I WAS WORRIED. POOR THING.
PLEASE! MISS ANIMAL LOVER HERE FORWARDED ME THE LINK--
WHAT IS *WRONG* WITH ALL OF YOU?!
PEOPLE ARE *DEAD!* PART OF A BUILDING GOT *BLOWN UP* IN THE CITY! AND YOU'RE GOING ON ABOUT ALL OF THIS *STUPID*, TRIVIAL--
NO! DON'T YOU *CARE* ABOUT--
BACK OFF, PARKER.
ABOUT WHAT? PEOPLE WHO DIED TWO DAYS AGO?
YOU GET THIS WORKED UP OVER *EVERY* DEATH IN THE WORLD? IN HAITI? SOMALIA?
OR ONLY FOR EIGHT--MOSTLY WHITE--NEW YORKERS?
THAT'S RIGHT. SO LET US HAVE OUR TRIVIAL @#$%. MAYBE THAT'S HOW SOME OF US DEAL.
DANG, SAJANI, EASE UP. HEY, PETE...
...COME WITH ME. THERE'S SOMETHING YOU SHOULD KNOW. HORIZON'S ALREADY ON THE CASE.
HEY, UATU.* WHATTYA MEAN?
YOU'LL SEE. SOMETHING MAX AND I'VE BEEN WORKING ON.
*DEAR MARVEL HANDBOOK WRITERS, UATU'S A BOY GENIUS NAMED **AFTER** THE WATCHER. HE'S NOT **THE** WATCHER.--STEVE.*

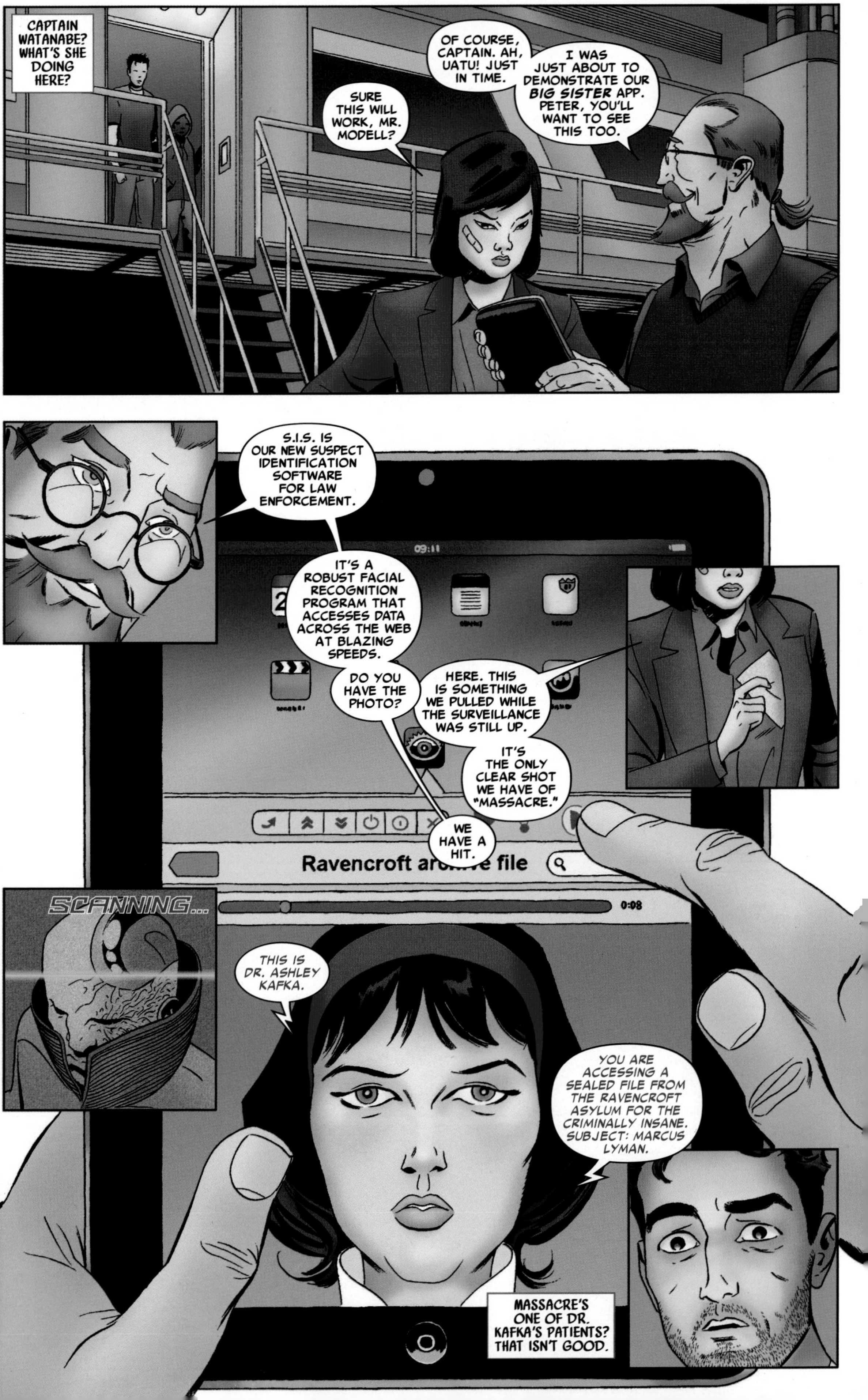
CAPTAIN WATANABE? WHAT'S SHE DOING HERE?
SURE THIS WILL WORK, MR. MODELL?
OF COURSE, CAPTAIN. AH, UATU! JUST IN TIME.
I WAS JUST ABOUT TO DEMONSTRATE OUR BIG SISTER APP. PETER, YOU'LL WANT TO SEE THIS TOO.
S.I.S. IS OUR NEW SUSPECT IDENTIFICATION SOFTWARE FOR LAW ENFORCEMENT.
IT'S A ROBUST FACIAL RECOGNITION PROGRAM THAT ACCESSES DATA ACROSS THE WEB AT BLAZING SPEEDS.
DO YOU HAVE THE PHOTO?
HERE. THIS IS SOMETHING WE PULLED WHILE THE SURVEILLANCE WAS STILL UP.
IT'S THE ONLY CLEAR SHOT WE HAVE OF "MASSACRE."
09:11
WE HAVE A HIT.
Ravencroft archive file
SCANNING...
0:08
THIS IS DR. ASHLEY KAFKA.
YOU ARE ACCESSING A SEALED FILE FROM THE RAVENCROFT ASYLUM FOR THE CRIMINALLY INSANE. SUBJECT: MARCUS LYMAN.
MASSACRE'S ONE OF DR. KAFKA'S PATIENTS? THAT ISN'T GOOD.

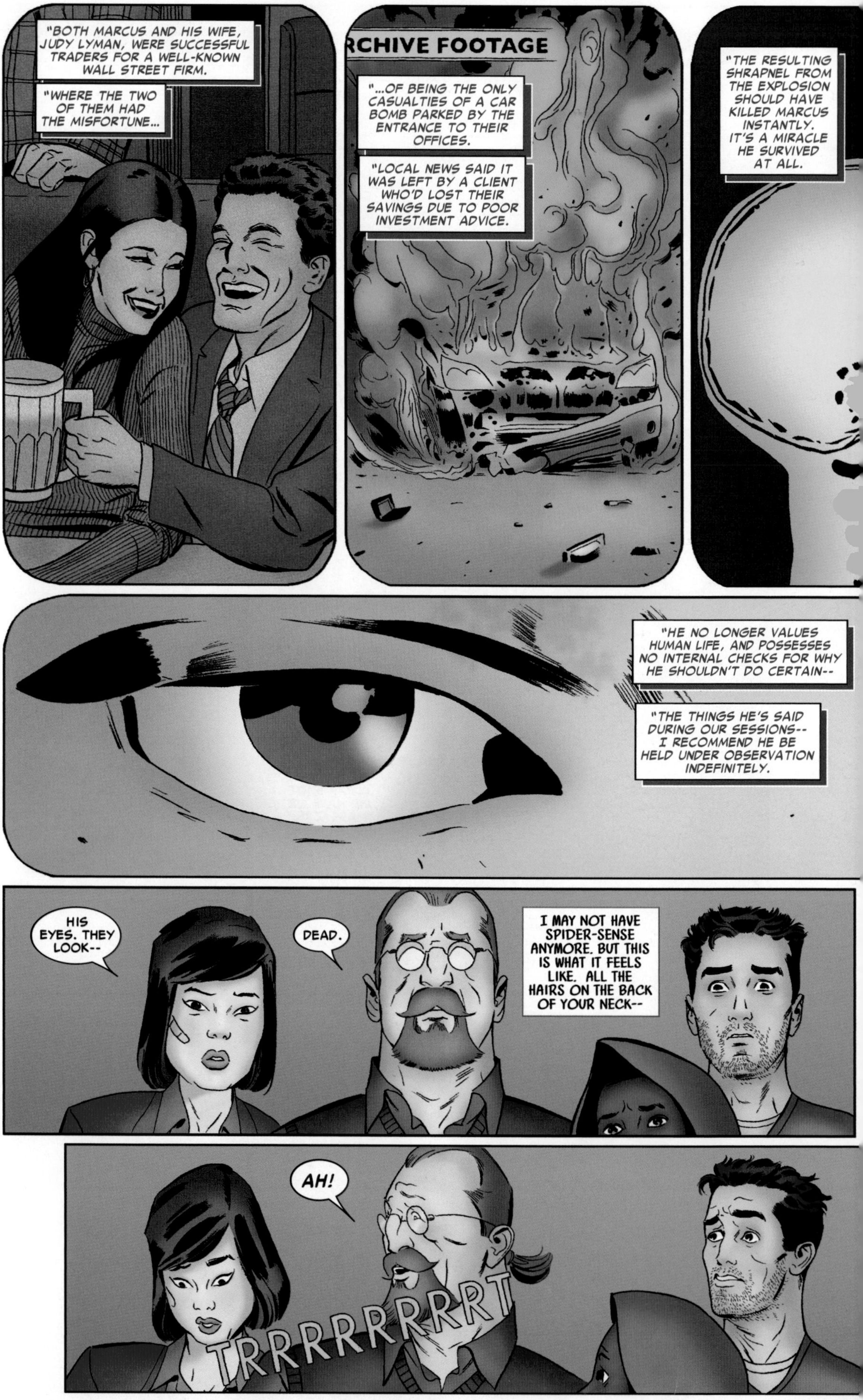
"BOTH MARCUS AND HIS WIFE, JUDY LYMAN, WERE SUCCESSFUL TRADERS FOR A WELL-KNOWN WALL STREET FIRM.
"WHERE THE TWO OF THEM HAD THE MISFORTUNE...
ARCHIVE FOOTAGE
"...OF BEING THE ONLY CASUALTIES OF A CAR BOMB PARKED BY THE ENTRANCE TO THEIR OFFICES.
"LOCAL NEWS SAID IT WAS LEFT BY A CLIENT WHO'D LOST THEIR SAVINGS DUE TO POOR INVESTMENT ADVICE.
"THE RESULTING SHRAPNEL FROM THE EXPLOSION SHOULD HAVE KILLED MARCUS INSTANTLY. IT'S A MIRACLE HE SURVIVED AT ALL.
"HE NO LONGER VALUES HUMAN LIFE, AND POSSESSES NO INTERNAL CHECKS FOR WHY HE SHOULDN'T DO CERTAIN--
"THE THINGS HE'S SAID DURING OUR SESSIONS-- I RECOMMEND HE BE HELD UNDER OBSERVATION INDEFINITELY.
HIS EYES. THEY LOOK--
DEAD.
I MAY NOT HAVE SPIDER-SENSE ANYMORE. BUT THIS IS WHAT IT FEELS LIKE. ALL THE HAIRS ON THE BACK OF YOUR NECK--
AH!
TRRRRRRRRT

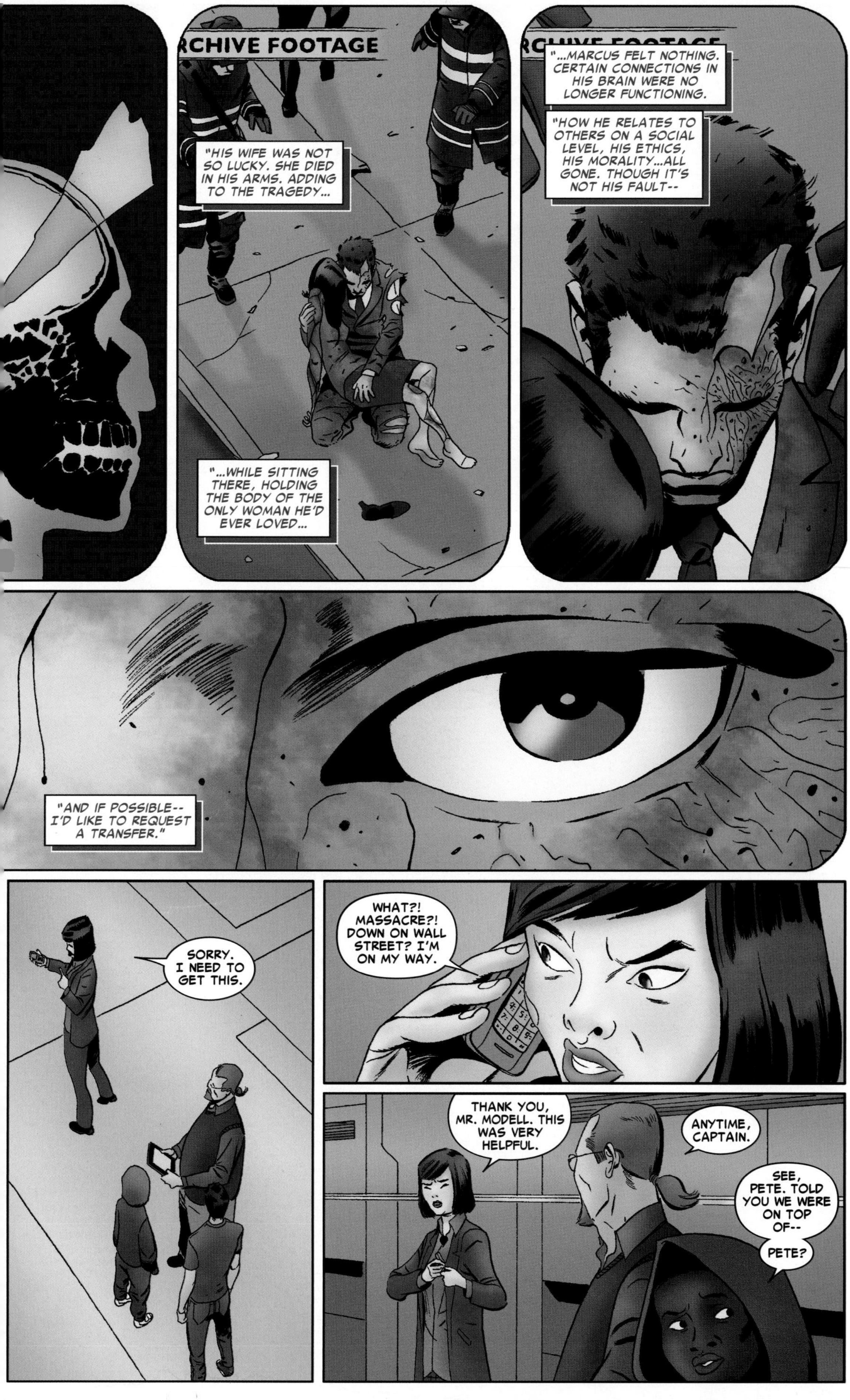
ARCHIVE FOOTAGE
"HIS WIFE WAS NOT SO LUCKY. SHE DIED IN HIS ARMS. ADDING TO THE TRAGEDY...
"...WHILE SITTING THERE, HOLDING THE BODY OF THE ONLY WOMAN HE'D EVER LOVED...
"...MARCUS FELT NOTHING. CERTAIN CONNECTIONS IN HIS BRAIN WERE NO LONGER FUNCTIONING.
"HOW HE RELATES TO OTHERS ON A SOCIAL LEVEL, HIS ETHICS, HIS MORALITY...ALL GONE. THOUGH IT'S NOT HIS FAULT--
"AND IF POSSIBLE-- I'D LIKE TO REQUEST A TRANSFER."
SORRY. I NEED TO GET THIS.
WHAT?! MASSACRE?! DOWN ON WALL STREET? I'M ON MY WAY.
THANK YOU, MR. MODELL. THIS WAS VERY HELPFUL.
ANYTIME, CAPTAIN.
SEE, PETE. TOLD YOU WE WERE ON TOP OF--
PETE?

GOT THE AREA CORDONED OFF. NO PRESS.

ALL THE NEARBY BUILDINGS EVACUATED, JUST IN CASE.

GOOD. HOW MANY THIS TIME, CHIEF?

SEVEN HOSTAGES.

DAMN. I WANT TO MAKE MYSELF PERFECTLY CLEAR, PRATCHETT.

THAT THING INSIDE IS A *THREAT!* A *MENACE!* AND WHATEVER HAPPENS TODAY...

...IT DOESN'T LEAVE HERE *ALIVE!*

MARCUS? IS THAT *YOU?* WHY ARE YOU DOING THIS?

I DON'T KNOW. CURIOSITY MAYBE? OUTSIDE OF JUDY, ALL I HAD WAS THIS FIRM.

YOU PEOPLE ARE THE CLOSEST THING I HAVE TO A FAMILY. AND STILL? NOTHING.

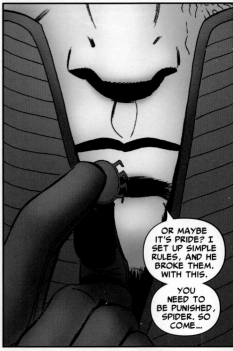

OR MAYBE IT'S PRIDE? I SET UP SIMPLE RULES, AND HE BROKE THEM. WITH THIS.

YOU NEED TO BE PUNISHED, SPIDER. SO COME...

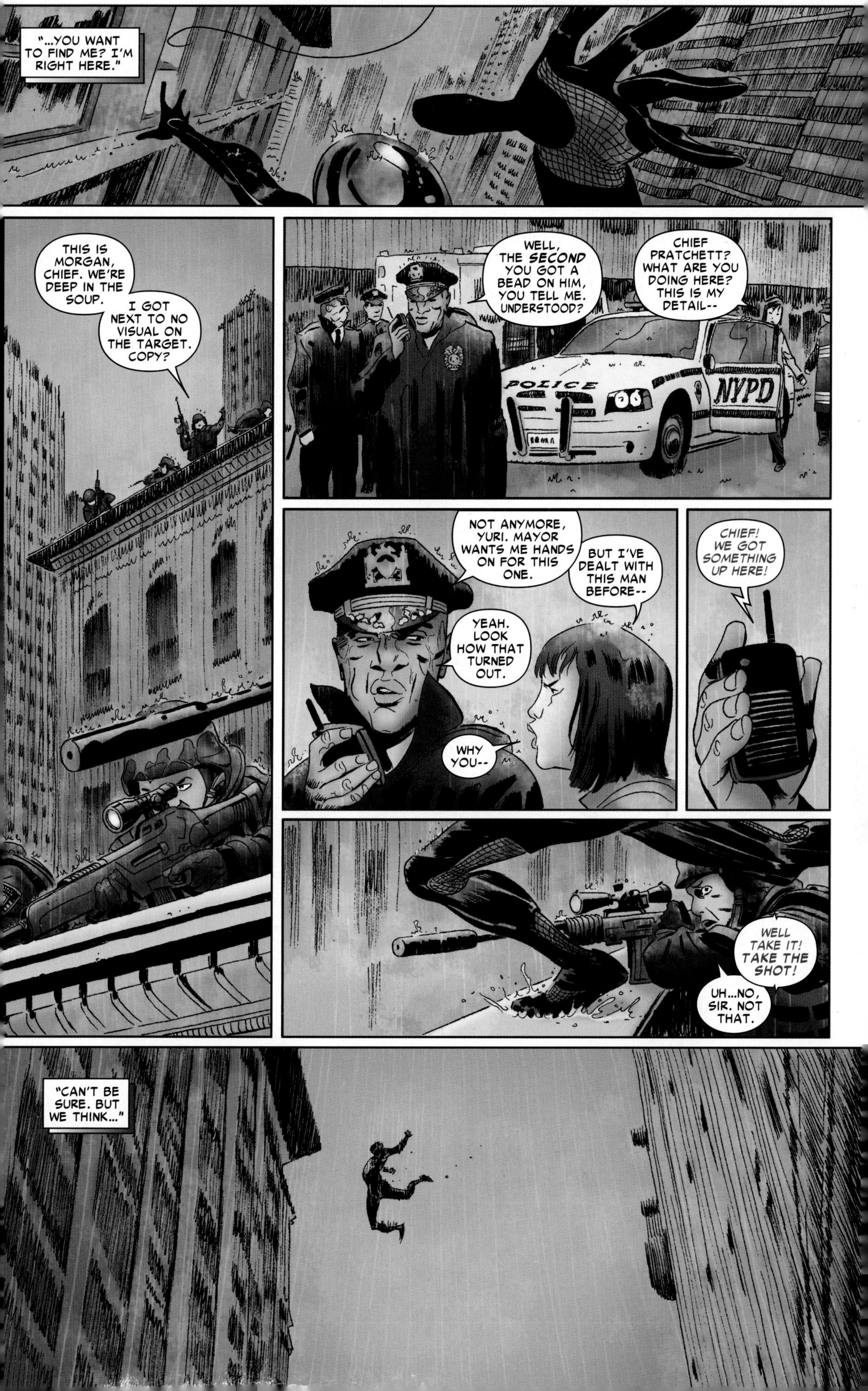
"...YOU WANT TO FIND ME? I'M RIGHT HERE."
THIS IS MORGAN, CHIEF. WE'RE DEEP IN THE SOUP.
I GOT NEXT TO NO VISUAL ON THE TARGET. COPY?
WELL, THE SECOND YOU GOT A BEAD ON HIM, YOU TELL ME. UNDERSTOOD?
CHIEF PRATCHETT? WHAT ARE YOU DOING HERE? THIS IS MY DETAIL--
POLICE
NYPD
NOT ANYMORE, YURI. MAYOR WANTS ME HANDS ON FOR THIS ONE.
BUT I'VE DEALT WITH THIS MAN BEFORE--
YEAH. LOOK HOW THAT TURNED OUT.
WHY YOU--
CHIEF! WE GOT SOMETHING UP HERE!
WELL TAKE IT! TAKE THE SHOT!
UH...NO, SIR. NOT THAT.
"CAN'T BE SURE. BUT WE THINK..."

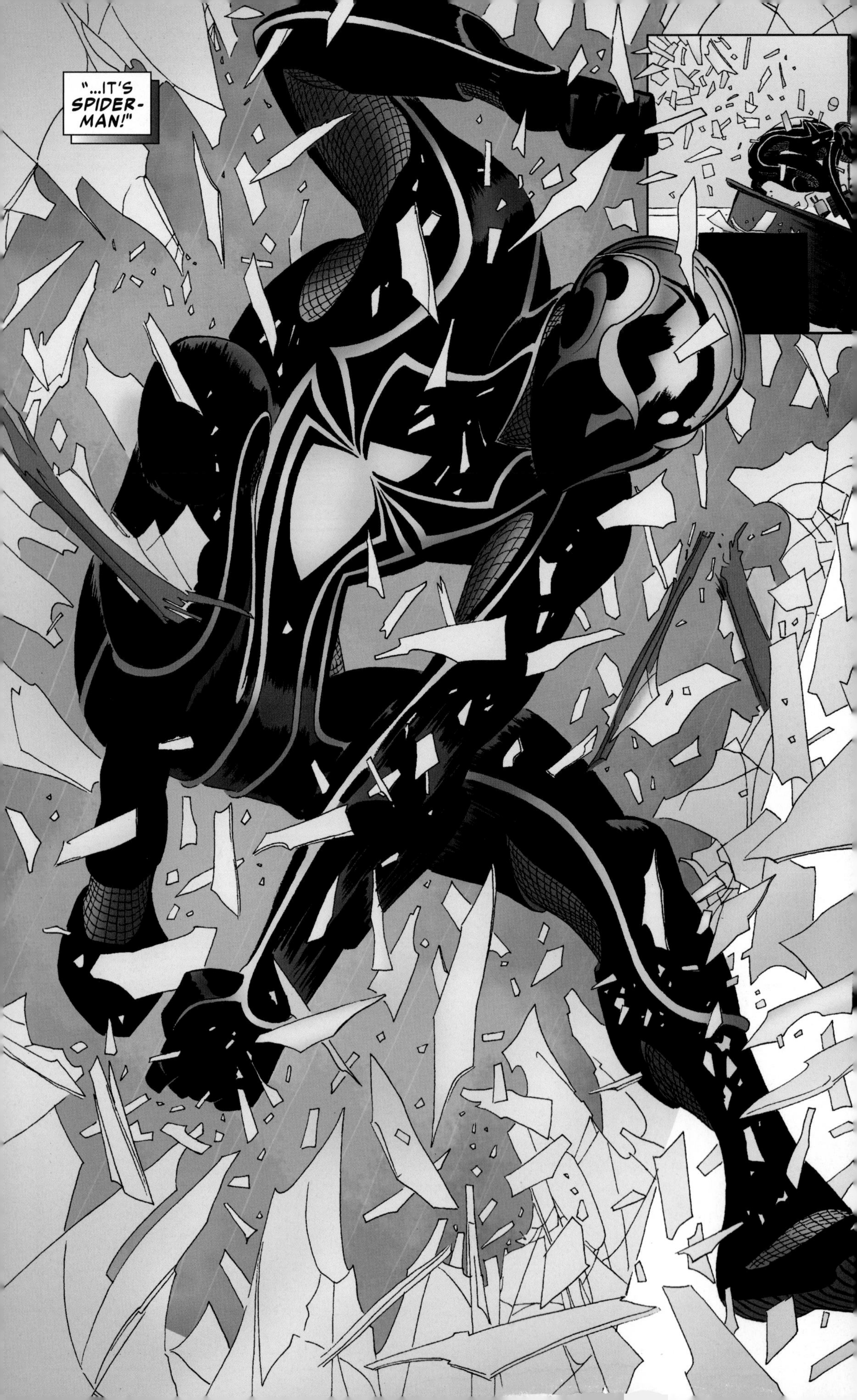
"...IT'S SPIDER-MAN!"

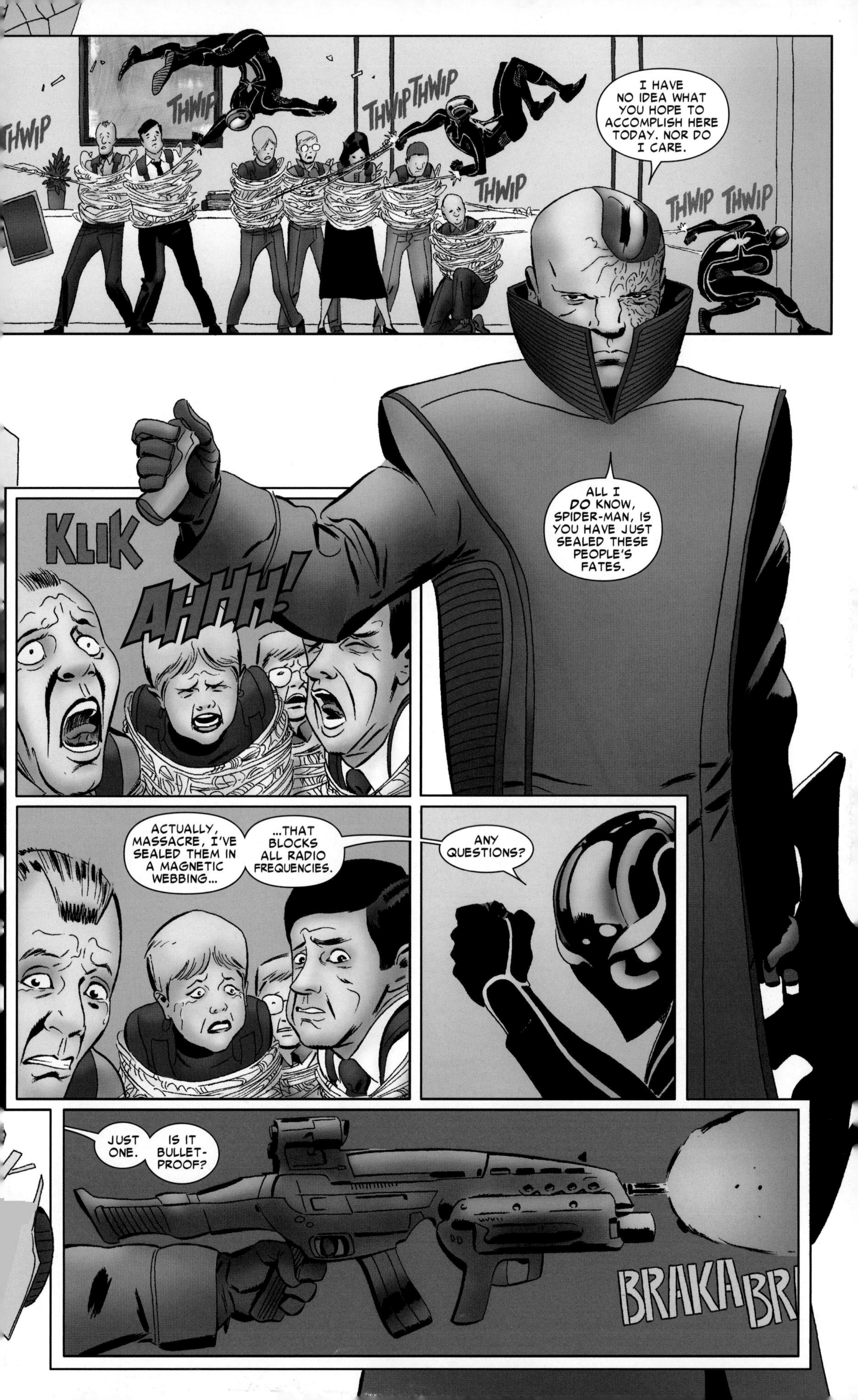
THWIP
THWIP
THWIPTHWIP
THWIP
THWIP THWIP
I HAVE NO IDEA WHAT YOU HOPE TO ACCOMPLISH HERE TODAY. NOR DO I CARE.
KLIK
AHHH!
ALL I DO KNOW, SPIDER-MAN, IS YOU HAVE JUST SEALED THESE PEOPLE'S FATES.
ACTUALLY, MASSACRE, I'VE SEALED THEM IN A MAGNETIC WEBBING...
...THAT BLOCKS ALL RADIO FREQUENCIES.
ANY QUESTIONS?
JUST ONE.
IS IT BULLET-PROOF?
BRAKABR

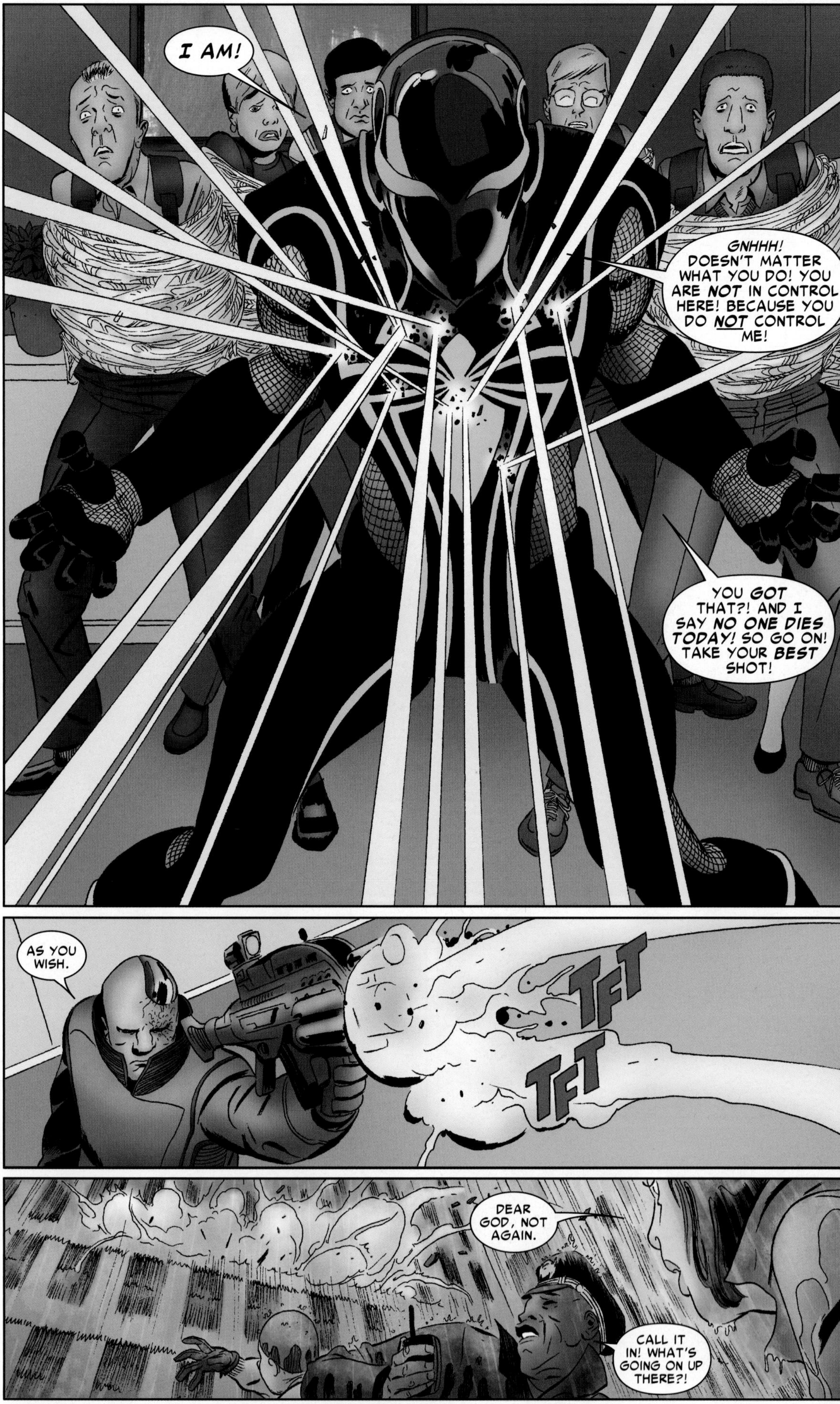
I AM!
GNHHH! DOESN'T MATTER WHAT YOU DO! YOU ARE NOT IN CONTROL HERE! BECAUSE YOU DO NOT CONTROL ME!
YOU GOT THAT?! AND I SAY NO ONE DIES TODAY! SO GO ON! TAKE YOUR BEST SHOT!
AS YOU WISH.
TFT
TFT
DEAR GOD, NOT AGAIN.
CALL IT IN! WHAT'S GOING ON UP THERE?!

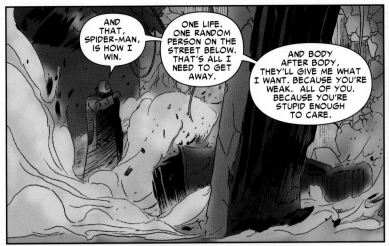

AND, THAT, SPIDER-MAN, IS HOW I WIN.

ONE LIFE. ONE RANDOM PERSON ON THE STREET BELOW. THAT'S ALL I NEED TO GET AWAY.

AND BODY AFTER BODY, THEY'LL GIVE ME WHAT I WANT. BECAUSE YOU'RE WEAK. ALL OF YOU. BECAUSE YOU'RE STUPID ENOUGH TO CARE.

THINK AGAIN.

IMPOSSIBLE!

WRONG. IT'S EASY TO KILL. TO DESTROY. THERE'S MILLIONS OF WAYS TO DO IT.

BUT THERE IS ALWAYS A WAY TO WIN.

AND I'M A PRETTY SMART GUY. FROM HERE ON OUT--I'LL FIND IT. EVERY TIME.

REALLY? NINE PEOPLE STRAPPED TO GELIGNITE A BLOCK AWAY.

YOU'LL NEVER GET TO THEM IN TI--

THWIP

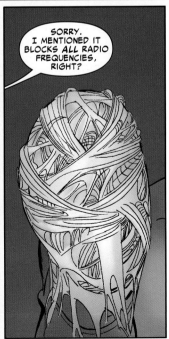

SORRY. I MENTIONED IT BLOCKS ALL RADIO FREQUENCIES, RIGHT?

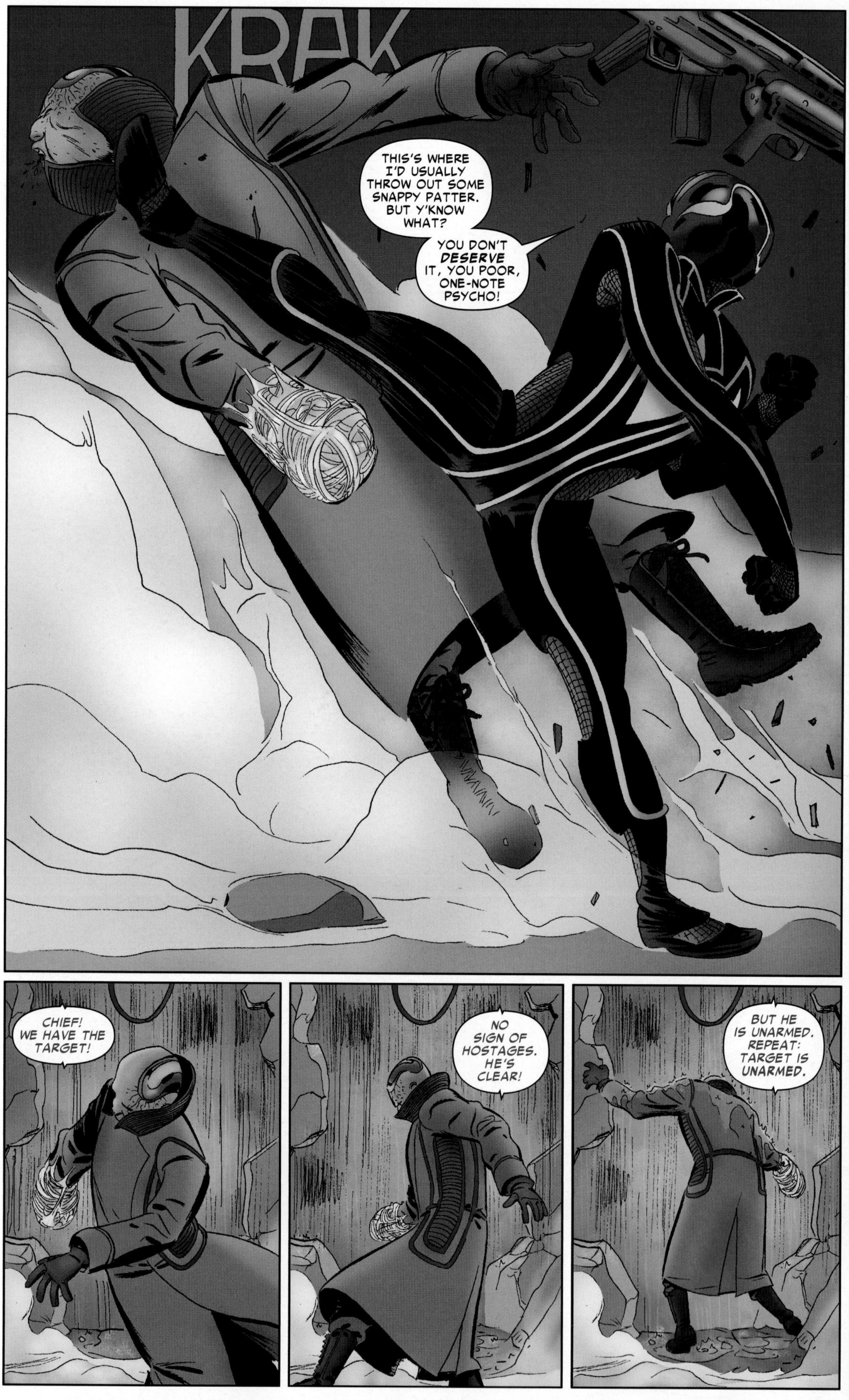
KRAK
THIS'S WHERE I'D USUALLY THROW OUT SOME SNAPPY PATTER. BUT Y'KNOW WHAT?
YOU DON'T DESERVE IT, YOU POOR, ONE-NOTE PSYCHO!
CHIEF! WE HAVE THE TARGET!
NO SIGN OF HOSTAGES. HE'S CLEAR!
BUT HE IS UNARMED. REPEAT: TARGET IS UNARMED.

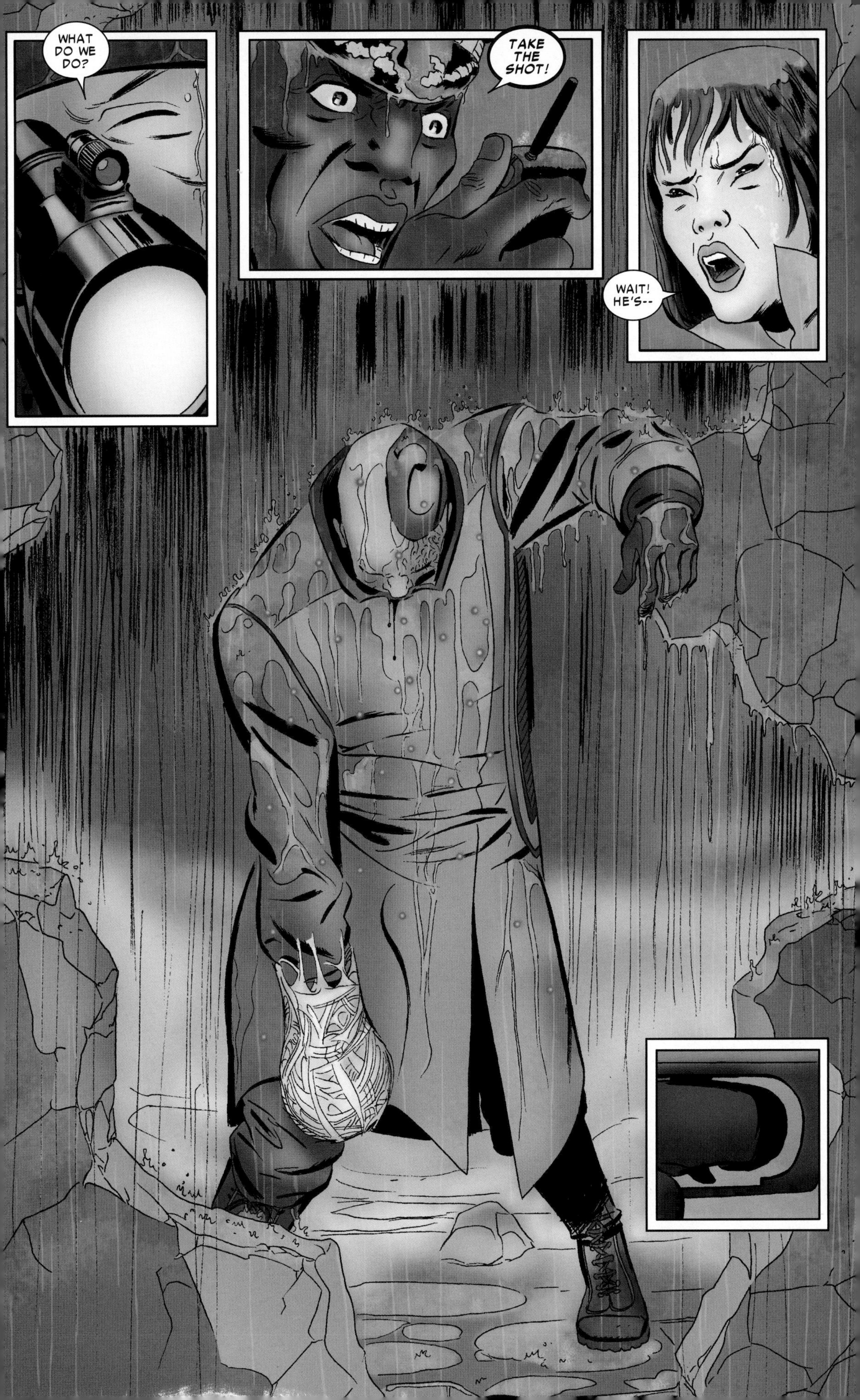
WHAT DO WE DO?
TAKE THE SHOT!
WAIT! HE'S--

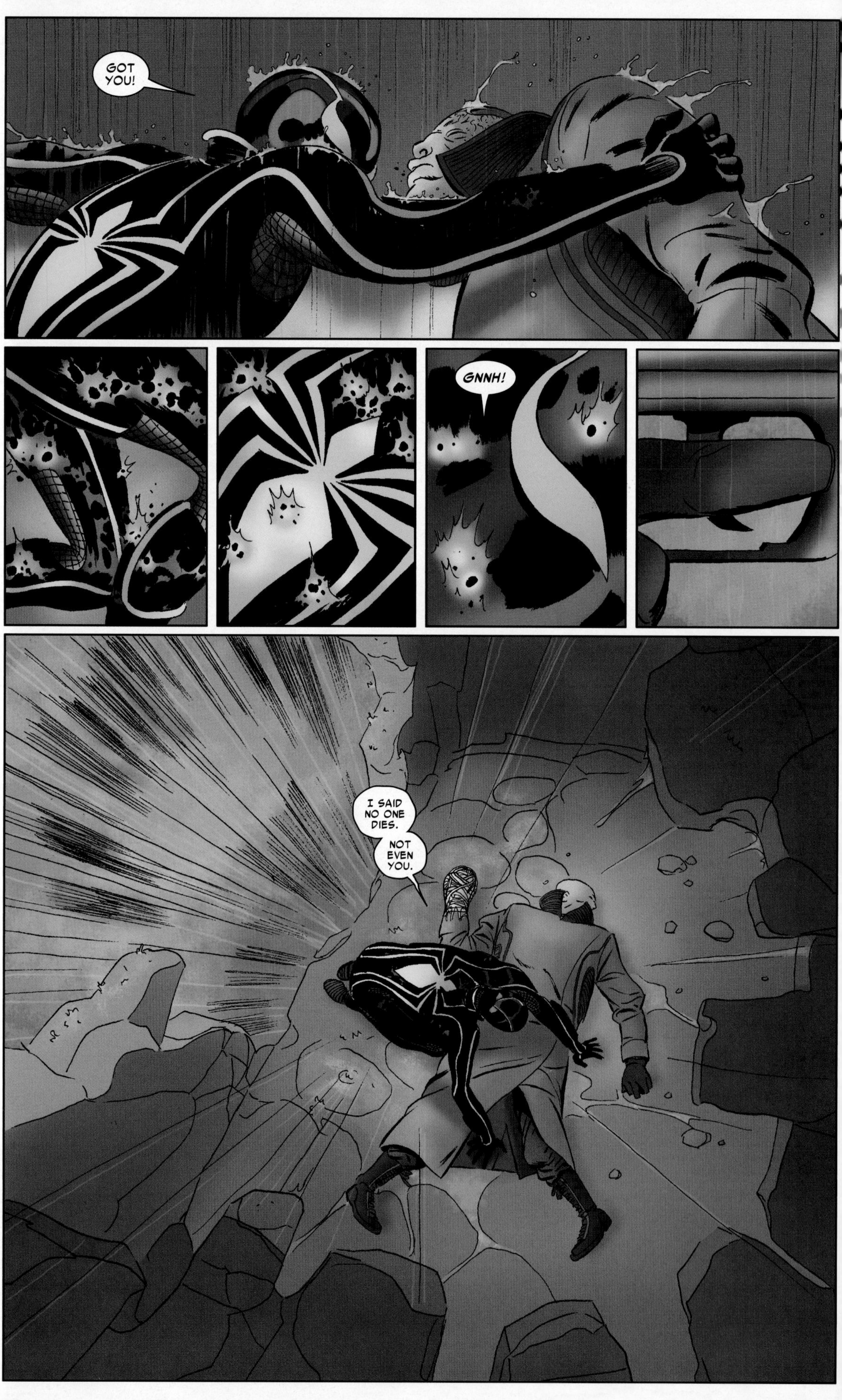
GOT YOU!
GNNH!
I SAID NO ONE DIES.
NOT EVEN YOU.

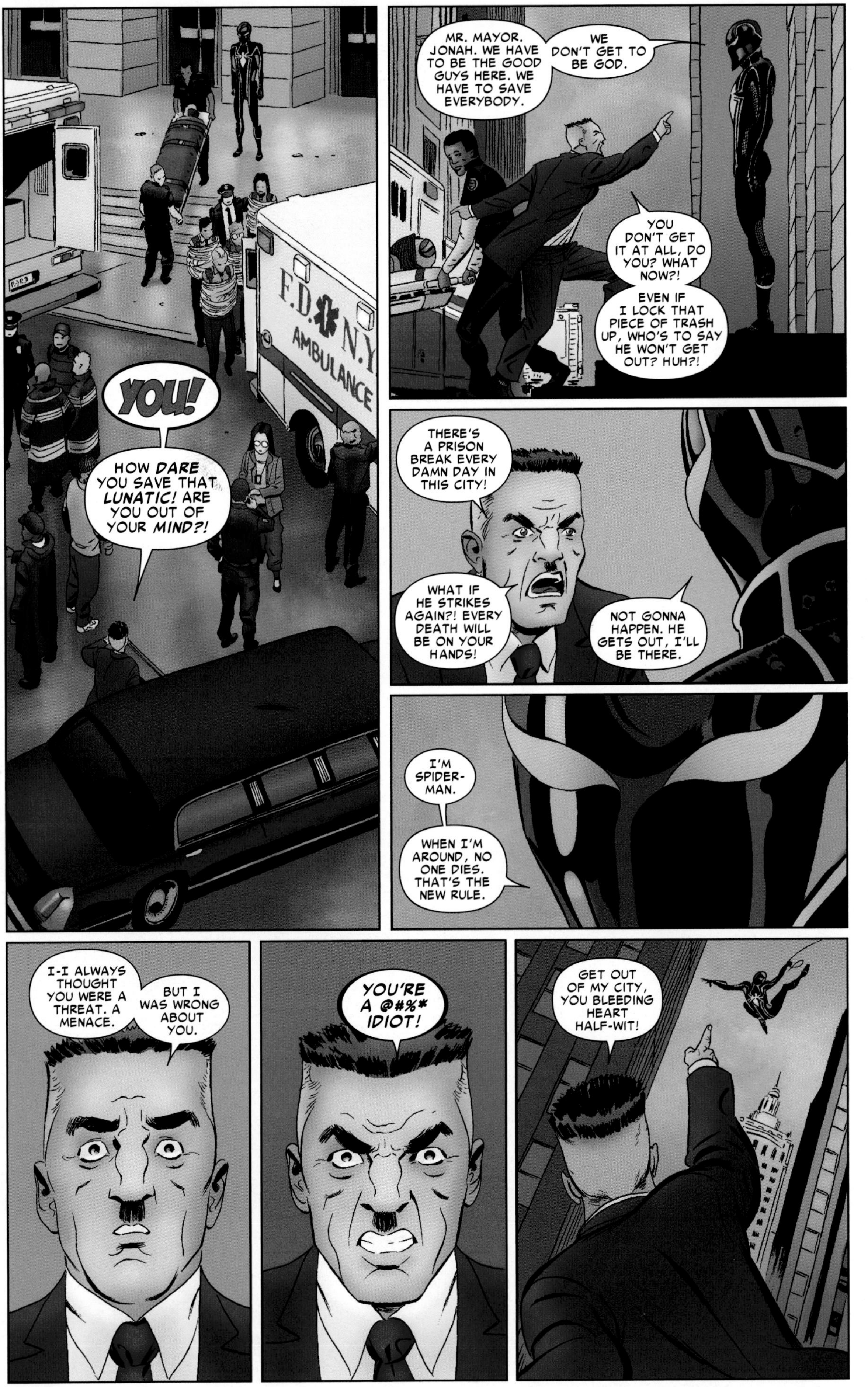
YOU!
HOW DARE YOU SAVE THAT LUNATIC! ARE YOU OUT OF YOUR MIND?!
F.D.N.Y. AMBULANCE
MR. MAYOR. JONAH. WE HAVE TO BE THE GOOD GUYS HERE. WE HAVE TO SAVE EVERYBODY.
WE DON'T GET TO BE GOD.
YOU DON'T GET IT AT ALL, DO YOU? WHAT NOW?!
EVEN IF I LOCK THAT PIECE OF TRASH UP, WHO'S TO SAY HE WON'T GET OUT? HUH?!
THERE'S A PRISON BREAK EVERY DAMN DAY IN THIS CITY!
WHAT IF HE STRIKES AGAIN?! EVERY DEATH WILL BE ON YOUR HANDS!
NOT GONNA HAPPEN. HE GETS OUT, I'LL BE THERE.
I'M SPIDER-MAN.
WHEN I'M AROUND, NO ONE DIES. THAT'S THE NEW RULE.
I-I ALWAYS THOUGHT YOU WERE A THREAT. A MENACE.
BUT I WAS WRONG ABOUT YOU.
YOU'RE A @#%* IDIOT!
GET OUT OF MY CITY, YOU BLEEDING HEART HALF-WIT!

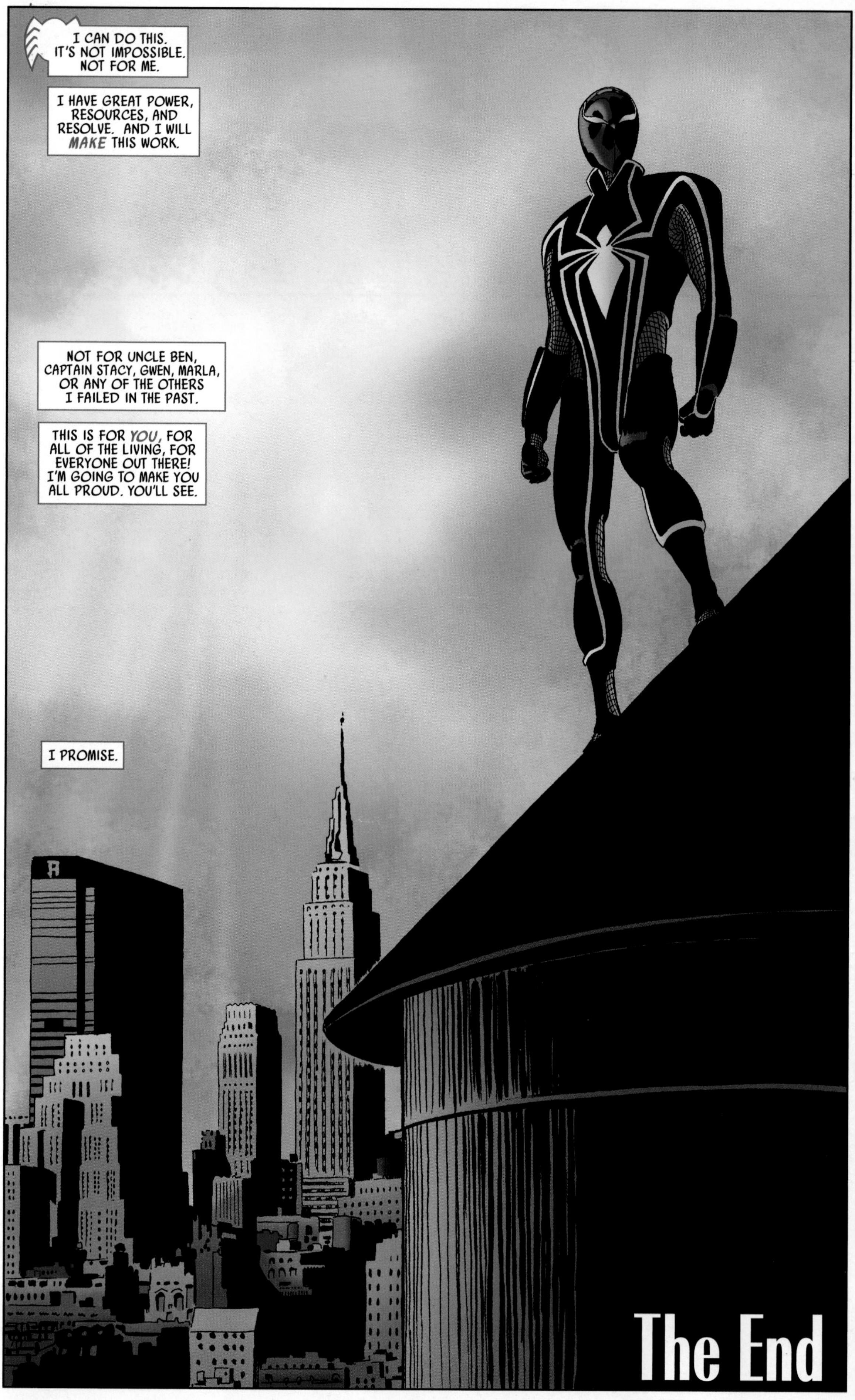
I CAN DO THIS. IT'S NOT IMPOSSIBLE. NOT FOR ME.
I HAVE GREAT POWER, RESOURCES, AND RESOLVE. AND I WILL *MAKE* THIS WORK.
NOT FOR UNCLE BEN, CAPTAIN STACY, GWEN, MARLA, OR ANY OF THE OTHERS I FAILED IN THE PAST.
THIS IS FOR *YOU*, FOR ALL OF THE LIVING, FOR EVERYONE OUT THERE! I'M GOING TO MAKE YOU ALL PROUD. YOU'LL SEE.
I PROMISE.
The End

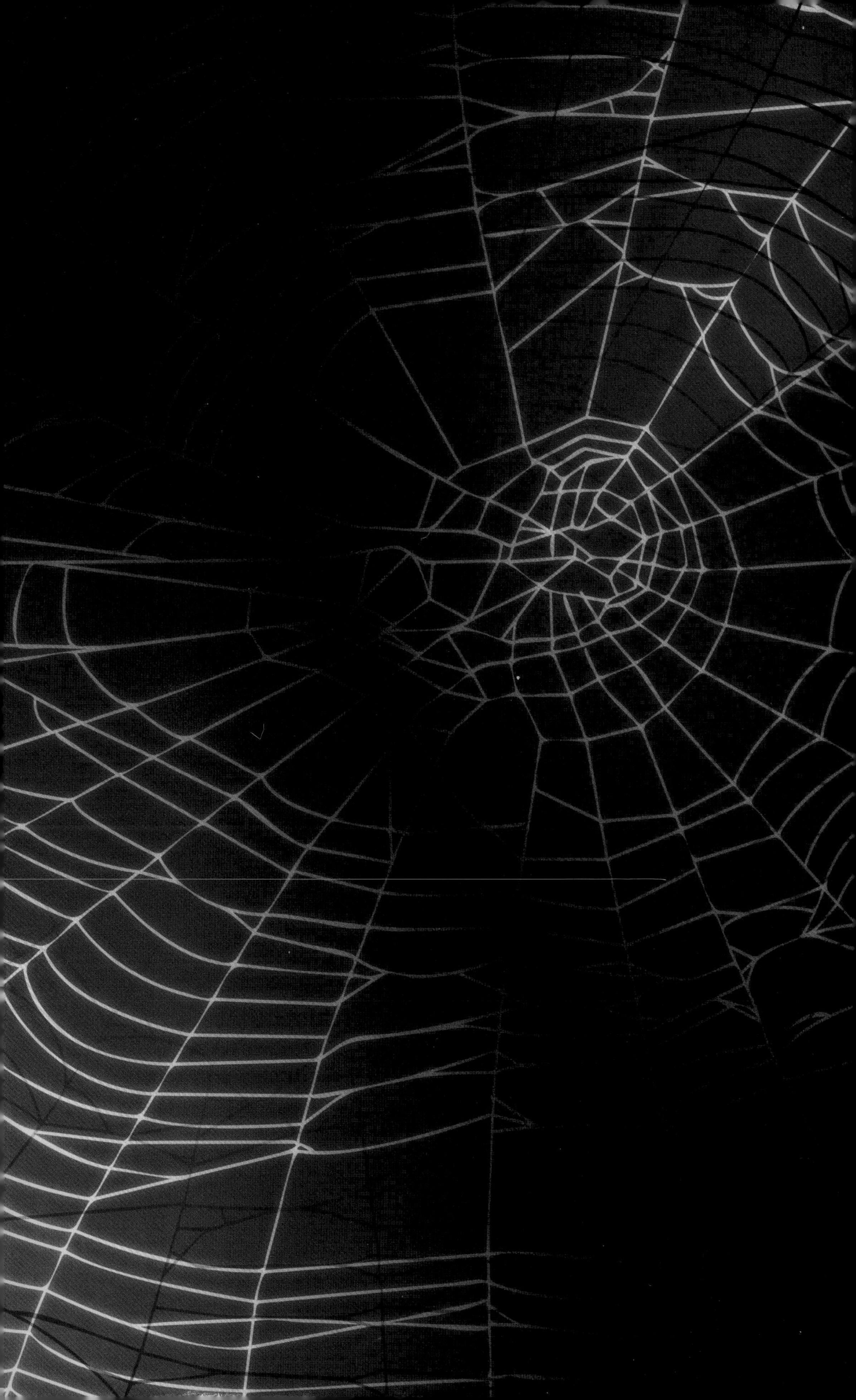

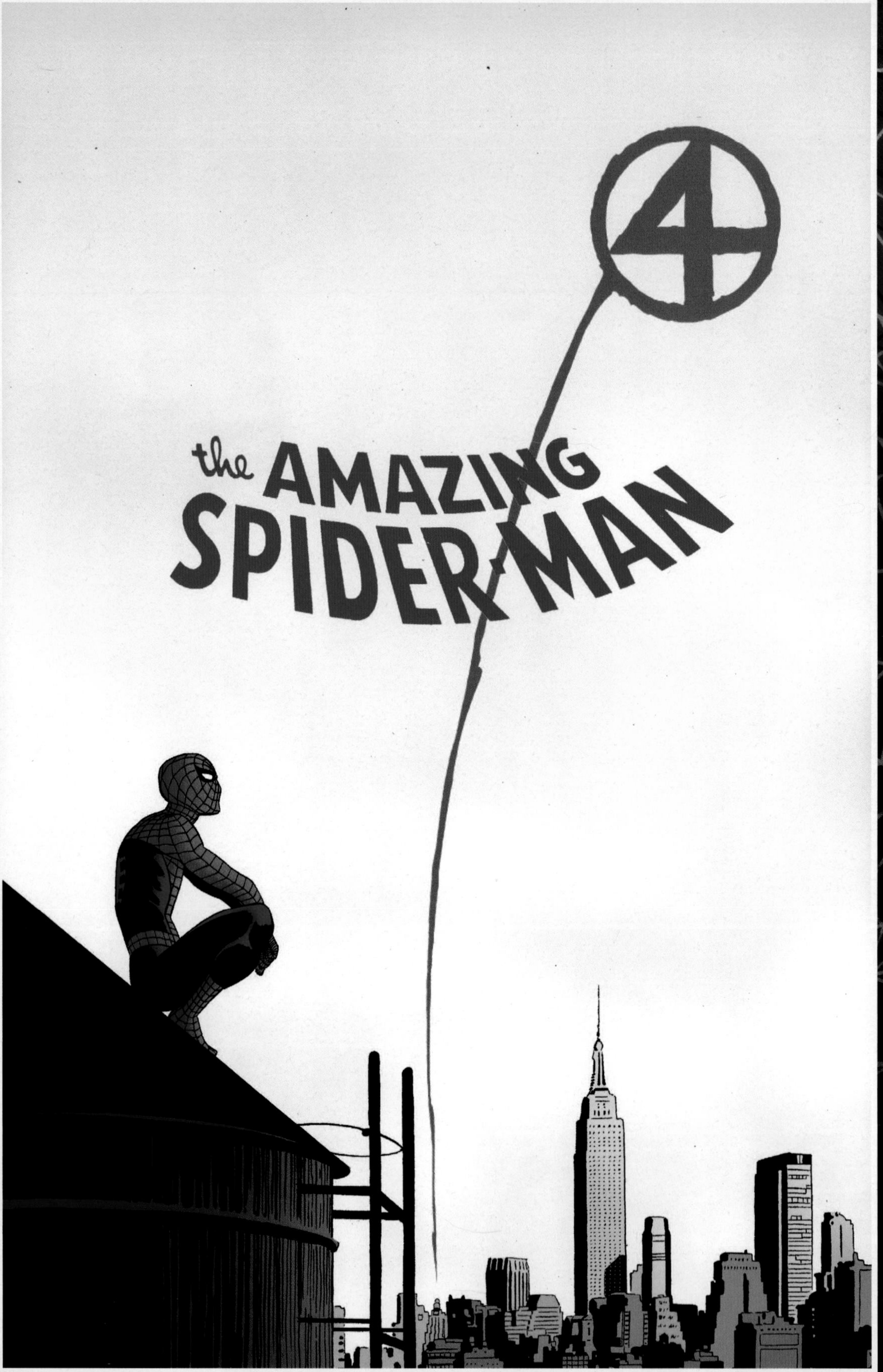
the AMAZING SPIDER-MAN

AMAZING SPIDER-MAN #657
COVER BY MARCOS MARTIN

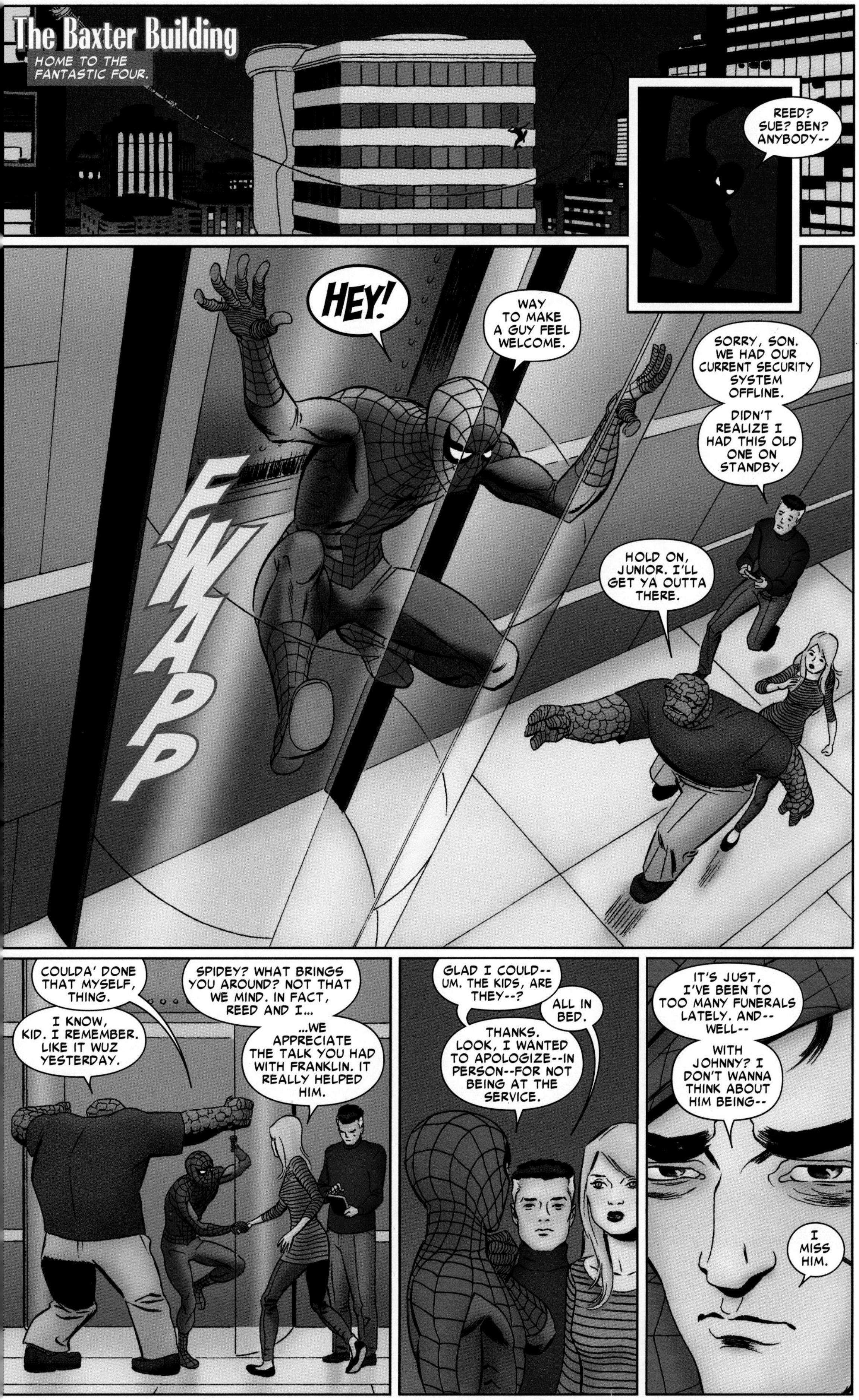

The Baxter Building
HOME TO THE FANTASTIC FOUR.
REED? SUE? BEN? ANYBODY--
HEY!
FWAPP
WAY TO MAKE A GUY FEEL WELCOME.
SORRY, SON. WE HAD OUR CURRENT SECURITY SYSTEM OFFLINE.
DIDN'T REALIZE I HAD THIS OLD ONE ON STANDBY.
HOLD ON, JUNIOR. I'LL GET YA OUTTA THERE.
COULDA' DONE THAT MYSELF, THING.
I KNOW, KID. I REMEMBER. LIKE IT WUZ YESTERDAY.
SPIDEY? WHAT BRINGS YOU AROUND? NOT THAT WE MIND. IN FACT, REED AND I...
...WE APPRECIATE THE TALK YOU HAD WITH FRANKLIN. IT REALLY HELPED HIM.
GLAD I COULD-- UM. THE KIDS, ARE THEY--?
ALL IN BED.
THANKS. LOOK, I WANTED TO APOLOGIZE--IN PERSON--FOR NOT BEING AT THE SERVICE.
IT'S JUST, I'VE BEEN TO TOO MANY FUNERALS LATELY. AND-- WELL--
WITH JOHNNY? I DON'T WANNA THINK ABOUT HIM BEING--
I MISS HIM.

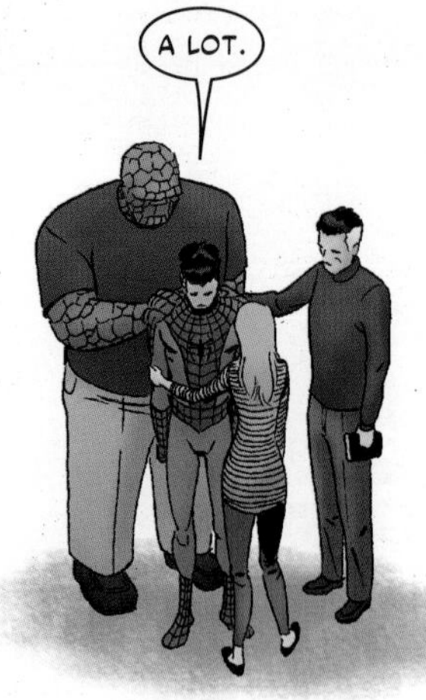
A LOT.

TORCH SONG

DAN SLOTT WRITER

MARCOS MARTIN, TY TEMPLETON NUNO PLATI & STEFANO CASELLI ART

MUNTSA VICENTE, JAVIER RODRIGUEZ NUNO PLATI & MARTE GRACIA COLORS

VC'S JOE CARAMAGNA LETTERER

ELLIE PYLE ASSISTANT EDITOR

STEPHEN WACKER SENIOR EDITOR

AXEL ALONSO EDITOR IN CHIEF

JOE QUESADA CHIEF CREATIVE OFFICER

DAN BUCKLEY PUBLISHER

ALAN FINE EXECUTIVE PRODUCER

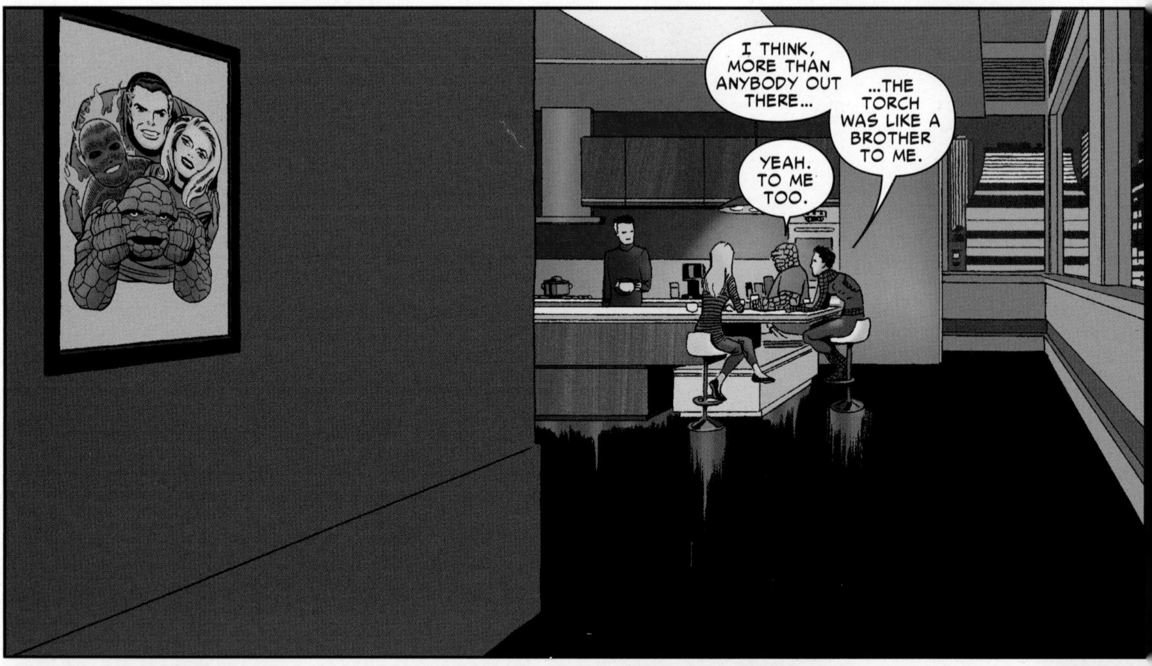
I THINK, MORE THAN ANYBODY OUT THERE...
...THE TORCH WAS LIKE A BROTHER TO ME.
YEAH. TO ME TOO.

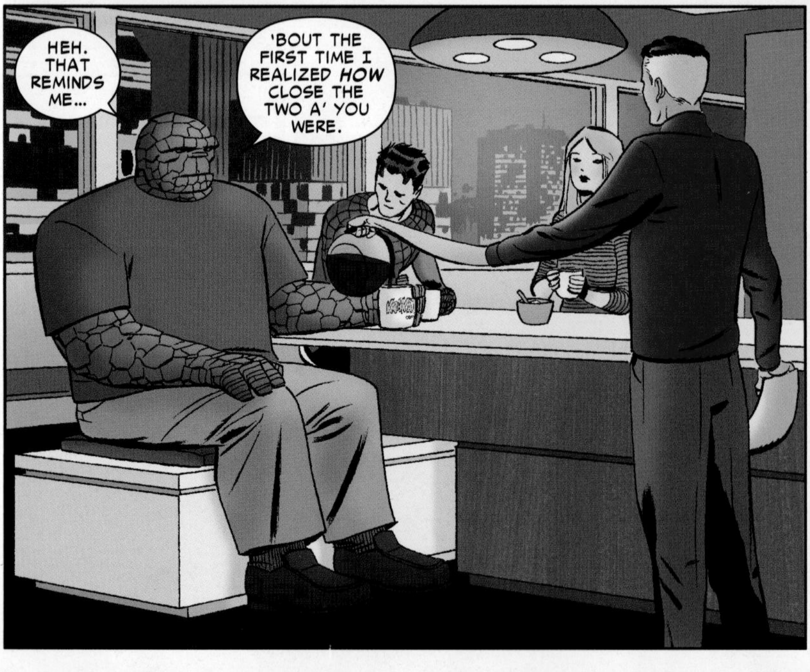
HEH. THAT REMINDS ME...
'BOUT THE FIRST TIME I REALIZED *HOW* CLOSE THE TWO A' YOU WERE.

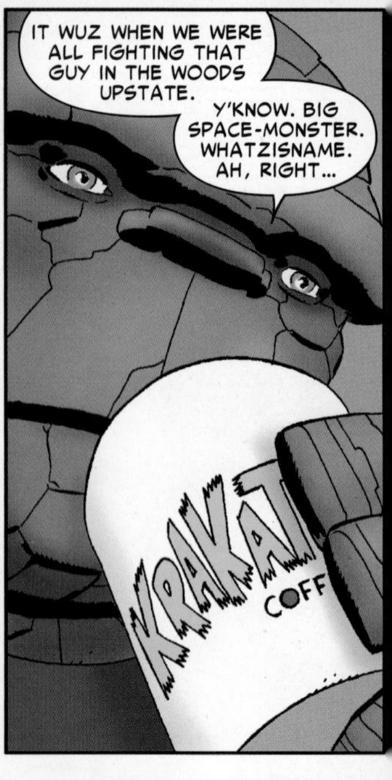
IT WUZ WHEN WE WERE ALL FIGHTING THAT GUY IN THE WOODS UPSTATE.
Y'KNOW. BIG SPACE-MONSTER. WHATZISNAME. AH, RIGHT...
KRAKAT
COFF

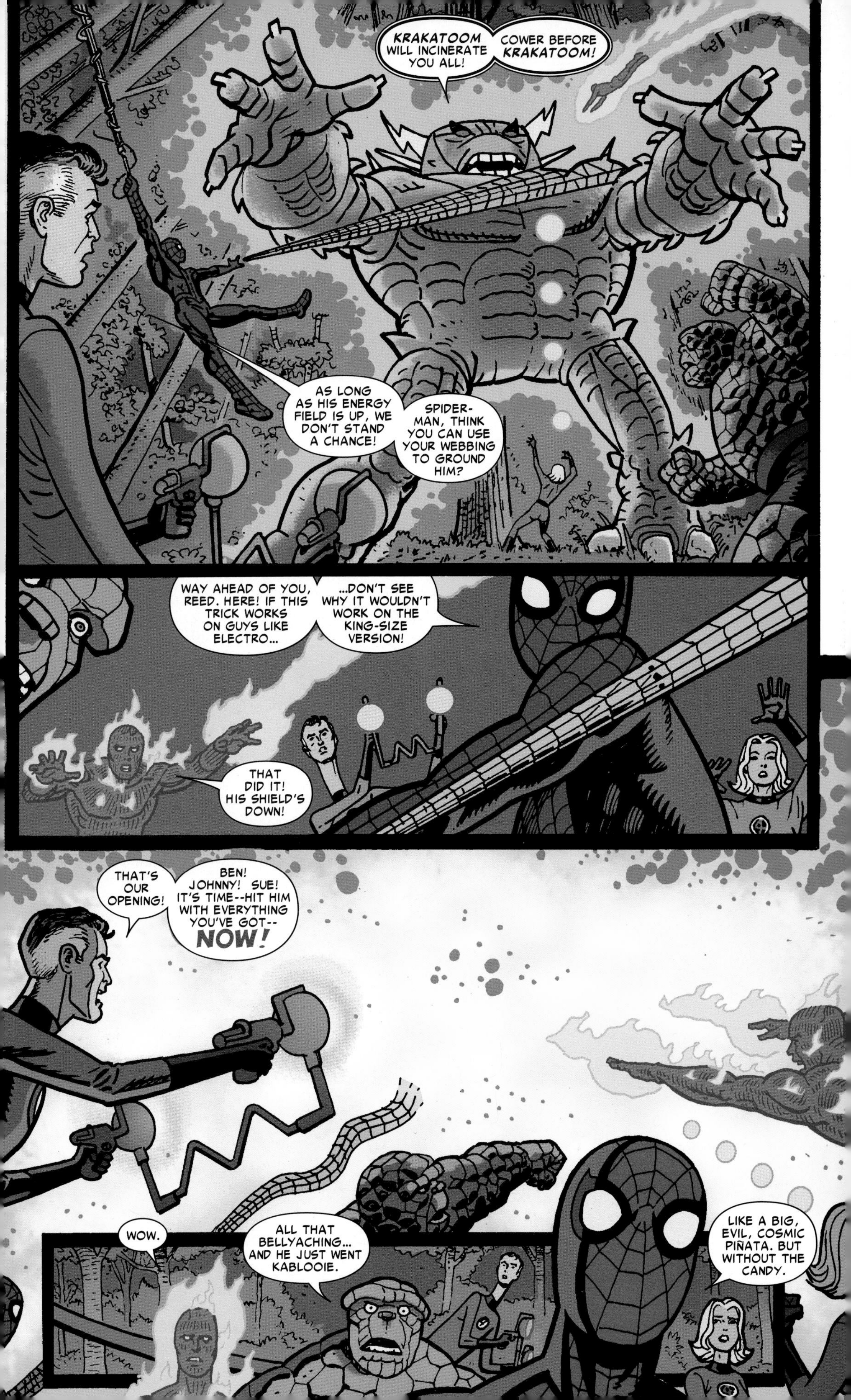
KRAKATOOM WILL INCINERATE YOU ALL!
COWER BEFORE KRAKATOOM!
AS LONG AS HIS ENERGY FIELD IS UP, WE DON'T STAND A CHANCE!
SPIDER-MAN, THINK YOU CAN USE YOUR WEBBING TO GROUND HIM?
WAY AHEAD OF YOU, REED. HERE! IF THIS TRICK WORKS ON GUYS LIKE ELECTRO...
...DON'T SEE WHY IT WOULDN'T WORK ON THE KING-SIZE VERSION!
THAT DID IT! HIS SHIELD'S DOWN!
THAT'S OUR OPENING!
BEN! JOHNNY! SUE! IT'S TIME--HIT HIM WITH EVERYTHING YOU'VE GOT-- NOW!
WOW.
ALL THAT BELLYACHING... AND HE JUST WENT KABLOOIE.
LIKE A BIG, EVIL, COSMIC PIÑATA. BUT WITHOUT THE CANDY.

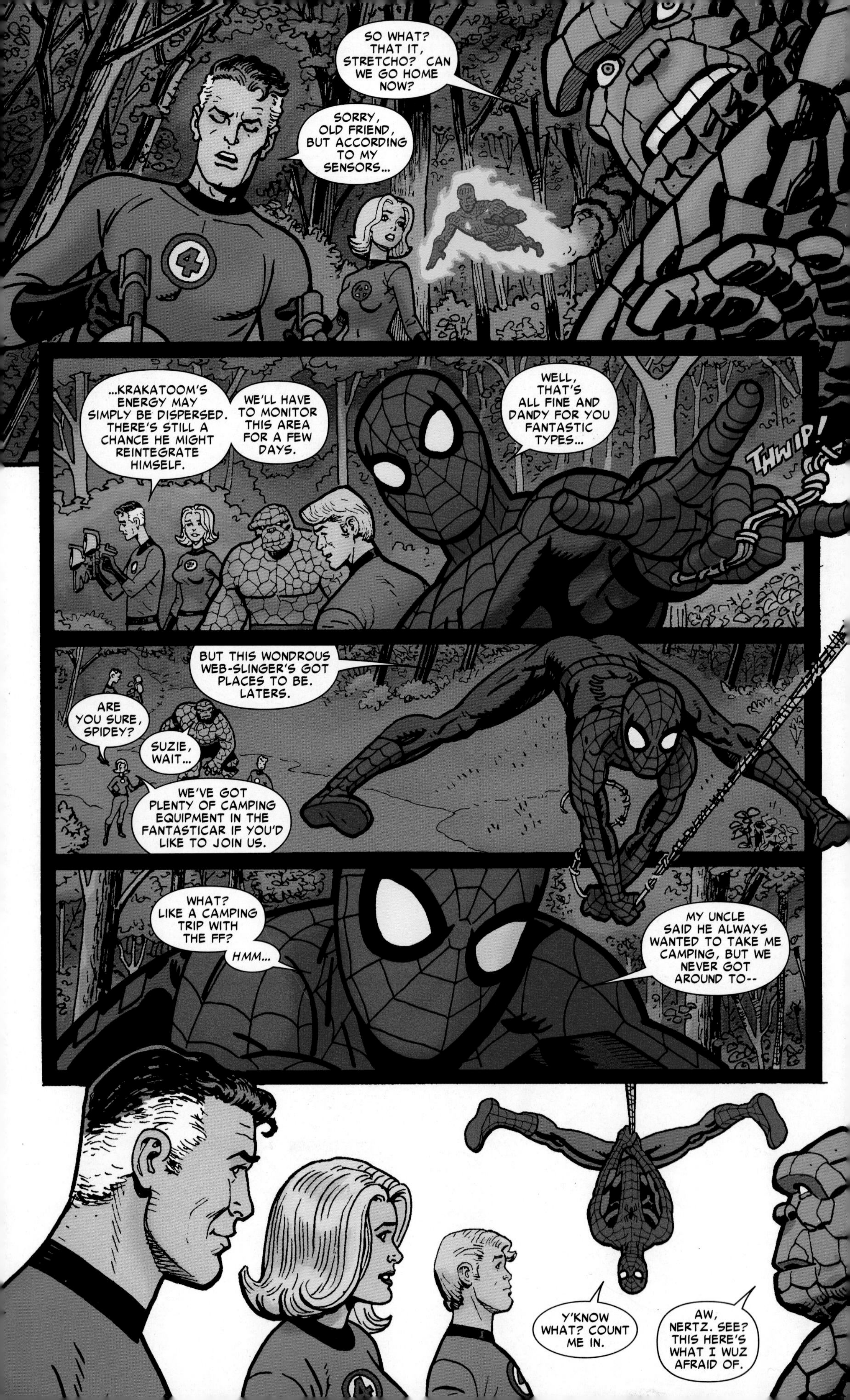

SO WHAT? THAT IT, STRETCHO? CAN WE GO HOME NOW?
SORRY, OLD FRIEND, BUT ACCORDING TO MY SENSORS...
...KRAKATOOM'S ENERGY MAY SIMPLY BE DISPERSED. THERE'S STILL A CHANCE HE MIGHT REINTEGRATE HIMSELF.
WE'LL HAVE TO MONITOR THIS AREA FOR A FEW DAYS.
WELL, THAT'S ALL FINE AND DANDY FOR YOU FANTASTIC TYPES...
THWIP!
BUT THIS WONDROUS WEB-SLINGER'S GOT PLACES TO BE. LATERS.
ARE YOU SURE, SPIDEY?
SUZIE, WAIT...
WE'VE GOT PLENTY OF CAMPING EQUIPMENT IN THE FANTASTICAR IF YOU'D LIKE TO JOIN US.
WHAT? LIKE A CAMPING TRIP WITH THE FF?
HMM...
MY UNCLE SAID HE ALWAYS WANTED TO TAKE ME CAMPING, BUT WE NEVER GOT AROUND TO--
Y'KNOW WHAT? COUNT ME IN.
AW, NERTZ. SEE? THIS HERE'S WHAT I WUZ AFRAID OF.

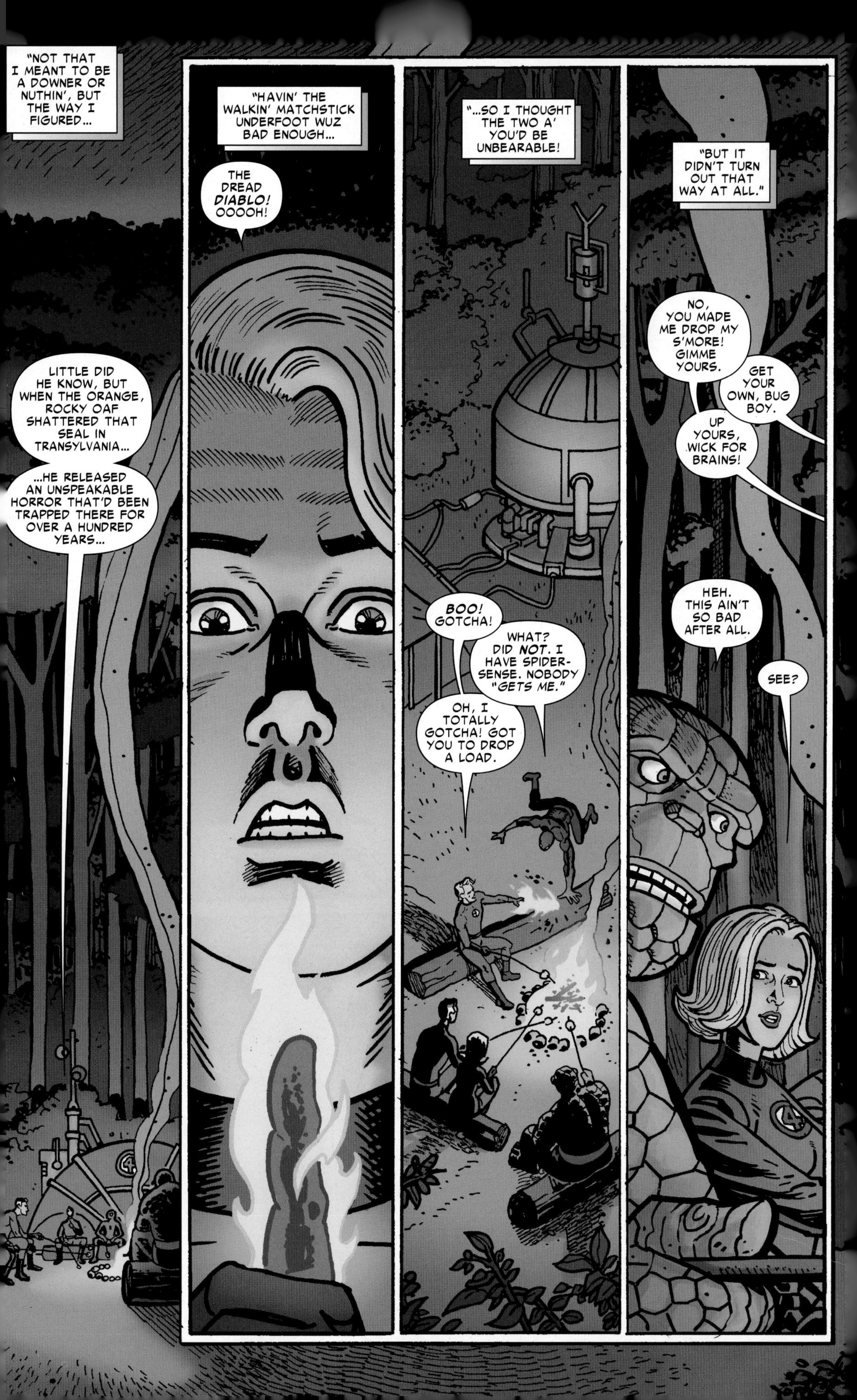
"NOT THAT I MEANT TO BE A DOWNER OR NUTHIN', BUT THE WAY I FIGURED...
LITTLE DID HE KNOW, BUT WHEN THE ORANGE, ROCKY OAF SHATTERED THAT SEAL IN TRANSYLVANIA...
...HE RELEASED AN UNSPEAKABLE HORROR THAT'D BEEN TRAPPED THERE FOR OVER A HUNDRED YEARS...
"HAVIN' THE WALKIN' MATCHSTICK UNDERFOOT WUZ BAD ENOUGH...
THE DREAD *DIABLO!* OOOOH!
"...SO I THOUGHT THE TWO A' YOU'D BE UNBEARABLE!
BOO! GOTCHA!
WHAT? DID **NOT**. I HAVE SPIDER-SENSE. NOBODY *"GETS ME."*
OH, I TOTALLY GOTCHA! GOT YOU TO DROP A LOAD.
"BUT IT DIDN'T TURN OUT THAT WAY AT ALL."
NO, YOU MADE ME DROP MY S'MORE! GIMME YOURS.
GET YOUR OWN, BUG BOY.
UP YOURS, WICK FOR BRAINS!
HEH. THIS AIN'T SO BAD AFTER ALL.
SEE?

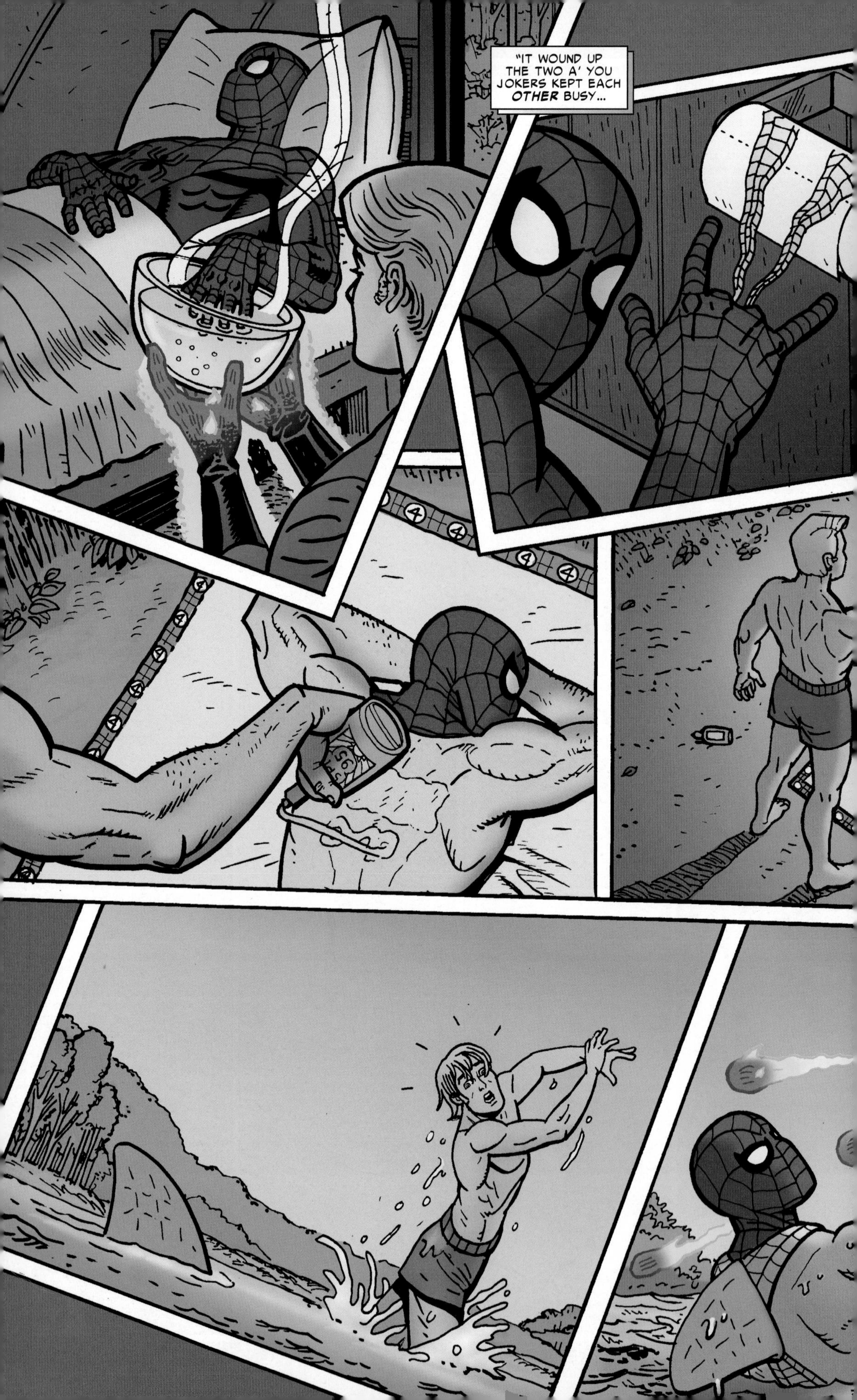
"IT WOUND UP THE TWO A' YOU JOKERS KEPT EACH OTHER BUSY...

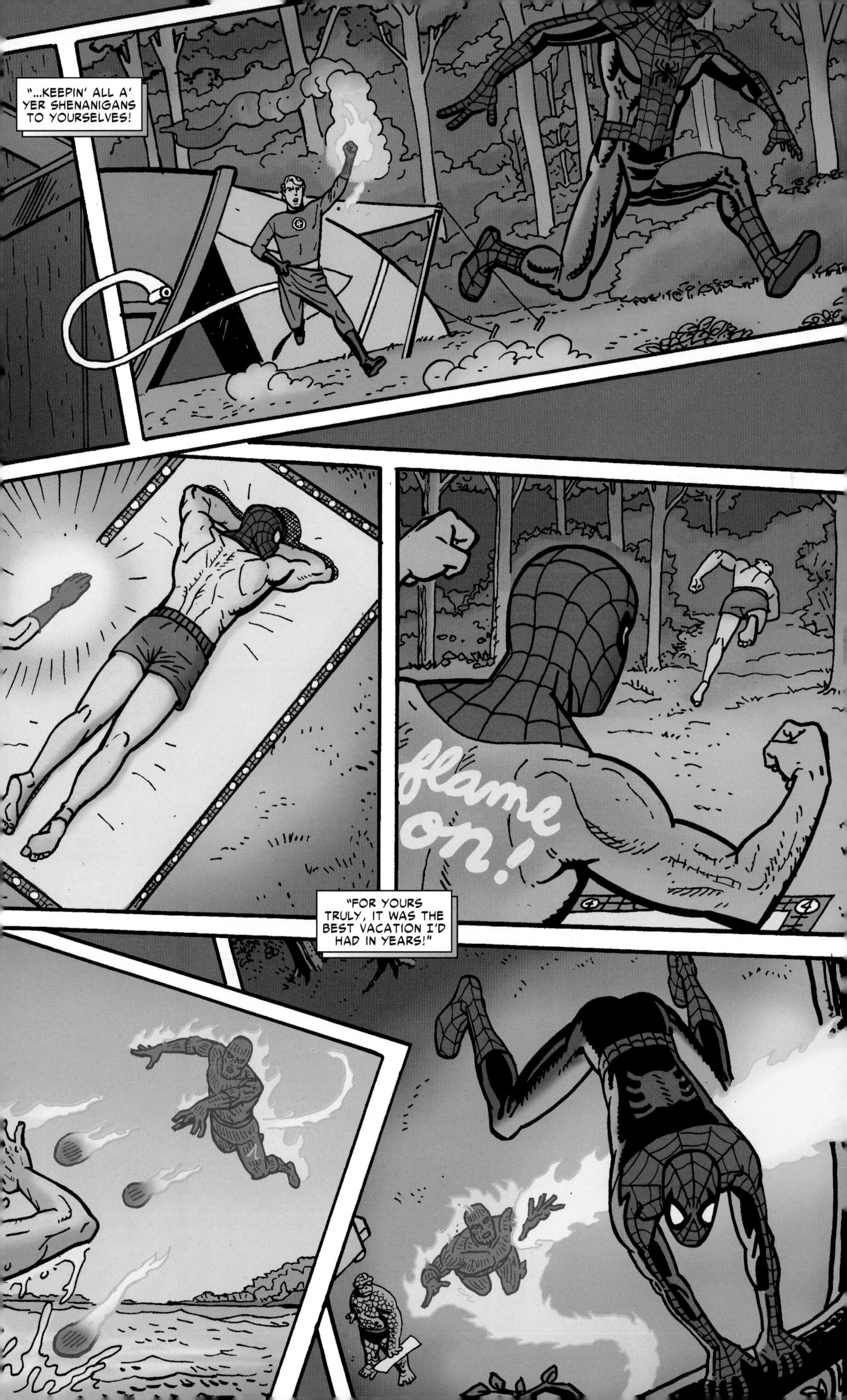
"...KEEPIN' ALL A' YER SHENANIGANS TO YOURSELVES!
flame on!
"FOR YOURS TRULY, IT WAS THE BEST VACATION I'D HAD IN YEARS!"

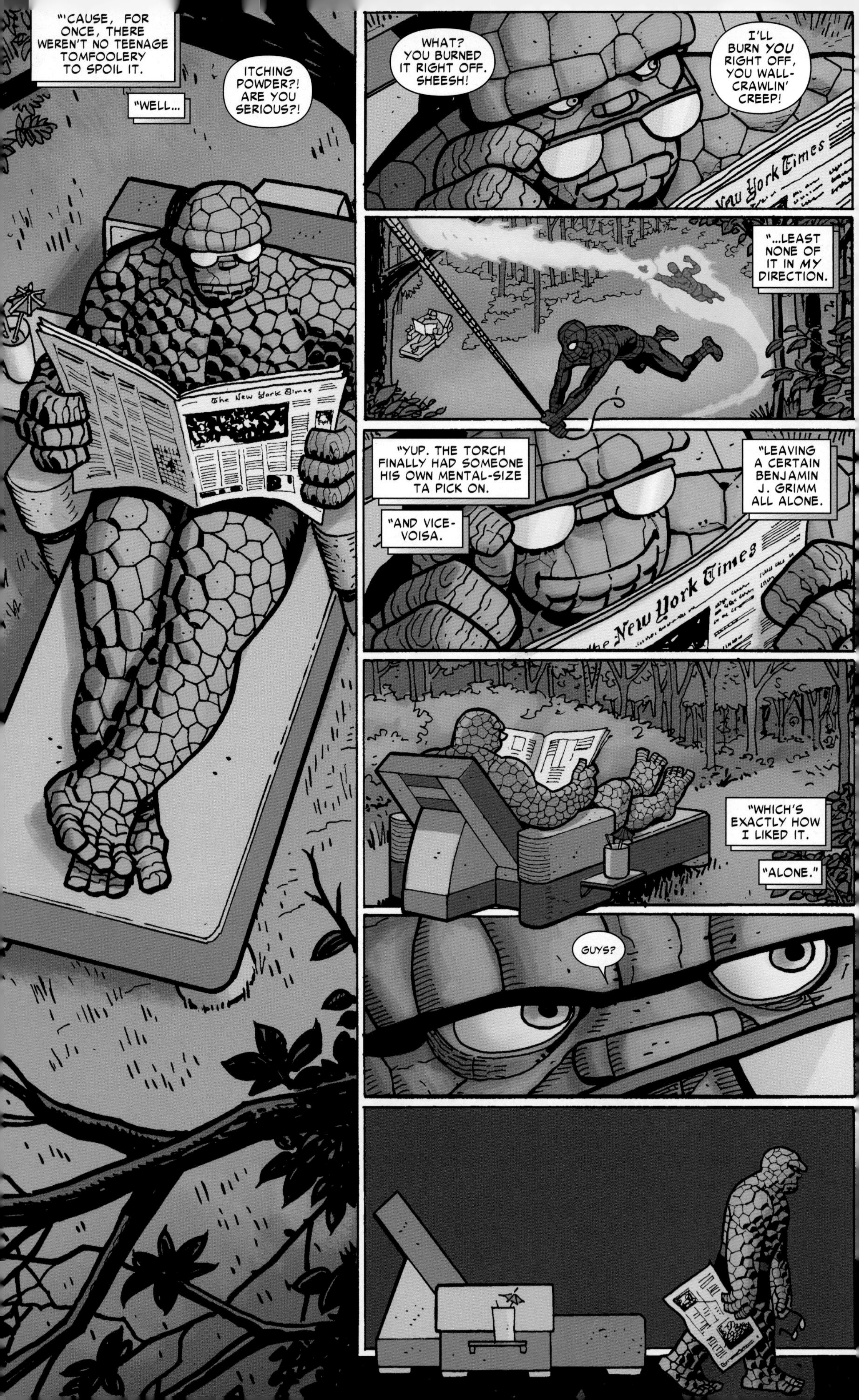
"'CAUSE, FOR ONCE, THERE WEREN'T NO TEENAGE TOMFOOLERY TO SPOIL IT.
"WELL...
ITCHING POWDER?! ARE YOU SERIOUS?!
WHAT? YOU BURNED IT RIGHT OFF. SHEESH!
I'LL BURN YOU RIGHT OFF, YOU WALL-CRAWLIN' CREEP!
"...LEAST NONE OF IT IN MY DIRECTION.
"YUP. THE TORCH FINALLY HAD SOMEONE HIS OWN MENTAL-SIZE TA PICK ON.
"AND VICE-VOISA.
"LEAVING A CERTAIN BENJAMIN J. GRIMM ALL ALONE.
"WHICH'S EXACTLY HOW I LIKED IT.
"ALONE."
GUYS?

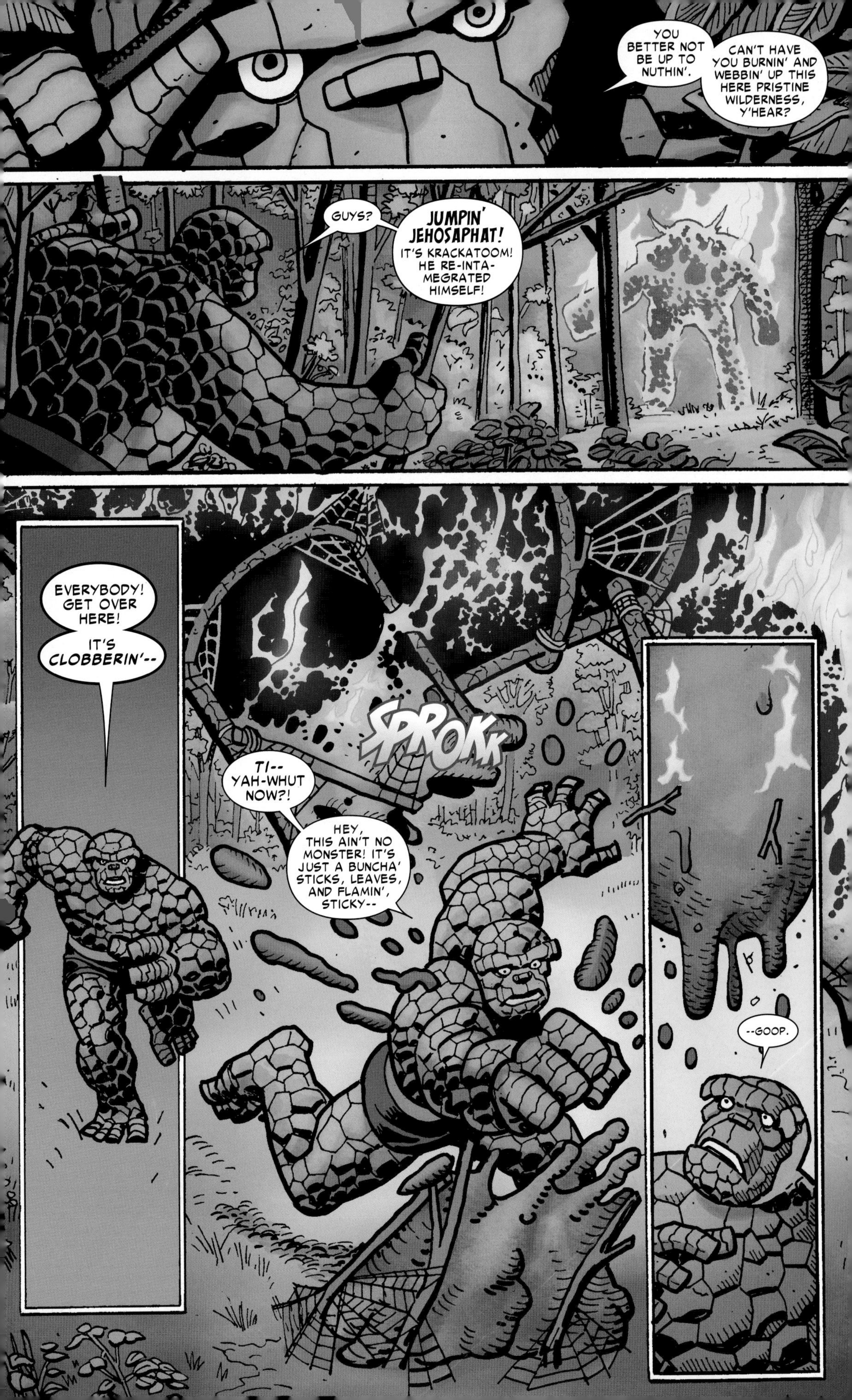

YOU BETTER NOT BE UP TO NUTHIN'.
CAN'T HAVE YOU BURNIN' AND WEBBIN' UP THIS HERE PRISTINE WILDERNESS, Y'HEAR?
GUYS?
JUMPIN' JEHOSAPHAT! IT'S KRACKATOOM! HE RE-INTA-MEGRATED HIMSELF!
EVERYBODY! GET OVER HERE!
IT'S CLOBBERIN'--
SPROKK
TI-- YAH-WHUT NOW?!
HEY, THIS AIN'T NO MONSTER! IT'S JUST A BUNCHA' STICKS, LEAVES, AND FLAMIN', STICKY--
--GOOP.

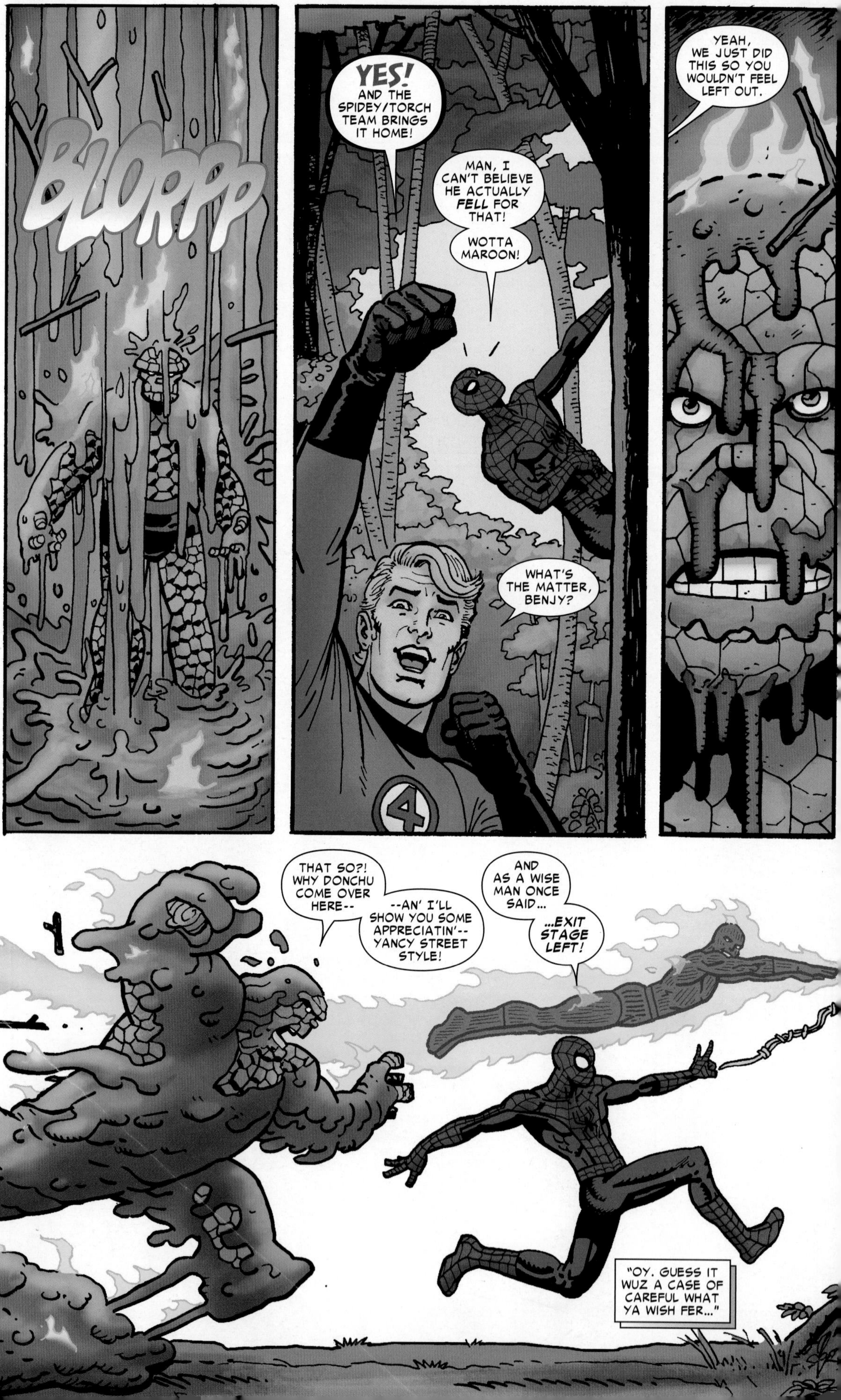
BLORPP
YES! AND THE SPIDEY/TORCH TEAM BRINGS IT HOME!
MAN, I CAN'T BELIEVE HE ACTUALLY FELL FOR THAT!
WOTTA MAROON!
WHAT'S THE MATTER, BENJY?
YEAH, WE JUST DID THIS SO YOU WOULDN'T FEEL LEFT OUT.
THAT SO?! WHY DONCHU COME OVER HERE--
--AN' I'LL SHOW YOU SOME APPRECIATIN'-- YANCY STREET STYLE!
AND AS A WISE MAN ONCE SAID...
...EXIT STAGE LEFT!
"OY. GUESS IT WUZ A CASE OF CAREFUL WHAT YA WISH FER..."

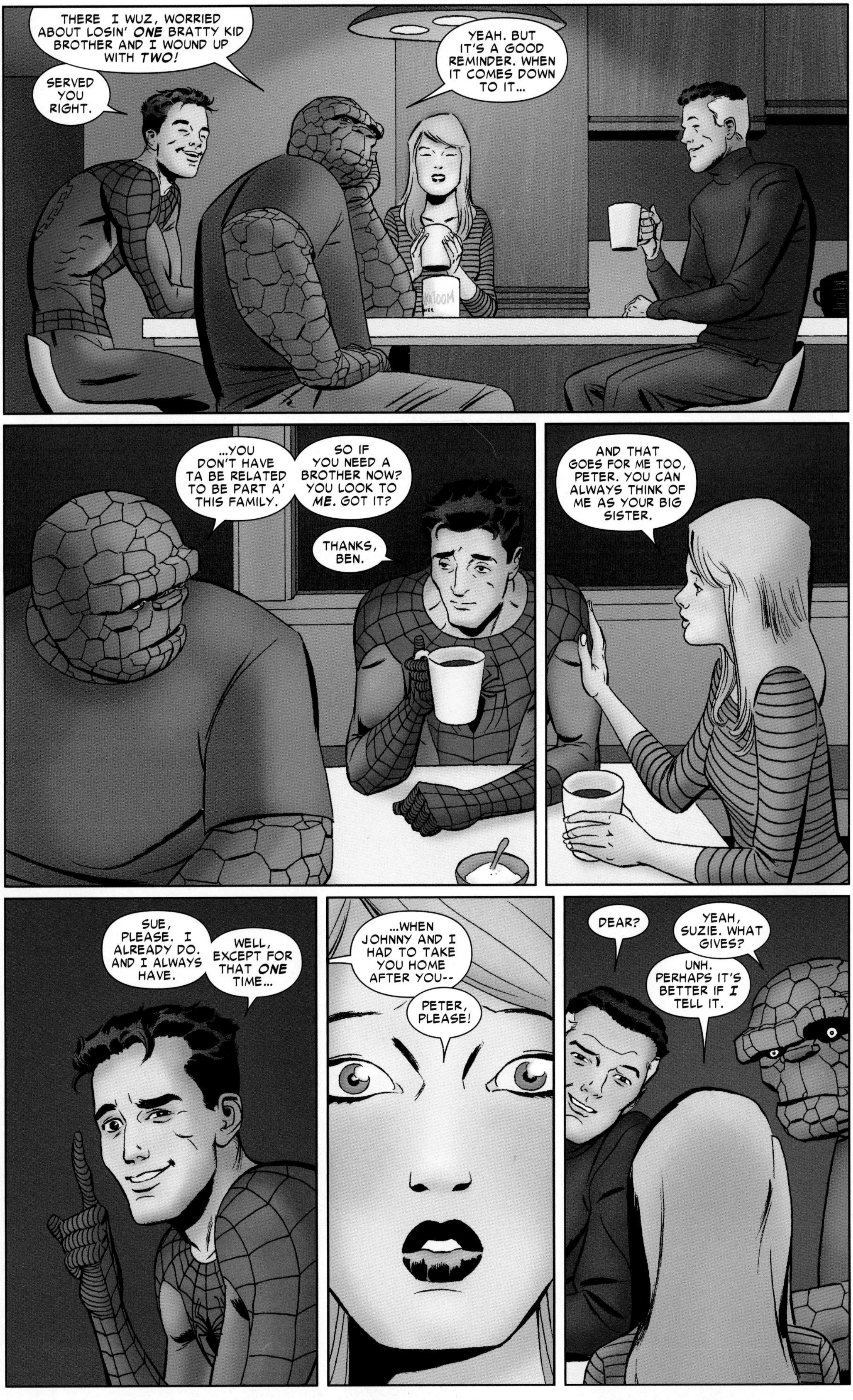
THERE I WUZ, WORRIED ABOUT LOSIN' ONE BRATTY KID BROTHER AND I WOUND UP WITH TWO!
SERVED YOU RIGHT.
YEAH. BUT IT'S A GOOD REMINDER. WHEN IT COMES DOWN TO IT...
...YOU DON'T HAVE TA BE RELATED TO BE PART A' THIS FAMILY.
SO IF YOU NEED A BROTHER NOW? YOU LOOK TO ME. GOT IT?
THANKS, BEN.
AND THAT GOES FOR ME TOO, PETER. YOU CAN ALWAYS THINK OF ME AS YOUR BIG SISTER.
SUE, PLEASE. I ALREADY DO. AND I ALWAYS HAVE.
WELL, EXCEPT FOR THAT ONE TIME...
...WHEN JOHNNY AND I HAD TO TAKE YOU HOME AFTER YOU--
PETER, PLEASE!
DEAR?
YEAH, SUZIE. WHAT GIVES?
UNH. PERHAPS IT'S BETTER IF I TELL IT.

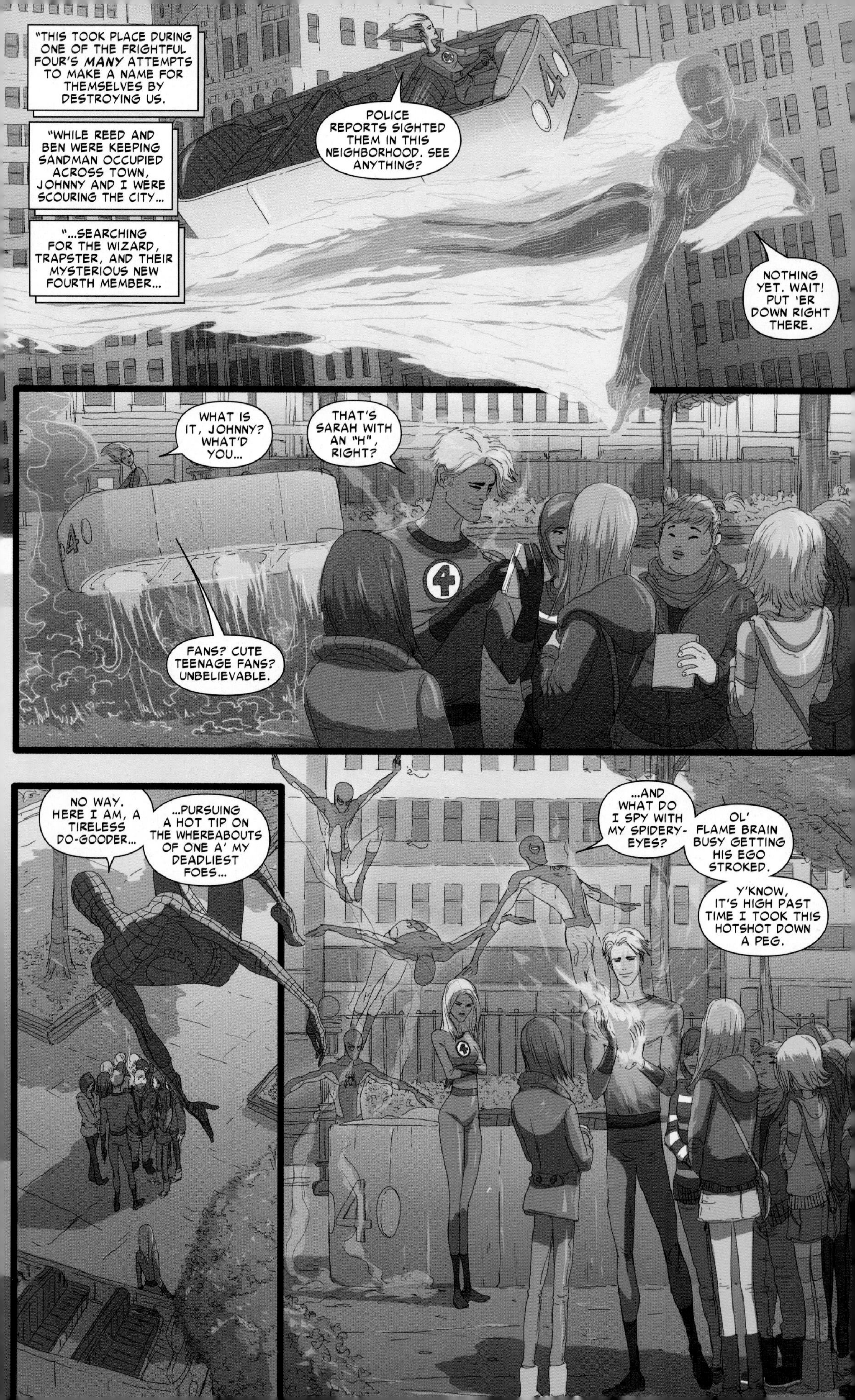
"THIS TOOK PLACE DURING ONE OF THE FRIGHTFUL FOUR'S MANY ATTEMPTS TO MAKE A NAME FOR THEMSELVES BY DESTROYING US.
"WHILE REED AND BEN WERE KEEPING SANDMAN OCCUPIED ACROSS TOWN, JOHNNY AND I WERE SCOURING THE CITY...
"...SEARCHING FOR THE WIZARD, TRAPSTER, AND THEIR MYSTERIOUS NEW FOURTH MEMBER...
POLICE REPORTS SIGHTED THEM IN THIS NEIGHBORHOOD. SEE ANYTHING?
NOTHING YET. WAIT! PUT 'ER DOWN RIGHT THERE.
WHAT IS IT, JOHNNY? WHAT'D YOU...
THAT'S SARAH WITH AN "H", RIGHT?
FANS? CUTE TEENAGE FANS? UNBELIEVABLE.
NO WAY. HERE I AM, A TIRELESS DO-GOODER...
...PURSUING A HOT TIP ON THE WHEREABOUTS OF ONE A' MY DEADLIEST FOES...
...AND WHAT DO I SPY WITH MY SPIDERY-EYES?
OL' FLAME BRAIN BUSY GETTING HIS EGO STROKED.
Y'KNOW, IT'S HIGH PAST TIME I TOOK THIS HOTSHOT DOWN A PEG.

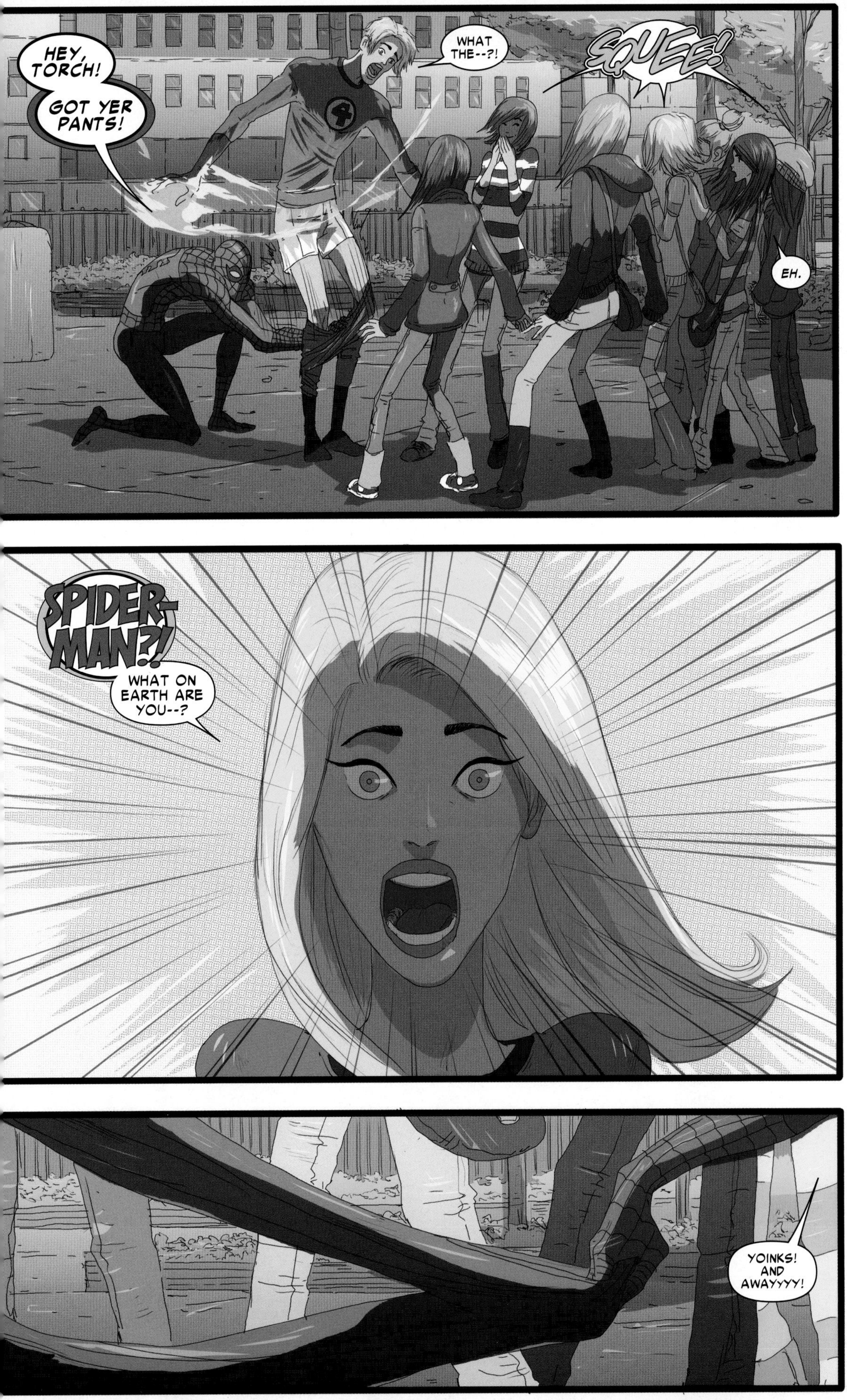
HEY, TORCH!
GOT YER PANTS!
WHAT THE--?!
SQUEE!
EH.
SPIDER-MAN?!
WHAT ON EARTH ARE YOU--?
YOINKS! AND AWAYYYY!

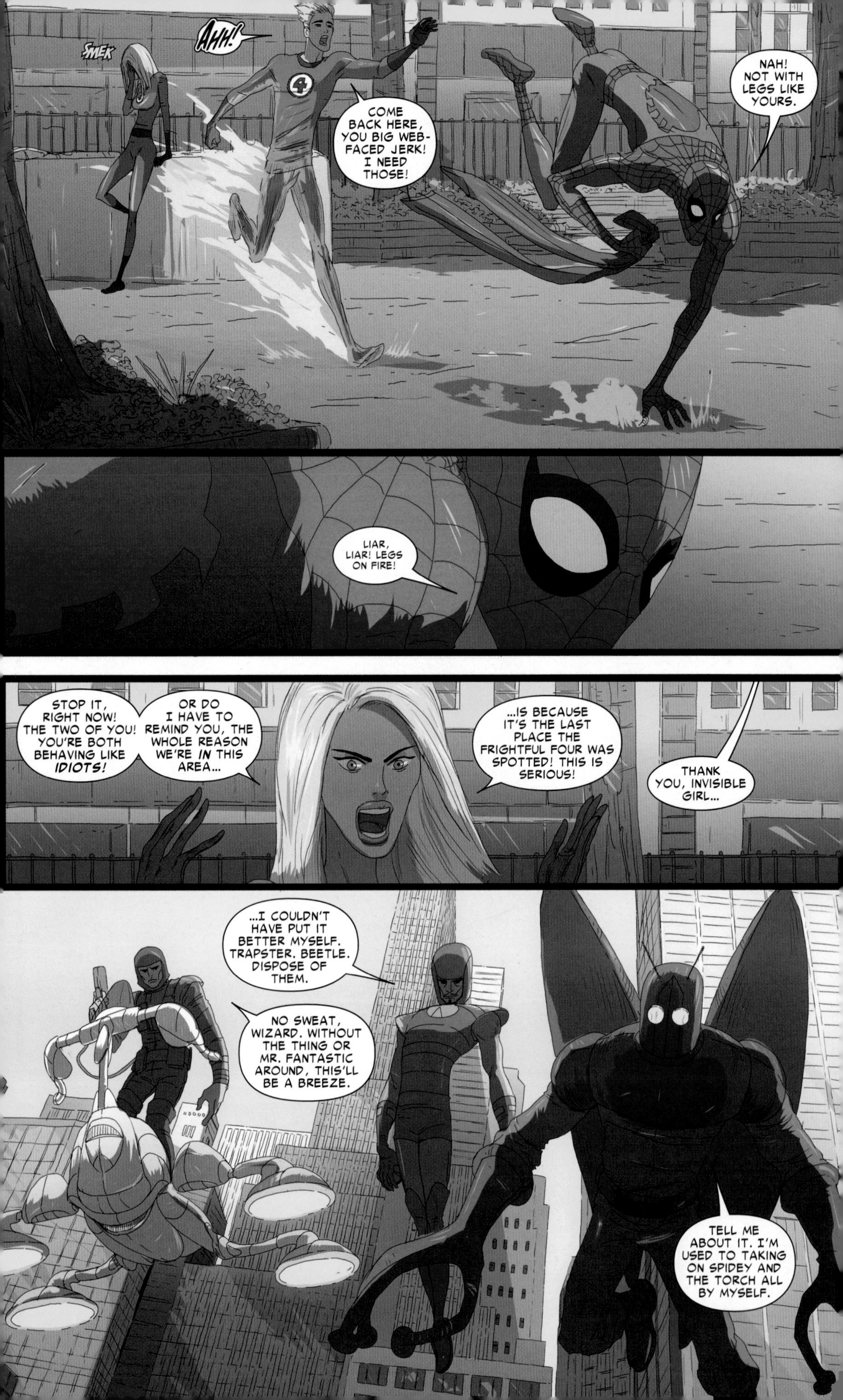
SMEK
AHH!
COME BACK HERE, YOU BIG WEB-FACED JERK! I NEED THOSE!
NAH! NOT WITH LEGS LIKE YOURS.
LIAR, LIAR! LEGS ON FIRE!
STOP IT, RIGHT NOW! THE TWO OF YOU! YOU'RE BOTH BEHAVING LIKE IDIOTS!
OR DO I HAVE TO REMIND YOU, THE WHOLE REASON WE'RE IN THIS AREA...
...IS BECAUSE IT'S THE LAST PLACE THE FRIGHTFUL FOUR WAS SPOTTED! THIS IS SERIOUS!
THANK YOU, INVISIBLE GIRL...
...I COULDN'T HAVE PUT IT BETTER MYSELF. TRAPSTER. BEETLE. DISPOSE OF THEM.
NO SWEAT, WIZARD. WITHOUT THE THING OR MR. FANTASTIC AROUND, THIS'LL BE A BREEZE.
TELL ME ABOUT IT. I'M USED TO TAKING ON SPIDEY AND THE TORCH ALL BY MYSELF.

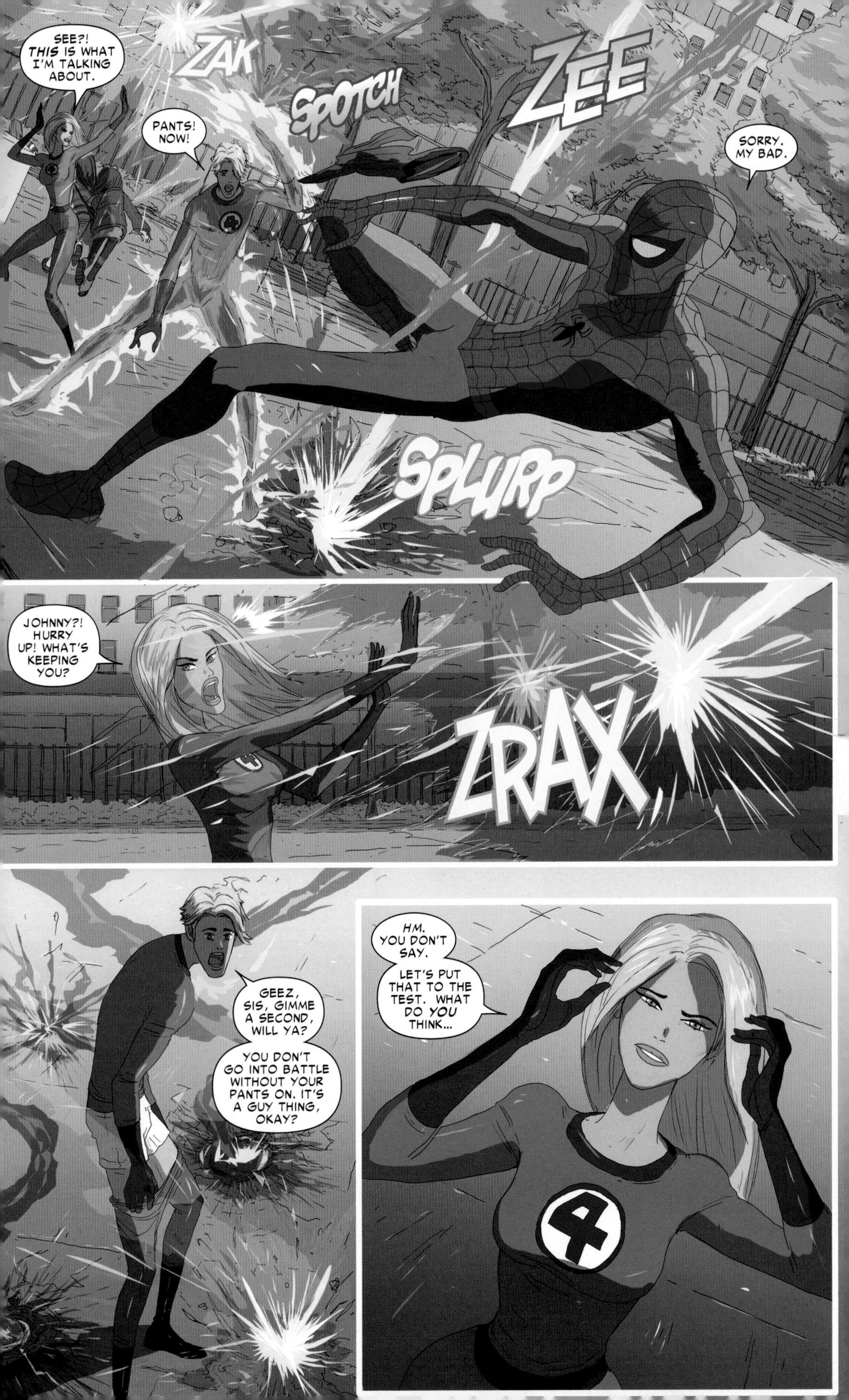
SEE?! THIS IS WHAT I'M TALKING ABOUT.
ZAK
SPOTCH
ZEE
PANTS! NOW!
SORRY. MY BAD.
SPLURP
JOHNNY?! HURRY UP! WHAT'S KEEPING YOU?
ZRAX
GEEZ, SIS, GIMME A SECOND, WILL YA?
YOU DON'T GO INTO BATTLE WITHOUT YOUR PANTS ON. IT'S A GUY THING, OKAY?
HM. YOU DON'T SAY.
LET'S PUT THAT TO THE TEST. WHAT DO YOU THINK...

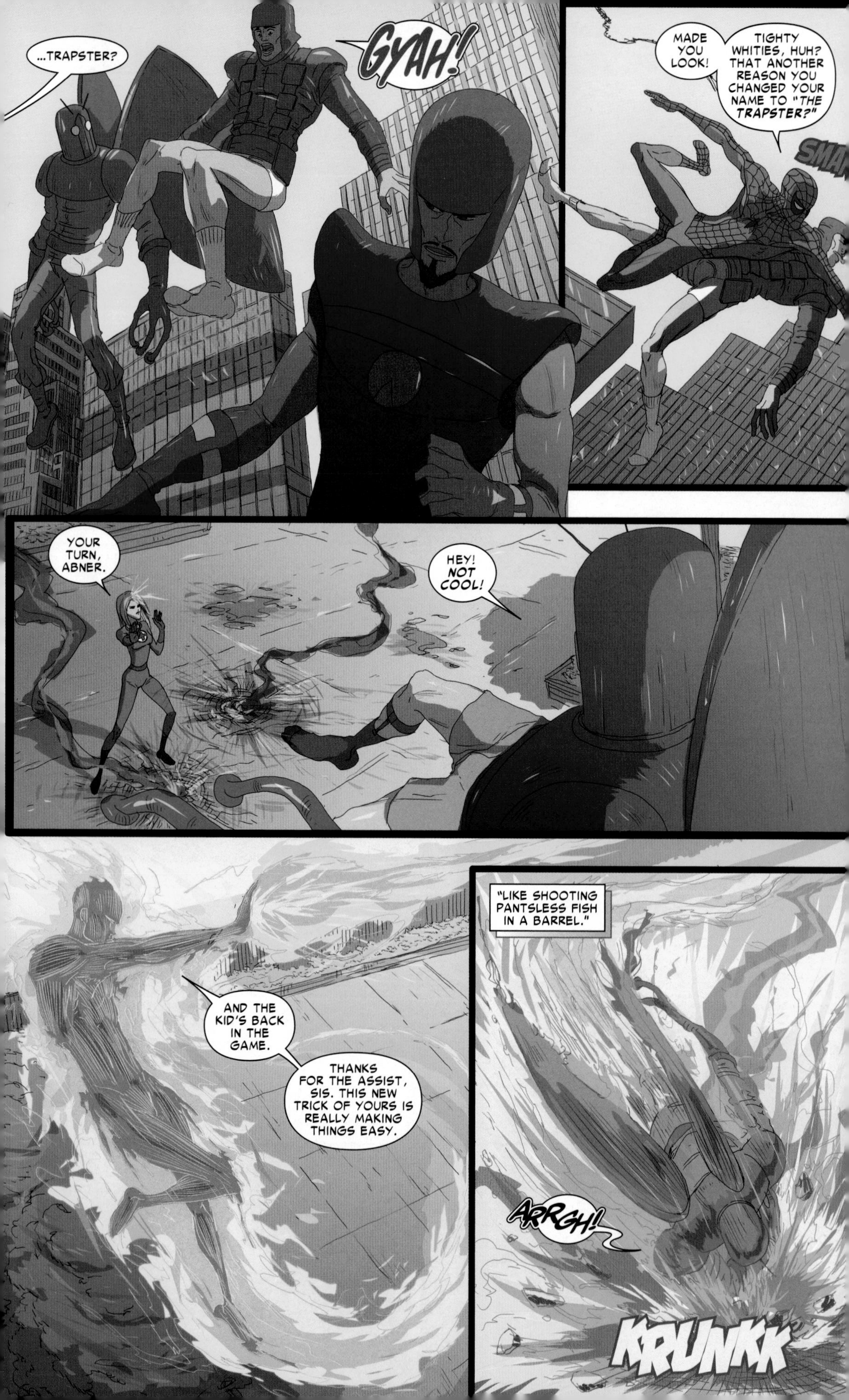
...TRAPSTER?
GYAH!
MADE YOU LOOK!
TIGHTY WHITIES, HUH? THAT ANOTHER REASON YOU CHANGED YOUR NAME TO "THE TRAPSTER?"
YOUR TURN, ABNER.
HEY! NOT COOL!
AND THE KID'S BACK IN THE GAME.
THANKS FOR THE ASSIST, SIS. THIS NEW TRICK OF YOURS IS REALLY MAKING THINGS EASY.
"LIKE SHOOTING PANTSLESS FISH IN A BARREL."
ARRGH!
KRUNKK

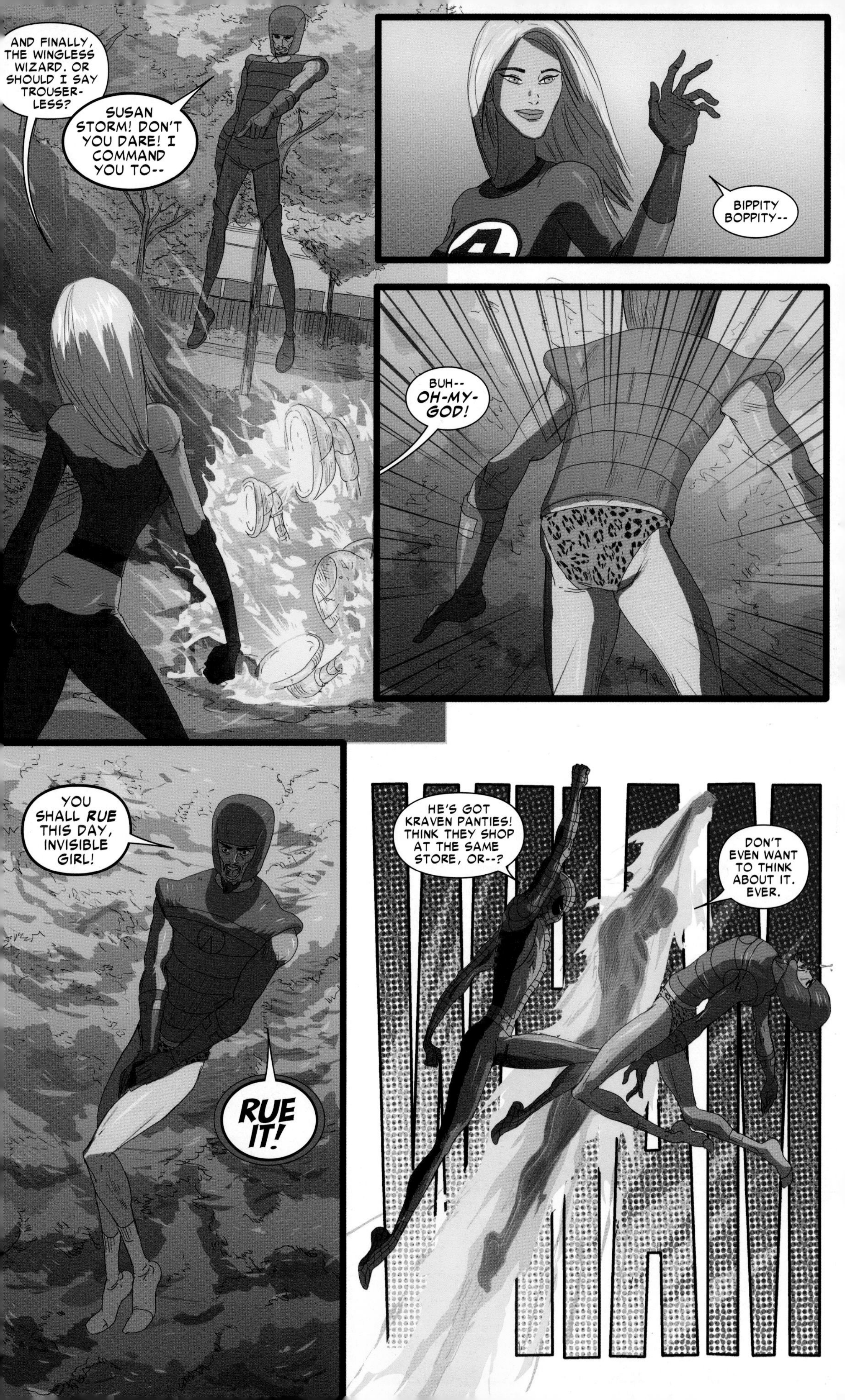

AND FINALLY, THE WINGLESS WIZARD. OR SHOULD I SAY TROUSER-LESS?
SUSAN STORM! DON'T YOU DARE! I COMMAND YOU TO--
BIPPITY BOPPITY--
BUH-- OH-MY-GOD!
YOU SHALL RUE THIS DAY, INVISIBLE GIRL!
RUE IT!
HE'S GOT KRAVEN PANTIES! THINK THEY SHOP AT THE SAME STORE, OR--?
DON'T EVEN WANT TO THINK ABOUT IT. EVER.

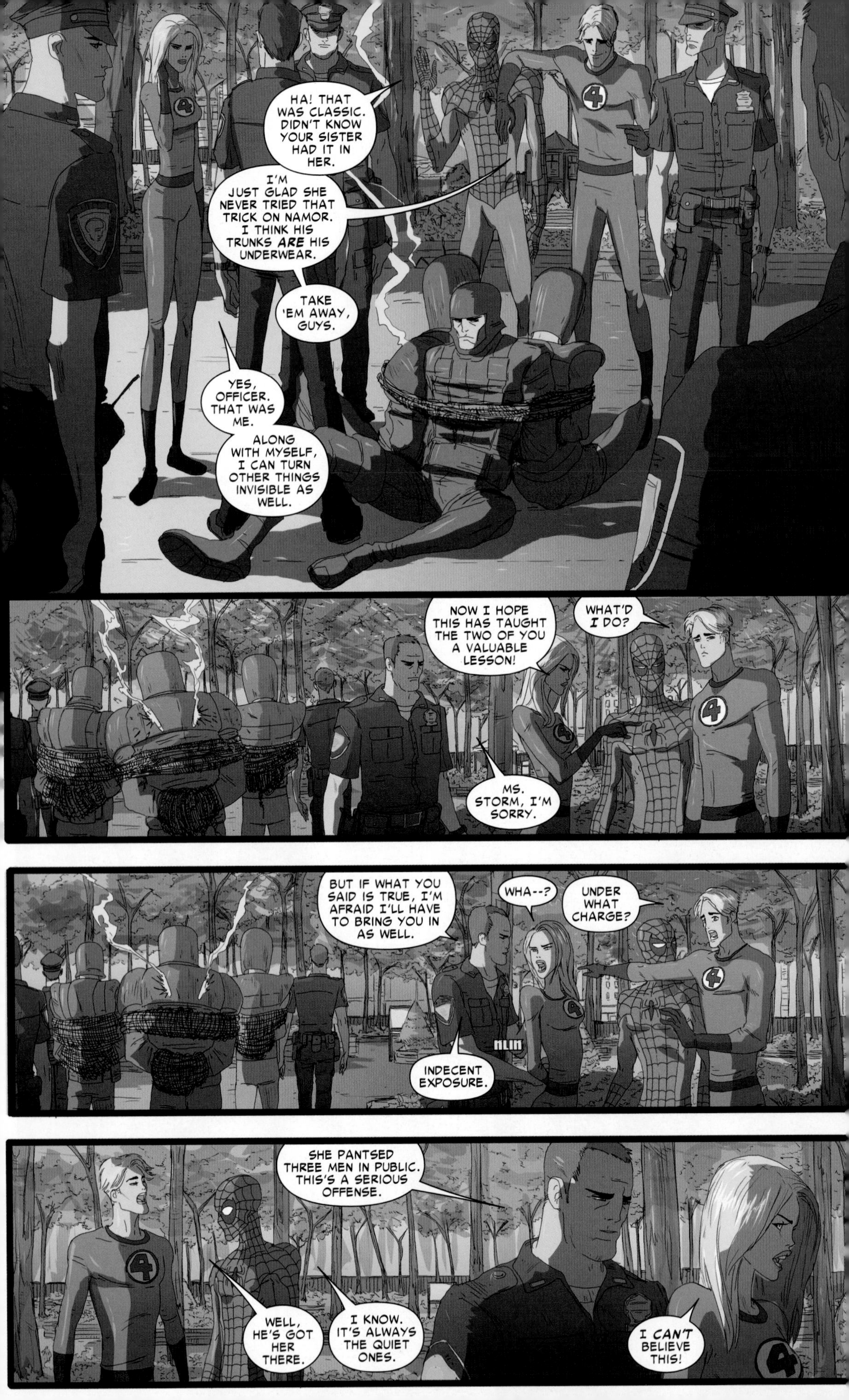
HA! THAT WAS CLASSIC. DIDN'T KNOW YOUR SISTER HAD IT IN HER.
I'M JUST GLAD SHE NEVER TRIED THAT TRICK ON NAMOR. I THINK HIS TRUNKS *ARE* HIS UNDERWEAR.
TAKE 'EM AWAY, GUYS.
YES, OFFICER. THAT WAS ME.
ALONG WITH MYSELF, I CAN TURN OTHER THINGS INVISIBLE AS WELL.
NOW I HOPE THIS HAS TAUGHT THE TWO OF YOU A VALUABLE LESSON!
WHAT'D *I* DO?
MS. STORM, I'M SORRY.
BUT IF WHAT YOU SAID IS TRUE, I'M AFRAID I'LL HAVE TO BRING YOU IN AS WELL.
WHA--?
UNDER WHAT CHARGE?
INDECENT EXPOSURE.
SHE PANTSED THREE MEN IN PUBLIC. THIS'S A SERIOUS OFFENSE.
WELL, HE'S GOT HER THERE.
I KNOW. IT'S ALWAYS THE QUIET ONES.
I *CAN'T* BELIEVE THIS!

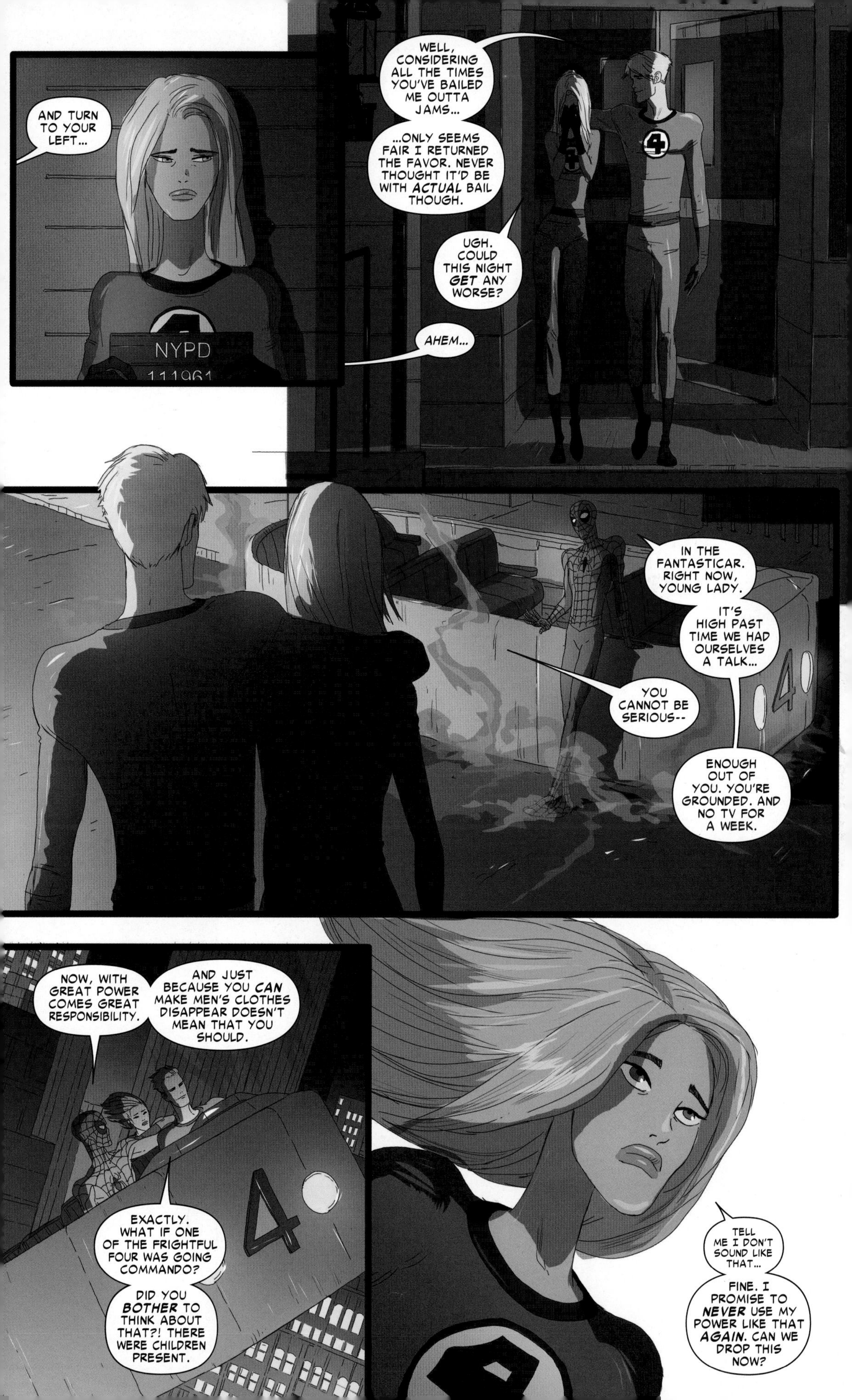
AND TURN TO YOUR LEFT...
NYPD
111961
WELL, CONSIDERING ALL THE TIMES YOU'VE BAILED ME OUTTA JAMS...
...ONLY SEEMS FAIR I RETURNED THE FAVOR. NEVER THOUGHT IT'D BE WITH ACTUAL BAIL THOUGH.
UGH. COULD THIS NIGHT GET ANY WORSE?
AHEM...
IN THE FANTASTICAR. RIGHT NOW, YOUNG LADY.
IT'S HIGH PAST TIME WE HAD OURSELVES A TALK...
YOU CANNOT BE SERIOUS--
ENOUGH OUT OF YOU. YOU'RE GROUNDED. AND NO TV FOR A WEEK.
NOW, WITH GREAT POWER COMES GREAT RESPONSIBILITY.
AND JUST BECAUSE YOU CAN MAKE MEN'S CLOTHES DISAPPEAR DOESN'T MEAN THAT YOU SHOULD.
EXACTLY. WHAT IF ONE OF THE FRIGHTFUL FOUR WAS GOING COMMANDO?
DID YOU BOTHER TO THINK ABOUT THAT?! THERE WERE CHILDREN PRESENT.
TELL ME I DON'T SOUND LIKE THAT...
FINE. I PROMISE TO NEVER USE MY POWER LIKE THAT AGAIN. CAN WE DROP THIS NOW?

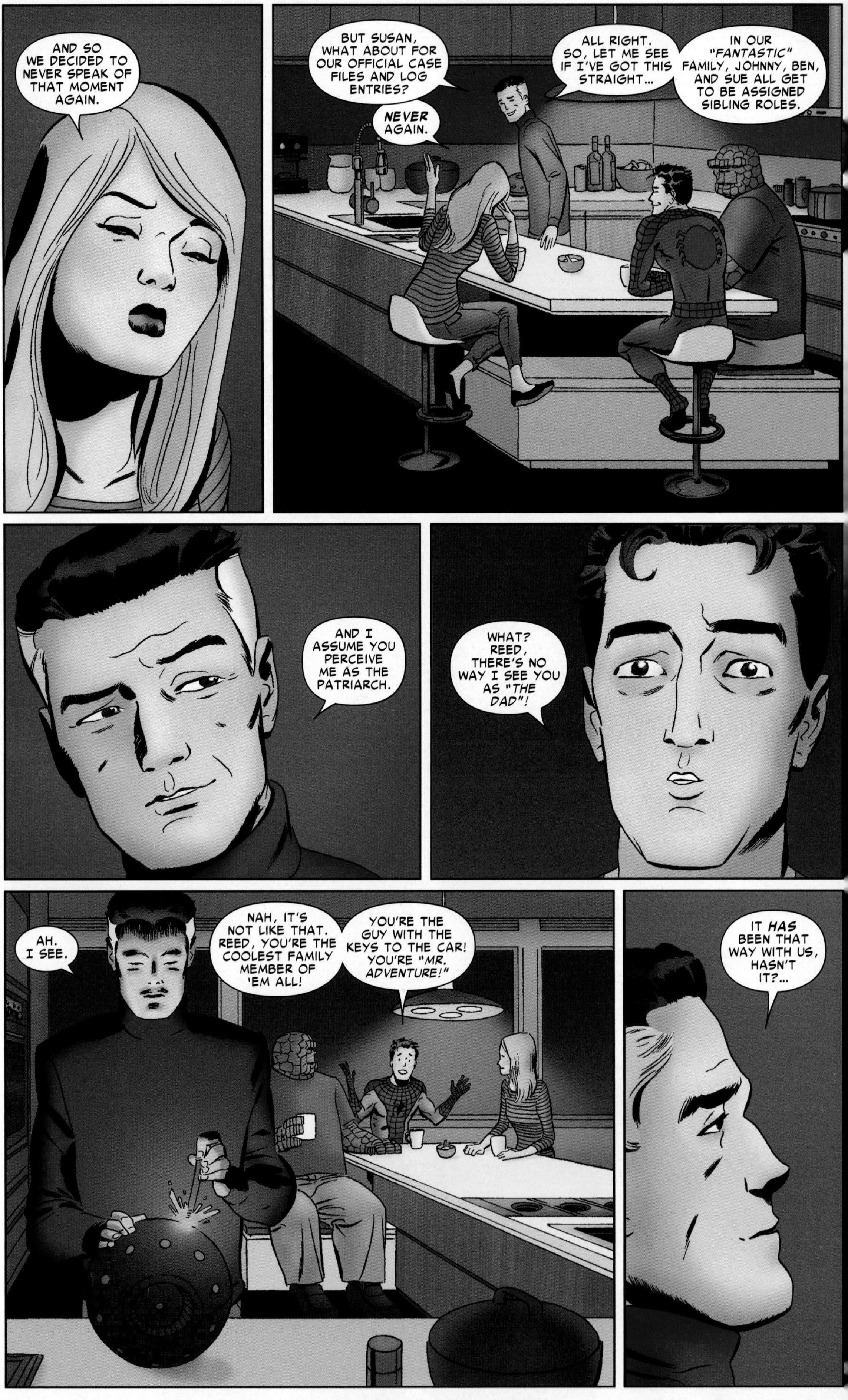
AND SO WE DECIDED TO NEVER SPEAK OF THAT MOMENT AGAIN.
BUT SUSAN, WHAT ABOUT FOR OUR OFFICIAL CASE FILES AND LOG ENTRIES?
NEVER AGAIN.
ALL RIGHT. SO, LET ME SEE IF I'VE GOT THIS STRAIGHT...
IN OUR "FANTASTIC" FAMILY, JOHNNY, BEN, AND SUE ALL GET TO BE ASSIGNED SIBLING ROLES.
AND I ASSUME YOU PERCEIVE ME AS THE PATRIARCH.
WHAT? REED, THERE'S NO WAY I SEE YOU AS "THE DAD"!
AH. I SEE.
NAH, IT'S NOT LIKE THAT. REED, YOU'RE THE COOLEST FAMILY MEMBER OF 'EM ALL!
YOU'RE THE GUY WITH THE KEYS TO THE CAR! YOU'RE "MR. ADVENTURE!"
IT HAS BEEN THAT WAY WITH US, HASN'T IT?...

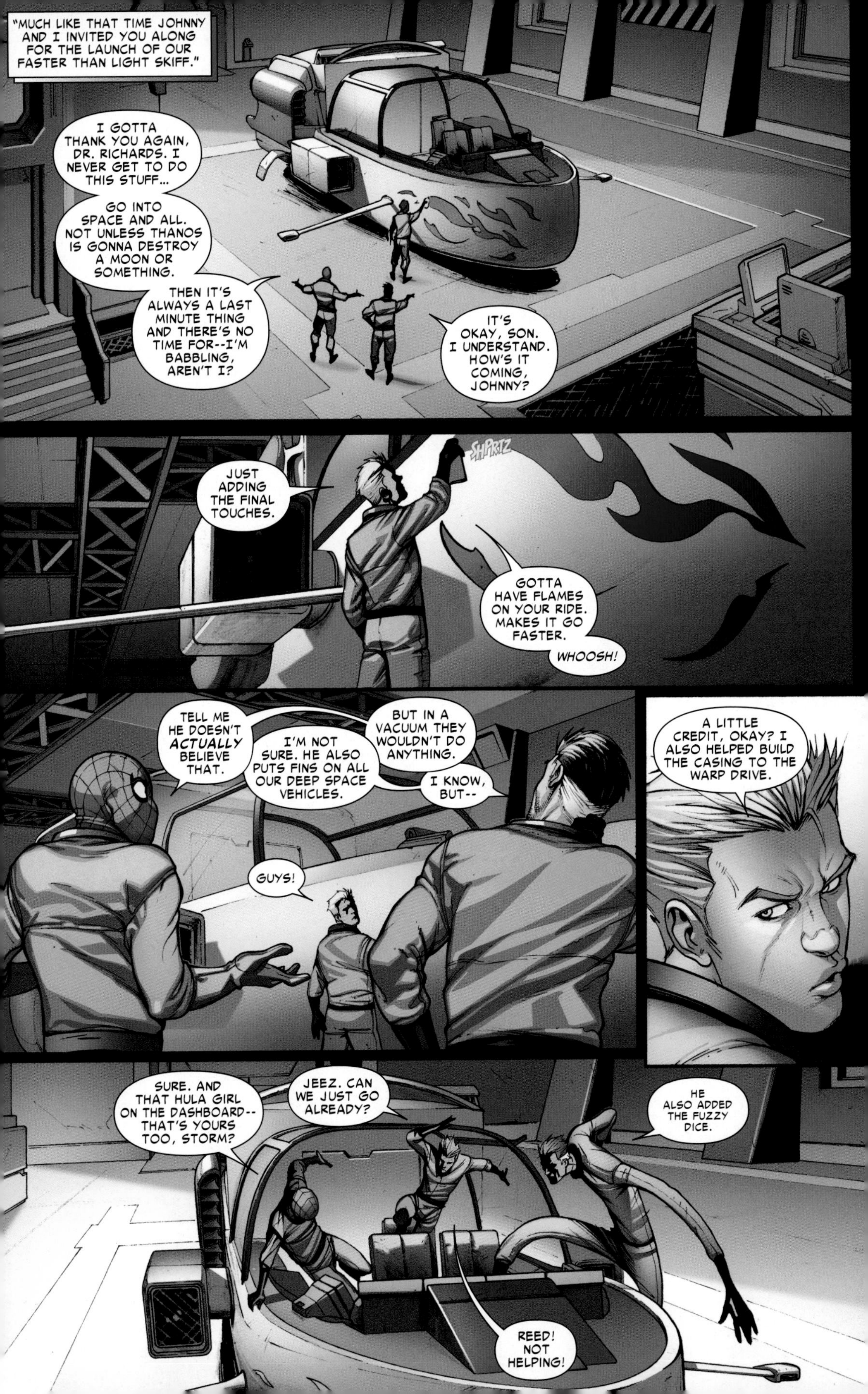
"MUCH LIKE THAT TIME JOHNNY AND I INVITED YOU ALONG FOR THE LAUNCH OF OUR FASTER THAN LIGHT SKIFF."
I GOTTA THANK YOU AGAIN, DR. RICHARDS. I NEVER GET TO DO THIS STUFF...
GO INTO SPACE AND ALL. NOT UNLESS THANOS IS GONNA DESTROY A MOON OR SOMETHING.
THEN IT'S ALWAYS A LAST MINUTE THING AND THERE'S NO TIME FOR--I'M BABBLING, AREN'T I?
IT'S OKAY, SON. I UNDERSTAND. HOW'S IT COMING, JOHNNY?
SHPRTZ
JUST ADDING THE FINAL TOUCHES.
GOTTA HAVE FLAMES ON YOUR RIDE. MAKES IT GO FASTER.
WHOOSH!
TELL ME HE DOESN'T ACTUALLY BELIEVE THAT.
I'M NOT SURE. HE ALSO PUTS FINS ON ALL OUR DEEP SPACE VEHICLES.
BUT IN A VACUUM THEY WOULDN'T DO ANYTHING.
I KNOW, BUT--
GUYS!
A LITTLE CREDIT, OKAY? I ALSO HELPED BUILD THE CASING TO THE WARP DRIVE.
SURE. AND THAT HULA GIRL ON THE DASHBOARD--THAT'S YOURS TOO, STORM?
JEEZ. CAN WE JUST GO ALREADY?
HE ALSO ADDED THE FUZZY DICE.
REED! NOT HELPING!

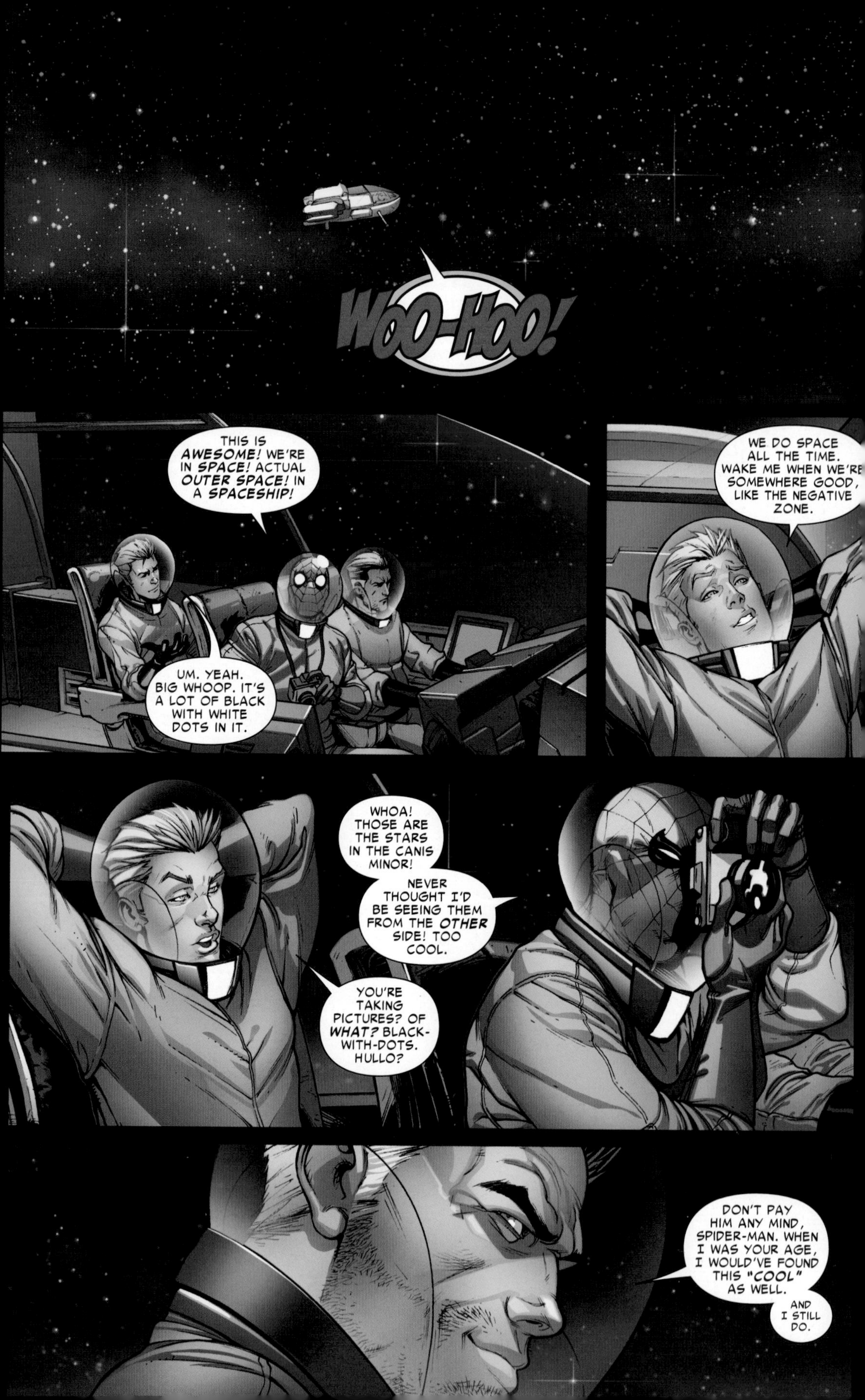
WOO-HOO!
THIS IS AWESOME! WE'RE IN SPACE! ACTUAL OUTER SPACE! IN A SPACESHIP!
UM. YEAH. BIG WHOOP. IT'S A LOT OF BLACK WITH WHITE DOTS IN IT.
WE DO SPACE ALL THE TIME. WAKE ME WHEN WE'RE SOMEWHERE GOOD, LIKE THE NEGATIVE ZONE.
WHOA! THOSE ARE THE STARS IN THE CANIS MINOR!
NEVER THOUGHT I'D BE SEEING THEM FROM THE OTHER SIDE! TOO COOL.
YOU'RE TAKING PICTURES? OF WHAT? BLACK-WITH-DOTS. HULLO?
DON'T PAY HIM ANY MIND, SPIDER-MAN. WHEN I WAS YOUR AGE, I WOULD'VE FOUND THIS "COOL" AS WELL.
AND I STILL DO.

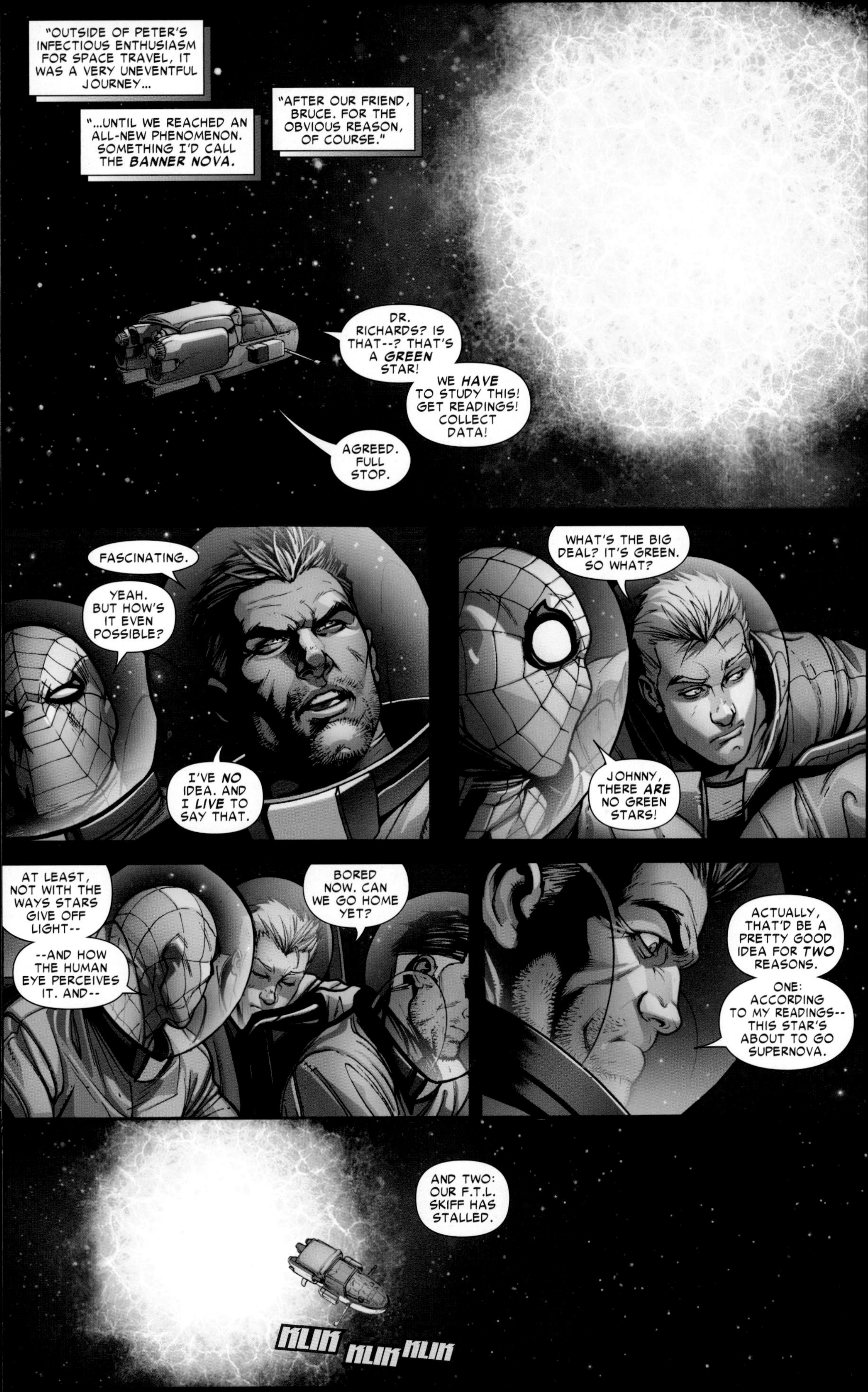
"OUTSIDE OF PETER'S INFECTIOUS ENTHUSIASM FOR SPACE TRAVEL, IT WAS A VERY UNEVENTFUL JOURNEY...
"...UNTIL WE REACHED AN ALL-NEW PHENOMENON. SOMETHING I'D CALL THE BANNER NOVA.
"AFTER OUR FRIEND, BRUCE. FOR THE OBVIOUS REASON, OF COURSE."
DR. RICHARDS? IS THAT--? THAT'S A GREEN STAR!
WE HAVE TO STUDY THIS! GET READINGS! COLLECT DATA!
AGREED. FULL STOP.
FASCINATING.
YEAH. BUT HOW'S IT EVEN POSSIBLE?
I'VE NO IDEA. AND I LIVE TO SAY THAT.
WHAT'S THE BIG DEAL? IT'S GREEN. SO WHAT?
JOHNNY, THERE ARE NO GREEN STARS!
AT LEAST, NOT WITH THE WAYS STARS GIVE OFF LIGHT--
--AND HOW THE HUMAN EYE PERCEIVES IT. AND--
BORED NOW. CAN WE GO HOME YET?
ACTUALLY, THAT'D BE A PRETTY GOOD IDEA FOR TWO REASONS.
ONE: ACCORDING TO MY READINGS-- THIS STAR'S ABOUT TO GO SUPERNOVA.
AND TWO: OUR F.T.L. SKIFF HAS STALLED.
KLIK KLIK KLIK

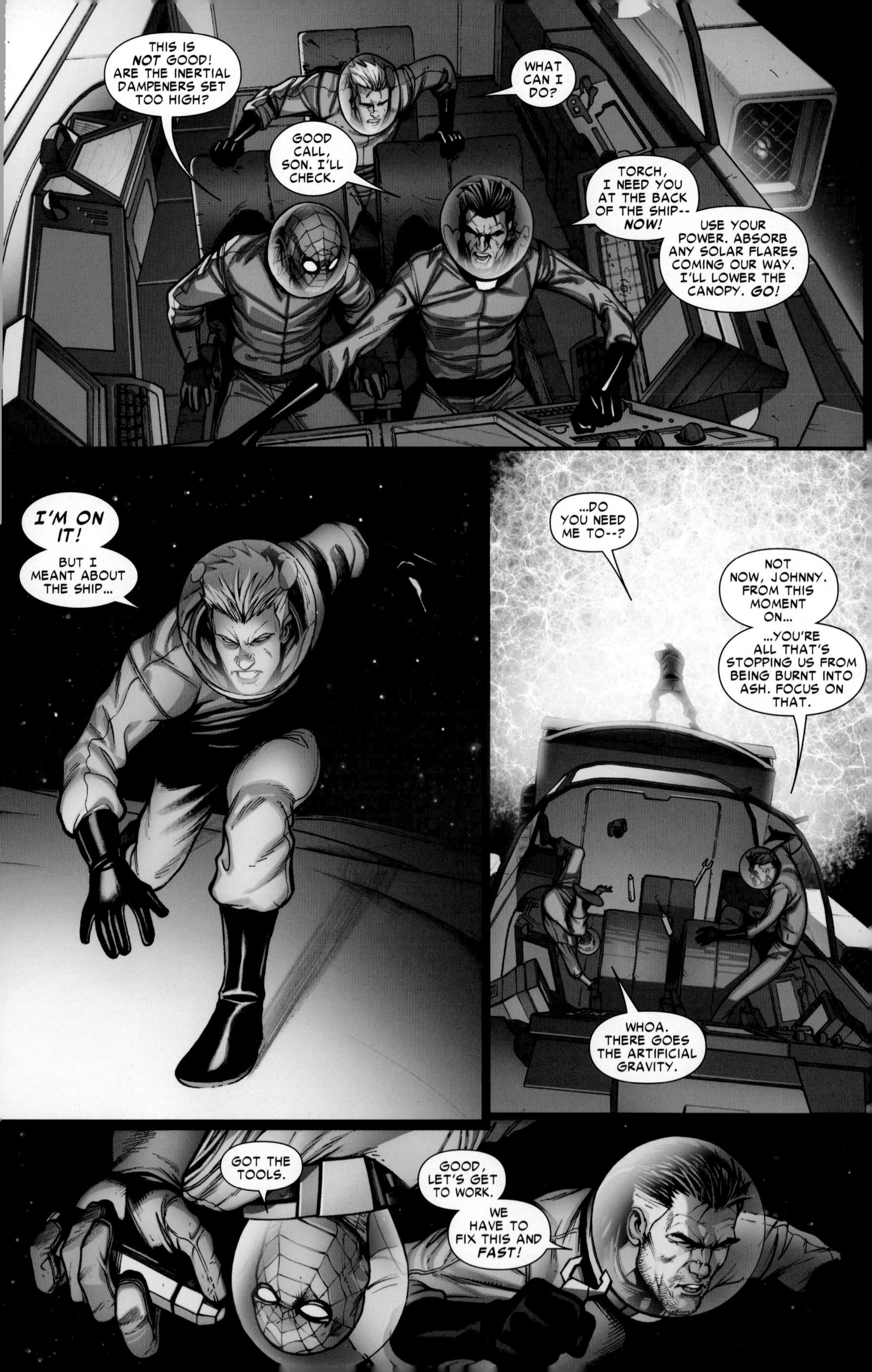

THIS IS NOT GOOD! ARE THE INERTIAL DAMPENERS SET TOO HIGH?
WHAT CAN I DO?
GOOD CALL, SON. I'LL CHECK.
TORCH, I NEED YOU AT THE BACK OF THE SHIP-- NOW!
USE YOUR POWER. ABSORB ANY SOLAR FLARES COMING OUR WAY. I'LL LOWER THE CANOPY. GO!
I'M ON IT!
BUT I MEANT ABOUT THE SHIP...
...DO YOU NEED ME TO--?
NOT NOW, JOHNNY. FROM THIS MOMENT ON...
...YOU'RE ALL THAT'S STOPPING US FROM BEING BURNT INTO ASH. FOCUS ON THAT.
WHOA. THERE GOES THE ARTIFICIAL GRAVITY.
GOT THE TOOLS.
GOOD, LET'S GET TO WORK.
WE HAVE TO FIX THIS AND FAST!

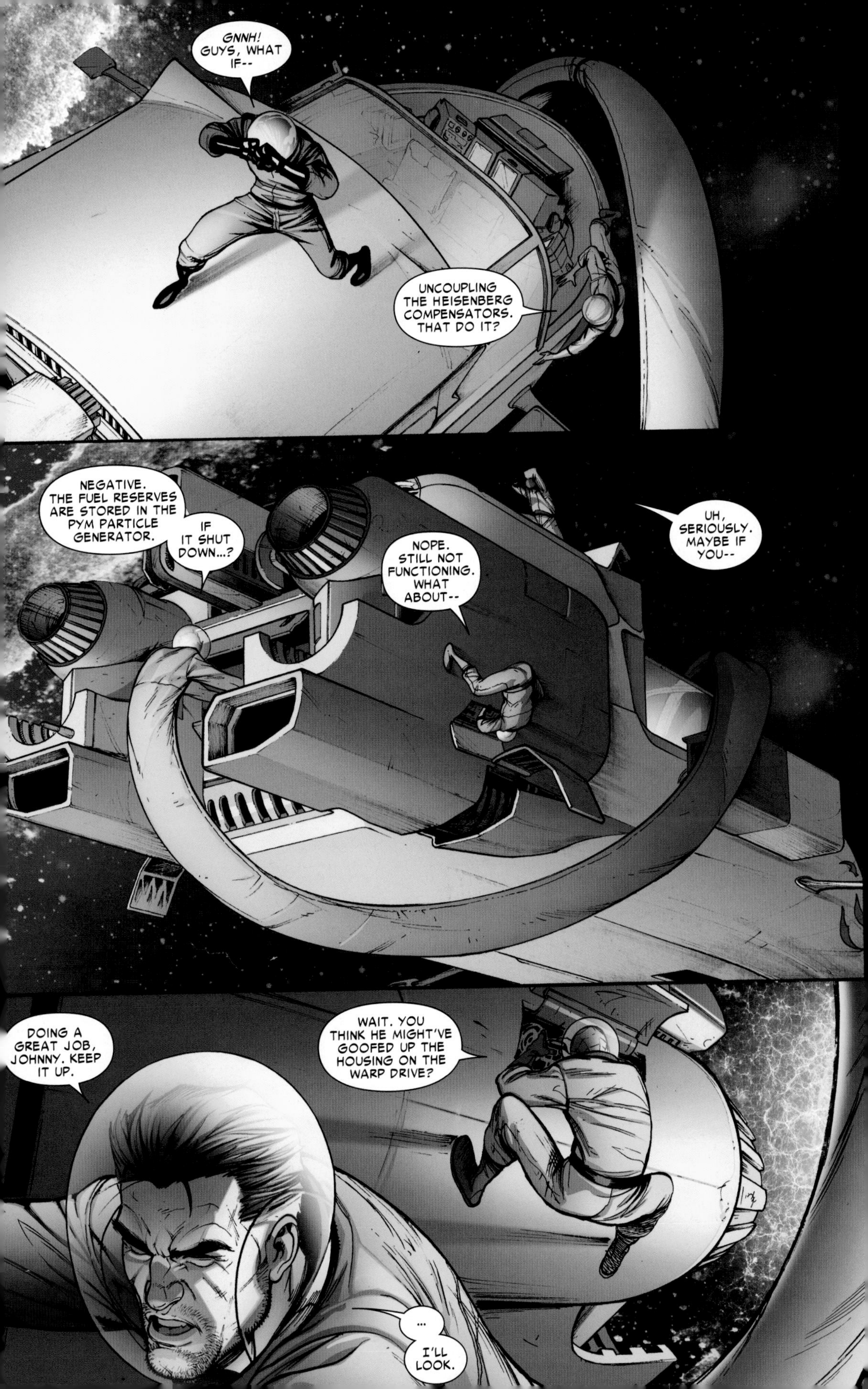
GNNH! GUYS, WHAT IF--
UNCOUPLING THE HEISENBERG COMPENSATORS. THAT DO IT?
NEGATIVE. THE FUEL RESERVES ARE STORED IN THE PYM PARTICLE GENERATOR.
IF IT SHUT DOWN...?
NOPE. STILL NOT FUNCTIONING. WHAT ABOUT--
UH, SERIOUSLY. MAYBE IF YOU--
DOING A GREAT JOB, JOHNNY. KEEP IT UP.
WAIT. YOU THINK HE MIGHT'VE GOOFED UP THE HOUSING ON THE WARP DRIVE?
...
I'LL LOOK.

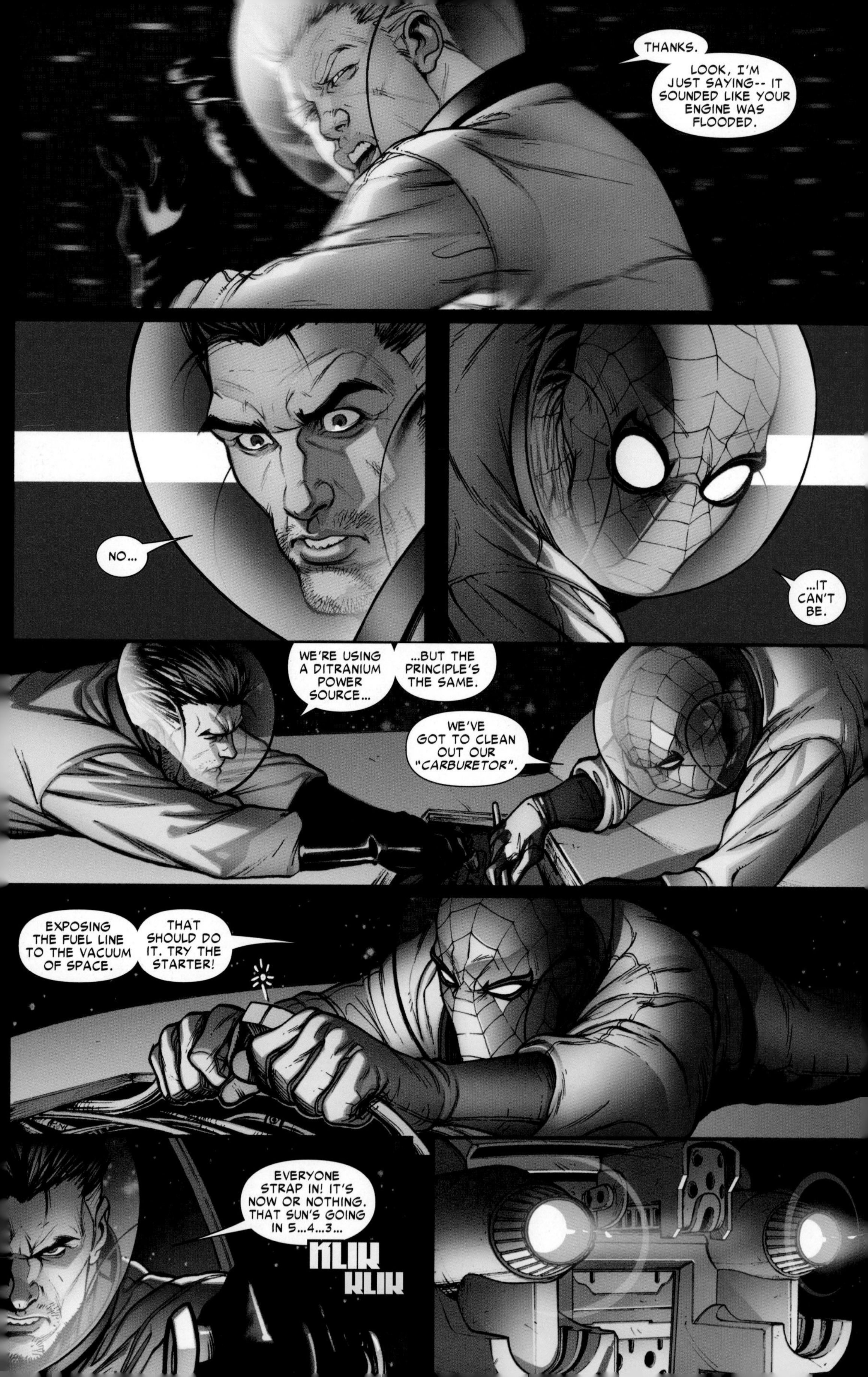
THANKS.
LOOK, I'M JUST SAYING-- IT SOUNDED LIKE YOUR ENGINE WAS FLOODED.
NO...
...IT CAN'T BE.
WE'RE USING A DITRANIUM POWER SOURCE...
...BUT THE PRINCIPLE'S THE SAME.
WE'VE GOT TO CLEAN OUT OUR "CARBURETOR".
EXPOSING THE FUEL LINE TO THE VACUUM OF SPACE.
THAT SHOULD DO IT. TRY THE STARTER!
EVERYONE STRAP IN! IT'S NOW OR NOTHING. THAT SUN'S GOING IN 5...4...3...
KLIK
KLIK

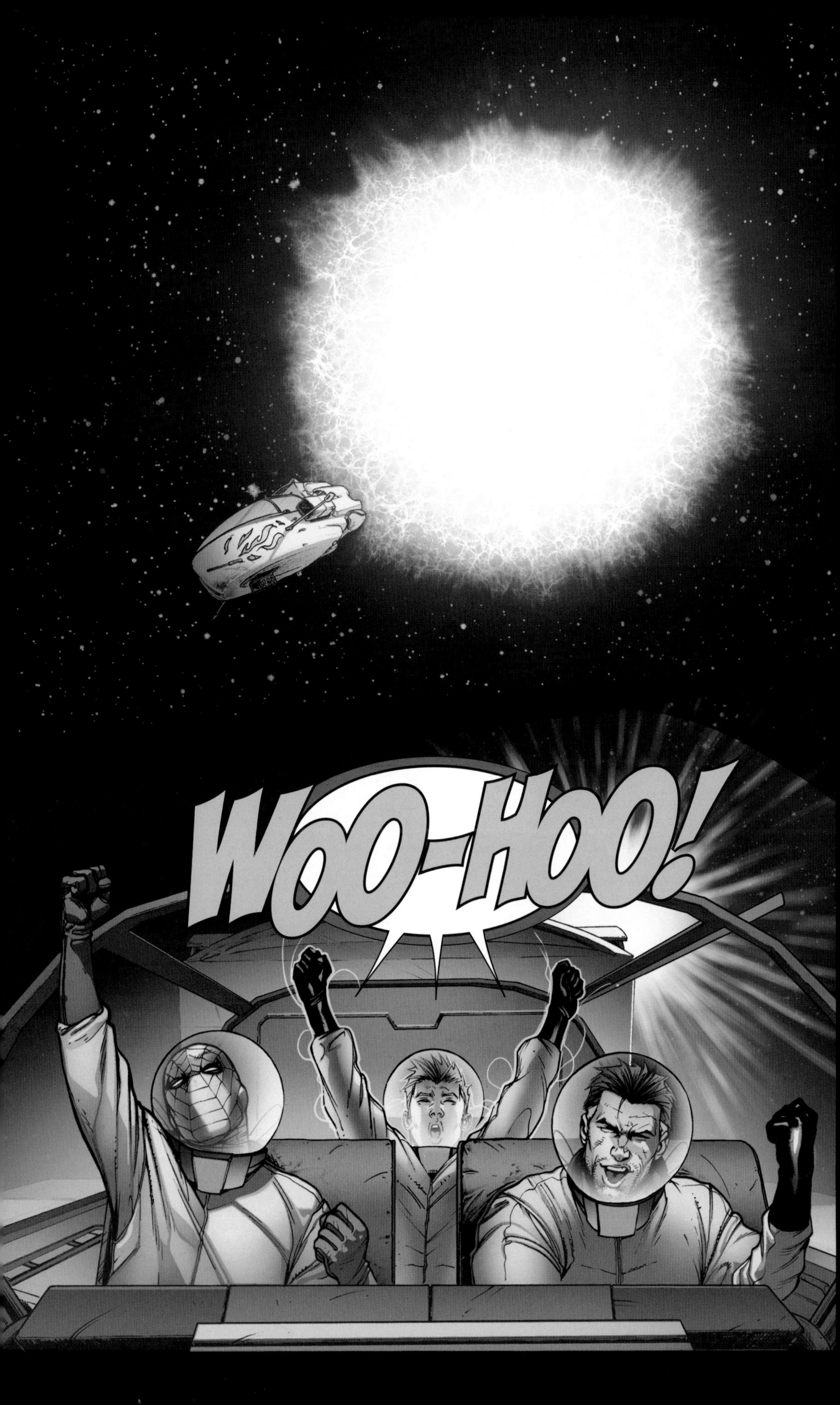
WOO-HOO!

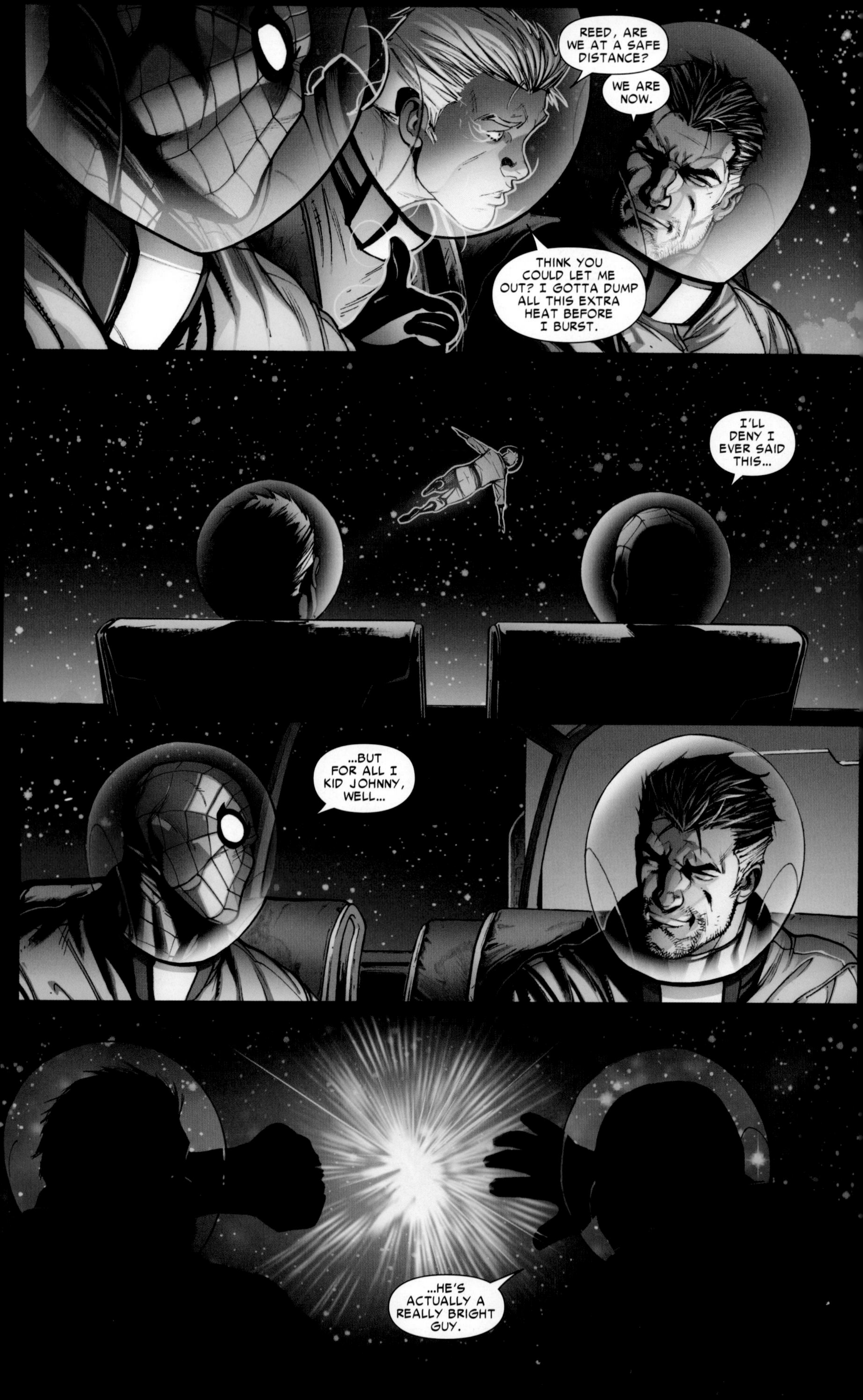
REED, ARE WE AT A SAFE DISTANCE?
WE ARE NOW.
THINK YOU COULD LET ME OUT? I GOTTA DUMP ALL THIS EXTRA HEAT BEFORE I BURST.
I'LL DENY I EVER SAID THIS...
...BUT FOR ALL I KID JOHNNY, WELL...
...HE'S ACTUALLY A REALLY BRIGHT GUY.

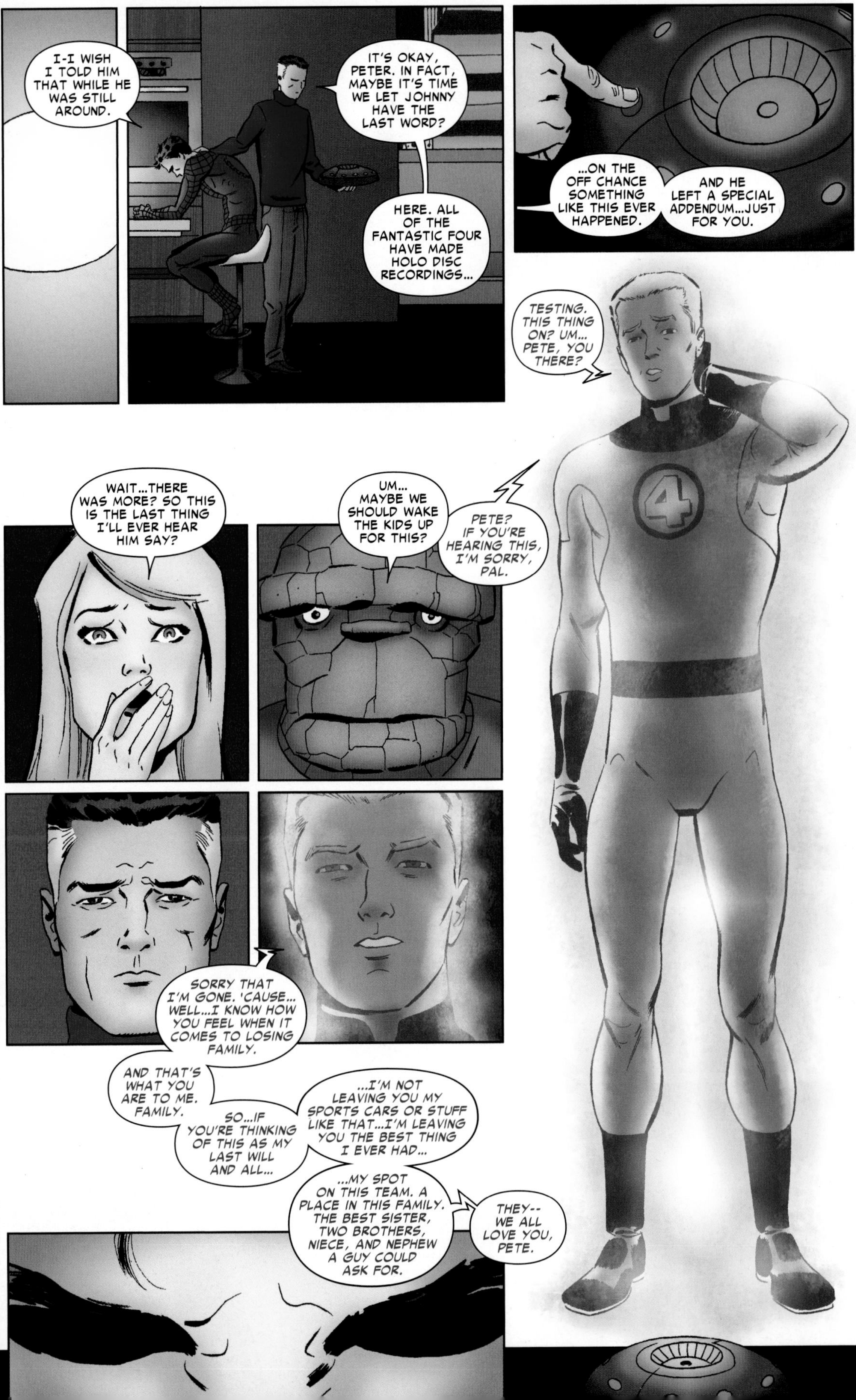
I-I WISH I TOLD HIM THAT WHILE HE WAS STILL AROUND.
IT'S OKAY, PETER. IN FACT, MAYBE IT'S TIME WE LET JOHNNY HAVE THE LAST WORD?
HERE. ALL OF THE FANTASTIC FOUR HAVE MADE HOLO DISC RECORDINGS...
...ON THE OFF CHANCE SOMETHING LIKE THIS EVER HAPPENED.
AND HE LEFT A SPECIAL ADDENDUM...JUST FOR YOU.
TESTING. THIS THING ON? UM... PETE, YOU THERE?
WAIT...THERE WAS MORE? SO THIS IS THE LAST THING I'LL EVER HEAR HIM SAY?
UM... MAYBE WE SHOULD WAKE THE KIDS UP FOR THIS?
PETE? IF YOU'RE HEARING THIS, I'M SORRY, PAL.
SORRY THAT I'M GONE. 'CAUSE... WELL...I KNOW HOW YOU FEEL WHEN IT COMES TO LOSING FAMILY.
AND THAT'S WHAT YOU ARE TO ME. FAMILY.
SO...IF YOU'RE THINKING OF THIS AS MY LAST WILL AND ALL...
...I'M NOT LEAVING YOU MY SPORTS CARS OR STUFF LIKE THAT...I'M LEAVING YOU THE BEST THING I EVER HAD...
...MY SPOT ON THIS TEAM. A PLACE IN THIS FAMILY. THE BEST SISTER, TWO BROTHERS, NIECE, AND NEPHEW A GUY COULD ASK FOR.
THEY-- WE ALL LOVE YOU, PETE.

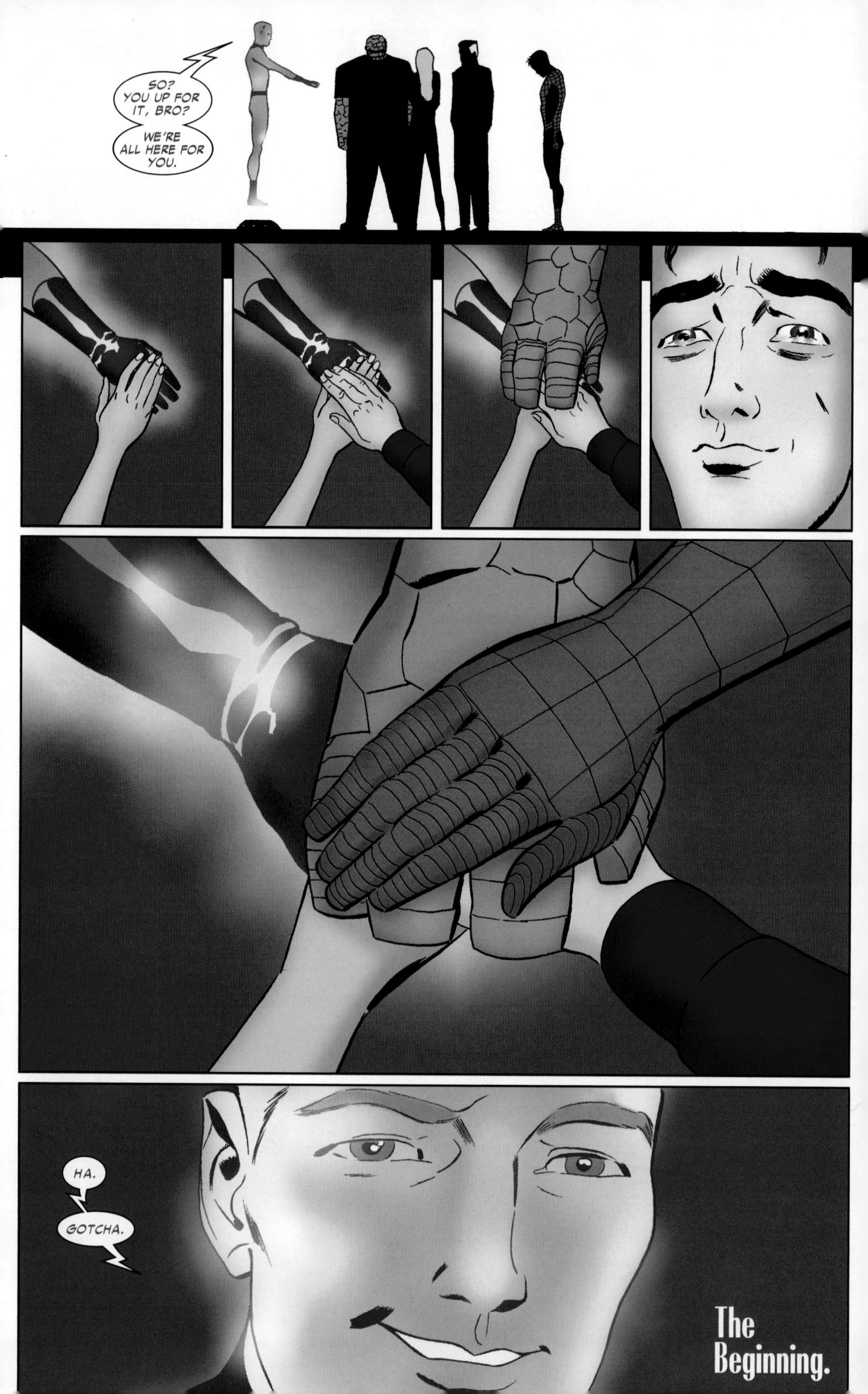
SO? YOU UP FOR IT, BRO?
WE'RE ALL HERE FOR YOU.
HA.
GOTCHA.
The Beginning.

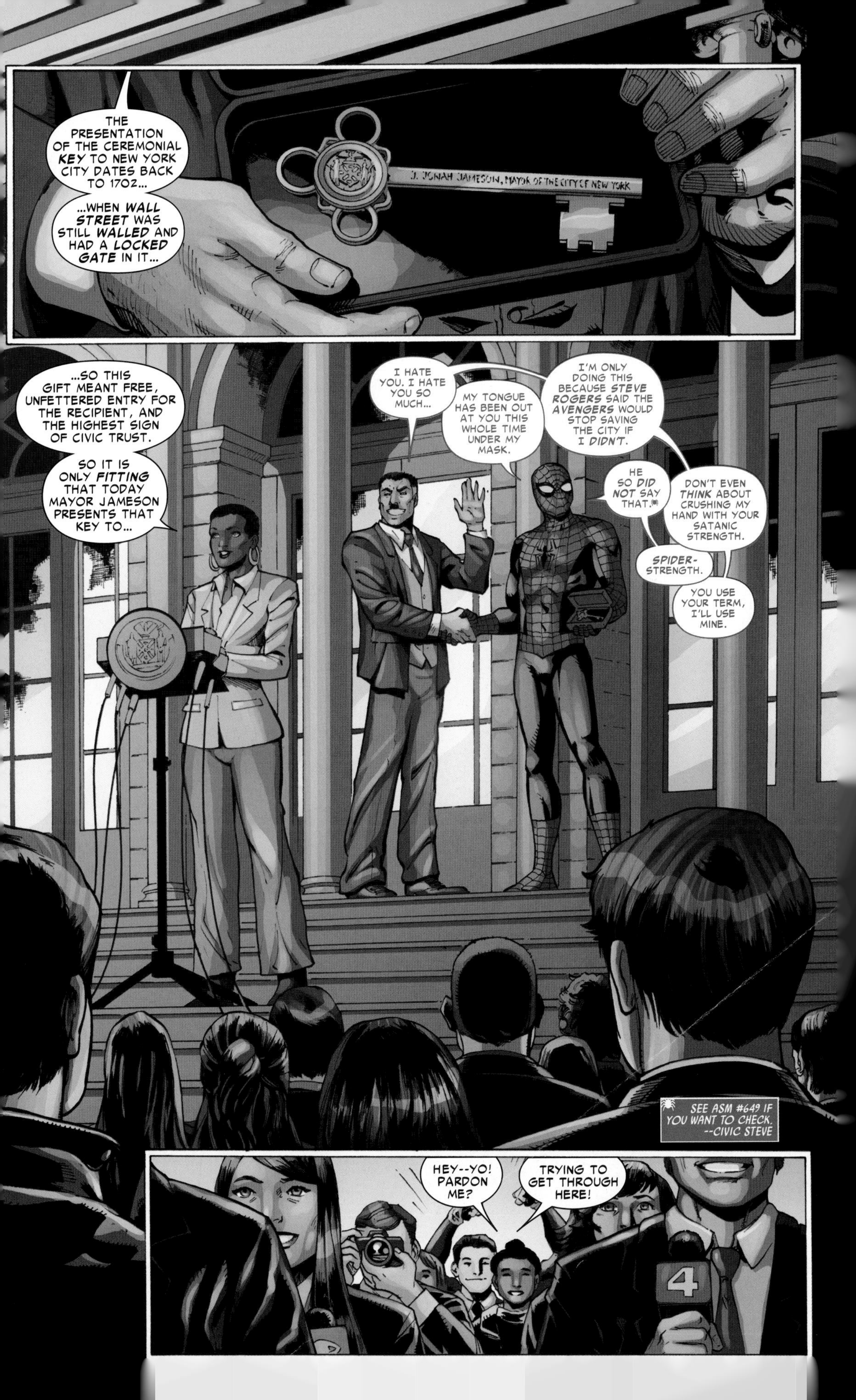
THE PRESENTATION OF THE CEREMONIAL KEY TO NEW YORK CITY DATES BACK TO 1702...
...WHEN WALL STREET WAS STILL WALLED AND HAD A LOCKED GATE IN IT...
J. JONAH JAMESON, MAYOR OF THE CITY OF NEW YORK
...SO THIS GIFT MEANT FREE, UNFETTERED ENTRY FOR THE RECIPIENT, AND THE HIGHEST SIGN OF CIVIC TRUST.
SO IT IS ONLY FITTING THAT TODAY MAYOR JAMESON PRESENTS THAT KEY TO...
I HATE YOU. I HATE YOU SO MUCH...
MY TONGUE HAS BEEN OUT AT YOU THIS WHOLE TIME UNDER MY MASK.
I'M ONLY DOING THIS BECAUSE STEVE ROGERS SAID THE AVENGERS WOULD STOP SAVING THE CITY IF I DIDN'T.
HE SO DID NOT SAY THAT.
DON'T EVEN THINK ABOUT CRUSHING MY HAND WITH YOUR SATANIC STRENGTH.
SPIDER-STRENGTH.
YOU USE YOUR TERM, I'LL USE MINE.
SEE ASM #649 IF YOU WANT TO CHECK. --CIVIC STEVE
HEY--YO! PARDON ME?
TRYING TO GET THROUGH HERE!
4

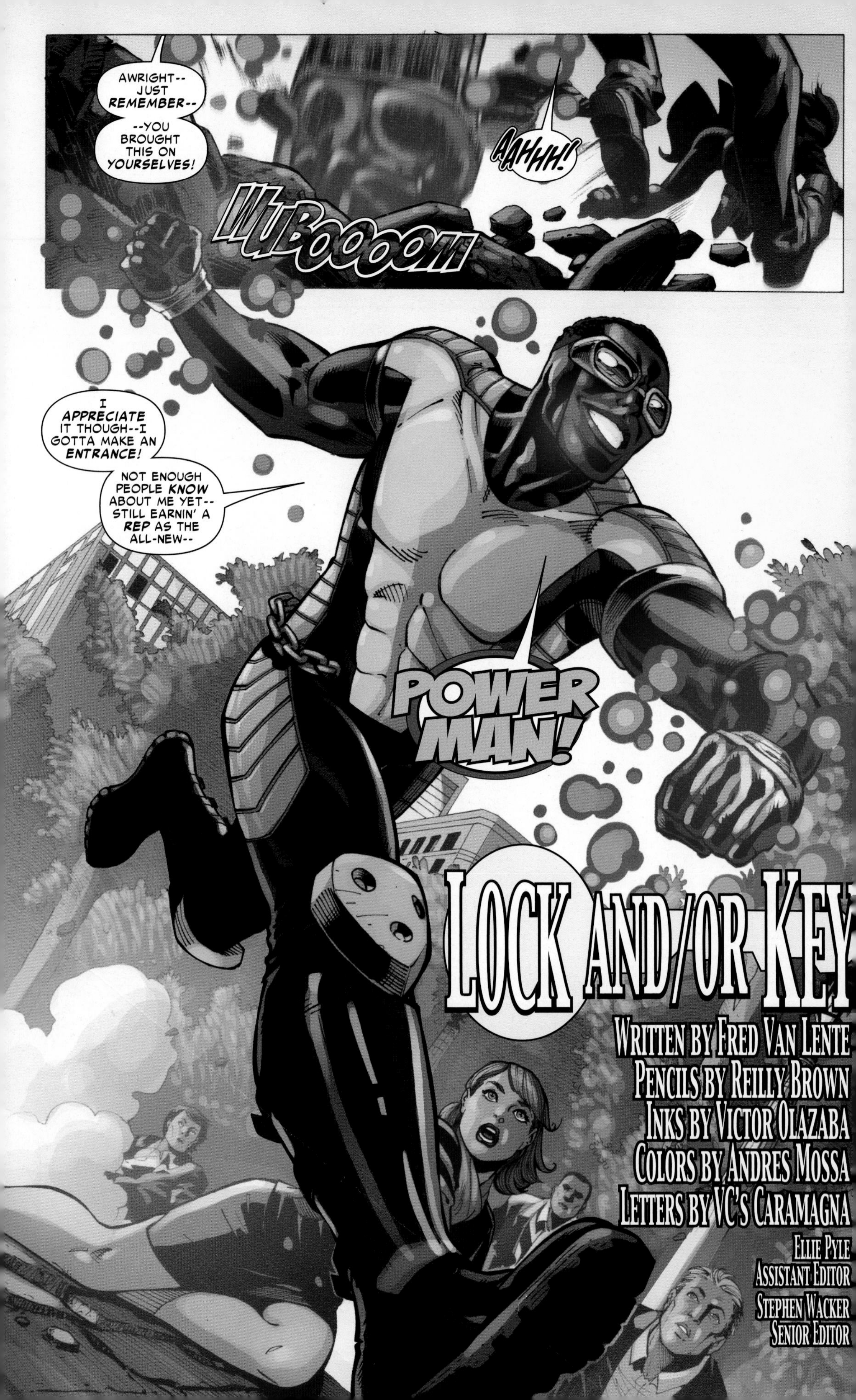
AWRIGHT-- JUST REMEMBER--
--YOU BROUGHT THIS ON YOURSELVES!
AAHHH!
WUBOOOOOM
I APPRECIATE IT THOUGH--I GOTTA MAKE AN ENTRANCE!
NOT ENOUGH PEOPLE KNOW ABOUT ME YET--STILL EARNIN' A REP AS THE ALL-NEW--
POWER MAN!
LOCK AND/OR KEY
WRITTEN BY FRED VAN LENTE
PENCILS BY REILLY BROWN
INKS BY VICTOR OLAZABA
COLORS BY ANDRES MOSSA
LETTERS BY VC'S CARAMAGNA
ELLIE PYLE
ASSISTANT EDITOR
STEPHEN WACKER
SENIOR EDITOR

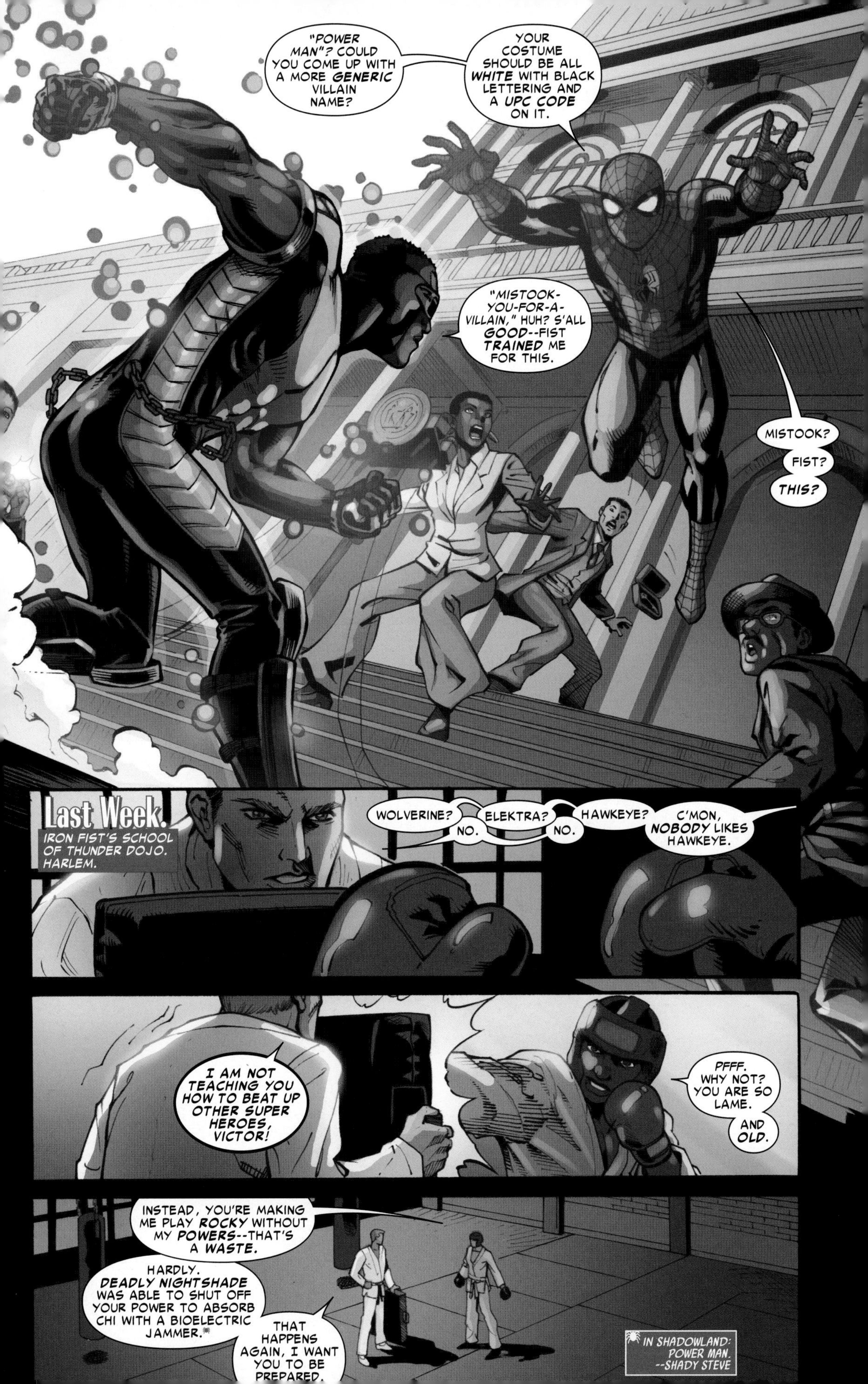
"POWER MAN"? COULD YOU COME UP WITH A MORE GENERIC VILLAIN NAME?
YOUR COSTUME SHOULD BE ALL WHITE WITH BLACK LETTERING AND A UPC CODE ON IT.
"MISTOOK-YOU-FOR-A-VILLAIN," HUH? S'ALL GOOD--FIST TRAINED ME FOR THIS.
MISTOOK?
FIST?
THIS?
Last Week.
IRON FIST'S SCHOOL OF THUNDER DOJO. HARLEM.
WOLVERINE?
NO.
ELEKTRA?
NO.
HAWKEYE?
C'MON, NOBODY LIKES HAWKEYE.
I AM NOT TEACHING YOU HOW TO BEAT UP OTHER SUPER HEROES, VICTOR!
PFFF. WHY NOT? YOU ARE SO LAME.
AND OLD.
INSTEAD, YOU'RE MAKING ME PLAY ROCKY WITHOUT MY POWERS--THAT'S A WASTE.
HARDLY. DEADLY NIGHTSHADE WAS ABLE TO SHUT OFF YOUR POWER TO ABSORB CHI WITH A BIOELECTRIC JAMMER.*
THAT HAPPENS AGAIN, I WANT YOU TO BE PREPARED.
*IN SHADOWLAND: POWER MAN. --SHADY STEVE

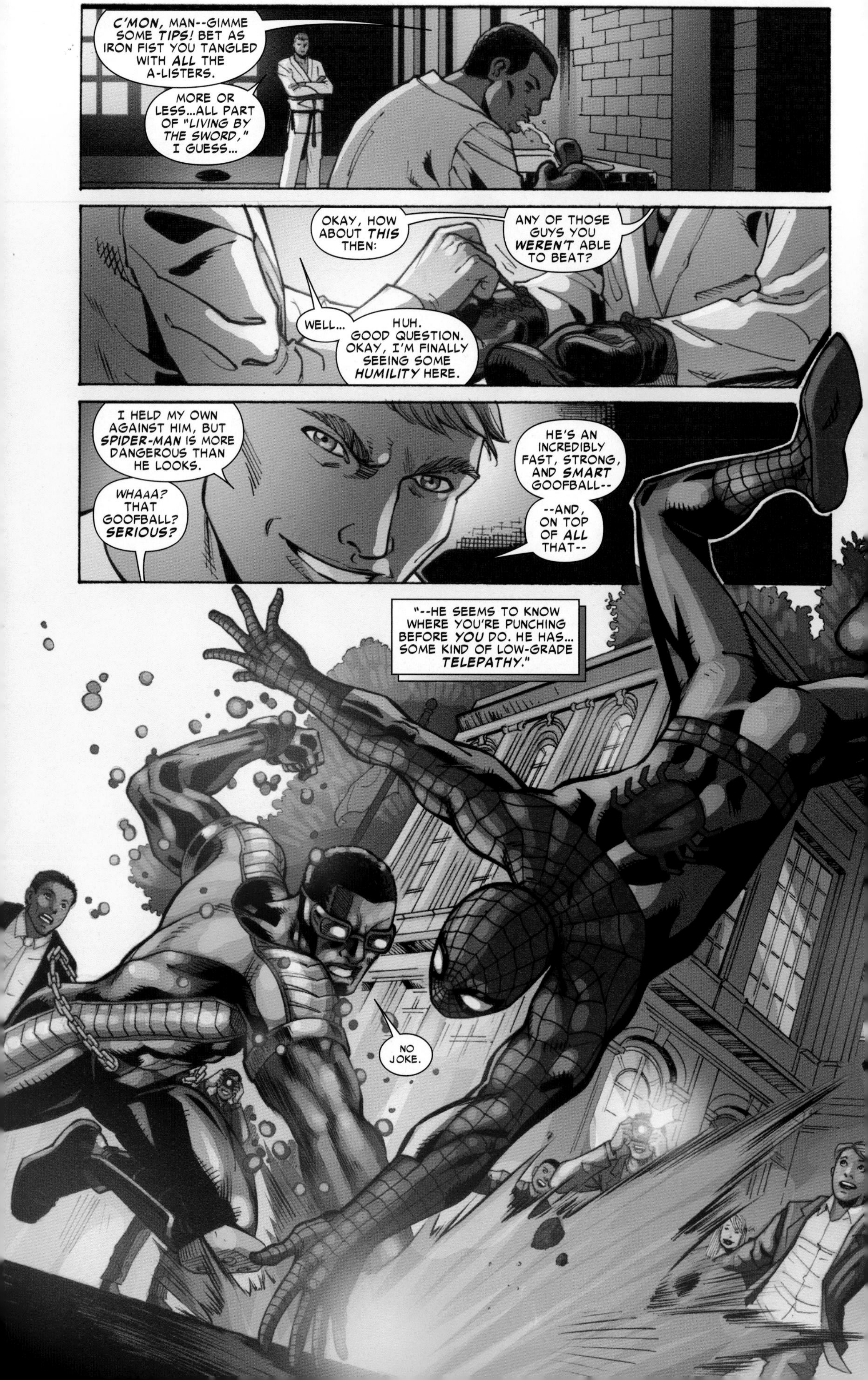
C'MON, MAN--GIMME SOME TIPS! BET AS IRON FIST YOU TANGLED WITH ALL THE A-LISTERS.
MORE OR LESS...ALL PART OF "LIVING BY THE SWORD," I GUESS...
OKAY, HOW ABOUT THIS THEN:
ANY OF THOSE GUYS YOU WEREN'T ABLE TO BEAT?
WELL...
HUH. GOOD QUESTION. OKAY, I'M FINALLY SEEING SOME HUMILITY HERE.
I HELD MY OWN AGAINST HIM, BUT SPIDER-MAN IS MORE DANGEROUS THAN HE LOOKS.
WHAAA? THAT GOOFBALL? SERIOUS?
HE'S AN INCREDIBLY FAST, STRONG, AND SMART GOOFBALL--
--AND, ON TOP OF ALL THAT--
"--HE SEEMS TO KNOW WHERE YOU'RE PUNCHING BEFORE YOU DO. HE HAS... SOME KIND OF LOW-GRADE TELEPATHY."
NO JOKE.

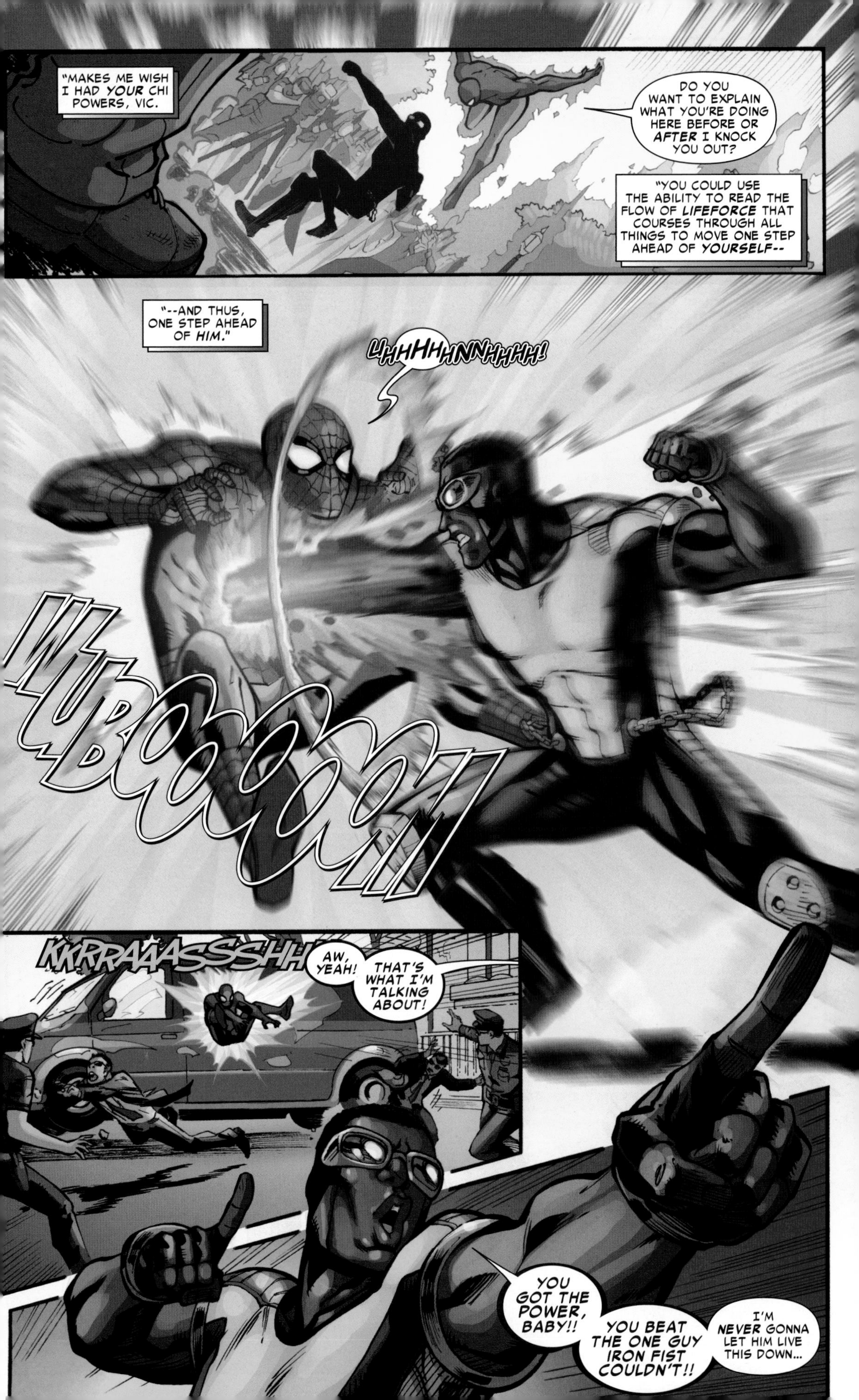
"MAKES ME WISH I HAD YOUR CHI POWERS, VIC.
DO YOU WANT TO EXPLAIN WHAT YOU'RE DOING HERE BEFORE OR AFTER I KNOCK YOU OUT?
"YOU COULD USE THE ABILITY TO READ THE FLOW OF LIFEFORCE THAT COURSES THROUGH ALL THINGS TO MOVE ONE STEP AHEAD OF YOURSELF--
"--AND THUS, ONE STEP AHEAD OF HIM."
UHHHHHNNHHHH!
WUBOOOOM
KKRRAAASSSHH
AW, YEAH!
THAT'S WHAT I'M TALKING ABOUT!
YOU GOT THE POWER, BABY!!
YOU BEAT THE ONE GUY IRON FIST COULDN'T!!
I'M NEVER GONNA LET HIM LIVE THIS DOWN...

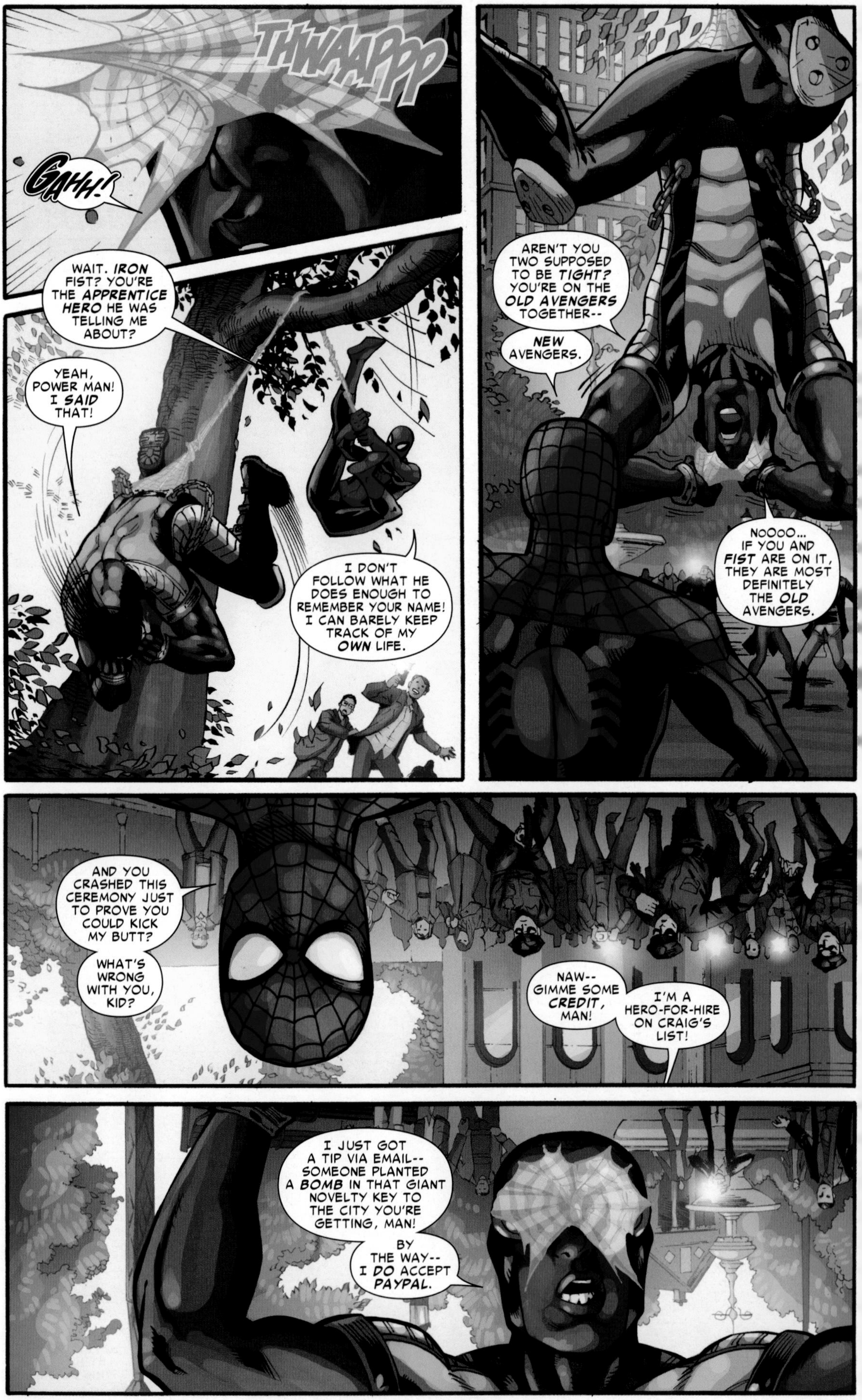
THWAAPPP
GAHH!
WAIT. IRON FIST? YOU'RE THE APPRENTICE HERO HE WAS TELLING ME ABOUT?
YEAH, POWER MAN! I SAID THAT!
I DON'T FOLLOW WHAT HE DOES ENOUGH TO REMEMBER YOUR NAME! I CAN BARELY KEEP TRACK OF MY OWN LIFE.
AREN'T YOU TWO SUPPOSED TO BE TIGHT? YOU'RE ON THE OLD AVENGERS TOGETHER--
NEW AVENGERS.
NOOOO... IF YOU AND FIST ARE ON IT, THEY ARE MOST DEFINITELY THE OLD AVENGERS.
AND YOU CRASHED THIS CEREMONY JUST TO PROVE YOU COULD KICK MY BUTT?
WHAT'S WRONG WITH YOU, KID?
NAW-- GIMME SOME CREDIT, MAN!
I'M A HERO-FOR-HIRE ON CRAIG'S LIST!
I JUST GOT A TIP VIA EMAIL-- SOMEONE PLANTED A BOMB IN THAT GIANT NOVELTY KEY TO THE CITY YOU'RE GETTING, MAN!
BY THE WAY-- I DO ACCEPT PAYPAL.

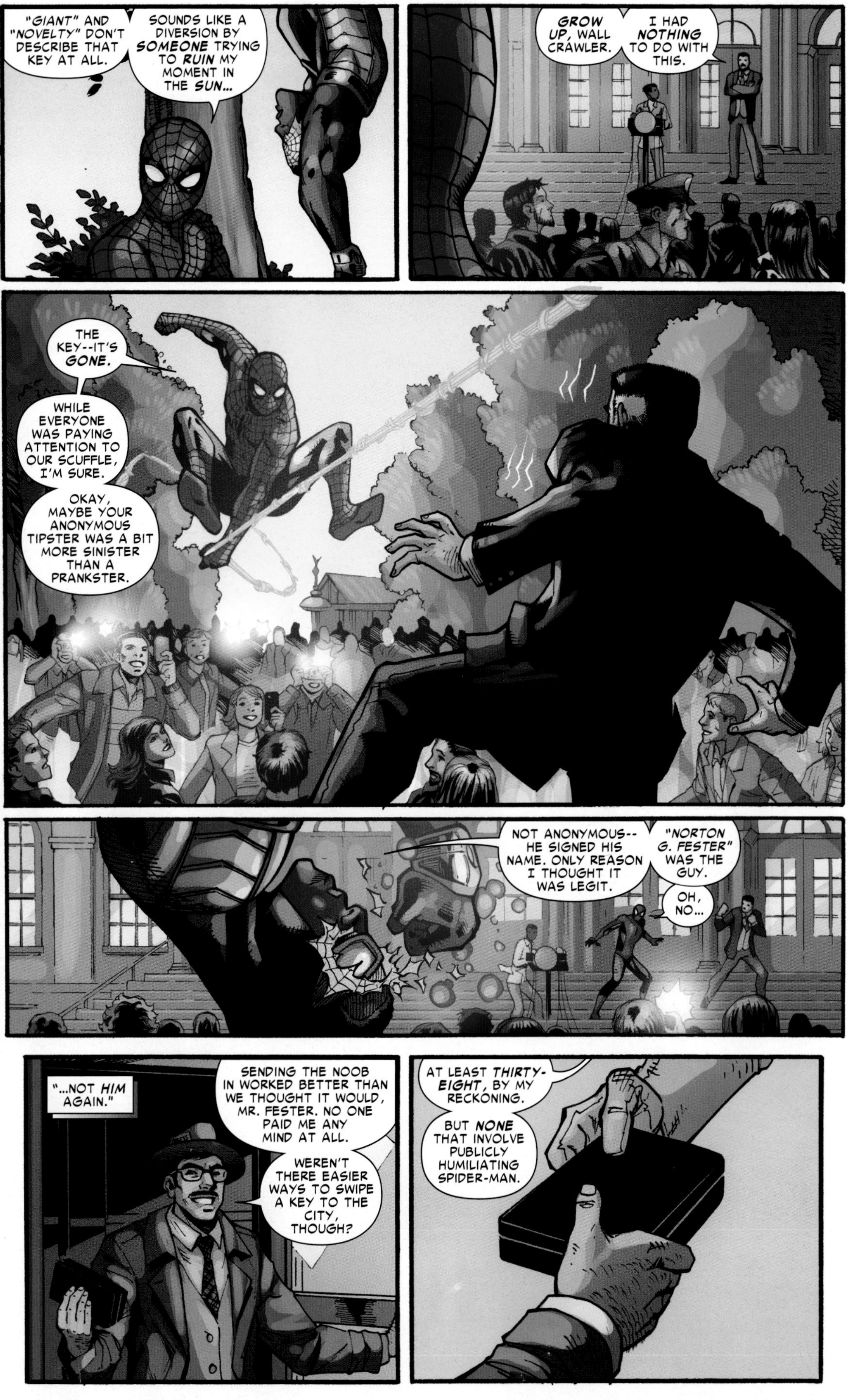
"GIANT" AND "NOVELTY" DON'T DESCRIBE THAT KEY AT ALL.
SOUNDS LIKE A DIVERSION BY SOMEONE TRYING TO RUIN MY MOMENT IN THE SUN...
GROW UP, WALL CRAWLER.
I HAD NOTHING TO DO WITH THIS.
THE KEY--IT'S GONE.
WHILE EVERYONE WAS PAYING ATTENTION TO OUR SCUFFLE, I'M SURE.
OKAY, MAYBE YOUR ANONYMOUS TIPSTER WAS A BIT MORE SINISTER THAN A PRANKSTER.
NOT ANONYMOUS-- HE SIGNED HIS NAME. ONLY REASON I THOUGHT IT WAS LEGIT.
"NORTON G. FESTER" WAS THE GUY.
OH, NO...
"...NOT HIM AGAIN."
SENDING THE NOOB IN WORKED BETTER THAN WE THOUGHT IT WOULD, MR. FESTER. NO ONE PAID ME ANY MIND AT ALL.
WEREN'T THERE EASIER WAYS TO SWIPE A KEY TO THE CITY, THOUGH?
AT LEAST THIRTY-EIGHT, BY MY RECKONING.
BUT NONE THAT INVOLVE PUBLICLY HUMILIATING SPIDER-MAN.

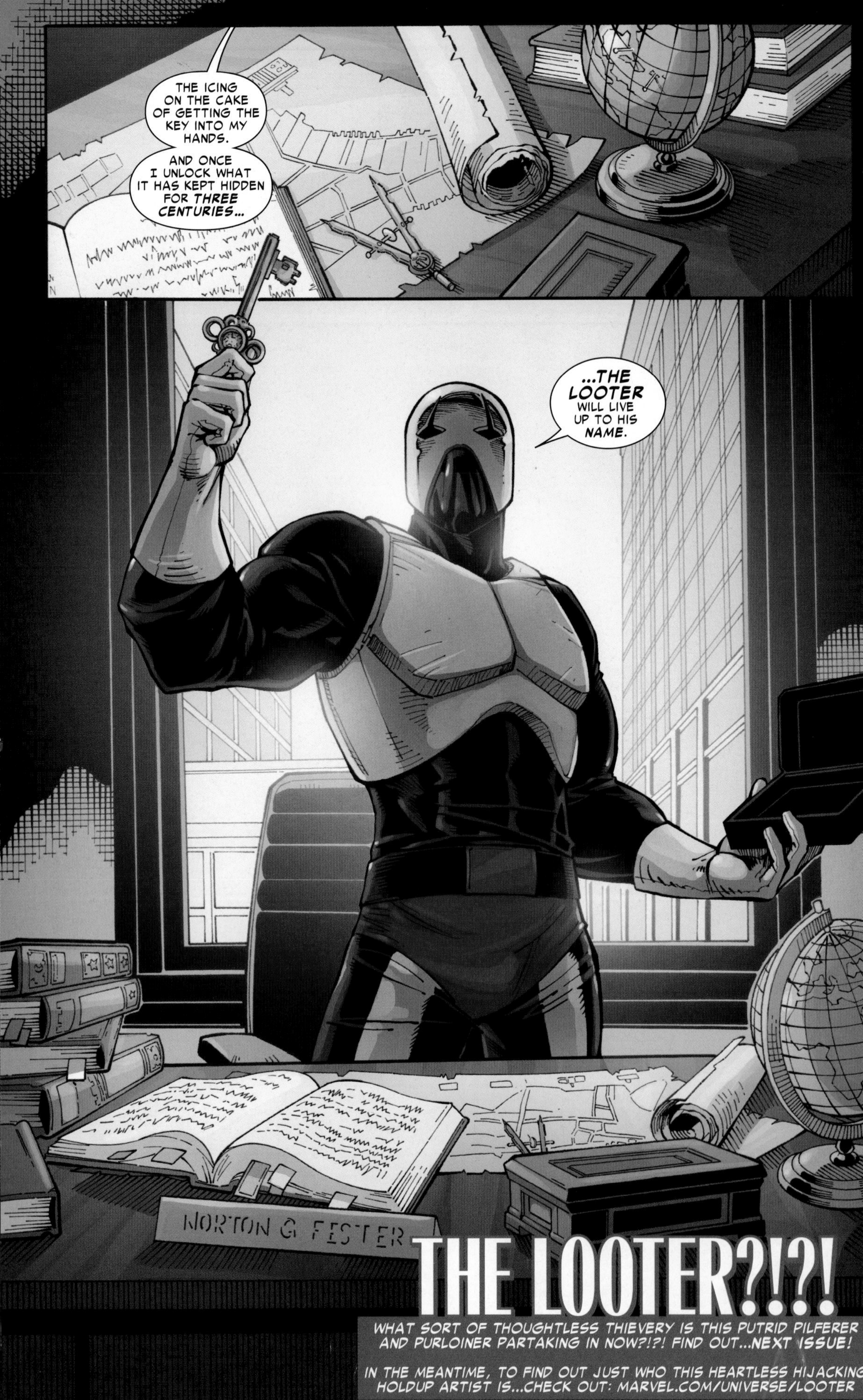
THE ICING ON THE CAKE OF GETTING THE KEY INTO MY HANDS.
AND ONCE I UNLOCK WHAT IT HAS KEPT HIDDEN FOR THREE CENTURIES...
...THE LOOTER WILL LIVE UP TO HIS NAME.
NORTON G FESTER
THE LOOTER?!?!
WHAT SORT OF THOUGHTLESS THIEVERY IS THIS PUTRID PILFERER AND PURLOINER PARTAKING IN NOW?!?! FIND OUT...NEXT ISSUE!
IN THE MEANTIME, TO FIND OUT JUST WHO THIS HEARTLESS HIJACKING HOLDUP ARTIST IS...CHECK OUT: MARVEL.COM/UNIVERSE/LOOTER

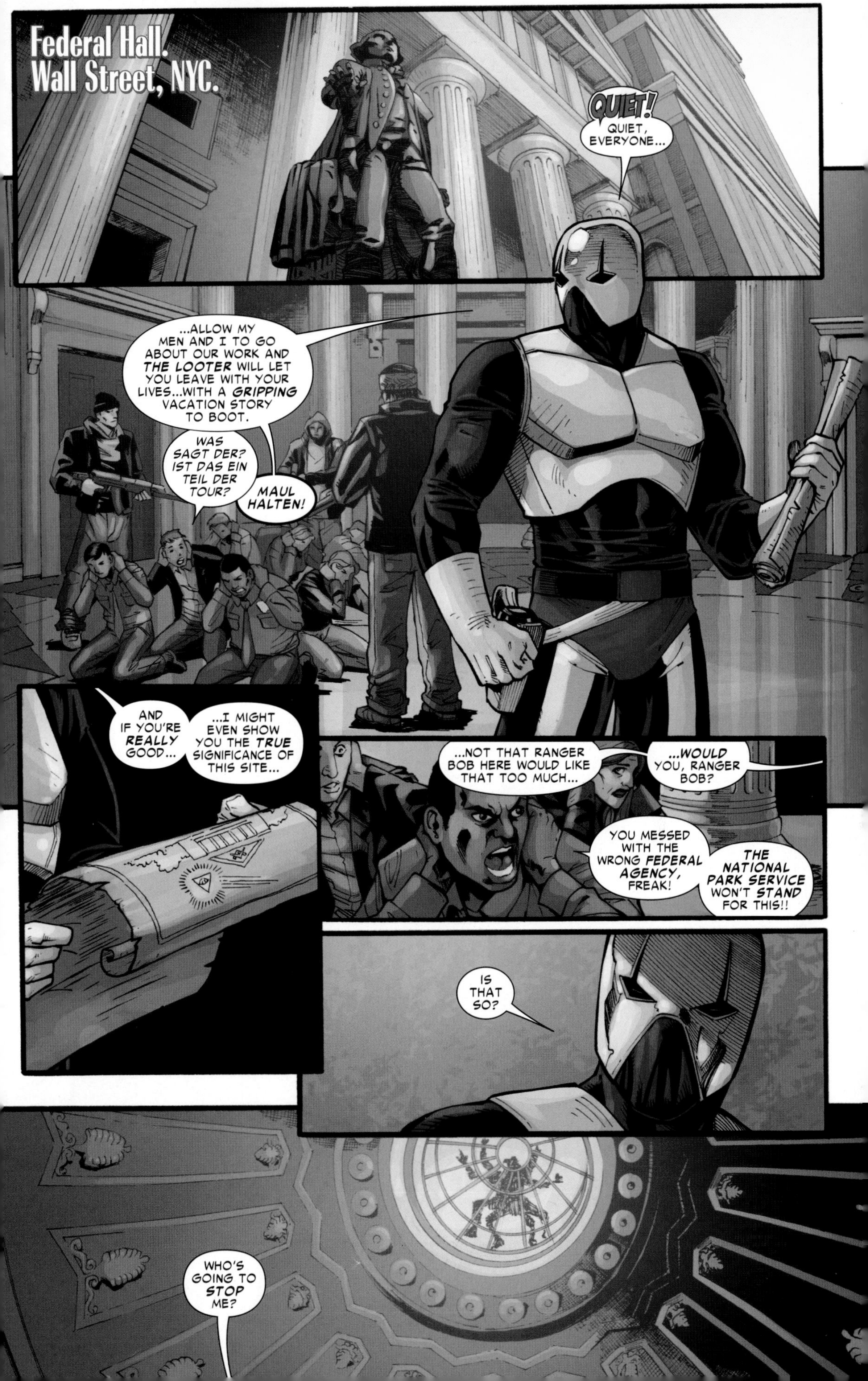
Federal Hall.
Wall Street, NYC.
QUIET! QUIET, EVERYONE...
...ALLOW MY MEN AND I TO GO ABOUT OUR WORK AND THE LOOTER WILL LET YOU LEAVE WITH YOUR LIVES...WITH A GRIPPING VACATION STORY TO BOOT.
WAS SAGT DER? IST DAS EIN TEIL DER TOUR?
MAUL HALTEN!
AND IF YOU'RE REALLY GOOD...
...I MIGHT EVEN SHOW YOU THE TRUE SIGNIFICANCE OF THIS SITE...
...NOT THAT RANGER BOB HERE WOULD LIKE THAT TOO MUCH...
...WOULD YOU, RANGER BOB?
YOU MESSED WITH THE WRONG FEDERAL AGENCY, FREAK!
THE NATIONAL PARK SERVICE WON'T STAND FOR THIS!!
IS THAT SO?
WHO'S GOING TO STOP ME?

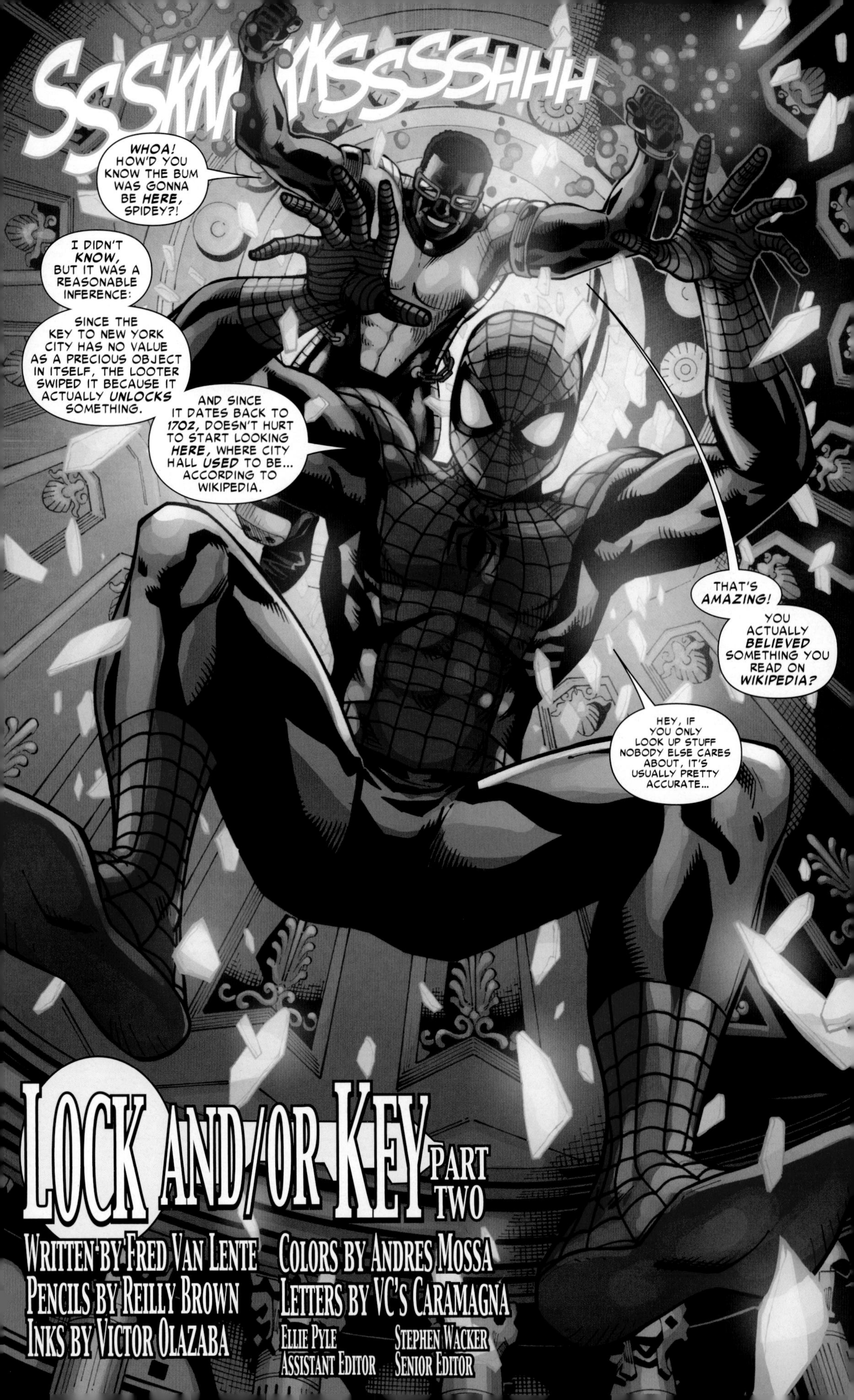
SSSKKKKKSSSSSHHH
WHOA! HOW'D YOU KNOW THE BUM WAS GONNA BE HERE, SPIDEY?!
I DIDN'T KNOW, BUT IT WAS A REASONABLE INFERENCE:
SINCE THE KEY TO NEW YORK CITY HAS NO VALUE AS A PRECIOUS OBJECT IN ITSELF, THE LOOTER SWIPED IT BECAUSE IT ACTUALLY UNLOCKS SOMETHING.
AND SINCE IT DATES BACK TO 1702, DOESN'T HURT TO START LOOKING HERE, WHERE CITY HALL USED TO BE... ACCORDING TO WIKIPEDIA.
THAT'S AMAZING!
YOU ACTUALLY BELIEVED SOMETHING YOU READ ON WIKIPEDIA?
HEY, IF YOU ONLY LOOK UP STUFF NOBODY ELSE CARES ABOUT, IT'S USUALLY PRETTY ACCURATE...
LOCK AND/OR KEY PART TWO
WRITTEN BY FRED VAN LENTE
PENCILS BY REILLY BROWN
INKS BY VICTOR OLAZABA
COLORS BY ANDRES MOSSA
LETTERS BY VC'S CARAMAGNA
ELLIE PYLE ASSISTANT EDITOR
STEPHEN WACKER SENIOR EDITOR

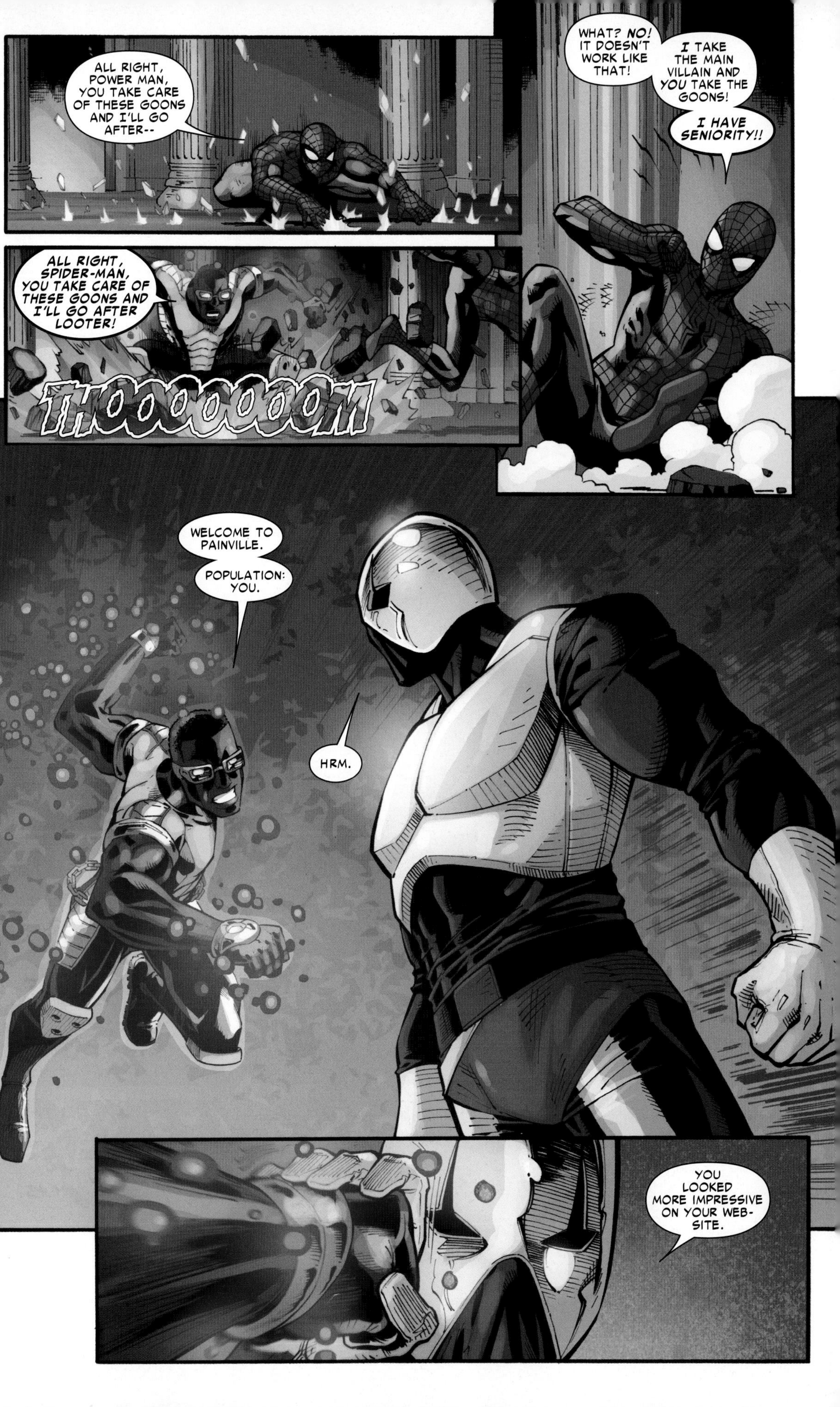
ALL RIGHT, POWER MAN, YOU TAKE CARE OF THESE GOONS AND I'LL GO AFTER--
ALL RIGHT, SPIDER-MAN, YOU TAKE CARE OF THESE GOONS AND I'LL GO AFTER LOOTER!
THOOOOOOOOM
WHAT? NO! IT DOESN'T WORK LIKE THAT!
I TAKE THE MAIN VILLAIN AND YOU TAKE THE GOONS!
I HAVE SENIORITY!!
WELCOME TO PAINVILLE.
POPULATION: YOU.
HRM.
YOU LOOKED MORE IMPRESSIVE ON YOUR WEB-SITE.

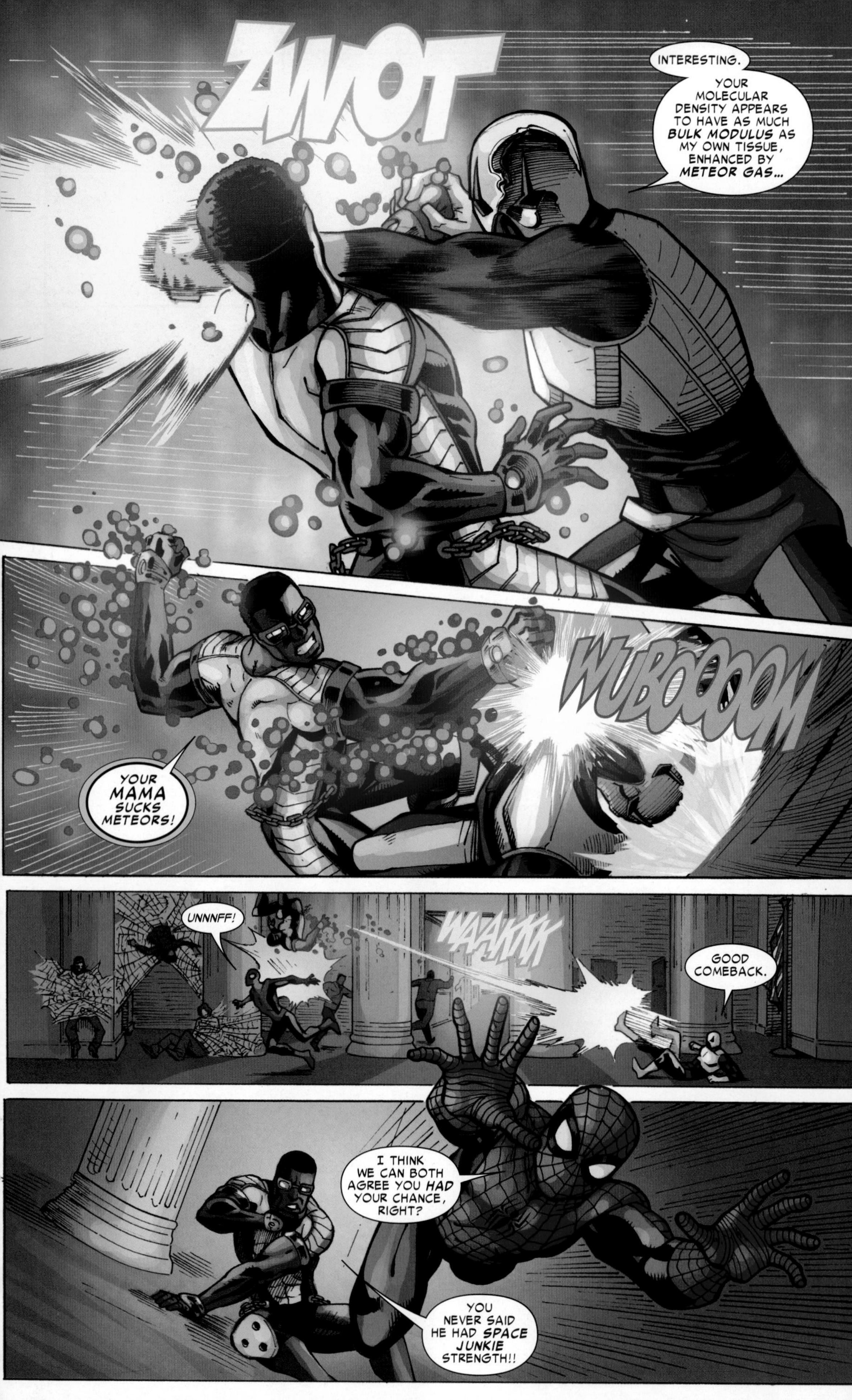
ZWOT
INTERESTING.
YOUR MOLECULAR DENSITY APPEARS TO HAVE AS MUCH BULK MODULUS AS MY OWN TISSUE, ENHANCED BY METEOR GAS...
WUBOOOOM
YOUR MAMA SUCKS METEORS!
UNNNFF!
WAAKKK
GOOD COMEBACK.
I THINK WE CAN BOTH AGREE YOU HAD YOUR CHANCE, RIGHT?
YOU NEVER SAID HE HAD SPACE JUNKIE STRENGTH!!

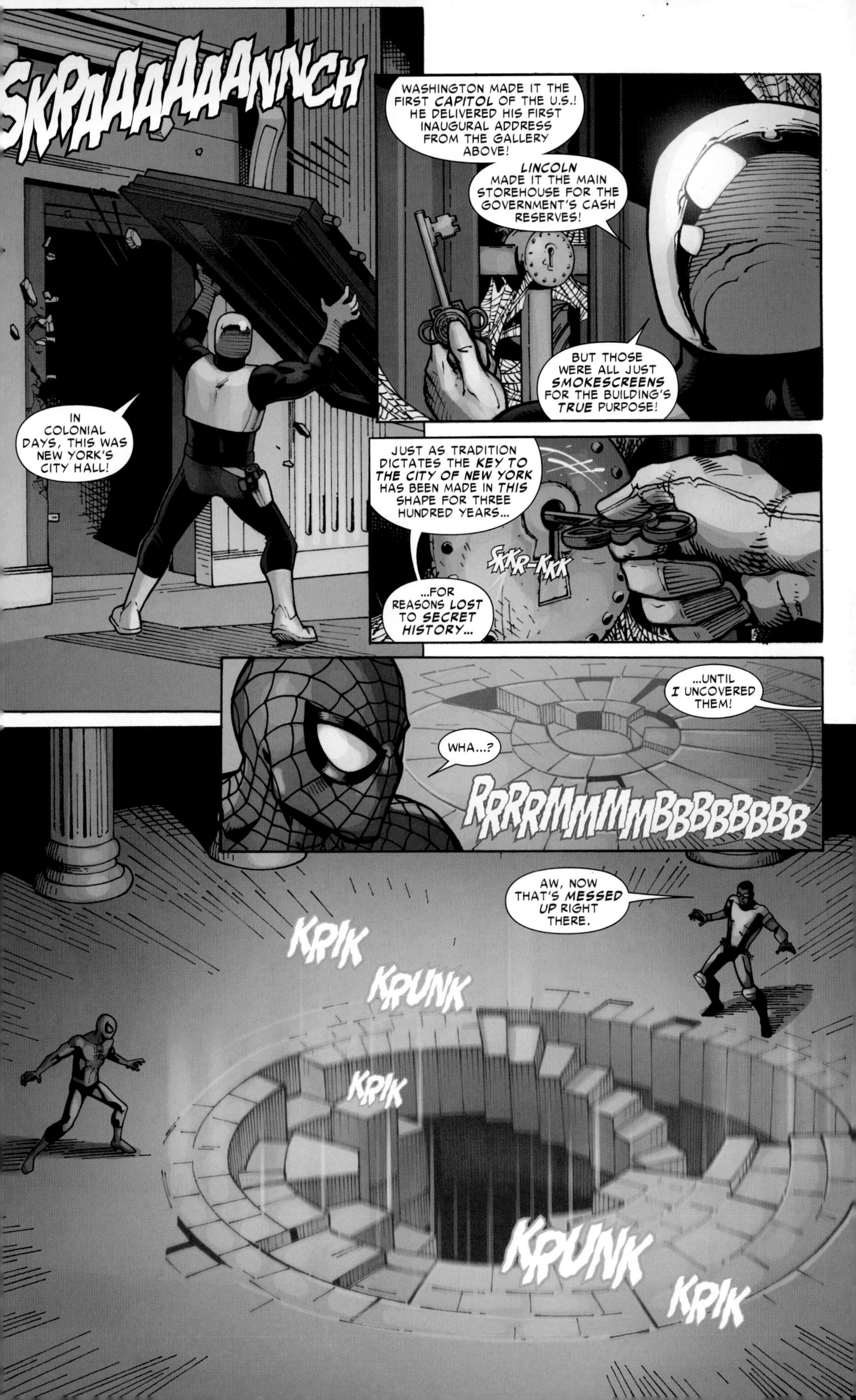
SKRAAAAAAANNCH
IN COLONIAL DAYS, THIS WAS NEW YORK'S CITY HALL!
WASHINGTON MADE IT THE FIRST CAPITOL OF THE U.S.! HE DELIVERED HIS FIRST INAUGURAL ADDRESS FROM THE GALLERY ABOVE!
LINCOLN MADE IT THE MAIN STOREHOUSE FOR THE GOVERNMENT'S CASH RESERVES!
BUT THOSE WERE ALL JUST SMOKESCREENS FOR THE BUILDING'S TRUE PURPOSE!
JUST AS TRADITION DICTATES THE KEY TO THE CITY OF NEW YORK HAS BEEN MADE IN THIS SHAPE FOR THREE HUNDRED YEARS...
SKKR-KKK
...FOR REASONS LOST TO SECRET HISTORY...
...UNTIL I UNCOVERED THEM!
WHA...?
RRRRMMMMMBBBBBBBB
AW, NOW THAT'S MESSED UP RIGHT THERE.
KRIK
KRUNK
KRIK
KRUNK
KRIK

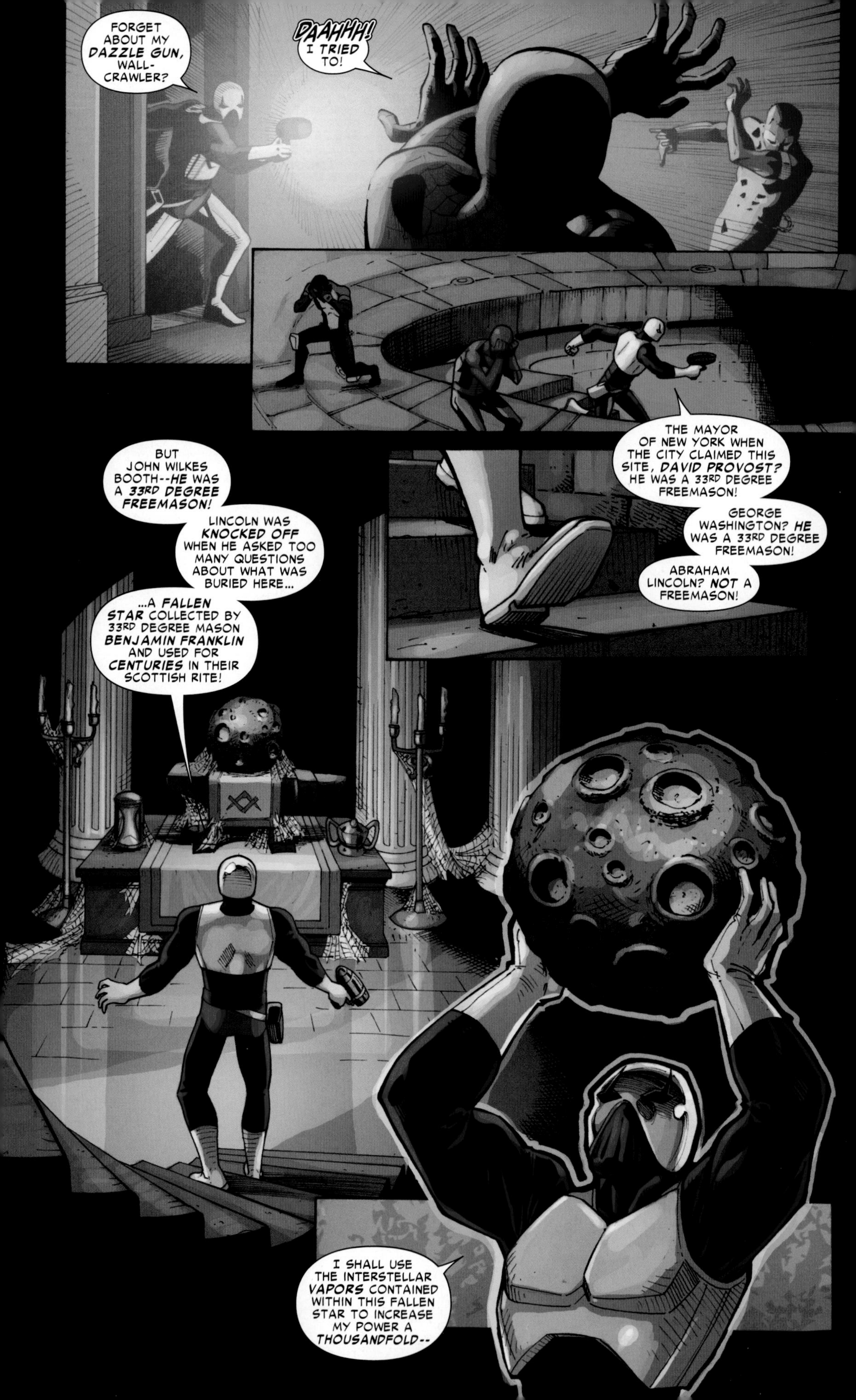
FORGET ABOUT MY DAZZLE GUN, WALL-CRAWLER?
DAAHHH! I TRIED TO!
THE MAYOR OF NEW YORK WHEN THE CITY CLAIMED THIS SITE, DAVID PROVOST? HE WAS A 33RD DEGREE FREEMASON!
GEORGE WASHINGTON? HE WAS A 33RD DEGREE FREEMASON!
ABRAHAM LINCOLN? NOT A FREEMASON!
BUT JOHN WILKES BOOTH--HE WAS A 33RD DEGREE FREEMASON!
LINCOLN WAS KNOCKED OFF WHEN HE ASKED TOO MANY QUESTIONS ABOUT WHAT WAS BURIED HERE...
...A FALLEN STAR COLLECTED BY 33RD DEGREE MASON BENJAMIN FRANKLIN AND USED FOR CENTURIES IN THEIR SCOTTISH RITE!
I SHALL USE THE INTERSTELLAR VAPORS CONTAINED WITHIN THIS FALLEN STAR TO INCREASE MY POWER A THOUSANDFOLD--

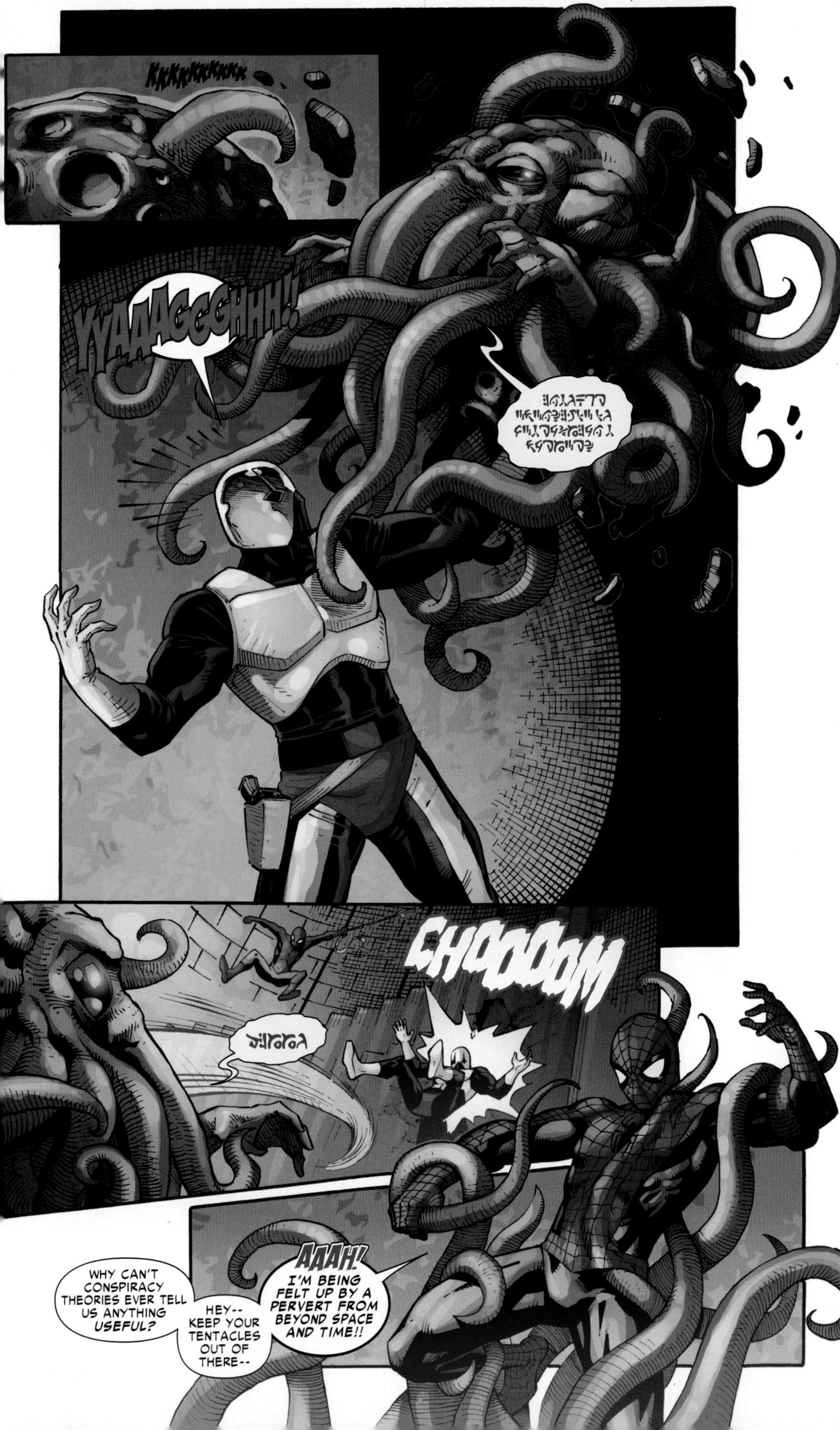

KKKKKKKKK
YYAAAGGGHHH!!
CHOOOOM
WHY CAN'T CONSPIRACY THEORIES EVER TELL US ANYTHING USEFUL?
HEY-- KEEP YOUR TENTACLES OUT OF THERE--
AAAH! I'M BEING FELT UP BY A PERVERT FROM BEYOND SPACE AND TIME!!

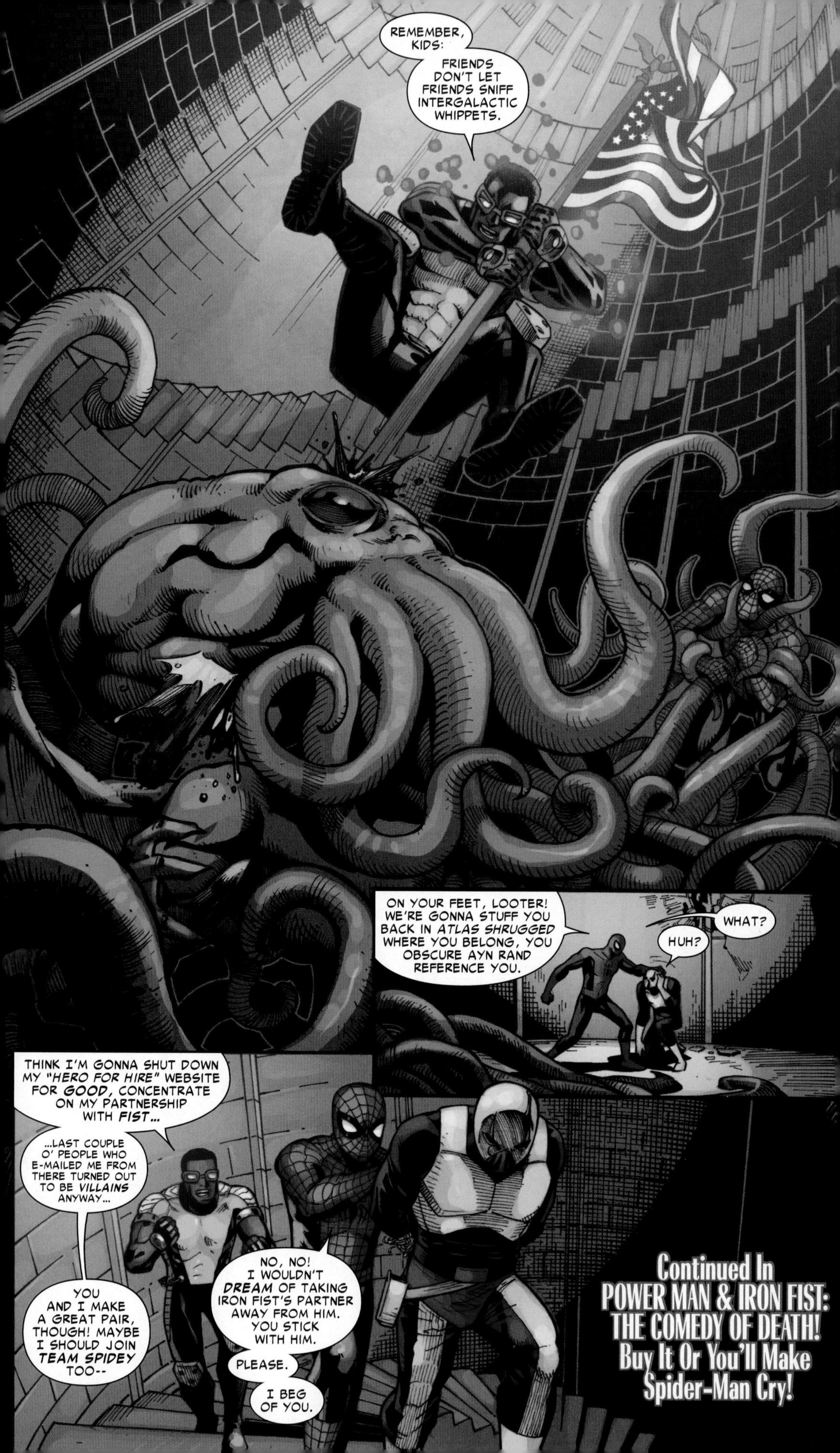
REMEMBER, KIDS:
FRIENDS DON'T LET FRIENDS SNIFF INTERGALACTIC WHIPPETS.
ON YOUR FEET, LOOTER! WE'RE GONNA STUFF YOU BACK IN ATLAS SHRUGGED WHERE YOU BELONG, YOU OBSCURE AYN RAND REFERENCE YOU.
WHAT?
HUH?
THINK I'M GONNA SHUT DOWN MY "HERO FOR HIRE" WEBSITE FOR GOOD, CONCENTRATE ON MY PARTNERSHIP WITH FIST...
...LAST COUPLE O' PEOPLE WHO E-MAILED ME FROM THERE TURNED OUT TO BE VILLAINS ANYWAY...
YOU AND I MAKE A GREAT PAIR, THOUGH! MAYBE I SHOULD JOIN TEAM SPIDEY TOO--
NO, NO! I WOULDN'T DREAM OF TAKING IRON FIST'S PARTNER AWAY FROM HIM. YOU STICK WITH HIM.
PLEASE.
I BEG OF YOU.
Continued In POWER MAN & IRON FIST: THE COMEDY OF DEATH! Buy It Or You'll Make Spider-Man Cry!

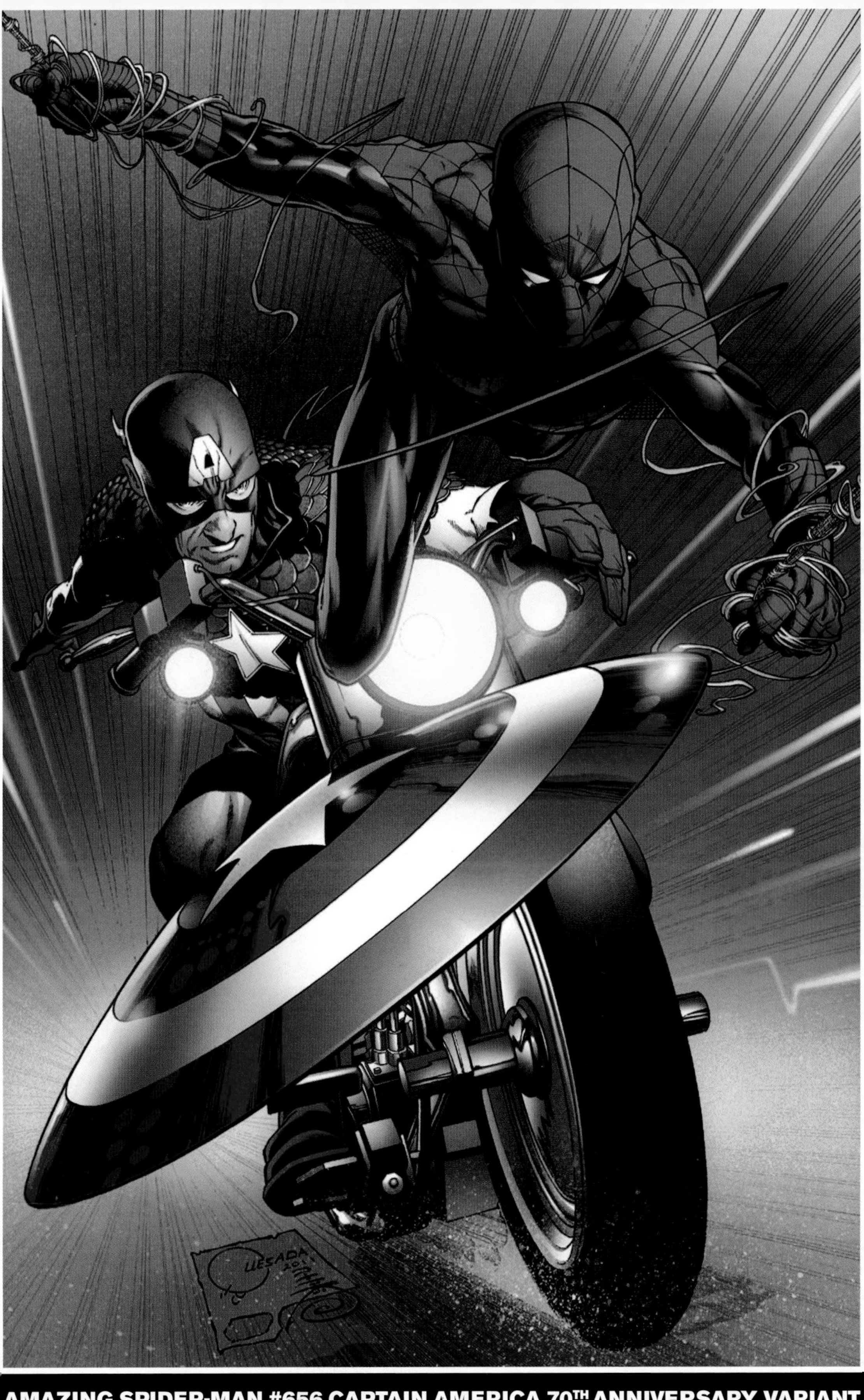

AMAZING SPIDER-MAN #656 CAPTAIN AMERICA 70TH ANNIVERSARY VARIANT

COVER BY JOE QUESADA, DANNY MIKI & RICHARD ISANOVE

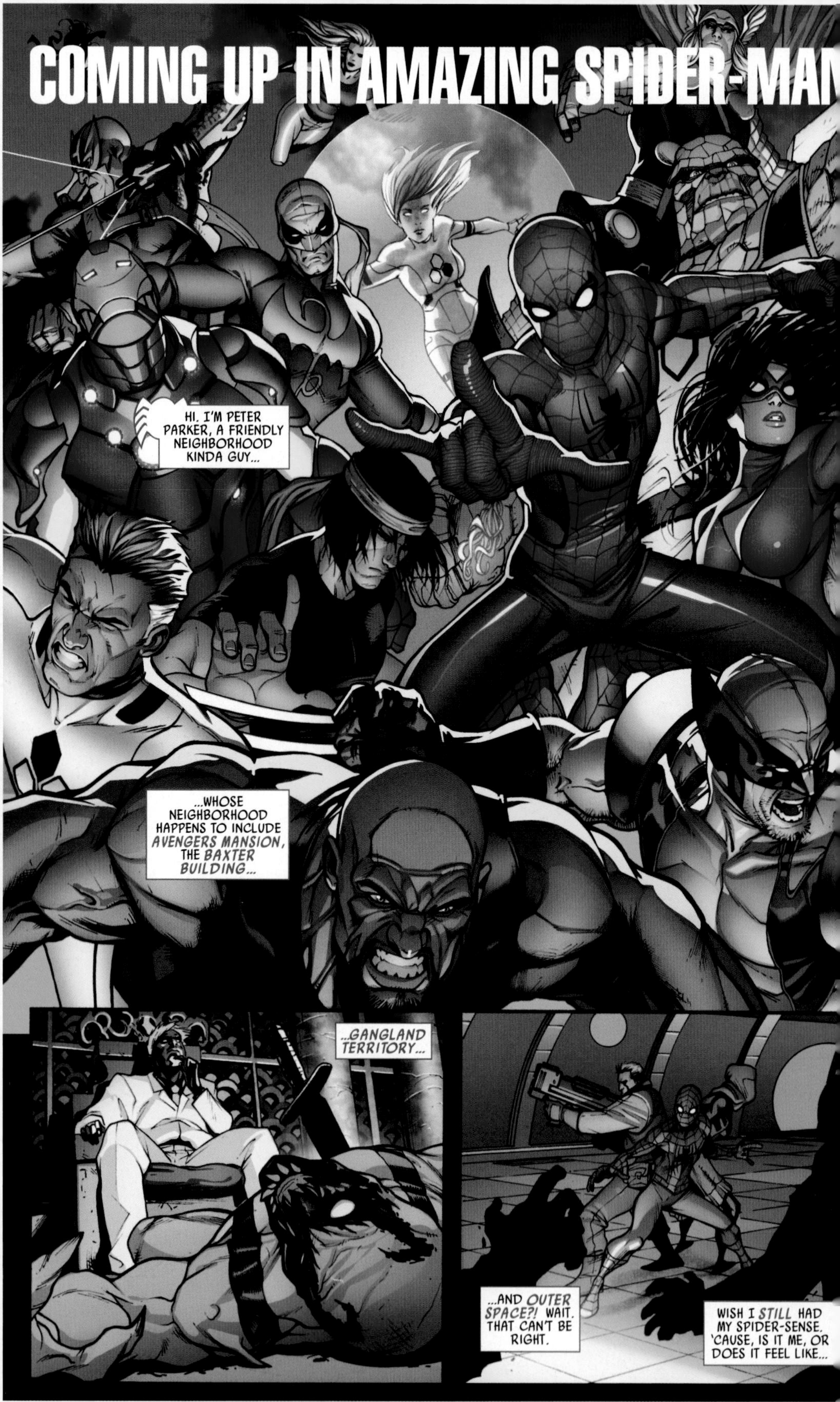
COMING UP IN AMAZING SPIDER-MAN
HI. I'M PETER PARKER, A FRIENDLY NEIGHBORHOOD KINDA GUY...
...WHOSE NEIGHBORHOOD HAPPENS TO INCLUDE AVENGERS MANSION, THE BAXTER BUILDING...
...GANGLAND TERRITORY...
...AND OUTER SPACE?! WAIT. THAT CAN'T BE RIGHT.
WISH I STILL HAD MY SPIDER-SENSE. 'CAUSE, IS IT ME, OR DOES IT FEEL LIKE...

AZING SPIDER-MAN #654.1 TEASER

TTEN BY DAN SLOTT, ART BY STEFANO CASELLI & MARTE GRACIA

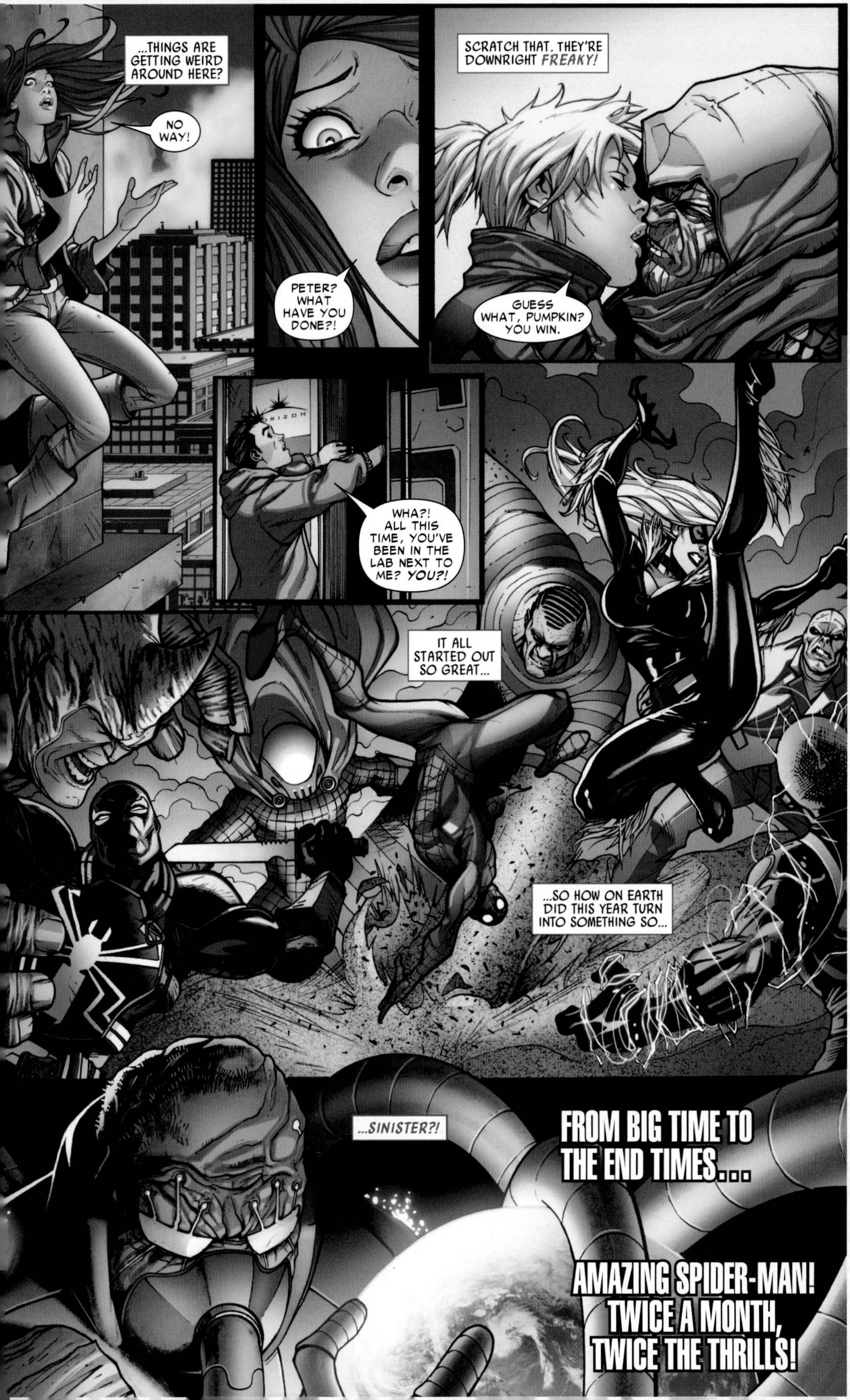

...THINGS ARE GETTING WEIRD AROUND HERE?
NO WAY!
PETER? WHAT HAVE YOU DONE?!
SCRATCH THAT. THEY'RE DOWNRIGHT FREAKY!
GUESS WHAT, PUMPKIN? YOU WIN.
WHA?! ALL THIS TIME, YOU'VE BEEN IN THE LAB NEXT TO ME? YOU?!
IT ALL STARTED OUT SO GREAT...
...SO HOW ON EARTH DID THIS YEAR TURN INTO SOMETHING SO...
...SINISTER?!
FROM BIG TIME TO THE END TIMES...
AMAZING SPIDER-MAN! TWICE A MONTH, TWICE THE THRILLS!

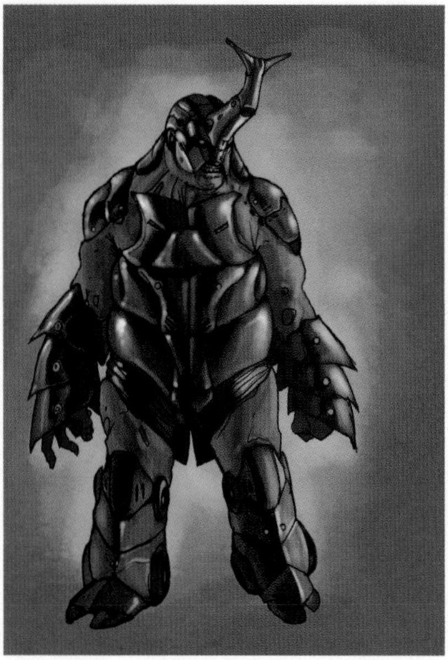

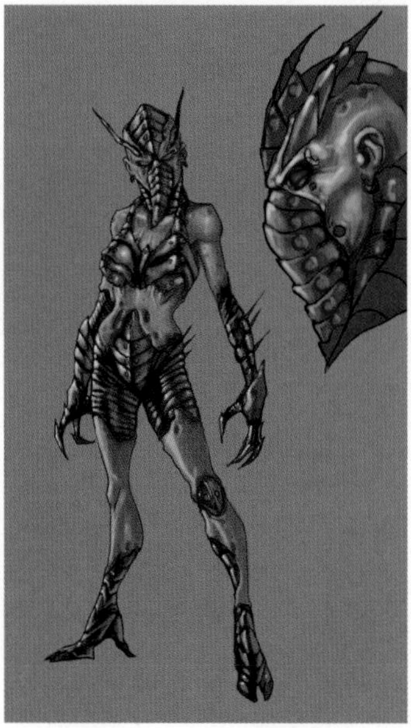

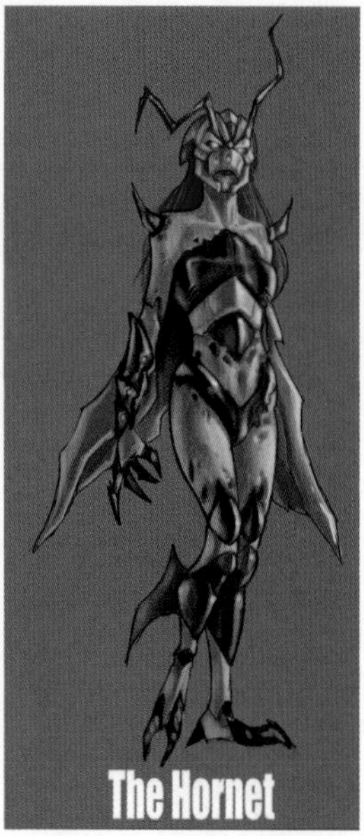
The Hornet

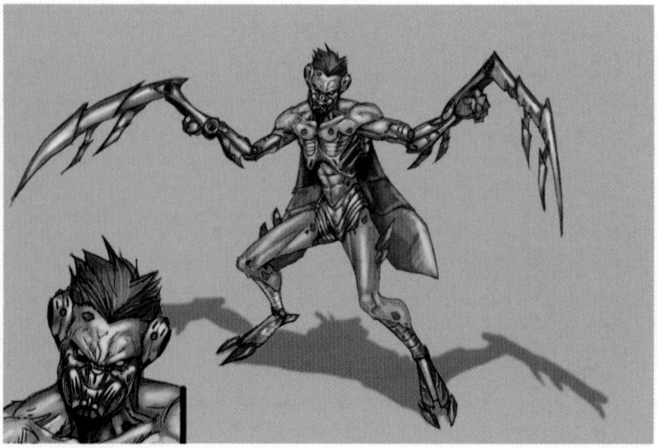

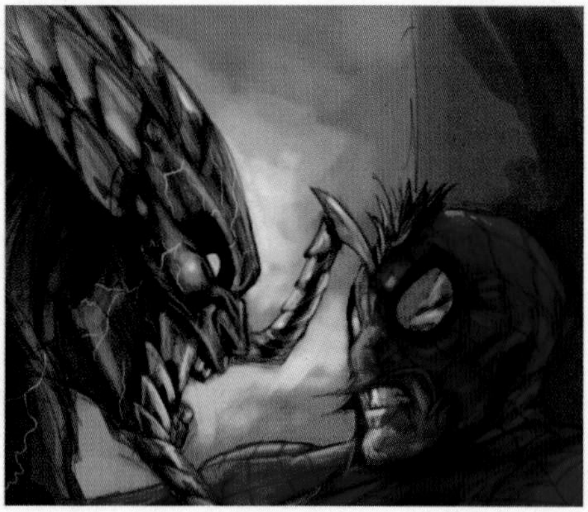

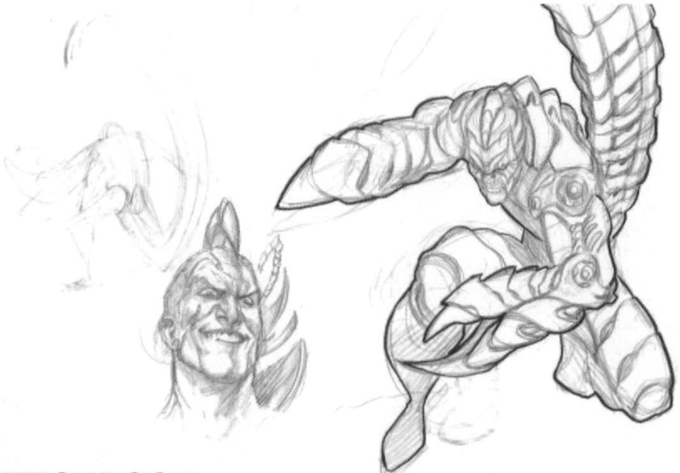

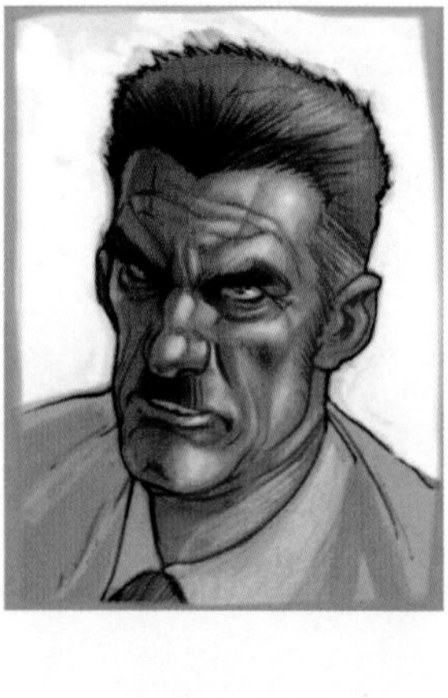

SKETCHBOOK
BY STEFANO CASELLI

SKETCHBOOK
BY STEFANO CASELLI

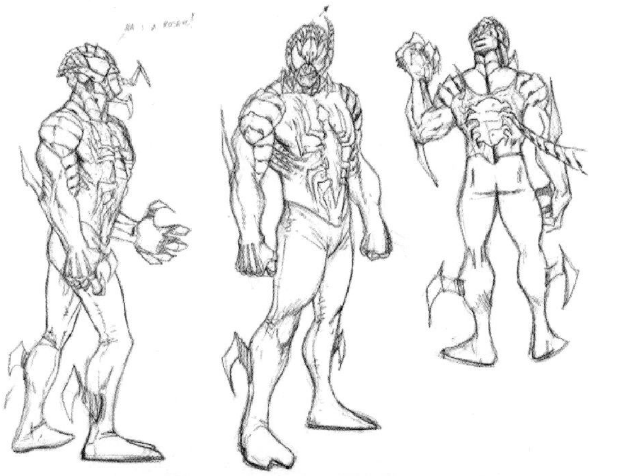

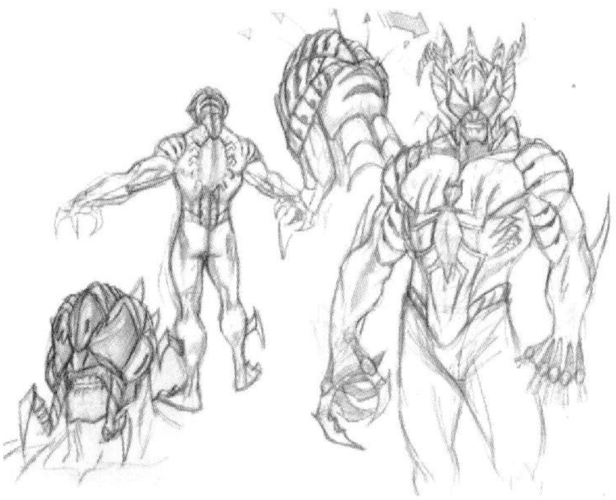

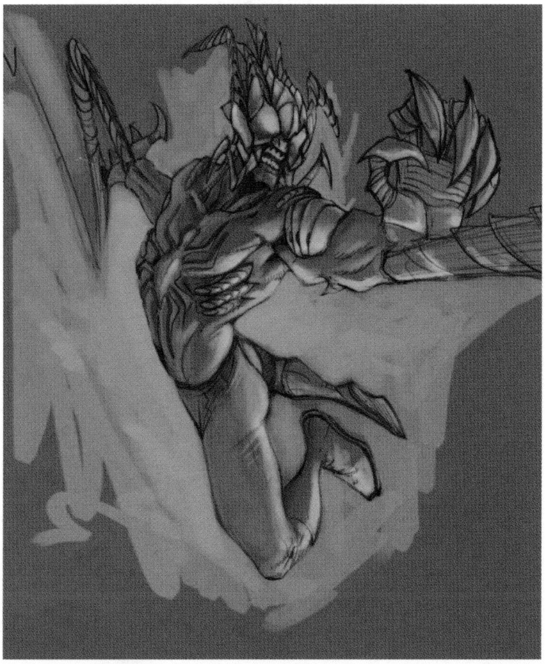

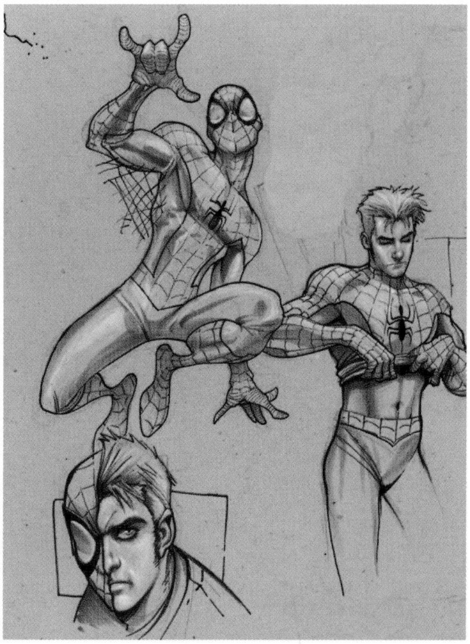

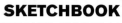

BULLETPROOF SPIDEY SUIT
BY MARCOS MARTIN

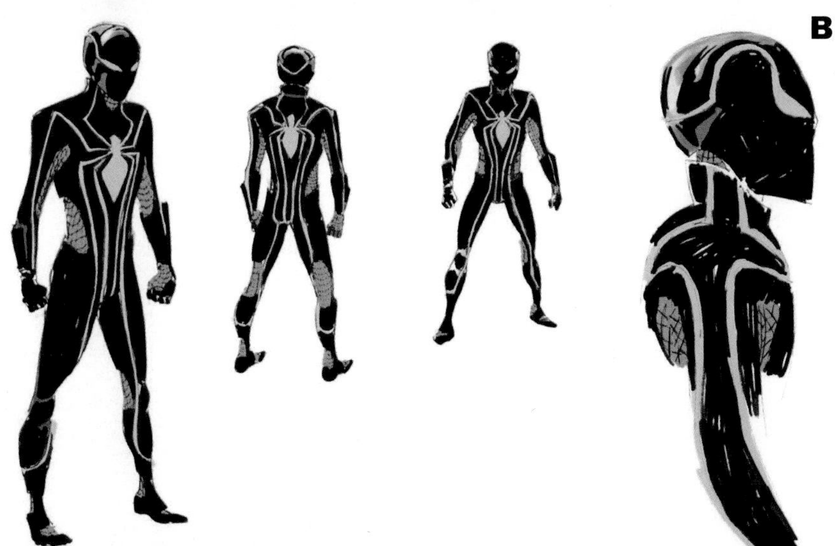

TO THE POINT

WITH SPIDER-MAN WRITER, DAN SLOTT

WE DISCUSS ALL THINGS SPIDER-MAN INCLUDING THE MARVEL POINT ONE ISSUE.

MARVEL: Why is your point one issue the perfect jumping on point for new readers?

DAN SLOTT: *NEW VENOM!* Since his very first appearance, Venom became a lot of fan's favorite Spidey villain. And over the years, after appearing in cartoon series, video games, toys, and a major motion picture, EVERYBODY out there knows Venom.

At the start of "BIG TIME," we saw that the Venom symbiote was forcibly removed off of its last host, Mac Gargan. Since then, the big unanswered question and a lot of fan speculation has been: Where's that suit going next? Who's going to be the next Venom? By AMAZING SPIDER-MAN #654, readers will know. And then, in AMAZING SPIDER-MAN #654.1, we'll have the perfect jumping on point for fans to see this new Venom in their first full-length adventure. You'll see how they work, what they're going to do with their powers, new takes on those powers, and what Venom's place in the Marvel Universe is going to be from now on.

MARVEL: Only a select few have worn the Venom symbiote and they've generally been some of the most memorable Spidey characters. What makes this new wearer such a perfect choice?

DS: In the past two decades, outside of Spider-Man, Eddie Brock, and Mac Gargan, most of Venom's hosts have been temporary-- just for an issue or a quick storyline. This next host, like Peter, Brock, and Gargan, is going to be a MAJOR status quo shift in the Venom saga. And, for the first time, the symbiote's going to a character we've seen in Spidey's supporting cast! That's BIG!

MARVEL: This new Venom may be friend or foe...so just what is his or her mission? And how does it draw them into conflict with Spidey?

DS: Okay, you've dragged it out of me. It's Aunt May. She's going to become Auntie-Venom. And Peter Parker's wheatcakes will now be laced with pure EVIL! Eeeeeevil!

Just kidding. How this new Venom is going to effect Spider-Man/Peter Parker is something readers are going to have to see for themselves over time. We gotta keep some secrets, right? But friend or foe? Good guy or bad guy? The answers to THOSE questions will be seen in AMAZING SPIDER-MAN #654.1!

MARVEL: Without giving away too much, what does this issue set up for the future?

DS: Lots. The second the Venom symbiote bonds with its new host, events are set in motion, and the clock starts ticking... If you're a Venom-fan, and you want to jump in at the beginning, the first time this new Venom goes into action, this issue is a great place to start!

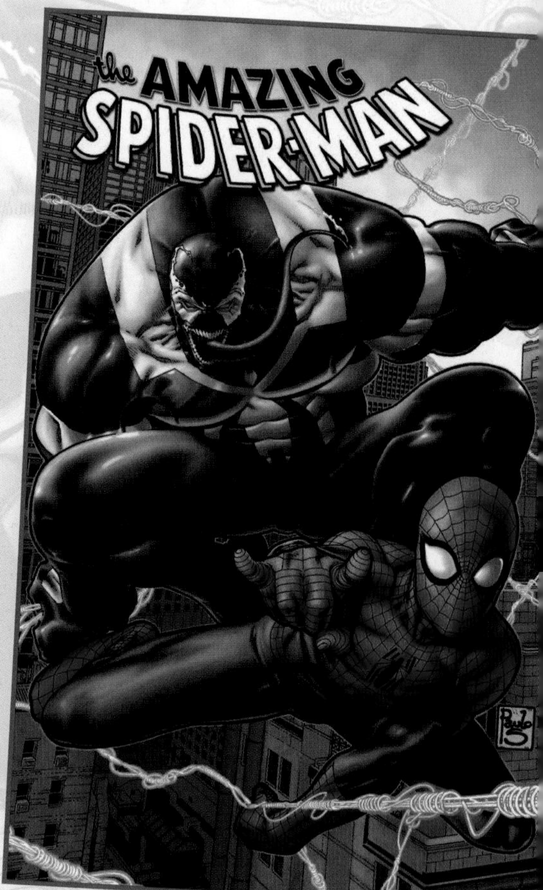
the AMAZING
SPIDER-MAN

Written by Dan Slott • Art by Humberto Ramos
Cover by Paolo Siqueira

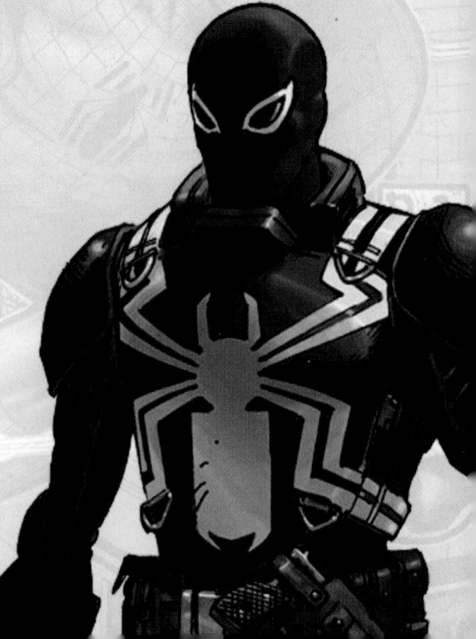